Johannes Friedrich Bleek, William Urwick

An introduction to the New Testament

Johannes Friedrich Bleek, William Urwick

An introduction to the New Testament

ISBN/EAN: 9783742895424

Manufactured in Europe, USA, Canada, Australia, Japa

Cover: Foto ©Lupo / pixelio.de

Manufactured and distributed by brebook publishing software (www.brebook.com)

Johannes Friedrich Bleek, William Urwick

An introduction to the New Testament

NOTICE TO SUBSCRIBERS.

———

EDINBURGH, *October* 1869.

MESSRS. CLARK have pleasure in forwarding to their Subscribers the Second Issue of the FOREIGN THEOLOGICAL LIBRARY for 1869, viz. :—

Keil's Introduction to the Old Testament (Vol. I.),

AND

Bleek's Introduction to the New Testament (Vol. I.),

oth of which, they trust, will be acceptable to British and American Students. The Second Volumes of each (completing them) are in the Press. The Second Volume of DELITZSCH on the *Hebrews* is also in the Press; and also the same Author's *Commentary on the Psalms*. The Publishers beg to call attention to the Imperial 8vo Edition of LANGE'S *Bible Commentary*, which they are publishing, and which will be supplied to Subscribers to *Foreign Theological Library* at 15s. each Volume.

CLARK'S

FOREIGN

THEOLOGICAL LIBRARY.

FOURTH SERIES.

VOL. XXIV.

Bleek's Introduction to the New Testament.

VOL. I.

EDINBURGH:
T. AND T. CLARK, 38, GEORGE STREET.

MDCCCLXIX.

PRINTED BY MURRAY AND GIBB,

FOR

T. & T. CLARK, EDINBURGH.

LONDON,	HAMILTON, ADAMS, AND CO.
DUBLIN,	JOHN ROBERTSON AND CO.
NEW YORK,	SCRIBNER AND CO.

AN INTRODUCTION

TO

THE NEW TESTAMENT.

BY

FRIEDRICH BLEEK.

EDITED BY
JOHANNES FRIEDRICH BLEEK,
PFARRER.

Translated from the German of the Second Edition,
BY THE
REV. WILLIAM URWICK, M.A.

VOL. I.

EDINBURGH:
T. & T. CLARK, 38, GEORGE STREET.
MDCCCLXIX.

TRANSLATOR'S PREFACE.

DR. FRIEDRICH BLEEK must be regarded as one of the most eminent and distinguished biblical scholars of the Evangelical Church in Germany. He was born July 4, 1793, at Ahrensbök, in Holstein. His father, who on the ground of health had exchanged the profession of notary for a business life, soon discovered the extraordinary gifts of his son, and, designing for him the career of a scholar, sent him for three years to the Gymnasium at Lübeck. There he pursued the study of the Greek and Latin classics, and began that of Hebrew; and, under the guidance of the learned and pious Director Mosche, evinced so strong a taste for ancient languages and history, that he gave up the idea of the law, and became in 1812 a student of philology and theology in the University of Kiel. Here his chief attention was directed to the philological departments of theological study. He afterwards spent three years, from 1814-1817, in the University of Berlin, where he imbibed a true love for theology under the influence of De Wette and Neander, and chiefly of Schleiermacher, who, with keen discernment and prognostication of his future career, was wont to say that he thought his friend was specially gifted with a *charisma* for Introduction to Holy Scripture. This was emphatically his *forte*, his *calling;* and to this, in the providence of God, he devoted his entire life. He passed the *examen pro ministerio* at Glückstadt, but he was soon recalled to Berlin by the Theological Faculty there, who recognised and appreciated his scientific earnestness, his love of truth, the thoroughness and simplicity of his nature, and the ability of his performances (some of which afterwards appeared in print), by giving him permission to lecture in public at the University, and conferring upon him the title of Professor-Extraordinary. His linguistic and exegetical exposition of Old and New Testament texts attracted the students by their thoroughness and clearness, and paved the way for his critical lectures on Old and New Testament Introduction. In 1829 he was called to the University of Bonn, on the Rhine, which was the scene of his uninterrupted labours for the remaining thirty years of his life. He died suddenly, of apoplexy, on the 27th February 1859, in firm reliance upon the grace of God in Christ, in whose service he had so faithfully employed the talent entrusted to him.[1]

Speaking of Bleek's great work on the Epistle to the Hebrews (1828-1840), DE WETTE said, "It is distinguished alike for comprehensive scholarship and thorough untiring diligence, for pure clear love of truth, and sound theological judgment, claiming thus the very first place among the exegetical works of our time;" and DELITZSCH has observed upon this, that "every one who knows the work will ratify De Wette's judgment." The other works of Bleek, his *Beiträge zur Evangelien-Kritik*, and his Lectures, are fully worthy of his first great work. Speaking of the last of the dissertations which came from his pen, DORNER says, "It is only another proof of the well-known pure and chaste perception and love of truth which guided Bleek in all his scientific inquiries, and of the comprehensiveness and thoroughness of his judgment. It is characterized by that

---

[1] See HERZOG'S *Real-Encyklopädie*, vol. xix., and *Conversations-Lexicon*, art. *Bleek*.

striking clearness and ease of scholarly exposition which makes us forget the laborious intricacy of thought implied, and the weighty *apparatus criticus* lying in the background, a clearness and ease which so signally marked him out as the MASTER of Old and New Testament criticism. All must admire the dignified and kindly tone in which he discussed adverse views, and the untiring patience with which he would still reason with his opponents who persevered in their objections after he had refuted them, and would enter into their arguments, in order to convince them that important data had been omitted in their reckoning. . . . Thanks be to God, who endowed His servant with this courageous faith adorning our Church, and who has given us, in his rare gifts, so rich and abiding a blessing! Thanks also, and peace to this *anima pia et candida!*"

As Biblical Introduction was Bleek's main and permanent calling in life, so his exegetical labours in the New Testament are fuller and more important than those on the Old. The work now presented in an English dress is distinguished by succinctness, clearness, accuracy, candour, love of truth, and, above all, reverence for the revelation of God in Christ, and for Holy Scripture as the record of that revelation. Attempts have been made to put upon Bleek the ban of rationalism, and to number him among the sceptical theologians of Germany; but a fair perusal of his works will furnish the best answer to such calumnies. "Bleek," says Prof. KAMPHAUSEN, "by his carefulness, his pure love of truth, and his unassuming humility, has done far more for biblical learning than any amount of rash self-assertion and oracular speaking could accomplish. Still, no one can fairly dare to reproach his investigations as in any way sceptical in their tendency. It was utterly impossible, for example, for Bleek to hesitate upon such a question as the authenticity of the fourth Gospel. His life and works bear witness to the fact, that positive faith in the truths of Christianity, and historical criticism of its sacred records, in no way exclude one another." He belonged to those theologians whom he himself describes in the Preface to his *Beiträge*—"Who, filled with love to the Lord and His Church, recognise an ever more thorough investigation of those normal beginnings and preparations for the faith which Holy Scripture and Scripture history furnish, as necessary to the confirmation and exposition of Christian doctrine, —who, susceptible to the recognition of Divine revelation, suffer themselves to be guided in their inquiries by no other law save that of truth,—and who, instead of identifying in an utterly unhistorical and irrational manner God's Word and Holy Scripture, regard it as their main task to discern the Word of God in Holy Scripture."

Bleek was indeed "filled with love to the Lord and His Church," and this love imparts to his thorough, clear, and candid investigations that humility and that reverence which befit his theme. The able and scholarly notes and additions of his son present to the reader the views of the latest German writers, with the bearing of Bleek's own opinions upon them; and though we do not follow him in all the conclusions to which he comes, we venture to predict that, as already in Germany, so in England, the work will take its rank as one of the very best text-books and safest guides which the theological student can select in the subject of New Testament Introduction.

HATHERLOW, CHESHIRE,
   24th July 1869.

CONTENTS OF VOL. I.

	PAGE
EDITOR'S PREFACE, ...	1

PRELIMINARY OBSERVATIONS—

    Meaning and Method of N. T. Introduction (§ 1-3), .   3

A. LITERATURE OF N. T. INTRODUCTION (§ 4-17)—

    § 4. The First Three Centuries A.D., . . .   12
    § 5. The Middle Ages, ...   14
    § 6. From the Reformation to the Middle of the Seventeenth Century, ...   15
    § 7, 8. From R. Simon to the Middle of the Eighteenth Century, ...   17
    § 9. Michaelis and Semler, ...   22
    Modern Literature, § 10-17—
        § 10. Main Topics of Investigation; Justification of Criticism, ...   24
        § 11-15. German Protestant Theology, . . .   26
        § 16. Roman Catholic Theologians, . . .   36
        § 17. English Biblical Critics, ...   37

B. DIVISIONS AND ORDER OF BOOKS IN THE N. T. AND THE NAME (§ 18), ...   39

C. THE RISE OF CHRISTIAN LITERATURE IN GENERAL (§ 19, 20),   42

D. LANGUAGE OF THE N. T. BOOKS (§ 21-25)—

    § 21. Not Latin, ...   49
    § 22. Not Aramaic, but Greek, ...   50

§ 22, 23. Proved (*a*) from the Character of the Primary Readers,	52, 53
§ 24. (*b*) From the Culture and Circumstances of the Writers,	56
§ 25. (*c*) From the Character of the Greek of the N. T.,	57

E. CHARACTER OF N. T. GREEK (§ 26-36)—

§ 26. Controversy between the Purists and the Hebraists,	58
§ 27. (1.) Development of the Greek Language; Rise of the κοινή,	60
§ 28. (2) and (3.) Spread of Later Greek in the East from the Time of Alexander the Great,	62
§ 29. (4.) Spread of Greek among the Jews: Influence of the Hebrew through the LXX., and of the Aramæan as the Vernacular of Palestine,	64

Language of the N. T. in Particular (§ 30-36)—

§ 30. (*a*) Its Affinity with later Greek generally,	66
§ 31. List of Works to be used as Helps for Studying N. T. Greek,	69
§ 32-35. (*b*) The Hebrew-Aramaic Element in N. T. Greek,	72
§ 36. Works bearing on the N. T.; Jewish Writers; Grammars; Concordances; Lexicons,	83
§ 37. APPENDIX.—Lists of the more Important Commentaries on the N. T.,	87

PART I.

ORIGIN OF THE SEVERAL BOOKS.

THE GOSPELS (§ 38-121).

Titles of the several Gospels, their Import and Significance (§ 38),	101

FACTS KNOWN CONCERNING THE FOUR EVANGELISTS. VARIOUS VIEWS HELD CONCERNING THE ORIGIN OF THE GOSPELS (§ 39-63)—

I. MATTHEW (§ 39-46)—

§ 39. Life of the Apostle Matthew,	104

CONTENTS.

	PAGE
§ 40, 41. Facts concerning a Hebrew Gospel by Matthew ("Gospel of the Hebrews"),	107
§ 42. Various Opinions concerning this,	116
§ 43. And concerning the Origin of this Gospel generally,	117

Relation of the "Gospel of the Hebrews" to the Greek Matthew—

§ 44. (1) and (2.) Affinity between the Two,	120
§ 45, 46. (3) and (4.) Priority of the Greek Matthew,	122

II. MARK (§ 47, 48), ... 126

III. LUKE (§ 49-55)—

§ 49. Life of Luke,	134
§ 50. Facts known concerning his Gospel,	138
§ 51. Its Relation to Marcion's Gospel,	139
§ 52. Various Opinions concerning this Relation,	143
§ 53, 54. Priority of our Luke,	145
§ 55. Views of Mayerhoff and the "Sächsische Anonymus,"	151

IV. JOHN (§ 56-63)—

§ 56-58. Life of the Apostle (a) apart from the Gospel,	155
§ 59, 60. (b) According to the Gospel,	163
§ 61-63. Controversy concerning the Genuineness of St. John's Gospel,	168

RELATION OF OUR FOUR GOSPELS TO EACH OTHER, BOTH AS TO CONTENTS AND HISTORICAL REPRESENTATION (§ 64-70).

Affinity between the Synoptics as contrasted with St. John—

§ 64. (1.) With reference to the Course of the History,	178
§ 65, 66. (2.) With reference to the Subject-matter,	181
§ 67. (3.) The Discourses and Miracles of Christ recorded,	188
§ 68. (4.) The Day of Christ's Death,	189
§ 69, 70. (5.) Style,	191

CONTENTS.

GENUINENESS OF ST. JOHN'S GOSPEL (§ 71-90)—

§ 71. (1.) The Journeys of Jesus to the Feasts in Jerusalem, ... 194
§ 72, 73. (2.) The Day of Christ's Crucifixion, . 198
§ 74, 75. (3.) The Controversies concerning the Passover in the Second Century, . . . 204
§ 76, 77, 78. (4.) The Discourses of Jesus. His Prophecies, ... 211
§ 79. (5.) Miracles, ... 219
§ 80. (6.) The Writer's Personality that of the Apostle John. (a) Nationality. (b) Greek Culture, . 222
§ 81. (c) His Dogmatic Views (Doctrine of the Logos), 227
§ 82. (d) His Universalism; the Independency of his Narrative, ... 230
§ 83, 84. (7.) The Witness of the Gospel itself; its Appendix, Ch. xxi. 232
§ 85-89. (8.) External Testimonies, . . . 236
§ 90. Theory of its Partial Genuineness, . . 250

FORMATION OF THE SYNOPTICAL GOSPELS (§ 91-112)—

§ 91. Attempts to explain the Harmony between the Three Synoptics; (a) by supposing a Primary Oral Gospel, ... 251
§ 92. By reference to a Work that formed their Common Basis, ... 254
§ 93-97. Dependence of *Mark* upon Matthew and Luke, ... 258
§ 98, 99. (1.)-(3.) *Matthew* and *Luke;* their Connection points to a Common Written Source or Sources, ... 275
§ 100. (4.) Conjectures concerning the Pre-Canonical Gospels, ... 281
§ 101, 102. (5.) Character of the *Primitive* Gospel, . 284
§ 103. (6.) Disappearance of the Pre-Canonical Gospels, ... 291
§ 104. (7.) Original Language of Matthew and Luke's Gospel, ... 291
§ 105. (8.) When Written, ... 292
§ 106, 107. (9.) Style, ... 294
§ 108. (10.) Religious Spirit and Genius of each Gospel, 299
§ 109, 110. (11), (12.) Conclusion as to their Origin. Their Integrity. Origin of the Gospel of the Hebrews, ... 304
§ 111. The Gospel of Mark, ... 308

CONTENTS.   xiii

	PAGE
§ 112. Note on the Griesbachian Theory, and the Mark Hypothesis in its present Form,	313

FURTHER INFERENCES CONCERNING THE ORIGIN OF ST. JOHN'S
GOSPEL (§ 113-118)—

§ 113. Time and Place of Writing,	316
§ 114. Whether Written Materials formed the Basis of the Discourses recorded,	319
§ 115. Design; not only Doctrinal, but also Historical,	322
§ 116, 117. Occasion,	327
§ 118. Integrity,	333

UNCANONICAL GOSPELS (§ 119-121), ... 334

THE ACTS OF THE APOSTLES (§ 122-131)—

§ 122. Title and Contents,	347
§ 123. Design,	349
§ 124-126. Sources,	355
§ 127. Use made of these Sources,	365
§ 128. Writer,	368
§ 129, 130. Historical Character of the Book,	370
§ 131. *Apocryphal Acts*,	376

THE PAULINE EPISTLES (§ 132-188).

ST. PAUL'S LIFE DOWN TO HIS FIRST STAY IN CORINTH
(§ 132-141)—

§ 132. Preliminary Remarks,	381
§ 133. Descent of the Apostle; his Name, Education, Life before his Conversion,	382
§ 134. His Conversion,	386
§ 135, 136. The Years immediately following his Conversion,	390
§ 137. *First* Great Missionary Tour,	395
§ 138. Council of Apostles,	398
§ 139. Paul's Opposition to Peter at Antioch,	402
§ 140, 141. *Second* Great Missionary Tour,	404

THE FIRST EPISTLE TO THE THESSALONIANS (§ 142), . . 410

THE SECOND EPISTLE TO THE THESSALONIANS (§ 143), . . 414

ST. PAUL'S LIFE, CONTINUED (§ 144, 145), . . . 418

THE EPISTLES TO THE CORINTHIANS (146-151)—

§ 146. Data of the Two Epistles; Second Visit of Paul
to Corinth, ... 423
§ 147, 148. *First Epistle*, ... 426
§ 149, 150. *Second Epistle*. Lost Letter between our
Two Epistles, ... 431
§ 151. Apocryphal Correspondence of St. Paul with
the Corinthians, ... 439

THE EPISTLE TO THE ROMANS (§ 152-154)—

§ 152. Time and Place of Writing, . . . 440
§ 153. Formation of the Roman Church, . . 441
§ 154. Occasion of the Epistle; its Contents; its Value;
its Genuineness; its Integrity, . . 444

EDITOR'S PREFACE.

 HAVE great pleasure in being able now to publish my sainted father's introduction to the *New Testament*, as a fit companion to his work on the *Old*. In it the reader will find the fruits of many years of faithful toil. My father first lectured upon this subject from four to six hours weekly, during the winter of 1822; and he revised and repeated his course of lectures four-and-twenty times, down to the winter of 1858. On reaching the Epistle to the Hebrews on this last occasion, he was suddenly taken away from that earthly calling to which he had, even to the last, amid severe attacks of illness, so faithfully and untiringly devoted himself. In his very first lecture he described Biblical Introduction as an *historical* science; and to the *historical method* he adhered throughout, as all his lectures show. The present work is for the most part a *verbatim* reproduction of these collegiate lectures of Bleek's. I have ventured only to make a few minor alterations, which do not in the least affect the subject-matter. The design of the few notes (marked *B*) which I have added, is simply to give the reader requisite references to works upon the point in hand; and if occasionally there be any deviations from this design, I hope he will forgive them. I have also inserted in the text names of works bearing upon the subject, which have been published since Bleek's death. The quotations have been revised and verified. The titles of those books which were not accessible to me I have marked with an asterisk, omitting this in those cases only where the statement of an author in another work, or of the publisher or editor,

seemed sufficiently to guarantee the accuracy of the title. For the rest, the same plan is adopted as in the O. T. Introduction, both works being closely connected, and very similar in plan and development. May this work, like the former, be a blessing! May it contribute to the promotion of a reverential and scientific, and at the same time of a liberal and unbiassed, criticism of Holy Scripture, and serve as a guide or directory to those who really and perseveringly strive after the full knowledge of the truth!

BONN, *September* 1861.

In preparing this *new edition*, I have followed substantially the same plan as that adopted in the second edition of the O. T. Introduction. The work has been divided into sections, and a few abridgments and corrections have been made; but with these exceptions, it appears in the same form as in the first edition. For the convenience of students, however, I have added a *resumé* of exegetical literature (§ 37), several quotations from authors referred to in the History of the Canon, and a few notes referring to the latest works upon the subject. These additions occur partly in notes, and partly in the text, and are enclosed in brackets. Owing to my remoteness from any public library, and partly to want of time, some points worthy of notice may have escaped me, or may not sufficiently have been investigated; but I hope that omissions of this kind are not numerous, and will not in any way impair the value attaching to Bleek's work in the judgment of many.

WINTERBURG, SYNOD. DISTRICT OF SOBERNHEIM,
May 1866.

PRELIMINARY OBSERVATIONS

CONCERNING THE MEANING AND METHOD OF NEW TESTAMENT INTRODUCTION.

§ 1.

THE theological study for the prosecution of which this treatise is intended, is pursued in wider or narrower compass, and under various names. From the middle of last century, downward to the present time, the commonest name for it has been "New Testament INTRODUCTION;" besides this, the designation "HISTORY of the New Testament" has frequently been used. Neither title accurately defines the sphere and limits of the study, or of the topics it includes; but the former is more expressive than the latter. An "Introduction" to the N. T. denotes essentially the same as an "Introduction" to other writings of antiquity. By an Introduction to any ancient work, we understand dissertations and inquiries prefixed to the text in printed editions, or coming first in oral expositions of the book, for the purpose generally of instructing the reader or hearer concerning certain points and bearings, the knowledge of which is necessary, or at least very desirable, in order to the right understanding of the treatise as a whole, and of its several parts: dissertations, for instance, concerning the author, his personal history and surroundings, the time and circumstances of his composition, and so on. Such introductory dissertations become the more necessary where the historical relations and phenomena of the work are very distinctive and peculiar, and where it concerns any special eras or events; but they are more or less needful even where this is not the case, in order to enlighten the hearer or the reader, and to enable him to understand the work in question.

This holds true to a certain extent, though only partially, of modern works, because we ourselves, as contemporaries, are surrounded by the same relations, and must in some degree be acquainted with the circumstances and events of our day. Facts which we are ignorant of, and which it is desirable we should know, are generally stated by the author himself in his preface, and any further introduction is usually unnecessary. But the need for such an introduction arises soon after, indeed sometimes immediately after, the appearance of a work, especially if the events and circumstances of the time are closely connected with the subject treated of, or if the author has seen fit to conceal his own position and relationships. Much more is such an introduction requisite in the case of works written in places, circumstances, or times unknown to us or distant from us, as *e.g.* in the case of the Greek and Latin classics. Here it is usual to prefix a longer or shorter introduction before the more direct exposition of the text. And, in like manner, it is customary to prefix to the several books of Holy Scripture brief essays or statements concerning their origin, their authorship, their design and contents, their genuineness and integrity, the works used in the exposition, etc.

It often happens that the knowledge requisite to the right understanding of the works of antiquity bears not only upon a single treatise, but upon many, belonging to one and the same class, written by the same author, or belonging to the same nation; and in this case an Introduction may be written which bears upon and embraces the whole. This is true, for example, with reference to the Greek tragedians and dramatists, the Greek prose writers, the Roman historians, and so on, or the residue of Greek or Roman literature generally; such dissertations as we actually have in the literary history of each of these countries. Such a comprehensive review is very useful in the study of the several works included, because it helps us to understand the place which each work holds in relation to the others, and to the whole department of literature to which it belongs, whether it be literature of a certain epoch, on a certain subject, or belonging to one and the same nation.

Now these remarks are specially true of Holy Scripture, in both the Old Testament and the New, whether viewed together or taken separately. The Scriptures of the N. T. (to confine our attention to these) belong to one and the same department of Christian authorship. They are all the works of writers who belong to one and the same epoch, viz. the very first years of Christianity,—writers who were closely and variously connected with each other, and who had all of them the same end in view,—namely, to awaken and to strengthen Christian faith, to unfold the truths of Christianity, and to apply them to the hearts and consciences of men. The style or character of the Greek in which they severally wrote, possesses alike an internal affinity and a distinctiveness of its own, when compared with the Greek of heathen and classical writers. And consequently the several books, when viewed together, form that series of Scriptures which had already, in the beginning of the second century of the Christian era, attained exclusive reverence side by side with the O. T. as part of Holy Scripture, possessing normative authority in the determination of Christian faith and the regulation of Christian conduct, and which afterwards have had one and the same history in reference to text, to circulation, and to use. It must therefore be a useful and right procedure, and thoroughly in keeping with the end in view, to examine the books of the N. T. together, as forming one complete whole; for by such a comprehensive treatment of them alone can adequate light be obtained, whereby we may be able to discern the distinctive peculiarities of each portion in relation to and comparison with the rest.

§ 2.

This consideration of the N. T. as forming one complete whole has already been variously prosecuted, and has now for a long time constituted a distinct department of theological study, usually under the name of NEW TESTAMENT INTRODUCTION, — thus forming one department of INTRODUCTION TO THE BIBLE, the other department being Old Testament Introduction. This title does not certainly afford a very accurate definition of the study before us; for one and another writer have included under it subjects which others have omitted, and which may be more appropriately transferred to other departments of theological study. Among these collateral topics, which more properly belong to other branches of Christian investigation, the following in particular may be named:

(*a.*) The political and religious history of the nation to which the N. T. writers for the most part belong, together with Bible chronology, and the physical and topographical character of the country in which they lived. A general exposition of this subject is certainly very requisite to the right understanding of the sacred books; and we find it treated of in the older works on Biblical Introduction, and in some more modern works of English theologians. But by German theologians the treatment of this subject has been quite excluded from Biblical Introduction, and has been assigned a province of its own, like that of Jewish history and Bible archæology and geography. And it is doubtless well that it is so; because any adequate and accurate examination of it would occupy too much space, and other topics more directly connected with the N. T. books would have to be too much curtailed.

(*b.*) The inquiry concerning the DIVINE ORIGIN and INSPIRATION of the sacred writings. This subject was in early times usually included in Scripture Introduction. Most theologians, however, in Germany now exclude it, as belonging more properly to the department of Christian doctrine; and in Bible Introduction they view the question concerning the origin and history of the sacred books in the *human aspect* of it simply, in order thus to establish a fit basis for the dogmatic treatment of the subject. This separation of the two spheres of inquiry seems certainly to be just and appropriate.

(*c.*) The development of principles and laws to guide us in the detecting corruptions and establishing true readings in the text of the N. T., and to help us in understanding N. T. phraseology; in a word, N. T. CRITICISM and HERMENEUTICS. These might indeed find an appropriate place in an Introduction to the N. T.; but they cannot be thoroughly and advantageously considered, without expounding the rules of criticism and hermeneutics generally, which should not be taken for granted as known. This would lead us too far away from our more direct subject; and it is therefore more appropriate to limit our Introduction in these points simply to an exposition of the historical relations, the character of the language, and the structure of the text, of the several books of Scripture.

It thus seems appropriate to exclude from the department of Introduction, strictly so called, scientific investigations connected with Holy Scripture, so as to give to our inquiry simply an *historical* character. Only thus shall we be able to define and mark out our subject as a distinct theological study. Biblical Introduction has often been regarded as a congeries of various branches of knowledge, which have, no doubt, a common connection and bearing, but which cannot be given any defined unity; and the department of study which would appropriate them seems itself to be very clearly defined side by side with other studies equally bearing upon Holy Scripture. It has long been felt not only desirable, but needful, definitely to mark out the special province and task of theological studies generally, and of Biblical Introduction—specially of N. T. Introduction—in particular. Now, amid all differences of treatment, one main topic of N. T. Introduction is universally held to be *an inquiry into the origin of the several books as the works of Christian writers.* This is a purely historical inquiry. But in order to give unity to the topics treated of, we must contemplate them simply, or at least mainly, from an historical point of view, and N. T. Introduction generally must be regarded as an historical study.[1] It must therefore be looked upon as a history of the N. T. books, severally and collectively, from the time when they were written down to our own day.[2]

N. T. Introduction may be regarded as a part of the history of Christian literature; but a part which, as it concerns the earliest written documents of Christendom forming the basis of Christian faith, claims our attention in a different manner and in a far higher degree than does the entire remaining range of Christian literature. It stands in the same relation to all following Christian literature, as the exposition of N. T. theology stands to the history of Christian Doctrine afterwards, or the life of Christ and His apostles to Church History in general. Though, as I have said, "Introduction" has to do mainly with the human element or aspect of the N. T. writings, still the greatest importance must be attached to it, because it furnishes the basis whereon alone we can form a correct estimate of what we possess in those writings —writings which we reverence as the primary and original witnesses of our Christian belief—whether they have such

---

[1] I have adopted this plan in my Lectures on Biblical Introduction during the past thirty years. The purely historical method has been advocated of late publicly, and with increasing earnestness, by CREDNER, REUSS, GUERICKE (2d ed.). It has been also espoused by HUPFELD, *Ueber Begriff und Methode der sog. biblischen Einleitung*, Marb. 1844, who himself adopted it in his Academic Lectures. [Cf. Hupfeld's latest dissertation on the subject, entitled "*Nochein Wort über den Begriff der sog. bibl. Einl.*," *Stud. u. Krit.* 1861, pp. 3–28.]

[2] We must renounce the purely historical character of Biblical Introduction, and admit into it dogmatic inquiries, if with HEINR. HOLTZMANN ("*Ueber Begr. u. Inhalt d. bibl. Einleitungswissenschaft,*" *Stud. u. Krit.* 1860, pp. 410–416) we include in it the comparison and harmonizing of the assured results of historical criticism with the dogmatic views of evangelical theologians concerning the canonical books. (See p. 6, *h.*) HOLTZMANN regards Canonicity as an essential part of Introduction, and as forming its concluding topic. So also does BAUR, *Theol. Jahrbücher*, 1850 and 1851. EWALD, moreover (*Jahrbücher d. bibl. Wissensch.* iv. 14 sqq.), includes not only the Doctrine of the Canon, but Hermeneutics and Criticism, in Biblical Introduction.

an origin, and have been preserved in their genuineness and integrity to such an extent, as to justify us in still and ever attributing to them this high authority.

Judging from the description we have now given of the special study before us, the ordinary title *Introduction to the N. T.* may perhaps seem too general, and not sufficiently defined. Still I would retain it, now that it has become naturalized among us, as a technical designation of our subject. Attempts have of late, indeed, been made more accurately to describe it by the title " Historico-critical Introduction to the N. T." But we would rather abide by the simpler name "N. T. Introduction." As to the other title which I mentioned at the outset, viz. " History of the N. T.," this and similar titles—*e.g. Critical History of the N. T.* (R. SIMON); *Collective History of the N. T.* (GUERICKE, ed. 2); *History of the Holy Scriptures of the N. T.* (HUPFELD and REUSS)—might perhaps be more descriptive of the character and range of our inquiry. But even these terms do not accurately define it. A "History of the N. T." might, for example, include the history of its spread throughout the world; of the various translations of it, old as well as new; of its use and interpretation; and of its moral and religious bearing upon the nations who have received it. Thus the range of our subject would become far too wide, at least for our Academic Lectures, and the topics included under the title would either be not touched upon at all, or only briefly alluded to; and the main topics would still concern the origin of the several books, their collection into one whole, and the history of the text of them. If, however, a title be preferred which expressly denotes the *historical* character of our investigation, I should choose this as most appropriate—CRITICAL HISTORY OF THE N. T., or OF THE N. T. CANON. Still, as I have said, I would rather retain the title, INTRODUCTION TO THE N. T.

§ 3.

As to the division of our subject, and the order in which each part should be considered, what we have already said indicates what will be most conformable to the end in view. Two main divisions have indeed been proposed, viz. GENERAL and SPECIAL Introduction; the latter being simply investigations concerning the origin of each particular book, and the former including all other topics belonging to N. T. Introduction,—namely, the history of the uniting of the several books in one collection, the history of the Text, of Manuscripts, Editions, Versions, etc. Accordingly many (*e.g.* MICHAELIS, DE WETTE, and others) give to General Introduction the precedence of Special in the order of consideration. But this arrangement is inconvenient and unnatural. It appears to me much more in order to inquire into the origin of the several books composing the N. T. first, and then to devote our attention to the history of the N. T. as a whole, and to the history of its text. I have therefore for many years treated of N. T. as well as O. T. Introduction in this manner, dividing it into three main parts, and prefixing thereto a few preliminary sections. These preliminary sections refer to the following topics :—

A. A review of what has already been done towards the critical history of the N. T. Canon, either in Introductions which have been published going over the entire ground, or in Investigations upon separate parts of our subject which have marked an epoch in the advance of Biblical knowledge.

B. A brief consideration of the various parts into which the N. T. is divided, and of the order of the several books upon which our inquiry is to be employed.

C, D, and *E.* A general dissertation concerning the rise of Christian literature generally, concerning the language in which the N. T. books have been handed down to us, its originality and distinctive character.

The three main divisions of the work which follow these preliminary sections are as follows :—

I. HISTORY OF THE ORIGIN OF THE SEVERAL BOOKS OF THE N. T.: An inquiry as to *when, by whom, on what occasion,* and *with what design* these books were severally written ;

and *whether we now have them in essentially the same form*, as to contents and extent, in which they first came from the hand of their authors.

II. HISTORY OF THE N. T. BOOKS COLLECTIVELY, or of THE NEW TESTAMENT CANON AS SUCH, ITS FORMATION AND CONSOLIDATION: An inquiry as to when and how first a collection of Christian writings, possessing special rank and authority above other writings, was formed; and what, if any, changes as to its range and its estimation this collection of writings has undergone, either as a whole or with reference to any of its parts.

III. GENERAL HISTORY OF THE TEXT OF THE N. T.: A review of the alterations the text has undergone in the course of time, and of the efforts which have been made to purify it from false readings, and to re-establish it in its genuineness. These inquiries naturally follow those concerning the History of the Canon, because the questions which they involve have to do not so much with this or that particular book, but with all the books together.

This division consists of three sections:—

(1.) *External History of the Text*: Concerning alterations in the outward form of the text having no influence upon its internal structure; changes affecting the written characters, the punctuation, the modes of division, and the like.

(2.) *Internal History of the Manuscript Text*: An inquiry whether the text of the N. T. books as we now have it has been maintained in its integrity, pure and unadulterated, since these books were first composed; or whether, through the carelessness or wilfulness of transcribers, they have been liable to similar corruptions with other manuscript memorials of antiquity. We shall then have to mention the earliest and most important witnesses and standards of the N. T. text in various centuries, especially the Greek Manuscripts and the Ancient Versions.

(3.) *History of the Printed Text* or *Editions* of the N. T.

A. GENERAL ACCOUNT OF THE LITERATURE OF NEW TESTAMENT INTRODUCTION.[1]

§ 4.

The importance of prosecuting investigations concerning the N. T. Canon and its several parts was felt in the Church as early as the first century, contemporaneously indeed with the formation of the Canon. The collection of the N. T. books into one complete whole did not take place (as we shall see in the second part of this work) precisely at the same time with the composition of the several books, but somewhat later, when at least most of the several books were already extant, and after what is strictly called the apostolic age; and upon its first formation it was not finally closed, but some centuries elapsed before it attained such a fixedness that the Church (or at least by far the greatest part of the Church) finally adopted as its own those books which now make up the N. T., to the exclusion of all others from that collection. Down to that time there had been a certain hesitation or wavering in the Church's judgment concerning some of those books. While received by a section of the Church and by many Church doctors as of equal value and authority with the rest, and therefore as forming part of the N. T. Canon, some books were rejected, or at least assigned a lower rank, by another section of the Church and by other Church doctors. Judgment upon this question was determined almost solely by the view taken of the origin of these writings, of the genuineness or spuriousness of the books which claimed to have been written by apostles, and of the relationship in which the author (if not an apostle) stood to

---

[1] See E. F. K. ROSENMÜLLER (*ob.* 1835), *Handbuch f. d. Literatur d. bibl. Kritik u. Exegese*, Gött. 1797–1800, in four parts, but not completed. For works on Introduction to the whole Bible, i. pp. 51–115; to the N. T., i. pp. 157–186. CREDNER, *Einl. in d. N. T.* i. pp. 6–52 : *Geschichte d. Einl. in d. N. T.* HUPFELD, *Begr. u. Methode d. bibl. Einl.* pp. 39–88. FERD. CHRIST. BAUR, *Die Einl. in d. N. T. als theol. Wissenschaft*, etc., in *Baur and Zeller's theol. Jahrb.* 1850, iv.; 1851, i. 3.

the first disciples of our Lord. Questions concerning the genuineness, and indeed the origin, of these writings must have arisen very early; and those doctors of the Church who recognised and maintained the authority of some books which others rejected, were obliged to vindicate themselves by asserting and proving the apostolic origin of the books they espoused. Indeed, the true and orthodox Church was obliged to do this in opposition to certain heretical sects, who rejected the books which the Church received, and branded them as spurious or interpolated. Hence it is that we find many affirmations on this subject scattered through the writings of the theologians of the second and third centuries,— in IRENÆUS, TERTULLIAN, CLEMENS ALEX., and especially in ORIGEN. These Fathers are content for the most part simply with an appeal to the tradition of the early Church. But in cases where this was not itself unanimous, or was not considered sufficiently certain, they endeavour to establish the proof from internal evidence. DIONYSIUS, bishop of Alexandria (*ob.* 264), seems to have been especially distinguished as a critic among the early Fathers, as appears from fragments of his treatise on the Apocalypse which have come down to us. We find notices of the critical judgments of the earlier Fathers concerning some N. T. books in Eusebius (*Church History*, circ. 324), and in JEROME (*ob.* 420), in his work, *De viris illustribus s. Catalogus scriptorum ecclesiasticorum*, and in many other works. The books of the N. T. as to the authorship of which doubt existed even at this time in the Church, and concerning which there was uncertainty whether they were of equal authority with the rest, were the Epistle to the Hebrews, the Revelation, the two Epistles of St. Peter, the second and third Epistles of St. John, and the Epistles of James and Jude. By small parties in the Church other books also were objected to, viz. the writings of St. John generally (even the Gospel), the Gospel of St. Matthew, the two other Gospels, and the Pastoral Epistles; so that the church had to vindicate the direct or indirect apostolic origin and authority even of these.

§ 5.

But after the fourth century, when the N. T. Scriptures in their present form were received almost unanimously by the whole Church, and when the Church had to contend but little, if at all, with heretical parties who rejected certain portions, the stimulus was lost which obliged the Church to maintain a living consciousness of the grounds whereon the adoption into the Canon of the several books rested. People contented themselves, without inquiry, with the traditional belief; at the most, the opinions of some of the earlier Fathers, *e.g.* Jerome and Augustine, were cited and arrayed without further inquiry into the matter, and very seldom were any opinions advanced at variance with the generally received view. Two works, however, may be named among the writings of this period—both belonging to the sixth century—which bear at least partially upon the subject of N. T. Introduction.

(*a.*) *De partibus divinae legis,* by JUNILIUS, an African bishop, about the middle of the sixth century. Book i. of this work treats, among other things, of the manner in which the different books of Holy Scripture are written, of the value attached to them respectively, of their authors, and how they might be known, and of their division and arrangement. In this work Junilius propounds views concerning the authority of several books even of the N. T. differing from the generally received opinion of the Church at the time. *Vid.* History of the Canon, § 252.

(*b.*) *De institutione divinarum scripturarum,* by CASSIODORUS,—a man who, having held high offices of state in Rome, in his later years (when he was about seventy) devoted himself to a monkish life in a cloister in Calabria built by himself (*ob. circ.* 562). Here he composed this work for the instruction of the monks, when he was about ninety years old. A great part of this work (ch. i.-xvi.) is occupied with directions concerning the study of Holy Scripture, and treats of many topics connected with Biblical Introduction. In the preface he speaks of this part of his work as *introductorios libros.* It does not contain any independent and critical investigations:

the author abides by the decisions of earlier orthodox doctors of the Church, especially Jerome and Augustine. Still the work was very generally used in the Western Church as an Introduction to the Bible down to the time of the Reformation.

§ 6.

At the time of the Reformation there awoke in the Church the desire to draw from the purest springs, even from Holy Scripture, the doctrines of the Christian faith—from Holy Scripture in the original tongues—because previously, and for the most part (with but few exceptions) in the West, the Latin version only had been in use. This in turn led to closer investigation as to the origin of the several books and their relation to each other, with regard to their value, and the authority attaching to them. Attention was turned to the various opinions of the early patristic writers concerning the N. T. Canon and its component parts; and this led on to more independent investigation and thought. This was the case in the era of the Reformation with many theologians who remained within the pale of the Catholic Church,—in particular, with ERASMUS of Rotterdam (*ob.* 1536), and another opponent of the Lutheran Reformation, CAJETAN (Thomas de Vio von Gaeta, *ob.* 1534), both of whom distinguished themselves by opinions concerning the authorship and canonical authority of several books of the N. T. differing from the traditional views. It was also the case with the great leaders of the Reformation themselves, with CALVIN, and above all with LUTHER, who did not hesitate to pronounce judgment concerning some of the N. T. books differing from the prevailing and traditional opinion, with a freedom which nothing but his firm and manly faith in Holy Scripture and Christian truth could have given him. The books concerning which these and other theologians, Catholic as well as Protestant, objected, or at least expressed doubts, were the Epistle to the Hebrews, the Revelation, the Epistles of James and Jude, and 2d Peter.

Still there was not yet a thorough historical and critical investigation of the entire N. T. Canon and of its several parts. But the opinions put forth by the theologians named concerning the books specified had no abiding influence; nor did the spirit of independent investigation thus manifested find much approval or imitation either in the Catholic or in the Evangelical Church. The N. T. Canon was confirmed and ratified by the Council of Trent in the same form in which it had been received in the Church since the fifth century. Protestants also inclined to the opinion that the Canon should be maintained in this its integrity, and they feared to give expression to any doubt regarding it; all the more because, in opposition to the Catholic Church, they regarded Holy Scripture as the only sure and pure spring whence the doctrines of the Christian faith can be drawn. The works on Introduction, therefore, in the sixteenth century, and during the first half of the seventeenth, abide by traditional views regarding the origin of the books of Holy Scripture.

Belonging to the sixteenth century, the works of two Catholic theologians may here be named, both of which relate to the Old and New Testaments.

(*a.*) That by the Dominican SANTES PAGINUS (born at Lucca, *ob.* 1541), entitled *Isagoge ad sacras literas*, Lucca 1536, and other ed. He recommends the study of Scripture in the original, treats in the N. T. of the relation between the Greek text and the Latin versions, and lays down exegetical rules for the exposition of Holy Scripture.

(*b.*) That by another Italian Dominican, SIXTUS SENENSIS (of Sienna, *ob.* 1569), *Bibliotheca sancta ex præcipuis catholicæ ecclesiæ auctoribus collecta*, Venice 1566, fol., and often republished—last at Naples 1742. In contrast with the method hitherto adopted by the Catholic Church, the author draws a distinction between canonical books of the first and of the second rank; but he rejects all doubt as to the authenticity of the several books, or as to the genuineness of certain passages of Scripture, appealing to the authority of the (Catholic) Church in proof of the unimpugned integrity of the traditional text, and strongly advocating the Vulgate in preference to the more modern Protestant translations. Nevertheless the book, which is rich in literary lore, met with much approval even among Protestants.

During the seventeenth century, in the Protestant Church, the two following works on Scripture Introduction appeared: (*a*) that by the Lutheran theologian MICHAEL WALTHER (General Superintendent of East Friesland), *Officina Biblica*, Leipzic 1636 (last ed. 1703); and (*b*) that by JOH. HEIN. HEIDEGGER, a theologian of the Reformed Church, Professor of Theology at Zurich (*ob*. 1698), *Enchiridion biblicum*, Zurich 1681 (5th ed. Jena 1723). Both these works treat of the O. and N. T., and were much in use for a long time, being very serviceable, though they contain no independent critical inquiries as to the origin and history of the books of Holy Scripture. A much greater freedom and independence of opinion concerning the origin of certain books is to be found at this period among Socinian and Arminian theologians. Among the latter we may specially name HUGO GROTIUS (of the Netherlands, *ob*. 1645).

§ 7.

But, as distinctively making an epoch in Biblical Introduction—indeed, as the father and founder of this study—we must give precedence to the French Catholic theologian RICHARD SIMON (*ob*. 1712), who also treated both of the O. T. and of the N. T., but in two separate works. Being already known as the author of several works, chiefly upon dogmatic subjects and archæology, he published in 1678 at Paris an Introduction to the O. T. entitled *Histoire critique du Vieux Testament*,—a work which excited great attention and caused much controversy: it was soon proscribed in France, but in Holland it was several times reprinted. He afterward published the following works upon N. T. Introduction :—

(*a*.) *Histoire critique du texte du N. T., où l'on établit la Vérité des Actes sur lesquels la Religion Chrétienne est fondée,* Rotterdam 1689, 4to.[1] The object of the work seems to be

[1] Ch. i.–iv. treat of the authenticity of the N. T. books generally, and of spurious books; ch. v.–xix. of the several N. T. books in order;

rather to vindicate the historical traditions of the Catholic Church concerning the origin of the N. T. books, than to advance any new or individual views on the subject; nevertheless, by the learned array of different theories already advanced in ancient and more modern times, it gave a decided impulse to further investigation. He polemically argues against Protestant theologians, who, rejecting Catholic tradition, maintained the exclusive authority of Holy Scripture, because he advocates a lax theory of inspiration in opposition to the strict doctrine held generally in the Protestant Church of that period, and because he grants that the text of the N. T. books may in process of time have been liable to corruptions and alterations, like the works of other ancient and classical writers. Among the other works of Simon, the following may be named:—

(*b.*) *Histoire critique des versions du N. T., où l'on fait connoître quel a été l'usage de la lecture des Livres Sacrés dans les principales Eglises du monde*, Rotterdam 1690, 4to. Here he examines not only the old versions as critical witch. xx.-xxii., answers to objections against the N. T. books, advanced by Jews and other opponents of the Christian religion; ch. xxiii.-xxv. on the inspiration of the N. T.; ch. xxvi.-xxviii. on the style of the N. T. and N. T. Greek; ch. xxix.-xxxiii. (end) on the Greek manuscripts of the N. T. The treatment of these various subjects is by no means as uniform as one might expect in a full introduction to a critical history of the N. T. The chapters (v.-xix.) especially which deal with the separate books contain no thorough investigations whatever concerning the origin of these writings. The author contents himself with citing and discussing the contradictory statements and opinions of the Fathers and of the heretics of the first few centuries, and those of more modern theologians of various creeds. He advances no judgments of his own, for fear perhaps of giving offence by the statement of opinions contrary to generally received views; and on subjects about which there had not already been much controversy, his observations are brief and incomplete, *e.g.* in inquiries concerning the Pauline epistles, the chronology and occasion of them, etc. He deals more at length with the discussion of particular passages which were topics of controversy in ancient or more modern times, *e.g.* 1 John v. 7. But even here he does not avow his own opinions if they are not in harmony with the views sanctioned by the Catholic Church, except indeed where he finds precedents for his views in the Catholic Church itself.

nesses for the N. T. text, as is usual in N. T. Introductions since, but also the more modern translations; and (as the title indicates) he uses these as witnesses to prove how widely the study of the N. T. had spread in various nations. This is a very learned and still highly valuable book; it betrays, however, the Catholic theologian by the very preponderating judgment in favour of the Vulgate in comparison of later Protestant translations, especially the Lutheran.

(c.) *Nouvelles observations sur le texte et les versions du N. T.*, Paris 1695, 4to, containing supplements to the two other works.[1]

(d.) *Histoire critique des principaux commentateurs du N. T. depuis le commencement du Christianisme jusques à nôtre tems*, Rotterdam 1693, 4to. This work is esteemed the best of Simon's writings, of permanent and universally recognised value; it indicates vast learning and extensive acquaintance with the commentaries on the N. T. from the earliest time downwards, with an acute and thorough judgment, prompted and expressed with moderation, though not always doing justice to Protestant interpreters.

I may here name two other works of French theologians which may be regarded as Biblical Introductions treating of the O. and N. T. together,—I mean those of DU PIN and CALMET: (a) LOUIS ELLIES DU PIN (member of the Sorbonne, and Prof. of Philosophy at Paris, *ob.* 1719), *Dissertation préliminaire ou Prolégomènes sur la Bible;* it first appeared as a supplement and first volume of his work *Nouvelle bibliothèque des auteurs ecclesiastiques* (Paris 1686),

---

[1] A German translation both of the *History of the Text* and of the *Versions of the N. T.* was published by a minister at Quedlinburg, HEINR. MATTH. AUG. CRAMER, entitled *Richard Simon's Kritische Schriften über das N. T.*, with preface and notes by J. S. SEMLER, Halle 1776-80, 3 vols. 8vo,—the first containing the history of the text, and the two others that of the versions. The supplementary matter contained in the *Nouvelles observations* (which is a scarce book) is inserted in the proper place; and thus with Semler's notes, and many other additions, this German translation is a better work than the original. [A translation in English of the *History of the Text*, also of the *History of the Versions*, was published in London in the years 1689-90.—TR.]

and afterwards as a distinct work, Paris 1699, 2 vols. 4to (vol. i. on the O. T., vol. ii. on the N. T.). The author gives a fair summary of what had been done in Biblical Introduction down to his time, with a tolerable candour of judgment. R. SIMON, in a work published long after his death, criticised Du Pin severely: the book is entitled, *Critique de la Biblioth. des auteurs ecclesiast. et des Prolegomènes de la Bible publiez par M. du Pin*, etc., Paris 1730, 4 vols. 8vo. [DUPIN's History of the Canon, and Writers of the O. and N. T., was published in English in 1700.—TR.] (*b*) AUGUSTIN CALMET (a Benedictine of the Congregation of St. Maurus, abbot of Senones in Lothringen, *ob*. 1757), *Dissertations, qui peuvent servir de prolegomènes de l'écriture sainte*, which he had prefixed to his commentaries on the several books, collected and published separately, Avignon 1715, 5 vols. 8vo; much enlarged, Paris 1720, 3 vols. 4to; in Latin by MANSI, Lucca 1729, fol.; in German, with notes by J. L. MOSHEIM, 2d ed. Bremen 1744, 6 vols. 8vo. [An English edition of this work was published by Parker at Oxford, 1726.—TR.] These Prolegomena contain investigations concerning the origin of the several books of Holy Scripture, together with historical and geographical inquiries: they are not very profound, but still are very useful.

§ 8.

In Germany, towards the end of the sixteenth and the beginning of the seventeenth century, several works on N. T. Introduction appeared, which, though valuable, contain little to advance our knowledge on this subject.[1]

---

[1] Among these we may name (*a*) that by JOH. HEINR. MAI (Prof. of Greek and Oriental Languages at Giessen, *ob*. 1732), *Examen historiæ criticæ N. T. a Richardo Simone vulgatæ*, Giessen 1694, 4to; ed. 3, 1708, 4to. It is a running criticism upon Simon's work, which the author endeavours to answer, yet shows but little fairness of judgment. The work, however, was much esteemed in its time. (*b*) JOH. GEORG PRITIUS (principal minister at Frankfort-on-the-Maine, *ob*. 1732), *Introductio in lectionem N. T., in qua, quæ ad rem criticam, historiam, chronologiam, geographiam, varias antiquitates tam sacras quam profanas*

Far more valuable materials for a critical history of the N. T. were furnished in the valuable *Prolegomena* which the English theologian Dr. JOHN MILL prefixed to his critical edition of the N. T. (Oxford 1707, fol.), and which were published separately (with many notes) by DAN. SALTHEN, Konigsberg 1733, 4to. These *Prolegomena* consist of two parts: the first gives a history of the collection, and treats of the authorship of the several books, together with the writings of the apostolic Fathers, and the various apocryphal books of the N. T.; and the second, which is far more comprehensive, endeavours to trace the history of the N. T. text through successive centuries. In the first part the author is very conservative, maintains the views generally received in the Church as to the origin of the several books, and vindicates them against objectors. This, indeed, was generally considered the appropriate task of critical works on the N. T., because the absolute correctness of those views was presupposed. As to the text of the N. T., moreover, the tendency in the German Protestant Church was to take for granted the perfect integrity of the received text as presented in the German editions. But in this department the second part of MILL'S prolegomenon, and the N. T. text following, would convince any unbiassed reader that such a presupposition is unjustifiable; that in the course of time the text of the N. T. books, like the text of other ancient writings, had been subject to many corruptions at the hands of transcribers; and that these

pertinent, breviter et perspicue exponuntur, Leipsic 1704, 12mo. No new opinions are advanced in this book; but it is a useful and much prized manual, giving much information in a small compass upon the subjects named in the title. It has been often republished, and especially with many additions by CARL GOTTLOB HOFMANN (Prof. at Wittenberg), Leips. 1737, 8vo, 1764. (*c*) JUSTUS WESSEL RUMP or RUMPÆUS (first tutor at the Gymnasium at Dortmund), *Commentatio critica ad libros N. T. in genere*, with a preface by Carpzov, Leips. 1730, 4to; ed. 2, 1757. The author treats of the subjects pertaining to N. T. Introduction in general, intending afterwards to publish a special introduction to the several books; but death prevented him. This volume contains, not indeed new investigations, but a diligent collection and careful arrangement of those already made, with additions of much that is interesting and but little known.

had been retained in the printed editions, so that an effort must be made to purify the text. Soon after Mill, special attention was given to this department—the criticism of the text—in Protestant Germany. The Wurtemburg theologian JOH. ALB. BENGEL (*ob.* 1752), in his critical edition of the N. T. (1734), endeavoured to purify the received text, which he regarded as authentic, by very laborious and scientific investigations. His endeavours in this department were followed up by those of JOH. JA. WETSTEIN (*ob.* 1754), in his critical edition of the N. T. 1751–52. The elaborate Prolegomena to this work[1] contain very valuable materials for the history of the N. T. text, in the description given of Greek manuscripts, old versions, and early editions; and also lay down hermeneutic and critical rules. Neither of them, however, enters upon the consideration of the origin of the several books, or the history of the Canon.

§ 9.

But a few years afterwards, and from the middle of the eighteenth century, Biblical investigations in Protestant Germany entered upon this sphere also in a freer and more independent manner than had been ventured upon or thought allowable for the two previous centuries. This corresponded with the revolution in theology which then took place, with the letting go of a strictly defined dogmatic form, and the growing prevalence of a freer dogmatic spirit. The conception of Inspiration was held in a milder and laxer manner than it had hitherto generally been among German Protestants; and it became less a matter of comment and reproach for men to hold and to avow views concerning the human origin of the Canon, different from those which had prevailed in the Church in some cases from the earliest times. J. D. MICHAELIS and SEMLER stand foremost for their inquiries in this direction as it regards the N. T. The former wrote a full Introduction to the N. T.; but the labours of the latter in this department are to be found scattered through various works.

[1] Published separately: *Wetstenii Prolegg. in N. T. Notas adjecit, etc.* J. S. SEMLER. Halle 1764.

JOHN DAV. MICHAELIS (tutor at Halle 1739, at Göttingen 1749, *ob.* 1791), *Einleitung in die göttlichen Schriften des Neuen Bundes,* Götting. 1750; 2d ed. 1765; 3d ed. 1777; 4th ed. 1788, 2 vols. 4to.[1] This work found great acceptance in Protestant Churches generally, as well as throughout Germany. In the fourth edition the first part of the work is on *General,* and the second part on *Special* Introduction. The first part begins with an inquiry concerning the genuineness and inspiration of the N. T. Scriptures, and touches (though not in an orderly way) upon most subjects since included in Scripture Introduction; but there is no separate chapter upon the history of the Canon. The chapters, however, upon the ancient versions, and upon the language of the N. T., are very rich and valuable. As to the canonicity of the several books, which with him is one with their inspiration, Michaelis betrays more doubt and hesitation in his later editions than in his first, with reference especially to the Revelation, the Epistle to the Hebrews, the Epistles of James and of Jude, and the Gospels of Mark and Luke. He does not, however, dispute the genuineness of these books. In parts the work is characterized by breadth of view; but cool caution is the prevailing characteristic.

JOHN SOLOMON SEMLER, a contemporary of Michaelis, was Professor of History and Latin Poetry at Altdorf, and afterwards of Theology at Halle (*ob.* 1791). He wrote no distinct work on N. T. Introduction; but he exerted a very powerful influence in this sphere by various treatises, some of which were works edited by him with preface and ad-

---

[1] This work has been translated into several languages—into Dutch, French (by Chenevière, 1822), and English twice,—first upon the issue of the 1st ed.; and a second time when the 4th ed. appeared, by HERBERT MARSH (Prof. at Cambridge, and afterwards Bishop of Peterborough, *ob.* 1839), Cambridge 1793, with many notes, alterations, and additions; but in the *Special* Introduction, upon the first three evangelists only. These additions were subsequently translated into German by E. F. K. Rosenmüller: *H. Marsh's Anmerkungen und Zusätze zu Michaelis Einleitung, etc.,* Gött. 1795; 1803, 2 vols. 4to. This work includes the manuscript annotations of Michaelis himself; and in vol. ii. a dissertation by Marsh upon the origin of the first three Gospels.

ditions, *e.g.* Wetstein's Prolegomena, the German translation of R. Simon's critical works, and *Oeder's* treatise upon the Apocalypse (1769); and others were composed by himself.[1]

§ 10.

The main point upon which Semler insists is the distinction between the N. T. writings or the Canon, and the word of God therein contained; between the local and temporal in Holy Scripture, and the divine and universally applicable, which he takes to be whatever ministers to the moral welfare of mankind. Finding, as he thinks, very little of this latter element in the Apocalypse, he holds that the Apostle John was not its author; but with this exception, he does not enter upon any critical investigations concerning the origin of the N. T. books. But, as was to be expected, the lax view of inspiration and of the Canon which he espoused, tended to arouse freer inquiry into the genuineness and integrity of the human sources of holy writ. From the time of Michaelis and Semler, accordingly, the historical and critical study of the Scriptures, especially of the N. T., has been prosecuted with great zeal and industry by German theologians. Much labour has been devoted to the criticism of the text, because abundant material for this was presented in the accurate comparison of Greek manuscripts and other early testimonies; these were classified and arranged according to their intrinsic worth, in order to purify the text, and to restore it as far as possible to its original form. Among the labourers in this field may be named GRIESBACH, MATTHÆI, LACHMANN, TISCHENDORF, and others. Much labour has also been given to more exact investigations—

---

[1] Among the latter may be named: (*a*) *Apparatus ad liberalem N. T. interpretationem*, Halle 1767; (*b*) *Vorbereitung zur theol. Hermeneutik* (vols. iii. and iv. entitled *Hermen. Vorbereitung*), 4 vols. Halle 1760–69,—the two last vols. containing dissertations upon the Greek text, and manuscripts of the N. T; (*c*) *Abhandlung von freier Untersuchung des Canon*, in 4 parts, Halle 1771–75, containing many essays and elaborate answers to objectors who had taken exception to the early parts.

conducted independently of ecclesiastical views—concerning the origin of the several books. The genuineness of the Apocalypse was closely contested and vindicated; then the relationship subsisting between the three first Gospels, and the bearing of this upon the authorship of each; then the origin and genuineness of St. John's Gospel; also concerning the author of the Epistle to the Hebrews; the chronology of the book of the Acts, and of the epistles of St. Paul; concerning the genuineness of these, especially of 1st Timothy, and of the Pastoral Epistles generally; as to the James and the Jude who wrote the epistles bearing their names; as to the connection between 2d Peter and Jude, and the genuineness of the former; and at length in the present century, the question has been mooted as to the historical character of the historical books of the N. T. generally—the Gospels and the Acts of the Apostles.

The fact cannot be concealed or denied, that in our day these investigations have assumed a most reprehensible character. Not only are the questions mooted, At what time was such and such a book composed? what are the proofs of its integrity and genuineness?—but the N. T. as a whole is called in question. It cannot be denied that the views which some modern critics, especially of the Tübingen school (of which Baur was the head), have zealously endeavoured to promulgate, would, if adopted, utterly undermine the historical basis of our evangelical and Christian belief. It is easy to understand how those whose Christianity is real and heartfelt are thus led to look with suspicion and mistrust upon all critical inquiry in this sphere, and to fall back upon and abide by the old ecclesiastical theories. Yet such a proceeding can be justified only upon the principle of the Roman Catholic Church, according to which all tradition sanctioned by the hierarchy must be received as indisputable authority; a principle which militates against the fundamentals of Protestantism, and which we, as Protestants, cannot assent to. Protestant theology cannot, without belying itself, surrender the right and the duty of submitting ecclesiastical tradition in general—that bearing upon the origin of Holy

Scripture in common with the rest—to a fair, a free, and a scientific examination; nor can it set up any limits to this examination beyond what faithfulness to historical truth and veracity demands. We may look forward to the results of these investigations without fear or anxiety; for the purer and the firmer our faith in Christ and in the truth of Christianity, the less shall we imagine that the sacred documents of our religion have any need to fear free inquiry as to their origin and their history carried on in the spirit of truth. We may confidently cherish the hope that misconceptions in this sphere, as in time past they have been, so in the future will be, adjusted and removed by more thorough investigation; and that what now perhaps seems to us threatening will by closer examination cease to be so, either because it will find its refutation, or because it will appear that this or that which hitherto we had regarded as an essential adjunct of our Christian faith, is after all only something non-essential. The mistakes which criticism has made can be rectified only by criticism; a healthy and honest criticism must be brought to bear upon false criticism and its manipulations; and this can only be accomplished when we are actuated in our inquiries by the spirit of truth, when we set up no notions in a reactionary spirit which have still to be proved and justified, and when we do not hesitate to allow that opponents are right even in points differing from received views, provided an unbiassed and thorough investigation teaches us that they are really right.

§ 11.

In reviewing the wider literature of N. T. Introduction, we shall notice first what we find in the Protestant Churches of Germany after Michaelis and Semler. Towards the end of the eighteenth and the beginning of the nineteenth century, Introductions to the N. T. were published by HAENLEIN, SCHMIDT, and EICHHORN.

HEINR. KARL ALEX. HAENLEIN (Prof. of Theol. at Erlangen, and from 1808 Director of the Protestant Consistorium at Munich, *ob.* 1829), *Handbuch der Einleitung in die*

Schriften des N. T., Erlangen 1794-1800; 2d and im proved ed. 1801-9, 3 vols. Vol. iii. contains the Special Introduction. Vols. i. and ii. treat of General Introduction, the authenticity, integrity, and trustworthiness of the N. T. books, but not in a very satisfactory manner. The work generally does not present anything very striking or profound; it is rather an exposition of what had already been said on subjects connected with Biblical Introduction, and is generally of a conservative and apologetic character, though with many concessions; the author simply claiming for traditional views a preponderating probability.

JOHN ERNST CHRISTIAN SCHMIDT (Prof. of Church History at Giessen, *ob.* 1831), *Historisch-kritische Einleitung ins N. T.*, 2 vols. 8vo, 1804-5,—a work marked by pleasing exposition and easy superficiality. It begins with a few short cursory essays on the N. T. books generally, followed by an inquiry concerning their authorship and admission into the Canon, and a history of the text, including an examination of the ancient MSS. as witnesses for the text. Remarks upon the later apocryphal books conclude the work. The investigation is often of a sceptical and unsatisfactory character. He suggests doubts even as to the origin of some books which had hitherto been regarded as genuine, *e.g.* of 2d Thessalonians and 1st Timothy, and more decidedly pronounces 2d Peter to be spurious.

EICHHORN's work[1] is very clever, and marked by many acute and sometimes brilliant combinations, but for the most part it will not stand proof. He has expended much pains-

[1] John Gottfr. Eichhorn (born 1752, *ob.* 1827 when Prof. at Göttingen, previously at Jena), *Einleitung in das N. T.*, 5 vols. 8vo. The first three vols., which appeared 1804-14, contain the Special Introduction (vol. i.) to the ancient Gospels generally, and to our first three canonical Gospels; (vol. ii.) to the Acts and St. John's writings; (vol. iii.) to the other N. T. epistles. Vols. iv. and v., which appeared in 1827, contain the General Introduction, in three chapters not very well divided,—viz. 1. Importance of the N. T., its preservation, compilation, canonicity, genuineness, and language of its books; 2. History of the text and MSS.; 3. Materials for the critical study of the N. T. (including the old versions and printed editions).

taking industry upon the three first Gospels, endeavouring by very ingenious hypotheses concerning their origin to explain their mutual connection, and this, as he thinks, conclusively. He had before treated of this subject in a dissertation (in his *Allgemeinen Biblioth. d. bibl. Litter.* v. [1793], p. 761 sqq.), which he greatly enlarges here. But Eichhorn's method of exposition has many vital blemishes and defects, which have now for long time been acknowledged. Many things which he endeavours to establish are utterly untenable, *e.g.* his attempt to trace the formation of the Canon to Marcion. He does not, however, impugn the authorship of the Gospels as written by those whose names they bear, and he maintains the genuineness of all the writings attributed to St. John; and so with most of the other books, save the Epistle of Jude, 2d Peter, and the three Pastoral Epistles. He was the first who endeavoured to prove that none of the three Pastoral Epistles, though Pauline, were written by St. Paul.

The work of LEONARD BERTHOLDT (Prof. and University Preacher at Erlangen, *ob.* 1822), which treats of the O. and N. T. together, and very awkwardly, is less important and independent. Still it is useful, because particularly on certain topics in the Special Introduction it arrays together and discusses the various views maintained, though with great verbosity: it is more notable (as Baur rightly says) for prolixity than for profundity.[1]

§ 12.

Of far greater importance is the much shorter work of WILH. MART. LEBER. DE WETTE (*ob.* 1849), *Lehrbuch*

[1] *Historisch-kritische Einleitung in sämmtliche kanon. u. apokr. Schriften des A. u. N. T.*, 6 parts, Erlangen 1812-19. The first two parts contain General Introduction, the four others Special, the O. and N. T. books being classified and examined side by side; *i.e.* the Gospels and Acts after the historical books of the O. T., and the Apocalypse after the prophets. The examination of the several books is very unequal, and by no means proportioned to the importance of the subjects discussed; that, for instance, of the Gospel by St. John, and that of the Acts, being quite out of proportion short.

der *historisch-kritischen Einleitung in die kanonischen Bücher des N. T.*, Berlin 1826; 5th ed. 1848; 6th ed. revised by MESSNER and LUENEMANN, 1860.[1] This work is very useful both as a handbook and as a help in lectures; it is marked by precise and comprehensive exposition, and sums up with brevity all the literature of the past and present, bearing upon the subjects treated of. The three last editions contain many additions enhancing the usefulness of the work, especially in the sections upon the old versions, and upon the Gospels. The latest investigations, moreover, down to the date of the edition, are carefully noted and reviewed. The author's inquiry in the first edition was decidedly sceptical; for, actuated by a desire to find out truth, he endeavoured, in investigating the origin of the several books, to go no further and to come to no more conclusive opinion than the data before him seemed to justify. Hence he left many doubts and difficulties attaching to received views concerning the origin of several books unanswered and unsolved. In later editions, however, he has moderated or retracted much that he had before advanced, and more distinctly avows his own positive opinions.

For example, in the case of St. John's Gospel, about the origin of which he had expressed himself very sceptically in his early editions, in the fifth edition he decidedly takes the side of the espousers of its genuineness. The doubts expressed in earlier editions as to the genuineness of 2d Thessalonians he retracts altogether, but not as to the Epistle to the Ephesians, nor as to the Pastoral Epistles, for in his last edition he clings more decidedly than ever to the supposition of their non-Pauline authorship; and among the Catholic Epistles he not only holds the spuriousness of 2d Peter, but the genuineness of 1st Peter also and of James he considers doubtful. In spite of this, however, it is very instructive, and much to be recommended as a handbook.[2]

---

[1] The fifth edition of De Wette was translated into English by the Rev. Fred. Frothingham of Portland, Maine, in 1858.

[2] It forms the second part of his *Lehrbuch der historisch-kritischen Einleitung in die Bibel, A. u. N. T.* In this part we find the Special

§ 13.

The following are the works of other German Protestant theologians treating of N. T. Introduction alone. I name them in the order in which they have appeared:—

1. HEINR. AUG. SCHOTT (of Jena, *ob*. 1835), *Isagoge historico-critica in libros Novi Fœderis sacros*, Jena 1830.[1] This work contains in the notes much valuable material, but for precise and valuable material it is far behind that of De Wette. As to the author's opinions, he endeavours to avoid all extreme views, and to reconcile the established conclusions of modern critics with traditional views, without directly referring to the former. Hence he is often led to propound strange and improbable hypotheses, *e.g.* concerning 2d Peter, the Pastoral Epistles, and the Apocalypse. The book cannot be regarded as an addition to our knowledge.

2. KARL AUG. CREDNER (Prof. at Giessen, *ob*. 1857), *Einleitung in das N. T.*, Halle 1836. A work distinguished, like De Wette's, by a pleasing and comprehensive exposition, based upon a diligent study of the various sources of information, and containing much that is original and acute, but at the same time much that is untenable and erroneous. For example, he takes a very artificial view of the three Pastoral

---

Introduction to the N. T., and inquiries as to the origin of the several books; but the history of the books collectively is given in the first part with the history of the O. T. Canon, and there we must look for the history and literature of N. T. Introduction, and for particulars concerning the names, the parts, the divisions of the N. T. books. It is thus a matter of regret that the second part does not form a complete work on N. T. Introduction, but demands a reference in many points to the first part. The second part is in two divisions, viz. General and Special Introduction,—the latter discussing the origin of the several books, and the former consisting of three sections: (1) the language of the N. T.; (2) the old versions; (3) the criticism of the text, where we find not only a history of the text, but a theory of textual criticism propounded.

[1] The work begins with the Special Introduction, occupying three-fourths of the whole. The General Introduction consists of two parts: 1. *De indole et auctoritate librorum N. Fœderis*; 2. *Historia textus N. F. critica*. With two maps: 1. Map of the missionary tours of the apostles as described in the N. T.; 2. Palestine in the time of Christ.

Epistles, which he considers partly genuine and partly spurious. Since, however, he has pronounced the whole to be spurious. The first two Gospels he holds in their present form not to have been the works of Mark and Luke, though he thinks that certain writings of these men formed the basis of them. He is a warm espouser of the genuineness of St. John's Gospel, but he attributes the Apocalypse and 2d and 3d John to an author other than St. John. He maintains the spuriousness of 2d Peter.[1]

3. CH. GOTTHOLD NEUDECKER (of Gotha), *Lehrbuch d. historisch-kritischen Einleitung in das N. T. mit Belegen aus den Quellenschriften und Citaten aus d. älteren und neuen Litteratur*, Leips. 1840. The author deals with Special Introduction only. He adopts the latest critical investigations, but he lacks a truly scientific spirit, and consequently Biblical knowledge is not advanced. He also lacks comprehensiveness of exposition; the text is inconveniently overladen with long notes.

4. ED. REUSS, *Die Geschichte der heiligen Schr. N. T.*, Halle 1842; second and enlarged edition, 1853; 4th ed. 1864.[2]

[1] The work is comprehensively planned as a history of the N. T., and divided into six parts: 1. History of N. T. Introduction; 2. History of the Origin of the N. T. Writings; 3. History of the Canon; 4. History of the Circulation of the N. T., or its Translations (not only the ancient ones); 5. History of the Text, (*a*) written, (*b*) printed; 6. History of Interpretation. Vol. i. (and the rest has not appeared) treats of parts 1 and 2. The same author has since published *Beiträge zur Einleitung in die biblischen Schriften*, 2 vols., Halle 1832, 1838. Vol. i.—*Die Evangelien der Petriner oder Judenchristen*—contains much valuable matter; but the views advocated as to the use in the early Church of several apocryphal Gospels, especially the so-called Petrine Gospel, are utterly false and mistaken. Vol. ii.—*Das alttestamentliche Urevangelium*—treats of the quotations from the O. T. in Matthew and in Justin Martyr, and presents laborious and independent investigations, in which, however, the main points are overlooked, and erroneous results arrived at. [We must also name his work entitled *Zur Gesch. d. Kanons*, Halle 1847, with many dissertations intended to prepare the way for the Introduction. In place of this, G. VOLCKMAR (Prof. at Zurich) has edited and published CREDNER's papers, with some additions of his own, under the title of *Gesch. d. N. T. Kanon*, Berlin 1860.]

[2] In five books, after the manner of Credner's work: 1. History of the

The author aims at a full history of the N. T. In book i. he deals with the canonical literature and with the apocryphal and spurious books, together with some of the works of the apostolic Fathers, without drawing any marked line of distinction between these and the canonical books. The second edition is far superior to the first in matter and extent, and the exposition bears more of the character of an investigation in contrast with the first edition, which only gave the results of investigation; but the work has lost its theological and critical character, for it is sceptical rather than positive and theistic. The author often speaks concerning the weightiest points—*e.g.* the genuineness of St. John's Gospel—in a very vacillating manner; still it is a work that should be known in the present state of Biblical inquiry.

5. HEINR. ERNST FERDINAND GUERICKE. After several *Beiträge* on N. T. Introduction,[1] he published a complete work, entitled *Historisch-kritische Einleitung in das N. T.*, Leips. 1843. This work afterwards appeared under the title, *Gesammtgeschichte des N. T. oder N. T. Isagogik*, 1854; but the substance of the work remains unchanged, and the author abides by the criticisms and opinions expressed categorically in his *Beiträge*, espousing and maintaining all traditional views even in reference to 2d Peter, which, on the strength of external evidence, he seemed to regard as non-Petrine in his *Beiträge*.

6. "*Einleitung ins N. T.*, from the MSS. of SCHLEIERMACHER and notes of his lectures, with a preface by FRIED. LÜCKE, published by G. WOLDE, private teacher at Göttingen," Berlin 1845 (vol. iii. of Schl.'s Literary Remains, vol. viii. of the first division of his *Sämmt. Werke*). These lectures contain much that is interesting, but many assertions and views that are untenable.[2]

Origin of the N. T. Books; 2. History of the Canon; 3. History of the Text; 4. History of the Translations; 5. History of Exegesis.

[1] (*a*) *Beiträge zur hist.-krit. Einleitung ins N. T.*, being a criticism of De Wette's Handbook, Halle 1828. It bears chiefly on Matthew, Acts, 2d Thessalonians, Ephesians, and the Pastoral Epistles. (*b*) *Fortgesetzte Beiträge*: first part, the Apocalypse, 1831.

[2] I. General Introduction: 1. History of the Canon; 2. Relation between *our* N. T. Text and the Original Text. II. Special Introduc-

§ 14.

Most of the scholars here named, especially De Wette, Guericke, and Reuss, have, in the later editions of their works, controverted the analytic and destructive views espoused by the TÜBINGEN SCHOOL. FERD. CHRIST. v. BAUR, of Tübingen (*ob.* 1860), may be called the father and founder of this school. Having written critically upon separate books of the N. T.—the Pastoral Epistles and the four Gospels—he published two extensive works, collecting (for the most part unaltered) his previous dissertations, and adding new matter. These works were: (*a*) *Paulus, der Apostel Jesu Christi*, Stuttg. 1845, in which he endeavours to demonstrate not only the unhistoric character of the Acts of the Apostles, but the spuriousness also of most of the Pauline Epistles, allowing four of them only to be genuine (Galatians; 1st and 2d Corinthians; Romans, with the exception of the last two chapters). He also regards the Epistle of James as spurious. (*b*) *Kritische Untersuchungen über die kanonischen Evangelien, ihr Verhältniss zu einander, ihren Charakter und Ursprung*, Tüb. 1847, wherein he endeavours in like manner to prove that the Gospels collectively are not to be regarded as historical works, but as writings indicative of the different tendencies of the parties then developing themselves in the early Church—the Petrine and the Pauline parties—and not written by the men whose names they bear, but in the second century, the fourth Gospel being the latest, and evidently designed as the exponent of a dogmatic tendency in the Church. Baur has repeated these views in the essay "*die Einl. in das N. T.*,"

tion, in six chapters: 1. The Pauline Epistles, of which (as in a separate work, 1807) he holds 1st Timothy not genuine, 2d Timothy and Ephesians doubtful; 2. The Four Gospels—he places the three first after the apostolic age, and in their present form not by the men after whom they are named, but he firmly maintains the apostolic authorship of the fourth Gospel, and assigns it a place far above the others; 3. The Acts; 4. The Catholic Epistles, of which he regards 2d Peter as spurious, James probably not genuine, 2d and 3d John as doubtful; 5. The Epistle to the Hebrews; 6. The Apocalypse, which he does not consider to have been the work of the Apostle John. There then follows a third part (III.) concerning the literary history and the sources of the N. T.

Theol. Jahrbücher x. (1851, part iii.)—where he distinctly pronounces his opinion as to the spuriousness of all the Catholic Epistles—and elsewhere.¹

Many of Baur's pupils — ZELLER, HILGENFELD, and others—have espoused views concerning the N. T. books substantially the same as his, for the most part in *Baur u. Zeller's Theol. Jahrb.* (16 vols. 1842-57), and since 1858 in *Hilgenfeld's Zeitschr. f. wissensch. Theol.* They do not indeed coincide with their master in every particular, *e.g.* in holding (as far as I can judge) all the shorter Pauline Epistles to be spurious; and in some other points they differ from him and from each other. But there are certain main points in which they are one with him, and differ from almost all other theologians, even from those of a critical bias,— namely: (*a*) they hold that the authors of all the historical books of the N. T. set forth and strive to forward certain tendencies, and that this is especially true of the fourth Gospel; (*b*) while maintaining that the Apocalypse is the work of the Apostle John, they hold that he wrote neither the Gospel nor the epistles which bear his name, and that the fourth Gospel is one of the latest writings in the New Testament, having been written not before the middle of the second century.² For particulars concerning their views, see the history of the several books. I may here name another work belonging to this school by ALB. SCHWEGLER (of Tübingen, *ob.* 1857): *Das nachapost. Zeitalter in den Hauptmomenten seiner Entwickelung*, 2 vols. Tüb. 1846. This

---

¹ [BAUR's treatise, *Das Christenthum u. die christl. Kirche der drei ersten Jahrhunderte*, Tüb. 1853, 2d ed. 1860, presents a summary of the results of his criticism. See also his *Vorlesungen über neutest. Theologie*, published by FERD. FRIED. BAUR, Leipz. 1864.]

² As a guide to help us in deciding the standing-point of the Tübingen school, an essay (written to recommend their views) entitled *Die Tübinger hist. Schule* will be found in SYBEL's *Hist. Zeitschrift*, 1860, pp. 90-173. See also a pamphlet of Baur's, *Die Tüb. Schule u. ihre Stellung zur Gegenwart*, Tüb. 1859, 2d ed. 1860. See, on the other side, RITSCHL, *Ueber geschichtl. Methode in der Erforschung des Urchristenthums*, in the *Jahrbb. f. Deutsche Theologie*, 1861, pp. 429-459; and in the correspondence between Ritschl and Zeller in SYBEL's *Zeitschr.* 1861, pt. 3, and 1862, pt. 3.

work should be named here, because it deals with the N. T. writings as part of the early Christian literature. The author not only places the N. T. books in order and side by side with other Christian works of the two first centuries, but puts most of them in the post-apostolic age, as far down as the middle of the second century, when he holds the fourth Gospel was written; yet he also attributes the Apocalypse to the Apostle John.

§ 15.

There have not been wanting many able and zealous opponents of the opinions of this school, from its beginning and onwards, even within the pale of the Evangelical Church, some of whom, however, go too far in endeavouring to maintain all the old and received views concerning the origin of the N. T. books. Among these may be named (besides GUERICKE) HEINR. W. J. THIERSCH. Two works of his bear upon this subject, viz.: (*a*) *Versuch zur Herstellung des hist. Standpunkts für d. Kritik d. N. T.*, Erlangen 1845. This work, which is partly directed against Baur, is indeed "a polemic treatise," but is not calculated to establish the historic standing-point in opposition to the Tübingen school. The standing-point which the writer assumes is that of the Church in the fourth century: this he advocates as the only true one, and as that which prevailed from the first century. He advocates his opinions in the spirit of the Roman Catholic rather than in that of the Protestant Church, and he sometimes ventures to adopt the most unnatural and forced explanations of the phenomena of these early times, and the opinions of ecclesiastical writers concerning them. (*b*) *Die Kirche im apost. Zeitalter u. die Entstehung der N. T. Schriften*, Frankf. and Erlangen 1852. This treatise is more moderate in tone, and the views put forth are modified in comparison of the former work, but it is of essentially the same character: it lacks an unbiassed spirit of investigation, and the author's views are for the most part unnatural, and quite improbable.

I conclude this review of modern works on N. T. Introduction in the German Protestant Church with the mention of a small treatise of my own, *Beiträge zur Einleitung und Auslegung der heiligen Schrift.*, first vol. *Beiträge zur Evangelien-Kritik*, Berlin 1846, in which the genuineness of St. John's Gospel is vindicated in opposition to Baur. I would also name as a useful manual a work by JOHN KIRCHHOFER (of Schaffhausen), *Quellensammlung zur Geschichte des N. T. Kanons bis auf Hieronymus*, Zurich 1844. Considering the material here collected, this is a very useful book, though Biblical criticism may not be much advanced by it.

§ 16.

A few Roman Catholic theologians have taken part in the movements of German theology and in the sphere of N. T. Introduction during the past half century; but their works, as far as they are worthy of notice, relate only to the questions of General Introduction. We may name in particular HUG, also FEILMOSER, SCHOLZ, MAIER, REITHMAYR.

a. JOH. LEONH. HUG (Prof. at Freiburg, *ob.* 1846, aged eighty-one). *Einl. in die Schriften des N. T.*, Tüb. 1808, 4th ed. 1847. The first part contains *General Introduction*, and presents learned and acute investigations, especially in the sections on the history of the text, and the old versions, where his labours may be designated excellent. The section on the age and genuineness of the N. T. contains many acute and clever remarks upon the internal character of the N. T. writings, and the historical circumstances and relations presupposed in them; also the testimonies of heretics in the first century, which had been but little noticed before, all the stress having been laid upon the sayings of orthodox theologians. The second part, on *Special Introduction*, contains much that is distinctive, acute, and worthy of notice. But the author does not write here with so much freedom and impartiality: in considering the authorship of the several books, he seems fettered by the received views of his Church, and endeavours to vindicate these views very learnedly and acutely. The work, written in a pleasant style, with a vein of wit and humour running through it, has had a wide circulation even among Protestant theologians. It was, when in the 2d ed., translated into English by D. G. WAIT, London 1827, and by *D. Fosdick, jun., New York. It was translated into French by CELLERIER Fils, *Essai d'une introduction critique au N. T.*, 1823.

 b. ANDR. BENED. FEILMOSER (Prof. at Innspruck, afterwards at Tübingen, *ob.* 1831), *Einl. in die Bücher des N. T.*, Innspr. 1810; 2d ed. Tüb. 1830, greatly enlarged and altered, though the character of the work remains the same. The General part is short, and follows the Special Introduction, wherein the author diligently makes use of the labours of others, even of Protestant theologians, with much acuteness and discernment, and (for a Catholic) with much candid impartiality.

 c. J. M. AUGUSTIN SCHOLZ (Prof. at Bonn, *ob.* 1852), *Einl. in die H. SS. des A. u. N. T.* The first part (Cologne 1845) is on General Introduction—both Testaments together; the fourth part, which was to contain the Special Introduction to the N. T., has not appeared. Among the nine sections of Part 1 the most important is the eighth, *Beschaffenheit des Textes*, which treats of the MSS. and versions.

 d. ADALB. MAIER (of Freiburg), *Einl. in die Schriften des N. T.*, Freib. 1852. I. Special Introduction; II. General Introduction: 1. History of the Canon; 2. History of the Text.

 e. F. X. REITHMAYR, *Einl. in die Kanonischen Bücher des N. T.*, Regensb. 1852.

 [*f.* The latest work by a Catholic theologian is that of GABRIEL JOA. B. GÜNTHER (Prof. of Theol. in Prague), *Introductio in sacros N. T. libros historico-critica et apologetica*, 1863.]

§ 17.

 New Testament Introduction has of late been undertaken in England according to the German method. This has been done especially by Dr. SAMUEL DAVIDSON (who was Prof. at the Independent College, Manchester) in an able manner from a scientific point of view, *An Introduction to the*

New Testament, 3 vols. 1848–51. The author gives attention to the investigations of German theologians generally down to the latest that have appeared, and manifests much acuteness and thoroughness. But the work which has been most generally and widely used in England since 1820 is HORNE's Introduction.

THOMAS HARTWELL HORNE (*ob.* 1862), *An Introduction to the Critical Study and Knowledge of the Holy Scriptures*, London 1818, 3 vols. This work treats not only of the O. and N. T. together, but of exegetical and other auxiliary sciences, Biblical geography, antiquities, and hermeneutics. It has passed through several editions, and the last (the 10th ed. 1856) is in four large and closely printed octavos. The venerable author, in order to bring the work in its completeness up to the present standard of knowledge, has called to his aid two other scholars who are well acquainted with the German literature of the subject, viz. (*a*) DAVIDSON, the writer of the second volume, which contains a Special Introduction to the O. T.; and (*b*) SAM. PRIDEAUX TREGELLES (of Plymouth), the editor of the fourth volume, which treats of the N. T., and which he has made a new and independent work. The first part is a very thorough and valuable introduction to textual criticism, based upon the author's own investigations: we wish this part were translated into German. The work in this new edition has justly won a scientific reputation; but it has lost its unity, because the different editors are of different tendencies in their theological views concerning Holy Scripture — Horne himself and Tregelles holding stricter views than Davidson. Many views and opinions of the latter have been strongly objected to by English theologians, and by his fellow-editors, who have parted company with him; and the second volume has been entrusted for revision to another English scholar — Dr. Davidson's revision being now an independent work. See my review of it in the *Theol. Stud. u. Krit.* 1858, Parts 2 and 3.

J. H. SCHOLTEN (Prof. at Leyden), *Historisch-kritische Einleitung in die Schriften des N. T.* (for use in academic lectures), 1853; 2d ed. Leyden (Leips. by Weigel), 1856.

B. DIVISIONS AND ORDER OF BOOKS IN THE N. T. AND THE NAME.

§ 18.

The collection of writings to which our attention is to be directed contains twenty-seven different books, some of which are EVANGELIC, presenting to us Christ Himself—His life, His works, His teaching, from His birth to His death, His resurrection and His ascension; and others are books wherein the apostles and others of our Lord's first disciples are set forth in their labours during the first few years after Christ's ascension. The writings of this second class were designated by the early Church APOSTOLIC (τὰ ἀποστολικά or οἱ ἀπόστολοι), in distinction from the "evangelic" writings. See § 243.

Of the evangelic writings the N. T. contains four, the four GOSPELS, called after Matthew, Mark, Luke, John. These always have stood at the beginning of the collection, and usually in the order in which we have named them.[1]

The APOSTOLIC writings, in the sense above explained, are *twenty-three* in number:—

1. *One* Historical Book, giving an account of the acts and sufferings of some of the apostles, and of other Christian teachers, from the time of Christ's ascension to St. Paul's imprisonment in Rome—the so-called *Acts of the Apostles*

---

[1] In a few manuscripts only of the old Vulgate (Vercell., Veron., Corbijensis, Brix., Palat., Monac.), and in a codex Græco-Latinus (Cantabrig.), and in the manuscript of the Gothic version, John immediately follows Matthew, and then the two others,—thus placing the two written by apostles first. Mark comes after Luke, and is therefore placed last. [The following order also occurs in one MS. and several Latin versions: Matthew, John, Mark, Luke. Origen and the Syriac MS. edited by CURETON, 1858, give another order, viz. Matthew, Mark, John, Luke. *Vid.* CREDNER, *Gesch. d. N. T. Kanon*, p. 93, and VOLKMAR, *ib.* p. 393, where the Conc. Eph., Cyrill. Al., Theodoret, and the Apostolic Constitutions are erroneously appealed to as witnesses for the order—Matthew, John, Mark, Luke. In the two last Mark is at the end, in the two first it is not named.—B.]

(πράξεις τῶν ἀποστόλων) by St. Luke, a continuation or supplement to his Gospel.

2. *Twenty-one* Epistles, viz. :

a. Thirteen by the Apostle PAUL; and of these, (α) nine addressed to Christian Churches—one to the Romans, two to the Corinthians, one each to the Galatians, Ephesians, Philippians, Colossians, and two to the Thessalonians; (β) four to individuals, viz. two to Timothy, and one each to Titus and Philemon. The four Epistles named first (Romans, 1st and 2d Corinthians, Galatians) are sometimes called the *larger*, and the rest the *smaller* Pauline Epistles; the three Epistles to Timothy and Titus, being addressed to the companions of the apostle, with directions to them how as pastors they are to feed the Christian fellowship, are called the *Pastoral Epistles*.

b. An anonymous epistle with the superscription TO THE HEBREWS, which has for the most part been reckoned among the Pauline Epistles.

c. Seven so-called *Catholic* or *General Epistles* by other specially named disciples of our Lord,—one by JAMES, two under the name of PETER, three by JOHN, and one by JUDE.

3. One Prophetic Book—the *Apocalypse* or *Revelation of John*.

The apostolic books occur in the order in which we have named them, in the Vulgate, in most editions of the Greek Testament, and in many Greek MSS. In these last, however, we find many differences. (*a*) The Acts is sometimes put after the Pauline Epistles, and sometimes after the General Epistles. (*b*) The General Epistles occur in the oldest and in most Greek MSS. containing the whole N. T. before the Pauline Epistles, *i.e.* between the Acts and the Pauline Epistles; and thus they are placed in the editions of Lachmann and Tischendorf. (*c*) The Epistle to the Hebrews is placed in some of the oldest Greek MSS. after 2d Thessalonians and before 1st Timothy—between the epistles addressed to Churches and those addressed to individuals. In Luther's translation, and most editions of it, the Epistle to the Hebrews is quite separated from the Pauline Epistles, and the Epistles of James and Jude from the other General Epistles; 1st and 2d Peter, and 1st, 2d, and 3d John immediately follow Philemon; then come Hebrews, James, Jude, with the Revelation. The reason of Luther's deviation from the usual arrangement we shall see in the History of the Canon.

The usual name for the entire collection which contains these several writings is THE NEW TESTAMENT, *Novum Testamentum*, ἡ καινὴ διαθήκη. The two parts of which it consisted were called in the early Church τὰ εὐαγγελικά and τὰ ἀποστολικά, or τὸ εὐαγγέλιον and οἱ ἀπόστολοι. Both these parts were already united in the beginning of the third century, and (in distinction from the Holy Scriptures of the Old Testament, which contained the history of the old covenant) were together called *Novum Testamentum* in the Latin Church.[1] Διαθήκη in the Greek Bible answers to בְּרִית, in the sense of a covenant between God and men, presented by God for man's acceptance. As διαθήκη in Greek usually means Testament, the Vulgate renders it by *testamentum* both in the books translated from the LXX. and in the N. T. In the Latin Church, accordingly, this word *testamentum* came to mean a mutual covenant between God and men. *Testamentum* was the name usually given in the Latin Church to the Holy Scriptures of both covenants, just as in the Greek Church they were called ἡ παλαιὰ καὶ ἡ καινὴ διαθήκη [2] as an abbreviation of αἱ γραφαὶ τῆς παλαιᾶς καὶ τῆς καινῆς διαθήκης (Origen, *de Princip.* iv. 1). Not until later was *Fœdus* (*vetus et novum*) now and again used in the same sense, nor was it ever widely used. *Testamentum* is the name historically established, which is therefore to be retained.

[1] See TERTULLIAN, *adv. Praxeam*, xv. 20; *adv. Marc.* iv. 1; *duos deos dividens* (Marcion) *alterum alterius* INSTRUMENTI, *vel quod magis usui est dicere*, TESTAMENTI.

[2] Καινὴ διαθήκη (בְּרִית חֲדָשָׁה), the covenant mediated by the Redeemer, is named in Jer. xxxi. 31. The term *instrumentum* for *testamentum* occurs in Rufinus, *expos. symb. apost.*, "novum et vetus instrumentum;" also in TERTULLIAN, *adv. Marc.* iv. 1, and even in AUGUSTINE, *de civ. Dei*, xx. 4, side by side with *testamentum*. Vid. BLEEK'S *Einl. ins A. T.* 31.

C. CONCERNING THE RISE OF CHRISTIAN LITERATURE IN GENERAL.

§ 19.

The men who are named as the writers of the N. T. books, either expressly in the books themselves, or in their superscriptions, and according to Church tradition, are all of them disciples of Christ, either directly (and thus St. Paul must be viewed) or indirectly, having received their knowledge in turn from other of our Lord's disciples, as in the case of Mark and Luke. None of these writings were attributed to Christ Himself as author. And yet the question has at different times been mooted, why Jesus Himself did not leave behind Him any written works. As all that lays claim to the name of Christian must be referred to Christ as the "author and finisher of our faith," it would seem as if much certainty and confirmation would have been given to the foundations of our faith had He Himself left behind Him a summary of His doctrine for all future generations, and as if by this means untold controversies might have been avoided. But had this been done, Christ could hardly have been what He was, and what we esteem Him to be. We might naturally expect that a lawgiver such as Moses, who had to enjoin upon the people committed to his charge obedience to a law made up of precepts ramifying into many particulars of duty, would be careful to define these by committing them to writing; and so with any worldly wise leader who sought to establish his own philosophical system. But this we could not expect in Christ. He came into the world not to establish a new law, like that of Moses, composed of a mass of complicated and for the most part external observances, nor to bring into vogue a new system of doctrine, but to save mankind,—to secure for them justification in the sight of God, and full redemption,—to renew in them a new and right spirit, the spirit of penitence and humility, of holiness and love. This certainly implied and required the doctrine of the Lord, but a different kind of doctrine from that given in a mass of legally defined enactments, or in a strictly defined system of doctrinal formularies. But all this required not the doctrine of the Lord only, but His entire manifestation, His incarnation, His holy life, His death, His resurrection and ascension. As we could hardly think (to name a merely human instance) that the great character and influence of a Socrates could have been increased by his having committed his doctrine himself to writing, still less can we believe this of Christ. It would be a very distorted picture of Him were we to fancy Him artificially committing to paper the subject-matter of His teaching, or writing down the substance of His discourses for the sake of preserving them, instead of propounding them orally in living conversation according as the occasion required.

It cannot be denied that Christ might, had He so pleased, have committed to writing, or allowed to be written on some special occasion, or to meet some particular need, what might serve as a means of instruction or admonition, of warning or comfort, to some one who was absent, and that this might have been preserved to us. But it is certain nothing of the kind has come down to us. There is indeed a short so-called "Epistle of Christ" to a king Abgarus of Edessa, professing to be a reply to a letter of Abgarus to Him.[1] Both letters, in Greek, occur in EUSEBIUS, *H. E.* i. 13,—a translation (according to him) from a Syriac original preserved in the archives of Odessa. It has long been perceived that these letters are apocryphal, and regarded as spurious in the Syrian Church; and it is a matter of question whether the narrative,

---

[1] The story is as follows:—Abgarus, who is sick and can obtain relief from no physician, writes to Jesus. He had heard of Christ's marvellous acts of healing, and infers that He must be either God or God's Son; he therefore asks Jesus to come to him, and free him from his sufferings, because (as he had heard) Jesus was oppressed with the lying in wait of the Jews. Jesus, in His reply, praises Abgarus because he had believed in Him without having seen Him, but that He cannot come, seeing that He must among the Jews accomplish all for which He was sent; but after His ascension He will send one of His disciples to the king, who shall free him from his sufferings.

though repeated by subsequent writers, has any real and historical basis whatever. *Vid.* the passages from ancient writers quoted by GRABE, *Spicileg. Patrum*, i. p. 1 sqq.; FABRICIUS, *Codex apocr. N. T.*, i. p. 316 sqq.

At a later period there were other writings in circulation bearing the name of Christ, but they have since been lost, and they must have borne on the very face of them the impress of spuriousness. They seem to have been put in circulation by certain heretical sects, and never to have been recognised by the Church. AUGUSTINE speaks against them in the *De consensu evangelistarum*, i. 9, 10, from which it would appear that they treated partly of magic, and were in the form of letters by Christ to the Apostles Peter and Paul, and could not therefore claim to have been written by Christ during His life on earth. (*Vid.* FABRICIUS, as before, p. 303 sqq.)

We may therefore regard it as certain that we possess no epistles or other writings by Christ during His sojourn on earth, and that in the first century of the Christian era none such existed; for had they then existed, they would have been handed down to us. Pretty early, however, there seems to have been among Christ's disciples, after His ascension, some activity in writing and authorship. Not, indeed, that they immediately prepared (either individually or collectively) a full and detailed exposition of Christian faith and morals, or with the deliberate purpose of providing a compendium of Christian doctrine, and an authoritative standard of Christian conduct for all future time; but when they wrote, it was with a definite purpose in view, just as when they taught orally, to give an exposition, when they were at a distance from those whom they wished to influence, and whom they had not the opportunity of teaching by word of mouth. When we examine the books preserved to us in the N. T., we find that they consist of two classes,—the *historical* or narrative series, and the *epistolary* series, to which last the Apocalypse may be added, because it is composed in the form of a letter to the Churches of Asia Minor. To one or other of these classes all those writings belonged (those which have not come down to us as well as those which have) which were composed in the Christian Church for the use of its members in the early years after Christ's ascension. The first of these two classes of writings was probably composed before the latter, though the historical books which have come down to us do not for the most part belong to an earlier age than the epistles.

§ 20.

Gospels describing the life and works of the Redeemer were undoubtedly the earliest historical writings in the Christian Church. We cannot tell whether anything in the way of history was written of Him during His life: the probability is there was not. Immediately upon His ascension, accounts of Him were circulated far and wide by His disciples by word of mouth. "They ceased not to preach and to teach Jesus Christ." Afterwards, when the several offices in the Church came to be more clearly defined, one of these offices was distinguished by the name EVANGELIST, εὐαγγελιστής (Eph. iv. 11; Acts xxi. 8). Those believers probably were so named whose province it was as itinerants to preach Jesus as Messiah and Saviour, and to do this by narrating the facts of His life and works, and by repeating His discourses. These evangelists would, some of them, be immediate disciples of Christ, who, though not among the inner circle of apostles, were followers of our Lord for a longer or shorter time during His earthly sojourn, and had seen His works and heard His teaching. Others of them doubtless received their information concerning Him from eye-witnesses and hearers of our Lord. Their preaching did not consist in giving a full and consecutive account of Christ's life in all its particulars, but in relating the more remarkable events and discourses of Jesus,—those best known to them, and which they considered best suited, as occasion required, to awaken and confirm the faith of men in Jesus as the Christ, the Son of God; and thus they would not call special attention to the chronological order of particulars.

The first evangelistic writings were probably of the same

character. It may be taken for granted that these began to be made immediately after Christ's ascension, though only as accounts of certain portions of His life and ministry, or as collections of His discourses and sayings, made some of them for a special purpose and on a special occasion, and others without this. Some of them, moreover, would be written by eye- and ear-witnesses of the events and discourses related, and some of them by others who committed to writing the testimony of eye-witnesses. Some, no doubt, would be written by those who filled the office of evangelist as above described, and some by those who had heard the gospel from their lips. The composition of connected and consecutive histories of our Lord's life and ministry was not attempted probably until the middle of the first century. We learn from Luke i. 1–4, that when this evangelist wrote, there were several of these connected evangelistic writings. He speaks of many (πολλοί) who already "had taken in hand to set forth in order (ἀνατάξασθαι) a history of those things which are most surely believed among us." From the manner in which he speaks of them, it would appear that these earlier Gospels (so far as Luke knew them) were not written by apostles or immediate disciples, but by other believers who had received their accounts from immediate disciples. And it is very probable on other grounds, as we shall hereafter see, that the first attempt to compose in writing a full and connected account of our Saviour's public life was not made by an apostle, but by some disciple who availed himself of the oral narratives of the apostles and first disciples, and of the smaller narratives (already drawn up) of Christ's discourses, and of particular portions of gospel history, and endeavoured to arrange these into an historically connected whole. The first attempt of this kind would soon be followed by others. The writer would be influenced thereto by special needs or wishes, either of the Church collectively or of individuals; and this last was the case with St. Luke, who wrote his Gospel in the first instance for a certain Theophilus. Remembering the great interest attaching to such records, they would soon spread beyond the range for which they were primarily intended. Still we can understand how, when the more complete Gospels appeared in the Church, the first writings of this kind, being imperfect and fragmentary, would be less read, and would gradually disappear, even though among them there might have been one or another written by an immediate disciple and follower of our Lord. When once the gospel history began to be written, and a new need arose, one of these first disciples might be induced (by the presence of other imperfect Gospels giving prominence to a few only of the more obvious facts of our Lord's life) to undertake a consecutive history of the Redeemer's life and work, and to give prominence to other facts which had in those other writings been overlooked.

Somewhat later, after the first gospel histories had appeared, accounts would probably be written of the acts and lives of the apostles and first disciples, and of the history of the Church generally after our Lord's ascension. As the gospel indeed spread rapidly in various countries, such accounts would at once be written—accounts of the journeys and labours of the missionaries, composed by themselves or their companions in travel, and intended in the first instance perhaps for the mother Church, by whom they had been sent, or from whom they had gone forth; and communications would be sent from one Church to another concerning their external position and their internal state and experience,— communications generally from the newly formed Church to the mother Church, which had laboured for its formation. These accounts and communications would soon multiply so as to call for a fuller and more connected history of the progress of the kingdom of God since the ascension of our Lord,—concerning the establishment, the growth, and the general life of the Churches in various places. Thus it was that the author of the Acts of the Apostles felt himself called upon, by the desire and needs of the same Theophilus for whom he had written the Gospel, to give a full and consecutive account of the progress of Christian history. We know not whether any similar histories of the apostles and early Churches preceded this; but judging from the form in which the work is written, it is very probable that the author of the book of the Acts, in writing his treatise, made use of previous accounts of certain events and discourses.

As to the *second* class of N. T. writings—the EPISTLES—the rapid spread of the Christian Church, and the multiplication of particular fellowships in different places, must have afforded abundant cause for correspondence, (*a*) between individual teachers and members, (*b*) between Churches and individual believers who were connected with them, but absent, and (*c*) between Churches of different countries. In Acts xv. 23-29 a letter is preserved which the mother Church in Jerusalem—" the apostles, elders, and brethren "—sent to the Churches in Syria and Cilicia, with reference to the freedom of Gentile Christians from the observances of the Jewish law. And in Acts xviii. 27 we are told that when Apollos was about to pass into Achaia, the Christians at Ephesus wrote a letter of recommendation for him to the brethren there.

The epistles, however, which form separate books in the N. T., are all of them the letters of individuals, of Christian teachers, either to particular persons, or to Christian Churches in particular places or scattered over a wide district. Most of them are written by the Apostle Paul. From this apostle it is that we might beforehand expect a wide-spread correspondence, more than from any other of the recognised Christian teachers of that age. He it was who (with his companions) laboured more abundantly than they all, to carry the gospel beyond the borders of Judaism, and to found Churches in various lands. He naturally kept up a close intimacy with the Churches which he had founded, and felt, moreover, a lively interest in those who had received the gospel first, not from himself, but from his friends and fellow-helpers. And we can easily understand how his generous heart would find abundant occasion, for the sake of travelling brethren, or in the varying circumstances of these Churches, to speak with them from a distance, and would embrace any opportunity that offered, either through his companions or by a private hand, to send them words of love, of instruction and admonition, of warning and of comfort, appropriate to their present need. The epistles of St. Paul in the New Testament, written to various Churches, are of this kind, and those addressed to particular persons are of the same character.

Influenced apparently by the example of St. Paul, other apostles and leading teachers in the early Churches wrote epistles to the believers; as, for instance, the author of the Epistle to the Hebrews, and the writers of the Catholic Epistles. These last are not addressed to any local Church or circumscribed circle of readers, as are the epistles of St. Paul, and hence they are of a more general and less epistolary character.

D. CONCERNING THE LANGUAGE OF THE N. T. BOOKS.

§ 21.

The books of the N. T., as we possess them, are written in Greek. It has, however, been a matter of dispute whether this was their original language, or whether any of them are translations from other languages. Concerning two of them, several Catholic scholars have endeavoured to prove that they were originally written in Latin: viz. BARONIUS (Cardinal, *ob.* 1607) and others concerning the Gospel of Mark; and BELLARMINE (*ob.* 1621), SALMERO (Jesuit in the sixteenth century), and A LAPIDE (*ob.* 1637), concerning the Epistle to the Romans. These opinions are now generally regarded as groundless.[1]

[1] This seems to be indicated in a note appended to St. Mark's Gospel in the Peschito: "This is the end of the holy Gospel preached by Mark, who preached in Roman at Rome,"—a remark which probably has reference to a written version of the Gospel; and it occurs at the end of some Greek MSS. also. As to the Epistle to the Romans, it is said in a note at the end of some Syrian MSS. that it was written in Roman,' רומאית, *i.e.* in Latin. But these notes and additions, though widespread, are not to be relied upon: they are the work of later copyists or readers, and were based upon the opinion that writings addressed to Roman Christians must have been written in Latin. It was generally

The Jesuit *Joh. Harduin* of Paris (*ob.* 1729), in his commentary on the N. T. (Haag 1741, fol.), goes still further; for he endeavours to prove that most of the N. T. books were originally written in Latin, at least that they were issued by their authors in this language. Such a supposition, suggested only for the purpose of elevating the Vulgate, as authenticated by the Catholic Church, to a higher place, needs only to be mentioned to be dismissed.[1]

§ 22.

But the question may with greater plausibility be raised, whether the N. T. writings were not, some of them at least, composed in the language which was the vernacular of the Palestinian Jews in the time of Christ and His apostles. This language is called in the N. T. "the Hebrew tongue" ('Εβραϊστί, John v. 2, Rev. ix. 11, xvi. 16; or τῇ 'Εβραΐδι διαλέκτῳ, Acts xxi. 40, xxii. 2, xxvi. 14). We must not

supposed—and, as we shall hereafter see, not wholly without reason—that St. Mark's Gospel was written for Romans. It must at least be granted that these books *might* first have been written in Latin. But they might just as probably have been written in Greek, because Greek was well known and in use, as in other countries, so also in Rome at the time: it was understood by all educated persons, and was spoken by many. (*Vid.* WETSTEIN, *N. T.* ii. p. 18; CREDNER, *Einl.* i. 2, p. 383.) The authors of the Christian Scriptures might therefore reasonably take it for granted that their works in Greek could be read and understood by all Romans. The Epistle of IGNATIUS to the Romans is written in Greek, and DIONYSIUS OF CORINTH wrote his work *adversus Hæreses* in this language. It is evident, however, from the character of the Greek itself in the two N. T. books named, that they are not translations from a Latin original, and there is no hint whatever of their existence during the first century in Latin. In the case of St. Mark's Gospel, the existence of such an original at a later period was asserted, and it was supposed that certain fragments in the libraries of Prague and Venice were in Mark's own handwriting. But this opinion is now generally acknowledged untenable, because the fragments there are only parts of an old Latin translation of Mark. (*Vid.* JOS. DOBROWSKY, *Fragmentum Pragense Ev. S. Marci, vulgo autographi,* Prag 1778.)

[1] *Vid.,* in answer to HARDUIN, S. J. BAUMGARTEN, *Vindiciæ textus Græci N. T. contra Hard.,* Halle 1742, 4to; MICHAELIS, *Einl.* i. p. 107 sqq.

understand by this, as many in past times were wont to do, the old Hebrew, but, as is now generally allowed, the *Aramæan*, or *Syro-Chaldaic*, which is akin to the old Hebrew, and belongs to the same stem, but is a distinct dialect. The Jews had partially adopted this dialect when they were in exile among the Aramæan nations; and after their return to Palestine it gradually became the prevailing one, both in conversation and in writing. Regarding two books of the N. T., it was generally thought that they had been originally written in Hebrew (*i.e.* in Aramæan), and were translated from that language into Greek; I mean the Gospel of St. Matthew and the Epistle to the Hebrews. As to the Gospel of St. Matthew, there is an opinion traceable as far back as the early part of the second century, that the apostle wrote in Hebrew, and that his Gospel was subsequently translated into Greek by another hand. And as to the Epistle to the Hebrews, we find the opinion as early as the end of the second century (CLEMENS ALEX. in EUSEBIUS, *H. E.* vi. 14), that it was written in the language of the Palestinian Jews, and was translated into Greek by some one else than the author. (*Vid.* Bleek on the Hebrews, i. 6-8.)

In more modern times some scholars have suggested the same supposition in reference to other books of the N. T., especially the Gospel of St. John.[1] BOLTEN (Pastor in Altona, *ob.* 1807), in his translation of the N. T. Scriptures (eight parts, 1795-1806), held the same opinion regarding the Apocalypse, and together with BERTHOLDT believed that the N. T. epistles were all of them originally written in Aramæan. The notion in this sweeping application of it is decidedly false, and it is probable in reference to none of the N. T. books. I would here briefly remark on this point, that in support of the opinion, reference is made (*a*) to the Greek of the N. T. as being very Hebraistic and Aramæan in its character, as if this were best explained by the supposition that it is a translation from a Hebrew or Aramæan

---

[1] See CL. F. SALMASIUS (Prof. at Leyden, *ob.* 1653), *De Hellenistica Commentarius* (1643), p. 258; *Pfannkuche* (Prof. at Giessen, *ob.* 1833), in EICHHORN'S *Allgem. Bibl. d. bibl. Litt.* viii. 367.

original. Some even fancy that they can trace mistakes of the translators in certain passages, arising from their misreading of certain words in the original. (*b*) The supposed want of a Greek education, and of any facility in writing Greek, on the part of the authors. (*c*) The supposed incapacity of those addressed to read or understand Greek. As to this last argument, it is clear that the language known and spoken by the persons addressed must have decided the writers in what language to address them, and must have led them to write in Greek. Aramæan was at the time the prevailing language of Judea, and of the neighbouring provinces northwards towards Syria, and eastwards in Mesopotamia and Babylon. But in the countries wherein Christianity spread, in Asia Minor and Europe, it was little known: most of the Jews even who sojourned in these countries were ignorant of the vernacular of Palestine, and the few who understood it had little or no occasion to use it. Since the reigns of Alexander the Great and his successors, Greek had become more and more common in these countries: even where it was not the vernacular, it was imported by states founded or at least repeopled by Alexander with Greek-speaking people; and in all states of any importance it was at least understood. (See §§ 28, 29.) This was especially the case with the ex-Palestinian Jews. Greek was so common among them, not only in Alexandria and Greece itself, but in other countries, that they usually read the Scriptures in that Greek translation which, originating in Alexandria, was widely circulated among the Jews of the dispersion. Now if we contemplate the N. T. books in reference to their purpose and the persons addressed, as far as this is indicated in their titles or otherwise, we find that, in the case of by far the most of them, there was nothing obliging the writers to adopt Aramæan, but, on the contrary, everything prompting them to use Greek. As to the Pauline Epistles, the Churches addressed were some of them European, and some of them in Asia Minor, where Aramæan was little known even by the Jewish settlers, while to the Gentiles it was utterly unknown; and though these Pauline Churches were composed partly of

Jewish and partly of Gentile Christians, the Gentile element prevailed. The individuals to whom the epistles of St. Paul are addressed were not Palestinians, nor even Jews by birth: 1st Peter is expressly addressed to Christians of Asia Minor, the Epistle of James to readers beyond Palestine, Jude to readers whose residence is unnamed; and so with 1st John, though it is generally recognised that this epistle was addressed to Christians in Asia Minor, and chiefly to Gentile believers. The Apocalypse is expressly (ch. ii. iii.) addressed to the Churches of Asia Minor. St. John's Gospel was written in Asia Minor, and in the first instance for the use of Christians there; St. Mark, as we have already said, was probably intended for Romans; and St. Luke's Gospel and the Acts are addressed to Theophilus, of whom (though we know little) it is universally acknowledged that he did not belong to a Jewish country, nor to the Jewish nation.

§ 23.

As to those two writings, the *Gospel of St. Matthew* and the *Epistle to the Hebrews* (for which even in early times a Hebrew original was supposed), considering their primary design, it would appear more appropriate had they been originally written in Aramæan, for both writings seem to have been primarily intended for believing Jews in Palestine. Yet this inference is not a necessary one. In the time of Alexander the Great, Palestine was certainly less under the dominion of Greeks, and more free, than many neighbouring countries; but afterwards, under the alternate rule of the Ptolemies and Seleucidæ, many towns in Palestine and in the neighbouring districts which previously belonged to Jews had been occupied by Hellenistic residents, and Greek had become the prevailing language. Among these towns, Josephus names in the west, *Cæsarea*, which was almost wholly occupied by Hellenists (*B. J.* iii. 9, 1), and *Gaza* (*Ant.* xvii. 11, 4); in Peræa, *Gadara* and *Hippos* (*Ant.* xvii. 11, 4). The knowledge of Greek must certainly have spread still more among the Jews of Palestine from the time when their land came under the dominion of the Romans (B.C. 63), either as in parts wholly subject to them, or as indirectly under their influence. Greek was certainly the language in which the Jews conversed or corresponded with their conquerors, and which the Roman governors used when they sat as judges, or otherwise held intercourse with the people. It was doubtless the language in which Jesus spoke before Pilate. Another circumstance which would certainly tend to promote the use of Greek among the Jews, was the fact that many foreign Jews, who with their families had been wont to speak Greek, sojourned in Palestine often for a long time, and in some cases were settled there. This was especially the case in Jerusalem, and in other large business towns in the land. These settlers retained the use of Greek in general intercourse, and this would certainly tend to make the home-born Jews acquainted with it. In Acts vi. 9 mention is made of a synagogue of the Libertines, Cyrenians and Alexandrians, *i.e.* Jews who had obtained their freedom from Cyrene and Alexandria, and who had settled in Jerusalem : Greek would be certainly the language used in this synagogue, and the LXX. version of the O. T. Scriptures would be the Bible read and expounded. There were doubtless in Jerusalem, and in the large towns of Judea and Galilee, other such synagogues for Grecian Jews. These Greek-speaking Jews were called Ἑλληνισταί, *Grecians* (Acts vi. 1, ix. 29), in distinction from the Hebrews, who still adhered to the use of the Aramæan, and cherished a strong preference for it, though Greek was not unknown by them. In Acts xxi. 40, for example, we are told that St. Paul, having obtained permission to address the multitude in Jerusalem, beckoned with the hand in order to obtain silence, and that the silence and attention were increased when they heard him speaking to them in the Hebrew tongue. The common people, who were for the most part home-born Jews, felt more kindly affected towards the apostle when, instead of speaking to them in Greek, he addressed them in Hebrew; and this implies that they must for the most part have understood both languages: they expected to be addressed as usual in Greek, and were pleasingly surprised to hear the Hebrew.[1]

The use of the Septuagint also among the Palestinian Jews of this period must not be overlooked. The old Hebrew had for many years been a dead language among them; and the knowledge of it, so far as was needed for the reading of Scripture, was confined almost exclusively to the learned. In the time of Christ there were probably no written translations of the sacred books in Aramæan; certainly there were none of any repute or wide circulation. The Palestinian Jews therefore, who, though unlearned, wished to study Holy Scripture, would have recourse to the Septuagint, and would read this version of it; and the consequence would be, that they would adopt and have most confidence in the Greek when conversing upon religious subjects; and in books upon such subjects, Greek would be the language used even by Palestinian Jews.

What is thus true of Palestinian Jews generally, is specially applicable to the Jewish Christians of that age. The narrative in Acts vi. shows that there were many Greek-speaking Jews among the first Christians in Jerusalem; and they probably were as numerous in proportion in other Jewish towns where the gospel gained a footing. Among the believing Jews who recognised in Jesus the Messiah and Saviour promised of God in the O. T., there prevailed a much closer searching of the Scriptures of the O. T. than among the bulk of the Jewish people; and we may take it for granted that most of them, the Hebrews among them as well as the Grecians, used as a rule the Greek translation, while comparatively few resorted to the Hebrew original; and thus even among the Hebrews, Greek would be fully understood, especially in connection with religious subjects.

Under these circumstances, a Christian teacher might choose the Greek language for a treatise intended specially for Palestinian Jews or Jewish Christians, without having any reason to fear that it would on this account fail of its

---

[1] Concerning the spread of Greek as a spoken language in Palestine, see Hug, ii. § 10, ed. 3, pp. 30–56.

immediate object. The writer would be fully warranted in believing, when he wrote in Greek, that he would be understood not only by the Hellenists, but by all Scripture readers in Palestine, including those whose vernacular was still the Aramæan. Nevertheless we must allow that, in writing exclusively for Palestinian Jews, an author might choose Aramæan, and that if he did write in this language he would be understood even by members of Hellenistic families; because we can hardly doubt but that, in intercourse with Hebrew-speaking Jews among whom they lived, they would acquire some knowledge of Aramæan. Hence, in reference to the Gospel of Matthew and the Epistle to the Hebrews, we must examine more closely the question as to whether the Greek in which they have come down to us was the language in which they were originally written. But as to those books which were written exclusively or mainly for readers beyond the borders of Palestine and other Aramæan-speaking districts, we cannot suppose that their authors would ever have published them in Aramæan; for had they done so, they could not expect the majority of their readers to understand them.

§ 24.

Some scholars have supposed that the Apostle Paul thought out his epistles in Aramæan, and employed an interpreter to translate them into Greek, and that thus they were circulated among the various Churches; and so in reference to the rest of the N. T. authors. But, from what we have already said, there is evidently no ground for the supposition that the Apostle Paul and the other N. T. writers had not a sufficient knowledge of Greek to think out and compose their epistles or other writings in this language, whether they wrote them themselves or only dictated them. Least of all is there any ground for this idea in the case of St. Paul; for he was born at Tarsus in Asia Minor, one of the main centres of Greek literature and culture, and his writings and speeches contain indications of his acquaintance with the Greek poets. How could he have made the missionary tours which he did in

Asia Minor and Greece, if he had not been familiar with Greek? How could he have spoken at the Areopagus at Athens (Acts xvii.)? As to Peter and John, and Mark also, we know that they lived and laboured for a considerable time in Greek-speaking cities and countries, so that we cannot doubt that they too knew Greek well. From what we have said as to the spread of Greek in Palestine, it is moreover evident that James, and Jude, and Matthew must have had sufficient knowledge of Greek not only to speak it, but also (though not perhaps perfectly) to write it. As to Luke, he was not even a Jew by birth (Col. iv. 14; cf. v. 11); and we have no reason to suppose that he belonged to any other Aramæan-speaking nation.

§ 25.

The Greek of the N. T. books itself bears witness against this notion of an Aramæan original. The Hebrew and Aramæan colouring of N. T. Greek is quite natural if we suppose the several authors wrote in Greek, but is not accounted for by the supposition that they are the work of a Greek translator. There are, indeed, some parts of the historical books which must obviously be referred to an Aramæan original,—as, for example, Christ's discourses and those of His apostles in Judea and Galilee. As to these, we may reasonably presume that they were originally spoken in Aramæan, and perhaps that they were primarily written down in this language; and in reference to two addresses in the early part of the book of the Acts, we have clear traces that this was the case. But it by no means follows that the authors of the N. T. books wrote originally in Aramæan. As to the Acts, this idea has never been entertained. Nor is there any ground for it in reference to the Gospels. We shall find that even as to Matthew there are indications which almost forbid the notion that it is a translation from an Aramæan original. We shall also find that in reference to the Hebrews there are internal grounds which amply prove that it was primarily composed in Greek; and the same is true of the other epistles and the Apocalypse. As to these books, the idea that they were written in Hebrew was not entertained in the early Church.

E. THE CHARACTER OF NEW TESTAMENT GREEK AS COMPARED WITH CLASSICAL GREEK, AND GREEK LITERATURE GENERALLY.

§ 26.

During the latter half of the seventeenth century and the first half of the eighteenth, a controversy was carried on with more or less vigour between the PURISTS on the one side and the HEBRAISTS or HELLENISTS on the other: the first maintaining that the Greek of the N. T. writers is pure, and answers to the classical, free from solecisms and barbarisms of every kind, and especially from Hebraisms; and the latter asserting that these things are to be attributed to the Greek of the N. T. writers to a very considerable extent.[1] The Purists supported their views mainly upon dogmatic grounds, holding that divinely inspired Scripture must be perfect in its language, and composed in the purest and most classic style: they considered the notion of "barbarisms" in the N. T. as offensive, and even as blasphemy against the Holy Ghost. They endeavoured to prove by examples from the classics that words and phrases in the N. T. which

[1] Among the Purists may be named SEB. PFOCHEN (of Amsterdam, born at Friedberg in the Wetterau: *Diatribe de linguæ Græcæ N. T. puritate*, Amst. 1629, 2d ed. 1633, 12mo), JAC. GROSSE (Pastor at Hamburg, in various works, Hamburg 1640–42), and others. Some of the later Purists were CHR. SIGISM. GEORGI (Prof. of Theology at Wittenberg: *Vindiciarum N. T. ab Ebraismis libri tres*, Frankfort and Leipsic 1732; *Hierocriticus N. T. sive de stylo N. T. libri tres*, Wittenberg 1733; and *Hierocritici N. Fœderis Pars II., sive controversiarum de latinismis N. T. libri tres*, Wittenberg and Leipsic 1733, 4to), JOH. CONR. SCHWARZ (*Commentarii crit. et philolog. linguæ Gr. Novi Fœderis divini*, Leipsic 1736, 4to), and EL. PALAIRET (1752). Among the Hebraists of this period I may mention JOH. MUSÆUS (Prof. of Theology at Jena, ob. 1681, in two treatises published in 1641–42), DAN. HEINSIUS (Prof. of History at Leyden, *Exercitatio de lingua Hellenistica et Hellenistis*, 1643, 8vo), THOMAS GATAKER (Fellow of Trin. Coll. Cambridge, *De*

were regarded as Hebraisms were perfectly good and pure Greek. By the pains they took, and by the industry of others roused by their example, though not to advance so strict a view of N. T. Greek, very clever philological compilations of passages were made which are still very useful, and are almost essential to a right judgment of the question; for they prove that much usually regarded as Hebraistic may be explained according to the usage of pure Greek. But besides the fact that much in the N. T. was passed by and left by them unexplained, they were often content with finding the same expressions in the Greek classics which occur in the N. T., without considering whether they were used in the same connection or in the same sense. They referred for the most part to later Greek writers, *e.g.* to the Byzantine historians, whose Greek the language of the N. T. had already influenced. They confined themselves to the consideration of lexical particulars, of single words and phrases, and took little or no notice of the general tone and colour of the language, or (with the exception of GEORGI) of its grammatical aspect. The Hebraists, on the other hand, also pushed their views too far. Yet there were some scholars who took a middle course, and who maintained on the whole correct views of the relation subsisting between the Greek and Hebraistic elements.[1]

But it was too much the fashion with writers on this side,

novi Instrum. stylo dissertatio, 1648), JOH. VORST (Librarian at Berlin, *De Hebraismis N. T. commentarius*, Amst. 1658-65).

Most of the earlier treatises upon this subject, down to the end of the seventeenth century, will be found collected (*a*) by JAC. RHENFERD (born at Mühlheim a. d. Ruhr, Prof. of Oriental Languages at Franecker), *Dissertationum philol. theol. de stylo N. T. syntagma*, Leeuwarden 1702, 4to; and (*b*) by VAN DEN HONERT (Prof. of Theol. at Leyden), *Syntagma dissertatt. de stylo N. T. Græco*, Amst. 1703, 4to. For the history of the controversy, see WINER, *Neutest. Grammat.* ed. 6, p. 12 sqq.; PLANCK, *Einl. in die theol. Wissenschaften*, ii. (1795) 43 sqq.; STANGE, *Theol. Symmikta* (1802), 295 sqq.; MORUS, *super hermeneutica N. T. acroases acad.*, ed. EICHSTAEDT, i. (1797) 216 sqq.

[1] Among these, at the outset of the controversy, we may name THEOD. BEZA (in his *N. T.* on Acts x. 46: *Digressio de dono linguarum et apostolico sermone*) and HEINR. STEPHANUS (in the *Præfatio* to his edition

to put down at once as Hebraisms all words and expressions which did not answer to classical usage; whereas, in order to a correct appreciation of the character of N. T. Greek, it is necessary to observe the relation of the Greek then usually spoken and written to what is properly called classical Greek. CLAUDIUS SALMASIUS, indeed, gave some attention to this; but the inquiry was not fully prosecuted until long afterwards, especially by STURZ, H. PLANCK, WINER, and others.[1]

§ 27.

Upon this subject I content myself with offering the following remarks:

1. It is well known that the Greeks, as far back as we possess any records concerning them, were divided into several states, each of which had its own peculiarities of language in the use of certain letters, words, and forms of expression, etc.; so that there were several dialects in Greek, the peculiarities of which were apparent in their literature. A few only of those dialects were fully developed, viz. the

of the N. T. 1576), neither of whom deny Hebraisms in the N. T., but who maintain that these give expression and beauty to the N. T. language. So also J. H. MICHAELIS (*Dissertatio de textu N. T. Græco*, Halle 1707) and ANT. BLACKWALL (*The Sacred Classics Defended and Illustrated*, London 1727, 1731, 2 vols. 8vo; translated into Latin, with notes, by CHRISTOPH. WOLLE, Leipsic 1736, 4to). To these we may add J. H. BÖCLER (Prof. at Strasburg and afterwards at Upsala: *de lingua N. T. originali*, 1642), J. OLEARIUS (of Leipsic: *de stilo N. T. liber*, Coburg 1672, 4to; 1721, 8vo), JOH. LEUSDEN (of Utrecht: *de dialectis N. T. singulatim de ejus Hebraismis*, 1670, 4to; republished by FISCHER, Leipsic 1754, 1792).

[1] SALMASIUS, *De Hellenistica commentarius, controversiam de ling. Hellenistica decidens et plenissime pertractans Originem et Dialectos Græcæ ling.*, 1643. F. W. STURZ (Rector in Grimma, and before Prof. at Gera, ob. 1832), *de dialecto Alexandrina*, Leipsic 1786, 4to; also *de dialecto Macedonica et Alexandrina*, Leipsic 1808. II. PLANCK (at Göttingen, ob. 1831), *de vera natura atque indole orationis Græcæ N. T.*, Göttingen 1810, 4to; reprinted in the *Commentatt. theol.* of ROSENMÜLLER, MAURER, and FULDNER, i. 112 sqq. WINER, *Neutest. Gramm.* 6th ed. pp. 11-38.

Doric, with its kindred dialect the *Æolic;* and the *Ionic*, with its more fully developed branch the *Attic*. But remembering the close connection between these various states, and the wide circulation of the standard works of any one state among them all, we find that the different writers did not each adhere to his own dialect, but wrote in that dialect which was specially appropriated by this or that topic. Thus, through the influence of Homer, the Ionic dialect was usually adopted in epic poetry, and the Doric for lyric poetry. The Attic dialect afterwards became the most general and fashionable in written works generally, when Athens had obtained for herself the leadership of all Greece, and had become the centre of Greek science and literature; so that the youth of Greece, in all its states, were taught it, and became familiar with it in their scientific pursuits. The Attic dialect thus became the most general and universal, at least with prose writers. But they did not adopt this dialect with all its peculiarities: they rejected much that was distinctive of it in its grammatical forms and uses of words, together with much they had been familiar with in their own or other dialects. Besides this blending of the Attic with much that had been found useful in the other dialects, many innovations were made, unknown at least in prose,—modifications in the meanings of words, changes by lengthening or shortening the word-forms, the formation of new words, especially of compounds, the adoption of many forms of expression before unknown except in some of the poets, but which now came to be commonly used in prose. Thus much that had been familiar only to one or two dialects was adopted into the written language. The Greek of these writers, moreover, had since the time of Alexander the Great been much influenced by the Macedonian dialect. The Macedonians were a people akin to the Greeks, whose language was very similar to the Doric dialect, though with many peculiarities of its own. By the subjection of all Greece to the one Macedonian dominion, the various Greek states would of course be more blended than ever in their intercourse and language, and the Macedonian dialect would considerably influence the Greek; much that was peculiar thereto would be adopted gradually into ordinary conversation among the people, and afterwards would find its way into their literature. Hence we find in the later Greek authors, while they adopt the Attic dialect, many variations from the Attic Greek of Thucydides, Xenophon, Plato, Demosthenes, and others. This form of Greek, which we find in the later prose writers from Aristotle downwards, has been called by lexicographers ἡ Ἑλληνική, *i.e.* common Greek, or ἡ κοινή (διάλεκτος), in contrast with the old and pure Attic; and the writers adopting this later Greek are called οἱ Ἕλληνες, οἱ κοινοί, and sometimes οἱ νῦν, οἱ πολλοί.[1]

§ 28.

2. By the conquests of Alexander the Great and their results, Greek was spread far beyond the limits within which it had hitherto been used, even into Egypt and the conquered countries of Asia. Many Greek towns and settlements were founded in these lands by Alexander and his successors; and older cities were rebuilt, re-established, and repeopled with Greeks. Among these may be named Alexandria in Egypt; Seleucia, Ktesiphon, Sittace, Carrhæ, on the Tigris and Euphrates; Gadara, Hippos, and others, in the east of Galilee; Antioch in Syria; and many others. Greek was the court language of Alexander's successors, the Ptolemies and Seleucidæ. Now the Greeks who settled in these cities belonged, like the Greek soldiers in Alexander's army, to various states; and we may therefore conclude that the Greek spoken would not be any one form or dialect in its purity, but a blending of the peculiarities of several dialects,

---

[1] To this class belong THEOPHRASTUS, POLYBIUS, APOLLODORUS, DIONYSIUS OF HALICARNASSUS, DIODORUS SICULUS, ARTEMIDORUS, PLUTARCH, ARRIAN, APPIAN, PAUSANIAS, DIO CASSIUS, HERODIAN, and others. Some later writers among the Sophists and Rhetoricians endeavour to imitate the pure Attic in their works (Ἀττικισταί, Ἀττικίζοντες); *e.g.* DIO CHRYSOSTOMUS, ARISTIDES, LIBANIUS, ÆLIAN, and others, also to some extent LUCIAN and THEMISTIUS; but this being artificial, gives a tone of affectation to their style: it is not the natural form of the language in its historical development at the time.

in which the Macedonian element would be the prevailing one. The Greeks, in these new or newly peopled cities, still pursued the study of Greek literature; they had Greek schools, and Greek was their written as well as spoken language. Above all, ALEXANDRIA became in time the head and centre of Greek literature generally, which was prosecuted there under the Ptolemies with great zeal, even down to the middle of the third century of the Christian era, and afterwards. Here, however, Greek as a written language retained the same character which it had in Greece itself. Its main basis was Attic, but in the modified form already described of the later Greek writers; and it appropriated no small element of the Doric and Macedonian dialects, and many useful popular forms of expression. By the zealous prosecution of literary and grammatical studies, the language here attained a more definite and fixed character than it had at the same time in other places, and influenced in no small degree the language spoken in other centres of population. Hence Greek as a written language, in this its latest form, was spoken of as the *Alexandrine dialect.*

3. In those parts of Asia and Africa which Alexander and his successors conquered, Greek was not only employed as the language of conversation and of writing by the colonists, but it became familiar to the home-born inhabitants who were not Greeks. Greek, however, would not supplant the native and aboriginal language: among the smaller populations, and in country parts, the vernacular would still hold its ground. But in the large commercial towns, which kept up intercourse with Greece or with Greek settlements, the knowledge of Greek would spread, and gradually become universal among the educated. Thus, *e.g.*, in Syria at the close of the fourth century, Greek was the prevailing language in all the large towns; but in the country Syriac still lingered, and has continued ever since. These non-Hellenic peoples became acquainted with Greek at first only by intercourse with the Hellenes, and they knew it only in the Hellenic dialect. But in time the more educated began to study Greek literature generally, and made use of Greek in

writing. And thus it came to pass, that both in speaking and in writing, they gave up the peculiarities of expression and the grammatical forms of their own vernacular, and made use of Greek, according to the extent of their knowledge.

§ 29.

4. And now, as to the JEWS, we have already seen (§ 22) that in the time of Christ and His apostles Aramæan was the ordinary vernacular of Palestine. Still, Greek had for a long time been making way in all but the most retired places, and was understood and spoken by most Jewish residents in Jerusalem, and in the maritime and commercial towns. The Jews of the διασπορά, moreover, earlier than those in Palestine, had become familiar with Greek; and living, as they did, among Greek-speaking people, they adopted it both in conversation and in writing. This was specially the case with many Jews in Alexandria and its neighbourhood, who, as soon as Greek literature began to be cultivated there, seem to have taken part in its pursuit. Most of the writings first published there in Greek were certainly the work of Jews. One of the earliest and most important of these works was the translation of the Book of the Law, which was followed by translations of the other sacred books of the Jewish Canon. The Greek in this translation is undoubtedly the κοινή, as it had been adopted in Alexandria both in speaking and in writing. But, as is generally the case with translations from a foreign language, if the translator does not deal very freely with the original, many of its peculiarities of grammatical construction and manner of expression, modifications of the meanings of words and phrases, are adopted and intertwined; and thus the Greek of the LXX., though in a different degree in different books, contains many Hebraisms. It was almost a necessity that it should be so; because some of the religious representations and conceptions of the O. T. could hardly have been expressed in Greek, if the translator confined himself solely to the Greek words and phrases in common use among the Greeks, and in their ordinary meaning.

This translation was widely circulated among the Jews in other lands; not only among the Jews of the dispersion in Greek-speaking countries, but even in Palestine itself, first by the Hellenistic residents, and gradually by the home-born Hebrews. As the knowledge of the old Hebrew had declined, this translation was made use of by most readers of the sacred books; and many had obtained their knowledge of Scripture in our Lord's time solely from the Septuagint. This was with many the only work in Greek which they read and knew. And hence we see how it was that the Greek of the LXX. influenced so decidedly the style of Jewish works in Greek generally, both in foreign countries and in Palestine, especially when their works dealt with subjects akin to those of the sacred books. Greek works composed by Jews represent just that type of the language which had been adopted in Alexandria, and which in the Septuagint had been more or less tinged with Hebraisms. These works, at the same time, contain provincialisms and phrases peculiar to the several districts in which the writers lived; the Jews having for the most part obtained their first knowledge of Greek not only from the Septuagint, but from the people among whom they dwelt—from intercourse with them rather than by reading. In Palestine, again, and among the Aramæan-speaking Jews, Greek must have been variously modified by the old vernacular of the people, by the adoption into Greek of Hebraistic words, by changes in the meanings of Greek words and expressions, according to the analogy of the Aramæan, and by altered grammatical constructions. And thus we might naturally expect that the style of works in Greek, composed by Palestinian Jews, would be characterized not only by *Hebraisms* borrowed from the Septuagint, and arising from its frequent use, but also by *Aramæisms*, so far as Aramæan differed from the old Hebrew; and this is a point which has in past times been too little considered. But we cannot expect to find traces of this distinctively Aramæan style, save in works composed by Jews whose ordinary vernacular was Aramæan. It could hardly be traced in the works of Alexandrine Jews, or of Jews living

VOL. I. E

in other Greek-speaking lands, because with them Aramæan was not their mother tongue, and many of them did not understand it. For the rest, however, the linguistic character of works composed by Jews would be more or less distinctive and marked, according to the different degrees of general, and especially of Hellenistic, culture in the several writers.

Among those who gained their knowledge of Greek, apart from the Septuagint, by intercourse with the people around them, the influence of the Hebrew would be manifest chiefly in grammatical constructions; and in addition to the Alexandrine type of the Septuagint, the popular language which they had acquired would tinge their works. We should naturally expect to find the style of literary Greek as it had latterly moulded itself into that called κοινή, together with a greater freedom from the influence of Hebraisms and Aramæisms (at least in grammatical forms), among those who had grammatically studied Greek, and had read the Greek authors copiously. Among Palestinian Jews, this was specially the case with Josephus. He had prosecuted the grammatical and literary study of Greek, and had practised the writing of it with great elegance and correctness. He speaks of himself as in this respect an exception to the rest of his countrymen. Among the Alexandrine Jews, however, this culture was common. In Alexandria there was a continual influx of men of various nations and religions. They were thrown more together, and Greeks learned the Jewish religion and the literature of the Israelites quite as much as the Jews learned Greek literature. The Alexandrine Jews had adopted the Greek of books as their language to a greater extent than their countrymen anywhere else, and they could therefore write more purely and fluently; and this we observe in Philo and in the book of Wisdom.

§ 30.

5. In accordance with what has now been remarked, it is clear that the Greek with which the Christian writers belonging to the Jewish nation in the apostolic age were acquainted, and in which they spoke and wrote, must have

been moulded in a similar manner, and with similar variations, according to the writer's place of residence, and the extent of his Greek knowledge; and this we find in the N. T. books. As was to be expected, we find that the Greek (and this is true of all the books) is of that later kind called κοινή, whether as a written or spoken language. Several peculiarities of later Greek are noticeable,—namely, that words and phrases are adopted from various dialects, and many expressions that had not before been generally employed in writing; earlier forms are lengthened or abbreviated; words which had been seldom used, or used only in poetry, had come into general use; new words had been coined, especially as compounds, and the signification of many words had been modified.[1]

Owing to the extended intercourse between men of diffe-

[1] Of the last-named characteristic παρακαλεῖν may be named as an instance. It means generally "to call to;" in Attic Greek, "to call hither" to an assembly, or to the help of gods or men, or "to invite" to an entertainment; but in later Greek (especially in Hellenistic Greek) it means "to exhort," "to comfort" any one who is present, or supposed to be present, either by request or admonition, by comforting or warning; so in the LXX., in the O. T. Apocrypha, in PHILO, and often in the N. T. Again, ὀψώνιον, "that which is purchased," but afterwards, and in the N. T., "pay;" ἀποτάσσεσθαι, "to refuse a thing," renunciare, valedicere (whereas in earlier Greek, ἀποτάσσειν = "to set apart," "to distribute"); ἀνακλίνειν, ἀνακεῖσθαι, and ἀναπίπτειν, with a special reference "to recline at table;" ἐν τρέπεσθαι, c. acc., "to be afraid of anything," or "to be timid before any one."

Of altered words peculiar to later Greek, or more frequently used therein, may be named: βασίλισσα (which occurs in Xenophon, but not usually until later) for βασίλεια; λευχνία, "a lamp," instead of λύχνος; ἐυχύνειν for ἐκχέειν; δεκατοῦν (Alexandrine) for δεκατεύειν; ψεῦσμα, which occurs in PLATO, but did not come into ordinary use till later; ἀροτριᾶν for ἀροῦν, "to plough." Diminutives, to denote the bodily organs: as ὠτίον or ὠτάριον for οὖς; τὰ ῥίνια, "the nostrils," for ἡ ῥίς, and others. Adjectives in ινός: as πρωϊνός for πρώϊος, καθημερινός for καθημέριος. New words formed, especially compounds: as ὁδηγεῖν (already occurring in the Attic tragedians, but not in prose till later); ἀποκεφαλίζειν (DIO CASSIUS); οἰκοδεσπότης; ἀνταποκρίνεσθαι; αἰχμαλωτίζειν, -τίζεσθαι (for which the grammarians would say αἰχμάλωτον ποιεῖν and γίνεσθαι); ἀντίλυτρον (not occurring in Greek authors);

rent countries, several words belonging to other languages are adopted into later Greek,—not only words which were names of things not known before, and for which there was no name in Greek, but other terms likewise, and in cases where there was no such need. After the Romans obtained dominion over the Greeks, many Latin words and Latin forms of expression began to be adopted into Greek, just as before many Egyptian and Persian words were adopted. Examples of these occur in the N. T. There was a controversy in the first half of the eighteenth century concerning the presence of Latin words in the N. T., and carried on between Joh. Erhard Kapp and Siegm. Friedr. Dresig on the one side, and Chr. Siegm. Georgi on the other; the latter denied that there were any such Latin words in the N. T.[1]

ὁμοιάζειν, παρομοιάζειν (first in the N. T.); ἀρχιτελώνης; ἀρχισυνάγωγος; δωδεκάφυλον.

Grammatical forms: Accusative ὑγιῆ (for ὑγίεα, Attic ὑγιᾶ); the accus. plur. τοὺς βασιλεῖς (for βασιλέας). The gen. and dat. of δύο, δύο, δυσί, instead of the dual form δυοῖν. For the third person plural of the perfect, the ending -αν instead of -ασι; as ἔγνωκαν, John xvii. 7; εἴρηκαν, Rev. xix. 3, and often in the LXX. According to the Greek grammarians, these forms were used in Chalcis as well as Alexandria. For the third plur. of the historic past, the ending -οσαν, which in the *Etymologicon Magnum* is called a Bœotian form. It often occurs in the LXX. and in the Byzantines; in the N. T., Rom. iii. 13; in an O. T. quotation, ἐδολιοῦσαν (for ἐδολίουν); according to Lachmann, Tischendorf, Buttmann; also in John xv. 22, 24, εἴχοσαν for εἶχον. The noun ἔλεος is with the Greeks always masculine, 2d decl.—ὁ ἔλεος, but in the LXX. and the N. T. usually τὸ ἔλεος, 3d decl. See Planck; Winer, § 2, p. 21 sqq.; Eichhorn, iv. § 13; Schott, § 123; De Wette, § 6 b, note a; Klausen, *Hermeneutik d. N. T.* (Leips. 1841), p. 339. But the examples given in these works, even in Winer, need still more careful sifting.

[1] The dissertations on both sides will be found in Georgi's *Hierocriticon*, Part ii. Of Persian words in the N. T. may be named, ἀγγαρεύειν, Matt. v. 41, xxvii. 32; γάζα; μάγοι; παράδεισος; and perhaps μεγιστᾶνες. Of Latin words may be named κεντυρίων; κολωνία; λεγεών, ὁ; πραιτώριον; κουστωδία; τίτλος (John xix. 19, in the other Gospels ἐπιγραφή); μάκελλον, 1 Cor. x. 25 (*macellum*, from *mactare*); φραγελλοῦν, *flagellare*; κῆνσος; κοδράντης; σπεκουλάτωρ; σιμικίνθιον. Latin forms adopted: ἐργασίαν δοῦναι, *operam dare*, Luke xii. 58; ἔχε με παρῃτημένον, Luke xiv. 18, = *habe me excusatum*; συμβούλιον λαμβάνειν, *consilium capere* (five times in Matthew); τὸ ἱκανὸν ποιεῖν τινι, Mark xv.

§ 31.

Before proceeding further, I will here briefly enumerate two classes of helps for students in examining the Greek of the N. T. :—

I. The old Greek grammarians and lexicographers (see De Wette, § 9, note). There is much in the home-born grammarians of Greece which helps to explain rarer words and forms, especially those which pertain to the several dialects, and concerning the relation of words of later usage to the older Greek, especially to the Attic. Light is thus thrown upon N. T. Greek. I name therefore those which are most useful in connection with the N. T. Of most value for N. T. Greek is the work of PHRYNICHUS (surnamed *Arabs*, of Bithynia, a Rhetorician and Sophist, about A.D. 180), entitled *Eclogae nominum et verborum Atticorum*, with the additions of its last editor LOBECK (Leipsic 1820). Three Alexandrines must be named belonging to the end of the fourth or the beginning of the fifth century: 1. AMMONIUS, περὶ ὁμοίων καὶ διαφόρων λέξεων, *de affinium vocabulorum differentia*, edited, with a learned commentary, by VALCKENAER (Leyden 1749; again, with additions by SCHÄFER, Leipsic 1822; and with short notes by C. FR. AMMON, Erlangen 1787). 2. HESYCHIUS, the author of a glossary explaining obsolete expressions and provincialisms. There is only one manuscript of it, in Venice; the best edition of it is that by ALBERTI and RUHNKEN, Leyden 1746-66, with corrections and additions by NIC. SCHOW, Leipsic 1792. A new edition of Hesychius has been begun by MORITZ SCHMIDT, of which vols. i.-iii. have appeared, Jena 1857 sqq. The explanations specially referring to the N. T. (*Hesychii glossae sacrae*) have been edited separately by JOH. CHR. GOTTL. ERNESTI, Leipsic 1785. 3. CYRILLUS ALEXANDRINUS, author of a glossary like that of

15, and also in POLYBIUS and APPIAN = *satisfacere alicui*, "to content or please any one." Cf. DE WETTE, § 6 *b* ; MICHAELIS, pp. 173-177.

Hesychius, which was published, with many similar works, at Lyons 1600, fol., Paris 1679, fol. The greater part of it is to be found in CHR. FRID. MATTHÄI, *Glossaria Graeca minora et alia anecdota Graeca*, Moscow 1775, 4to; with a glossary to the Pauline Epistles. MATTHÄI published another glossary on the Epistles of John, according to Moscow MSS., in his *Lectiones Mosquenses* (Leipsic 1779), ii. p. 71 sqq. The following works belong to a much later time, but much may be found in them bearing upon N. T. Greek: 1. PHOTIUS, Patriarch of Constantinople in the ninth century, author of the so-called *Bibliotheca* or μυριο-βίβλον. Here we specially name his *Lexicon* or *Onomasticon*, edited by GOTTF. HERMANN, Leipsic 1808, 4to, and according to another MS., by PORSON, Leipsic 1823, 8vo. 2. The *Etymologicon Magnum*, edited by GAISFORD, Oxford 1848, fol. 3. SUIDAS, probably of the 11-12th century. The best edition used to be that of LUD. KÜSTER, Cambridge 1705, 3 vols. fol.; new editions were issued by BERNHARDY (2 vols., Halle 1853), and by GAISFORD, Oxford 1834, 3 vols. fol. 4. FAVORINUS or VARINUS of Umbria, *ob.* 1537, the author of an elaborate lexicon, compiled from old lexicographers, grammarians, and schoolmen, published at Rome 1523, fol., and at Basle 1538, and at Venice, 1712, fol. The explanations of SUIDAS and FAVORINUS bearing upon the N. T. (*glossae sacrae*) have been collected and edited by ERNESTI, Leipsic 1786, royal 8vo. 5. ZONARAS, a Greek historian of Constantinople in the beginning of the twelfth century. A lexicon of his was edited by J. A. H. TITTMANN, Leipsic 1808; *Zonarae glossae sacrae*, enlarged by FRIEDR. WILH. STURZ, Grimma 1818-20, 4to. I would also mention a *Glossarium Graecum, in N. T. libros, e MSS.* ed. Leyden 1735, which Alberti adopted in his edition of Hesychius. WETSTEIN in his *Novum Testamentum*, and Schleusner in his *Lexicon in N. T.*, have both given much from these Greek lexicographers.

II. As to more modern collections of various Greek authors, in explanation of N. T. Greek, which for the most part advocate the pure character of the N. T. books, they are some of them very clever, and are valuable as helps in studying N. T. Greek. 1. WETSTEIN, in his edition of the N. T. (1751), gives numerous quotations from various Greek writers; and though there is much that is superfluous and badly arranged, there is very valuable material which only requires revision. Before Wetstein's time there were other collections of various authors: two by LAMB. BOS (Prof. of Greek at Franecker), viz. *Observatt. miscell. ad loca quædam N. T.*, Franecker 1707; and *Exercitatt. philologicæ, in quibus Novi Fœderis loca nonnulla ex auctoribus Græcis illustrantur*, Franecker 1700. 2. GE. RAPHELIUS (Pastor and Superintendent at Lüneburg, *ob.* 1740) collected certain passages from Xenophon, Polybius, and Arrian; also from Herodotus; in three treatises, Hamburg 1709-31, which after his death were collected in one work, entitled *Annotatt. in Sacram Scripturam, historicae in V., Philol. in N. T. ex Xen., Pol., Ar. et Her. collectae*, Leyden 1747, 2 vols. 3. JAC. ELSNER (*ob.* 1750), *Observatt. sacrae in N. Fœderis libros, quibus plura illorum Librorum loca ex Auctoribus potissimum Græcis et Antiquitate exponuntur et illustrantur*, 2 vols., Utrecht 1720-28. 4. JO. ALBERTI (Prof. of Theol. at Leyden, *ob.* 1762), *Observatt. philol. in sacros N. Fœderis libros*, Leyden 1725. Soon after Wetstein, several similar collections appeared, namely: (*a*) ELIAS PALAIRET (a French preacher in London, *ob.* 1765), *Observatt. philol. crit. in sacros N. F. libros*, Leyden 1752, and under the title *Spec. exercitatt. philol. crit. in sacros N. T. libros*, London 1755. The author was a Purist, yet his collections contain much that is useful. (*b*) GE. DAV. KYPKE (Prof. of Oriental Languages at Königsberg), *Observatt. sacræ in N. F. libros*, Breslau 1755, 2 vols. This is among the best of these collections. (*c*) Quo-

tations from Diodorus Siculus only, by Csp. Friedr.
Munthe (Rector at Copenhagen, *ob.* 1763), *Observatt.
philol. in sacros N. T. libros ex Diod. Sic. collectæ,* etc.,
Copenhagen 1755. A very valuable collection of the
same kind from Josephus was made by Jo. Tob.
Krebs (preacher at Grimma, *ob.* 1782), *Observatt. in
N. T. e Fl. Josepho,* Leipsic 1755; and before this by
Jo. Bapt. Otte (Archdeacon at Zurich), *Spicil. s.
excerpta ex Fl. Josepho ad N. T. illustrationem,* Leyden
1741. Bretschneider has largely quoted from
Josephus in his *Lexicon in N. T.* Lastly, a very useful collection of passages from Philo by Christoph.
Fried. Lösner (Prof. of Bibl. Philol. at Leipsic, *ob.*
1803), *Observatt. ad N. T. e Philone,* Leipsic 1777,
with a supplement by Ad. Friedr. Kühn; *Spicil. C.
F. Loesneri observationum ad N. T. e Philone,* Pforta
1785. Before this, a very accurate and valuable
collection of passages from Philo in explanation of the
Epistle to the Hebrews had been published by Jo.
Bened. Carpzov (Prof. of Theol. at Helmstädt, *ob.*
1803), *Sacræ exercitatt. in S. Paulli Ep. ad Hebr. ex
Philone,* Helmstädt 1750, 8vo.

§ 32.

Let us now briefly consider the influence of the Hebraic
Aramæan upon the language of the N. T. That it must
influence it, is evident when we remember the nature of the
subjects treated of, and the connection between the N. T.
and the revelation of the Old. It would have been impossible to give expression to all the religious conceptions and
Christian ideas of the N. T. had the writers strictly confined
themselves to the words and phrases in use among the Greeks,
and with the significations usually attached to them. These
Christian ideas were quite unknown to the Greeks, and they
had never formed phrases suitable to give expression to them.
On the other hand, most of these ideas and conceptions already existed in germ in the O. T., and were more or less
familiar to the Jews by means of appropriate designations.

Hence they would be best expressed for Greek-speaking Jews in the words by which they had been rendered in the Septuagint. These expressions would naturally be chosen and spread by those teachers who were of Jewish extraction and education, and would, of course, be adopted generally to denote Christian ideas. Many of these expressions, moreover, had been ordinary Greek words, whose meanings had been made fuller and higher when applied among the Jews to religious subjects, and which retained these meanings when adopted by the Christian Church, or were again modified and further elevated, just as the ideas and conceptions of the O. T. revelation were modified and elevated by Christianity. Hence it frequently came to pass, that when a Greek word in its ordinary signification corresponded with a Hebrew or Aramæan word, the derived and developed meanings attaching to the latter would be transferred to the former, and the Greek word would be used in the higher sense of the Hebrew or Aramæan word, although this meaning had before been unknown to Greek usage.

Among words of this character in the N. T. we may especially name ὁ Χριστός, τὸ πνεῦμα, ὁ λόγος, ὁ διάβολος, βασιλεία τοῦ Θεοῦ and τῶν οὐράνων, υἱὸς τοῦ ἀνθρώπου, ἡ σωτηρία, ἀπώλεια, σωζόμενοι, ἀπολλύμενοι, δικαιοῦσθαι, πίστις, εὐαγγελίζεσθαι, εὐαγγέλιον, ἐκκλησία, οἱ ἅγιοι (קְדֹשִׁים), ἐκλεκτοί, ἐκλογή, καλεῖν, κλητός, χάρις, χάρισμα; κοινός (not only, as among the Greeks, "common," "ordinary," "usual," but also as = חֹל, "profane," "unclean," as contrasted with what was holy, ἅγιος, and hence κοινοῦν, with the signification "to make profane," "to pollute"); κόσμος, as "the world," in contrast with the kingdom of God and the things pertaining thereto; εἴδωλον, "an idol," and its compounds; εἰδωλόθυτον, εἰδωλολάτρης, -λάτρεια, and εἰδωλεῖον, "an idol's temple;" αἰών for "world," like עוֹלָם, αἰών οὗτος and ἐκεῖνος corresponding with the later Jewish forms עוֹלָם הַזֶּה and עוֹ' הַבָּא, which was already common among the Hebrew Jews in the time of Christ and His apostles; so also the plural οἱ αἰῶνες, "the world" (Heb. i. 2, xi. 3; 1 Tim. i. 17), like the rabbinical עוֹלָמִים; τὸ ἔσχατον τῶν ἡμερῶν,

אַחֲרִית הַיָּמִים; ἄγγελος, "angel," like מַלְאָךְ, literally "messenger;" ὀφείλημα, as meaning "the guilt of sin," like the Aramæan חוֹב, because sin in the Bible is felt and regarded as a debt incurred against God: the word does not occur among the Greeks in this sense, nor does the expression ἀφιέναι ὀφειλήματα, Matt. vi. 12, = the Aramæan שְׁבַק (לְ) חוֹבַיָּא, Ps. xxv. 18. To these may be added the terms peculiar to the Christian Church, such as εὐαγγελίστης, ἀπόστολος in the distinctively N. T. sense, ἀποστολή, and others.

Examples similar to those here given, and for the most part extensions and elevations of the meaning of certain Greek words, or a putting new meanings into them as occasion required, occur in all the N. T. books, whether written by Palestinian Jews or by writers living in Greek-speaking countries, and independently of any difference in the general culture of the authors, or in their acquaintance with Greek.

§ 33.

We find this, however, not only where the want of appropriate expressions in ordinary Greek necessitated the remodelling of words and phrases, but also in cases where there was no lack of words in ordinary Greek to express the thought intended. This was, for the most part, owing to the Septuagint. The Seventy often translated the Hebrew literally, and word for word, into Greek: they (*a*) put such Greek words for Hebrew as corresponded therewith literally, and then transferred to the Greek the derived meaning attaching to the Hebrew, though this meaning never belonged to the Greek word in its ordinary use; and (*b*) they translated Hebrew forms of expression verbally into Greek, forming in Greek a construction after the pattern of the Hebrew, which had before been quite unknown. Now, by the frequent reading of the Septuagint, these expressions would become familiar to the Jews, and would be employed by them in conversation and in writing, without their being conscious of anything strange or non-classical in them. This was the case also with many words and phrases of the Palestinian vernacular, the Aramæan: those Jews who spoke it as their mother tongue, when they adopted Greek, would translate these Aramæan phrases literally into Greek, and thus make Greek compounds and constructions quite inconsistent with classical usage, so that Greeks themselves could hardly at first understand them.

We find this to be the case in those N. T. writers who belonged to the Jewish nation, and had been educated among them. We find Hebraic Aramæan words adopted into the Greek, as many Latin words and words of other languages were: thus, ἀμήν; ἀλληλούϊα; ὡσαννά (הוֹשִׁיעָה־נָּא); κορβᾶν, Mark vii. 11, = קָרְבָּן, and with the Aramæan affix κορβανᾶς, Matt. xxvii. 6; σατᾶν, 2 Cor. xii. 7, and with the Aramæan affix σατανᾶς; κόρος and βάτος, with Greek terminations = בַּת, בֹּר; σάτον = סְאָה, Aram. סָאתָא. Again, from the Aramæan ἀββᾶ, אַבָּא; μαμωνᾶς, מָמוֹן, מָמוֹנָא; ῥαββί, ῥαββωνί (Mark x. 51), ῥαββουνί (John xx. 16) = רַבִּי, רַבּוּנִי; ῥακά, רֵיקָא, Matt. v. 22; μαραναθά, 1 Cor. xvi. 22; also μεσσίας = מְשִׁיחָא; πάσχα; σίκερα, שֵׁכָר, Luke i. 15.

Greek words and phrases in the N. T. formed after the pattern of the Hebrew:—

'Ρῆμα = דָּבָר, and used as indefinitely, e.g. Luke i. 65; πάντα τὰ ῥήματα ταῦτα = "all these things," Luke ii. 15; ἴδωμεν τὸ ῥῆμα τοῦτο τὸ γεγονός, i. 37, cf. Gen. xviii. 14.

"Ἄνεμοι, of the four quarters of the heaven, in the N. T. and LXX.; οἱ τέσσαρες ἄνεμοι, like the Hebrew אַרְבַּע רוּחוֹת.

'Εξομολογεῖσθαι, only in later Greek, = confiteri, "to confess:" this is in the Hebrew הוֹדָה. The same Hebrew word means also "to confess to any one," especially to God, praising Him; and this meaning has been transferred to the Greek in the LXX. and N. T.

Τὰ σπλάγχνα = רַחֲמִים, "the inward parts," especially the nobler: the Hebrew word is used to denote the affections whose seat was supposed to be in the nobler viscera—tender love, pietas, and compassion: the LXX. have rendered this by σπλάγχνα, and thus the word occurs in the N. T. to denote sympathy and pity. In classical Greek, τὰ σπλάγχνα is also used to express strong emotion, but it is used of wrath as well as of love, and only by the poets: the use of the word in the N. T. is certainly derived from the Hebrew. In the first three Gospels the verb σπλαγχνίζεσθαι is used in the sense of רָחַם, "to feel tender and pitiful love," "to sympathize;" but this word does not occur in this sense in classical Greek, nor even in the LXX. In 2 Macc. vi. 8 σπλαγχνίζειν is used in the sense of σπλαγχνεύειν, "to consume the entrails of beasts offered in sacrifice." The use of the verb with the signification to sympathize originated in the Christian Church.

Ἀνάθεμα also appears in later Greek with the signification of the Attic ἀνάθημα (both from ἀνατίθημι), of that which is consecrated to God. In the MSS. of the LXX. both forms occur interchangeably, but as used in Scripture generally they are distinct: ἀνάθημα (Luke xxi. 5) denotes offerings consecrated to God, but ἀνάθεμα answers to the Hebrew חֵרֶם, which also denotes what is set apart to God, and consecrated to Him, but in such a manner that it can never be applied to human uses, on account of its total destruction; hence ἀνάθεμα denotes cursing, and is applied to the objects of divine malediction. Hence we have in the LXX. and N. T. the verb ἀναθεματίζειν = הֶחֱרִים, "to curse," "to devote to cursing,"—a verb which does not occur in classical Greek.

Ἐρωτᾶν = שָׁאַל, and hence not only meaning "to ask," but "to beg."

Εὐλογεῖν, not only, as in classical Greek, "to praise any person or thing," "to speak good of it," but also "to bless," like בֵּרֵךְ.

Ὁδός = דֶּרֶךְ, אֹרַח, and, like these Hebrew words, of a course of conduct or action; and so the verb περιπατεῖν = הָלַךְ, הִתְהַלֵּךְ. Σκάνδαλον is a later and Alexandrine form for σκανδάληθρον (a stumbling-block): in the LXX. and N. T. it is used for מִכְשׁוֹל and other words, to denote what serves for seduction in a moral and religious sense, so that a person is entangled, stumbles, or falls—"obstacle," "offence;" and hence in the N. T. the verb σκανδαλίζειν, -ίζεσθαι, which does not occur in the LXX.

CHARACTER OF N. T. GREEK. 77

Νυμφή, "bride," = כַּלָּה; in Hellenistic Greek, as in Hebrew, also used for "daughter-in-law" (Matt. x. 35; Luke xii. 35); and so in the LXX. (Judg. xix. 5) νύμφιος stands for "son-in-law," = חָתָן.

Ἱλαστήριον, Heb. ix. 5, = כַּפֹּרֶת.

Ὁ νόμος = הַתּוֹרָה, of the Jewish law as a whole.

Γλῶσσα, not only, as in classical Greek, for language or dialect, but often, especially in Revelation, of nations of various languages, like לָשׁוֹן, Isa. lxvi. 18, and oftener לְשָׁן in the book of Daniel, whence this use of it is derived.

Γλῶσσαι πυρός, Acts ii. 3, = לְשֹׁנוֹת אֵשׁ, Isa. v. 24.

Πᾶσα σάρξ = כָּל־בָּשָׂר.

Τὸ σπέρμα τινός = the descendants of any one; this occurs also in classical Greek, but the frequent use of the expression in the N. T. is owing probably to the O. T. use of זֶרַע.

Στόμα μαχαίρης, Heb. xi. 34, = פִּי חֶרֶב,

Ὀφθαλμὸς πονηρός, Mark vii. 22, Matt. xx. 15, = "envy," "jealousy," like the Hebrew עַיִן רָעָה and רַע בְּעֵינֵי פ׳.

Πρόσωπον τῆς γῆς, Luke xxi. 35, = פְּנֵי הָאָרֶץ.

Ζητεῖν τὴν ψυχήν τινος, Matt. ii. 20, as in the LXX. for בִּקֵּשׁ נֶפֶשׁ פ׳.

Ἄρτον φαγεῖν or ἐσθίειν, Matt. xv. 2, 2 Thess. iii. 8, etc., = אָכַל לֶחֶם, of eating generally.

Λαμβάνειν πρόσωπον = נָשָׂא פָנִים. This expression would be quite strange and incomprehensible to a Greek. From it are formed the compounds, προσωπολημπτεῖν, Jas. ii. 9; προσωπολήμτης, Acts x. 34; προσωπολημψία, three times used by St. Paul (Rom. ii. 11; Eph. vi. 9; Col. iii. 25), and in Jas. ii. 1.

Τίθεσθαι ἐν τῇ καρδίᾳ ἑαυτοῦ, "to consider anything," = שִׂים בְּלֵב.

Γεύεσθαι θανάτου,—an expression which a Greek might use, but which never occurs in Greek authors, yet often in the N. T. and by different writers: it had evidently become common among the Greek-speaking Jews, because among later Jewish writers in Hebrew the corresponding expression טְעַם מוֹתָא often occurs.

Ὁ καρπὸς τῆς κοιλίας σου, Luke i. 42, = פְּרִי בִטְנֶךָ, Deut. xxviii. 4.

Ἐξέρχεσθαι ἐκ τῆς ὀσφύος τινος, Heb. vii. 5, "to spring from a certain progenitor," = יָצָא מֵחַלְצֵי פ״, Gen. xxxv. 11, 2 Chron. vi. 9.

Συντηρεῖν or διατηρεῖν ἐν τῇ καρδίᾳ, Luke ii. 19, 51, according to Dan. vii. 28 (מִלְּתָא בְּלִבִּי נְטָרֵת).

Hebraisms of this kind occur more or less frequently in all the N. T. books.

§ 34.

The peculiarities of the Hebrew and of the Aramæan, in their relation to the Greek, for the most part coincide; because the old Hebrew of the O. T. influenced in no small measure the Aramæan of the Jews, both as regards the use of words and the formation of phrases. In some places it is not easy to determine whether a peculiar mode of expression in the N. T. has come from the old Hebrew by way of the LXX., or from the vernacular spoken in Judea at the time. It may be supposed that the same peculiarities which were adopted by the Palestinian writers through their vernacular, occurred to the Alexandrine writers through the LXX. Generally, however, I think we may take it for granted that the language of all Jews, whether Palestinian or Grecian, when they wrote upon religious subjects, was influenced by the language of the LXX. and of the old Hebrew much more than by the Aramæan. WINER thinks otherwise, and, as it seems to me, wrongly.

But it would be different in the case of writings translated into Greek direct from the Aramæan. Here the influence of this dialect would be very marked, and would far outweigh that of the old Hebrew. This, however, was not probably the case with any of our N. T. books, not even with the first canonical Gospel, but only with certain portions of the historical books, *e.g.* the early part of the book of the Acts, and perhaps the early Gospels in their original conception or form. As to the discourses of Christ recorded in the Gospels, they were probably most of them spoken in Aramæan, and perhaps first recorded thus. And the same probably was the case with the discourses of the Acts delivered in Jerusalem; so that in explaining them we must resort to the Aramæan, even though the writings in which we now have them were originally composed in Greek. Still we could not suppose that Aramæan peculiarities would be very prominent in their influence upon the Greek, unless the discourses in question had been rendered literally and word for word: they would not be so marked if fidelity of narration be supposed to have consisted in giving the sense, and not the very words and forms.[1]

§ 35.

The Hebrew and Aramæan have moulded in some degree the *grammatical construction* of the Greek. Many verbs which of themselves govern the accusative or dative in ordinary Greek are followed by prepositions: thus, προσκυνεῖν is followed in older Greek by the accusative of the object, and in later Greek by the dative; in the N. T. and LXX. in both ways, and sometimes with ἐνώπιον, or ἔμπροσθέν τινος, or ἔμπροσθεν τῶν ποδῶν τινος. Ἀκολουθεῖν, instead of the dative, has sometimes ὀπίσω τινος, like πορεύεσθαι (ἔρχεσθαι, ὑπάγειν) ὀπίσω τινος, and this is formed after the manner of הָלַךְ אַחֲרֵי פ׳ (הָלַךְ). Φεύγειν ἀπό τινος, or ἀπὸ προσώπου τινος, like בָּרַח (or נוּס) *sq.* מִן or מִפְּנֵי. Προσέχειν (with or without ἑαυτῷ) ἀπό τινος, often in the N. T., and the LXX. 2 Chron. xxxv. 21 (חָדַל מִן), Lev. xxii. 2 (נָזַר in *Niphal*), and often in Ecclesiasticus. Ὀμνύναι ἐν τινι, "to swear by any one" (Matt. v. 34, etc.), like נִשְׁבַּע בְּ; in classical Greek, on the contrary, it is followed by the accusative. Ὁμολογεῖν ἐν τινι, Matt. x. 32, Luke xii. 8, formed after the analogy of הִזְכִּיר בְּשֵׁם יהוה, *e.g.* Ps. xx. 8. Κρύπτειν τι ἀπό τινος, often in the N. T. and in the LXX. after the Hebrew הִסְתִּיר followed by מִן or מִפְּנֵי; in classical Greek, κρύπτειν τινα, εἶναι εἴς τι = הָיָה לְ. Ποιεῖν ἔλεος μετά τινος, Luke i. 72, x. 37, = עָשָׂה חֶסֶד עִם פ׳. Δέκα δύο,

---

[1] These remarks apply not only to examples of the kind already given, but equally to those still to be presented.

Acts xix. 17, xxiv. 11, and in the LXX. instead of δώδεκα, like שְׁנֵים עָשָׂר.

Special modes of expression, such as: εἰ in a negative oath, Mark viii. 12, ἀμὴν λέγω ὑμῖν εἰ δοθήσεται, so frequently in the LXX. after the manner of the Hebrew אִם, but quite contrary to Greek usage; προστίθεσθαι, with the infinitive of another verb, Luke xx. 11; προσέθετο ἕτερον πέμψαι δοῦλον (Mark xii. 4, πάλιν ἀπέστειλεν . . . ἄλλον δοῦλον), Luke xx. 12, Acts xii. 3, as with the Hebrew יָסַף, which the LXX. have often imitated. The *casus obliqui* of the relative pronoun are expressed in Hebrew by the personal pronoun (as a suffix) with אֲשֶׁר preceding. And so we find it in the Greek of Matt. iii. 12, οὗ τὸ πτύον ἐν τῇ χειρὶ αὐτοῦ, "in whose hand is the winnowing fan;" Rev. vii. 2, οἷς ἐδόθη αὐτοῖς; ver. 9, ὃν ἀριθμῆσαι αὐτὸν οὐδεὶς ἐδύνατο. So also ὅπου . . . ἐκεῖ (Rev. xii. 14) corresponds with the Hebrew שָׁם . . . אֲשֶׁר.

The plan in Hebrew of joining to the finite verb the infinitive absolute of the same verb, for the sake of emphasis, is followed in N. T. Greek by joining the verb with a verbal noun: *e.g.* Luke xxii. 15, ἐπιθυμίᾳ ἐπεθύμησα; John iii. 29, χαρᾷ χαίρει, *impense laetatur*; Acts iv. 17, ἀπειλῇ ἀπειλησώμεθα αὐτοῖς, "let us strictly forbid them;" and so often in the LXX.

In Hebrew adjectives are used less frequently than substantives, and the qualifying thought is expressed by a substantive in the genitive following. This method is followed by Jewish writers in Greek generally, and we find it in the N. T.: for example, Luke iv. 22, λόγοι τῆς χάριτος; xvi. 8, οἰκονόμος τῆς ἀδικίας; xviii. 6; Eph. v. 2, εἰς ὀσμὴν εὐωδίας; Rev. xiii. 3; Rom. i. 26, πάθη ἀτιμίας; Acts ix. 15, σκεῦος ἐκλογῆς for σκεῦος ἐκλεκτόν. By this construction the thought is expressed more fully and graphically, and with greater emphasis. When a personal genitive has to be added to the thought thus expressed, it is attached to the genitive noun, though it refers to the whole expression or to the governing word (Gesenius, § 119, 6). We find a similar construction in Rev. xiii. 3, ἡ πληγὴ τοῦ θανάτου αὐτοῦ ἐθεραπεύθη. And, in like manner (though Winer judges differently, § 34, b), we may probably understand the expressions in Acts v. 20, πάντα τὰ ῥήματα τῆς ζωῆς ταύτης; Rom. vii. 24, ἐκ τοῦ σώματος τοῦ θανάτου τούτου. The expressions υἱοὶ τῆς βασιλείας, υἱοὶ τῆς ἀπειθείας (Eph. ii. 2; Col. iii. 6), υἱοὶ φωτός, υἱοὶ ἡμέρας (1 Thess. v. 5), ὁ υἱὸς τῆς ἀπολείας (2 Thess. ii. 3), are also Hebraistic.

As to prepositions, the frequent occurrence of בְּ in Hebrew and Aramæan has led to the corresponding use of ἐν in many cases where in classical Greek it would not occur: thus we find it when mention is made of the means or instrument by which anything is done, where the simple dative or διά with the genitive would be ordinarily used; e.g. ἀποκτεῖναι ἐν ῥομφαίᾳ; κράζειν ἐν φωνῇ μεγάλῃ; ἐκβάλλειν τὰ δαιμόνια ἐν τῷ ἄρχοντι τῶν δαιμονίων, Matt. ix. 34. Hence it happens that the distinction between ἐν and εἰς is not so marked as otherwise it would be.

Lastly, the Hebrew and Aramæan have given a very definite colouring to the style of the N. T. writers, especially in the historical books; the Hebrew through the Septuagint, which bears a very marked Hebraistic character, and the Aramæan as the still living vernacular of Palestine. This appears, for instance, in the absence of long sentences and periods in the narratives. In Hebrew and Aramæan the sentences are short, and the propositions simply stated one after another; and as this is the case also in the Septuagint, we need not wonder that it should be so in writers who were accustomed thus to express themselves in their mother tongue, or whose Greek reading was almost exclusively confined to the Greek Bible. Hence arises the meagre use or entire absence of Greek conjunctions, so nicely modifying and connecting the several sentences, and the frequent use of the simple καί, like the Hebrew וְ, even at the beginning of sentences. Still we find a great difference between the several writers in the style of their Greek generally, and even when the topics treated of do not lead to a Hebrew or Aramæan style. The PAULINE style is more periodic than that of the evangelists. The Greek of the Epistle of

JAMES is comparatively pure, and even elegant in some parts. Above all, the Epistle to the HEBREWS is distinguished by its beautiful style and the flow of its periods, which are constructed with great art, and (comparatively speaking) in very pure and well-chosen Greek. The Greek, too, in many parts of St. LUKE'S writings is very pure; for instance, in the latter half of the book of the Acts, and especially in the preface to the Gospel; but other parts, particularly in the Gospel, are very Hebraistic in their style. The most thoroughly Hebraistic, and consequently unclassical, in style of all the N. T. books is the Apocalypse, which is full of grammatical inaccuracies; and here it is not easy to mistake a Palestinian writer, who, with varied and learned culture, attained his knowledge of Greek, and his ability to write it, in his later years.

As to the most appropriate name for the Greek of the N. T. there has been much discussion. Some have called it ALEXANDRINE Greek, or the Alexandrine dialect; but this is inadmissible. We have seen, indeed, that the later Greek attained a determinate form and character in Alexandria and elsewhere; and hence we might speak of an Alexandrine dialect, though not in the sense of the older Greek dialects whereby the various tribes of Greece were distinguished. But this Alexandrine type formed only the basis or element of N. T. Greek. The name HELLENISTIC, which JUSTUS JOS. SCALIGER (*Animadv. in Chronologica Euseb.* p. 124) and JOH. DRUSIUS (on Acts vi. 6) recommend, is more appropriate. SALMASIUS strongly objects to it, but, at least partly, on insufficient grounds. DE WETTE also (§ 4) considers this name inappropriate, and so does TREGELLES (*Horne's Introduction*, 10th ed., iv. 21). Still I am inclined to retain it as the name most generally received; WINER also approves of it (§ 3, 26, note; *vid. Theol. Studien u. Krit.* 1858, p. 546). Ἑλληνίζειν and Ἑλληνιστής are used to denote foreigners who adopted Greek as their language; and thus, as we have already seen, the word Ἑλληνισταί is used, Acts vi. 1, ix. 29, to designate Greek-speaking Jews in Jerusalem, and to distinguish them, not indeed from native Greeks, but from 'Εβραίους. The name HELLENISTIC, therefore (not *Hellenic*, which is = κοινή), may be taken to denote the kind of Greek spoken or written by a Greek-speaking Jew, tinged as it would be more or less by a Hebrew or Aramæan style. This name, for which we might also use JEWISH GREEK, embraces, besides the writings of the N. T., the Septuagint and the apocryphal books of the O. T., and other Greek writings included in Jewish literature. If we would denote N. T. Greek alone, we must speak of it as the N. T. idiom.

§ 36.

I here append a few literary notices of the more modern grammatical and lexical works upon the language of the N. T., and of works containing excerpts or quotations from the later Jewish writers—the Targums, the Talmud, and the Rabbins—in explanation of the N. T., both as to its language and its subject-matter, and similar to those collections already referred to from Greek authors. In these later Jewish writers we find many expressions that were not fully formed when the O. T. was completed, but that were quite current in Jewish intercourse and writing in the time of Christ and His apostles, and that must have influenced the language of the N. T.; and thus an examination of these later Jewish writers is useful in the elucidation of N. T. Greek. Collections of quotations are given by the following scholars:—

JOHN LIGHTFOOT (Vice-Chancellor of the Univ. of Cambridge, *ob.* 1675) on the four Gospels, the Acts, 1st Corinthians, and part of Romans, first published in English, 1644; then in Latin at Cambridge, and by Carpzov at Leipsic, 1675. Lightfooti *Opera omnia*, 2 vols., Rotterdam 1686, fol.; ed. 2 by Leusden, Franecker 1699. Whole works edited by the Rev. J. R. Pitman, 13 vols. 8vo, 1825.

CHRIST. SCHÖTTGEN (Rector at Dresden), *Horæ Hebraicæ et Talmudicæ*, Dresden 1733-42, 2 vols. 4to: the first vol. only bears upon the N. T., and there texts of the N. T. in the order of the books are explained by the Talmud and the Rabbins, while vol. ii. treats of the Christology of the later Jews. Many illustrations from later Jewish writers will be found in WETSTEIN. The work of JOHN GERH. MEUSCHEN (General Sup. and Prof. of Theology at Coburg, *ob.* 1743), *Nov. Test. ex Talmude et antiquitt. Hebræorum illustratum*, Leipsic 1736, 4to, contains learned dissertations by J. A. DANZ, RHENFERD, and others, which bear more upon matters of fact and archæology than upon the language of the N. T.

As to *grammatical* works, the grammar of N. T. Greek, as distinct from Greek grammar generally, has been the subject of distinct works since the middle of the seventeenth century. The first who composed a grammar of the N. T. (in conjunction with that of the Hebrew of the O. T.) was A. T. GLASS: *Philologia sacra*, first in two books, Jena 1623, and afterwards 1636, in five books, the third of which is the *Grammatica sacra*, and the fourth contains additions thereto. He starts from the Hebrew, and what he says concerning the Grammar of N. T. Greek is more as an addition thereto, or appendix. Soon after him there appeared much fuller treatises: (*a*) by CASP. WYSS (Prof. at Zurich, *ob.* 1659), *Dialectologia sacra*, etc., Zurich 1650; and (*b*) by G. PASOR (Prof. of Greek at Franecker, *ob.* 1637), *Grammatica Græca sacra N. T. in tres libros distributa*, published, with emendations and additions by his son MATT. PASOR (Prof. at Gröningen), 1655. For an account of both works, see WINER, *Grammatik*, p. 5 sqq. In modern times, PH. H. HAAB was the first who again took up the subject, in his *Hebr.-griech. Grammatik zum Gebrauch für d. N. T.*, Tübingen 1815. But this was a very meagre work, and was supplanted by the superior labours of G. BENED. WINER (*ob.* 1858). His *Grammat. d. N. T. Sprachidioms als sichere Grundlage d. N. T. Exegese* appeared first at Leipsic 1822. A supplement was afterwards published in 1828, and both parts were blended in one in the fifth ed.

1844; 6th and enlarged ed. 1855, since translated into English. This work, which forms an epoch in N. T. exegesis, has not yet been excelled by any other. C. J. W. ALT's (minister at Eisleben and Hamburg) *Grammatica ling. Græcæ qua N. T. Scriptores usi sunt,* Halle 1829, is of less value. So also is that of ALEX. BUTTMANN, *Grammat. d. N. T. Sprachgebrauchs,* as an addition to Ph. Buttmann's Greek Grammar, Berlin 1859. *Vid.* the *Beiträge zur Kritik u. Grammatik des N. T.* by the same author in the *Theol. Stud. u. Krit.* 1858, pp. 474-516.

The lexical works on the Greek of the N. T. are of two kinds: (a) *Concordances,* wherein the words of the N. T. are alphabetically arranged, lists of places where each occurs, and the immediate connection given; (b) *Lexicons,* wherein the lexical material is arranged, the various senses in which the words are used stated, and thus the author's view of the various passages presented.

1. *Greek Concordances:* (a) by XYSTUS BETULEJUS (his German name was Sixtus Birken, Rector of the Gymnasium at Augsburg, *ob.* 1554), Basel 1546, fol.; (b) by HEINR. STEPHANUS (of Paris, *ob.* 1598), Paris 1594 and 1624; (c) by ERASMUS SCHMID (Prof. at Wittenberg, *ob.* 1637), entitled *N. T. Græci* ταμεῖον, *alliis Concordantiæ,* and published after his death, Wittenberg 1638, fol.,—a work for a long time widely used, and republished by CYPRIAN, Gotha 1717, again at Glasgow 1819, 2 vols. 8vo; (d) the newest and best, by KARL HERM. BRUDER: Ταμεῖον τῶν τῆς καινῆς Διαθήκης λέξεων, or *Concordantiæ omnium vocum N. T. Græci, primum ab Erasmo Schmidio editæ, nunc secundum critices et hermeneutices nostræ ætatis rationes emendatæ, auctæ, meliori ordine dispositæ,* Leips. 1842, 4to; *Editio stereotypa altera,* 1853. This is a very useful work, and a decided improvement upon all earlier concordances. It regards not only the *textus receptus,* but the text of other editions of the N. T. and

of the chief MSS.; hence many words and word-forms occur in it which are not in former concordances, and by certain signs it is indicated in what texts a word occurs in any special or figurative sense. There are other improvements and additions which render the work most acceptable and useful.

2. *Greek Lexicons to the N. T.* From the early part of the seventeenth century, and for a considerable time, that of GEORGE PASOR, *Lexicon Græco-Latinum in N. T.*, Herborn 1626, 7th ed. 1663, was generally used; latest edition, *cum animad.* J. F. FISCHERI, Leipsic 1774. During the first half of the eighteenth century two were published: (*a*) CHRIST. STOCK (Prof. of Oriental Languages at Jena, *ob.* 1733), *Clavis ling. sanctæ N. T.*, Jena 1725; ed. 5, ed. J. F. FISCHER, Leipz. 1752. (*b*) CHRIST. SCHÖTTGEN, *Novum Lexicon Graeco-Latinum in N. T.*, Leipz. 1746, who, like Hesychius, uses chiefly the O. T. and rabbinical works in explaining N. T. Greek; enlarged ed. by TOB. KREBS, Leipz. 1765; last ed. by GOTTLIEB LEBERECHT SPOHN, who adds references from the Syriac; Leipz. 1790, royal 8vo. Next we must mention that of J. F. FISCHER (Prof. of Classics at Leipsic, *ob.* 1799), *Prolusiones de vitiis lexicorum N. T. separatim antea, nunc conjunctim editæ*, Leipsic 1791. Soon afterwards appeared the work of J. FRIEDR. SCHLEUSNER (*ob.* 1831, Professor, etc., at Wittenberg), *Novum Lex. Græco-Latinum in N. T.*, Leipsic 1792, 2 vols., 4th ed. 1819. This work had in its time a wide repute and circulation, and it is still very useful on account of the valuable material therein collected; though, as a work, it is very deficient and crude, an almost countless number of meanings being put into each word. The works of WAHL and BRETSCHNEIDER, which appeared almost simultaneously, indicate a much better arrangement of material: (*a*) CHR. ABR. WAHL (*ob.* 1855 at Dresden), *Clavis N. T. philologica usibus scholarum et juvenum Theol. studios.*

accommodata, 2 vols., Leipsic 1822, 8vo ; ed. 3, *emendat. et auctior*, 1843, 4to. (*b*) CARL GOTTLIEB BRETSCHNEIDER (General Superintendent at Gotha, *ob.* 1848), *Lexicon manuale Græco-Lat. in libros N. T.*, 2 vols., Leipsic 1824 ; ed. 3, 1840. Each of these works has its distinguishing advantages. WAHL dwells chiefly upon the classical uses of words, BRETSCHNEIDER upon the Hellenic. The former is very full, almost too full, in its consideration of the particles ; the latter dwells much upon matters of fact, with much that is interesting from Josephus. On the whole, I prefer BRETSCHNEIDER ; but both works leave much still to be desired, and so does C. G. WILKE'S work, *Clavis N. T. philol. usibus schol. et juvenum Theol. studios. accommodata*, Leipsic 1841, 2d ed. 1850, and the shorter work of J. C. SCHIRLITZ (Prof. at the Gym. at Wetzlar), *Griech-deutsches Wörterbuch zum N. T.*, Giessen 1851, 2d ed. 1858. It is much to be regretted that two scholars who purposed treating on the N. T. lexically, H. PLANCK and WINER, did not accomplish their design. [GRIMM has re-edited WILKE'S *Clavis:* C. G. WILKII *Clavis N. T.*, etc. *Quem librum ita castigavit et emendavit ut novum opus haberi possit*, C. L. W. GRIMM. Also under the title, *Lexicon Graeco-Latinum in libros N. T. auctore C. L. W. Grimmio: Fasc.* 1, Leipz. 1862 ; *Fasc.* 2, 1864. To this last must now be added the able work of HERMANN CREMER, *Biblisch-theologisches Wörterbuch der N. T. Graecität*, Gotha 1868.]

Supplementary List, for the use of Students, of Critical Commentaries upon the N. T. Books. (By the Editor, J. F. BLEEK.)[1]

§ 37.

No. 1. *Works upon the entire N. T.*, over and above those named in § 31 and 36.—LAURENTINUS VALLA

[1] In this list, Bleek's Introduction to the O. T. is denoted by i. §, and the simple § always denotes the present work.—B.

(*ob. circ.* 1456: *Annotatt. in N. T.*, first published by Erasmus 1505); ERASMUS OF ROTTERDAM (*Annotatt. in N. T.*, 1516, and often; also *Paraphrases* of most of the books, from 1517); MARLORATUS (*N. T. Catholica expositio ecclesiastica*, etc., Paris 1561, and often); JOACHIM CAMERARIUS (*Comm. in N. Fœdus*, in Beza's edition of the N. T., 1642); BEZA (see § 298); GROTIUS (*Annotatt. in N. T.* in his *Opp. theol.*). The expositions of Valla, Erasmus, Camerarius, Vatablus, Castellio, Drusius, Camero, J. and Ludw. Cappellus, Grotius, and others, are collected in the *Critici sacri* (9 vols., London 1660, fol.), and in vols. iv. and v. of MATT. POOLE's *Synopsis criticorum* (5 vols. fol., Lond. 1669–76); and here, too, may be found the annotations of Estius, Gerhard, Hammond, a Lapide, Piscator (see i. § 50), and others. The annotations of HUGO GROTIUS may be found also in the polemical work of CALOV (*Biblia N. T. illustrata*, 2 vols. fol., Frankf. 1676; see i. § 53).

HAMMOND (*Paraph. and Annotations upon all the books of the N. T.*, Lond. 1653: in Latin, with additions by Clericus, Amst. 1698, fol.; Frankf. 1714); DE DIEU (*Animadverss. in libros N. T.*, 1633; and in the *Critica sacra*, Amst. 1693, fol.); A LAPIDE (see i. § 49); CALMET (see § 7, and i. § 49); the *Englische Bibelwerk*, originally in French, containing the annotations of all the best English critics (see i. § 55).

WOLF, *Curæ philol. et crit. in N. T.*, began to appear in 1725, and was published as a whole in 5 vols., Basel 1741. To this is added KÖCHER, *Analecta philol. et exeg. in 4 evang. quibus Wolfii curæ supplentur atque augentur*, Altenburg 1766, 4to; BENGEL (*Gnomon N. T.*, Tüb. 1742; ed. 2, 1759; ed. 3, 1773; new ed. by Steudel, Tüb. 1835–36; Berlin ed. 1860); WETSTEIN (see § 300); J. D. MICHAELIS (*Anmerkk. f. Ungelehrte* to his translation of the N. T., 4 parts, Gött. 1790–92; see i. § 54); J. G. ROSENMÜLLER (*Scholia in N. T.*, first in 1777, 6th ed. 1815–31).

HERM. OLSHAUSEN (*ob.* 1839), *Comm. über Bibl. sämmtl. Schriften des N. T.*, Königsb. 1830 sqq. Vol. i., the three first Gospels down to the account of our Lord's Passion, 1830; 4th ed., revised by Ebrard, 1853. Vol. ii., 4th ed., revised by Ebrard, 1862: Part i., the Gospel of John; Part ii., the account of our Lord's Passion; Part iii., the book of the Acts. Vol. iii., Romans and Corinthians; 2d ed. 1840. Vol. iv., Galatians, Ephesians, Colossians, 1st and 2d Thessalonians, 1840. Vol. v., Part i., Epistles to Philippians, Titus, Timothy, and Philemon, revised by Wiesinger, 1850; Part ii., the Epistle to the Hebrews, by Ebrard, 1850. Vol. vi., Part i., Epistle of James, by Wiesinger, 1854; Part ii., 1st Peter, by Wiesinger, 1856; Part iii., 2d Peter and Jude, by Wiesinger, 1862; Part iv., the Epistles of John, by Ebrard, 1859. Vol. vii., the Apocalypse, by Ebrard, 1853. [Most of these have been translated into English, and published in Clark's Foreign Theological Library, 1st series.]

H. A. W. MEYER, *Krit.-exeg. Komm. über das N. T.:* Part i. (first appeared in 1832), Matthew, 5th ed., Gött. 1864; Mark and Luke, 4th ed. 1860 and 1864: Part ii., Gospel of John, 4th ed. 1862: Part iii., Acts, 3d ed. 1861: Part iv., Romans, 4th ed. 1865: Part v., 1st Corinthians, 4th ed. 1861: Part vi., 2d Corinthians, 4th ed. 1862: Part vii., Galatians, 4th ed. 1862: Part viii., Ephesians, 3d ed. 1859: Part ix., Philippians, Colossians, and Philemon, 3d ed. 1865: Part x., Thessalonians, by Lünemann, 2d ed. 1859: Part xi., Timothy and Titus, by Huther, 2d ed. 1859: Part xii., Peter and Jude, by Huther, 2d ed. 1859: Part xiii., Hebrews, by Lünemann, 2d ed. 1861: Part xiv., Epistles of John, by Huther, 2d ed. 1861: Part xv., James, by Huther, 2d ed. 1863: Part xvi., the Revelation, by Düsterdieck, 1859.

DE WETTE, *Kurzgefasstes exeg. Handb. z. N. T.:* Vol. i.: 1. Matthew, 4th ed., by Messner, 1857; 2.

Mark and Luke, 3d ed. 1846; 3. Gospel and Epistles of John, 3d ed. 1846; 5th ed., by Brückner, 1863; 4. Acts, 3d ed. 1848. Vol. ii.: 1. Romans, 4th ed. 1847; 2. Corinthians, 3d ed., by Messner, 1855; 3. Galatians and Thessalonians, 3d ed. 1864; 4. Colossians, Philemon, Ephesians, Philippians, 2d ed. 1847; 5. Titus, Timothy, and Hebrews, 2d ed. 1847. Vol. iii.: 1. Peter, Jude, James, 3d ed., by Brückner, 1853; 2. Revelation, 3d ed., by Möller, 1862.

J. P. LANGE, with other scholars, has published *Theol.-homilet. Bibelwerk*, 1857 sqq., which contains all the N. T. excepting Revelation.

DE WETTE's *Uebersetzung* (see i. § 55), 4th ed. 1858. The 5th vol. of BUNSEN's *Bibelwerk*, edited by Holtzmann (Leipz. 1865), contains a translation of the N. T., with short annotations.

No. 2. *Works upon large portions of the N. T.*—JEROME; THEOPHYLACT (Archbp. of Bulgaria in the eleventh century); ŒCUMENIUS (on Acts, the Pauline and Catholic Epistles); CALVIN, on the whole N. T. except the Apocalypse; COCCEIUS (see i. § 52); J. CRELL (*Opp. exeg.* 1656, fol.); MORUS (*ob.* 1792), *Prælectiones*, published after his death; KOPPE (*ob.* 1791), *N. T. Gr. perpet. annotatt. illustr.*, vols. iii.–x., Gött. 1778 sqq.; continued by Heinrichs, Pott, Tychsen, and Ammon. Vols. i. and ii. on the Gospels were not published. BAUMGARTEN-CRUSIUS (*ob.* 1843), *Theol. Auslegung der Johann. Schriften* (Gospel and Epistles), 2 vols., Jena 1844–45; also his *Exeg. Schriften zum N. T.*, by Kimmel, Otto, and Schauer.

No. 3. *Works upon the Synoptical Gospels only.*—Besides those already named under 1 and 2: EUTHEMIUS ZIGABENUS, *Comment. in 4 Evv.*, Græce et Lat., ed. Matthäi, Leipz. 1792; H. E. G. PAULUS, *Commentar*, 1800, 2d ed. 1804–5, and *Exeg. Handb. über die drei ersten Evv.*, 1830–33; KUINŒL, *Commentarius in libros N. T. historicos;* EWALD (see § 92); BLEEK, *Synopt. Erklärung der drei ersten Evv.*, edited by Holtzmann, 2 vols., Leipz. 1862. See also THOLUCK *on the Sermon on the Mount*, 4th ed. 1856; and WICHELHAUS *on the History of the Passion in all four Evv*. (see § 68).

No. 4. *On Matthew only.*—ORIGEN; CHRYSOSTOM (*Homiliæ*); HILARIUS PICTAV.; JEROME; ELSNER (*Commentarius*, ed. Stosch, 2 vols. 1767); GRATZ (*Krit.-histor. Commentar.*, 1821-23); FRITZSCHE (*Quatuor Evangelia recensuit*, etc., i. Matthew, 1826).

No. 5. *On Mark only.*—VICTOR ANTIOCHENUS (circ. 400, ed. Matthäi, Moscow 1775); ELSNER, 1773; FRITZSCHE (4 *Evv.*, ii. Mark, 1830).

No. 6. *On Luke only.*—AMBROSE: STEIN (Halle 1830): *Selecta e scholis* VALCKENARII *in libros quosdam N. T.*, ed. Wassenbergh, i. Luke and Acts, 1815; ii. 1st Corinthians and Hebrews, 1817: BORNEMANN (*Scholia*, 1830).

No. 7. *On John.*—ORIGEN; CHRYSOSTOM; AUGUSTINE; EUTHYMIUS; LUTHER; MELANCHTHON; BEZA; F. A. LAMPE (*Comm. exeg. analyticus*, Amsterd. 1724-26, 3 vols. 4to); MOSHEIM (*Erklärung*, edited by Jacobi, Weimar 1777); KUINŒL (vol. iii. 1812, 3d ed. 1825); LÜCKE (see § 63); THOLUCK (1827, 7th ed. 1857); KLEE (1829); A. MAIER (2 vols. 1843, 1845); EWALD (see § 63); WEISS (*Johann. Lehrbegriff*, Berl. 1862); HENGSTENBERG (2 vols. 1862); GODET (2 vols., Paris 1865).

No. 8. *On the Acts.*—55 Homilies of CHRYSOSTOM; BUGENHAGEN (*Commentarius*, 1524); KUINŒL (vol. iv.); VALCKENÆR (see No. 6 and § 132).

No. 9. *On the Pauline Epistles, including Hebrews.*—THEODORET (*Opp.* ed. Schulze et Nœsselt, 3 vols., Halle 1771); J. FABER STAPULENSIS; ESTIUS (*In omnes Pauli et al. apostolorum ep. commentarius*, Douai 1614 sqq.); BUGENHAGEN (*Adnotatt. in epp. ad Gal., Eph., Phil., Col., Thess., Tim., Tit., Philem., et Heb.*, 1524, Romans 1521); SEB. SCHMID (*In Ep. ad Rom., Gal., et Col., una cum paraphr. ep. 1 ad Cor., utriusque ad 2 Thess., 1 Tim., Philem., et cantici Mariæ*, Hamb.

1704, 4to); S. J. BAUMGARTEN (Halle 1749–67); VON FLATT; EWALD (see § 132); BAUR (see § 14); and USTERI (*Paulin. Lehrbegriff*, 6th ed. 1851).

No. 10. *On the Ep. to the Romans.*—MELANCHTHON (*Adnotatt.*, 1522; *Commentarii*, 1540); LOCKE (London, 1742); CHR. FR. BÖHME (*Comment. perpet.*, Leipz. 1806); THOLUCK (Berlin, 5th ed. 1856); H. E. G. PAULUS (Heidelb. 1831); REICHE (Gött. 1833–4); C. F. A. FRITZSCHE (Halle 1836–43); RÜCKERT (2d ed. Leipz. 1839); A. MAIER (Freib. 1847); JOWETT (*Epp. to Thessalonians, Galatians, Romans*, Lond. 1856); PHILIPPI (2d ed. Frankf. 1855).

No. 11. *On the Epp. to the Corinthians.*—MOSHEIM (1762); VALCKENÆR; HEYDENREICH (*Comm. in 1 Cor.*, 2 vols., Marb. 1825–28); BILLROTH; RÜCKERT; NEANDER (see § 149); OSIANDER; HOFMANN (Nördl. 1862–64).

No. 12. *On the Ep. to the Galatians.*—AUGUSTINE (*expositio*, Opp. ed. Bened., tom. iii.); LUTHER (*cur.* Irmischer, Erlang. 1843–44); WINER (ed. 4, Leipz. 1859); H. E. G. PAULUS; RÜCKERT (Leipz. 1833); USTERI (Zurich 1833); SCHOTT (see § 155); HILGENFELD (Leipz. 1852); JOWETT; HOLSTEN (*Inhalt u. Gedankengang*, Rostock 1859); WIESELER (Gött. 1859); HOFMANN.

No. 13. *On the Ep. to the Ephesians.*—HOLZHAUSEN; MATTHIES (see § 170); F. K. MEIER (Berlin 1834); RÜCKERT (Leipz. 1834); HARLESS (Erlangen 1834, 2d ed. Stuttg. 1858); BLEEK (*Vorlesungen*, etc., Berl. 1865).

No. 14. *On the Ep. to the Philippians.*—RHEINWALD (Berl. 1827); MATTHIES (Greifsw. 1835); VAN HENGEL (*Comm. perp.*, Leyden 1838); HÖLEMANN (Leipz. 1839); WEISS (Berl. 1859).

No. 15. *On the Ep. to the Colossians.*—BÄHR (Basel 1833); BÖHMER (*Theol. Auslegung*, Bresl. 1835); HUTHER (Hamb. 1841); DALMER (Gotha 1858); BLEEK (Berl. 1865).

No. 16. *On the Thessalonians.*—Besides those already named by HOFMANN and JOWETT, may be mentioned PELT (*Perp. Comm.*, Greifswald 1830).

No. 17. *On the Pastoral Epistles.*—HEYDENREICH; MATTHIES (see § 173); MACK (see § 184); LEO (*Pauli ep. prima ad Tim.*, Leipz. 1837, and 2 Tim. 1850); MOSHEIM (Hamb. 1755, 4to); KUINŒL (*Explicatio ep. Pauli ad Tit.* in the *Commentatt. Theol.*, edd. Velthusen, Kuinœl, et Ruperti, 292 sqq.).

No. 18. *On the Ep. to Philemon.*—HAGENBACH (Basel 1829); H. A. PETERMANN (*ad fidem versionum or. vet. una cum earum textu originali græce*, ed. Berl. 1844); KOCH (Zurich 1846); BLEEK (Berl. 1865).

No. 19. *On the Ep. to the Hebrews.*—SCHLICHTING and CRELL (Rakau 1634; and *Crellii opp. exeg.*, vol. ii. 1656, fol.); BRAUN (Amsterd. 1705, 4to); J. BEN. CARPZOV (see § 31); JOHN OWEN (Lond. 1674); J. PEIRCE (*Paraphrase and Notes*, etc.); J. D. MICHAELIS (Frankf. 1780, 1786); VALCKENÆR; DAVID SCHULZ (Breslau 1818); CHR. FR. BÖHME (see § 197); KUINŒL (Leipz. 1831); H. E. G. PAULUS (see § 194); BLEEK (see § 189); THOLUCK (3d ed. 1850); DELITZSCH (Leipz. 1857); RIEHM (*Lehrbegriff*; see § 197).

No. 20. *On the General Epistles.*—Besides those named under Nos. 1 and 2, see CLEMENS ALEX. (*Adumbratt.*); DIDYMUS ALEX. (in the *Maxima bibl. Patrum*, London 1667, vol. iv. 320 sqq.); GRYNÆUS (*Explic. ep. cath.*, Basel 1593); J. BEN. CARPZOV (Halle 1790); AUGUSTI (see § 213); JACHMANN (see § 226).

No. 21. *On the Ep. of James.*—HERDER (see § 217); STORR (Tüb. 1784, 4to); HENSLER (Hamburg 1801); SCHULTHENS (Zurich 1824); SCHNECKENBURGER (see § 206); THEILE (Leipz. 1833); KERN (Tüb. 1838).

No. 22. *On the Ep. of Jude.*—HERDER (see § 217); HÄNLEIN (see § 217); SCHNECKENBURGER (*Beitr. zur Einl. i. N. T.*, p. 214 sqq.).

No. 23. *On 1st and 2d Peter.*—Jno. Gerhard (Jena 1641, 4to); Luther (on 1st Peter, *Werke*, ix. 624-833); Leighton; Hensler (Sulzbach 1813); Steiger (Berl. 1832); Weiss (*Petrin. Lehrbegr.*, Berl. 1855); Dietlein (on 2d Peter; see § 217).

No. 24. *On the Epp. of John.*—Augustine (*Tractat.* x.); Luther; Whiston (Lond. 1719); S. G. Lange (see § 223); H. E. G. Paulus (Heidelb. 1829); Lücke (Bonn 1825; 3d ed., revised by Bertheau, 1856); Düsterdieck (Gött. 1852-56); Ewald (see § 63); Weiss.

No. 25. *On the Book of the Revelation.*—Among the innumerable commentaries on this book,—see Lücke and De Wette (*Exeg. Handb.*),—I name Andreas of Cæsarea in Cappadocia (in the fifth cent.); Bossuet (Paris 1689); Vitringa ('Ανάκρισις, *Apoc. Jo. Ap.*, etc., Franecker 1705, 4to; ed. 3, Leucop. 1721, 4to); Abauzit (*Discourse, Historical and Critical, on the Revelation ascribed to St. John*, London 1730); Bengel (see § 230); Hartwig (see § 230); Herder (Μαρὰν ἀθά, etc., Riga 1779); Eichhorn (Gött. 1791); Zullig (§ 229); Ewald (1828 and 1862; see § 229); Hengstenberg (see § 229); Auberlen (see § 230); Lücke (§ 229); Bleek (see § 229). B.

[*Supplementary List of English and American Works on the N. T.*

No. 1. *On the N. T. at large.*—Harmony, Chronicle, and *Order of the N. T.*, by John Lightfoot, D.D. (*ob.* 1675); Works, vol. iii. *Introduction to the Study of the N. T.*, by Edw. Harwood, D.D. (*ob.* 1794), 2 vols. 8vo, 1773. *The N. T. arranged in Chronological and Historical Order*, by George Townsend, D.D., 2 vols. 8vo, new ed. 1838. Trapp, *Commentary*, new ed. 1865. *Doctrinal Harmony of the N. T.*, by E. W. Grinfield, 1824; also by the same, *Scholia Hellenistica in N. T.*, 1848. *Annotations on the N. T.*, by E. LEIGH (*ob.* 1671), fol., Lond. 1650. GELL's *Remains*, 2 vols. fol. 1676. BAXTER's *Paraphrase on the N. T.*, 1685. POOLE's *Annotations*, by various writers, 2 vols. fol. 1700, and 3 vols. 8vo, 1840. WHITBY's *Commentary*, 4th ed., 2 vols. fol. 1760. *The N. T. Explained*, by F. FOX (*ob.* 1738), 2 vols. 8vo. *Expository Notes*, by W. BURKITT, fol. 1752. *N. T. Compared with the Original*, etc., by JOHN LINDSAY, 2 vols. fol. 1736. GUYSE's *Practical Expositor*, 3 vols. 4to, 1739–52. *Brief Critical Notes*, by W. WALL, D.D., 1730. DODDRIDGE's *Family Expositor*, 6 vols. 4to, 1739. *Critical Conjectures on the N. T.*, by W. BOWYER, 1812. W. GILPIN's *Exposition of the N. T.*, 4to, 1790. *An Illustration of the Method of Explaining the N. T. by the early Opinions of Jews and Christians concerning Christ*, by W. WILSON, B.D. (*ob.* 1800), edited by Dr. TURTON, 8vo, 1838. *The Greek Testament, with English Notes*, by S. T. BLOOMFIELD, D.D., 2 vols. 8vo, 1841, 9th ed. 1855; *Recensio synoptica annotationis sacræ: A Critical Digest*, etc., 8 vols. 8vo, by the same. *Horæ Biblicæ Sabbaticæ*, by T. CHALMERS, D.D.; Posth. Works, vol. iv. NATHANAEL LARDNER, *Credibility*, etc.; Works, 5 vols. 4to, 1815. JEREMIAH JONES, *On the Canon of the N. T.*, 3 vols., Oxford 1827. The Commentaries of THOS. SCOTT, MATT. HENRY, ADAM CLARK, BARNES. Dean STANLEY, *Sermons and Essays on the Apostolic Age*, 1847. Dr. S. P. TREGELLES, *An Account of the Criticism of the N. T. Text*, 1854; see also HORNE's *Introduction*, above-named. F. H. SCRIVENER, *Introduction to the Criticism of the N. T.* Dr. SAMUEL DAVIDSON, *Introduction to the N. T.*, 3 vols. 1848–51; new ed. 2 vols. 1868. FREDERIC D. MAURICE, *Unity of the N. T.*, 1854. Dean ALFORD, *The N. T., with Notes and Introductions, Prolegomena*, etc., 4 vols. 8vo: Vol. i., *The Gospels*, 5th ed.; Vol. ii., *Acts to 2d Corinthians*, 4th ed.; Vol. iii., *Galatians to Philemon*, 3d ed.; Vol. iv., Part i., *Hebrews to 2d*

Peter, 2d ed.; Part ii., 1*st John to Revelation.* The
N. T., with Notes and Introductions, by CHR. WORDS-
WORTH, D.D.: Part i., *The Gospels;* Part ii., *The
Acts;* Part iii., *The Epistles of St. Paul;* Part iv.,
The General Epistles and Revelation: in 2 vols. imp.
8vo. B. F. WESTCOTT, *History of the N. T. Canon,*
new ed. 1867.

No. 2. *On the Gospels only.*—Abp. NEWCOME'S
Harmony, 8vo, 1802. J. MACKNIGHT, D.D., *Harmony
of the Gospels,* 1726; 2 vols. 8vo, 1819. GRESWELL'S
Harmony, 5th ed., Oxford 1856; and *Dissertations,* 2d
ed., 4 vols. 1837. ISAAC WILLIAMS, *On the Gospels,*
1842–50. FURNESS, *Jesus and His Biographers,* Phi-
ladelphia 1838. HENNELL, *Inquiry concerning the
Origin of Christianity,* 2d ed., Lond. 1841. W. H.
MILL, *On the attempted Application of Pantheistic Prin-
ciples to the Theory and Historic Criticism of the Gos-
pels,* Cambr. 1840–44. J. R. BEARD, *Voices of the
Church in reply to Strauss,* Lond. 1845. DA COSTA,
The Four Witnesses (translated from the Dutch), Lond.
1851. T. R. BIRKS, *Horæ Evangelicæ, or the Internal
Evidence of the Gospel History,* Lond. 1852. JAMES
SMITH (of Jordanhill), *Dissertation on the Origin and
Connection of the Gospels,* Edin. 1853. NORTON, *Inter-
nal Evidences of the Genuineness of the Gospels,* 3 vols.,
Camb. 1846–48. J. BROWN, D.D., *Discourses and
Sayings of our Lord,* 3 vols. 8vo, Edin. 1850. F. D.
MAURICE, *Unity of the Gospels.* F. M., *Anonymous
Notes on the Gospels and Acts,* Lond. 1838. Dean
GOODWIN, *Comm. on the Gospels,* 1857–61. ALEX.
ROBERTS, *Discussions on the Gospels,* 2d ed., Edin.
1864. WESTCOTT, *Introduction to the Study of the
Gospels,* 3d ed. 1867. G. P. FISHER, *Essays on the
Supernatural Origin of Christianity,* New York 1866.
C. A. ROW, *The Historical Character of the Gospels;
Journal of Sacred Lit.,* 1865–67. Abp. TRENCH,
Notes on the Parables, 9th ed. 1864; *Notes on the
Miracles,* 7th ed. 1860; *Studies in the Gospels,* 1867.

Bp. ELLICOTT, *Historical Lectures on the Life of our Lord*, 1860; (TISCHENDORF, Leipz. 1865.)

No. 3. *On St. Matthew only.*—CHRISTOPHER BLACKWOOD, *Exposition of Chap.* i.-x., 4to, Lond. 1659. J. LIGHTFOOT, *A Chorographical Century*, etc.; Works, vol. x. DAVID DICKSON, *A Brief Exposition of St. Matthew*, 12mo, Lond. 1651. ISAAC DE BEAUSOBRE, *A New Version of St. Matthew*, 8vo, Camb. 1790. DANIEL SCOTT, LL.D., *A New Version of St. Matthew*, Lond. 1741. Bp. PORTEOUS, *Lectures on St. Matthew*, 2 vols. 8vo, Lond. 1802. O. LODGE, *Lectures on St. Matthew*, Lond. 1818. Abp. SUMNER, *Practical Exposition of St. Matthew*, Lond. 1834. H. GOODWIN, *Commentary*, etc., 1859. CURETON's *Syriac Recension.*

No. 4. *On St. Mark.*—GEO. PETTER, 2 vols. fol., Lond. 1661. Bp. HINDS, *The Catechist's Manual*, 1829, 1855. M. BLAND, *Annotations*, Lond., Whittaker. KENRICK's *Biblical Essays.*

No. 5. *On St. Luke.*—Bp. THIRLWALL, *Translation of Schleiermacher on St. Luke, Introd.* R. WILSON, *Questions on St. Luke's Gospel*, Camb. 1830. Abp. SUMNER, Lond. 1833. J. FOOTE, *Lectures*, 2 vols. 8vo, Glasgow 1857. W. TROLLOPE, 12mo, 1849. OOSTERZEE, in *Lange's Bibelwerk*, Clark's For. Theol. Lib. Professor MILL, *The Historical Character of St. Luke's Gospel*, 1841.

No. 6. *On St. John.*—G. HUTCHESON, Lond. 1657. R. SHEPHERD, D.D., *Notes, Critical and Dissertatory, on the Gospel and Epp. of St. John*, 4to, Lond. 1796. C. C. TITTMANN, *Meletemata Sacra*, Leips. 1816; translated, 2 vols. 8vo, Edin. 1844. F. D. MAURICE, 1857. J. J. TAYLER, 1867.

No. 7. *The Acts of the Apostles.*—SAM. CRADOCK, *The Apostolical History*, fol., 1672. G. BENSON, 2 vols. 4to, 1756. R. BISCOE, *History of the Acts Confirmed*, 8vo, Oxford 1840. W. G. HUMPHRY, 8vo, Lond. 1847. Professor HACKETT, 8vo, Boston (U.S.) 1852, new ed. 1858. JAMES SMITH, Esq.,

Voyage and Shipwreck of St. Paul, 3d ed. 1866. J. A. ALEXANDER, New York 1857. See also ALFORD, WORDSWORTH, CONYBEARE and HOWSON, and other critical works before named.

No. 8. *On the Pauline Epistles.*—J. LOCKE (*ob.* 1704), *Paraphrase and Notes*, 4to, 1742. PALEY (*ob.* 1805), *Horæ Paulinæ*. CONYBEARE and HOWSON, *Life and Epistles of St. Paul*, 2 vols. 4to, 1841. T. LEWIN, *Life and Epistles of St. Paul*, 2 vols., Lond. 1851. BIRKS' *Horæ Apostolicæ*. Dr. SCHAFF's *History of the Apostolic Church*, New York 1854. (See *Acts*.)

No. 9. *The Epistle to the Romans.*—LOCKE, *Paraphrase and Notes*, Lond. 1733. J. TAYLOR, *Paraphrase with Notes*, 1745. T. CHALMERS, D.D., 4 vols. 8vo; Works, vols. xxii.-xxv. MOSES STUART, 1838. W. W. EWBANK, Lond. 1850. C. HODGE, D.D., 12mo, 1855. R. HALDANE, 3 vols. 12mo, 1842.

No. 10. *1st and 2d Corinthians.* — G. BILLROTH, translated by WILLIAM L. ALEXANDER, Edin. 1837. OLSHAUSEN, translated by J. E. COX, Edin. 1851. Dean STANLEY, 2 vols. 8vo, 3d ed. 1865. PEILE, Lond. 1848. C. HODGE, New York 1857.

No. 11. *Galatians.*—LUTHER, translated 1835. W. PERKINS, *Works*, vol. ii. Bp. ELLICOTT, *Critical and Grammatical Comm.*, Lond. 1854. Professor B. JOWETT, 2d ed. 1859. J. H. TURNER, New York 1855. H. T. J. BAGGE, Lond. 1856. J. B. LIGHTFOOT, 2d ed., Lond. 1866.

No. 12. *Ephesians.* — PAUL BAYNE, fol., Lond. 1643. C. HODGE, D.D., New York 1856. J. H. TURNER, D.D., 1856. Professor EADIE, Lond. 1854. Bp. ELLICOTT, 1855. J. L. DAVIES, *Epistles to Ephesians, Colossians, Philemon*, 1866.

No. 13. *Colossians.*—THOS. CARTWRIGHT, 4to, Lond. 1612. N. BYFIELD, fol., Lond. 1615. EDW. ELTON, 1620. Bp. DAVENANT, fol. 1630; translated by JOSIAH ALLPORT, 2 vols. 8vo, 1831. JOHN OWEN, Lond. 1672; new ed. 1841. JAMES PEIRCE, 4to,

1733. Professor EADIE, 1856. Bp. ELLICOTT, 1857. Bp. DANIEL WILSON, 8vo, Lond. 1845.

No. 14. *Philippians.*—HENRY AIRAY, 4to, 1618. JAMES PEIRCE. MANTON EASTBURN, New York 1833. H. S. BAYNES, Lond. 1834. Bp. ELLICOTT, 1857.

No. 15. *1st and 2d Thessalonians.*—Bp. JEWELL, 1583. R. ROLLOCK, *In epist. Pauli ad Thess.*, 8vo, Edin. 1598. JOHN PHILLIPS, *The Greek of the 1st Epistle*, Lond. 1751. W. SCLATER, Lond. 1616, 1629, 4to. T. K. BIRKS, *Bloomsbury Lectures*, 3d series, 1845. B. JOWETT, 2d ed. 1859. Bp. ELLICOTT, 1858.

No. 16. *The Pastoral Epistles.*—J. BARLOW and T. HALL on 2d *Timothy*, fol., Lond. 1632. A. S. PATERSON, 18mo, 1848. THOMAS TAYLOR, D.D., *on Titus*, fol., 1668. Bp. ELLICOTT, 1856.

No. 17. *Philemon.*—W. JONES, D.D., fol., Lond. 1635. DANIEL DYKE, D.D., 4to, 1618. W. ATTERSOLL, fol., Lond. 1833. Bp. PARRY, 12mo, London 1834. Bp. SMALRIDGE, Oxford 1734. C. J. ELLICOTT, 1857.

No. 18. *The Hebrews.*—R. ROLLOCK, *Analysis Logica*, Edin. 1605. N. GOUGE, 2 vols. fol., 1655. GEO. LAWSON, fol., 1662. JOHN OWEN, D.D., 4 vols. for 1668-74; edited by Dr. GOOLD, 7 vols. 8vo, 1854. MOSES STUART, 4th ed. 1837. DUKE OF MANCHESTER, *Horæ Hebraicæ*, 1835. S. H. TURNER, D.D., New York 1855. EBRARD'S *Comm.*, translated by J. FULTON, 1853. F. S. SAMPSON, New York 1856. FORSTER, *Apol. Authority of Ep.*, Lond. 1838.

No. 19. *St. James.*—RD. TURNBULL, 4to, Lond. 1606. T. MANTON, D.D., 4to, Lond. 1653; edited by T. M. MACDONOGH, 8vo, 1844. NEANDER, translated by H. C. CONANT, 12mo, New York 1852.

No. 20. *1st and 2d Peter.*—LUTHER, translated by NEWTON, 4to, Lond. 1581. W. AMES, 1641. N.

BYFIELD, *on* 1*st Peter*, 1637. JOHN ROGERS, *on* 1*st Peter*, fol., Lond. 1650. THOMAS SMITH, *Commentarius* (2*d Peter*), 1690. Abp. LEIGHTON (1*st Peter*), 2 vols. 8vo, 1829. J. E. RIDDLE (1*st Peter*), 1849, 8vo. ARCHIBALD SIMSON (2*d Peter*), 4to, Lond. 1632. T. ADAMS (2*d Peter*), fol., Lond. 1633. BROWN'S *Discourses*, 2d ed. 1839.

No. 21. *The Epistles of St. John.*—W. WHISTON, Lond. 1719. T. HAWKINS, 8vo, 1808. JOHN COTTON (1*st John*), fol., 1656. N. HARDY, *on* 1*st John*, 4to, Lond. 1656. (SANDER, 1851.)

No. 22. *St. Jude.*—L. RIDLEY, 16mo, Lond. R. TURNBULL, 4to, 1606. SAMUEL OTES, 4to, Lond. 1633. W. JENKYN, 4to, Lond. 1652; Glasg. 1783; edited by SHERMAN, Lond. 1839. T. MANTON, D.D., 4to, Lond. 1658. F. GARDINER, Boston (U.S.) 1856.

No. 23. *The Revelation.*—LORD NAPIER, 4to, Edin. 1645. T. BRIGHTMAN, 4to, 1609. JOSEPH MEDE, *Clavis Apoc.*, translated by R. MORE, 1643. JAMES DURHAM, fol., 1658; 4to, 1788. W. WHISTON, 4to, 1706. CHARLES DAUBUZ, fol., Lond. 1730. JAMES ROBERTSON, *Things New and Old*, etc., fol., 1730. MOSES LOWMAN [*ob.* 1752], *A Paraphrase and Notes*, etc., 2d ed. 4to, 1745. Dean WOODHOUSE, Lond. 1805. S. P. TREGELLES, 1844. MOSES STUART, 2 vols. 1845. ALEX. TILLOCH, *Dissertations Introductory*, 8vo, Lond. 1823. E. B. ELLIOTT, *Horæ Apocalypticæ*, 4th ed., 4 vols. 8vo, Lond. 1851. Canon WORDSWORTH, *Hulsean Lectures*, 1848. J. H. TODD, D.D., *Donnellan Lecture*, Dubl. 1846. Abp. TRENCH, *The Epistles to the Seven Churches*, 1861. ISAAC WILLIAMS, 8vo, Lond. 1852.]—TR.

PART I.

HISTORY OF THE ORIGIN OF THE SEVERAL BOOKS OF THE NEW TESTAMENT.

IN the inquiries now before us, we shall follow for the most part the order wherein the several books are arranged in most editions of the Greek Testament. Accordingly, we shall first examine the GOSPELS, which present the Redeemer in His life and works on earth, His death and resurrection, and onwards to His return to His Father in heaven. And then we shall consider the APOSTOLIC works, which present to us the apostles and other disciples of our Lord in their labours after His ascension: first, the only historical book, the ACTS OF THE APOSTLES; next the PAULINE EPISTLES; then the Epistle to the HEBREWS; next the CATHOLIC or GENERAL EPISTLES; and lastly, the REVELATION.

THE GOSPELS.

§ 38.

The N. T. contains four Gospels, which in the Greek editions and in most manuscripts are respectively entitled: εὐαγγέλιον κατὰ Ματθαῖον, κατὰ Μάρκον, κατὰ Λουκᾶν, κατὰ Ἰωάννην. The manuscripts present some differences in the titles: εὐαγγέλιον is wanting in Codex B, and the superscriptions are simply κατὰ Ματθαῖον, κατὰ Μάρκον, etc. Thus we find them also in the *Codex Sinaiticus* (ℵ); Codex D has only κατὰ Ἰ. prefixed to St. John's Gospel, and Codex F has this form in St. Mark and St. Luke's Gospels. Some Latin MSS. have simply *secundum Matthæum*, etc. In some other MSS. the titles are longer: τὸ κατὰ Ματθαῖον ἅγιον εὐαγγέλιον, or the like. But all the Greek MSS. have the κατά before the name; and that this was the usual way of naming them, at least from the second century downwards, is evident from the fact that the Fathers of that century and afterwards name the several Gospels thus. The name εὐαγγέλια for these books was certainly common in the middle of the second century. This is evident from Justin Martyr's words, *Apol*. i. 66: οἱ γὰρ ἀπόστολοι ἐν τοῖς γενομένοις ὑπ' αὐτῶν ἀπομνημονεύμασιν, ἃ καλεῖται εὐαγγέλια, οὕτως παρέδωκαν. We cannot tell whether these titles, the εὐαγγέλιον and the κατά with the name, were prefixed by the authors themselves. Considering the similarity of the titles, the probability is that they were prefixed when these writings were collected together as the four Gospels: either this form was then for the first time chosen, or, as is more likely, one or other of these writings had before, perhaps originally, been thus named, and similar titles were given to the rest.

As to the import of this title, the writings which narrate the history of Christ's life and work during His sojourn upon earth are called εὐαγγέλια, *i.e.* "glad tidings," because they narrate the fulfilment of those joyous promises which God the Lord (Jehovah) had given in the O. T. by the prophets. We find the verb εὐαγγελίζεσθαι in the LXX. answering to the Hebrew בִּשַּׂר, and describing the proclamation of salvation by the prophet, *e.g.* Isa. lx. 6, lxi. 1, and elsewhere; εὐαγγελιζόμενοι being used of those who were commissioned to preach it (Isa. xl. 9, lii. 7, etc.). In the N. T. εὐαγγελίζεσθαι and εὐαγγέλιον refer to the announcement of the fact that this salvation is nigh at hand, or that it has come in the person of the Redeemer, and that the establishment of the kingdom of God is now about to be realized. Hence the word εὐαγγελιστής. But this name was used (as we have already seen) with reference to a special office in the Church —with reference to those who were not teachers in any one fellowship, but who travelled from place to place preaching the promised Messiah and Saviour, and doing this chiefly by narrating the facts of His life and works, and by repeating His discourses and sayings. Thus, in Eph. iv. 11, evangelists are named among the Christian teachers, between apostles and prophets on the one hand, and pastors and teachers on the other; and in this sense mention is made, in Acts xxi. 8, of Philip the deacon as an evangelist (cf. Acts viii. 5). This name evangelist would afterwards be applied to those who composed written accounts of the life and works of Christ, and the treatise thus composed came to be called εὐαγγέλια. The word occurs in some of the Pauline epistles, where the apostle speaks of "his gospel" (Rom. ii. 16, xvi. 25; 2 Tim. ii. 8); but here we certainly cannot understand it as denoting a written work: indeed, in this sense it does not seem to occur in Scripture, though we have an approach to this signification in Mark i. 1 (ἀρχὴ τοῦ εὐαγγελίου Ἰησοῦ Χριστοῦ).

The expression εὐαγγέλιον κατά τινα means *Evangelium* (*i.e.* history of Christ) "according to the account given by Matthew," etc., and this was probably intended to denote the actual author of each Gospel. It does not indeed positively denote that the Gospel "according to Matthew" was composed by him; it might simply signify that the gospel recorded was that given by Matthew orally, and committed to writing by some one else. The word κατά is used still more indefinitely in the titles of some apocryphal Gospels, *e.g.* εὐαγγέλιον καθ᾽ Ἑβραίους, κατ᾽ Αἰγυπτίους, where it can only signify the gospel as it was received by the Hebrews or Egyptians. As to the N. T. Gospels, κατά was taken by the Manichæan Faustus (*vid.* Augustine, *contra Faustum*, xxxii. 2) to denote merely the person from whom the account was primarily received, and some modern scholars have understood the word thus (*vid.* De Wette, § 78, note *b*),—as, for example, CREDNER (§ 89, note) and SCHLEIERMACHER in the case of Matthew and Mark. But the expression may with equal propriety be taken to denote the actual author, —as *e.g.* in DIODORUS SICULUS, ἡ καθ᾽ Ἡρόδοτον ἱστορία;

EPIPHANIUS, *Hær.* viii. 4, ἡ κατὰ Μωϋσέα πεντάτευχος; and so often in later writers. We may with the greatest probability conclude that they who put these titles to the Gospels used κατά in this sense; for the early Fathers, who quote from the Gospels, thus understand the title. Some have erroneously supposed κατά to be an imitation of the Hebrew ל when prefixed to the name of an author, *e.g.* לְדָוִד in the superscriptions to the Psalms. It is much simpler to explain it from the analogy of later Greek usage. Matthew, Mark, Luke, and John are thus named in these titles as the authors of the Gospels. As to the question whether they really were the authors, and as to the time and object of their writing, it will be most in keeping with our purpose to consider first these Gospels collectively—not the three first only, but all four successively. We shall first state what we know from external testimony, from history, concerning these four men, as to their personal character and career, concerning the style of writing adopted by them, including a survey of the main views which in ancient and modern times have been put forth as to the origin and genuineness of their writings. Having done this, we shall be prepared to consider the internal form and structure of the several Gospels, each by itself and by comparison with the rest, and to inquire what are the conclusions concerning their origin to which we are led.

§ 39.

THE FIRST GOSPEL says nothing concerning its authorship beyond what the title states. The author does not personally come forward, nor does he give us any hints as to who he is, and what his circumstances are. In the title, however, and in Church tradition, MATTHEW is named as the author; and this is supposed to be the Matthew who is named in the four lists of the apostles which the N. T. contains: Matt. x. 3; Mark iii. 18; Luke vi. 15; Acts i. 13. The name, which etymologically seems = מַתִּיָה, from יְתַן, מִתַּי, *donum Jovæ*, [according to others = אֲמִתַּי, Treumann, John i. 1,] occurs elsewhere only once in the N.

T., namely Matt. ix. 9. According to this latter passage, Matthew was a tax-gatherer at Capernaum, and he is called in the list of apostles in Matthew ὁ τελώνης. In the ninth chapter we are told that, as he sat at the receipt of custom, Jesus spoke to him, and commanded him to follow Him; and that he at once obeyed, and followed Him. What is here recorded does not of necessity refer to the first approach of Matthew to the Redeemer, but simply to his call to be His disciple in the stricter sense, so that from that time he became Christ's constant follower.

What is related in the first Gospel concerning Matthew is told concerning LEVI, a tax-gatherer, in Luke v. 27 and Mark ii. 14, who is called by Mark "the son of Alphæus;" and the account is in the same place as in the first Gospel, viz. immediately after the narrative of the healing of the paralytic, and before the supper at which Jesus met a number of publicans, and the discourse following thereupon concerning Christ's eating and drinking with publicans and sinners, and the fact that His disciples did not fast. Hence it is generally supposed that Matthew and Levi were different names for one and the same man.[1] This certainly might be so. It was not unusual among the Jews for the same person to have two different names. We might suppose that he who as a tax-gatherer bore the name of Levi was afterwards called Matthew as an apostle, because in all the four lists this name is given to him.[2] Still there were some who held very early in the Church the opinion that Matthew and Levi were different persons. The Gnostic HERACLEON considered that they were two different disciples of Jesus (in Clemens Alexandrinus, *Strom.* iv. p. 502 C, ed. Sylb. : Ματθαῖος, Φίλιππος, Θωμᾶς, Δευΐς, καὶ ἄλλοι πολλοί); and so did ORIGEN (*c. Cels.* i. 13), for he speaks of Levi as one of Christ's disciples in the more general sense merely; and so

---

[1] Thus the *Const. Apost.* viii. 22, EUTHYMIUS ZIGAB., and others, together with most modern expositors.

[2] GUERICKE's opinion (stated in ed. i. p. 234, note 2, and still held by him to be possible, ed. ii. p. 109, note 3), that both names have etymologically the same meaning, is untenable.

also many later expositors, such as GROTIUS and others (*vid.* DE WETTE, § 97, *a*). The similarity of the two accounts has been variously explained: *e.g.* by MICHAELIS, who supposes that Levi was a superintendent tax-gatherer and Matthew a subordinate officer, that Jesus called both at the same time—Matthew to the office of apostle, and Levi to be His disciple in a more general sense; or by NEANDER, who thinks that Matthew was the tax-gatherer called, but that the supper was in the house of Levi, another tax-gatherer, who followed Jesus afterwards,—and that thus Mark and Luke confused the two; or by SIEFFERT, who thinks that the author of the first Gospel confounded two different accounts, viz. the call of Matthew to the apostleship, and that of Levi to more general discipleship to Christ,—transferring to the former what properly belonged only to the latter event.

The opinion formed upon this point will depend much upon the view taken concerning the origin of the first Gospel, and its relation to Mark and Luke. I would here simply observe the fact that Mark and Luke name Matthew in their lists of the apostles without the least intimation that he is the same with Levi, whose call they had before related, and without even calling him a tax-gatherer. This rather points to the probability that these two evangelists were not themselves aware of an identity between the apostle Matthew and the publican Levi. Notwithstanding this, however, it might have been so, though we can hardly speak with certainty upon the question. We have, at any rate, no reason to doubt that Matthew was originally a tax-gatherer, as he is described in the first Gospel, and in the list of the apostles there given.

As to Alphæus the father of Levi (Mark ii. 14), an Alphæus is named in all four lists of the apostles as the father of James the Less; and this Alphæus is probably the same with Klopas (John xix. 25), the husband of the sister of our Lord's mother. CREDNER thinks that this Alphæus was the same with the father of Levi, and he therefore describes Matthew as, on his mother's side, a near kinsman of Jesus. But no reference whatever is made in the N. T.

to any kinship between Matthew and our Lord, nor is there any mention of such a relationship in Church tradition; and supposing the identity of Levi and Matthew, we must conclude that the Alphæus named by Mark as the father of Levi, was a different person from Alphæus the father of James the Less.

The N. T. contains nothing concerning the subsequent life of the Apostle Matthew. We learn from Acts i. 13 that he was still among the apostles in Jerusalem after the ascension; but he is not again mentioned in the book of the Acts nor in the epistles, and the accounts of Church historians concerning him are not very trustworthy. The story is first given in EUSEBIUS (iii. 24), that after he had preached the Gospel to the Hebrews (the Jews in Palestine) he went elsewhere (ἐφ' ἑτέρους), but whither Eusebius seems not to have known. Later writers name various countries in which he laboured: Ethiopia (so Rufinus, x. 9; Socrates, *II. E.* i. 19, and others); Macedonia (so Isodorus Hispal. *de vita et morte sanct.* c. lxvii.); afterwards Parthia, India, Arabia. Later historians describe him as suffering martyrdom in Ethiopia or Persia, and the Catholic Church keeps the 21st September (and the Greek Church the 16th November) as the day of his martyrdom. But we can put no reliance on these suppositions; for the early Church historians clearly knew nothing of such a martyrdom of the apostle, and Heracleon (in Clemens Alexandrinus as before) expressly names him among those who died a natural death. No special weight, indeed, can be attached to the story of Clemens Alex. himself (*Pædag.* ii. 1, p. 148 D), that he led an ascetic life, ate no animal food, but only grain, fruits, and vegetables.

§ 40.

This Matthew is expressly named by PAPIAS (who is reckoned among the apostolic Fathers) as a writer of one of the Gospels. Papias was bishop of Hierapolis in Phrygia. According to an account of him in the *Chronicon Alexandrinum,* he seems to have lived until the year 164 A.D., when he died at Pergamos as a martyr, in the reign of Marcus Aurelius.[1] He seems to have attained to a good old age, and his birth and youth were probably in the first century. IRENÆUS (*adv. Hær.* v. 33, in Euseb. iii. 39) calls him ἀρχαῖον ἄνδρα, a friend (associate or contemporary, ἑταῖρον) of Polycarp, a hearer of John (Ἰωάννου ἀκουστήν), by whom must certainly be meant John the apostle, and not (as Credner, § 38, note, supposes) another John. Eusebius indeed asserts, in opposition to Irenæus, that it is clear from Papias' own words that he had not seen or heard any of the apostles. But this does not appear in the words which Eusebius quotes in proof of his statement. Papias had composed a treatise (long since lost) entitled λογίων κυριακῶν ἐξήγησις, in five books, wherein he had collected the more important facts of our Lord's life and teachings, and (as he says himself in the preface) not copying other writings, but putting on record the oral tradition which he himself had heard from the πρεσβύτεροι, and had remembered; whence it would appear that he had been a scholar of the πρεσβύτεροι. By the πρεσβύτεροι (as is evident from the connection) he meant the earliest Christian teachers, who had been the immediate disciples of the Lord—apostles and others who had themselves heard the Lord—and of whom he names two, Aristion, and a presbyter John, not the apostle. It would appear, from the manner in which he speaks of them, that he did not personally know these two; yet, according to his words, we can hardly doubt that he had known and heard some of our Lord's immediate disciples, one of whom it is quite possible may have been the Apostle John, whose ἀκουστήν Irenæus says he was, though from the words of Papias given by Eusebius this does not appear, and he had not probably expressly stated the fact himself in his treatise elsewhere. His acquaintance and intercourse, however, with the first disciples of our Lord, must have been in his early youth, and long before he wrote his work. This he did evidently in his riper years, for he says that he arranges in it ὅσα ποτὲ παρὰ τῶν πρεσβυτέρων καλῶς ἔμαθον καὶ

[1] *Vid.* RETTIG, *Theol. Stud. u. Krit.* 1831, p. 766.

καλῶς ἐμνημόνευσα. The work was probably written about the middle of the second century, but we cannot be certain about this. In this compilation Papias may have written honestly indeed, but not critically; so that Eusebius may have felt himself justified in describing him as a very narrow-minded man, σφόδρα σμικρὸς τὸν νοῦν, which may not perhaps refer, as some have thought, simply to his gross chiliastic views. In our editions of Eusebius mention is also made of Papias in iii. 36, and there he calls him ἀνὴρ τὰ πάντα ὅτι μάλιστα λογιώτατος καὶ τῆς γραφῆς εἰδήμων. But the whole of this passage is wanting in the best MSS., and has been doubtless interpolated by later copyists, as Valesius long ago concluded.

Now this Papias somewhere in his work, as Eusebius tells us—perhaps in the preface—mentions Matthew by name as the author of a Gospel, but in the Hebrew language, which each one interpreted as well as he could.[1] This statement has been variously interpreted. Scholars of old took τὰ λόγια συνεγράψατο, as a matter of course, to denote a work upon the life of Christ, like our Gospels, of which our first canonical Gospel was a Greek translation. But in modern times several have thought that the expression simply refers to a writing wherein Christ's discourses only were collected.[2] But there is nothing in the manner in which Papias expresses himself to justify this supposition: he would certainly have expressed himself as he does, if he meant an historical work

---

[1] Ματθαῖος μὲν οὖν Ἑβραΐδι διαλέκτῳ τὰ λόγια συνεγράψατο, ἡρμήνευσε δ᾽ αὐτὰ ὡς ἦν δυνατὸς ἕκαστος. For συνεγράψατο some read συνετάξατο, and for ἦν δυνατός some read ἡ δύνατο.

[2] SCHLEIERMACHER was the first to adopt this view (*Ueber die Zeugnisse des Papias von unseren beiden ersten* EVANGELIEN, *Theol. Stud. u. Krit.* 1832, p. 735 sqq., reprinted in his theological works, ii. p. 361; and *Einl. i. N. T.* p. 240), and after him LACHMANN (*De ordine narrationum in evangeliis synopticis, Stud. u. Krit.* 1835, p. 577), CREDNER (*Einl.* § 88, and in his supplement to Part i. p. 752), WEISSE (*die evang. Gesch. krit. u. philos. bearbeitet*, 2 vols. Leipsic 1838, i. 29 sqq.), WIESELER (*Chronol. Synopse der vier Evang.*, Hamb. 1843, p. 304), EWALD (*Jahrb. d. bibl. Wiss.* ii. 201 sqq.), REUSS (§ 186). [WEISS, *Stud. u. Krit.* 1861; MEYER; HOLTZMANN, *Die Synopt. Evang. ihr Ursprung u. geschichtl. Charakter*, Leipz. 1863, pp. 248 sqq.]

like our N. T. Gospels, if he were referring to a writing whose contents were those of our Greek Gospel according to Matthew. Schleiermacher takes the second clause of Papias' statement, the ἑρμηνεύειν, to denote a sort of writing which explained the original collection of discourses by Matthew, which gave " the cream of the history," *i.e.* the facts and circumstances whereby the discourses might be explained. But this certainly is not what Papias says: the ἡρμήνευσε clearly refers to the Ἑβραΐδι διαλέκτῳ, and can only mean an interpreting of this work, which was written in a language which most Christians little understood,—either written interpretations, or the explanations given by teachers, or discovered by the readers themselves. The words τὰ λόγια συνεγράψατο give no warrant for the translation, " a collection of discourses," as has already been rightly remarked (*e.g.* by De Wette, § 97, *a*, note *b*; Ebrard, *Krit. d. ev. Gesch.* 767). The word λόγιον, both in classical and Hellenistic Greek, is used not of any simple statement, but of a divine declaration; and τὰ λόγια τοῦ Θεοῦ in Heb. v. 12 stands, like ὁ λόγος τοῦ Θεοῦ, for the entire revealed word of God, and (according to the connection of Christian doctrine) for the gospel. Papias therefore here uses the name τὰ λόγια of the entire Gospel, without making any distinction between the historical narrative and the discourses of Christ. It is evident that what Eusebius quotes from Papias concerning Mark, refers to him as the writer of a Gospel, viz. that he had not written ὥσπερ σύνταξιν τῶν κυριακῶν ποιούμενος λογίων. By this, I say, he could only have meant, as he had before said, that Mark had not written τάξει τὰ ὑπὸ τοῦ Χριστοῦ ἢ λεχθέντα ἢ πραχθέντα. In like manner, in the title of the work of Papias the κυριακὰ λόγια do not mean merely Christ's discourses; for we have clear evidence that it contained other narratives of gospel history, of which the discourses did not form the main part. And τὰ λόγια τοῦ Θεοῦ or κυριακά are used in a similar manner by the Fathers.

It is thus certain that Eusebius understood the words of Papias in this sense, as denoting a Hebrew (Aramæan) original of our Greek Gospel of Matthew. Eusebius had already said (iii. 24) that Matthew, after having preached to the Hebrews, resolved to give his Gospel to others, and wrote it in his mother tongue (πατρίῳ γλώττῃ γραφῇ παραδούς). From this and other ancient testimonies it is clear that in the early Church—indeed, from the middle of the second century—it was generally thought that the Apostle Matthew had written a Gospel in the vernacular of Palestine. Thus before Eusebius did IRENÆUS, iii. 1 (in Euseb. v. 8), and ORIGEN (in Euseb. vi. 25); and after Eusebius, JEROME (Præf. in Matt. and *de viris illustr.* c. iii.), EPIPHANIUS, CHRYSOSTOM, AUGUSTINE, and many others; whereas none assert the contrary, viz. that the evangelist wrote his Gospel in Greek. This coincides with what Eusebius observes (v. 10) concerning Pantænus, an Alexandrine divine about the middle or after the middle of the second century, that he had been told of him that he had gone among the Indians (probably the inhabitants of southern Arabia), and there had found the Gospel of Matthew, which the Apostle Bartholomew, who preached among them, had left there "in Hebrew" (Ἐβραίων γράμμασιν). He does not say that this Hebrew Gospel was the original, but Eusebius unquestionably understood it thus. Still this story is not implicitly to be relied on. The statement, however, that our Gospel according to Matthew had been written in Hebrew, occurs at the end of several Greek MSS., and also in the Peschito; and this opinion was also held in the Syrian Church (*vid.* Credner, i. 73).

Now, as to the relation which this Hebrew work bears to our Greek Gospel, explain ἡρμήνευσε, κ.τ.λ. as we may, nothing definite is stated in Papias. If we understand the expression to denote a written translation, it must mean a plurality of such versions, and different translators. But it is hardly likely that so early as the time of Papias there were many translations already made, and we should have to suppose that Papias had in his mind several Greek Gospels which more or less resembled the Aramæan original, and might be regarded as translations of it. In this case his words would imply that there was not in his time one recognised Greek

Gospel which was regarded as above all others an authentic translation, and which was thus regarded by the Church in his time. Again, if we take ἡρμήνευσε, κ.τ.λ. to mean that each one endeavoured in teaching and reading to interpret the Hebrew work as best he could, the words of Papias contain nothing about a Greek translation as a written work; and we may with great probability suppose that Papias said nothing regarding it in the course of his work, otherwise Eusebius would not have failed to notice it.

But there cannot be any doubt that, at the very least, from the end of the second century downwards, our first canonical Gospel was regarded as the only authentic translation of the Hebrew work of Matthew. Still, down to the end of the fourth century no ecclesiastical writer makes the slightest allusion to the author of this translation. Some modern scholars hold that Matthew himself wrote the Greek translation side by side with the Hebrew original. This is the view of Bengel, Schott, Guericke, Olshausen. But none of the ancients give the slightest hint of this. JEROME, however, says (*de viris illustr.* c. iii.): *quod quis postea in Græcum transtulerit non satis certum est.* Different opinions have since been suggested: (*a*) that the translator was James the Lord's brother (thus the *Synopsis Scripturæ sacræ,* and the postscript to several Greek MSS. of the Gospel); or (*b*) that he was John (thus Theophylact, Euthymius Zigabenus, and the postscripts and *scholia* to other Greek manuscripts). Still we cannot attach any importance to these opinions, because they are of so late a date, and seem not even to have been known to the earlier Church writers.

§ 41.

As to the Aramæan work which Papias knew, and which he describes as a work of the Apostle Matthew, it would be of use and would be circulated in those places and among those Churches only where Aramæan was known, *i.e.* among the Hebrew Christians in Palestine and its neighbourhood. And we find that it was so. Most of these

Christians held a Christianity which was more or less of a Judaizing character. The Jewish Christians of Judea in the apostolic age seem to have been more or less decidedly opposed to the Apostle Paul and his phase of doctrine. Notwithstanding their faith in Jesus as the Christ, they seem to have maintained the obligation of the Jewish law even as regarded certain ceremonies, and many of them held that the observance of it was necessary to justification before God and to salvation; so that they not only obeyed it themselves, but enforced obedience to it upon all Christians, even upon those who never had been Jews. Hence their views concerning the person of Christ were narrower than those of other Churches; and they did not believe in the miraculous conception of Jesus, or in His pre-existence, or if in the former, not certainly in the latter. These Jewish Christians held their ground after the destruction of Jerusalem, and became a distinct sect, living some of them to the east of the Dead Sea and the Jordan, and some in the neighbourhood of Beroea in Syria. In the end of the second century, mention is made of them by writers of the Church under the designation EBIONITES, or Ebionists. Later, at the end of the fourth century, another sect of these Jewish Christians is spoken of under the name of NAZARENES (or Nazarites) by Jerome and Epiphanius. Epiphanius, indeed, mentions both these sects. The Nazarenes were nearer in doctrine to the Churches at large than were the Ebionites: they obeyed the Mosaic law as far as it could be obeyed now that the temple was destroyed; but they did not, like the Ebionites, impose this upon other Christians; and they took a higher view of Christ's person, believing in the miraculous conception.

By the testimony of Church writers from Irenæus downwards, we know that these Jewish Christians received only *one* of the Gospels as of ecclesiastical authority, viz. the Aramæan Gospel, which they attributed to Matthew as the author, and which is generally called εὐαγγέλιον καθ' Ἑβραίους, because it was in use among Hebrew Christians. Irenæus (*adv. Hær.* i. 26, iii. 11) says that the Gospel of Matthew only was in use among them; Eusebius (*H. E.* iii. 27) calls the Gospel which they received the εὐαγγέλιον καθ' Ἑβραίους. Jerome also says the same thing. He found this Gospel which the Nazarenes and Ebionites used (*Comment. ad* Matt. xii. 13 [1]) in Hebrew—or, as he elsewhere says,[2] in Syro-Chaldaic with Hebrew characters—at Cæsarea Stratonis in Palestine, in the library which Pamphilus, the friend of Eusebius, had founded there; and another copy among the Nazarenes at Berœa, from which he copied, and which he translated into Greek as well as Latin (*ad* Matt. *passim; de viris illustr.* c. ii. and iii.). In the passage *de viris illustr.* c. iii., he seems to take it for granted that this was the original of Matthew. But in his commentary on Matthew, which was written afterwards, and in his still later work *adv. Pelag.*, he simply says that it was generally supposed to be the original of Matthew, or the work of Matthew. Epiphanius distinguishes between the Gospel of the Nazarenes and that of the Ebionites. He says of both, that they presuppose the Gospel of Matthew in the Hebrew original; but he describes that of the Ebionites as a mutilated copy of Matthew's Gospel, which began with the account of the baptism of John (*Hær.* xxx. 3, 13 sqq., in De Wette, § 64, note *a*). Of the Nazarenes, on the contrary, he says that they retained Matthew's Gospel in its integrity (πληρέστατον) as it had been originally written in Hebrew (*Hær.* xxix. 9, in De Wette, *ib.*); but as he adds that he is uncertain whether it contained the genealogy from Abraham to Christ (Matt. i. 1–17), it would appear that Epiphanius did not know, or knew but slightly, this Nazarene Gospel, and had no copy of it by him, so that we can hardly suppose that (as possessed by them) it corresponded with our Gospel of Matthew. Otherwise, indeed, we might

---

[1] *In Evangelio, quo utuntur Nazareni et Ebionitæ, quod nuper in Græcum de Hebræo sermone transtulimus, et quod vocatur a plerisque Matthæi authenticum.*

[2] *Adversus Pelagianos*, iii. 1 : *In Evangelio juxta Hebræos, quod Chaldaico quidem Syroque sermone, sed Hebraicis litteris scriptum est, quo utuntur usque hodie Nazareni, secundum apostolos, sive, ut plerique autumant, juxta Matthæum, quod et in Cæsareensi habetur bibliotheca.*

harmonize with this what Theodoret (*Hæret. fab.* ii. 1) says, who clearly distinguishes two different classes of Ebionites, one of which denied and the other acknowledged the miraculous birth of Christ; and he says that the former adopted the Gospel καθ' Ἑβραίους only, but the latter the Gospel of Matthew. Still Theodoret does not seem to have had any exact knowledge of the matter, and his statement may have been only an inference from the combined statements of Irenæus and Eusebius concerning the Gospel used by the Ebionites. We may, at any rate, conclude from what Epiphanius says, that the Hebrew Gospel was not of one and the same form among all the Jewish Christians of Palestine. We should be led to this conclusion by comparing the different accounts given by Epiphanius (*Hær.* xxx. 13) and by Jerome (on Isa. xi. 1, in De Wette, § 65, *a*, note *b*) of the narrative (in the Ebionite and Nazarite Gospel) of the baptism of Christ, when He came up out of the water; though, according to the quotations given by Epiphanius from the Ebionite Gospel, the narrative in our Greek Matthew would seem to resemble *this*, rather than what Jerome found in the copy which he had received from the Nazarenes of Berœa. We learn from the doctors of the orthodox Church of the first century, that the Gospel καθ' Ἑβραίους was made use of as an authority by Hegesippus, Ignatius, and (with quotations from it under this title) by Clemens Alexandrinus and Origen (*vid.* De Wette, § 64, *a*, note *a*): still Origen leaves it with the reader to decide whether it was authoritative, and to what extent (ἐὰν δὲ προσίεταί τις τὸ καθ' Ἑβραίους εὐαγγέλιον; *si tamen placet alicui suscipere illud non ad autoritatem, sed ad manifestationem propositæ quæstionis*); so that he clearly distinguishes it from our four canonical Gospels. So still more clearly does Eusebius, who in his main statement concerning the N. T. Canon (*H. E.* iii. 25) merely says of the Gospel καθ' Ἑβραίους, that some (*i.e.* some Church writers) reckoned this Gospel which was used by the believing Hebrews among the writings of the second rank (the νόθα or ἀντιλεγόμενα).

§ 42.

As to the relation of this Hebrew Gospel to our Greek Gospel of Matthew, various views have in modern times been held. Many maintain that our Greek canonical Gospel was the original, and was of apostolic authorship. On this I make the following historical observations:—

In the early Church, from the end of the second century downwards, we find our Greek Gospel recognised universally and without contradiction as a genuine work of the Apostle Matthew; and equally general was the opinion (as we have seen) that Matthew originally wrote in Hebrew, *i.e.* Aramæan. The doctors of the Church down to the end of the fourth century do not attempt to explain how it came to pass that the Aramæan Gospel used by the Jewish Christians of Palestine (and which these latter attributed to Matthew, without contradiction on the part of the orthodox doctors of the Church) presented so many discrepancies when compared with our Greek Gospel. Still the apostolic authorship of our canonical Gospel, as written by Matthew, was not denied by those sects who did not grant the canonical authority of this or the other three Gospels,—by the Marcionites, for example, and others. The Manichæans, however, or at least Faustus the Manichæan, at the end of the fourth century, denied that our Gospel was composed by Matthew, in proof of which he referred not only to the title κατὰ Ματθαῖον, but to the fact that the apostle speaks of himself in the third person (see Augustine *c. Faustum*, xvii. 1). This, however, had no influence with the Church generally, and the Gospel was still regarded as the genuine work of the Apostle Matthew, and without the belief in a Hebrew original being disputed until the time of the Reformation. The first who ventured to doubt this latter opinion were Erasmus and Cajetan, and they were supported by the Protestant theologians generally, who maintained the originality of the Greek Matthew mainly for dogmatic and apologetic reasons, fearing that on the opposite supposition the authority of the Greek Gospel as maintained by the Church would be endangered. Many Catholic theologians, on the contrary, in opposition to the

Protestants, and to their assertion of the supreme authority of Holy Scripture in matters of faith, and in order to demonstrate the necessity of the Church's authority, urged the recognition of a Hebrew original, according to the early ecclesiastical tradition.[1]

MICHAELIS, on the contrary, among Protestants, declared himself as a believer in an Aramæan original; and HUG, among Roman Catholic theologians, against the testimony of Papias and the early Church, endeavoured to prove a Greek original. Many Protestant theologians have espoused this latter view, e.g. Paulus, Fritzsche (and others; see Credner, § 43 fin.), and especially HARLESS.[2] Others have endeavoured to blend both opinions by the supposition that Matthew wrote his Gospel in both languages, or at least issued it thus, —the Greek translation having been prepared by another apostolic man under his superintendence.[3]

§ 43.

In these conflicting views concerning the original language of this Gospel, it is assumed that the work as we have it, in its range and construction, was the work of the Apostle Matthew. But in modern times, during the past thirty or forty years, criticism concerning this Gospel has taken another turn; and it has been questioned whether, as we have it, it can fairly be considered as the work of this

---

[1] Among Protestants of the Lutheran Church especially, who endeavoured to maintain that Matthew's Gospel was written originally in Greek, may be named M. FLACIUS (Prof. at Wittenberg, and afterwards at Jena, ob. at Frankfort 1575: *N. T. ex vers. Des. Erasmi cum glossa compendiaria*, Basel 1540, fol., Frankfort 1659) and JOHN GERHARD (Prof. at Jena, ob. 1637: *Annott. posthumæ in ev. Matth.*).

[2] Erlanger Programm, 1841: *Lucubratt. Evangelia canonica spectantium pars prima. Fabula de Matthæo Syro-Chaldaice conscripto.*

[3] This was held by J. C. SCHWARZ (*Solœcismi discipulorum J. Chr.*, etc., Cob. 1730, 4to, p. 49), BENGEL (*Gnomon N. T.* 1742), GUERICKE, SCHOTT, OLSHAUSEN (*Bibl. Comment.* i., Königsb. 1830), THIERSCH. EBRARD also says (*Wissensch. Kritik d. evang. Gesch.*, Frankfort 1841, 1842), "The translation was made under the eye and with the assistance of the apostle."

apostle, whether he had any hand in its composition, and whether it bears any relation to the Hebrew treatise of Matthew mentioned by Papias, and to the Gospel καθ' Ἑβραίους. At the time of the Reformation, the ANA-BAPTISTS asserted that, as this Gospel seemed to have been composed originally in Greek, it could not be the same with that which (according to Papias) Matthew wrote in Hebrew.[1] This opinion was little thought of at the time; but of late it has been again espoused by German Protestant theologians, who maintain that our Gospel was not written by Matthew, and was not a translation of any Aramæan work. The course of critical inquiry had for a long time been preparing the way for this view, and many hints at it have at different times been given. DAVID SCHULZ was the first, however, to state the reasons which led him to the conclusion that Matthew was not the author, in his *Bemerkungen über den Verf. des Ev. nach Matthæus,*—a supplement to his treatise, *Die Christl. Lehre vom heiligen Abendmahl nach den Grundtexte des N. T.*, Leipsic 1824, pp. 302–322. Schulz did not propound any positive view of his own upon the question. Heydenreich (in Winer's *Krit. Journal,* iii. 1825) advocates Matthew's authorship in answer to Schulz, as Theile, C. F. A. Fritzsche, and others have done. Negative views on the subject continued to spread, however; but a genuine work of Matthew in Aramæan, containing our Lord's discourses, was supposed to have formed the basis of our Greek Gospel.[2]

The controversy concerning the truth of the Gospel narratives generally, as prosecuted by DAV. FRIEDR. STRAUSS in his *Leben Jesu,* was not without its influence upon this

---

[1] S. SIXTUS SENENSIS, *Biblioth. sancta,* vii. 2, p. 924; in Credner, i. p. 95.

[2] The following scholars agree (though with various modifications) in maintaining this theory in its main points:—R. E. KLENER, *recentiores de authentia Ev. Matth. quæstiones recensentur,* etc., Gött. 1832, 4to. F. L. SIEFFERT, *ueber den Ursprung des ersten kanon. Ev.,* Königsb. 1832, who endeavours to separate the later additions in the Greek from the original Hebrew elements. SCHLEIERMACHER, *ueber das Zeugniss des Papias,* etc., 1832; and *Einl. in das N. T.* LACHMANN, *Studien u. Krit.* 1835. WEISSE, *evang. Gesch.* NEANDER, *Leben Jesu.* M. SCHNECKENBURGER,

question. This work it was which called forth the treatises above named of NEANDER and WEISSE. Strauss, together with BRUNO BAUER (*Kritik d. evang. Gesch. der Synoptiker*, 3 vols., Bremen 1841–42), asserts the entirely unhistorical character, as of the other Gospels, so of this, and thus of course denies its apostolic authorship. A. F. GFRÖRER (*Gesch. des Urchristenthums*, 2d part, also entitled *die heilige Sage*, Stuttg. 1838) endeavours to prove this on internal grounds.

Among the scholars who have endeavoured to vindicate the Gospel of Matthew against the objections thus urged against it, may be named—OLSHAUSEN, in his *bibl. Commentar;* in *Tholuck's litter. Anzeiger*, 1833, No. 14; and in three essays, *Apostolica Ev. Matt. origo defenditur*, Erlangen 1835–37 : GUERICKE, Beiträge i., *u. Einl. i. d. N. T.* Ebrard (as before) regards the Gospel as a correct and authentic translation from the original Hebrew of Matthew : HEINR. AUG. W. MEYER, in his *Commentar über Matt.;* and others : *vid.* De Wette, § 98, *a*, note.

FRANZ DELITZSCH, *die Entstehung des Matthäus-Evang.*, in *Rudelbach u. Guericke's Zeitschr. f. d. gesammte luther. Theol. u. Kirche*, 1850, iii. pp. 456–494. He considers the Gospel καθ' Ἑβραίους as a later work, and our Greek Gospel (according to external evidence) to be a true but free Greek translation of an Aramæan original by Matthew, lost since the middle of the second century, and composed during the last thirty years of the first century. This Greek translation, he thinks, was made in the country east of Jordan, in confirmation of which he refers to Matt. xix. 1.

DE WETTE, in his *Einl. ins N. T.*, urged from the outset objections against the apostolic origin of our Gospel, and in his latest editions has confirmed them, though he does not *ueber den Ursprung der ersten Kanon. Ev., ein krit. Versuch*, reprinted from Klaiber's *Studien*, Stuttgard 1834. He has developed the arguments which seem most to tell against the apostolic authorship of the Gospel in its present state with great clearness and acuteness. CREDNER, § 88, 89. F. H. KERN, in the Tübingen *Zeitschr. f. Theol.* 1834, ii. pp. 1–132 ; 1835, ii. pp. 133–138. SCHOTT, besides his *Isagoge*, in a dissertation published by DANZ since his death, *ueber die Authenticität des Kanon Ev. nach Matt. benannt*, Leipsic 1837. And others.

suggest any positive theory as to the author, and his relation to Matthew. He firmly denies, however, that it was translated from the Aramæan Gospel καθ' Ἑβραίους.

The theologians of the modern Tübingen school take another view. They regard the Aramæan Gospel mentioned by Papias—the εὐαγγέλιον καθ' Ἑβραίους—though not composed by the Apostle Matthew, yet the oldest and original Gospel. This, they believe, was at an early date translated into Greek, various modifications having been made in it, until at length it attained its present form in our canonical Gospel before the middle of the second century (according to Baur, about the year A.D. 130 or 140); and they hold that in that last revision of it many elements were introduced to give it an aspect of universality, in contrast with the narrow Judaizing character which it at the outset bore. Thus BAUR himself explains his views in his *Krit. Untersuchungen über die kanon. Ev.*, etc., Tüb. 1847, pp. 570-621. And in like manner SCHWEGLER (in his review of De Wette's *Einl.* in *Zeller's theol. Jahrbb.* 1843, iii. pp. 550-564; and in his *Nachapost. Zeitalter*, i. 199-216, 241-259). ZELLER and others of this school agree in the main with this view, which is, however, decidedly false.

§ 44.

The questions—*first*, whether our first Gospel was originally written in Greek, or in Aramæan, so that what we have is a translation; and *secondly*, whether it can in either case be regarded as a work of Matthew the apostle—cannot be fully answered without a comparison of it with the other canonical Gospels, with Luke and Mark as well as with John; and we must therefore postpone for the present a final answer. But we may, without any special reference to the other Gospels, consider the relation of our canonical Gospel to the Gospel καθ' Ἑβραίους, because the ancients have given us hints as to the contents and form of this Hebrew Gospel.[1] The following conclusions on this point

[1] The statements of the early writers concerning the Hebrew Gospel, and the fragments of it which they have quoted, are collected in DE

may be stated, some of them with certainty, and the rest with great probability.

1. The Hebrew Gospel used by the Judaizing Christians in Palestine and the neighbourhood, from the end of the second to the beginning of the fifth century, and which they described as the work of Matthew the apostle, was in some respects very similar to our Greek Gospel of Matthew, yet was marked by many differences and peculiarities of its own. This is evident from the citations which the writers of the Church give from it, which are in certain parts wholly different from what our Greek Gospel contains. There is truth, however, in the remark that the Church writers were likely to refer to just those passages which were different from the canonical Gospel; and we must not conclude, from the relation of these parts to our Gospel, that the two works were similarly contrasted throughout. We may rather infer that the points of resemblance predominated; otherwise the Church writers themselves, especially Jerome (who knew the work well), could not have held, or even have supposed, that the Hebrew Gospel was the original work of the apostle. That the two works differed in some important particulars, is evident from the fact that Jerome was obliged to translate the Hebrew Gospel not only into Latin, but also into Greek.

2. According to the dates presented to us, we may conclude that, from the end of the second to the beginning of the fourth century, the Gospel καθ' Ἑβραίους had a determinate form and contents, which for the most part coincided with that of Matthew; to such an extent at least, that though it presented many points of difference, we might with the greatest probability suppose that the one work was immediately dependent upon the other. From what we have remarked under the first head, it is clear that our Greek Gospel could not have been, strictly speaking, a translation of the Hebrew Gospel. Scholars who take this view have in their minds, not the Hebrew Gospel which Epiphanius and Jerome knew, but the Hebrew Gospel in its supposed original form.

WETTE, § 64, 65; KIRCHHOFER, pp. 448–465; CREDNER, *Beiträge*, i. 380; FABRICIUS, *Cod. apocr. N. T.* i. 355; GRABE, *Spicileg. Patr.* i. 15.

It is certainly clear, from the statements and quotations of Epiphanius and Jerome, that the Hebrew Gospel in their time was not precisely the same among all the Judaizing sects, and in all places; and from this it is inferred that some of these Jewish Christians must in course of time have admitted alterations in the Gospel which they had received. As we cannot tell how early such changes began to be made, we might infer that all the differences between the Greek Gospel and the Hebrew pointed out by Epiphanius and Jerome were owing to these alterations in the latter, and that the Aramæan Gospel in its original form coincided with our Matthew. But considering the dates lying before us, this is not likely. Down to the end of the fourth century we find no traces of such differences among the copies of the Hebrew Gospel. If these copies were in such a state that, according to Epiphanius, the gospel *infantiæ* was wanting in the Ebionite Gospel, while it was inserted in another—probably the Nazarene Gospel—it is not likely that the early writers in the Church could have regarded the Gospel used by these different sects of Jewish Christians as one and the same, or have spoken of it by one and the same name as the Gospel καθ' Ἑβραίους. The Gospel thus described by the Church Fathers from the end of the second to the beginning of the fourth century, by CLEMENS ALEX., ORIGEN, EUSEBIUS— thus referred to and quoted by them—must have been a well-known writing, with settled and determinate contents, like our canonical Gospel. There may have been slight differences in different manuscripts and in different countries, but none of any importance.

§ 45.

3. Now, *if* the Aramæan Gospel, as the writers of the Church knew it before the end of the second century, were the original work of Matthew the apostle, our canonical Greek Gospel cannot have been in any true sense a translation of it, but only a free version of it in Greek. But an unbiassed consideration will lead us to the conclusion that this supposition is very improbable. For,

(*a.*) What was distinctive of the Gospel of the Hebrews, according to the references of the earlier Church writers, was by no means apostolic, but was rather apocryphal in its character when compared with our Greek Gospel of Matthew. For example, according to ORIGEN (*in Joann.* tom. ii. c. vi.), the following saying of Christ's is found in it : ἄρτι ἔλαβέ με ἡ μήτηρ μου, τὸ ἅγιον πνεῦμα, ἐν μιᾷ τῶν τριχῶν μου καὶ ἀπένεγκέ με εἰς τὸ ὄρος τὸ μέγα Θαβώρ; and CLEMENS ALEX. (*Strom.* ii. p. 380, ed. Sylburg.) gives us the following from it as a saying of Christ's which is enigmatical in its form : ὁ θαυμάσας βασιλεύσει καὶ ὁ βασιλεύσας ἀναπαυθήσεται.

(*b.*) What was distinctive of this Gospel as compared with our Greek Matthew, is of such a character that, if it were apostolic, it could hardly have been omitted from a Greek version of it ; nor could it have been altered, as it must have been if our Greek Matthew were derived from it. As the matter stands, a comparison of the two leads rather to the conclusion that our canonical Gospel was the earlier and the more original. ORIGEN, for example (*in Matt.* tom. xv.), tells us how the conversation of Christ with the rich young man (Matt. xix. 16-23) was given in the Hebrew Gospel. It says that when Jesus told him to sell his goods and give to the poor, and then to follow Him, the rich young ruler "scratched his head:" that Jesus said to him, "How can you think that you have obeyed all, when it is written in the law, 'Love thy neighbour as thyself,' and yet so many of thy brethren, sons of Abraham, are clothed in rags, dying of hunger, while thy house is filled with goods, and nothing given?" And lastly, that Jesus spoke the words, "How hardly shall they that have riches," etc., not to the disciples generally, as in our Matthew (ver. 19), but to Peter only, addressing him, "Simon, son of Joanna." And yet there is so great a similarity between the two accounts, that we are led rather to the conclusion, that what the Gospel of the Hebrews presents in an altered form was preceded by the narrative as recorded in our canonical Matthew. And so in other places.

The Gospel of the Hebrews contains, moreover, places which, differing from our Matthew, remind us rather of St. Luke's Gospel; and this tells rather for the priority of the Greek Matthew. It has, for example, as Jerome (*de viris illustr.* c. xvi.) tells us, a saying of Christ's to be found (as Jerome also observes) in the Ignatian Epistle to the people of Smyrna (ch. iii.), viz. where Jesus, after His resurrection, tells His disciples to handle Him, and see that He is not a disembodied spirit. This is essentially the same with what we find in Luke xxiv. 39, but it does not occur in our Matthew. Had it originally belonged to Matthew's Gospel, it is unaccountable why the translator or editor should have left it out; but we can easily understand how a reviser of our canonical Gospel might borrow and insert such a saying from another source. Again, according to Epiphanius (*Hær.* xxx. 13), at the beginning of the Ebionite Gospel, in the account of John the Baptist's ministry, it is said of him: ὃς ἐλέγετο εἶναι ἐκ γένους Ἀαρὼν τοῦ ἱερέως, παῖς Ζαχαρίου καὶ Ἐλισάβετ; which corresponds with what Luke records in ch. i. Now if this, too, had belonged to the original text of Matthew, a Greek translator or reviser could have had no motive to omit it; but it is very easy to see how a reviser of our canonical Gospel who was acquainted with Luke's Gospel would insert it, as giving a more exact account of the person and parentage of the Baptist. And so in other instances.

(*c.*) Our canonical Gospel was, as its title and universal tradition testify, attributed to Matthew, but the author does not in any part of it expressly say so, or hint at the fact. Now it is otherwise in the Hebrew Gospel. In the form in which (according to Epiphanius) the Ebionites had it, it laid claim to be an apostolic Gospel, and the work of Matthew (see Epiphanius, *Hær.* xxx. 13, where it appears that in the account of the choosing of the apostles the first person occurs—ὃς ἐξελέξατο ἡμᾶς); and Matthew, moreover, is given prominence in one of Christ's discourses. The same was certainly the case in the Nazarene Gospel which Jerome found at Cæsarea. Hence he says of this Syro-Chaldaic

Gospel of the Nazarites (*adv. Pelagian.* iii. 1) : *secundum apostolos, sive ut plerique autumant, juxta Matthæum.*

§ 46.

4. The result which these facts lead to is confirmed by another consideration which cannot escape observation, viz. that the basis of the Hebrew Gospel must have been a Greek text. (*a.*) The usual food of John the Baptist is called honey-cakes (ἐγκρίς) instead of locusts (ἀκρίδες, Matt. iii. 4, Mark i. 6), at least in the Ebionite Gospel, as Epiphanius tells us (*Hær.* xxx. 13), evidently with reference to the food of the Israelites in the wilderness (Ex. xvi. 31; Num. xi. 8). Now this term has obviously been suggested by the ἀκρίδες in the Greek Gospel; whereas such a confounding of words and alteration in an original Aramæan text, and without reference to the Greek, could not be explained, for in the Greek only are both things called by similarly sounding words. (*b.*) According to Jerome, the name of Barabbas was explained in the Gospel καθ' Ἑβραίους (*quod scribitur juxta Hebræos*) as *filius magistri eorum*. Now the true etymological signification of Barabbas is בַּר אַבָּא, *filius patris;* but in that explanation it is regarded as = בַּר רַבָּן, *filius magistri nostri*. Such a mistaken explanation could not be accounted for if the name had been rightly written in Hebrew. But the Greek form of the word is Βαραββᾶν, which appears thus always in the Greek Matthew (xxvii. 16, 17, 20, 21, 26),—the word in all these places being in the accusative; and the inventor of that interpretation must have mistaken this for the true and original form of the name (cf. Paulus, *theol.-exeg. Conservatorium*, i. 143, 1822; Credner, *Beitr.* i. 405; my *Beitr.* p. 61). This explanation of the word is itself perhaps a later interpolation in the Hebrew Gospel, but it could not have been suggested unless the word in that Hebrew Gospel was written ברבן in mistake for its proper form ברבא or בראבא; and such a mistake was not likely to have been made by a slip of the pen, but is most naturally explained as a blundering retention of the accusative in the Greek.

Putting all these considerations together, it follows, with the highest probability, that the Aramæan Gospel καθ' Ἑβραίους was neither the original of our Greek Matthew, nor its basis, but was, on the contrary, itself derived from our canonical Gospel, and written in Aramæan for the sake of the Hebrew Christians. But what are we to make of the statement of Papias, that Matthew wrote a Gospel in the Hebrew tongue? If this statement be regarded as valid, we must conclude that Papias meant an Aramæan Gospel of Matthew different from the Gospel καθ' Ἑβραίους, which had already disappeared and was lost. But the words of Papias, to all appearance, denote a writing which was still extant at the time; and if we compare the statements of writers who immediately followed him, it is, to say the least, very probable that the Aramæan work meant by Papias was the same with the Gospel καθ' Ἑβραίους, which the Hebrew Christians and some of the writers in the Church assigned to Matthew. It would hardly be likely, if the true original of Matthew's Gospel were still extant in the time of Papias, that an Aramæan translation of our Greek Gospel would be required among the Hebrew Christians. We are therefore driven to the conclusion that the statement of Papias, and of some Church writers who followed him, that Matthew himself wrote a Gospel in Hebrew, was based upon a misconception. The possibility of this cannot be denied. For if, besides the Greek Gospel called after Matthew, there already existed an Aramæan Gospel the same in substance, it might easily be supposed that the latter was the original, when in reality the former was.

§ 47.

The SECOND of our canonical Gospels contains no statement whatever concerning its author: he does not appear personally, any more than in the first Gospel. But in the title or superscription prefixed to the Greek manuscripts and to the old versions, together with Church tradition generally, MARK is named as the writer. This Mark was, according to tradition, the person who bears this name in the book of the Acts and in the epistles. His original Jewish name was JOHN, but to this was added the Roman name Mark, according to a custom not unusual among the Jews. Thus in Acts xii. 12, 25, xv. 37, he is called Ἰωάννης ὁ ἐπικαλούμενος (ἐπικληθεὶς, καλούμενος) Μάρκος; and simply Ἰωάννης, Acts xiii. 5, 13; and Μάρκος only; Acts xv. 39. It is clear from the connection that the same person is referred to in all these places. In the epistles the name Mark only occurs, and so generally in the Fathers. Living out of Palestine in his later years, he dropped the Jewish name, and was called simply Mark. He was by birth a Jew, and his mother, named MARY, had a house in Jerusalem (Acts xii. 12). We there are told that Peter, when miraculously delivered from prison, went to that house, where many of the believers were gathered together praying. It is thus clear that this Mary, with her family, already belonged to the Christian fellowship. From what is told us, we cannot say whether she had been a disciple during the lifetime of our Lord, or whether she had not been converted until after the resurrection and ascension. Epiphanius (*Hær.* li. 6) and the Pseudo-Origen (*de recta fide in Deum*) suppose that Mark was one of the Seventy; but little importance can be attached to this statement, because a very early witness, Papias (Euseb. *H. E.* iii. 39), expressly says: οὔτε γὰρ ἤκουσε τοῦ Κυρίου οὔτε παρηκολούθησεν αὐτῷ. Still the position which the mother of John Mark evidently held in the early Church by no means obliges us to suppose, as Schleiermacher does (*Stud. u. Krit.* 1832, p. 760; *Works*, ii. 386), that Papias in this statement must have meant another of the name, and not John Mark.

The narrative in the Acts leads us to suppose that there was a personal relationship between Mark's mother and family and the Apostle Peter: this, moreover, appears from the fact that Peter calls Mark his son (1 Pet. v. 13, ἀσπάζεται ὑμᾶς . . . Μάρκος ὁ υἱός μου). It is not likely, as some have supposed, that this refers to another Mark, a literal son of the apostle's; John Mark, the son of Mary, is meant, whom the apostle calls "his son" in a spiritual sense, perhaps because he was converted and baptized by him. It appears from Col. iv. 10 that he was nephew (ἀνεψιός) of Barnabas. By Barnabas probably he was first brought into connection with the Apostle Paul. According to Acts xii. 25, when Paul and Barnabas were returning to Antioch, after having fulfilled their mission as the conveyers of a collection from the Church at Antioch to that of Jerusalem during a dearth, Mark accompanied them. He was still at Antioch when Paul and Barnabas were starting upon their first missionary tour, and he accompanied them as subordinate minister (ὑπηρέτης, Acts xiii. 5). He travelled with them from Antioch through Seleucia to Cyprus, and went through this island with them. But when Paul and Barnabas went thence into Asia Minor, Mark departed from them in Pamphylia and returned to Jerusalem (Acts xiii. 13, xv. 38); and, as is evident from the latter passage, he did this in opposition to Paul's will, probably simply because he lacked courage to bear the hardships to which such a missionary journey must have exposed him. In contemplating another missionary tour, Paul was unwilling to take Mark (whom again we find at Antioch) with them; and the contention between him and Barnabas upon this point was so sharp, that they departed asunder one from the other, at least for this journey. Paul went again through Syria and Cilicia, and from thence into other districts of Asia Minor, and into Europe; and Barnabas sailed with Mark into Cyprus (Acts xv. 39-41).

Mark's name does not again occur in the book of the Acts, but he is mentioned not only in 1 Pet. v. 13, but in some of St. Paul's epistles; and thence it appears that he had again been received into the friendship of this apostle, and had been serviceable to him in the ministry. He was with St. Paul during his imprisonment in Rome, when he wrote the Epistles to Philemon and to the Colossians (Philem. 24; Col. iv. 10, where St. Paul names him with others as his συνεργοὺς εἰς τὴν βασιλείαν τοῦ Θεοῦ, οἵτινες ἐγενήθησαν μοι παρηγορία). Mark seems then to have had it in his mind to leave Rome and to go into Asia Minor, for the apostle writes

(Col. iv. 10), περὶ οὗ ἐλάβετε ἐντολάς· ἐὰν ἔλθῃ πρὸς ὑμᾶς, δέξασθε αὐτόν. When St. Paul wrote the second Epistle to Timothy (likewise from Rome, but probably during a second imprisonment), Mark was not with him, but was not far from Timothy in Asia Minor; and St. Paul tells Timothy when he comes to bring Mark with him, "for he is profitable to me for the ministry" (2 Tim. iv. 11).

When 1st Peter was written, Mark must have been with Peter in Babylon or its neighbourhood. This epistle (as we shall see) was not certainly written at a very early date, though we cannot exactly say when; perhaps between the writing of that to the Colossians and of 2d Timothy, so that in the interval Mark must have visited Peter at Babylon. According to Church tradition, he was afterwards in close connection with Peter at Rome (Euseb. *H. E.* ii. 25) as his interpreter. In the passage where Papias is quoted (Euseb. iii. 39) Mark is called ἑρμηνευτὴς Πέτρου, and this upon the express testimony of a still older witness, the Presbyter John, who was one of Christ's own disciples; and in the strength of this, the later Church writers, *e.g.* Irenæus (*adv. Hær.* iii. 10), Tertullian (*adv. Marc.* iv. 5), Eusebius (*H. E.* v. 8, and *Chronicon ad A.* 2 et 3, Claud.), Jerome (*de viris illustr.* c. 8; *Epist.* cl., *ad Hedibiam, Quæst.* xi.), and others, give him this title.

Fritzsche (*in Marcum Prolegg.* p. xxvi.) and Thiersch (*Versuch zur Herstellung*, etc., p. 181) decidedly err in taking Mark's office as ἑρμηνευτής, to mean only that he committed to writing the Apostle Peter's words. That he did this is certainly stated in that passage of Papias, and by other writers; but the term ἑρμηνευτής, or in Latin *interpres*, does not properly mean this: it denotes one who came between the apostle and those to whom he spoke, when he could not speak in a language which they could understand. It is not very probable, moreover, though it is generally taken for granted, that the language into which Mark interpreted St. Peter's words was Greek, St. Peter speaking only in Aramæan. Peter, without doubt, knew Greek sufficiently well to make himself understood in that language, for it must have been in this language that he conversed with Cornelius the Roman centurion. Latin was probably the language for which Mark acted as interpreter, and he probably had learned this during his residence at Rome with St. Paul. Greek was indeed generally understood in Rome, but the popular language was Latin; and among the poorer classes, with whom chiefly Peter would have to do, there were but few who understood Greek.

There is, moreover, no reason for supposing, as some have conjectured (*e.g.* Grotius, *Præf. in Marc.*; Cotelerius, *ad Constitutt. Apost.* ii. 57; Kienlen, *Theol. Stud. u. Krit.* 1843, ii. 423), that St. Peter's companion and interpreter Mark, after whom the second Gospel is named, while the same with him named in 1st Peter, was not the same with the Mark spoken of in St. Paul's epistles and in the Acts as John Mark, the companion in travel of Paul. As we have already seen, Acts xii. 12 implies a close relationship between the family of John Mark and the Apostle Peter.

Besides Rome, Egypt has been named as the sphere of Mark's ministry; and here he is said to have been the first to preach the gospel, and to have founded the Church at Alexandria.[1] We have no reason to doubt this; but his residence in Egypt must have been in his later years, after the death of the Apostles Paul and Peter. Jerome is the first who refers to Mark's death, which he says (*de vir. ill.* c. viii.) took place in the eighth year of Nero (61-62 A.D.), and that he was buried at Alexandria. But this is too early a date, for Peter did not probably die until after this, and Irenæus tells us (*adv. Hær.* iii. 1) that Mark outlived Peter. Still less can we attach any importance to the statements of later writers, such as Nicephorus (*H. E.* ii. 43), that he died a martyr, being slain by the mob in Alexandria: earlier writers, and even Jerome, clearly knew nothing of this.

---

[1] Eusebius (ii. 16) first names this as a tradition (φασί), and after him Epiphanius (*Hær.* li. 6), Jerome (*de vir. ill.* c. viii.), the *Chronicon Alex.*, and others.

§ 48.

Papias is the first who speaks of a written work by Mark,[1] and he bases what he says upon the witness of the Presbyter John. Still, as Eusebius gives the extract from Papias, it is not clear how far the words of the Presbyter John go. The entire passage is commonly taken as the statement of the Presbyter John; and accordingly this early witness, who was a contemporary of Mark's, speaks as follows: "Mark, the interpreter of Peter, carefully committed to writing, as his memory served him, the words and works of Christ, but not in chronological order.[2] For he did not himself hear the Lord, nor did he follow Him, but, as is said (ὡς ἔφην), the Apostle Peter, who taught according to the needs of his hearers, without giving a consecutive narrative of our Lord's history. Mark therefore did not err, for he committed to writing what he remembered. He was careful on one point, viz. to leave out nothing that he had heard, and to falsify nothing." But Tholuck is of opinion,[3] and justly, as I think, that the entire statement does not belong to the Presbyter John. It is very probable that the ὡς ἔφην is not his, but the word of Papias, who thus refers to an earlier passage in his work. We cannot with certainty say how far the words of the Presbyter John extend—whether the words of Papias begin with οὔτε γὰρ ἤκουσε, or before that with οὐ μέν τοι

---

[1] Euseb. iii. 39: Καὶ τοῦτο ὁ πρεσβύτερος ἔλεγε· Μάρκος μὲν ἑρμηνευτὴς Πέτρου γενόμενος, ὅσα ἐμνημόνευσεν, ἀκριβῶς ἔγραψεν· οὐ μέν τοι τάξει τὰ ὑπὸ τοῦ Χριστοῦ ἢ λεχθέντα ἢ πραχθέντα. Οὔτε γὰρ ἤκουσε τοῦ Κυρίου, οὔτε παρηκολούθησεν αὐτῷ· ὕστερον δὲ, ὡς ἔφην, Πέτρῳ, ὃς πρὸς τὰς χρείας ἐποιεῖτο τὰς διδασκαλίας, ἀλλ' οὐχ ὥσπερ σύνταξιν τῶν κυριακῶν ποιούμενος λογίων. Ὥστε οὐδὲν ἥμαρτε Μάρκος οὕτως ἔνια γράψας ὡς ἀπεμνημόνευσεν. Ἑνὸς γὰρ ἐποιήσατο πρόνοιαν, τοῦ μηδὲν ὧν ἤκουσε παραλειπεῖν, ἢ ψεύσασθαί τι ἐν αὐτοῖς. Ταῦτα μὲν οὖν ἱστόρηται τῷ Παπίᾳ περὶ τοῦ Μάρκου. Περὶ δὲ τοῦ Ματθαίου ταῦτ' εἴρηται, κ.τ.λ. (Here follow the words already quoted, § 40, concerning Matthew.)

[2] οὐ τάξει, when used in reference to an historical treatise, can only mean, "not in the chronological order wherein the individual had done them." Schleiermacher (*Stud. u. Krit.* 1832, p. 759) takes it to mean, that he had disconnectedly jotted down everything in an isolated manner; but this is too strong.

[3] *Die Glaubwürdigkeit d. evang. Gesch.*, ed. 1, p. 243, note.

τάξει. In the latter case, the statement of the Presbyter John would simply be, that "Mark, the interpreter of Peter, had carefully committed to writing what he recollected;" in the former case, this statement would be further referred by him to "the things which Christ had said and done," and he would further observe that Mark had not written these things τάξει. In either case, the statement that Mark had received the material of his work from the discourses of Peter which he had heard, would belong to Papias, and not to the Presbyter John; though the first part of the passage, which contains the Presbyter's words, may be taken as implying this.

Still it may be doubted whether the entire passage, including the statement of John and of Papias, really refers to our Gospel of Mark, or to some other writing. It is certain that Eusebius, who has preserved for us the entire passage, takes it to apply to our Gospel; and thus it has been almost universally understood. But in modern times many scholars have doubted, and even denied this.[1] It must be admitted that the words, when applied to our Gospel, present some difficulty. They suggest to our minds a work wherein the gospel narratives are told one after another without order, just as Peter had related them at different times, according to the needs of his hearers; but our Gospel of Mark, viewed by itself, has the aspect of a continuous and consecutive history. Still, Papias, or before him the Presbyter John, may have spoken of Mark's Gospel in comparison with some other Gospel held in higher esteem, *e.g.* that of Matthew, and may have explained the difference of arrangement of some particulars in Mark by the supposition that he had not written chronologically. But what specially confirms the reference of the statement to Mark's Gospel, is the fact that subsequent writers make no mention of any other work of Mark's, but clearly mean our Gospel when they similarly refer to St. Mark's treatise; and they also trace this back to the oral teachings of the Apostle Peter as its source, and

---

[1] SCHLEIERMACHER, CREDNER (§ 56), SCHWEGLER (*nachapost. Zeitalter*, i. 457-460), and BAUR (*kanon. Evang.* p. 536 sqq.).

even attribute to this apostle a share in its composition. Thus Irenæus, Clemens Alex., Origen, Eusebius, Jerome, and others, with various modifications.[1] Nevertheless the discrepancies among these writers concerning the time and place of writing, and the part of the Apostle Peter in it, show that they had no further information upon the subject. Clemens Alex. (*adumbratio in* 1 *Peter*), Eusebius (*H. E.* ii. 15), and Jerome (*de viris illustr.* c. viii.), represent Mark as writing his Gospel during the lifetime of Peter, and at the request of Peter's hearers; and according to the two last named writers, Peter himself sanctioned and recommended it. To this, too, the statements of Clemens Alex., in the sixth book of his *Hypotyposen*, have been supposed to refer, but according to a false interpretation; for Clemens himself (as Eusebius informs us, vi. 14) says, that when Peter heard of the undertaking, he neither hindered nor encouraged it. Jerome (*ad Hedibiam, Quæst.* xi.) speaks as if Peter had actually dictated the Gospel to Mark. The older Irenæus (*adv. Hær.* iii. 1; cf. Euseb. v. 8) says distinctly that Mark wrote his Gospel after the death of Peter and of Paul (μετὰ τὴν τούτων ἔξοδον); and this corresponds with the still earlier statement of the Presbyter John and Papias (supposing that their statement refers to our Gospel), viz. that Mark wrote from memory (ὅσα ἐμνημόνευσεν, ὡς ἀπεμνημόνευσεν): they would not have expressed themselves thus had they meant that Peter was still alive when Mark wrote, and that Mark could have consulted him concerning it.

As to the PLACE of writing: at the end of some Greek manuscripts Rome is named, and in others Alexandria or Egypt. The latter statement, that Mark completed his Gospel in Egypt at the request of his disciples there, occurs also in Chrysostom (*in Matt. Homil.* i.); but most of the Fathers presuppose or expressly name Rome.

No doubt whatever is expressed by any writer as to the authorship of this Gospel until we come down to very recent times.[2]

---

[1] *Vid.* DE WETTE, § 99 *b*, note *a;* CREDNER, § 52.
[2] Excepting we thus regard what has already been stated, that some

In modern times, as we have already said, Schleiermacher, Credner, Schwegler, Baur, have advocated the opinion that the work of Mark referred to by the Presbyter John and by Papias was not our Gospel; and that our Gospel was the work of some one who took St. Mark's Gospel as his guide, and made free use of it. Gfrörer [1] also argues against the composition of our Gospel by Mark. It cannot be denied, however, that the external evidence is thoroughly in favour of St. Mark's authorship; and supposing that the statements of the Presbyter John and of Papias really refer (as is most probable) to our Gospel, its genuineness as written by Mark must be regarded as established upon the incontestable witness of an almost contemporary Christian writer.

As to the language of this Gospel: according to the statement of some manuscripts and the opinion of a few Catholic theologians, it was originally written in Latin; but this is (as we have shown) quite untenable (§ 21). Equally untenable is the supposition of Wahl (*Magazin für alte, besd. morgenl. Litteratur*, 3d part, 1790), that the Gospel being composed in Egypt, was originally written in Coptic. The Greek and Latin Fathers unanimously testify that the Gospel was originally written in Greek, and no one now can fairly doubt it.

§ 49.

The THIRD canonical Gospel differs from the other two, in the fact that the author speaks of himself. Still he does this only at the outset, when he describes the design he has in view in composing the following work, and names the person for whom he writes, viz. a certain Theophilus. He does not personally appear in the course of his Gospel any more than do the two first evangelists in theirs, and even in the preface he does not speak of himself by name. The Acts of the Apostles, in the beginning of it, is described as

take the Petrine Mark to be a different person from the Pauline Mark, i.e. John Mark.

[1] *Gesch. d. Urchristenth.* ii. Hauptthl., *die heil. Sage*, 2 Abth., Stuttg. 1838.

a supplement to the Gospel, and as if a second part of one and the same historical work. It also is written in the first instance for Theophilus. Yet the writer does not name himself there either. In the second half of this latter work, however—in his account of more than one of St. Paul's missionary tours—the apostle and his companions in travel are spoken of in the first person, so that the narrator must himself have been one of the company. Still he never names himself; and it is, as we shall presently see, a matter of question whether this first person was the author of the Gospel and the Acts himself, or some one else whose account the author of these writings incorporated into his work in its original form.

In the title of the Gospel, however, as we find it both in the Greek MSS. and in the old versions, as well as in the Fathers universally, LUKE is named as the writer. Of his personal history little certainly is known. It is clear, from the introduction to the Gospel, that he could not have been among our Lord's first disciples;[1] for he distinguishes himself from those who were eye-witnesses and participators in the events he is about to record, and he ranks himself among those who had received their information from the accounts given by those eye-witnesses. It is, I think, clear from Col. iv. 14 compared with ver. 11, that Luke was not by birth a Jew; for St. Paul evidently distinguishes him with Epaphras and Demas from those of his fellow-labourers who were of the circumcision (οἱ ὄντες ἐκ περιτομῆς). Many, however, think otherwise.[2] The probability is, that Luke

---

[1] According to the PSEUDO-ORIGINES, De recta in Deum fide, sect. 1, EPIPHANIUS, Hær. li. 11, and others, he was one of the 70 disciples; and THEOPHYLACT (in Lucam, xxiv. 13) is of opinion that he was one of the two disciples to whom Jesus appeared after His resurrection on their way to Emmaus, the other of whom was Cleopas. HUG seems inclined to adopt both these conjectures, but manifestly without warrant.

[2] e.g. J. N. TIELE, Theol. Stud. u. Krit. 1858, iv. pp. 753-766: he does not allow the force of the texts referred to, and he maintains Luke's Jewish descent on the ground of the Hebraistic character of both his works. This, however, is only partially traceable, and can be otherwise explained. See § 107.

before his conversion to Christianity had adopted Judaism as a proselyte of the gate, attending Jewish services, and keeping the law, though he had not been circumcised.[1]

Some have supposed that Luke is the same with the Lucius who is mentioned in Acts xiii. 1, Rom. xvi. 21: in the former place as " of Cyrene, and among the prophets and teachers who were at Antioch" when Paul started upon his first missionary tour with Barnabas and Mark; in the latter place with Jason and Sosipater, συγγενεῖς of Paul's, from whom he sends greetings, and who must have been with him at Corinth when he wrote the epistle. Origen mentions this as the opinion of many (*in Ep. ad Rom.* xvi. 21); and it is espoused by some modern critics, even still by Tiele (as before, p. 766), who considers it not improbable. But this is evidently a mistake; if for no other reason, obviously because Lucius, though a συγγενής of the apostle, was certainly a Jew by birth: it is, moreover, very improbable that Paul would name the same person at one time Lucius, and at another time Luke. The name Luke or Lucas is probably an abbreviation for Lucanus, like Silas for Silvanus.

As to Luke's birthplace, Eusebius describes him as an Antiochian, and others repeat this. We know not on what ground this opinion rests, but it is not on the face of it improbable.[2] Modern scholars, *e.g.* Eichhorn, Kuinœl (*Evv. Marci et Lucæ*, ed. 2, Lpz. 1817), Credner, have supposed that this opinion rests upon the supposed identity of Luke and Lucius (Acts xiii.); but this is hardly probable, because, though Lucius is there spoken of as among the Christian prophets at Antioch, he is called a Cyrenian, *i.e.* a native of Cyrene.

---

[1] Cf. ISIDORUS HISPAL., *De vita et obitu sanctorum*, c. lxxxii.: Lucas Antiochenus . . . natione Syrus, arte medicus, Græco eloquio eruditus, quem plerique tradunt proselytum fuisse, et Hebræas litteras ignorasse.

[2] EUSEB. *H. E.* iii. 4, τὸ μὲν γένος ὢν τῶν ἀπ' 'Αντιοχείας; JEROME, *præf. in Matt.* and *de vir. ill.* c. vii.; ISIDORE HISPAL.; THEOPHYLACT, *in Lucam procem.*; EUTHYMIUS ZIGABENUS, *præf. interpr. Luc.*; NICEPHORUS, *H. E.* ii. 43; and others.

It is a matter of greater certainty that he afterwards resided at Rome. He was there when Paul, now a prisoner there, wrote his Epistles to the Colossians and Philemon (Col. iv. 14; Philem. 24); and subsequently, when 2d Timothy (iv. 11) was written. It would seem that then he was permanently settled in Rome, and earned his livelihood as a physician there; for in Col. iv. 14 he is called Λουκᾶς ὁ ἰατρός. It was not until long afterwards (first in Nicephorus Kallistus in the fourteenth century, *H. E.* ii. 43) that he was said to have been also a distinguished painter, and to have taken portraits of Christ, of Mary, and of the chief apostles. This is merely a legend of the later Roman Catholic Church, though many miracle-working pictures of the Virgin had been exhibited before this, which Luke was said to have painted. But considering the time when this statement was first broached, we can only regard it as a fable, the origin of which cannot be traced. Perhaps it arose by confounding some later Christian painter who bore the name of Luke, and who made pictures of Christ or of Mary, with the Evangelist.

The texts referred to in St. Paul's epistles show that Luke enjoyed personal intercourse with the apostle during his residence in Rome. In Philem. 24 Paul describes him, together with Marcus, Aristarchus, and Demas, as his συνεργούς, and in Col. iv. 14 he calls Luke ὁ ἀγαπητός. In 2 Tim. iv. 11 he says, "Only Luke is with me," *i.e.* Luke only of his more immediate friends and fellow-helpers. A very close personal relationship between Luke and Paul seems to be intimated before this in the passages already referred to in the Acts, where the first person plural is used in the account of the apostle's journeys. The most obvious inference would seem to be, that the writer himself was in these cases in St. Paul's company. This was the view usually taken in early times, *e.g.* by Irenæus (*adv. Hær.* iii. 14, 1; see Credner, p. 125). Still there is much to favour the opinion that the writer is here making use of the narrative of some one else, which he partly adopts in its original form, retaining even this communicative mode of narration (see

§ 124). We cannot therefore refer with certainty to these expressions in the Acts as throwing light upon the facts of Luke's life.

As to Luke's history subsequently to the reference in 2 Tim. we have no reliable evidence. Eusebius seems to have known nothing, and the conjectures of later writers are hardly worth notice. Jerome (*de vir. ill.* c. vii.) intimates that his bones were brought from Achaia to Constantinople in the twentieth year of Constantius : there must therefore have been a tradition then current that he had died in Achaia. In some old editions of Jerome's work it is added, "vixit octoginta et quatuor annos, uxorem non habens;" but this is wanting in all the early MSS., and is no doubt an interpolation. Isidorus Hispal. (*de vita et obitu sanctorum*, c. lxxxii.) also mentions the removal of Luke's bones to Constantinople, but he says they were brought from Bithynia; and in the *Martyrolog. Romanum* this is said to be the country where he died. Gregory Nazianzen is the first who names Luke among the Christian martyrs (*Orat.* iii. *adv. Julianum*); and Nicephorus (*H. E.* ii. 43) states that he preached the gospel in Greece, and that while there he was hanged upon an olive tree, in the eightieth year of his age. But this must be regarded as a legend of late origin, without any historical value.

§ 50.

In the works of the Fathers which have come down to us mention is made of Luke as an evangelist, not indeed so early as of Matthew and Mark, but at the end of the second century, and then with clear reference to our third Gospel, which has ever since been incontestably attributed to him. So unanimous an opinion must have had for its basis the earliest tradition of the Church. As to the time and place of writing, and the materials he made use of for his history, there seems to have been no tradition in the early Church. The references on these points which we find in patristic writings can be regarded only as conjectures, based upon what was known or believed concerning his personal history, or upon supposed hints in the writings attributed to him.

Thus, when Irenæus (*adv. Hær.* iii. 14), Eusebius (*H. E.* iii. 4), Jerome (*de vir. ill.* c. vii.), tell us that Luke received the substance of his Gospel from the apostles, this is simply an inference from the manner in which he speaks concerning his work in the preface. Irenæus indeed hints (iii. 1) that Luke committed to writing the gospel preached by Paul, and Tertullian says that his Gospel was generally attributed to Paul; but these are obviously mere conjectures, supposed to be sanctioned by the relationship in which Luke stood to the apostle. Hence, too, it has been supposed, that when Paul speaks of "*his* gospel" (Rom. ii. 16, xvi. 25; 2 Tim. ii. 8), he means Luke's Gospel: thus Origen thought (Euseb. vi. 25); and Eusebius himself (iii. 4), and Jerome (*de vir. ill.* c. vii.), give this as the generally received opinion (see De Wette, § 101 *b*, note *a*). Equally conjectural is Jerome's statement (*Præf. ad Matt.*), that Luke wrote his Gospel in Achaia and Boeotia (*Lucas ... in Achajæ Boeotiæque partibus volumen condidit*), which harmonizes with the tradition already referred to concerning the place of his death.

§ 51.

Among the gospel writings of the first century which were not recognised by the Church at large, there was one which bore a striking resemblance to St. Luke's, and which was therefore regarded as closely related thereto: this was the *Marcionite Gospel*. The relation of this work to our Luke has of late been a matter of much controversy, and the decision of this question is of no small importance in arriving at a just conclusion concerning the origin and historical authority of our canonical Gospel. We may as well discuss this question now, before entering upon the wider inquiry concerning the relation of Luke's canonical Gospel to the Gospels of Matthew, Mark, and John.

Marcion was the founder of a gnostic and anti-Jewish sect. He was son of a bishop of Sinope in Pontus, and lived in the first half of the second century. He was distinguished for his zeal in Christian piety, and by his strictly ascetic life. He regarded Christianity as the only divine revelation, refusing to recognise Judaism as such. Judaism he attributed not to the most high God, the Author of Christianity, but to another and lower being, whom he considered the creator of the material world, and whom he named δημιουργός, *creator*. He therefore industriously sought to give prominence to the discrepancies between Christ's sayings and O. T. teaching, and maintained that the doctrines of Christianity, as moulded and defined by the Church, were corrupted by the intermixture of many extraneous elements, borrowed chiefly from Judaism, and from which they should be purified. For these opinions his own father excommunicated him, and he betook himself to Rome. Here he arrived at the beginning of the reign of Antoninus Pius, about A.D. 140, and afterwards met Polycarp, who had made a journey thither. The followers of Marcion had, like him, a biblical canon of their own, which of course included Christian scriptures only, *one* Gospel and ten Pauline Epistles, the Pastoral Epistles being excluded. The Marcionite Gospel contained in its title no intimation of its having had any human authorship, or as to who the writer was. The only knowledge we have of it is derived from the references made to it (which, however, are very copious), direct or indirect, by the Fathers in their polemics against Marcion.[1] We cannot indeed with certainty infer from the citations of the Fathers what this Gospel contained, and what it did not contain, for they presuppose this as already known to their readers; and some of them, especially Tertullian, make use of this Gospel recognised by the Marcionites themselves in combating the Marcionite doctrines. Still the references we find, if carefully studied, suffice to show us not only the general characteristics, but the main contents, of this work, in its relation to our canonical Gospels. This much at least may with certainty be ascertained, that it was closely

---

[1] Our main sources of information are: TERTULLIAN, *adv. Marcion*, l. iv., and EPIPHANIUS, *Hær.* xlii.; also PSEUDO-ORIGINES (*Dialogus de recta fide*), JEROME, and others. See *Ev. Marcionis ex auctoritate vet. monumentorum descr.*; A. HAHN, in Thilo's *Cod. apocr. N. T.*, i. 401–486; DE WETTE, § 71, *b*, note *c*.

akin to our third Gospel, that it contained hardly anything which is not to be found in Luke, but was deficient in much that Luke contains.

Thus Luke i. and ii., containing the preface and the history of Christ's infancy, were wanting; also ch. iii. iv., concerning the Baptist, the baptism of Jesus, the temptation, and the genealogy. It began with the statement of date given in iii. 1, which was immediately followed by the account of the healing of the demoniac in the synagogue at Capernaum, iv. 31 sqq., together with that of the opposition of the people of Nazareth, iv. 16–30. Various sections of our Luke also were wanting in the course of the work; certainly ch. vii. 29–35, concerning the perverseness of those who were satisfied neither with the asceticism of the Baptist, nor with the contrasted manner of life practised by the Son of man; ch. xiii. 1–9, the sayings of Jesus concerning the Galileans slain by Pilate, and those on whom the tower in Siloam fell; also the parable of the fig-tree; xiii. 29–35, the declaration of Jesus concerning those who should come from various regions and sit down in the kingdom of God; His answer respecting Herod, when they endeavoured to persuade Him to leave that neighbourhood, and the lament over Jerusalem; xv. 11–32, the parable of the prodigal son; xviii. 31–34, the prophecy of Jesus concerning what was about to befall Him, in fulfilment of O. T. prophecies; xix. 29–48, the account of the triumphal entry into Jerusalem, and the cleansing of the temple, with a reference to O. T. prophecy; xx. 9–18, the parable of the faithless labourers in the vineyard, in which the mission of the Son of God is described as a repetition and continuance of the sending of earlier divine messengers, His rejection and the punishment of His enemies being already prophesied in the O. T.; xxii. 35–38, Christ's words to His disciples concerning the fulfilment of O. T. prophecy in Him; very probably xxii. 42–46, concerning the agony in Gethsemane; xxii. 49–51, how one of the disciples cut off the ear of the high priest's servant; and probably many others, such as xvii. 5–10; also the concluding verses of Luke concerning the ascension.

Certain passages, moreover, were wanting in the sections which the Marcionite Gospel had in common with Luke : *e.g.* xi. 30-32, the reference to Jonah and the queen of Sheba ; xi. 49-51, concerning the sending of the prophets, and the guilt of their blood coming upon that generation ; xx. 37, 38, where Moses is referred to as a witness for the resurrection of the dead ; xxi. 21, 22, where the days of vengeance are represented as coming in fulfilment of all that had been written ; xxii. 16, concerning keeping the passover in the kingdom of God ; xxii. 30, Christ's words, that His disciples should sit on thrones judging the twelve tribes of Israel; xxiii. 43, Christ's words to the penitent thief, " To-day shalt thou be with me in paradise ; " xxiv. 44, latter part, about the fulfilment of all that was written in the law of Moses, in the prophets, and in the Psalms concerning Him ; and other texts.

In the portions, moreover, which Marcion had in common with Luke there were many discrepancies, some of which might be regarded as ordinary variations, such as might be found between the various MSS. of our Gospel, but which in other cases seriously affect the sense. For example, in ch. xvi. 17, instead of " It is easier for heaven and earth to pass than one tittle of the law to fail," Marcion in his Gospel reads, " It is easier for heaven and earth, the law and the prophets, to fail, than one tittle of the word of the Lord ; " ch. xiii. 28, instead of the words, " When ye shall see Abraham, and Isaac, and Jacob, and all the prophets, in the kingdom of God," Marcion reads, "When ye shall see all *the righteous* in the kingdom of God ; " and instead of the words which follow, ὑμᾶς δὲ ἐκβαλλομένους ἔξω, these, ὑμᾶς δὲ ἐκβαλλομένους καὶ κρατουμένους ἔξω ; ch. xxi. 32, instead of " This *generation* shall not pass away till all be fulfilled," Marcion has " *Heaven and earth* shall not pass away till all be fulfilled ; " ch. iv. 34, where, in the words of the demoniac to Jesus, the Ναζαρηνέ is left out, as probably in xviii. 37 and xxiv. 19 the ὁ Ναζωραῖος and the τοῦ Ναζωραίου ; ch. viii. 19, where what Luke introduces as part of his own narrative concerning Christ's mother and brethren, Marcion inserts as a statement made by certain Jews who were present, as in ver. 20.

Marcion's Gospel seems to have contained very little that is not to be found in our Luke. In ch. viii. 21, before Christ's words, "My mother and my brethren are they who hear the word of God, and do it," we find the words which occur in Matthew, "Who are my mother and my brethren?"

§ 52.

Now, as to the nature of the relationship between the two Gospels, the Fathers generally supposed that Marcion was acquainted with our Gospel of Luke, and adapted it to his dogmatic system by certain omissions and interpolations; and this was the generally received opinion down to the last decade of the eighteenth century, taken for granted as a matter of course, and not requiring further proof. The first who rejected this view was Semler, who propounded the opinion (which is the opposite of Tertullian's) that our Luke and the Marcionite Gospel were two different recensions of one and the same original, and that the latter was among the many evangelical histories from which the Catholic Church afterwards selected the four which are canonical. Löffler also adopted this view.[1] Others subsequently maintained that Marcion's Gospel was one of the sources which Luke made use of in the composition of his Gospel.[2]

Storr, on the contrary, had already opposed these theories,

---

[1] SEMLER, first in the notes to the German ed. of R. Simon's *Krit. Hist. d. Textes d. N. T.* (1776), and afterwards elsewhere. JOSIAS FRIEDR. CHR. LÖFFLER (ob. 1816), *Marcionem Paulli epistolas et Lucæ evang. adulterasse dubitatur* (Frankfurt a. O. 1788, 4to); reprinted in the *Commentatt. theol.*, edd. Velthusen, Kuinœl, et Ruperti, i. (1794), pp. 180–218.

[2] Thus did H. CORRODI (*Versuch einer Beleucht. d. Jüd. u. Christl. Bibelkanons*, ii. [Halle 1792], p. 158 sqq.), J. E. C. SCHMIDT (*Einl. i. N. T.*), EICHHORN, BERTHOLDT, and others. SCHMIDT had previously thrown out the suggestion, that the Marcionite Gospel might have been the genuine Gospel of Luke, and that ours had been enlarged by a later hand (in Henke's *Magazin f. Rel.-Phil. Exegese u. K. Gesch.* vol. v. part iii. pp. 468–526),—an opinion which he afterwards modified as above.

and had adopted the patristic view. He was followed by
Hug, Paulus, and others, and by the two Roman Catholic
theologians Arneth and Gratz. The Protestant theologians
H. Olshausen and Hahn, in the prosecution of a still more
thorough and comprehensive investigation, arrived at the
same conclusion.¹ The matter was thus for a long time
considered settled; and even some who had formerly espoused
another view (*e.g.* Gieseler and De Wette) were led to adopt
this, the old belief of the Fathers, which now again became
general in Germany.²

But a reaction has again taken place, led by Schulz and
Schleiermacher. The theologians, too, of the later Tübingen
school—Schwegler, Baur, and even Ritschl—have endeavoured to establish the priority of Marcion's work. These
scholars agree (the two last more decidedly than Schwegler)
in regarding the Marcionite Gospel as the earlier, and our
canonical Gospel as the later, compiled from the former after
Marcion's time, with revision and enlargement. Dav. Schulz
(*Theol. Stud. u. Krit.* 1829, iii. pp. 586–595) speaks rather
angrily of the investigation of Hahn and Olshausen and their
conclusions, without advancing any distinct theory of his own.
It is evident, however, that he considers the Marcionite Gospel
an independent work. Schleiermacher (*Einl. i. N. T.* pp.
64, 197, 214), without fully entering into the question, expresses himself strongly against the notion that Marcion

---

¹ STORR, *über d. Zweck d. evang. Gesch. u. d. Briefe Johannis*, Tüb.
1786, pp. 254–265; H. E. G. PAULUS, *Theol.-exeg. Conservatorium*
(Heidelb. 1822), pp. 12, 115, 146 sqq.; MICH. ARNETH (Prof. at
Linz), *über die Bekanntsch. Marcions mit unserm Canon d. neuen Bundes
u. insbesondere über das Evang. desselben*, Linz 1809, 4to; A. GRATZ,
Krit. Untersuchungen über Marcion's Evang., Tüb. 1818; HERM.
OLSHAUSEN, *die Echtheit d. vier canon. Evang.*, etc., Königsb. 1823, pp.
105–214; AUG. HAHN, *das Evang. Marcions in seiner ursprüngl. Gestalt*,
etc., Königsb. 1823. These two scholars were pursuing their investigations at Königsberg at the same time independently of each other, and
yet they arrived at substantially the same conclusions.

² GIESELER, in a review of Hahn's treatise in the *Hall. allg. Litt. Z.*
1823, p. 225 sqq., and *K. Gesch.* i. § 45; DE WETTE, *Einl. i. N. T.* §
70–72.

made use of our Gospel, and mutilated that of Luke. He suggests, moreover, the possibility that his Gospel may have been an earlier edition of Luke's. Ritschl and Baur differ simply in the fact that, according to the former, the revision was made in the interest of anti-Marcionite opinions; and according to the latter, the aim of the redactor was to give to the original Gospel, which was wholly Pauline, a form suitable for Jewish Christians, by introducing Judaizing references, and thus to guard it against an apparently Pauline onesidedness. This difference is unimportant. Such views, however, could not long be maintained, but had to give way to more unbiassed, exact, and comprehensive inquiries, prosecuted partly by the same parties. Harting (*Quæstionem de Marcione*, etc., Utrecht 1849) and Volkmar (*das Evang. Marcions*, Leipz. 1852) endeavoured to vindicate the old Patristic view. Hilgenfeld (*Krit. Untersuchungen*, etc., Halle 1850) maintains that Luke's Gospel was the original, and that Marcion moulded it to suit his doctrinal views. He thinks, however, that our Gospel is the result of a redaction made after Marcion's time. See also G. Fr. Franck (*Stud. u. Krit.* 1855, 296-364). Influenced by these writings, Baur has somewhat modified his earlier view: for instead of holding that the Marcionite Gospel was the original one, he allows that Marcion altered the original Luke out of love for his dogmatic system; but he maintains that the author of our third Gospel greatly altered the original Luke, and that this was done after Marcion's time, adding the sections ch. i., ii., iv. 16-30, etc. Ritschl has withdrawn his earlier view, and now pronounces his judgment in favour of the priority of our canonical Gospel (*Theol. Jahrbb.* 1851, pp. 528-533), and so also does Zeller (*ibid.* p. 337); and certainly they are right.

§ 53.

We cannot here enter minutely upon the discussion of this topic; I shall therefore content myself with the following remarks:—

1. If the Marcionite Gospel were an older work which

Marcion adopted, it must have been in use in the Church before him, together with the other evangelical histories; and it would be so also after him, at least in some places. But not the slightest hint of this has come down to us; and it is clear that none of the Fathers who speak of the Marcionite Gospel, from the end of the second century downwards (*e.g.* Irenæus, Tertullian, etc.), had any idea that this Gospel was used either before or after Marcion's time by any but the followers of Marcion.[1] This fact of itself makes it highly probable that the Gospel in question originated with the Marcionites, or with Marcion himself: we cannot account for its origin elsewhere in any probable or reasonable way. It does not appear, moreover, that Marcion or his followers, in their controversies with the orthodox Fathers, ever referred to the supposed fact, or asserted that their Gospel had been used by the earlier Fathers.

2. Seeing that (wholly apart from the question of its origin) this Marcionite Gospel never seems to have been esteemed or reverenced by the Church at large, it is in the highest degree improbable that, after the rise of the Marcionites, and in opposition to the opinion and practice of the Church, any one should choose it instead of any other, in order to introduce into it Judaistic elements, and thus make it a Gospel for general use in the Church. There were not wanting other Gospels, which treated, with equal or greater fulness than does our Luke, of Christianity in its relation to Judaism and the O. T. revelation.

3. As the first two chapters of our Luke are wanting in the Marcionite Gospel, so also is the preface (i. 1-4); and therefore, on the supposition that the Marcionite Gospel was the original work, or the basis of our Luke, this preface could not have proceeded from the original author, but must have been the work of some subsequent interpolater or reviser. Baur himself, in his work on Mark (1851), takes this view,

---

[1] TERTULL. *adv. Marc.* iv. 5 : *Marcionis vero (evangelium) plerisque nec notum; nullis notum, ut non eo damnatum. Habet plane et illud ecclesias, sed suas; tam posteras quam adulteras. . . . Marcione scilicet conditore vel aliquo de Marcionis examine.*

and holds that these two whole chapters, including the preface, did not belong to the original Luke. But this is in the highest degree improbable. If our Luke had been compiled from the Marcionite Gospel after Marcion's time, this revision and the preface must have been made after the middle of the second century. Now the preface certainly speaks of other evangelic histories already in existence; but on the face of it, it conveys the impression that it was not composed at so late a date, but only in the second generation of Christendom, while the Christian tradition was springing still fresh and new from its fountainhead, and that the composition of evangelic histories had not long begun. A writer in the latter half of the second century could hardly have said concerning the facts of gospel history, τῶν πεπληροφορημένων ἐν ἡμῖν πραγμάτων, and περὶ ὧν κατηχήθης λόγων, κ.τ.λ. It is utterly improbable that any evangelist who only appropriated (and this fully and even word for word for the most part) the treatise of another which he had before him, adding to it only a few facts or discourses, could have spoken of his undertaking as the preface speaks, ἔδοξε κἀμοὶ παρηκολουθηκότι ἄνωθεν πᾶσιν ἀκριβῶς καθεξῆς σοι γράψαι, κ.τ.λ.

4. Irenæus and Tertullian both intimate that Marcion was acquainted with our Luke as well as with the other Gospels, that he knew it to be a Gospel reverenced in the Church, and that he rejected it solely upon the ground that in his view it contradicted the doctrines of Christianity; so that it is quite impossible that it could have received the form it has, wherein it differs from the Marcionite Gospel, after Marcion's time. It is clear, from what Tertullian says (*de carne Christi*, c. ii.; *adv. Marcionem*, iv. 4), that Marcion in a letter of his had acknowledged that he himself had previously received the same Gospels as the Church, and had subsequently come to the conclusion that these Gospels did not present the gospel of Christ in its purity, but from a Jewish and therefore distorted point of view; that, moreover, he thus felt himself called upon to restore the gospel narrative to its purity. He referred (according to Tertullian, *adv. Marc.* iv. 3) to the declarations of St. Paul, Gal. ii., concerning the apostles,

"*ut non recto pede incedentes ad veritatem evangelii,*" and concerning "*pseud-apostolos quosdam pervertentes evangelium Christi;*" applying these words to the condemnation "*eorum evangeliorum, quæ propria et sub Apostolorum nomine eduntur vel etiam Apostolicorum, ut scilicet fidem, quam illis adimit, suo conferat.*" There can be no doubt that by the Gospels *Apostolorum* here named Marcion meant those of Matthew and John, and by the Gospels *Apostolicorum* those of Mark and Luke. This is further evident from what is said in the preceding chapter, where we read, *Nobis fidem ex Apostolis Johannes et Matthæus insinuant, ex Apostolicis Lucas et Marcus instaurant.* Other passages also from Irenæus and Tertullian (see De Wette, § 72, c, note d) clearly show that they were familiar with statements of Marcion expressly intimating that he knew our Gospels, and rejected them because he believed that, being written with a Jewish bias, they distorted the pure apostolic gospel. This, too, was obvious from a work of Marcion's called *Antitheses*, wherein he set forth the contrast between the law and the gospel, Christianity and Judaism, and thus endeavoured to vindicate his views.[1] He therefore expressly found fault with the canonical Gospel of Luke, *ut interpolatum a protectoribus Judaismi* (Tertull. iv. 4); and he seems to have made no secret of it, that his purpose was to re-write or amend this Gospel.

That Marcion knew our Gospel of Luke, is evident further from the following fact. In the account of the discourse of Jesus in the synagogue at Nazareth (Luke iv. 16), the references to the history of Elisha and Elijah (vers. 24–27) are wanting in Marcion's Gospel; according to Epiphanius (*Schol.* xlviii.), Marcion had put ver. 27 (referring to the cure of Naaman the Syrian) in another place, viz. in the account of the healing of the ten lepers (ch. xvii. 14). It is usually supposed (by Hahn, p. 189; De Wette, § 71, b, note c) that Tertullian (*adv. Marc.* iv. 35) read the passage in question in its right place in Marcion's Gospel. But Ritschl (p. 119) has rightly shown that, judging by the manner in

---

[1] See HAHN, p. 105 sqq.; and the *Antitheses Marcionis gnostici, liber deperditus, nunc quoad ejus fieri potuit restitutus*, Königsb. 1823.

which Tertullian expresses himself, it is very improbable that he found these words thus placed in the Gospel of Marcion, but only in Marcion's *Antitheses;* so that either Epiphanius was mistaken, or the words had been introduced by the Marcionites into their Gospel at that other place subsequently to Tertullian's time. It is highly probable that Marcion, when he quoted the words in his *Antitheses*, had the Gospel of Luke before him, where they occur in their right connection; and the fact that they do not occur in his Gospel is in keeping with his rule of excluding all references to O. T. history.

§ 54.

5. A candid consideration shows it to be in the highest degree probable that the Marcionite Gospel was not an older writing which Marcion found before him, but one which Marcion himself compiled, to suit his views, from the other Gospels, and especially from St. Luke. A careful comparison of his Gospel with our Luke, and especially of the character and tenor of the sections and verses omitted, leads us to this conclusion. The omitted passages all of them present facts or statements which Marcion could not reconcile with his views concerning the essentials of Christianity and the person of Christ; and he therefore felt himself justified in concluding that they could not have belonged to the genuine gospel history, but had been interpolated by Judaizers. He excludes all passages in which the gospel history is brought into harmony with O. T. revelation,—in which the N. T. is represented as the fulfilment of O. T. prophecies,—in which Christ is described as springing from the Jewish nation, and of human parentage, and partaker of human weaknesses,—in which the kingdom of God is represented as a feast or supper, or as a kingdom for Israel,—in which Christ describes God, after the manner of the O. T., as an avenging judge. These are all passages which contradict Marcion's distinctive doctrines; and considering what we have already urged, there can hardly be a doubt that Marcion expunged them from love to his system.

6. When we consider the manner in which Marcion has

dealt with the epistles, we need not be surprised that he should have had no qualms of conscience in thus "purifying and improving," as he would consider it, the gospel history, and in particular St. Luke's treatise. He recognised Paul alone as a true apostle; and his Canon included St. Paul's epistles alone (omitting the Pastoral Epistles), together with the one Marcionite Gospel. But the text of these epistles, as given by him, presents many omissions of isolated passages and longer sections which are found in the canonical version received by the Church; and even Irenæus (*adv. Hær.* i. 29, ed. Grabe) blames him for his mutilation of the text to suit his dogmatic system. Some of these alterations are only ordinary and accidental variations (see De Wette, § 34, *b*, note *b*); but others are far too important, and correspond too exactly with his system, to be thus accounted for. In all such cases, it is indubitably clear that Marcion's Canon never could have been the original and genuine text. Thus the two last chapters of the Epistle to the Romans (xv. xvi.) are wanting; and it is quite improbable, as Baur suggests, that these chapters are spurious, and were added to the epistle after Marcion's time. There were gaps also in the middle of the epistle, as Tertullian's references show. The entire section ch. x. 5–xi. 32, showing that the Jews were not utterly cast away, and containing many O. T. quotations, was wanting; and so also was ch. viii. 11–ix. *fin.*, at least probably the greater part;[1] and again ch. i. 17 : καθὼς γέγραπται· ὁ δὲ δίκαιος ἐκ πίστεως ζήσεται.[2] Important passages were wanting also in the

---

[1] For instance, after quoting Rom. viii. 11, TERTULLIAN (*adv. Marc.* v. 14) says : *Salio et hic amplissimum abruptum intercisæ scripturæ, sed apprehendo testimonium perhibentem Apostolum Israeli, quod quidem zelum Dei habeant* (Rom. x. 1–4). ... *Atquin exclamat,* " *O profundum divitiarum,*" etc. (Rom. xi. 33). *Unde illa eruptio? Ex recordatione scilicet scripturarum, quas retro revolverat, ex contemplatione sacramentorum, quæ supra disseruerat in fidem Christi ex lege venientem. Hæc si Marcion de industria erasit, quid Apostolus ejus exclamat?*

[2] TERTULL. c. xiii. : *Cum dicit* "*justitia Dei in eo revelatur ex fide in fidem*" (Rom. i. 17a), *sine dubio et evangelium et salutem justo deo deputat, non bono.* ... *Quoniam et* "*iram*" *dicit* "*revelari de cœlo super impietatem,*" etc. (Rom. i. 18).

Galatians, and to a less extent in the other Pauline Epistles (Hahn, p. 51). It may, indeed, be doubtful whether this or that passage was really wanting, because Tertullian's aim is not to show what was wanting in Marcion, but rather to refute Marcion by passages retained in his own Canon; and he takes for granted that his readers know how the matter really stood as to these omissions. But concerning several passages the inference from his statement and those of Epiphanius is most clear. It is beyond question that the Marcionite text of these epistles contained many alterations and significant omissions when compared with the then generally received text, which could not have been accidental, nor already made in Marcion's time (in which case they would be traceable in some other MSS. of the epistles), but must have been produced by a designed recension and revision made probably by Marcion himself, conformably with his distinctive doctrines. The fact, however, that his version of the epistles contains these omissions and variations, is a strong confirmation of the opinion that his Gospel stands in a similar relationship to our Luke.

§ 55.

7. I will now briefly notice the objections urged against this view of the Marcionite Gospel.

(*a.*) If Marcion, it is asked,[1] knew our Gospels, and wrote his in this manner, why did he not choose St. John's Gospel as his text, which would have far better accorded with his doctrines than St. Luke? It is clear from Tertullian (*adv. Marc.* iv. 3) that he knew St. John's Gospel;[2] but it has with correctness been said in reply, that according to his system he could not have adopted even St. John's Gospel without alteration.[3] O. T. sayings are often quoted in St. John as fulfilled by N. T. facts. St. John's Gospel, moreover, being throughout from one fount and of one type, would be

---

[1] So argue CORRODI, EICHHORN, SCHULZ, SCHLEIERMACHER, and others.
[2] See my *Beitr. zur Ev. Krit.* pp. 222 sq., 279.
[3] OLSHAUSEN, p. 371 sqq.; HAHN, p. 269 sqq.

much more difficult to alter than St. Luke's. But the most conclusive answer is, that Marcion must, to begin with, have felt a prejudice against St. John's Gospel, bearing as it did the name of a Jew-apostle—of one of those whom he supposed that St. Paul blamed in Gal. ii.; indeed, he seems, according to Tertullian,[1] to have expressly used this argument to justify his rejection of this Gospel. He would, on the contrary, naturally have a prejudice in favour of St. Luke's Gospel, seeing that it was the work of one who did not belong to the Jewish race, and who was a friend and companion of St. Paul, whom alone he acknowledged as truly an apostle. Still, as he found even in his work much that was opposed to his views of Christ's person, and of Christianity in its purity, he regarded these as falsifications and interpolations, and thought he was purifying the Gospel by expunging them. Whether he attributed this adulteration to Luke himself, or regarded the passages in question as later interpolations, we cannot with certainty say; it made little difference to him whether they arose the one way or the other. Perhaps, however, he considered them to be Luke's own; and he therefore did not describe *his* Gospel when it was complete as Luke's, but gave to it the name of no human author,—merely the title εὐαγγέλιον, as we may with tolerable certainty conclude from Tertullian, *adv. Marc.* iv. 2.

(*b.*) It has been urged that Marcion's Gospel is characterized by a better arrangement and more consecutive connection than St. Luke's Gospel, and that accordingly St. Luke's is the altered and interpolated edition, the Marcionite Gospel being the original. It must certainly be granted that, as in the three first Gospels in common, so especially in St. Luke, some of the words and works of Christ are related in a connection different from that to which they belonged. This is just what we might expect in Luke, judging from what he tells us in his preface, viz. that he knew of many gospel

---

[1] After the words quoted in § 53, we read, *Porro etsi reprehensus est Petrus et Johannes et Jacobus, qui existimabantur columnæ, manifesta causa est.*

narratives longer or shorter, and drew from them the materials for his narrative. It was therefore quite possible for a later reviser, influenced by a certain dogmatic bias, to alter and transpose Luke's Gospel, so as to obviate this apparent want of order and arrangement; and we should be quite wrong to infer from this the priority of his revised work. This may be illustrated in the case of the narratives, ch. iv. 16–30 and iv. 31–37. In Luke, ch. iv. 16–30 stands at the head of the account of Christ's Galilean ministry, recording how Jesus taught in the synagogue at Nazareth, and was rejected; and this is immediately followed by the account in vers. 31–37 of the healing of the demoniac at Capernaum. These two sections are (as we learn from Tertullian, iv. 7, 8) recorded by Marcion in the opposite order; and this seems to be more appropriate to what we read in ver. 23, "What we have heard done in Capernaum, do also here in thy country." But it is much easier to believe that Marcion, noticing this, altered Luke's order, than that a later reviser altered Marcion's order for Luke's. Luke probably put ch. iv. 16–30 first, because he wished to show how it was that Jesus took up His abode at Capernaum, and not at Nazareth. Possibly he found the two accounts thus arranged in the narratives of others before him, and adopted it without observing that the first implied a previous visit to Capernaum. At any rate, the narrative in Marcion is greatly abridged and altered to suit his system, so that it certainly could not have been the original account; and it is equally improbable that any original and independent Gospel would have begun the history of Christ with the account of the healing of the demoniac at Capernaum. Marcion joined the κατῆλθεν εἰς Καφαρναούμ (Luke iv. 31) with the statement of iii. 1. Now this κατῆλθεν is natural and appropriate in Luke, but not in Marcion, who adopted it to denote Christ's coming down from heaven. Volkmar has very acutely endeavoured to establish from this the priority of our Luke. The same thing might be shown in the case of other passages, which we cannot here stay to discuss.

(c.) Some have endeavoured to show that Marcion's

Gospel contains what is as little in harmony with his system as anything to be found in Luke which he had omitted. This is certainly the case. But, considering his mode of procedure, we cannot be surprised that logical sequence does not characterize his work throughout. He allowed much to remain which on his principles he ought to have expunged, both in the Pauline Epistles and in the Gospel; and he then resorted to forced and unnatural explanations (Hahn, p. 49). We therefore find that the later Marcionites did not hesitate further to alter or omit passages contradicting their system, and contrary in their view to the pure doctrine of Christ, which Marcion had illogically allowed to remain (see Hahn, 31 sqq.). That Marcion's followers adopted this mode of procedure does not prove that it was his; but it makes us less scrupulous in attributing it to him, especially when we are led to the same opinion by other facts.

We cannot here go further into particulars. What we have said will suffice to guide us to a right conclusion. This phenomenon of the Marcionite Gospel is of no little weight in favour of our canonical Gospel of St. Luke. It proves that in Marcion's time, in the first half of the second century, it was not only in use in the Church, but was held in pre-eminent esteem as the work of such a man as Luke, of whom we might have supposed, judging from his non-Jewish extraction and his connection with the apostle of the Gentiles, that he would have been the last to have represented Christianity as dependent on Judaism; and hence that Marcion was led to cling to his Gospel rather than the others as the basis of his system.[1]

---

[1] Among the contrary views which have been advanced regarding the third canonical Gospel may be named: (*a*) that of MAYERHOFF (*Hist.-krit. Einl. in die Petrin. Schriften, nebst einer Abhandlung über den Verf. der Ap. Gesch.*, Hamb. 1835), who attributes this Gospel and the Acts to Timothy; (*b*) that of the anonymous author of a work entitled *Die Evang., ihr Geist, ihre Verf. u. ihr Verhältniss zu einander*, Leipz. 1845, who attributes it to Paul himself in conjunction with Luke, circ. 57–58 A.D., and in contrast with Matthew's Gospel.

§ 56.

The *fourth* Gospel is, both in its title and by the tradition of the Church, attributed to the Apostle JOHN [1] as its author. Considering first the references which the N. T. contains to him personally, and apart from his connection with the Gospel, we find that he was the younger brother of the Apostle James the elder, who was beheaded by Herod Agrippa (Acts xii. 2),—both brothers being the sons of Zebedee and Salome. That Salome was their mother, is evident from a comparison of Matt. xxvii. 56 with Mark xv. 40. Among the Galilean women present at the crucifixion, Matthew names (*a*) Mary Magdalene, (*b*) Mary the mother of James and Joses, and (*c*) the mother of Zebedee's children. Mark in the same connection names the two first, and the third he calls Salome.

Zebedee their father followed the occupation of a fisherman on the Sea of Galilee (Matt. iv. 21), either at Bethsaida, as the Fathers usually supposed, or at some other place along the coast. His family does not seem to have been in very needy circumstances. According to Mark i. 20, Zebedee seems to have been assisted in his occupation, not only by his sons, but by μισθωτούς; and the manner in which Salome is spoken of in the first three Gospels indicates that the family were respectable and in good circumstances. We find her in company with the Lord on His journeys, among the women who ministered to Him of their substance (Matt. xxvii. 55, 56; Mark xv. 40, 41), who followed Him to Golgotha, and prepared spices to embalm Him (Mark xvi. 1). According to this last-named text, she was among the women who received the first tidings of the Lord's resurrection. See also Matt. xx. 20 sqq., where she asks Jesus that her sons may have the two foremost places in the kingdom of God.

The call of John to be a disciple of the Lord is related in Matt. iv. 21, Mark i. 19, Luke v. 9–11. Luke's account differs slightly from that of Matthew and Mark, but not so much as to oblige us to suppose that he is referring to a

---

[1] 'Ιωάννης is a Græcized form of the Hebrew יְהוֹחָנָן,—a name frequently occurring in the O. T. = Jehovah is gracious.

different time and occasion: all three agree that John and his brother James were engaged with their father at their employment as fishermen by the Sea of Galilee when our Lord called them. The narrative does not forbid, but rather sanctions, the supposition that these disciples were already acquainted with the Lord. From the time of his call it would appear, from all three evangelists, that John was among the closest and most constant companions of Jesus, and with his brother James and Peter was admitted to a closer intimacy with Him than the rest of the twelve. Jesus allowed these three only to accompany him when He raised Jairus' daughter (Luke viii. 51; Mark v. 37); they alone were with Him upon the Mount of Transfiguration (Matt. xvii. 1; Luke ix. 28; Mark ix. 2); and they only were allowed to be near Him in the agony in Gethsemane (Matt. xxvi. 37; Mark xiv. 33).

A short and passing but interesting notice of John occurs in Mark iii. 17, where we are told that Jesus gave to him and his brother the name βοανηργές, בְּנֵי רֶגֶשׁ, "the sons of thunder,"—not, as the Fathers supposed, because of any special gifts of eloquence possessed by them, but on account of a certain impetuosity and natural ardour of character, and a fiery zeal in asserting and carrying out what they knew. This disposition was manifested in an eagerness to coerce, even by forcible means, those who were unfavourable to their views and wishes, which was incompatible with the principles and spirit of the kingdom of God. Thus in Luke ix. 51-56, when the inhabitants of a Samaritan village refused to receive Jesus, the sons of Zebedee desired Him to call down fire from heaven upon them, as Elias did. We have another indication of this zeal (though not unmixed with selfishness) in Luke ix. 49, 50, Mark ix. 38-40, where John tells the Lord that they had forbidden one who was casting out devils in His name, because he did not join His disciples.

After our Lord's ascension we find John frequently named among the apostles, and especially in connection with Peter. At his side he was when Peter healed the impotent man in the temple (Acts iii.). He with Peter was imprisoned on account of this miracle, and was miraculously delivered (ch. iv.). After the martyrdom of Stephen, and when the gospel had been successfully preached in Samaria by Philip the deacon, John with Peter was appointed to go thither on the part of the apostles, to bestow upon the believers the gift of the Holy Ghost. He returned with Peter to Jerusalem after they had laboured in Samaria, and preached the gospel in many places around (Acts viii. 14-25). John must have remained in Jerusalem a considerable time; for Paul found him there when he came with Barnabas to tell the apostles concerning the spread of the gospel among the Gentiles, and his manner of preaching it (Gal. ii. 1 sqq.). This journey of Paul (Acts xv.) must be dated (according to the testimony of the Galatian epistle) about seventeen years after his conversion, and more than twenty years after Christ's death. The high position which John then occupied in the Church appears in the manner in which Paul speaks of him, together with Peter and James the Lord's brother. He describes the three as τοὺς δοκοῦντας στύλους εἶναι, and with them chiefly did he consult and negotiate concerning the freedom of the Gentile Christians from the yoke of the Jewish law.

We have no trustworthy evidence to tell us how long John remained in Jerusalem after this. He is not mentioned in the account (Acts xxi. 17 sqq.) of Paul's last visit to Jerusalem; and many (*e.g.* Credner and Lücke) have inferred from this that John was not then there. But the uncertainty of such an inference is clear from the fact that in Acts xv. no mention is made of him, though we know from Gal. ii. that he was there on that occasion. Still less can we conclude that, if absent on occasion of Paul's last visit, he had permanently left Jerusalem. The probability is that he did not finally leave Jerusalem until circumstances compelled him; not perhaps until the disquiet and alarm which the Roman war brought with it had reached Judea.

§ 57.

All the Fathers, from the middle of the second century downwards, agree in their belief that John spent the latter part of his life in proconsular Asia, and at Ephesus. Lützelberger[1] has endeavoured to prove that this tradition is unhistorical, but on utterly weak and insufficient grounds. One thing, however, which he urges is apparent, viz. that the apostolic Fathers make no mention of John at Ephesus, even in places where we might have expected that they would, as *e.g.* in the Epistles of Ignatius, bishop of Antioch, who was martyred at Rome under Trajan, A.D. 115. It is very strange that in his Epistle to the Ephesians (ch. xii.) he should congratulate them that Paul had gone forth from them to martyrdom, and that they had been praised by Paul in his epistle, without referring to the privilege they enjoyed in the residence of John among them. And in writing to the Trallians (ch. v.), he says he is not an apostle like Peter and Paul, but makes no mention of John. In the Epistle to Polycarp also, where we certainly might have expected it, John is not named. This argument appears strong; for we certainly might expect that in his admonitions to the Christians at Ephesus to obey their overseers, and in his warnings against false teachers, John would be referred to had he lived a considerable time among them. But when we have strong and clear evidence on the other side, this *argumentum e silentio* cannot outweigh it. John had died only a few decades of years before, and we cannot say that it was absolutely necessary that Ignatius should have mentioned him: he may not yet have been so generally known and esteemed as were Peter and Paul. To this we must add that the genuineness of the Ignatian epistles is doubtful. There are two recensions of them, which present many differences,—the one a shorter, and the other a longer. The latter is greatly interpolated; but it is in this only that the words quoted from the Epistle to the Trallians occur; and we may be almost certain that they are not original, and are therefore of no weight here. The passage quoted from the Epistle to the Ephesians certainly does occur in the shorter recension; but the

---

[1] *Die kirchl. Tradition über den Ap. Joh. u. seine Schriften in ihrer Grundlosigkeit nachgewiesen*, Leipz. 1840; and on the other side, my *Beitr. z. Ev. Krit.* 88–90, 224.

genuineness even of this recension is very doubtful. Cureton has published (London 1845) a version of this and two other Ignatian epistles, which he discovered in Syriac, wherein this epistle appears in a much shorter form: it wants ch. xi., xii., xiii., and the greater part of xiv. We cannot be sure that this Syriac recension is older than the Greek; but Bunsen's researches (*Ign. u. seine Zeit.*, Hamb. 1847) make this very probable. Considering these facts, we should be by no means justified in receiving that passage from the Greek recension as conclusive against generally received facts.

The two chief witnesses *for* the apostle's residence in Asia Minor are Polycrates and Irenæus. The former was bishop of Ephesus about the end of the second century, and belonged to an important family, distinguished in the Church, for among his kindred he could number seven bishops. His testimony therefore is weighty, and in a letter to the Roman bishop Victor he expressly says that John died at Ephesus.[1] Irenæus was at the same time bishop of Lugdunum in Gaul; but by birth he was certainly a Greek of Asia Minor. He had seen Polycarp at Smyrna. In a letter to Florinus (Euseb. v. 20), he says that he remembers the place where Polycarp had eaten and spoken, and that his incoming and outgoing, his whole manner of life, was vividly in his mind's eye. He also says (*adv. Hær.* iii. 3) that he had, when a child, seen Polycarp. He says in the former place that he remembered Polycarp's words to the people, telling them how he had conversed with John, and the others who had seen the Lord; and we cannot doubt that he meant the *Apostle* John, especially if we compare another remark of Irenæus' in a letter to Victor (Euseb. v. 24), to the effect that Polycarp persisted in celebrating Easter in a certain way, because he had always thus celebrated it with John the disciple of the Lord, and the other apostles. Irenæus, moreover, refers to one or more old presbyters whom he had himself conversed with, and whom he describes as disciples of the apostles, Poly-

---

[1] EUSEB. *H. E.* v. 24: Ἰωάννης ὁ ἐπὶ τὸ στῆθος τοῦ Κυρίου ἀναπεσών, ὃς ἐγενήθη ἱερεὺς τὸ πέταλον πεφορεκὼς καὶ μάρτυς καὶ διδάσκαλος· οὗτος ἐν Ἐφέσῳ κεκοίμηται.

carp being evidently one of those referred to (see Olshausen, *Echtheit d. 4 kanon. Ev.* p. 219 sqq.). Irenæus appeals to their testimony as to the teaching of John the Lord's disciple, and says that they had intercourse with John in Asia, that John abode among them till the time of Trajan (*reg.* A.D. 98-117), and that some of them had seen not only John, but other apostles (*adv. Hær.* ii. 39). Irenæus is therefore a very important witness for the residence of the Apostle John in proconsular Asia; and his testimony, together with that of Hypocrates, must be regarded as conclusive, confirmed as it is by the statements of Clemens Alex. (*quis dives salv.* c. xlii.), Origen (in Euseb. iii. 1), Eusebius (*ib.*), and others.

St. John's residence in Ephesus probably began subsequently to the Apostle Paul's ministry, and peradventure after his death. We know not whether he came direct from Jerusalem to Ephesus, or whether he stayed and took up his residence at other places on his way. Concerning his manner of life, and his labours at Ephesus, we have a few intimations, but they are not fully authenticated. He is said to have been engaged in controversy with the Judaizing heretic Cerinthus. Irenæus tells us (*adv. Hær.* iii. 3; cf. Euseb. iii. 28, iv. 14) that once, when St. John was going to the bath, he found Cerinthus there before him, and immediately turned away, saying, "Let us fly, lest the bath in which Cerinthus the enemy of truth is, fall upon our heads." The trustworthiness of this story is much disputed. It may be apocryphal; still there are not sufficient grounds to warrant our rejecting it: for it is quite conceivable that, in his later years, the natural ardour and impetuosity which characterized the apostle, sanctified by his intercourse with his Saviour, and by the working of the Spirit, now and then broke forth. Clemens Alex. (*quis dives salvetur*, xlii.; in Euseb. iii. 23) illustrates another trait in his character, by the story of a youth whom he committed to the care of a bishop for spiritual instruction, but who was led astray by bad companions, and became captain of a band of robbers. John, suffering himself to be taken captive by the band, by his presence and exhortation won back the wanderer, who became a notable example to the Church of penitence and renewal. According to the testimony of an anti-Montanist writer, Apollonius (Euseb. v. 18), John raised a dead man to life at Ephesus. The mention of this, however, is too brief and passing for us to attach any importance to it.

The early writers of the Church unanimously testify that St. John lived to a great age. He must have lived at least to the end of the first century, because Polycarp, who himself died as a martyr about the year 167, and at an advanced age, knew him personally, and had eaten in his company (see above). Irenæus says that he died in the reign of Trajan (*adv. Hær.* ii. 39, iii. 3). Polycrates says that he died at Ephesus, and his grave was wont to be pointed out there (Euseb. vii. 25). Jerome tells us (*in Ep. ad Gal.* vi. 10) that the apostle, when in his old age he could no longer walk, was wont to be carried into the assemblies of the Church, where he would continually repeat the words, "Little children, love one another."

§ 58.

We have still to consider a tradition current in the Church from the end of the second century, that St. John was banished from Ephesus by the Roman Emperor for a considerable time to Patmos, an island in the Ægean Sea. The Fathers seem to have had no historical information concerning this; their statements concerning it are uncertain and discrepant. According to Clemens Alex. (*quis dives salv.* xlii.), it was in his time generally believed, but he does not give the name of the emperor; he merely says, that after the tyrant's death John returned to Ephesus. Origen also (*in Matt.* tom. xvi.) simply refers to the tradition that John was banished to Patmos by the king of the Romans on account of his testimony to Christ. Both these Fathers probably meant Domitian, whom Eusebius (*H. E.* iii. 18, 20, and *Chronicon ad annum* 14 *Domit.*), Jerome (*de vir. ill.* ix.), and others name in this connection. Tertullian relates (*de præscr. hær.* xxxvi.) that St. John, after he had been plunged in boiling oil without sustaining any injury, was banished to the island (*in insulam*). But the plunging in boiling oil took place, according to him, in Rome, and from Rome he supposes the apostle was banished. This is certainly false, and is not confirmed by any contemporary or subsequent writer, so that nothing can with certainty be known from Tertullian's statement. He does not name the emperor in whose reign it happened; still some have inferred from another passage in his works that he had Domitian in his mind, for in *Apologet.* v. he says that Domitian tried at first to imitate Nero's tyranny, but that he soon abandoned this, and the exiled were recalled. Still it is a question whether Tertullian really had St. John in his mind here. Epiphanius (*Hær.* li. § 12, 33), on the other hand, puts the banishment and return of St. John in the reign of Claudius (A.D. 41–53). This is obviously false and unhistorical.

Rev. i. 9 is referred to generally by early Christian writers as pointing to this event, and they suppose that the revelation was made to John during his exile at Patmos. But it is possible that the story altogether may have arisen out of this passage, and not from a tradition independent of this; and in this case the question would arise, whether this passage affords sufficient ground for the story (see § 237). Here I will venture only two remarks.

(*a.*) Against the supposition that John was exiled in the reign of Domitian, a not unimportant argument may be advanced from the silence upon the subject of the earliest Christian historian, Hegesippus, who lived in Rome in the reign of Marcus Aurelius, about A.D. 170. He says that Domitian summoned some descendants of Judas, the Lord's brother, but immediately released them, and by an edict put a stop to the persecutions of the Christians (Euseb. iii. 20). Now, had Hegesippus known anything of a banishment of St. John, he could hardly have failed to notice it here; and Eusebius, when he speaks of this banishment, would certainly have referred to Hegesippus, whom he often quotes. When once, however, Rev. i. 9 was taken as referring to a banishment to Patmos, this might easily be referred to a banishment in Domitian's reign, because Domitian did punish certain Christians with banishment, though seemingly with banishment from Rome only, as may be inferred from Tertullian, *Apologet.* v.; Euseb. iii. 18; Dio Cassius, lxvii. 14, lxviii. 1.

(*b.*) Whatever historical basis there may be for the alleged banishment of St. John, the tradition concerning it, even supposing that it arose solely from Rev. i. 9, could not have become so general if there had not been a general knowledge or belief that he resided in these parts; and thus the tradition serves at least to confirm this general belief.

§ 59.

In our summary of St. John's life and history thus far, we have refrained from any reference to the fourth Gospel, which bears his name. Now, mention is often made in this Gospel of a "disciple whom Jesus loved" (ὃν ἠγάπα (ἐφίλει) ὁ Ἰησοῦς)—xiii. 23, xix. 26, xx. 2, xxi. 7, 20 sqq.; and if we compare xxi. 24 with v. 20, it is evident that this disciple is described as the writer of the preceding Gospel. It cannot be doubted that by this "beloved disciple" the Apostle John—to whom the title and ecclesiastical tradition ascribe the Gospel—is meant. In the early Church it was universally taken for granted that this expression denotes the Apostle John, and this has been maintained hitherto down to our time as a matter not requiring further proof. This proof, however, we must not now omit; for Lützelberger maintains that Andrew, Simon Peter's brother, is the disciple meant. His reasons for this opinion are very meagre. Andrew is frequently mentioned by name in the fourth Gospel (i. 41, 45, vi. 8, xii. 22), but not in any way to sanction the supposition that the Gospel was his, or that he is the same with the person described as "the beloved disciple" in the latter part of the treatise. Our reasons for taking this "beloved disciple" to be John are as follows:—

1. Judging from the relation which this "beloved disciple" is represented as occupying towards the Lord Jesus, it is evident that he was not only among the apostles, but was one of that still narrower circle who were specially

intimate with the Lord, and whom He favoured with His special confidence. We learn from the first three evangelists that Andrew was not one of these, but that they were Peter and the two sons of Zebedee only (see § 56). It is therefore highly probable that one of these three was "the beloved disciple."

2. It could not have been Peter, because he is often mentioned in this Gospel not only by name, but in distinction from this "beloved disciple" (xiii. 24, xx. 2 sqq., xxi. 7, 20 sqq.). The choice, therefore, is between the two sons of Zebedee.

3. That it could not have been James (who was probably the elder), but John, is evident (*a*) from the universality of the testimony of the early Church, which cannot be explained save upon the supposition that it had an historical basis. (*b*) According to Acts xii. 2, James suffered martyrdom by the hand of Herod Agrippa; but according to John xxi., "the beloved disciple" must have reached a great age, as according to universal tradition was the case with St. John. We learn, moreover, from John xxi. 23, that a saying of the Lord concerning "the beloved disciple" was interpreted to the effect "that that disciple should not die," but should live to the coming of the Lord; and accordingly in reference to St. John we find the notion prevailed, at least in the fourth century and afterwards, that he did not really die, but simply slumbered in his grave (see Credner, p. 220). This notion evidently had its origin in that saying of Christ's, and it therefore confirms the belief that "the beloved disciple" was John. Taking for granted the genuineness of the Gospel as composed by "the beloved disciple," the following arguments against James and in favour of John as the person meant, may be urged:—(*c*) The Gospel was written at a much later date than that to which James lived. (*d*) It bears internal marks of having been written by one who was no longer resident in Palestine, but who had now for some time been living among Greeks, which, according to tradition (see § 57), was the case with John; whereas James, so far as we know, never perma-

nently left Judea. (e) When the evangelist names the Baptist, he never thinks it necessary (as Credner, p. 209, has observed) to distinguish him from John the Apostle by calling him ὁ βαπτιστής, although he distinguishes between the two apostles called Judas, by speaking of the one as "Judas, not Iscariot;" and he speaks of Simon as Simon Peter, or Peter, and not simply as *Simon*, save in ch. i. 42, 43, when he first introduces him. Now, if the writer were not the Apostle John himself, we should certainly expect that, like the Synoptics, he would have distinguished John the Baptist by this appellation from John the Apostle. If, on the contrary, the writer was the apostle himself, he would not have felt the need of this. Herein, I observe in passing, we have an important argument for the genuineness of the Gospel. (f) Lastly, we find that "the beloved disciple" appears in the Gospel in company with Peter— xx. 2–8, xxi. 7, xviii. 15, 16. The "other disciple" (ἄλλος μαθητής), who followed the Saviour after His betrayal into the house of Annas, and obtained admittance for Peter, was clearly "the disciple whom Jesus loved." Now, after the ascension in the Acts of the Apostles, we find John frequently in company with Peter (see § 56).

§ 60.

If we now consider what the fourth Gospel tells us concerning John, we find, first of all, that a personal acquaintance subsisted between him and Annas the high priest. We there read: ὁ δὲ μαθητὴς ἐκεῖνος ἦν γνωστὸς τῷ ἀρχιερεῖ. This may mean either "he was known to him," or "was related to him." Taking the words simply in the first sense, it is not likely that this acquaintanceship, which secured for John unhindered admission to the house of Annas, was merely a personal friendship between the two: it must have been rather some connection between the two families; probably they were related to each other: and this is confirmed by the fact that John's relations were by no means obscure or mean. A testimony for the priestly kinship of John is supposed to lie in the words of Polycrates (in Euseb. v. 24;

see § 57, note). But it is very doubtful whether Polycrates here refers to John's natural descent and parentage, or only figuratively to his relation to Christ and the Church. If he meant the former, the expression ἐγενήθη ἱερεὺς τὸ πέταλον πεφορεκώς seems very inappropriate and inexact; for even if he belonged to the high priest's family, he would have no right to wear the πέταλον, unless he were himself discharging the duties of the high priest.

It is with great probability supposed that, previous to his following Jesus, John was in the Baptist's company, and was one of the two disciples who, according to John i. 35–42, when the Baptist bore witness to Jesus as the Son of God, followed Him, and abode with Him that day. One of them is expressly named as Andrew, Simon Peter's brother, who in turn led his brother to Jesus. The name of the other is not given; but, as was supposed by Chrysostom, and by almost all expositors since, it was most probably the evangelist himself. Besides the manner in which the writer of this Gospel is wont to refer to, or rather conceal himself, the minuteness with which the very hour of the day is mentioned leads most naturally to the conclusion that the writer was one of those immediately concerned.

On that occasion, John and the other disciple Andrew abode with the Saviour one day only. They probably soon returned to Galilee and resumed their wonted employment, until the Lord saw them again by the Sea of Galilee, and chose them as His permanent followers (according to the Synoptics; see § 56). No intimation is given in the Gospel concerning John's age when he was first called. The general supposition has always been that he was very young; and this is very probable, for he seems to have outlived all the other apostles. We know not how long he had been with the Baptist, nor how he came to be his disciple, neither what interval elapsed between his first and his second call. The latter (on the Sea of Galilee) certainly must have taken place before Christ's journey to the passover at Jerusalem recorded in John ii. 13 sqq. Thenceforward he seems never to have been absent from the side of his Lord, and soon he became the most trusty of His disciples. In the first three Gospels we find him in the closest intimacy with the Lord; and still more is this the case in the fourth, where, as we have seen, he is continually called "the disciple whom Jesus loved." He sat at table with Him, and lay in His bosom at the last supper which the Lord partook of with His disciples before His passion; and the Fathers therefore called Him ἐπιστή-θιος. He followed the Saviour, after His betrayal, into the dwelling of the high priest Annas (John xviii. 15). But the most beautiful and affecting proof of His love that Jesus gave him was when, as He hung upon the cross, He committed His mother to his care, telling her that for the future the apostle would be for her in place of a son, and telling him that she was to be as his own mother; "and from that hour that disciple took her to his own home" (εἰς τὰ ἴδια). This incident seems also to imply that the family of John were not in needy circumstances; for Christ would not have put the burden of providing for His mother upon one whose means were inadequate thereto.

We must here notice the view of Wieseler (*Theol. Stud. u. Krit.* 1840, p. 648 sqq.), that John and his brother James were very near kin to our Lord, their mother being sister to our Lord's mother. This he infers from John xix. 25. Μαρία ἡ τοῦ Κλωπᾶ is usually taken as standing in apposition with ἡ ἀδελφὴ τῆς μητρὸς αὐτοῦ; and thus the difficulty arises of two sisters having the same name, though, to obviate this, it may be supposed that they were only step-sisters. Wieseler, on the contrary, takes Μαρία ἡ τοῦ Κλωπᾶ to denote a different person from the sister of Christ's mother, and thus four women would here be mentioned. He thus takes "His mother's sister" to denote Salome the mother of James and John, who is mentioned in Matt. xxvii. 56, Mark xv. 40, as one of the women who accompanied Jesus on the way to Golgotha. This view has certainly much to recommend it; it is clever and plausible, but it is hardly probable (see Neander, *Pflanzung u. Leitung*, 4th ed. ii. 609). For in this case we should certainly expect the copula καί before Μαρία ἡ τοῦ Κλωπᾶ, as it occurs between the first and second named, and between the last named and the preceding. We might equally expect some remark on the part of the evangelist himself, intimating that " His mother's sister " was the mother of the disciple whom Jesus loved, and some hint of this relationship between the sons of Zebedee and the Lord in the other Gospels, or in the early tradition of the Church. But nothing of the kind occurs.

It appears from the fourth Gospel that John saw Jesus several times after the resurrection, first in Jerusalem, then in Galilee, and on the Sea of Tiberias. Here we find him again at work with the other disciples at their old employment, when the risen Jesus showed Himself to them. John was the first to recognise Him; and Jesus made a statement in reference to John which was wrongly taken by some in the Church as a prophecy that this disciple should not die, but should live to the coming of the Lord. This is related in ch. xxi. And yet even after his death, the opinion, as we have seen (§ 59), was entertained by some that he was still alive.

§ 61.

If we now examine the Gospel which bears the name of this Apostle John, we shall find that, apart from ch. xxi., it lays claim (and herein it differs from the three other Gospels, even from Matthew) to be the work of an eye-witness, to be the work of the Apostle John himself, the most beloved among our Lord's disciples.

This has usually been taken as self-evident; but of late here and there one has represented it as doubtful, or has spoken of it as if it were a mere supposition, as in the case of Matthew's Gospel, resting simply upon the title κατὰ Ἰωάννην, and upon Church tradition. But this is not the case. We have already shown that "the beloved disciple" in the fourth Gospel was undoubtedly the Apostle John, and this beloved disciple is expressly described (ch. xxi. 24) as the writer of the Gospel. It is indeed very probable, as we shall hereafter see, that this twenty-first chapter is not from the pen of the evangelist, but was added by another hand. Still we shall see that this addition must have been made very early, and that the Gospel was publicly circulated with it from the first; so that it must be regarded as a primary witness of one who was personally known to the writer of the Gospel, though not a statement of the evangelist himself. Other parts of the Gospel, however, testify that it is the work of the beloved disciple. The words καὶ ἐθεασάμεθα τὴν δόξαν αὐτοῦ in ch. i. 14 represent the writer unmistakeably as one of our Lord's immediate disciples. This is also evident in what is said of the piercing of the Lord's side, xix. 35: καὶ ὁ ἑωρακὼς μεμαρτύρηκεν, καὶ ἀληθινὴ αὐτοῦ ἐστὶν ἡ μαρτυρία· κἀκεῖνος οἶδεν ὅτι ἀληθῆ λέγει, ἵνα καὶ ὑμεῖς πιστεύσητε. Weisse (*Ev. Gesch.* i. 99, xi. 327), Lützelberger (p. 205), and Tobler have thought that the writer here refers only to the testimony of another who was an eye-witness, and on whose veracity he relied.[1] Weisse thinks that there is a reference to 1 John v. 6, confirming the truth of the statement that blood and water flowed from the side of Jesus; and he therefore takes the passage as a proof that the writer of the Gospel was a different person from the writer of the epistle, which he attributes to the Apostle John. This is so very far-fetched and improbable, that even the opponents of the genuineness of the Gospel decline to adopt it. The mode of expression in the passage would be utterly unnatural if the writer were not referring to what he had himself seen,

---

[1] So also Köstlin (*Theol. Jahrbb.* 1851, p. 207), Hilgenfeld (*die Evang. nach ihrer Entstehung*, p. 341, *Zeitschr. f. wissensch. Theol.* 1859, p. 414), Ewald, Weizsäcker, and others. Köstlin and Hilgenfeld urge the use of the more remote demonstrative ἐκεῖνος. The manner in which Steitz (*über den Gebr. des Pron.* ἐκεῖνος im 4 *Ev.*; *Stud. u. Krit.* 1859, pp. 497–506, and *ibid.* 1861) combats Hilgenfeld's argument is objected to by Alex. Buttmann (*ib.* 1860, pp. 505–536; cf. *Zeitschr. f. wiss. Theol.* 1862, pp. 204-216) upon philological grounds. But Buttmann recognises (what Hilgenfeld disputed) that "in a direct narration any one who speaks of himself in the third person may use ἐκεῖνος with reference to himself, because every form of expression appropriate to a sentence in the third person may in this case be adopted." If the writer meant an eye-witness who was not himself, he would have said, "we know," as in xxi. 24, and not "he knows" (Bleek, jun.).

if by the ἑωρακώς he did not mean himself. We cannot doubt that here that "beloved disciple" is meant who is spoken of immediately before (vers. 25-27),—to whom Jesus as He hung upon the cross commended His mother. (See also § 83, 84.)

We shall hereafter see how clear the evidence is, that at least before the middle of the second century this Gospel was widely circulated and generally received as an apostolic treatise; indeed, we have already seen (§ 53) that Marcion, for example, must have found it thus held in esteem by the Church at large. We do not, however, meet with any express statements affirming that John was the writer in the works of the Fathers until a somewhat later date, towards the end of the second century; and what they tell us upon this point seems to rest more upon conjecture and inference on their part, than upon trustworthy and historical tradition. All who mention the subject agree in stating that John wrote his Gospel late in life, during his residence in proconsular Asia, and after the first three Gospels had appeared. His design they represent in two different ways,—either to supplement the other Gospels, or to counteract certain heresies. Irenæus takes the latter view of the apostle's aim; Clemens Alex. and (though somewhat differently) Eusebius take the former. Irenæus describes John as the latest of our evangelists, and as writing his Gospel during his residence at Ephesus (*adv. Hær.* iii. 1), with special reference to the errors of Cerinthus and the so-called Nicolaitanes (iii. 11). Clemens Alex. (*Hypotypos.* in Euseb. vi. 14) says that John, the last of our evangelists, perceiving that τὰ σωματικὰ δεδήλωται in the other Gospels, at the request of his friends, and moved by the Spirit of God (πνεύματι θεοφορηθέντα), composed a πνευματικὸν εὐαγγέλιον. Eusebius himself (iii. 24) describes it as the prevailing opinion (φασί), that John was led to the composition of his own Gospel by the incompleteness of the others. But he puts the matter rather differently from Clemens Alex.: "John received the other Gospels, and recognised their truth; but he missed in them an account of the events of the first period of Christ's public ministry, which (observes Eusebius) was really the case, for they record the events of only one year of Christ's ministry, *i.e.* after the Baptist's imprisonment : therefore it is said that John determined to treat in his Gospel of this period which was passed over in silence by the first three evangelists."

These statements form the basis of the later observations of the Fathers, who repeat them with a few slight modifications. See, for example, Theodore of Mopsuestia (*ob.* circ. 428) in the *Catena in Joh.*, ed. Corder. p. 706. According to Epiphanius (*Hær.* li. § 12), John was ninety years old when he wrote his Gospel. According to Jerome (*Proœm. in Matt.*), he wrote it during his residence in Asia; for there heretical sects were being formed, and all the bishops of Asia and deputies of many churches urged him *altius scribere* concerning the divinity of Christ. These statements can hardly be regarded as testimonies of historic value.

As to the place of writing, besides the old opinion that it was Ephesus, Patmos also has been named (in the *Synopsis scripturæ sacræ*, in the Pseudo-Hippolyt. *de* xii. *apostolis*, in Theophylact, and in many Greek MSS.) ; but this opinion belongs only to a much later period than the other.

§ 62.

The genuineness of this Gospel was called in question at a comparatively early date. Not by Marcion : he rejected it, indeed, together with our canonical Gospels; but he did not deny that it was written by the Apostle John. On the contrary, he regarded its authorship (as the work of a Jew) as one reason why it should be rejected (see § 55). It was questioned by a small party in the Church itself. Even Irenæus (*adv. Hær.* iii. 11) speaks of some who *illam speciem non admittunt, quæ est secundum Joannis Evangelium, i.e.* the kind of Gospel which the Johannine presents. We find the passage in the Latin version only, and it is not very clear. It is evident, however, that reference is made to those who disapproved of the manner in which Christian doctrine is presented in the fourth Gospel, and who therefore refused to acknowledge its canonical authority ; for

Irenæus adds, *simul et Evangelium et Propheticum repellunt Spiritum*, referring in the *Propheticum* to their rejection of the Apocalypse. The probability is that these persons (unlike Marcion) denied the apostolic authorship of the Gospel. They were, it would appear, none other than those of whom Philastrius and Epiphanius speak. Philastrius (bishop of Brescia, *ob.* 387 ; *Hær.* lx.) speaks of those *qui Ev. secundum Joannem et Apocalypsin ipsius non accipiunt*, but who attributed it to the heretic Cerinthus. Epiphanius (bishop of Salamis in Cyprus, *ob.* 403) is more explicit. He speaks (*Hær.* li.) of a sect in Asia Minor, particularly in Thyatira in Lydia, who rejected both the Apocalypse and the Gospel of John, regarding both as the works of Cerinthus. They referred (in support of their opinion) to the discrepancies between the fourth and the other Gospels: that, according to it, Jesus during His public ministry attended two passovers, whereas the other evangelists mention only one; again, that after the prologue and the witness of the Baptist to Christ, it relates the call of several disciples, the return of Jesus to Galilee, and the marriage feast at Cana, whereas the other evangelists describe Him as forty days in the wilderness and tempted of the devil, and as afterwards going to Galilee and there choosing His disciples, etc. They endeavoured also critically to prove the spuriousness of the Gospel upon internal grounds. There is every reason to suppose, however, that their objections against St. John's Gospel primarily arose from other causes,—from a cold, apathetic temperament which scorned all enthusiasm, and especially that of the Montanists, who believed that the Paraclete promised by Christ had appeared in Montanus, and had given him true revelations (hints of this we find in Irenæus),—and because they could not adopt the doctrine of the Logos, as is evident from what Epiphanius says, who appropriately invented for them the name *Alogi*. They seem to have been of an Ebionite tendency, and to have assumed the more definite aspect of a sect chiefly through their opposition to the Montanists in their neighbourhood. (See my *Beiträge z. Ev. Krit.* pp. 207-211.) In other respects, even according to Epiphanius, they do not seem to have departed from the doctrine of the orthodox Churches, who do not appear to have excommunicated them.

These objections seem to have had no influence upon the judgment of the Church at large, and were espoused by a very small party only. The genuineness of the Gospel was generally recognised from the end of the second century down to the Reformation, and from the Reformation down almost to the close of last century. At the end of last century, and the beginning of this, attacks began to be made upon the apostolic authorship of this Gospel. Those of Evanson (1792) and Eckermann (in Kiel, *ob.* 1836) were unimportant. More minutely, but more frivolously, Erh. F. Vogel (*ob.* 1823) attacked the Gospel in an anonymous work entitled *Der Evangelist Johannes u. seine Ausleger vor dem jüngsten Gericht*, Leipz. 1801. More becoming and seriously, G. K. Horst, 1803; H. H. Cludius, 1808; and H. Ch. Ballenstedt, 1812, wrote against it. (See in De Wette, § 109 *a*, note *a*).

Bretschneider's (*ob.* 1848) attack excited greater attention. It was entitled *Probabilia de Evang. et epp. Joannis Apost. indole et origine*, Leipz. 1820. He argues at length from internal and external grounds, from the form of the Gospel in itself, and from its relation to the other three, that it could not have been the work of the apostle, but of another writer in his name, about the beginning or middle of the second century. This attack called forth many replies, especially that of J. T. Hemsen (*die Authentie d. Schriften des Ev. Joh.*, Schlesw. 1823); see in LÜCKE, *Commentar*, 3d ed. i. 99.

Bretschneider felt obliged, in the preface to the second edition of his *Dogmatik*, 1822, to avow that he had suggested his doubts only by way of inquiry, and in order to call forth a satisfactory proof of the genuineness of St. John's Gospel, which to him seemed imperfect. This object he had attained. But explanations such as these leave a doubt upon the mind whether and how far the author himself has been convinced of the invalidity of his former objections. These objections seem ever and anon to subside for a while, and then to break forth anew. Hence we find them re-asserted in Dav. Strauss' *Leben Jesu*, 1835-6. Strauss does not attempt any historico-critical investigation concerning the origin of our fourth Gospel, but endeavours to show that its contents—the discourses of Jesus, and the events recorded of Him—are quite unhistorical and mythical, full of inner contradictions and improbabilities; so that it could never have been the work of an eye-witness and participator in the events recorded, least of all of the most beloved disciple of the Lord. In the preface to the third edition of his first volume (1838) he admitted that, owing to the arguments of Neander and De Wette, he hesitated concerning the genuineness of this Gospel; but he soon withdrew this confession, and avowed himself more distinctly than ever against even the possibility of its apostolic origin, and to this he adheres in his fourth edition.

Among the works which Strauss' book called forth, I may here mention that of Weisse, who distinguishes between a genuine Johannine kernel or substratum in our Gospel, and a later recension. He attributes to St. John certain essays containing discourses of Jesus, sayings of the Baptist, together with the prologue and some other portions; but he considers our Gospel, and the entire narrative it contains, as the work of a later hand, and he regards its historical value as far below that of the three other Evangelists, among whom he thinks Mark stands first as the most original and trustworthy, both in its accounts of particular occurrences, in its consecutive history, in the character of the discourses it records, and in the picture it gives of Christ's whole life. Weisse maintains this view in his work entitled *Die Evang.-Frage in ihrem gegenwärtigen Stadium*, Leipzic 1856.

This notion of Weisse, that material provided by the Apostle John formed the basis of the ampler work, which was written in full by a disciple of the apostle's, had been advanced by other scholars before him (see De Wette, § 110, *e*, note *a*), and has been advocated since his work by

Schenkel and Schweizer.[1] Schenkel thinks that two sets of discourses came from St. John's hand,—the one the discourses found scattered through ch. i.-xii., and the other the farewell discourses: the history linking together these discourses he takes to have been by a later hand. Schweizer also recognises a twofold authorship, but in a different way: he thinks that, besides ch. xxi., the narratives of events in Galilee (ii. 1–12, iv. 44–54, vi. 1–26), and a few minor interpolations (xix. 35–37, xviii. 9, xvi. 30, ii. 21, 22), are by a later hand, but that the rest is the work of the Apostle John, and possesses a thoroughly historical character.

§ 63.

Views such as these, though advocated with great acuteness and nicety, especially by Schweizer, have not been regarded with much favour, nor been generally adopted. The attention of theologians was soon turned in another direction, viz. to the attacks made by the Tübingen school upon the genuineness of the Gospel as a whole. This school is unanimous in attributing the Apocalypse to St. John, but in regarding the Gospel which bears his name as quite unhistorical, and as the work of a Gentile Christian about the middle of the second century, who wrote not with an historical, but a dogmatic, end in view. These it considers ascertained truths. Schwegler (*ob.* 1857), in his *Montanismus u. die ch. Kirche des 2 Jahrh.*, Tübingen 1841, pp. 183–221, endeavours to prove that the Gospel was written about A.D. 150 in Asia Minor, and owed its origin to the same theological movement as Montanism, in opposition to the Judaiz-

---

[1] SCHENKEL, *über die neuesten Bearbeitungen des Lebens Jesu*, Theol. Stud. u. Krit. 1840. AL. SCHWEIZER, *das Ev. Joh. nach seinem innern Werthe*, etc., 1841. [Schenkel, in his *Characterbild Jesu*, 1864, regards the entire Gospel as far removed from the apostle, and holds that it was published about A.D. 110-120, from the accounts of the character of Jesus which had been formed from the influence and teaching of John in Ephesus, speculatively coloured by the rising *gnosis* of the time. J. H. SCHOLTEN (*Het Evangelie naar Johannes, Kritisch historisch onderzoek*, Leyden 1864) dates the Gospel circ. A.D. 140, but considers that it subsequently received many interpolations.]—B.

ing tendencies of the age; and in his *Nachapost. Zeitalter*, ii. 346-376, he puts St. John's Gospel last, as the culmination and focus of doctrinal development in Asia Minor in the post-apostolic age. Baur himself (*ob.* 1860), in his *Krit. Untersuchungen über die kanon. Evv.* 1847, pp. 77-389, and in the *Theol. Jahrbb.* 1844, 1847, 1851, puts forth the following view: The fourth Gospel was not written with an historical aim, but in advocacy of certain doctrinal ideas; and the writer made use of the Gospel tradition already before him, especially in the first three Gospels, in a very free and arbitrary way. The author, who was not certainly a Jew by birth, lived in Asia Minor, or more probably in Alexandria, in the second century, at a time when the Church was agitated and divided by conflicting parties, by the gnostic controversies, by that concerning the doctrine of the Logos, by that concerning Easter, and by those of Montanism. Zeller also advocated these views in the *Theol. Jahrbb.* 1845, 1847; also Hilgenfeld (*das Ev. u. die Briefe Joh.*, etc., 1849; *die Evv. nach ihrer Entstehung*, 1854; and in his *Zeitschr. f. wis. Theologie*, 1859), who thinks that our fourth Gospel presupposes the end of Gnosticism, and was written in the second quarter of the second century, probably in Asia Minor, by a highly accomplished Gentile Christian.

My remarks in my *Beitr. zur Evang.-Kritik*, Berlin 1846, were directed mainly against Baur's and Zeller's dissertations. I endeavour both to answer their objections, and positively to establish the genuineness and historical veracity of the Gospel by external and internal arguments, by the construction of the Gospel itself, and its relation to the other Gospels. What Baur and Zeller have again advanced in the *Theol. Jahrb.* of 1847 is of little weight. Other scholars have replied to the objections of Baur and his school. Among these I may name G. A. Hauff, *Theol. Stud. u. Krit.* 1846, pp. 550-629; Ebrard, *das Ev. Joh.*, etc., Zur. 1845, and *Wissensch. Kritik der evang. Gesch.*, 2d ed., Erl. 1850, pp. 828-947; Guericke, in the 2d ed. of his *Einl. ins N. T.*; Georg. Karl Mayer, *die Echtheit des Ev. nach Joh.*, Schaffhausen 1854. De Wette, in the earlier editions of his *Einl.*

ins N. T., and even in the fourth, expressed himself very sceptically concerning St. John's Gospel. He allows, on the one hand, that in its doctrinal and historic contents it bears the stamp of originality and apostolicity; and he thinks, on the other hand, that much in it indicates a later point of view. He does not therefore pronounce any decided verdict; but in his fifth edition he expresses himself (with special reference to my *Beiträge*) decidedly in favour of its genuineness, as also did Credner (*Einl. ins. N. T.*, but not in his *Gesch. des N. T. Kanon*, 1860), Schleiermacher, and Lücke in his commentary. Reuss does not adopt the sceptical view, but thinks that the argument for the Johannine authorship, though not strictly conclusive, is, critically speaking, only barely possible.

[The notion of a partial genuineness, or indirect apostolic authorship, has again been advanced in various forms. According to Ewald (*Jahrbb. d. bibl. Wissenschaft*, iii. 146-174, v. 178-207, x. 83-114; *die Johann. Schriften übers. u. erklärt*, Gött. 1861), John, in writing his Gospel, made use of the hand, and perhaps the head, of a trusty friend, who afterwards (but not during the apostle's lifetime) appended ch. xxi., and dealt with the work more independently; on which account he speaks of what the apostle had narrated as an eye-witness in the third person, *e.g.* xix. 35 (see § 61). Originally it was intended for only a small circle of readers. Weizsäcker (*Untersuchungen über die Evang. Gesch.*, Gotha 1864) thinks that this Gospel was composed by a disciple of St. John, under his guidance, and after his prelections or addresses in the congregation, long after the Synoptics, but not later than the end of the first century, and that the comment or interpretation of facts has often been confounded therein with the historical recollection of them.

J. T. Tobler, the author of the work entitled *Die Ev.- Frage im Allgem. u. die Joh.-Frage insbesondere*, first published anonymously 1858, considers that the author was Apollos (= the writer of the Epistle to the Hebrews), who made use of the apostolic (Johannine) information. See also his dissertation in Hilgenfeld's *Zeitschr. f. wiss. Theol.* 1860, p. 169 sqq.]—B.

THE RELATION OF OUR FOUR GOSPELS TO ONE ANOTHER, WITH REFERENCE PARTICULARLY TO THEIR CONTENTS.

§ 64.

All the four Gospels give us an account of Christ's public ministry, or at least of certain facts occurring during His public ministry, from His baptism onwards to His resurrection, and His subsequent appearances to His disciples. Matthew and Luke give us, in addition to this, an *evangelium infantiæ*, relating certain circumstances attendant upon His miraculous birth, and (in Luke) relating also to His youth. Mark and Luke have also at the end a short notice of His ascension; whereas Matthew and John tell us nothing of the way in which Christ separated Himself from His disciples, and returned to His Father in heaven.

For the rest, however, and in most other particulars, the first three Gospels bear a close affinity with each other, both as to their contents and arrangement,—an affinity very different from that which they severally bear to the Gospel of John. Each of the first three has much that is peculiar to itself; but when compared with St. John, they appear but three different modifications of one and the same story, which St. John tells over again, but in a different manner, and with many and essential additions.

1. This is evident, first, with reference to the general tenor of the history. Apart from the *evangelium infantiæ*, which Mark does not give, their narrative divides itself into three parts. The first includes an account of the beginning of our Lord's public ministry, of the ministry of the Baptist, of the baptism of Jesus and His temptation: Matt. iii. 1–iv. 11; Mark i. 1–13; Luke iii. 1–iv. 13. In the second part all three tell us of the return of Jesus to Galilee, and then give a series of connected narratives concerning Christ's teaching and miracles in this district and the parts surrounding, without any intimation that during this time He also visited Judea and Jerusalem: Matt. iv. 12–xviii. 35; Mark

i. 14–ix. 50; Luke iv. 14–ix. 50. Throughout this part, and especially in its later sections, the accounts of the three evangelists coincide, both as to the events narrated, and as to the order in which they are told. Hereupon they all three at once pass to the last journey of Christ from Galilee to Jerusalem, to that feast of the passover at which He was crucified: in Matthew from ch. xix. 1 onwards; in Mark from ch. x. 1; in Luke from ch. ix. 51. The third and last part thus contains the events and circumstances of this journey, Christ's triumphal entry into Jerusalem, the various events which were enacted in Jerusalem itself during the days between the entry and the passion of the Lord; and finally, the history of the passion, and of the Lord's resurrection.

Now, if we turn to St. John's Gospel, we find (*a*) that Christ's public ministry, during the interval between the baptism and the last passover, was not confined to Galilee, but that the residence in Galilee, as narrated by the Synoptics, was interrupted by certain journeys to Jerusalem; and (*b*) that Christ does not seem to have come up to the last passover from Galilee to Jerusalem direct, but left Galilee some months before.

To enter into particulars. According to John, during the first period of His public ministry, after the testimony of the Baptist concerning Him, and the meeting of some of His disciples with Him, Jesus went to Galilee (i. 44, ii.); and having wrought His first miracle at Cana, went to Capernaum (ii. 12), which, according to the Synoptics also, seems to have been Christ's usual place of residence in Galilee. Then St. John tells us that He went up to Jerusalem to the passover; and on this occasion the cleansing of the temple and the visit of Nicodemus took place (ii. 13–iii. 21). While still in Judea, He heard that the Pharisees were observing Him, and He returned through Samaria to Galilee (iv. 1 sqq.). The Galileans received Him, because they had seen the miracles which Jesus had wrought at the feast of the passover (iv. 35),—a clear proof that He had not been unobserved or disesteemed at Jerusalem (cf. ii. 23). According to v. 1, Jesus goes a second time to Jerusalem, on occasion of a Jewish feast, and awakens the hostility of the Jews by working a miracle on the Sabbath. He therefore returns again to Galilee, where we find Him in ch. vi. 1 sqq., and according to ver. 4, at a time when the feast of the passover was nigh. He walks in Galilee, and not in Judea, because of the opposition of the Jews (vii. 1). Here he remains nearly to the time of the feast of tabernacles, which was held six months after the passover (vii. 2). During this feast He goes up again to Jerusalem (ver. 10), and appeared openly to the people, both during the feast and afterwards (vii. 14 sqq.). There we find Him at the feast of the dedication, which took place two months later (x. 22). It does not appear in St. John's account whether Jesus spent this interval of two months at Jerusalem, or whether during it He returned to Galilee. We might suppose the former, seeing that the latter is not expressly mentioned. It is clear, however, from what follows in St. John, that after the feast of the dedication Jesus did not return to Galilee until the last passover: for after the feast of the dedication, Jesus went to the other side Jordan, to the place where the Baptist John at first baptized (x. 40), which probably was not far from Jerusalem; and from thence, being summoned by Martha and Mary, He came to Bethany, close by Jerusalem, where He raised Lazarus to life (ch. xi.). Thence, in order to avoid the lying in wait of the Jews, He retired to a village called Ephraim, in the wilderness of Judea (in the neighbourhood of Bethel, xi. 53, 54); and six days before the passover He returned to Bethany (xii. 1), and on the day following made His triumphal entry into Jerusalem (xii. 12 sqq.). Upon this follows, as in the first three evangelists, the history of the passion, of His crucifixion, and the appearances after His resurrection. According to St. John, therefore, between Christ's last journey from Galilee to Jerusalem and His triumphal entry there was an interval of several months—of four at least from the time of the feast of dedication, and of six if we reckon from the feast of tabernacles—which was spent partly in Jerusalem and partly in the neighbouring district. And yet, according to the three first Gospels, viewing their account alone, it would seem as if Jesus went from Galilee to Jerusalem to the last passover only a short time before it began; that He had previously remained in Galilee and the neighbourhood continuously, having taken up his abode there at the beginning of His public ministry. We thus find a striking coincidence between the several accounts given by the first three evangelists, viewing their history as a whole, of our Lord's ministry down to the last passover; but the Gospel of John presents marked and very obvious differences.

§ 65.

2. There is a close affinity between the three first evangelists *in the subject-matter of their narrations,* both as regards the discourses and sayings of Christ which they record, and other facts of His life. Each has some things peculiar to himself, but the points of agreement preponderate. Matthew and Luke give each an independent account of Christ's birth and infancy, and this is wholly wanting in Mark. In the first part, the preliminary account of the outset of Christ's ministry, all three give the same incidents, and in the same order, viz. an account of John the Baptist and his ministry, the baptism of Jesus, His fasting and temptation, and His return to Galilee. In Luke the genealogy of Jesus is inserted between the baptism and the temptation.

In the second part, Christ's ministry in Galilee and the parts surrounding, most of the events narrated are given by all three evangelists, or at least by two out of the three, and comparatively few are told by any one of them alone. MARK has here only two short accounts of miracles peculiar to himself, viz. vii. 32-37, viii. 22-26, and the brief parable (iv. 26-29). We do not find in Mark some things which are common to Matthew and Luke, viz. the healing of the nobleman's son at Capernaum, the visit of the disciples of John to Jesus, the sermon on the mount, and many sayings of Christ; for Mark gives very few of Christ's discourses in comparison of the other evangelists, and in proportion to the length and other contents of his Gospel. Peculiar to MATTHEW in this part is the account of the *stater* in the fish's mouth, xvii. 24–27; the healing of two blind men and of a dumb demoniac, ix. 27–34: many sayings of Christ, partly parables—that of the tares, xiii. 24–30, with its explanation, vers. 36–42; of the unmerciful servant, xviii. 21–35: many sayings in the sermon on the mount, ch. v.–vii., and in the address to the twelve, ch. x.; that concerning Peter, xvi. 17–19; and others. There is wanting in Matthew, in this part, the following sections, which Mark and Luke have in common: the healing of the demoniac at Capernaum (Mark i. 21-28; Luke iv. 31-37); the account of the choosing of the twelve apostles (Mark iii. 13-19; Luke vi. 12, 13); the incident in Mark ix. 38 sqq., Luke ix. 49, 50; and a brief summary of Christ's journey through Galilee, begun on the day after the healing of Peter's wife's mother (Mark i. 35-39; Luke iv. 42-44). Peculiar to LUKE, in this part, is the raising the widow's son at Nain, vii. 11-17, and viii. 1-3; the anointing of Jesus in Simon's house, vii. 36-50 (which perhaps was the same with the anointing at Bethany, Matt. xxvi. 6-13, Mark xiv. 3-9). The accounts Luke gives of the unfriendly reception of Jesus in the synagogue at Nazareth, iv. 16-30, and of the call of Peter, James, and John, v. 1-11, probably refer to the same events, which are somewhat differently told in Matthew, xiii. 54-58, iv. 18-22, and Mark vi. 1-6, i. 16-20. There is wanting in Luke all that Matthew and Mark insert between the feeding of the 5000 and that of the 4000, including this latter and what immediately follows (Matt. xiv. 22–xvi. 12; Mark vi. 45–viii. 21); the walking on the sea, the discourse concerning the washing of hands, the healing the daughter of the woman of Canaan, the feeding of the 4000, and the warning concerning the leaven of the Pharisees.

Some of the works and discourses of Christ are not told by the three evangelists in the same order, but there is a striking coincidence between them. Especially towards the end of this part (Matt. xvi. 13, Luke ix. 18, Mark viii. 27, and onwards), all three narrate, first, how Jesus asked His disciples what men said of Him; secondly, Peter's confession concerning Him; thirdly, the prophecy of Jesus concerning His betrayal and death; fourthly, the transfiguration six or eight days afterwards, and the healing of a demoniac whom the disciples could not heal; fifthly, the foretelling of His death repeated; and lastly, Matthew having inserted the account of the *stater* in the fish's mouth, Christ's condemnation of the question or thought of the disciples, which of them should be greatest. Hereupon they all, and especially Matthew, add many sayings of Christ, each peculiar to each; and then, in all three, the triumphal entry of Jesus into Jerusalem leads on to the feast at which He was crucified. In the various sections of this part the three evangelists link together certain facts and events: *e.g.* (*a*) the stilling of the tempest, and the healing of the demoniac in the country of the Gergesenes (Matt. viii. 18-34; Mark iv. 35-v. 20; Luke viii. 22-39); (*b*) the healing of the man sick of the palsy, the calling of the publican, and the feast, with the discourses following (Matt. ix. 1-17; Mark ii. 1-22; Luke v. 17-39); (*c*) the healing of the woman with the issue of blood, and the raising of Jairus' daughter (Matt. ix. 18-26; Mark v. 22-43; Luke viii. 41-56); (*d*) two narrations concerning the charge brought against Jesus and His disciples of breaking the Sabbath (Matt. xii. 1-14; Mark ii. 23-iii. 6; Luke vi: 1-11); (*e*) the sayings of Herod and others concerning Jesus, and the feeding of 5000 (Matt. xiv. 1-21; Mark vi. 14-44; Luke ix. 7-17), where Matthew and Mark have inserted the account of the Baptist's imprisonment and beheading, which is briefly told by Luke a little earlier (iii. 19, 20). The coincidence and agreement become still more striking when we compare any two of these three evangelists together, especially when we compare Mark with either Matthew or Luke (see § 94 sqq.).

In the third part, relating to the journey of Jesus from Galilee to Jerusalem, Luke has a long section, ix. 51—xviii. 14, which, as thus placed, is peculiar to him: it contains many facts, and especially parables and other sayings of Christ, some of which Matthew gives in other places, but most of which are peculiar to Luke. For instance, Christ's rebuke of the sons of Zebedee concerning the inhospitable Samaritan village, ix. 51-56; the sending forth, instruction, and return of the seventy, x. 1-20; Martha and Mary, x. 38-42; the words of Jesus regarding the Galileans and those on whom the tower in Siloam fell, xiii. 1-5; the healing of the man with the dropsy on the Sabbath, xiv. 1 sqq.; the cleansing of the ten lepers, xvii. 11-19. Among the parables peculiar to Luke are—the good Samaritan, x. 30-37; the great supper, xiv. 15-24; the prodigal son, xv. 11-32; the unjust steward, xvi. 1-13; the rich man and Lazarus, xvi. 14-32; the Pharisee and publican, xviii. 9-14; also xi. 5-8, xiii. 6-9, xviii. 12 sqq.

After this long section in Luke, which we find after that place in his Gospel where he begins his account of Christ's journey to Jerusalem, we find other incidents recorded which occurred previous to Christ's triumphal entry (xviii. 15-xix. 28); and this is pretty much the same as that told by the two other evangelists, and placed by them immediately after the account of Christ's Galilean ministry (Matt. xix. xx.; Mark x.). Mark has nothing in this part peculiar to himself; Luke alone gives the account of Zaccheus in Jericho (xix. 1-10), and the parable of the pounds (vers. 11-28), which is wanting in Mark, and resembles that of the talents in Matthew (xxv. 14-30). There is wanting in Luke (*a*) Christ's discourse concerning marriage and divorce (Matt. xix. 1-9; Mark x. 1-12); (*b*) Christ's answer to the mother of James and John (Matt. xx. 20-28; Mark x. 35-45). Peculiar to Matthew in this part is (*a*) xix. 10-12 and (*b*) xx. 1-16, the parable of the labourers in the vineyard. All the other narratives in this part are told similarly and in the same order by the three evangelists.

A great similarity is observable in the Synoptics in the following part, which treats of *Christ's triumphal entry into Jerusalem, and the events of the first days of His residence there*, down to the point when the history of the passion begins (Matt. xxi.–xxv.; Mark xi.–xiii.; Luke xix. 29–xxi. 38). But little here is peculiar to any one evangelist.

Nothing is peculiar to Mark. Matthew gives a saying of Christ's, xxi. 14–16; the parable of the two sons, xxi. 28–32; the parable of the marriage of the king's son, xxii. 1–14; and other parables and sayings of Christ in the latter part of His discourse concerning the coming of the Son of man, ch. xxiv. xxv., some of which we find in that section which Luke has peculiar to himself. Here, however, peculiar to Matthew are the parable of the ten virgins (xxv. 1–13), and the account of the final judgment (xxv. 31–46). Peculiar to Luke are xxi. 34–38 and xix. 39–44. There are wanting in Luke the narrative concerning the withering of the barren fig-tree (Matt. xxi. 17–22; Mark xi. 11–14, 19–26), and Christ's answer to the lawyer's question concerning the great commandment (Matt. xxii. 34–40; Mark xii. 28–34, though this may be the same as Luke x. 25). Matthew is wanting in the account of the widow's mite, which Mark and Luke insert between our Lord's discourse against the Pharisees, and that concerning the end (Luke xxi. 1–4; Mark xii. 41–44). Everything else in this section is told by all three evangelists, and in the same order.

After Christ's eschatological discourse, which closes this part, all three evangelists narrate the decree of the Sanhedrim to put Jesus to death as the beginning of *the history of the passion* (Matt. xxvi. xxvii.; Mark xiv. xv.; Luke xxii. xxiii.). In this part especially they narrate the same facts, circumstances, and sayings of Jesus, and for the most part in the same order. Luke has very little indeed that differs from Matthew and Mark. Peculiar to Mark is xiv. 51, 52 only, concerning the young man with the linen cloth; and he omits nothing which we find told by Matthew and Luke in common. Matthew omits nothing which Mark and Luke have in common. Matthew and Luke have each of them something peculiar to his own Gospel:—*Matthew*—ch. xxvii. 3–10, the remorse and suicide of Judas; xxvii. 24, 25, Pilate's declaration as he washed his hands; xxvii. 62–66, the setting a watch at the sepulchre. *Luke*—ch. xxiii. 4–15, Pilate and Herod; xxiii. 27–32, Christ's words to the weeping women; xxiii. 39–43, the penitent thief; also xxii.

24-30, Christ's rebuke of ambition in His disciples, though we find a similar narration in an earlier part of the history in Matthew and Mark.

The last chapters of the three Gospels, *concerning the resurrection and the appearances of the risen Jesus* (Matt. xxviii.; Mark xvi.; Luke xxiv.), present, when compared together, many more differences and peculiarities. Matthew alone tells of the bribing of the watch by the Sanhedrim (vers. 16-20); the assembling of the disciples in Galilee in obedience to Christ's command, and the last words which He spake to them there. Luke tells of the two disciples journeying to Emmaus, of Christ's appearance to the eleven gathered together, and of the ascension (vers. 13-53); parallel to this in Mark, but in a more cursory manner, we have vers. 12-20; vers. 15-18 containing some final words of Christ to His disciples, which are peculiar to Mark.

§ 66.

Putting together now all that each of the first three evangelists has peculiar to himself and different from the other two, we find that it falls very far short of that which they all or any two of them have in common; and this will strike us all the more, if we compare *St. John's Gospel* with them. In the account which John gives of our Lord's public ministry, the events of His Galilean ministry occupy by no means so large and prominent a place as do those of His various journeys up to the feast to and from Jerusalem, together with His abode in Jerusalem at the outset. John mentions only four events connected with Christ's Galilean ministry: (*a*) the miracle at Cana, ii. 1-11; (*b*) the healing of the son of the βασιλικός at Capernaum, iv. 47-54; (*c*) the feeding of the 5000, and (*d*) the walking on the sea, vi. 1-21; with the following discourse of Christ with the Jews and His disciples, vers. 22-71. The two last (without the discourse) are related by the other evangelists likewise; the miraculous feeding by all three; the walking on the sea by Matthew and Mark: the second is not improbably the same with Matt. viii. 5-13, Luke vii. 1-10; the first is peculiar to John. John tells nothing of all the other works and words of the Lord Jesus in Galilee told us by the first three evangelists; and we find nothing in these of all that John relates concerning Christ's works during His earlier residence in Jerusalem,—concerning, *e.g.*, the healing of the impotent man at the pool of Bethesda (v. 2 sqq.), and the opening the eyes of one born blind (ix. 1 sqq.).

We find nothing said in John of the events narrated by the first three evangelists on occasion of Christ's journey to Jerusalem before the last passover (Matt. xix. xx.; Mark x.; Luke ix. 51–xix. 28); and in them no mention is made of the greatest of all Christ's miracles upon that occasion, viz. the raising of Lazarus (John xi.). The greatest similarity and coincidence is to be found, however, in the narrations of all four in the closing scenes of the history: *e.g.* the anointing at Bethany, John xii. 1–8, Matt. xxvi. 6–13, Mark xiv. 3–9 (Luke vii. 36–50); the triumphal entry into Jerusalem, John xii. 12 sqq., Matt. xxi. 1 sqq., Mark xi. 1 sqq., Luke xix. 29 sqq.; the treachery of Judas, and how Jesus at the last supper pointed him out as the traitor; how Christ foretold the denial of Peter; the betrayal; the cutting off the ear of the high priest's servant, and other facts.

Yet even in this section John has several things peculiar to himself, and not narrated by the first three evangelists. In his account of the events of the last evening before the passion, He says nothing of the institution of the holy communion, which the first three evangelists narrate; but relates instead the symbolic washing of the disciples' feet, which is omitted by them. In his account of the events of the following day, he mentions Christ's trial before Annas; but the three others His appearance before the assembled Sanhedrim in the house of Caiaphas. John also tells of a cleansing of the temple, not, like the first three evangelists, on occasion of Christ's last visit to Jerusalem, but at the outset of His public ministry (ii. 13–22).

What holds true of the outward acts and miracles of our Lord as related by the several evangelists, is still more fully applicable to the discourses and sayings of Christ which they record. In Mark, prominence is given to the various facts of Christ's life; while His discourses, especially His longer ones, are omitted. Matthew and Luke record each of them certain discourses not elsewhere to be found; but most that Matthew gives is found in Luke, and most that Luke tells occurs in Matthew, though sometimes (as we have already seen) in different connections and in different places. In John, however, the case is different. Prominence is here given to the discourses, and we find in him but few sayings of Christ which can be regarded as identical with those told by the first three evangelists—at least short sentences only.[1] But as to the longer discourses, those which Matthew and Luke give are not found in him; and those which he gives are not found in them, even when the same events and circumstances are narrated. The Synoptics, for example, do not give the discourse which in John follows the miraculous feeding of the multitude and the walking on the sea (vi. 22-71); and in the account of the last supper and of our Lord's passion, John gives long discourses which do not occur in the Synoptics, while the Synoptics relate certain words and sayings of Jesus which John omits.

§ 67.

Not only are our Lord's discourses, which St. John records, different from those given by the Synoptics; but their entire character, their form and contents, are peculiar, and convey to our minds a somewhat different impression of the character of our Lord's teaching. As to their form, their conversational character as mutual discourse and dialogue with others is retained more vividly and strikingly in John than in the discourses given by the Synoptics; e.g. Christ's conversation with Nicodemus, with the woman of Samaria, with the Jews after the feeding of the 5000, etc.: the conversational form of discourse is given comparatively seldom, and more briefly, in the Synoptics. The discourses

---

[1] Thus John xii. 25 (Matt. x. 39, xvi. 25; Luke ix. 24, xvii. 33; Mark viii. 35), xiii. 20 (Matt. x. 40), xiii. 16, cf. xv. 20 (Matt. x. 24). See also iv. 44 (Matt. xiii. 57; Mark vi. 4; Luke iv. 24).

which they record consist mainly of short, proverbial, sententious sayings, arranged together one after another, and sometimes blended with similitudes and with parables. The discourses in John also contain similitudes; but they do not consist so much of sententious sayings, nor do they contain so many fully elaborated parables: we find in them simple metaphors, or comparisons only. Jesus calls Himself the vine, His Father the husbandman, His people the branches; again He says, "I am the door," "I am the good shepherd;" but no elaborate parables, such as that of the sower or the good Samaritan, occur in John. As to the subject-matter of the discourses, those in the Synoptics set forth either the relation of the kingdom of God to the world, in its nature, its spread, its beginnings, its development or its completion in the second coming of the Son of man in His glory, or describe the duties resting upon those who would enter the kingdom of heaven and partake of its bliss. But those recorded by St. John refer chiefly to the dignity and glory of the Son of God, and His relation to the Father, both before and after the incarnation, together with the character of those who follow Him, and would be His true disciples, and be brought by Him to the Father. The discourses which St. John records are of a more speculative character, while those in the Synoptics are more popular and practical. Christ's promises concerning the triumph of God's kingdom upon earth, and the second coming of the Son of man, are not so definite and circumstantial as in the Synoptics: they occur rather in hints and figures. His prophecies, too, concerning His sufferings, His death, and His resurrection, are less explicit, and given in similitudes only, in St. John. (See § 78.) And as to the character of Christ's miracles as recorded by St. John, we find this difference: he makes no mention whatever of the cure of demoniacs, so often related by the first three evangelists.

§ 68.

The seeming difference between St. John and the Synoptics with reference to *the day of Christ's crucifixion*, in its relation to the feast of the passover, is equally striking and important. All the four evangelists agree as to *the day of the week* on which the crucifixion took place, viz. Friday; for on the previous evening the Lord had celebrated the last supper with His disciples, *i.e.* on the Thursday evening, which was reckoned by the Jews as part of the following day. But there is a difference in the relation of this Thursday evening and Friday to the annual passover. The feast of the passover was fixed according to *the day of the month only*, not for any particular day of the week. It continued seven days from the 15th of Nisan to the 21st; but the 14th of Nisan came to be reckoned in the feast, which thus was said to last eight days, as we learn from Josephus (*Antiq.* ii. 15, 1). Of these seven or eight days two only were specially sacred, being of a sabbatical character, viz. the 15th of Nisan (as the first, or if we reckon the 14th Nisan, the second day) and the 21st or last day. The first great day began with the eating of the paschal lamb on the evening of the 14th of Nisan, *i.e.*, according to Jewish reckoning, at the beginning of the 15th.

Now, according to the first three evangelists, Jesus ate the last supper with His disciples as the passover, and at the time legally fixed among the Jews for the celebration of the passover (Matt. xxvi. 17, 19, 20; Mark xiv. 12, 16, 17; Luke xxii. 7, 8, 11, 13); and accordingly the Friday on which He was crucified would be the 15th of Nisan, the great day of the feast. But in St. John it is distinctly represented that the Lord was crucified on the day before the great feast day, on the 14th of Nisan, and consequently that He ate the last supper with His disciples a day before the time fixed for the celebration of the passover. According to John's account, the 15th of Nisan, the great day of the feast, coincided *that year* with the weekly Sabbath (our Saturday); and the day before (*i.e.* the Friday) would be the preparation day both for the weekly Sabbath and for the great feast day (see xiii. 1, 29, xviii. 28, xix. 14, 31).

Various modes of reconciliation have been proposed in order to obviate this difficulty. Some explain the passages in the Synoptics so as to make them also say that Jesus celebrated the passover a day before its legal time, and that He was crucified on the 14th of Nisan;[1] and others try to bring St. John's statements into accord with the Synoptics, so as to make John say that Jesus was crucified on the 15th of Nisan, and that His last supper was held at the proper time for the passover.[2] But an unbiassed examination of the statements of the Synoptics and of St. John proves that both these explanations are alike untenable; see my *Beitr. zur Ev. Kritik*, pp. 107-139. A thorough exegesis will not suffer us to deny that we have here a real difference between the narrative of the Synoptics and that of St. John.

§ 69.

5. As to the style of writing and the language used, we find that the first three evangelists have much in common, so that when we have read the Greek of one, we shall not find much that is strange or different in the Greek of the others; *e.g.* many frequently recurring expressions and modes of speaking in Matthew recur in Mark and Luke. But John's Gospel presents to us much that is peculiar to itself and different from the Synoptics. His manner of writing, indeed, like that of the Synoptics, is very simple, and free from lengthy and elaborate periods; but in the selection and use of words, and in the construction, we find much less of a Hebraistic

---

[1] So often in early writers, and of late by MOVERS, *Zeitschrift für Philos. u. kathol. Theologie*, viii. 71 sqq., and G. K. MAYER. The latter says that the words τῇ πρώτῃ ἡμέρᾳ τῶν ἀζύμων (Matt. xxvi. 17 ; Mark xiv. 12) mean "the day *before* the feast ;" but this is unnatural, nay impossible : for even if πρῶτος does sometimes stand for πρότερος, and with a genitive, in the sense that anything is first in relation to some other thing, and = that it is before it (*e.g.* John i. 15, 30, xv. 18), still ἡ πρώτη τῶν ἀζύμων cannot mean "the day immediately before the beginning of the ἄζυμα," but "the first day of the ἄζυμα ;" and the entire history in the Synoptics confirms this.

[2] *e.g.* THOLUCK (on John xiii. 1), HENGSTENBERG (*Ev. K. Z.* 1838, Nos. 98-102; and his *Comm. in loc.*); WIESELER (*Chronol. Synopse der vier Evv.*, Hamb. 1833; and in *Reuter's Repertorium*, 1849), and in a different manner JOH. WICHELHAUS (*Comm. on the Sufferings of Christ*, Halle 1855).

colouring than in the Synoptics. We find this even in the sections which John and the Synoptics have in common. Like differences are indeed traceable among the Synoptics themselves, in the narrations or discourses which they have in common; but there is nevertheless a great similarity not only generally, but in particulars also, — a coincidence in the use of the very same words and constructions, especially in Mark as compared with Matthew and Luke, and also between these latter. For examples of this, see De Wette, § 79, *b*, note *a*. A coincidence also occurs sometimes in the very text of O. T. quotations, made by more than one of them; and this is especially traceable in quotations which differ somewhat both from the Hebrew and the LXX.: see Matt. iii. 3, Luke iii. 4, Mark i. 3; Matt. xi. 10, Luke vii. 27, Mark i. 3; Matt. xv. 8, 9, Mark vii. 6, 7 (see my *Beitr.* pp. 173–175). John, on the contrary, even in those narrations which he has in common with the other evangelists, has much more that is distinctively characteristic, and very seldom coincides in expression with any of them, unless in an exceptional way; *e.g.* xii. 3, μύρον νάρδου πιστικῆς, as coincident with Mark xiv. 3.

§ 70.

This general relationship of the Gospels to each other— that on the one hand of St. John to the other three, and that on the other hand of the Synoptics to each other—must somehow correspond with the origin of these several writings as to time, place, and authorship; and this correspondence has been variously explained. In virtue of this relationship between St. John and the Synoptics, even the early writers of the church supposed that the fourth Gospel was intentionally written as supplementary to the other three,—intended either as a πνευματικὸν εὐαγγέλιον, in contrast with the others, which were styled τὰ σωματικά, or to give an account of the early ministry of Jesus (omitted by the others) down to the time of the Baptist's imprisonment (see § 61). Whether and how far such a supposition is admissible, we shall hereafter consider (§ 116). It is clear, however (we may here remark), that these explanations suggested by the ancients are partly inadequate, and partly (in the last-named particular) erroneous. St. John's purpose cannot have been simply to fill up gaps in Christ's history left by the Synoptics, because he treats in full of the sufferings, the death, and the resurrection of Christ, which are fully narrated by the other three. And even with reference to his account of Christ's ministry previous to the passion, we cannot suppose that all that he relates occurred previous to the history given in the Synoptics, for in this case St. John and the Synoptics could have nothing in common; whereas at least the miraculous feeding of the 5000, and the walking on the sea, are common to him and them. There is not, moreover, the slightest hint in John that the writer meant to omit that portion of Christ's history which immediately preceded His passion, because it had been narrated by the others. No explanation, moreover, could on this supposition be given of the strange circumstance that three evangelists should unanimously pass by one and the same portion of our Lord's life. Indeed, there is not the least intimation of such an omission; on the contrary, Matthew (iv. 17) speaks of the beginning of Christ's public ministry (ἀπὸ τότε ἤρξατο ὁ Ἰησοῦς κηρύσσειν καὶ λέγειν μετανοεῖτε, κ.τ.λ.), and what follows is closely connected with this. Still less are those differences explained which we have already indicated between St. John and the Synoptics, both as to the day of the crucifixion and as to other points in the course of Christ's public ministry.

In judging of the relation subsisting between the four Gospels generally, and of the three first to one another, it is of greater importance to decide which of the accounts presented to us is the most exact, and corresponds best with the actual course of the history. For the history given by the Synoptics, it may be said we have three witnesses. Still we must recollect that two of them were not Christ's immediate disciples; the third, that of Matthew, was generally attributed to that apostle, but it lays no claim in itself to be an apostolic work (see § 39). The fourth Gospel, on the other hand, is not only attributed to the Apostle John by its title and universal tradition, but itself claims to be the work of the most intimate and beloved disciple of the Lord (see § 61). If this be so, we have every reason to conclude that we have in it the truest and exactest account of any doubtful portion of the history; and our duty will be as far as possible to explain how it came to pass that the other evangelists give in any way a different account, and how it is that they all three essentially agree in the manner of their narration. But before entering upon this, the question must be decided whether the fourth Gospel really is what it claims to be,— whether it is really the work of the Apostle John, or only the work of one who wrote in his name, and forged it as his. We have seen that the latter opinion is not new, but was held even in the second century by the *Alogi*, and likewise that in modern times it has been zealously espoused in various quarters; indeed, this question as to the genuineness of the Gospel of John may be regarded as *the main question of N. T. criticism in our day*. Considering its bearing upon our view of the other three evangelists, and upon the relationship subsisting between them, it will be well for us to make this question the topic of our inquiry now.

CONCERNING THE GENUINENESS OF ST. JOHN'S GOSPEL.

§ 71.

1. Let us examine the relation between the account given by St. John and that given by the Synoptics concerning our Lord's journeys to Jerusalem to the feasts (§ 64). Weisse rejects St. John's account, and holds that the Synoptics distinctly teach that Jesus spent the whole of His public life in Galilee and the parts adjacent, until the journey to Jerusalem on occasion of the last passover. Baur also (*Kanon. Evv.* p. 126 sqq.) regards the accounts in the fourth Gospel of earlier journeys to Jerusalem as wholly unhistorical. He does not deny that, if this be so, the apostolic authorship of the Gospel cannot be maintained. But a careful and unbiassed inquiry certainly favours St. John's account, not only

as the more probable, but as the more exact, and as even confirmed by certain hints in the Synoptics. It would seem, on the face of it, unlikely that during His public ministry Jesus should never have gone up to Jerusalem on occasion of any of the great annual feasts. Even had His ministry lasted one year only, this would have been improbable, considering the manner in which He, and His disciples after His ascension, obeyed the national law, which obliged all male Israelites to appear before Jehovah in the temple three times a year. But, as I have said, we find in the Synoptics indications which lead us to infer that Jesus during His public ministry must have paid visits either longer or shorter to Jerusalem, in order to preach to and convert the inhabitants of the city. For example, the declaration, Luke xiii. 34, 35, Matt. xxiii. 37, 38 : Ἱερουσαλὴμ, Ἱερουσαλὴμ, ... ποσάκις ἠθέλησα ἐπισυνάξαι τὰ τέκνα σου ... καὶ οὐκ ἠθελήσατε, κ.τ.λ. These words occur in both Gospels, though in different connections; but in both places they are evidently addressed to the inhabitants of Jerusalem, who are meant by "thy children," and not, as Baur thinks, to the Jews in general,—an explanation evidently unnatural, and considering its place in the Gospels, and the whole sentence, quite untenable. Baur himself, indeed, seems at length to have acknowledged the force of our argument;[1] and he endeavoured accordingly to prove, (a) that the passage in Luke is not genuine (because it does not occur in Marcion's Gospel; but see my arguments, § 53 sqq.); (b) that the language may have been that of one of the prophets speaking in God's name, and thus naturally occurred to Jesus in this form,

[1] *Theol. Jahrbb.* 1847, pp. 99, 100; cf. *Kanon. Evv.* p. 127, note. See also STRAUSS, *Das Leben Jesu*, 1864, No. 40 : "Here all subterfuges are vain, and we must confess, 'If these are really the words of Jesus, He must have been in Jerusalem oftener and longer than would appear from the accounts in the Synoptics.'" SCHENKEL, *Characterbild Jesu*, Anhang i., endeavours to explain this and other hints in the Synoptics concerning a longer and more frequent ministry of Christ in Jerusalem, by saying that Jesus went but once, and that before the last passover, to Judea, but that His residence there was somewhat protracted, and that during it He often visited Jerusalem.

and that the ποσάκις simply denotes the succession of prophets and messengers who had been sent. This explanation, however, is so evidently a last resort in order to escape the embarrassment in which Baur felt himself placed, that we need not carry the argument further. Even supposing that the words had been those of some earlier prophet, Jesus could not Himself have appropriated them had He not personally and frequently laboured in Jerusalem. This remark applies also to the acute supposition of Strauss (*Leben Jesu*, p. 249; *Zeitschr. f. wiss. Theol.* 1863, p. 84), that Jesus here adopts the words of the personified Wisdom of God, quoted from some lost writing in which the Wisdom of God was introduced as speaking. What we read in Matt. xxiii. 34, 35, might indeed be supposed to have belonged to some such work, as the parallel passage Luke xi. 49 sq. shows (see Bleek, *in loc.*); but even if this be so, the quotation does not extend beyond ver. 35. Ver. 39 certainly does not belong to it; and it is most natural to regard ver. 36 as an application on the part of the Lord Himself of what had gone before, especially as (also in Luke xi. 51) the words, "Verily, I say unto you," are introduced. Whatever similarity there be between vers. 37 and 34 is explained partly by the similarity of the subject, and partly as a reference made by Jesus Himself to the words cited in ver. 34. Ver. 37 cannot by any fair device be construed as part of the quotation.

In addition to this passage, though not so decisive, we find other hints in the Synoptics of the Lord's visits to Jerusalem as recorded by St. John. For instance, among the members of the Sanhedrim we find Joseph of Arimathea named as a disciple of Christ (Matt. xxvii. 57–59; Luke xxiii. 50–53; Mark xv. 42–45): he resided in Jerusalem, and had a grave there; and the probability is that Jesus had met him there on occasion of a previous stay in the city. Again, we learn from Luke x. 38–42 how close the intimacy of Jesus was with the family at Bethany; and this seems to imply that He had been in Jerusalem and the neighbourhood previous to His last passover. Compare also Luke ii. 41, Acts x. 29, and other passages.

This also must be considered: Suppose for a moment that, as Bretschneider and Baur hold, the fourth Gospel was composed by some writer in the second century, not as an historical work, but merely in advocacy of certain dogmatic views; we should surely expect that with reference to Christ's history he would follow the generally received tradition as embodied in the Synoptics, instead of inventing such an apparently different account of the whole course of His life, —thus unnecessarily creating hindrances to the reception of his work, and defeating the end he had in view. If nothing had been heard of Jesus visiting Jerusalem during His public ministry and before His passion, a person who wished to write a Gospel under the pretext of apostolic authority might at once foresee that, to invent anything so strange and contradictory, would at once awaken suspicion, and seriously tell against his entire work. He certainly would, under such circumstances, have followed the generally received history; for there would be no occasion to depart from it in order to advocate his dogmatic views. Baur, indeed, thinks (*Kanon. Evv.* 126–128) that the design of the fourth Gospel was to represent the conflict of Light with unbelief, and that the author was therefore obliged to represent Jesus as often in Jerusalem, the centre and seat of unbelief, and the headquarters of Jewish hostility. But even this would by no means be a reason sufficient to account for the writer so aggravating the difficulty of his task, by inventing various journeys to Jerusalem which he knew were untrue. Even if he had no regard to historical truth, it would have been easier for him to have represented Jesus in conflict with the Jews in Galilee, or to have prolonged Christ's residence in Jerusalem at the last passover; and thus he would not so manifestly have contradicted and set at nought the generally received view. Supposing, therefore, according to Church tradition, that the fourth Gospel was written after the Synoptics, or at least at a time when the narrative of our Lord's life had attained the settled form in which we find it in the Synoptics, nothing could have induced the writer to give an account so different from the generally received narrative, but the conviction that it was true; and we cannot see how he could have entertained such a conviction if his account did not actually correspond with the facts of the history.[1]

§ 72.

2. The same holds true of the difference (pointed out in § 68) between John and the Synoptics concerning the day of Christ's death. According to the Synoptics, the Friday on which He was crucified was the 15th of Nisan; according to John, it was the 14th; and by the former, accordingly, Christ's last supper or meal with His disciples on the preceding evening is represented as, strictly speaking, the passover held at the time appointed for it among the Jews, but by the latter as a paschal meal held a day earlier. If John's account be incorrect, this might certainly be urged against the genuineness of his Gospel; for had Jesus really been crucified on the 15th Nisan, the great day of the feast, and had He really celebrated the passover at its legally fixed time the evening before, how could a trustworthy apostle, who had himself been with the Lord throughout all those scenes, have adopted and put forth a different and erroneous account? Bretschneider and others, upon the supposition of the correctness of the date in the Synoptics, make use of this as an argument against the genuineness of our fourth Gospel. We, on the contrary, urge it in proof of the genuineness of St. John, because both internal probability, and hints in the Synoptics themselves, favour the Johannine date as really the correct one. As to internal probability, the 15th Nisan was, according to the law, to be regarded as a Sabbath; indeed, in Lev. xxiii. 11, 15, it is expressly called a שַׁבָּת, and nothing was to be done in the way of worldly business on it any more than on the weekly Sabbath. The only difference between it and the weekly Sabbath was, that "what every man must eat" might be prepared (Ex. xii. 16); but in Lev.

---

[1] See my *Beitr.* pp. 94–99; NEANDER, *Leben Jesu*, ed. 4, pp. 252–257. What Baur urges in reply (*Theol. Jahrbb.* 1847, pp. 92–100) really contains nothing that demands further answer or investigation.

xxiii. 7, Num. xxviii. 18, even this exception is not mentioned. All references and statements in the writings of later Jews, especially in the Talmud, correspond with this ordainment of the law concerning Nisan 15th and similar high feast-days being kept as Sabbaths; and we may therefore hold it as certain that in the time of Christ this was the law and practice of the Jews, especially of the Pharisees and Jewish council, who insisted so strictly upon outward conformity to the letter of the law. We cannot therefore suppose that upon that day, and during the preceding night, which belonged to it, and shared its sabbatical character, all could have been transacted by the high council in Jerusalem, and at their instigation, which, according to the account in the Synoptics, really was transacted. For instance, (*a*) it is not at all probable that the Sanhedrim would have sent an armed band against Jesus on the holy night after the eating of the passover; indeed, it was expressly forbidden to carry arms on the Sabbath.[1] (*b*) It is hardly conceivable that on such a night the Sanhedrim would have sat in council to judge Jesus, for to hold a court of judgment on the Sabbath was expressly prohibited.[2] (*c*) It is utterly improbable that the crucifixion took place on the 15th Nisan; for it must have been a glaring violation of the sabbatical rest of the day, according to Jewish notions still in vogue, as can be expressly proved.[3] Baur has urged that the crucifixion was not the act of the Jews, but of the Romans; but it was the Jews with their Sanhedrim who urged on the Roman governor to it against his will. The Romans paid great respect to Jewish customs and religious scruples in such matters. See Josephus (*Ant.* xvi. 6, 2) with reference to the keeping of the Sabbath, where, in an edict of Augustus, it is provided that the Jews may live according to

---

[1] *Mischna tr. Schabb.* vi. 4. We find the same in JOSEPHUS; see MOVERS, *Zeitsch. f. Philos. u. kath. Theol.* viii. 66.

[2] *Mischna tr. Bezah.* v. 2; *Gemara Sanhedr.* fol. 35, 1; *Gemara Hieros. Chetub.* fol. 24, 4; *Moed Katon*, fol. 63, 1; see LIGHTFOOT on Matt. xxvii. 1.

[3] *Gemara Sanhedr.* fol. 35, 1; and MAIMONIDES, *in loc.*

their law, and shall not be obliged to do legislative acts upon their Sabbaths (ἐγγύας μὴ ὁμολογεῖν). It has been said that the fanatical zeal of the Jews against Jesus made them forget the violation of the Sabbath which His trial and crucifixion involved, or at least that ecclesiastical offenders might be condemned upon the feast-day (so Hengstenberg, Tholuck, Wieseler). There is no proof that this was the case; and even if it had been, neither it nor the fanaticism of the Jews would account for the execution of the two malefactors at the same time with Christ. There is no intimation leading us to conjecture that *their* misdeeds had been of an ecclesiastical character, or that there was any fanaticism hurrying on their execution. See my *Beitr.* pp. 140–148; and Movers, *Zeitschr. f. Philos. u. kath. Theol.* viii. 66 sqq.

Apart altogether, therefore, from St. John's Gospel, great difficulties beset the representation, apparently given in the Synoptics, as to the date of the Friday of our Lord's death. It would be wholly contradictory to all that is known of Jewish customs and notions at the time, as well as of Jewish law, to suppose that the Sanhedrim sat in judgment upon Jesus during the sacred night ushering in the 15th Nisan. We should have expected that, even if they had seized the opportunity afforded by the season to lay hands on Him, they would at least have kept Him in prison, and postponed His trial and crucifixion until after the feast, or until after the sabbatical 15th Nisan. Baur felt this difficulty, and suggests that perhaps the synoptic account is not wholly historical, and that the closing scenes of the life of Jesus must ever remain wrapped in dark obscurity. But he still holds that even if the synoptic date be unhistorical, this does not make St. John's narrative a whit more true; for that probably between Christ's betrayal and crucifixion there was no formally judicial examination, but merely a tumultuous assembly, which must not be judged of or estimated by the formal laws (p. 112; *Kanon. Evang.* p. 271). Baur does not expressly adopt this supposition, but this seems to be his meaning. In this case, St. John's account would be just as inexact as that of the Synoptics: both would be utterly unhistorical; all conjectures even regarding the Synoptics would be superfluous, and of course no inferences could be drawn from their harmony and agreement as to the genuineness or otherwise of the fourth Gospel.[1] The Synoptics, I say, would no longer be any standard whereby to judge of St. John; and yet Baur (inconsistent with himself) continually makes use of the Synoptics for this purpose throughout his attack upon St. John's Gospel, describing them as writers whose historical veracity cannot be called in question (*Theol. Jahrbb.* 1844, pp. 400, 633).

§ 73.

St. John's narrative upon this very point is quite clear and consecutive, and presents no difficulty when taken by itself. If Jesus was betrayed in the night following the 13th and beginning the 14th of Nisan, we at once understand the anxiety and hurry of the Sanhedrim in meeting to judge and condemn Him, and their evident eagerness to hasten on His execution before the 15th Nisan, which this year was a double Sabbath. Now this account in St. John is sanctioned and confirmed by many hints in the synoptical Gospels themselves. In Luke xxiii. 26, 27, we read that the Galilean women, when they returned from the sepulchre, prepared spices, and rested the Sabbath-day according to the commandment, and returned again to the sepulchre when the Sabbath was past. Now it would have been equally illegal for them to have prepared the spices on the day preceding the Sabbath, if that day were the 15th Nisan (see Ex. xii. 16; Lev. xxiii. 7; Num. xviii. 18). The same argument applies to the burial of Jesus by Joseph of Arimathea on the day of the crucifixion, and still more strongly to Luke xxiii. 26, Mark xv. 21, where it is said of Simon the Cyrenian, whom they compelled to bear the cross, that he was ἐρχόμενον ἀπ' ἀγροῦ, which clearly signifies that he was returning from his work

---

[1] This is applicable with still greater force to the opinion which HILGENFELD (*Paschastreit*, p. 154) is inclined to adopt, as suggested by JOST and others, viz. that there was no Sanhedrim properly so called in the time of Christ.

in the fields, which could hardly have been the case if that day had been the 15th Nisan, the sabbatical feast-day. The 15th of Nisan, moreover, could hardly have been called the παρασκευή before the Sabbath, being itself a Sabbath; and yet the day of Christ's death is called the παρασκευή, not only in St. John, but in the Synoptics also (Matt. xxvii. 62; Luke xxiii. 54; Mark xv. 42). Again, all four evangelists speak of the custom of releasing some prisoner on the day whereon Christ was crucified; and the probability is that this release was made on the day before the passover, that the person released might eat of the passover himself in celebration of his release. (See Bleek's *Beitr.* pp. 35, 136–149.) Baur calls these considerations unimportant (*Theol. Jahrbb.* 1847, p. 106), but he makes no attempt to explain these passages in the Synoptics on the supposition that the 15th Nisan was the day of Christ's death. The Apostle Paul (1 Cor. xi. 23) says that the Lord Jesus instituted the holy communion "the same night in which He was betrayed." Now if this had been the 15th of Nisan, we certainly might have expected him to have described it also as the night in which the passover was celebrated. According to Jewish tradition, moreover, Jesus was crucified on the day before the passover (עֶרֶב הַפֶּסַח); and this is often stated in the Talmud (*Sanhedrin,* fol. 43, 1, and elsewhere).

If, indeed, the Friday on which Christ was crucified was the 15th Nisan, it is quite inexplicable that a later writer, said to belong to the second century, should have given an account so contradictory to what must in this case have been the universal tradition of the Church. Bretschneider and Baur have suggested explanations of this; but what they urge is in the highest degree unnatural, and indeed impossible. Baur even has admitted this, and has since resorted to another explanation, suggested by Strauss (*Leben Jesu,* § 85), viz. that the writer of the fourth Gospel aimed at representing Christ as the true Paschal Lamb (see ch. xix. 31 sqq.), and therefore described His death as having occurred on Nisan 14th, on the evening of which day the passover lamb was killed. As Jesus, moreover, could not, in his view, have celebrated the passover on the evening of the 14th Nisan, after He was Himself offered as the true Paschal Lamb, he could not describe the last supper as a passover (so Hilgenfeld, Schenkel, and Weizsäcker, p. 560). But I take it to be quite improbable that any such motive as this could have led the evangelist arbitrarily to give an incorrect and unhistorical account; for had Christ been offered on the 15th Nisan, he could still have represented Him as the true passover. If, on the other hand, there be any force in this reason, we might, in the strength of it, refer to St. Paul's statement, 1 Cor. v. 7, καὶ γὰρ τὸ πάσχα ἡμῶν ἐτύθη Χριστός, as confirming St. John's account. This is an argument used by some, but I do not attach any importance to it. Baur inconsistently objects to it. Lastly, if the evangelist was led by such a motive deliberately to falsify the received and true account, he would have been particular in specifying the exact hour of the day in which, according to the law, the paschal lamb was to be killed, as that wherein Christ's death took place. But St. John does not do this. Supposing, on the other hand, that the day of Christ's death was, as St. John represents, the 14th Nisan, we can easily see how a representation like that of the Synoptics might nevertheless arise in the Church. The testimony alike of the Synoptics and of St. Paul (1 Cor. xi. 23 sqq.) shows that, at the evening meal eaten by our Lord with His disciples on the night before His crucifixion, He instituted the holy communion in remembrance of His death, and with reference to, and in the place of, the Jewish passover. Thus the notion might easily arise, that He held this evening meal on the very night whereon the Jews kept their passover, though really, in anticipation of His sufferings, He held it a day earlier. An account of our Lord's passion written upon this supposition would seem to represent that Jesus was crucified upon the first day of the feast. But we have seen that many expressions in the Synoptics themselves are inconsistent with this; and these lead us to suppose that even the Synoptics had, as the basis of their narrative, an account which represented (if it did not expressly name) the 14th Nisan, and not the 15th, as the date of Christ's death. By a misunderstanding, however, there came to be incorporated with this the notion that Jesus ate the last supper with His disciples at the hour legally instituted for the Jewish passover; and in the Synoptics, as we now have them, both representations, though non-coincident, yet, unconsciously to the evangelists, lie side by side. It is not improbable, moreover, that some of Christ's words recorded by the Synoptics as spoken by Him on the day and night before His crucifixion, originally had reference to the fact that Jesus was about to hold the last supper before the time legally appointed among the Jews for the passover. See Matt. xxvi. 18, ὁ καιρός μου ἐγγύς ἐστιν· πρὸς σὲ ποιῶ τὸ πάσχα μετὰ τῶν μαθητῶν μου; and Luke xxii. 15, ἐπιθυμίᾳ ἐπεθύμησα τοῦτο τὸ πάσχα φαγεῖν μεθ' ὑμῶν πρὸ τοῦ με παθεῖν.

Taking all together, we have complete evidence for the genuineness and correctness of St. John's account with regard to this point; and this, in turn, is a very strong argument that the writer was one well acquainted with the facts and order of the history, and with Jewish customs and relations—a very strong testimony for the genuineness of the fourth Gospel.[1]

§ 74.

3. I would here advert to another point which has of late been strongly urged as an argument against the genuineness of St. John's Gospel, and against the correctness of his account of the day of Christ's death:[2] I mean *the controversies concerning the keeping of the passover in the second century*. There were in the latter part of that century two different views and practices in the Church with reference to

---

[1] See USTERI, *Commentat. crit.*, in qua Ev. Jo. genuinum esse ex comparatis 4 Evv. narratt. de cœna ultima et passione J. Chr. ostenditur, Zür. 1823.

[2] By BRETSCHNEIDER, and especially by SCHWEGLER (*Montanismus*, p. 191), BAUR (*Theol. Jahrbb.* 1844, pp. 638–659; 1847, pp. 120–183; 1848, p. 264 sqq.; 1857, p. 240 sqq.), and HILGENFELD (*Der Paschastreit der alten Kirche nach s. Bedeut. f. die K. Gesch. u. f. die Ev. Forschung*,

a certain feast about the time of the Jewish passover, which gave rise to several disputes.

(*a.*) So far as we know, the subject came to be discussed first between the Christians of proconsular Asia, and those of the West, especially in the Roman Church, about the year 160, when Polycarp, bishop of Smyrna, was in Rome, and argued this subject among others in conversation with Bishop Anicetus. Neither disputant convinced the other, but the good understanding subsisting between them remained undisturbed. (*b.*) Ten years later—about A.D. 170—the matter was discussed in Asia Minor. Claudius Apollinaris, bishop of Hierapolis in Phrygia (who had written a book against the Jews), declared the practice prevailing in Asia Minor erroneous, and Melito of Sardis vindicated it. (*c.*) The difference caused still greater excitement towards the end of the second century (circ. A.D. 190), when the Roman bishop Victor ordered the bishops of Asia Minor to adopt the Western practice; and when they declined doing so, cut them off from fellowship with the Church. The bishops of Palestine and of Pontus, of Gallia and Corinth, however, were in favour of the Western practice, but they did not ratify the haughty demand of the Roman bishop. Irenæus, on the contrary, strongly disapproved of it. The feast about which the dispute was, was held in Asia on the 14th Nisan, at the hour in which the Jews celebrated their passover (*i.e.* on the night which, according to Jewish reckoning, began the 15th Nisan); and hence the Christians of Asia Minor who followed this practice were called *Quarto-decimani* (τεσσαρεσκαιδεκατῖται). They argued that, according to Matthew's account, Jesus ate the passover at the same time with the Jews, on the 14th Nisan, and was crucified on the 15th.[1] Now it is certainly

---

Halle 1860). The history of these controversies, apart altogether from our Gospel, is so dark and difficult, that it is not easy to explain in few words even the point in dispute, to say nothing of thoroughly and satisfactorily exhausting the subject. I refer to my *Beitr.* p. 38 sq., 156–166, with the single remark that Baur's reply does not oblige me to retract anything that I have there advanced.

[1] APOLLINARIS, *Chron. paschale*, ed. Dindorf, i. p. 14: εἰσὶ τοίνυν οἳ

strange that this appeal to the testimony of Matthew in favour of a practice prevailing only in proconsular Asia, should be made by those among whom the Apostle John had so long lived and laboured; and still more strange that Polycarp, in justifying this practice in his argument with Anicetus, should have urged that he had often celebrated the feast thus with John and the other apostles whom he knew. Polycrates also, in an epistle to Victor,[1] refers to the Apostle John and other distinguished men of that early age in Asia, who all ἐτήρησαν τὴν ἡμέραν τῆς τεσσαρεσκαιδεκάτης τοῦ πάσχα κατὰ τὸ εὐαγγέλιον. This seems incompatible with the fact that John has stated the case differently from Matthew, saying that Jesus celebrated the last supper with His disciples, not on the day of the passover (*i.e.* the evening of the 14th Nisan, or, according to Jewish reckoning, the beginning of the 15th), but a day earlier; and this has been urged as a proof either that John's account does not differ from that of the Synoptics (so Hengstenberg, Tholuck, Wieseler, and others), or that the fourth Gospel, which gives such a different account, could not have been written by the Apostle John, nor have been recognised by Polycarp and the Christians of Asia Minor in the middle of the second century as his work.[2] This last argument is plausible, but upon closer examination it loses its weight. As to the different practice of the Eastern and Western Churches, it is usually represented as if from the beginning there was simply a difference in the time of

... λέγουσιν, ὅτι τῇ ιδ' τὸ πρόβατον μετὰ τῶν μαθητῶν ἔφαγεν ὁ Κύριος, τῇ δὲ μεγάλῃ ἡμέρᾳ τῶν ἀζύμων αὐτὸς ἔπαθεν καὶ διηγοῦνται Ματθαῖον οὕτω λέγειν ὡς νενοήκασιν· ὅθεν ἀσύμφωνός τε νόμῳ ἡ νόησις αὐτῶν καὶ στασιάζειν δοκεῖ κατ' αὐτοὺς τὰ εὐαγγέλια. See on this, my *Beitr.* p. 133, note, 165.

[1] IRENÆUS, *Ep. ad Victor.* in EUSEB. v. 24: οὔτε γὰρ ὁ Ἀνίκητος τὸν Πολύκαρπον πεῖσαι ἐδύνατο μὴ τηρεῖν, ἅτε μετὰ Ἰωάννου τοῦ μαθητοῦ τοῦ Κυρίου ἡμῶν καὶ τῶν λοιπῶν ἀποστόλων οἷς συνέτριψεν, ἀεὶ τετηρηκότα, κ.τ.λ.

[2] EUSEB. v. 24: Ἡμεῖς οὖν ἀρραδιούργητον ἄγομεν τὴν ἡμέραν μήτε προστιθέντες μήτε ἀφαιρούμενοι. Καὶ γὰρ κατὰ τὴν Ἀσίαν μεγάλα στοιχεῖα κεκοίμηται ... ἔτι δὲ καὶ Ἰωάννης ὁ ἐπὶ τὸ στῆθος τοῦ Κυρίου ἀναπεσών ... οὗτος ἐν Ἐφέσῳ κεκοίμηται ... οὗτοι πάντες ἐτήρησαν τὴν ἡμέραν τῆς τεσσαρεσκαιδεκάτης τοῦ πάσχα κατὰ τὸ εὐαγγέλιον.

the celebration of a certain feast in commemoration of the passion and the resurrection. It is supposed that in Asia Minor the feast of Easter began at the time fixed for the passover in the Jewish law, *i.e.* on the night of the 14th Nisan; whereas in the West it was customary to celebrate the resurrection on the Sunday and the passion on the preceding Friday, without reference to the Jewish feast. But this is incorrect. We find that the difference, when first mentioned, consisted simply in the fact that the Asiatic Christians *kept a certain feast on the night of the 14th Nisan, which the Westerns did not keep.* Thus it is described in the statement of Irenæus concerning Polycarp's argument with Anicetus, as a question τηρεῖν or μὴ τηρεῖν, and he speaks of οἱ τηροῦντες and οἱ μὴ τηροῦντες. It would appear, moreover, that this custom was one retained by tradition from the earliest times among the Eastern Christians; but it could not have been the celebration of a yearly feast in memory of the sufferings and the resurrection of our Lord, or of His institution of the holy communion. A long period elapsed before any yearly festivals came into vogue in celebration of the main events of gospel history. The resurrection was from the first celebrated every Sunday (which was called "The Lord's Day," Rev. i. 10), and the communion at every religious service. This feast was, originally, simply the celebration of the Jewish passover by the believing Jews. There can be no doubt that the Church at Jerusalem, consisting of Jewish Christians, still celebrated the temple worship after the ascension, and kept the Jewish passover at the legally appointed time, without any reference to the question whether the Lord ate His last supper with His disciples on this day or on the evening before; and the Jewish Christians in other parts, living far away from the temple, and after it was destroyed, still continued to celebrate a yearly passover feast, taking the place of the passover proper, and held at the same time. In those Churches where the Jewish element preponderated, the Gentile members also took part in this feast with their brethren; and this was probably the case with the Ephesian Church, which from the outset consisted mainly of Jewish Christians, as appears from the account of its origin (Acts xviii. 19 sqq., xix. 1 sqq., and Rev. ii. 1 sqq.). The passover was celebrated in this Church from the beginning, as also in many other Churches — even in those founded by St. Paul: cf. Acts xx. 6; 1 Cor. v. 6-8. Thus St. John found when he came to Ephesus; and he could have had no motive in altering or doing away with what he had already been accustomed to during his residence in Jerusalem. Even Paul could not have objected to take part in its celebration, judging at least from the way in which he kept the Jewish law even with reference to the Jewish festivals: see Acts xviii. 21, 18, xxi. 23-27; Rom. xiv.; 1 Cor. viii.-x. It would have been of no concern with St. John that Jesus had not eaten the last supper with His disciples on the day legally appointed for the passover, because the commemoration of this last supper was not originally, and did not for a long time after, become the main purpose of this Christian celebration of the passover. Baur thinks that one who (like the author of our fourth Gospel) recognised Jesus as the true Paschal Lamb (John xix. 36), could not any longer celebrate a Jewish passover. But even Paul, who also recognised Jesus as the true Paschal Lamb (1 Cor. v. 7), did not hesitate to celebrate the legally appointed Jewish passover when he was with Jews and Jewish Christians at Jerusalem.

This feast of the passover, or of a meal taking the place of the passover proper, had been celebrated in many Churches, especially in Asia Minor, not indeed in subserviency to the Jewish law, but from custom simply, long after the destruction of the temple and the extinction of Jewish rites thus brought about. But in some Churches (Pauline), wherein the Jewish element was but small, it was not kept. A different rule therefore guided the practice of different Churches in this, as also in other things, without giving any occasion for controversy. Controversy began when the desire arose to promote uniformity in the practices of the various Churches; and then the celebration of the Jewish passover was objected to. It was natural that those Churches who had long been accustomed to this celebration should appeal to the practice of their predecessors, and especially to that of the apostles who had lived among them, as we find Polycarp and Polycrates doing. In course of time, too, it might be expected that Christian thoughts and ideas would gather round this yearly celebration, and especially that the last supper of the Lord with His disciples would be associated with it. Judging from Polycarp's argument with Anicetus, there was no discussion as to the day of the month whereon Jesus ate this last meal with His disciples, still less to the witness of the evangelists on this point. But when the controversy had fully begun, it was natural that both parties should appeal to the Gospels recognised by the Church; and this we find to have been the case in the *second* era of the controversy, when the Quarto-decimans referred to the fact that, according to Matthew, Jesus had kept the passover with His disciples (see Apollinaris, above quoted); and their opponents urged in reply that Jesus had in previous years eaten of the passover with the Jews, but not in the last year, when He Himself was slain as the true Paschal Lamb.[1] These opposite arguments recognise alike the synoptic and the Johannine account, the interests of party leading each side to lay stress upon what seemed to tell in their favour. This was the manner in which the controversy, when fully matured, was conducted; but at first, as we have said, the simple question was whether the passover should be kept or not.

§ 75.

If this be a true account of the rise and progress of this controversy, it is clear that no argument can be deduced from it against the genuineness of St. John's Gospel. The apostle's knowledge that Jesus had eaten the last supper with His disciples not on the day legally fixed, but a day earlier, could not have obliged him to refuse to keep the yearly passover, as he had been wont to do at Jerusalem, among the Christians at Ephesus, who also were wont to

[1] CLEMENS ALEX. in the *Chron. paschale*, ed. Dindorf, pp. 14, 15; PETRUS ALEX. *ib.* pp. 10, 11; see HIPPOLYTUS, *ib.* p. 13.

celebrate it, for Jesus Himself had kept the passover in the earlier years of His ministry. It is likely, too, that the Christians of Asia Minor subsequently retained the custom simply because it had become a custom, and because of the opposition raised against it. They accordingly appealed to the practice of St. John, without any implication that the account of the passion given in the fourth Gospel was unknown or in any way suspected by them; because the practice of keeping the passover was at first, and for long after John's death, quite independent of the institution of the Lord's Supper, and of the day of the month upon which this took place. Subsequently, indeed, this reference was introduced, but not till long after St. John's death—not until the latter part of the second century, when the adherents of the practice naturally appealed to those parts of the Gospels which seemed in any way to sanction it, and endeavoured to bring any part which seemed to tell against them into harmony with it. Thus they were satisfied, like many modern expositors, to bring St. John's account into harmony with the Synoptics; because, though the representation he gives as to the exact dates runs throughout his narrative, there is no express statement on the point excluding the possibility of such a way of reconciliation. Still, when the second passover controversy arose (about A.D. 170), John's Gospel was known and its authority recognised by both parties; and this is evident from the words of Apollinaris.[1]

[1] Quoted § 74, note. My account of the matter is confirmed by DE WETTE (edd. 5 and 6, § 109, c, note d). WEITZEL also (Die christl. Passahfeier der drei ersten Jahrh., etc., 1848; and Stud. u. Krit. 1848, 805-858) urges the case still more decidedly in favour of our Gospel. EBRARD (Krit. der ev. Gesch. § 146) agrees with me, and so does STEITZ (Stud. u. Krit. 1858, pp. 721-809; 1857, pp. 741-782; 1859, pp. 716-740; and in Herzog's Real-Encykl. art. Pascha). They think that the second controversy (A.D. 170) referred to quite a different subject from those of A.D. 160 and 190. I cannot satisfy myself of the correctness of this view, and the conclusions based upon it; but it would lead us too far away from our subject to go into it further here. [They think that the Christians of Asia Minor celebrated the 14th of Nisan *as the day of Christ's death*. NEANDER (*Church History*, i. 513) is of a similar opinion, but he says that they kept the Jewish passover, and included in it the

§ 76.

4. Great exception has been taken in our day against *the discourses of Christ*, as given in St. John, viewed partly in themselves and partly in comparison with those given in the Synoptics, with reference alike to their form, their contents, the picture they give of the person of Jesus, their appropriateness to the circumstances of the time, and their uniformity and similarity with the discourses of other persons recorded in the Gospel, and with the style of the writer himself.[1]

With reference to this I observe as follows:—

(*a.*) There certainly is a marked difference between the discourses of Christ as given by the Synoptics and those recorded by St. John (see § 67); and this to some extent influences the general picture of Christ's character, as presented by them respectively. But the question is, whether the contrasted traits of character thus presented could have

commemoration of Christ's death; whereas WEITZEL and STEITZ consider that the festival was simply a Christian one, and that the point in dispute between the Asiatic Christians and the rest of the Catholic Church was merely one of ritual. This would be a still stronger testimony for the genuineness of St. John. It tells against this, however, that the Quarto-decimans, whose views are combated in the *Chron. Paschale* (see also the fragment of Apollinaris above quoted), held that the 14th Nisan was the day of Christ's last passover meal, and therefore celebrated that day with a passover feast. These Quarto-decimans, therefore, may be regarded as a Judaizing offshoot of the Quarto-decimans generally; and Apollinaris, who opposes them, may be ranked among the Catholic Quarto-decimans. Neander considers the fragment of Apollinaris as of doubtful genuineness. A full exposition of the various views upon the subject, upon the principles of the Tübingen school, will be found in HILGENFELD, *Paschastreit*, pp. 5-118.—B.]

[1] BRETSCHNEIDER urges this as a main argument against the genuineness of the fourth Gospel, and so does WEISSE; both giving the preference to the Synoptics. BRUNO BAUER (*Krit. d. ev. Gesch. des Joh.* 1840) endeavours to prove that the discourses, as given by St. John, could not possibly have been thus spoken at the time; but he regards those given by the Synoptics as equally unhistorical. F. v. BAUR endeavours to prove that they must have been forged by the writer of the Gospel, because they are blended with unhistorical statements, and are utterly improbable in themselves.

been blended in one and the same person, so that both pictures, both aspects, may be equally true. We find on examination that they can thus be blended. Reference has been made to the contrasted representations given us of the person and teaching of Socrates in Plato and Xenophon respectively: it is well known how greatly they differ. Some, supposing these irreconcilable, have held Xenophon's account only to be historically true, and have declared the Platonic Socrates to have been the creation of Plato himself.

The narrowness and erroneousness of this opinion is now acknowledged; for if Socrates were a teacher only, as Xenophon describes him, if he was not also the speculatist and philosopher that Plato describes, we could not explain how so many schools of speculative philosophy sprang from his teaching and influence.[1] Both descriptions of Socrates are true, and are only different aspects of one and the same character. Now if a wise man, who was merely human like Socrates, could thus present such manifoldness in unity that two of his pupils could give such contrasted yet true pictures of his teaching, surely the same is possible in the case of Christ—in the case of HIM whose office and work was to be the Redeemer of men of all shades of character and life; surely in His person and life there must necessarily have been a far richer fulness. We might naturally expect to find that, among His closest disciples, one would specially contemplate and give prominence to one aspect of His person and His work, and another to another aspect.

We have no right, therefore, to infer from the different pictures given by the evangelists of Christ's teaching and life, that any one of them must be unhistorical and unapostolic. As to St. John's Gospel in particular, we have no right thus to argue; for the synoptic discourses, both in their *form* and *contents*, do present resemblances to those in St. John; and in the Synoptics indications are not wanting to show that Jesus uttered discourses of the very kind that are

---

[1] SCHLEIERMACHER, *über den Werth des Sokrates alle Philosophen* (*Werke zur Philosophie*, ii. 287–308); BRANDIS, *Handb. der Gesch. der Griech.-Röm. Philosophie*, ii. 1, 21; H. RITTER, *Gesch. der Phil.* ii. 43.

recorded by St. John. As to *form*, Matt. xiii. 10 sqq. expressly intimates that Jesus did not adopt the parabolic style in discoursing with His disciples. The Saviour there remarks that He spake to the people in parables because otherwise they could not understand; and He draws a distinct line of demarcation between His discourses to the people generally and those to His disciples: cf. ver. 34; Mark iv. 11, 33, 34; Luke viii. 10. The discourses recorded in John were not indeed all of them addressed to the inner circle of His disciples: several of them were spoken to His adversaries among the Jews; and this suggests a difficulty, because in Matt. xiii. 34, Mark iv. 34, it is stated that He spoke to the people only in parables. This, however, cannot be taken as applying to all the conversations of Jesus with the people during His public ministry, but simply as denoting His usual style of addressing them. We shall hereafter consider how it is that the Synoptics give for the most part discourses of this parabolic kind. But supposing that John wrote his Gospel late in life, when Christ's parabolic discourses were already well known and recorded, this very circumstance would naturally lead him to put on record those others of Christ's discourses which were not so widely known.

And as to the *subject-matter* of these discourses, declarations of Christ are recorded in the Synoptics perfectly corresponding with what we find in John concerning the divine dignity of the Son of God, and His relation to the Father: see Matt. xi. 27, Luke x. 22 (a saying quite of the Johannine type); Matt. ix. 4 sqq. (Mark ii. 8; Luke v. 22), xvi. 16, 17, xxi. 37 (Mark xii. 6; Luke xx. 13), xxii. 41 sqq. (Mark xii. 35; Luke xx. 41), xxv. 31 sqq., xxvi. 64 (Mark xiv. 62), xxviii. 18-20, where He declares Himself the Son of God, and (Matt. xxii. 41-43; Mark xii. 35-37; Luke xx. 41) refers to His pre-existence. That special stress is laid upon these topics in the Johannine discourses, is just what we should expect from the character of John himself, and it is quite in keeping with what is told in the Gospel concerning him and his relation to the Lord. It is not only conceivable, but natural, that St. John should give preference to those discourses which set forth Christ's divinity and His relation to the Father,—the more so because the other discourses concerning the kingdom of heaven, and so on, were already widespread and well known in the Church; the parabolic form of these securing them a wider circulation.[1]

§ 77.

(*b.*) Bretschneider and others observe that the discourses of Christ in the fourth Gospel bear the same character and impress as the other portions of the Gospel, and even as the epistles of St. John. There is some truth in this, but it is of little weight as an argument against the genuineness of those discourses, still less against the genuineness of the Gospel. The Gospel itself testifies that St. John stood in a very close and self-surrendering position towards the Redeemer, and he must therefore have imbibed much of His spirit and manner of speaking. This is manifest where he speaks in his own person. Granting, moreover, the apostolic authorship, we need not, on the other hand, necessarily suppose that the discourses are recorded throughout in the *ipsissima verba* of Jesus. Jesus spoke in Aramæan, and John wrote in Greek; and the more fully the disciple was penetrated with the thoughts expressed by his Lord, the greater freedom would he feel in giving expression to those thoughts. Some of the discourses, too, are not given *in extenso*, but in outline; and the record of them must of course present somewhat of the idiosyncrasy of the writer, though they have not lost one whit of their historic correctness and truth, and cannot in any sense be regarded as the arbitrary composition of the evangelist himself. The same is true of the dialogues recorded by St. John, though, as we have already remarked (§ 67), they are much more lifelike and full than those recorded by the Synoptics. Weisse's opinion,

---

[1] E. A. BORGER (Prof. at Leyden, *ob.* 1820), *De constanti et æquabili J. Chr. indole, doctrina ac docendi ratione, s. commentatt. de Ev. Jo. cum Matt., Marco, et Luco comparato*, Haag 1816, Part i.; J. PARÉ, *de Jo. Ev. non prorsus dissimili prioribus Ev. nec ob dissimilitudinem repudiando*, Utrecht 1828.

which ranks those of the Synoptics above those of John, is very erroneous. Still John has not recorded all the conversations which he gives, in full; he has doubtless omitted many questions and answers, and added some. The phraseology, therefore, of the dialogues recorded may be in some degree tinged by the evangelist's own individuality.

It may, moreover, be worth while to mention that, according to ecclesiastical tradition, which is elsewhere confirmed, John wrote his Gospel late in life, and probably after the destruction of Jerusalem, fifty years after Christ's death; and we have no reason for thinking that he had committed Christ's discourses to writing before. The promise of the Lord, in John xiv. 26, that the Holy Spirit would bring all things to the disciples' remembrance, while fulfilled in his case, cannot be construed as denoting that the *ipsissima verba* would be repeated to them by rote in a magical and mechanical manner, but simply that Christ's discourses and sayings would be brought again fully to their remembrance in all their life-giving power, and in their fullest and highest import, so as to enable them to prosecute His work and teach His doctrine as He taught it. We cannot for a moment suppose that the longer discourses of Jesus were dictated by the Spirit word for word as Christ first uttered them, but simply that the apostle committed them to writing as the Holy Spirit helped him to remember them. The words in which the thoughts were recorded would therefore bear in some particulars the impress of the writer's individuality, though their full historical character would in no degree be impaired (see my *Beitr.* pp. 240-244). In order to make this clear, many instances from the discourses might be named which we have not room for here. I may remark, however, that the impugners of the Gospel, Bretschneider, and especially Baur, act very arbitrarily in importing into the discourses a meaning and reference utterly inappropriate, and which a candid consideration of them shows to be far removed from their real sense.

§ 78.

(*c*.) We shall further see how false is the notion that these discourses were merely composed unhistorically by the writer of the Gospel himself—like the Greek and Roman historians, who put orations of their own composing into the mouths of various characters—if we examine the shorter declarations and remarks of Christ which John records, and which bear upon the face of them a clearly historical character. As an instance of these, we may name John xiv. 31, where, in the middle of His longer discourse, Christ says to His disciples, ἐγείρεσθε, ἄγωμεν ἐντεῦθεν. It is evident that Jesus here calls His disciples to rise with Him from supper, and to go with Him to the Mount of Olives. We are not told whether they really did this, the remainder of the discourse being spoken on the way, or whether our Lord, constrained by His love to His disciples, still remained in conversation with them, unburdening to them the deep feelings of His heart. The latter conjecture is the more probable; but still the words produced a general movement among the disciples, who probably rose simultaneously. Thus they were impressed upon the memory of a disciple present at the time, and were inserted by him in the Lord's discourse, though they are quite unconnected with the context. But we could hardly conceive that a later writer, freely composing the discourse himself, would have interpolated such words, and thus interrupted the current of the address. He might indeed have put some such words at the end of the discourse, and then he would have added that Jesus did rise from the table with His disciples, or have explained how it was that, notwithstanding, they still remained there. Baur's explanation of this, like that of Strauss, is very improbable. He thinks that the writer borrowed these words from Matt. xxvi. 46, Mark xiv. 42, where Jesus, in the garden of Gethsemane, seeing the armed band approaching, says to His disciples, ἐγείρεσθε, ἄγωμεν· ἰδοὺ ἤγγικεν ὁ παραδιδούς με. It was very unlikely indeed that a writer who could "compose" such discourses as John xiii.–xvii. could be at such a loss as to cull words from another Gospel which, apart from their connection, are meaningless, and which have a special reference of their own, and to interpolate them in the wrong place, where they only interrupt the connection of the discourse.

The prophetic declarations of Christ, especially those referring to His sufferings and death, or at least thus explained by the evangelist, furnish in themselves, and when compared with the Synoptics, another striking evidence of the genuineness of the Gospel. In the Synoptics it would seem that Jesus made these declarations in the plainest terms, and not merely in figurative language, concerning His betrayal, His being delivered up to the Sanhedrim and the Gentiles, His being mocked, scourged, spit upon, and crucified, and His resurrection on the third day.[1] It is strange that, notwithstanding this explicitness, the evangelists frequently add that His disciples did not understand these sayings (Mark ix. 32, Luke ix. 45, and even Luke xviii. 34); and that when these things took place, both His death and His resurrection came upon them unexpectedly, and were matters of surprise to them. This suggests the supposition that perhaps the Synoptics do not give Christ's exact words, but a full statement of what they really meant, and that Jesus Himself had at the time couched His prophecies concerning His sufferings and His resurrection in figurative language. Now this is just the characteristic of the prophetic sayings of Christ upon these topics as given in St. John: see, for example, John vii. 33, 34, viii. 21, x. 11, 17, 18, xii. 23, 24, xiv. 1-4, 18, 19, 28, xvi. 16; see also v. 19, 20, vii. 6-8, xii. 8, iii. 14. These declarations clearly bear the impress of historical truth; and if Jesus spoke in this manner, it was not to be wondered at that the disciples did not understand His death or resurrection, to which their Master thus vaguely referred.

---

[1] Thus Matt. xvi. 21, Luke ix. 22, Mark viii. 31. The statements are in these places given only in indirect narrative. They are directly spoken in Matt. xvii. 22, 23, Mark ix. 31, Luke ix. 44, where, however, they are less explicit. Still more minute are Matt. xx. 18, 19, Mark x. 33, 34, Luke xviii. 31-33, where the spitting is expressly mentioned. See also Matt. xxvi. 32; Mark xiv. 28 and Matt. xii. 40.

These prophetic sayings are not such as a writer would have invented after the events had taken place.

Still more decisive are the declarations of our Lord, to which the evangelist himself adds an explanation with reference to future events. For instance ii. 19-21, λύσατε τὸν ναὸν τοῦτον, καὶ ἐν τρισὶν ἡμέραις ἐγερῶ αὐτόν. The evangelist explains these words as referring to the death and resurrection of Jesus. It may be doubted whether this explanation exhausts our Lord's meaning. I have stated my view in the *Theol. Stud. u. Krit.* 1833, ii. pp. 442-451. But no unprejudiced mind can have any doubt that the evangelist gives the words as the Lord spoke them, without adding to them or taking from them, in order to make them more obvious and explicit. The same remarks apply to John xii. 32, 33, where to the words of Jesus, κἀγὼ ἐὰν ὑψωθῶ ἐκ τῆς γῆς, πάντας ἑλκύσω πρὸς ἐμαυτόν, the evangelist adds, τοῦτο δὲ ἔλεγε σημαίνων ποίῳ θανάτῳ ἤμελλεν ἀποθνήσκειν. He obviously understands the ὑψωθῆναι ἐκ τῆς γῆς of the crucifixion. Here, too, it may be doubted whether this is the full meaning of our Lord's words; but there can be no doubt that the evangelist gives those words correctly, just as our Lord spoke them. See also John vii. 37-39.

Now we may at least infer that if prophetic sayings of this kind, in the recording of which after their fulfilment additions and alterations might have been made even unconsciously by the writer, are so correctly given, the other and fuller discourses are probably correctly recorded also. The recorded sayings of Christ which we have now examined furnish very strong evidence of the genuineness of the Gospel. It is quite improbable that sayings of this kind could have preserved their evidently unaltered form, had they passed through several hands or mouths before they were finally committed to writing. Bretschneider refers to these prophetic sayings (p. 14 sqq.), and allows that in John they are less explicit than in the Synoptics; but he does not say how he reconciles this with his view of St. John's Gospel. Baur also refers to them, but he does not in the remotest degree set aside the argument they undoubtedly furnish for the genuineness of the Gospel. It is surprising that he should think that these discourses cannot be received as genuine until we have beforehand proved the historical trustworthiness of the writer; when the fact is, we cannot conceive how the writer, even if he wished, could have written such discourses, and in such a form, if they had not been historically true. In the *Theol. Jahrbb.* of 1847, Baur does not again refer to this argument, though it is of the greatest importance in influencing our judgment as to the origin and genuineness of the Gospel. In his work on the Gospels (pp. 141, 142, note) he refers to my remarks on John ii. 19, but he does not answer my argument.

§ 79.

5. Modern opponents of the genuineness of St. John's Gospel have endeavoured to prove that the writer could not have been an eye-witness of the facts narrated, because these facts, as he records them, could not have happened. They argue partly from the nature of the facts themselves, and partly from the discrepancies or the silence of the Synoptics with reference to them; and they suppose either (as Bretschneider and formerly Strauss) that the narratives gradually grew into this form in the later tradition of the Church, or (as Baur and now Strauss) that the writer himself manipulated them into their present form in order to suit the ideas and dogmatic views which he sought to promulgate, making facts and sayings recorded in the Synoptics the groundwork of his stories. Thus, for example, Baur thinks that the evangelist compiled the story of the raising of Lazarus as the most marvellous, in comparison of the resurrections recorded by the Synoptics, out of those elements which Luke gives in his account of Martha and Mary (x. 48–52), and in the parable of the rich man and Lazarus (xvi. 19). The story of Christ washing the disciples' feet is said to be an exposition or illustration invented by St. John of Christ's two declarations, Matt. xx. 26, 27, Luke xxii. 26, 27, 28. Bretschneider's opinion is, that this washing of the feet was intended by the evangelist as a ceremony performed upon the disciples instead

of baptism, and that the story was invented by tradition, to show that the apostles had gone through a kind of baptism, and to illustrate the importance of baptism. We cannot here enter into details; but I content myself with offering the following remarks:—

(*a*.) The difficulties said to beset the Johannine narrations, and the supposed contradictions between them and the Synoptics, are not really found in them by an unprejudiced consideration of them, but are imported into them. Baur, for instance, contrasts the readiness with which the Samaritans received Christ, according to John (ch. iv.), with the opposition of the Samaritans to Him, according to Luke (ix. 52). But Luke is speaking of the inhospitality of a single Samaritan village (κώμη), whereas John tells of the reception of Jesus by the inhabitants of a certain city in Samaria. We might as well find an incompatibility between the statement that the preaching of Jesus was acceptable in Galilee, and the fact that the people of Nazareth rejected Him. John would naturally feel himself obliged to give this account of Christ's conversation with the woman of Samaria, and the events ensuing thereupon, because this was the first beginning of the success of the gospel among the Samaritans, which afterwards followed the labours of himself and Peter there (Acts viii. 14 sqq.).

(*b*.) We have already seen that St. John's narrative proves to be correct in some very important points wherein it apparently differs from the Synoptics. St. John is right, for example, in his account of Christ's several journeys to the feasts at Jerusalem, and in the day of the month when the last supper was partaken of, and when Jesus was crucified; in his version, too, of the Lord's prophecies concerning His death. All these together testify that the writer was well acquainted with the course of events, and correctly narrates them; and we thus are led reasonably to infer the trustworthiness of the writer in other parts of his Gospel, for which we have no special confirmation, and that these certainly were not (as is here supposed) manipulated and invented by him.

(*c.*) The opposers of this Gospel whom we have named, and others with them, would not lay such stress upon objections such as these, if their minds were not already prejudiced against this Gospel, on account of *the miracles* it records, and the dogmatic presupposition which they entertain against the possibility of such miracles. This is evident, and indeed avowed, in what Strauss says in the third edition of his *Life of Jesus*. He confesses that, perceiving the unmistakeable clearness of St. John's narrative, he was forced, in spite of himself, to doubt his own doubts concerning the genuineness of the Gospel, though he quickly suppressed and withdrew these misgivings. But a critic whose leading principle is of this kind, cannot certainly be given any credit for that doctrinal impartiality and freedom from all foregone conclusions which Strauss and other objectors claim. As to the miracles which John records, they do not essentially differ in kind from those related in the Synoptics; and they who reject the former equally reject the latter. But disbelievers in miracles have of late felt it necessary especially to attack and call in question the genuineness of St. John, because in his case we have (if he be really the writer) the testimony of an apostle and an eye-witness. This is not indeed the place to discuss miracles, or to vindicate their possibility and their appropriateness in the Gospel history.

I would briefly remark: *First*, That the conception of a miracle was in former times too strictly and absolutely defined, as if it only meant an event which absolutely violated the laws of nature; and I perfectly agree with the view put forth by Schleiermacher, and now generally adopted, viz. that a miracle is an event only relatively supernatural; not absolutely violating the laws which God has established, but brought about by a hidden co-operation (rarely exercised in this manner) of other and higher laws than those which appear in ordinary phenomena. *Secondly*, That the miracles of Christ are generally to be viewed as the result of the influence of the Divine Spirit, which dwelt in Him in all its fulness, operating upon nature. *Thirdly*, We must be content not to determine for ourselves beforehand, or *à priori*, how far this influence of God's Spirit may extend, and how far not: we must grant that it may operate not only on animate and human nature, but upon inanimate nature likewise. It is only self-deception to think that we can set up a barrier or line of demarcation, determining what miracles are possible and what impossible, or that it is by no means necessary to infer this from the character of the miracles themselves, trustworthily attested and recorded. It is quite unreasonable, on the ground merely that St. John's Gospel records miracles as wrought by Jesus, which do not come within our arbitrarily preconceived notion of a possible miracle, to deny to it that trustworthiness and historical genuineness which it so evidently possesses in many points. When we have every reason to recognise in the writer an immediate and trustworthy witness, an apostle, we must allow narrations of this kind which he gives to influence our conceptions of a miracle generally, and our views as to the nature of a possible miracle. *Fourthly*, It is not unimportant to observe, that the accounts given of miracles in the fourth Gospel are comparatively rare, and by no means so frequent as in the Synoptics; and this should awaken in the minds of persons who so argue a prejudgment in favour of St. John. In those cases, moreover, wherein a comparison can be instituted, the account given by St. John is much simpler than that in the Synoptics; and bearing in mind the comparatively late composition of the Gospel, this tells all the more in favour of the opinion that the writer was himself an eye-witness and participator. See, for example, the account of the walking on the sea, John vi. 15 sqq. (Matt. xiv. 22; Mark vi. 45), and of the voice from heaven, John xii. 28 sqq. (cf. my *Beitr.* pp. 102–105, 272).

§ 80.

6. Another argument urged against the genuineness of the fourth Gospel, is its supposed thoroughly Hellenistic and theological character, which is said to warrant the belief that it never belonged to the apostolic age, was not the work of a Palestinian Jew, nor even of one belonging to the Jewish

nation, but of a Gentile Christian of the second century. Let us test the main grounds upon which this argument and inference rest.

(*a.*) It is alleged that the writer could not have belonged in any way to the Jewish people, on account of the manner in which he repeatedly speaks of the Jews as strangers to him. He speaks of τὸ πάσχα τῶν Ἰουδαίων, ἑορτὴ or ἡ ἑορτὴ τῶν Ἰουδαίων, ὁ καθαρισμὸς τῶν Ἰουδαίων, ἄρχων τῶν Ἰουδαίων (ii. 6, 13, iii. 1, v. 1, vi. 4, vii. 2, xi. 55); the Jews are very often called generally οἱ Ἰουδαῖοι, when those of the nation are spoken of who were the opposers of Christ, and the chiefs of the people, not only in Judea proper, but even in Galilee (vi. 41, 52). The evangelist also (it is urged) makes Jesus speak of the Mosaic law as something strange to Him, as the law of His opponents, or of the Jews, viii. 17, ἐν τῷ νόμῳ τῷ ὑμετέρῳ γέγραπται; xv. 25, ὁ λόγος ὁ γεγραμμένος ἐν τῷ νόμῳ αὐτῶν; see also x. 34.[1]

We admit that these expressions are somewhat peculiar, and could not easily be explained or justified, as coming from a writer belonging to the Jewish nation, save upon the supposition that he wrote at a comparatively late date, at a time when the Christian Church had become independent, either separated from or disowned by the Jewish, and when he was living beyond the Jews' country, and among Greeks, and would feel that he had to write not so much for Jews, but rather for Greeks and Grecian Christians. But to hold that the Gospel was composed under these circumstances, is in exact accordance with the unanimous tradition of the Church. Admitting this, it seems to me quite natural that a disciple of the Lord, who had been a Jew by birth, should express himself thus: that having himself seen the hostility and persecution practised by the chiefs and others of the Jewish nation against the Lord, and against those who confessed His blessed name, in his account of the sufferings of Jesus, and His encounters with the Sanhedrim and individual Jews,

[1] BRETSCHNEIDER, pp. 91, 92; FISCHER, *Tüb. Zeitschr. f. Theol.* 1840, pp. 96–133; and BAUR, *Theol. Jahrbb.* 1844, pp. 623–625; *Kanon. Evv.* p. 317.

he should designate these persons not by name, but by the more general appellation which we find in the Gospel. See my *Beitr.* pp. 245-249.

The opponents of the Gospel are indeed right in inferring that, if these expressions tell against the genuineness of the Gospel, we must conclude that the author was not a born Jew. But there cannot be a doubt that the writer was a Jew both by birth and education. This is evident (*a*) from his knowledge of the Jewish law concerning the passover indicated in his account of the passion as compared with that of the Synoptics, the two first of whom were also Jews, and Jews of Palestine: (*b*) from the references so often occurring in the Gospel to the O. T., and to the accomplishment of O. T. prophecies in the events of Christ's life,—references which make the Gospel akin to that of Matthew, and which represent Jesus as the promised Messiah, *e.g.* ii. 17, xii. 14, 15, 37, 38, 39, xix. 24, 28, 36, 37; and in the recorded discourses of Jesus, xiii. 18, xv. 25, xvii. 12: (*c*) these O. T. quotations are made some of them from the LXX., but some of them direct from the Hebrew, which the writer himself renders directly into Greek; *e.g.* xii. 40 (Isa. vi. 10), xiii. 18 (Ps. xli. 10), xix. 37 (Zech. xii. 10), and perhaps other passages, which are not quite so evidently from the Hebrew (see my *Beitr.* 244). No Gentile Christian of the second century could be expected to have had such an acquaintance with the Hebrew text of the O. T., but only a native Jew, and one who had not been educated among Greeks, as *e.g.* at Alexandria, but who had been brought up, as St. John was, in Palestine.

It is of no avail to urge against this (as Bretschneider does), that the writer, when he mentions Hebrew words and Jewish customs, adds an explanation of his own (i. 39, 42, ii. 6, v. 2, xi. 18, xix. 40, and others). We might with equal propriety object against Mark as the writer of the second Gospel, for similar explanations are to be found in his Gospel. These explanations only show that the writer had Gentile and not Jewish or Palestinian readers chiefly in his mind. Bretschneider, Baur (*Theol. Jahrbb.* 1844, p. 635), and others, urge the mistakes which (they say) the author of the fourth Gospel makes in these Jewish matters, and which no Palestinian Jew could have fallen into. They refer to John i. 28 and iv. 5. In the former of these passages, according to what is proved to be the oldest text, the text of all the MSS. down to Origen's time, mention is made of a *Bethany* beyond Jordan, where John was baptizing; yet the only Bethany known to us was that close by Jerusalem. But it is evident from xi. 18 that the evangelist knew this Bethany; for he says that it was "nigh to Jerusalem, about fifteen furlongs off." We cannot therefore suppose that he meant to describe this place as "on the other side Jordan." We must assume either that he meant another place of the same name in Peræa (which is quite possible), or that this reading is a trifling error of a very early copyist, or of the evangelist himself, who, when about to write another name, perhaps Bethabara (as the *textus receptus* has it, but seemingly upon a conjecture of Origen's only), wrote by mistake the more familiar name Bethany. Baur's notion is really quite absurd (see my *Beitr.* 256), when he says that the author names here an imaginary Bethany beyond Jordan, because he wants to represent Jesus as coming from a Bethany to begin His public ministry, just as he represents Him as going into Jerusalem from a Bethany at the end! As to the other passage in ch. iv. 5, a Samaritan town is called Sychar. Judging from the connection, it is certain—though Delitzsch and Ewald[1] think differently—that Sichem is the place meant (שְׁכֶם, LXX. usually Συχέμ), and Sychar seems to have been an inexact pronunciation and writing of this name. But in the language of the Jews and Samaritans at the time this may have been the ordinary pronunciation, the liquids *m* and *r* being interchangeable. This indeed may have been a scornful manner of naming the place adopted by the Jews, either with reference to שִׁכֹּר, *drunk*, according to Isa. xxviii. 1-7, where the Ephraimites, in whose

---

[1] DELITZSCH, *Talmudische Studien*, in *Rudelbach and Guericke's Zeitschr.* 1856, p. 240. EWALD, *Jahrbb. d. bibl. Wiss.* viii. p. 255; and his Commentary, *in loc.*

tribe Sichem was, are described as drunken; or with reference to שֶׁקֶר, *falsehood*, as the idolatry of the Samaritans was regarded. Here again we may have merely a corruption in the pronunciation or spelling of the word, as Credner (*Einl.* p. 264) ingeniously suggests, explaining that the evangelist had dictated this portion of his Gospel to some one else, some Greek Hellenist of Ephesus, who found it easier, instead of Σιχέμ (Συχέμ), to write Συχέρμ, Συχάρ, like the Syrian Darmeschek instead of Dameschek (Damascus), and like the Palmyrean inscription αγαπητος for αγαπητος. However we explain it, the form Συχάρ does not help us to decide whether the writer were the Apostle John or another. Baur has also discovered a decisive proof in the words used concerning Caiaphas — he was ἀρχιερεὺς τοῦ ἐνιαυτοῦ ἐκείνου (John xi. 51, xviii. 13); whence he would infer that he believed that the office of high priest was merely a yearly one. But the expression does not mean this, nor is it likely that the writer, whoever he might have been, could have entertained such a meaning; see my *Beitr.* p. 257.

(*b.*) The doubt has been suggested whether a Galilean fisherman, such as John was, could have written a work in Greek, and so marked by Greek culture as the fourth Gospel. This objection is sufficiently answered by what we have said concerning the family circumstances and the later history of the Apostle John. The family of St. John, though that of a Galilean fisherman, was by no means obscure or poor. His mother's piety, which led her to cleave so closely to the Saviour's person, prompted her doubtless to instruct her sons early in life in the holy Scriptures; and this in itself would involve a certain degree of culture. That he may thus early have become acquainted with Greek, is evident from what we have said (§ 23, 28) respecting the spread of the Greek language in Palestine, and especially in Galilee. What is said in Acts iv. 13, viz. that the Sanhedrim had heard concerning Peter and John that they were unlearned and ignorant men (ἄνθρωποι ἀγράμματοί καὶ ἰδιῶται), cannot be urged against this; for this was simply a report that had reached the ears of the Sanhedrim, and the words simply mean that

Peter and John were not, like Paul, trained in the schools of the learned, and brought up at the feet of a Rabbi—that they had not received a systematic theological education. It by no means implies that they had received no instruction, or that they were ignorant of Greek. If John did not know Greek pretty well, he would hardly have chosen Asia Minor, and especially Ephesus, where Greek was commonly spoken even by Jews, as his permanent place of residence when he had to leave Palestine. During his residence there his knowledge of the language, in understanding it, in speaking, and in writing it, must have been quite matured, for he would hardly ever have occasion to speak or write in any other tongue.

§ 81.

(*c.*) The general dogmatic views of this Gospel, and especially its Christology, have been urged as a proof that it could not have been written by a Palestinian Jew like John. Bretschneider, for example, finds a strong objection against the Johannine authorship in the doctrine of the *Logos* as the eternal Word of God, who enlightened the world under the O. T., and became flesh in Christ. He thinks that no Palestinian Jew could have given such a representation of Christ, because the idea of the *Logos* was quite Alexandrine, the creation of Greek philosophy, and not adopted by Christians until long afterwards, when Greek philosophers were found within the pale of the Christian Church; whereas the Jewish Christians regarded the Messiah only as a man. This is mainly the view of Baur, Schwegler, and other scholars of that school, who hold that the theological standing-point of the fourth Gospel, especially its Christology, is quite different from what it must have been were it a work belonging to the apostolic age, and written by an apostle who was a Jewish Christian. They take it for granted that the view of Christ's person held by Jewish Christians in the apostolic age was exclusively the Ebionite view, which regarded Jesus simply as a man gifted with higher powers. They regard St. Paul's Christology as a higher stage of development which gained ground in the Church only after a long conflict; and the Johannine Christology, *i.e.* that which we find in the fourth Gospel, as a still later development.

We cannot here stay fully to examine what and how much truth there may be in all this: such an inquiry belongs properly to the sphere of N. T. theology. The following suggestions, however, will suffice for the discussion of the subject now before us. First, as to the doctrine of the *Logos* generally, we find the germ of it in the O. T., especially in Proverbs; we find it also in Ecclesiasticus; and still more fully elaborated, both as to form and terminology, in Philo, at a time previous to the composition of the fourth Gospel, even supposing it to have been the work of St. John. We find the same representation in the writings of Hebrew-speaking Jews, especially in the Targums, under the designation "the Word of Jehovah," מֵימְרָא דַיְיָ. We cannot therefore suppose that this was a dogma merely borrowed into the Alexandrine schools from Greek philosophy; we are rather led to the conclusion that it was not unknown, even with the very expression *the Word* of Jehovah or of God, to the Hebrew-speaking Jews of Palestine in the apostolic age. We are warranted to suppose that St. John himself had become familiar with this view in Palestine, without in any way coming into contact with the Alexandrine theology. But not to lay stress upon this, there is nothing unreasonable in the supposition that, when he came to reside at Ephesus, he would become acquainted with the theology of the Alexandrine Jews, and with this dogma as stated by them. The forms and terms of the Alexandrine theology would be known at Ephesus even before St. John came to reside there, and even in the Christian Church itself, through such men as the Alexandrine Jew Apollos, who had, we have reason to believe, been trained in the Alexandrine schools, and was not unacquainted with the writings of Philo, whether he was or was not the writer of the Epistle to the Hebrews.[1] If John, therefore, had obtained this idea of the *Logos* in

---

[1] Concerning the relation of the writer of the Epistle to the Hebrews to Philo, see my *Einl. z. Hebr. Br.* p. 398 sqq.

Palestine, or afterwards in Asia, we can easily understand his application of it to the person of Jesus,—thus blending the idea of the *Logos* with that of the Messiah and the Son of God.

We find that this idea was not strange even to the Apostle Paul, who was a man of Hebrew culture, though the term *Logos* is not thus technically used by him: see Col. i. 15 sqq.; Phil. ii. 6; 1 Cor. viii. 6, x. 4. The same idea is traceable in 1 Pet. i. 11, where the spirit of prophecy, speaking in the prophets, is called τὸ ἐν αὐτοῖς πνεῦμα Χριστοῦ. Indications of it are not wanting even in the Synoptics, in the discourses of Christ there recorded (see § 76); and this view of the person of Christ has, beyond doubt, its foundation and confirmation in some of Christ's own sayings. The Apocalypse witnesses how little the representation of the *Logos* and its application to Christ tells against a Palestinian writer. Bretschneider himself attributes this book to a Palestinian, which indeed cannot be doubted; and Schwegler, Baur, and that school, acknowledge it to be a genuine work of the Apostle John. Yet in the Revelation we not only have this representation of Christ (see i. 17, ii. 8, iii. 14), but the very term itself as His distinctive name, ὁ λόγος τοῦ Θεοῦ (xix. 13). Even if it could be proved that in the Christology of the fourth Gospel we found a later development of this doctrine than in St. Paul's writings, this would be no witness against its genuineness, because, on the supposition that St. John wrote it, it would still bear a much later date than St. Paul's epistles. But this view cannot be justified; for Baur is certainly wrong in supposing that he can trace a docetic element as the basis of the Christology of our Gospel, and that the subject of the history it contains is not the man Christ Jesus, but the *Logos*, who, though incarnate, is the absolute subject, and is only apparently clothed with a human corporeity. Baur refers to the prologue and ch. vii. 10, viii. 59, x. 39, xii. 36; but these texts by no means sanction his opinion. It must not be forgotten, moreover, that the evangelist uses the term *Logos* thus only in the outset of his Gospel, where he is himself the speaker, and is stating his views of Christ's relations to God. He never introduces it into Christ's discourses, nor into those of the Baptist or others which he records. This indirectly proves how utterly ungrounded the opinion is, that the evangelist puts his own ideas and words into Christ's mouth. Yet Baur refuses to see this (*Theol. Jahrbb.* 1844, p. 467).

§ 82.

(*d.*) Another ground of objection against the Apostle John in particular as the writer of our Gospel, is found [1] in the free, universalist spirit which pervades the work, as contrasted with the way in which John appears in Gal. ii. 9 in conjunction with the other apostles at Jerusalem, to whom the Judaizing party appealed. He there appears as narrow-minded as the rest; and he could not have been acquainted with those beautiful discourses, so free and broad in spirit, which the fourth Gospel contains. If he wrote the Gospel, he must himself have developed, and indeed made these discourses, though it is more natural to suppose that he continued to the end a narrow-minded Judaizing apostle. So Lützelberger argues. My reply is as follows:—It by no means appears, from the mention of John along with Peter and James in Gal. ii. 9 as τοὺς δοκοῦντας στύλους εἶναι—the chief men of the Jerusalem Church, with whom Paul conferred respecting the liberation of Gentile Christians from the law—that he was then a narrow-minded Judaizing Christian; indeed, there is nothing in the course of events which then transpired, as recorded in Gal. ii. and Acts xv., to sanction such a description of St. John. It would be unjust to describe even the Apostle Peter thus, judging from the part he takes at this time, and from what we are told of him in the Acts, and may infer from the epistle which is acknowledged as his. The Christian teachers in Jerusalem showed their readiness, as the result of those proceedings, to free their Gentile brethren from the bondage of the Mosaic law; and Paul does not in the least intimate that they did this by con-

---

[1] LÜTZELBERGER, p. 173; BAUR, *Theol. Jahrbb.* 1844, p. 653; *Kanon. Evv.* p. 329. See, on the other hand, my *Beitr.* pp. 249-256.

straint, or against their own convictions. Judging from the part that either Peter or John took in those proceedings, we have no reason to infer that they were actuated by a Judaizing spirit. It is remarkable that nothing is said in the Acts of John having taken any part in those proceedings; but this is quite in keeping with the contemplative spirit which characterizes the beloved disciple in the fourth Gospel. By virtue of this spirit, we may well imagine that he took no prominent part; and yet he was so esteemed and beloved in the circle of the apostles, that even a Paul recognised his importance and worth, as the mention of him in Galatians shows. Remembering this characteristic of the Apostle John, we can understand how it may have been that just *that* aspect of the Lord's person upon which he especially dwells, and that class of discourses which most deeply impressed him, were not much talked about or orally repeated by him before he wrote his Gospel, as were those discourses of another kind related by the Synoptics, and widely circulated in the Church.

This obviates another objection urged by Lützelberger, who thinks that, as John lived a considerable time with the other apostles at Jerusalem, the constant and mutual interchange of thought and experience between him and them must have moulded the apostolic tradition concerning Christ's life into such a oneness of spirit and uniformity, that any composition so individual and different from the common account as is the fourth Gospel in comparison of the Synoptics, could not have emanated from him. We have no right to infer any such uniformity of mind and development among the apostles, from the fact of their having lived and worked together in Jerusalem. Even Peter and James (the Lord's brother), when compared with each other, are found to have had peculiarities of their own; and we are not justified in supposing that, on account of John's long connection with them, he had not great individuality of his own too, and even in the views he took of Christ's person and work, as distinct from them and the other apostles. His peculiarly inward and contemplative disposition would enable him to live long with his fellow-apostles, who were of a more outward and demonstrative spirit, without feeling himself called upon to put forth his own views and to exchange them with theirs, unless special opportunity and occasion required. Least of all can we hold with Baur, that this long residence in Jerusalem would quite unfit him to be the author of a Gospel which relates (John xii. 20 sqq.) how, during Christ's life on earth, certain Greeks desired to see Him; for the fact itself, as there recorded, presents nothing that is strange or improbable. The fact that the Gospel, and especially Christ's discourses as recorded in it, breathe a free and universal spirit which does not limit the kingdom of God within the pale of Judaism, is of no avail as an argument against its apostolic origin, unless this liberal spirit was not the spirit of Jesus—unless Jesus Himself had never spoken thus. But we find the same broad spirit even in the Synoptics, and even in that Gospel which is usually regarded as specially Jewish in its tone—I mean the Gospel of Matthew; see ch. viii. 10–12, xxi. 43, xxiv. 14, xxviii. 19.

§ 83.

7. Bretschneider has found a special ground of objection against our Gospel in the manner in which the writer affirms the truth of his testimony, and the anxiety he shows on this point without giving his name. This, if anything, testifies conclusively to the genuineness of the Gospel. We have already seen (§ 59, 61), that both from the Gospel itself, and from a comparison of other facts stated in the N. T., we may with certainty conclude that the writer was the Apostle John. But a forger could not have calculated that his readers would take the trouble to find this out: he could not have expected that, when his work made its appearance suddenly, and without being heard of before, any one would imagine the writer to have been St. John. He would therefore have taken pains at least to intimate unmistakeably who the person was that he meant to simulate. But St. John, on the contrary, would be content to refer to himself as the writer only so as that those around who knew him and would read his Gospel would know who the writer really was; and as

the Gospel circulated, the writer's name would circulate with it. Hence we find that in the early Church no doubt whatever was entertained that "the beloved disciple," as the writer calls himself, was the Apostle John: there is not the slightest trace of any other opinion. This conviction, apart from the Gospel itself, rests upon a tradition contemporary with its first promulgation, which began with the testimony either of the writer himself, or of those who received the work from him. We thus have, in the very fact referred to, a proof that "the beloved disciple" was the Apostle John.[1] We have already shown (§ 59) that the manner in which John the Baptist is named in our Gospel witnesses to its composition by the Apostle John.

§ 84.

The conclusion of the Gospel (ch. xxi.), in its relation to what precedes, presents a very strong argument for the genuineness of the work. What we read in ch. xx. 30, 31, forms an apparent and appropriate close; and the writer of the Gospel, when he penned this, could not have had an idea that anything more would be added. Ch. xxi. is certainly a later addition, and the question arises whether it was made by the evangelist himself or by some other writer. Weitzel endeavours to prove the former. Grotius holds the latter, and conjectures that the addition was made by one of the elders of the Church at Ephesus after the apostle's death. He rightly refers to the conclusion of this twenty-first chapter, especially ver. 24: "This is the disciple which testifieth of these things, and wrote these things; and we know (οἴδαμεν) that *his* testimony is true." This could not have been written by "this disciple" himself, but by some one among his friends and pupils, who added this as confirmatory of the full trustworthiness of the foregoing work of the beloved disciple. It is quite improbable, as Zeller thinks (*Theol. Jahrbb.* 1847, p. 140), that a writer who wished himself to be taken as the author of the Gospel

---

[1] Compare K. L. WEITZEL, *das Selbstzeugniss des vierten Evan. über seine Person*, *Stud. u. Krit.* 1849, pp. 578–638.

would have expressed himself thus. Here we have a case quite different from ch. xix. 35, where the testifier himself expressly says that *he* knows that his testimony is true. In ch. xxi. 24 the writer expressly distinguishes himself from him who testifieth these things: the sentence is indeed in the third person, but those who know that his testimony is true is in the first person—"*we* know;" and the writer who thus speaks in his own name and that of others conjointly could not have intended it to be understood that he was the testifier, the evangelist. Most of those who acknowledge the genuineness of the Gospel agree with Grotius in his view of the twenty-first chapter; a few take only the last two verses of it as a later addition. And even among those who deny the genuineness of the Gospel, many hold that this last chapter is not by its author, but by a still later hand. Whatever, therefore, be our view of the genuineness of the Gospel (and supposing its genuineness, because, among many reasons, of the subject-matter and tendency of the narrative), we may conclude that ch. xxi. was not written till after the death of the "beloved disciple." Supposing the whole Gospel spurious, we should still have to come to the same conclusion, because it would be very improbable that the skilful author, if he added this chapter himself, should not have known its contents from the outset, and have incorporated them as part of his work. The closing verses of ch. xx. show that he could not thus have known them.

If this twenty-first chapter, then, was not added by the evangelist himself—and we yet find no hint that the Gospel was ever known in the Church without it (for it is found in all MSS. and versions)—we are justified in supposing that it formed part of it from the time when it began to be publicly known and circulated, and that the chapter was added by the person or persons who first made the Gospel public, and who had received it from the evangelist himself, whoever he may have been. This being so, we have in v. 24, where the evangelist is said distinctly to be the beloved disciple, the most authentic testimony possible both as to the writer and the genuineness of the Gospel,—a testimony which every unprejudiced critic must acknowledge to be of the highest value; and this argument holds true even if we take only the two last verses to be from another hand. Any one who still holds that the Gospel is spurious, must assume and believe not only that the author endeavoured falsely to make it appear that he was an eye-witness and a participator in the events he records, and did this with a very crafty and skilful hand, but also that another shared in the deception, and being let into the secret, added a false witness (perhaps by direction of the author) to the genuineness of the work, knowing that his witness was untrue, or at least that he was quite incompetent to bear any such testimony. Not a word need be said to show the utter improbability of such an assumption.

The proof furnished by this twenty-first chapter becomes still stronger when we consider the design of the narrative it contains. It is a standard assumption of Baur's school, that the main aim of the writer here was to extol John, as the apostle of the Churches in Asia Minor, above Peter, the apostle of the Roman Church.[1] Schwegler and Baur hold that this is the tendency of the entire Gospel; so that this appendix by a later hand was only intended to confirm and give still greater prominence to it. Yet these same scholars are of opinion that this Gospel was a blow struck in the passover controversies on the side of the Western, and especially the Roman Church, against the Asia Minor Churches; so that they must look upon this Gospel (which they regard as a party work written with a designed bias) as telling for the interests of one party in one respect, and for the interests of the opposite party in another,—a view which, on the face of it, cannot lay much claim to probability. Passing by this, however, we find that the narrative of ch. xxi. does not in the remotest degree sanction the notion that the writer (whether he narrates a traditional yet historical circumstance, or a fiction) seeks to depreciate Peter in order to give pro-

---

[1] So SCHWEGLER, *Montanismus*, p. 283; *Nachap. Zeitalter*, ii. 355–357; BAUR, *Theol. Jahrbb.* 1844, p. 626; ZELLER, *ib.* 1847, p. 141; STRAUSS, *Leben Jesu, f. d. Deutsche Volk*, p. 610.

minence to John. Had this been his object, how could he have told how Jesus three times gave to Peter the command, "Feed my sheep, feed my lambs" (vers. 15-17)?

The true design of the narrative is apparent in vers. 22-24. The opinion had spread in the Church, that after His resurrection Jesus had given John the promise that he should live until His second advent. The writer endeavours to correct this opinion by giving the exact words of the Lord on the occasion referred to,—words which, rightly understood, contained no such promise. What precedes is narrated on account of the connection. The entire narrative bears the impress of historic truth; and so do the prophetic words of Jesus to Peter, ver. 18. Probably the writer obtained it from an immediate disciple, perhaps from John himself. Such being the case, occasion and need to make known the facts with this design could only arise when the beloved disciple was very far advanced in years, or immediately after his death, and in order that his death might not become a pretext for disbelief in the words of the Lord, or in His prophecies concerning the future. It must have been written at least within half a century after; for, later than this, unbelief would not have based itself on this saying of the Lord's, even supposing that the saying was still known in the Church. The narrative itself, even apart from vers. 24, 25, is clearly intended as an addition or supplement to the Gospel; and thus it is a very important testimony that the Gospel was written still earlier (see my *Beitr.* pp. 179-181)

§ 85.

8. We have still to examine *the external testimonies for the fourth Gospel.*[1] In the first place, it is a universally recog-

---

[1] See my *Beitr.* pp. 201-226, 274-280; EWALD, *Jahrbb. der bibl. Wiss.* v. 178-208. Among the latest opposers of the Gospel, WEISSE admits that it is recognised by external testimony, and that, judging by this alone, every unprejudiced person must admit its authenticity. But BRETSCHNEIDER, SCHWEGLER, BAUR, ZELLER, and others, are of a different opinion, and hold that, before the middle, or indeed the end, of the

nised and established fact, that towards the end of the second century the fourth Gospel occupied a place side by side with the other three as a canonical work, and indeed as a work of the Apostle John. Thus it was esteemed by all sections of the Church—by the Alexandrine, the Syrian, the African, and the Roman Churches (see the *History of the Canon*, § 242). Among the Fathers to be adduced as witnesses to this, IRENÆUS (first presbyter, and afterwards bishop, of Lyons, *ob.* 202) stands foremost. He may be regarded as a witness concerning the Canon in Gaul, and, considering his origin, in Asia Minor likewise. Remembering the personal acquaintance which he had in his youth with many aged presbyters, and especially with Polycarp, who had himself heard and seen the Apostle John (§ 57), he stands prominent as a very valuable witness concerning such a treatise as our Gospel. Now he recognises it, in the same manner as his contemporaries, Clemens in Alexandria, and Tertullian in proconsular Africa, without hesitation as a genuine work of the Apostle John ; and he makes use of it as such. His firm conviction of its apostolic origin is unmistakeable. He is so convinced that the Church was right in recognising the *four* Gospels, that he looks upon this number as involving a moral necessity, and thinks that there could not have been more or less than just four Gospels, like the four divisions of the world, the four winds, the four cherubim.[1] However strange and exaggerated such a style of argument may seem to us,

second century, there is no trace to be found of the existence of our Gospel in the Church.

[1] *Hær.* iii. 11 : Ἐπειδὴ τέσσαρα κλίματα τοῦ κόσμου, ἐν ᾧ ἐσμὲν, εἰσὶ, καὶ τέσσαρα καθολικὰ πνεύματα, κατέσπασται δὲ ἡ ἐκκλησία ἐπὶ πάσης τῆς γῆς, στύλος τε καὶ στήριγμα ἐκκλησίας τὸ εὐαγγέλιον, καὶ πνεῦμα ζωῆς· εἰκότως τέσσαρας ἔχειν αὐτὴν στύλους, πανταχόθεν πνέοντας τὴν ἀφθαρσίαν καὶ ἀναζωπυροῦντας τοὺς ἀνθρώπους. Ἐξ ὧν φανερὸν, ὅτι ὁ τῶν ἁπάντων τεχνίτης Λόγος ὁ καθήμενος ἐπὶ τὰ χερουβὶμ . . . ἔδωκεν ἡμῖν τετράμορφον τὸ εὐαγγέλιον, ἑνί τε πνεύματι συνεχόμενον . . . καὶ γὰρ τὰ χερουβὶμ τετραπρόσωπα. . . . Τούτων δὲ οὕτως ἐχόντων, μάταιοι πάντες καὶ ἀμαθεῖς, προσέτι δὲ καὶ τολμηροὶ, οἱ ἀθετοῦντες τὴν ἰδέαν τοῦ εὐαγγελίου καὶ εἴτε πλείονα εἴτε ἐλάττονα τῶν εἰρημένων παρεισφέροντες τῶν εὐαγγελίων πρόσωπα.

it certainly proves how deeply the conviction was rooted in the mind of Irenæus, and of the Church in his time, concerning the trustworthiness of the four Gospels, and therefore of the genuineness of St. John; for such a view could hardly have been taken, if this, the fourth Gospel, had not already been for a considerable time known and acknowledged as a genuine apostolic treatise. We cannot understand how Schenkel (*Charakterbild Jesu,* Anhang No. 2), reversing the true argument and inference, can say that Irenæus, by his comparison of the four zones, etc., was led to the belief that the fourth Gospel was genuine.

POLYCRATES, bishop of Ephesus, may also be regarded as a witness for our fourth Gospel. He names John as ὁ ἐπὶ τὸ στῆθος τοῦ Κυρίου ἀναπεσών (Euseb. *H. E.* v. 24; see § 57, 74); and we cannot reasonably doubt, though Baur and Zeller do, that this distinctive appellation has reference to the manner in which John appears and is described in the fourth Gospel (xiii. 25, and especially in the addition ch. xxi. 20). It implies a recognition of the historical truth and genuineness of the Gospel, together with its appendix, on the part of Polycrates and the Church in the place to which he belonged.

The Gospel certainly had, even at this time, some opponents in a small anti-Montanist sect in Asia Minor, whom Epiphanius afterwards called the *Alogi,* and which appeared soon after the rise of Montanism, not long after A.D. 150, and continued for a considerable time (see § 62). Baur attached great weight to their opposition against St. John's Gospel; but Zeller allows that it cannot be brought forward as a testimony that there was anything like a tradition against the Gospel. From what is known concerning their objections, it is manifest that they found the Gospel acknowledged by the Churches in their parts as the work of the Apostle John, and that it had been thus acknowledged for some time. Had they known it as a fact that the Gospel had only lately made its appearance, it would have sufficed to have referred to this fact as an adequate reason for rejecting it; and they could not have attributed it as they did, confessedly without any historical reasons, to Cerinthus. They were led to the rejection of it by a cold, dry, rationalistic tendency of mind, a leaning towards the Ebionite view of the doctrine of Christ, and opposition to the dreamy enthusiasm of the Montanists, whose headquarters were Thyatira, and who looked upon Montanus as the Paraclete promised in St. John's Gospel. This proves how utterly untenable the supposition of Schwegler and Baur is, that the Gospel originated in one and the same theological movement as Montanism. It cannot be denied that Montanism, upon its rise in 150, found our Gospel already in the Church, and esteemed as a genuine and apostolic work. It must therefore have been thus known, esteemed, and circulated during the first half of the second century, though not perhaps so widely as it was subsequently, and particularly after the end of the second century. The fact that the anti-Montanist party attributed all St. John's writings, the Apocalypse as well as the Gospel, to Cerinthus, proves that they were in circulation together in the Church from of old, and that they regarded, not the time of their composition, but their authorship, as erroneous. Had the Gospel only appeared as the outgo of the Montanistic movement, it could not have been so immediately regarded as apostolic by the Montanists themselves, nor so unanimously received, and so soon held in reverence as apostolic by the Church at large, —indeed, by all save a small party in Thyatira.

§ 86.

We have already shown (§ 74, 75) that no just ground of objection against our Gospel, and its authorship by the Apostle John, can be found in the passover controversies of the second century. Still more unfounded is the opinion of Baur, Zeller, and others, that the Gospel was not in existence when these controversies began, but that it was first called into existence by these controversies. In proof that it was in existence when these controversies commenced, and was already regarded as a high authority in the Church, we have the two fragments of Apollinaris in the *Chron. Paschale*. Apollinaris himself took part in the second of these controversies, about the year 170. In the second fragment[1] there is an unmistakeable reference to the account of the piercing of Jesus' side, just as we find it recorded in John xix. 34; and this involves a recognition of this act as an historical fact, and thus of the genuineness of the Gospel. In the first fragment, which immediately precedes (see § 74, note), Apollinaris speaks of a στασιάζειν of the Gospels which would take place if, as the Quarto-decimans thought was the testimony of Matthew, Christ suffered on the 15th Nisan. This στασιάζειν does not mean, as Baur and others think, a contradiction between the Gospels and the Jewish law, but one of the Gospels between themselves; and this can only have reference to a contradiction between the Synoptics, and especially Matthew on the one hand and John on the other. This fragment therefore shows that these Gospels, John as well as Matthew, were already recognised as authorities, and by both the contending parties. But this could not have been the case had the fourth Gospel been in existence only a few years, and as the result of the first passover controversy. If it had really been thus recently forged, it could not have been received, at least by the Quarto-decimans of Asia Minor.

The reverence with which the Gospel was regarded by the Valentinians, one of the most important sects of the second century, confirms these external witnesses. They held it in high repute, and made frequent use of it; and there can be no doubt that the orthodox Church also recognised it: for Valentinus, when he founded his school, must have found it already thus esteemed, and occupying so high a rank as to lead him to adopt it as the basis of his distinctive views. Thus, again, we are led to the conclusion that at the beginning of the second century it must have been in high repute. Irenæus says that the members of this sect made special use of St. John's Gospel (*Hær.* iii. 11 : *hi autem qui a Valentino sunt, eo*

---

[1] *Chron. pasch.* p. 14: Ἡ ιδ´ τὸ ἀληθινὸν τοῦ Κυρίου πάσχα, ἡ θυσία ἡ μεγάλη, ὁ ἀντὶ τοῦ ἀμνοῦ παῖς Θεοῦ ... καὶ ὁ τὴν ἁγίαν πλευρὰν ἐκκεντηθείς, ὁ ἐκχέας ἐκ τῆς πλευρᾶς αὐτοῦ τὰ δύο πάλιν καθάρσια, ὕδωρ καὶ αἷμα, λόγον καὶ πνεῦμα, καὶ ὁ ταφεὶς ἐν ἡμέρᾳ τῇ τοῦ πάσχα, ἐπιτιθέντος τῷ μνήματι τοῦ λίθου.

quod est secundum Joannem plenissime utentes, etc.), and we find that this was so. Ptolemæus and Heracleon were two of the most distinguished followers of Valentinus, and both of them lived about A.D. 150. Ptolemæus, in an Epistle to Flora (Epiphan. *Hær.* xxxiii. 3), quotes John i. 3, without observation, as the declaration of "the apostle;" and Heracleon wrote a commentary upon the Gospel, from which Origen in his commentary on John quotes several extracts. The composition of a commentary on such a Gospel, is a proof not only of the commentator's high estimate, but of the esteem in which it must have been held among those for whom his commentary was intended. Considering this recognition of the Gospel by his disciples, we can hardly doubt that Valentinus himself recognised it, though Bretschneider, Baur, and others deny this; wrongly, however, because Tertullian expressly says that these Gnostics accepted intact the Canon of Scripture, disputing only its sense.[1] According to the newly discovered work of Hippolytus,[2] again, Valentinus appears as a witness for our Gospel.[3] It cannot be denied that Valentinus has borrowed his distinctive terminology in great part from the fourth Gospel. He lived in the first half of the second century, probably under Hadrian, and at Alexandria, whence about A.D. 140 he came to Rome, and died at Cyprus, *circ.* A.D. 160. Considering these testimonies, the notion is quite inadmissible which Bretschneider, Schwegler, Baur, and Zeller entertain, that St. John's Gospel was composed after the rise of the Valentinians, and with reference to them. Any one who examines the fragments of Heracleon's

---

[1] *De præscr. Hær.* xxxviii.: *Neque enim si Valentinus integro instrumento uti videtur, non calidiore ingenio quam Marcion? . . . Valentinus pepercit, quoniam non ad materiam scripturas sed materiam ad scripturas excogitavit.*

[2] E. MILLER, *Origenis Philosophumena*, Oxford 1851.

[3] VI. 32, where the devil is twice called ὁ ἄρχων τοῦ κόσμου τούτου (John xii. 31, xiv. 30, xvi. 11); vi. 35, where John x. 8 is quoted as the word of Christ. BASILIDES also is quoted as a witness (c. 125); see vii. 22, 27 (John i. 9, ii. 4). According to ZELLER (*Theol. Jahrbb.* 1853, p. 148) and others, these quotations are not those of Basilides and Valentinus, but of their disciples. See, however, WEIZSAECKER (p. 232), who allows this in the case of Valentinus.

VOL. I. Q

commentary, and considers to what distortions of meanings he must resort in order to give them a sense reconcilable to the notion that the Valentinians composed the Gospel, will be convinced. The Fathers, moreover, were so thoroughly opposed to these Gnostics in the middle of the second century, that, had the Gospel emanated from them, or made its appearance first among them, they would not have received it. It would not, on the other hand, have been held in such high repute by these Gnostics, if it had arisen in the orthodox sections of the Church after the time of Valentinus.

Schwegler, Baur, and Zeller think that the writer was neither a Valentinian nor an opponent of their gnosis, but one who occupied an intermediate position; and Schwegler regards the Gospel as an attempt to bring back these Gnostics into the Church, taking (as Baur also) the words μονογενής, ζωή, ἀλήθεια, χάρις, πλήρωμα, λόγος, φῶς, παράκλητος, as names of Æons, having reference to the Valentinian gnosis. But it is unreasonable and inadmissible to regard St. John's use of these words, which is by far the simpler, as the derived, and the artificial gnostic use of them as the original and primary. The true view, to which every consideration leads, is clearly that the Gnostics borrowed these terms from the Gospel, which was already recognised and esteemed, and made use of them as watchwords on which to hang the doctrines of their speculative system.

Marcion, who was contemporary with Valentinus, and the Marcionites, regarded the Canon differently from the Valentinians. He (as we have already seen, § 54) at first received the four Gospels, but he afterwards rejected that of John, chiefly because he supposed that Paul in Gal. ii. blamed John for certain Judaizing tendencies (Tertull. *adv. Marc.* iv. 3). But herein we have a proof that Marcion, when he formed his system, *i.e.* not later than A.D. 140, must have found this Gospel already in the Church, and recognised as the work of the Apostle John. For in the passage from Tertullian (see § 53) the Gospels *quæ propria et sub Apostolorum nomine eduntur* are not, as Zeller supposes, the apocryphal Gospels of Thomas, Matthias, Bartholomew, etc.

Marcion had no need to object to and reject these in opposition to the Church, for the Church itself rejected them, but the Gospels according to Matthew and John.

§ 87.

Another doctor of the same period, but belonging to the orthodox Church, was Justin Martyr, born about 89, ob. 161–168. He often quotes the Gospels, which seemingly, according to the analogy of Xenophon's *Memorabilia of Socrates*, he usually designates ἀπομνημονεύματα τῶν ἀποστόλων. He describes them as written by the apostles and their companions.[1] The supposition of some modern scholars,[2] that what Justin refers to and makes use of was some one distinct work, is clearly false. His own words[3] explicitly declare that they were more than one, and the citations themselves witness that all our four canonical Gospels were included. Now, among his quotations from the ἀπομνημονεύματα we find unmistakeably traces of our fourth Gospel. The most obvious of these is that in the *Apol.* i. 61 : καὶ γὰρ ὁ Χριστὸς εἶπεν· ἂν μὴ ἀναγεννηθῆτε, οὐ μὴ εἰσέλθητε εἰς τὴν βασιλείαν τῶν οὐρανῶν· ὅτι δὲ καὶ ἀδύνατον εἰς τὰς μήτρας τῶν τεκουσῶν τοὺς ἅπαξ γεννωμένους ἐμβῆναι, φανερὸν πᾶσίν ἐστι. The words here are not literally the same with those in John iii. 3–5 : ἀναγεννηθῆτε is used instead of γεννηθῇ ἄνωθεν, and βασιλείαν τῶν οὐρανῶν instead of βασ. τοῦ Θεοῦ, and some have concluded from this that Justin made his quotation from another source; Bretschneider, that the author of the Gospel borrowed from the same source as Justin. But these variations are of little moment when we remember that the Fathers seldom quoted Scripture verbatim and word for word. The coincidence is here so great, that both on this ground, and on account of the peculiar character of the

---

[1] *Dial. c. Tryph.* c. ciii. : ἐν γὰρ τοῖς ἀπομνημονεύμασι ἅ φημι ὑπὸ τῶν ἀποστόλων αὐτοῦ καὶ τῶν ἐκείνοις παρακολουθησάντων συντετάχθαι.

[2] Thus CREDNER, *Beitr.* i. 258 ; *Gesch. des N. T. Kanon*, p. 10 ; MAYERHOFF, *Einl. in die Petrin. Schriften*, p. 243 ; SCHWEGLER, *Nachapost. Zeitalter*, i. 216–223 ; and others.

[3] *e.g. c. Tryph.* ciii., cvi. ; and *Apol.* i. 66, see § 119.

whole passage, we need have no hesitation in affirming that Justin quoted from our Gospel. Schwegler with some plausibility refers part of Justin's quotation to Matt. xviii. 3 (which, however, by no means corresponds with it), and part to the *Clementine Homilies*, xi. 26, where the saying is quoted, with some additions indeed, but with the same variations from John. Baur, too, refers to this latter passage in the *Clementines*, and thinks that it is a quotation from the *Gospel of the Hebrews*, or from the *Gospel of Peter*, which is identical with this. Zeller, too, traces it back to the Gospel of the Hebrews. Even if this were the case, the greater probability would still be that the passage had been adopted in this latter work from the Johannine Gospel. But it is most likely that the author of the *Clementines* knew Justin's writings, and quoted the words of the quotation from him. We have other instances of this kind in the *Clementines*, iii. 55, xix. 2, where the command against swearing is given by blending Matt. v. 37 and Jas. v. 12, and in precisely the same words as in Justin, *Apol.* i. 16,[1]—the writer in the *Clementines* probably having Justin before him, and taking the quotation from him. At any rate, the declaration as we have it in John iii. 3–5 has so decidedly a Johannine colouring, and is so obviously in his style, that we can have no hesitation in regarding his Gospel as its original place. Other places in Justin indicate with still greater probability the use of our Gospel on his part.[2] I here mention the reference in *Apol.* i. 52 to Zech. xii. 10, where Justin takes the O. T. reference in a way quite different from the LXX., but closely resembling John xix. 37 : καὶ τότε ὄψονται εἰς ὃν ἐξεκέντησαν (see Semisch, p. 200). The inference from these

---

[1] *Homil. Clem.* xix. 2 : ἔστω ὑμῶν τὸ ναὶ ναί, καὶ τὸ οὒ οὔ· τὸ δὲ περισσὸν τούτων ἐκ τοῦ πονηροῦ ἐστίν. Justin : μὴ ὀμόσητε ὅλως· ἔστω δὲ ... τὸ δὲ περισσὸν τούτων ἐκ τοῦ πονηροῦ.

[2] *Dial c. Tryph.*: Οὐκ εἰμὶ ὁ Χριστός, ἀλλὰ φωνὴ βοῶντος (John i. 20). Ἥξει γὰρ ὁ ἰσχυρότερός μου, οὗ οὐκ εἰμὶ ἱκανὸς τὰ ὑποδήματα βαστάσαι. Also many references to the doctrine of the Logos; *e.g. Apol.* ii. : καὶ υἱὸς καὶ λόγος ἐστίν, ὃς τίνα τρόπον σαρκοποιηθεὶς ἄνθρωπος γέγονεν, ἐν τοῖς ἑξῆς ἐροῦμεν. *Exposit fid.*: Ὁ λόγος σὰρξ γενόμενος τοὺς οὐρανοὺς οὐκ ἔλιπε. See OLSHAUSEN, *Echtheit der Kan. Evv.* 304 ; DE WETTE, § 66, *a* ;

quotations plainly is, that as Justin describes the Ἀπομνημονεύματα as partly written by apostles, he had John in his mind, for one, as the writer of our Gospel. This testimony from Justin Martyr is very valuable, not only on account of the early age in which he lived, but also because of his travels in various districts, and among many Churches. We know from his own testimony, that besides Samaria, his birth-place, he had been at Rome, Alexandria, and Ephesus. He had therefore ample opportunity of learning the judgment of the Churches in many lands concerning the genuineness of our Gospel.

§ 88.

Tatian, the disciple of Justin, is by no means an unimportant witness, both as to his teacher's view and as to the Gospel itself. We find in his *Oratio ad Græcos* unmistakeable proofs (which Baur and Zeller do not venture, like Bretschneider, to deny) that he knew our Gospel.[1] It is amazing that Baur should think it strange that the εἰρημένον in c. xiii. is not distinctly predicated of the Apostle John. This surely was not by any means necessary, if Tatian knew that his readers generally were acquainted with the Gospel in which the words occurred. At any rate, he quotes them as a written authority, as the statement of a sacred and canonical book; and he could not have done so had he not regarded the Gospel in which he found them a genuine and apostolic work. The same acquaintance with and recognition of our Gospel is manifest in Tatian's Harmony of the Four Gospels —his *Diatessaron*. According to ancient testimony, Tatian wrote a εὐαγγέλιον διὰ τεσσάρων, which Eusebius (*H. E.* iv.

BINDEMANN, *Theol. Stud. u. Krit.* 1842, 478–482; SEMISCH, *Die apost. Denkwürdigkeiten des Märt. Justinus*, 1848, 155–205; LUTHARDT, in the *Zeitschr. f. Protest. u. Kirche*, 1856. See, on the opposite side, HILGENFELD, *Krit. Untersuchungen über die Evv. Justins*, Halle 1850; VOLKMAR, *Ueber Justin den Märt. u. sein Verhältniss zu unsern Evv.*, Zurich 1853.

[1] See c. xiii.: καὶ τοῦτό ἐστιν ἄρα τὸ εἰρημένον· ἡ σκοτία τὸ φῶς οὐ καταλαμβάνει (John i. 5). C. xix.: πάντα ὑπ' αὐτοῦ, καὶ χωρὶς αὐτοῦ γέγονεν οὐδὲ ἕν. C. v.: Θεὸς ἦν ἐν ἀρχῇ. Ib.: ὁ λόγος ἐν ἀρχῇ γεννηθείς.

29) calls συνάφειάν τινα καὶ συναγωγὴν τῶν εὐαγγελίων—a connected harmony of the Gospels. Eusebius intimates that it was widely used, even by the members of the catholic Church. It is evident from Theodoret (*Hæret. fab.* i. 20) that it was still widely known down to the beginning of the fifth century; for he says that he had found more than 200 copies of it among the Churches, but that they had been laid aside and our four Gospels used in their stead. Credner (*Beitr.* i. 437) and others are certainly wrong in supposing this *Diatessaron* to have been a distinct and independent Gospel. Upon this supposition the very title would be unmeaning,—a title which expressly intimates that the work was, as Eusebius says, a harmony of the four Gospels. As they were four in number, and must have been four which were highly esteemed in the Church, the fair and most probable inference is that they were our four canonical Gospels. Now there is a work of this kind still extant in Latin and in an old German version. This, which begins with the first verses of St. John's Gospel, is not certainly, judging by its construction, the genuine work of Tatian, though Tatian's work may have been used in its compilation: it is not perhaps even a translation from the Greek, but may have been written originally in Latin. But that St. John's Gospel must have formed one element in Tatian's work, may be inferred beyond doubt from the use which he makes of this Gospel in his *Oratio*. There was, moreover, a Syriac translation of the *Harmony*, which, as a later Syrian writer, Bar Salibi, informs us, began with the words, " In the beginning was the Word " (John i. 1). This Syriac translation must have been made at a comparatively early date; for Ephraem Syrus (*ob.* 378), who was not master of Greek, wrote a commentary on Tatian's *Diatessaron*, as the Syrian writer tells us.[1]

Contemporary with Tatian was THEOPHILUS, bishop of Antioch, from the year 169. He wrote (as Jerome informs

[1] See DANIEL, *Tatianus der Apologet.*, Halle 1837, pp. 87-111; and especially the careful inquiry of SEMISCH, *Tatiani Diatessaron, antiquissimum N. T. evangeliorum in unum digestorum specimen*, Breslau 1856.

us¹) a commentary upon the Gospels, in which he went through them synoptically, having before apparently written a Harmony of the four evangelists. Jerome takes it for granted that these four were our four Gospels, and we are warranted in supposing that Jerome himself knew the work. It certainly cannot be doubted that St. John's Gospel was included in it; because Theophilus, in his work which has come down to us, *ad Autolycum*, ii. 22, expressly says that this Gospel was part of Holy Scripture, and names John as a writer moved by the Holy Ghost.² Now this fact, namely, that soon after the middle of the second century more than one Christian scholar undertook the task of treating our four Gospels synoptically and in a Harmony, shows that these Gospels must already have been held in high repute in the Church, as distinguished from and above other writings of a similar kind; and the fourth Gospel in particular could not thus have been esteemed, if it had not already been recognised by the Church for a considerable time as a genuine and apostolic work.³

The heathen philosopher CELSUS, who lived in the latter half of the second century, is not an unimportant witness. Origen, in his *contra Celsum*, has preserved some fragments of his polemic against Christianity: ὁ λόγος ἀληθής. It is evident that his attack was mainly directed against the Gospels, and more than one passage leads us to infer that St. John's Gospel was one of the books assailed. Looking at any one passage by itself, this inference may be doubtful;

---

¹ *De viris ill.* xxv., and *Ep.* 151 *ad Algasiam: Theophilus . . . qui quatuor evangelistarum in unum opus dicta compingens ingenii sui nobis monumenta reliquit, hæc super hac parabola* (of the unjust steward) *in suis commentariis est locutus.*

² Ὅθεν διδάσκουσιν ἡμᾶς αἱ ἅγιαι γραφαὶ καὶ πάντες οἱ πνευματοφόροι, ἐξ ὧν Ἰωάννης λέγει· ἐν ἀρχῇ, κ.τ.λ.

³ MELITO of Sardis cannot be adduced as a witness, because the Latin translation of his Κλείς (published by PITRA, *Spicilegium Solesmense*, vols. ii. and iii., Paris 1855), which contains quotations from John xv. 5, vi. 54, xii. 24, is not genuine. See STEITZ, *Theol. Stud. u. Krit.* 1857, p. 584.

but taking all together, an unbiassed contemplation will leave no doubt that he had this Gospel in his mind. The inference is, of course, that this Gospel must have been widely circulated and generally held in esteem.[1]

§ 89.

We need not be surprised at finding no quotations from St. John's Gospel in the apostolic Fathers; for they do not usually make any quotations from the Gospels, though they certainly must have known them. There are indeed some passages which seem indirectly to refer to sayings in our Gospel, but we cannot affirm this with certainty. In the Ignatian Epistles, too, there are some very probable reminiscences;[2] but I do not attach any weight to them, because the genuineness and integrity of these Ignatian Epistles in the later editions is very questionable. There is an Epistle of Polycarp to the Philippians—the genuineness of which there is no reason, with Schwegler, Zeller, and others, to question, for Irenæus knew it[3]—which does not directly quote our Gospel. Still, it by no means follows from the tenor of the letter, which is short, that the Gospel was unknown to Polycarp. We may grant (as Lützelberger urges) that Irenæus never heard Polycarp speak of this work of the Apostle John's, and that he had no evidence that Polycarp had used it. But this amounts to nothing; for Irenæus knew nothing of Polycarp's writings beyond this one Epistle to the Philippians; and though in his youth he had often seen and heard Polycarp, he never seems to have had any close intercourse with him. It is not irrelevant to our design, however, to observe that in the Epistle of Polycarp, written probably in the beginning of the second century, among many references to N. T. epistles, there is an unmistakeable

---

[1] See OLSHAUSEN, *Echtheit der Kan. Evv.* pp. 349-355; LÜCKE, *Commentar*, 3d ed. i. 68.

[2] *e.g. ad Rom.* vii. (in the Syriac version also), cf. John vi. 32, 33, 51-53; *ad Philad.* vii., cf. John iii. 8; *ad Philad.* ix., cf. John x. 7, 9.

[3] *Adv. Hær.* iii. 3, and *ad Florinum* in EUSEB. *H. E.* v. 20.

one to 1 John iv. 3.¹ Eusebius,² too, says of Papias—and there is no reason why we should doubt—that he quoted as authorities 1st Peter and 1st John. Now Weisse, Schwegler, Baur, Hilgenfeld, Zeller, and Strauss unanimously question whether the first Epistle of John and our Gospel are by the same author; but of this there can be no doubt, as even the impugners of the Gospel generally allow (see § 223). These testimonies for the Epistle may accordingly be viewed as testimonies indirectly for the Gospel. Zeller indeed urges the silence of Papias with reference to St. John, and there were perhaps no express allusions in his writings thereto, like those to Matthew and Mark; for had there been any, Eusebius would probably have noticed it. But we know not in what connection Papias speaks of Matthew and Mark, and we cannot say whether there was any occasion at the same time to mention the Apostle John's Gospel.

Even in the N. T. itself we find indications of an acquaintance with our Gospel. It is very probable (*a*) that 2 Pet. i. 14 refers to the words of Christ in John xxi. 18, so that the writer of that epistle seems to have known our Gospel and its appendix, and to take for granted that his readers knew it; and (*b*) that Mark, in writing his Gospel, made use of St. John's here and there (§ 111). Still, as this is a disputed point, we do not attach any importance to it, because, as we have already shown, there is abundant evidence in the history of the Church during the first two centuries to show how utterly impossible, as well as untenable, is the notion that the fourth Gospel was not composed till after the middle of the second century: there is much, very much, in that history which is quite inexplicable upon the assumption of its spuriousness. My conviction at least is, that an unpre-

---

[1] Πᾶς γὰρ, ὃς ἂν μὴ ὁμολογῇ Ἰησοῦν Χριστὸν ἐν σαρκὶ ἐληλυθέναι, ἀντίχριστός ἐστιν. It is utterly futile and unreasonable to say, as BRETSCHNEIDER and LÜTZELBERGER suggest, that the author of 1st John made use of Polycarp; or, as Baur conjectures, that it was an anonymous saying current in the Church which both writers adopted.

[2] *H. E.* iii. 39 : Κέχρηται δ' ὁ αὐτὸς μαρτυρίαις ἀπὸ τῆς Ἰωάννου προτέρας ἐπιστολῆς, καὶ τῆς Πέτρου ὁμοίως.

judiced consideration of the external testimonies leads to the certain conclusion that our fourth Gospel was recognised as a trustworthy authority, and a genuine work, in the various Churches of Christendom before the middle of the second century.

It must, as we have seen, have existed and been known in the Church (a) before the Easter controversies; (b) before the appearance of the Valentinian Gnosis in Egypt and elsewhere; (c) before the rise of Montanism in Asia Minor; (d) before the time of Marcion himself. The position which the contending parties in all these controversies allowed to our Gospel, can be historically explained only upon the supposition that it was known and recognised as genuine in the Church at large some decades of years before the middle of the second century, if not from the very beginning of it; and this fact, in turn, can only be explained upon the supposition that it is a genuine and apostolic work. Our investigation has confirmed us in the stedfast conviction, which is unavoidably urged upon us ever and anon from different considerations, that this fourth Gospel is really the work of St. John, the trusted and beloved disciple of the Lord. Whatever, then, be difficult and strange in the history of this Gospel in the Church, in its contents or in its exposition, is only of such a nature as to become tenfold more difficult and more strange upon the supposition of a later and non-apostolic authorship.

§ 90.

We may therefore briefly examine and dismiss the view of Schweizer named in § 62. He thinks that not only the last chapter, but several sections in the course of the work, have been added by a later reviser; those parts even which have external evidence wholly in their favour, proving that the Church at large never knew the Gospel without them. This opinion, though advocated with great acuteness and nicety by Schweizer, is far more difficult and improbable than the corresponding belief with reference to the last chapter only. Supposing that John ended his Gospel with ch. xx., entrusting it during his lifetime to the circle of his disciples and friends, we can easily understand that after his death, when about to be circulated in the Church at large, one of his disciples may have added ch. xxi., so easily separated from the rest of the work, as clearly and without disguise distinguishing himself (ver. 24) from the writer of the Gospel.

But it is very difficult to conceive how any disciple could have ventured to make interpolations in the body of the work, without any intimation that these portions were not by the apostle, whom he nevertheless expressly names (xxi. 24) as the writer of the Gospel, "whose witness is true." Schweizer's theory implies too great artfulness on the part of this reviser: he must not only have interpolated his additions in the original apostolic work, but incorporated and blended them with it so closely, that at the end of his revision he could venture to describe it as the work of a disciple worthy of full trust. See also De Wette, § 110, 111.

Still more decisively do our investigations tell against the views of Weisse, Schenkel (*Stud. u. Krit.*, 1840), and others, who allow to the Apostle John a few materials only for this Gospel, *e.g.* the discourses given, attributing the historical narrative in which these discourses occur to a different hand. This theory virtually involves the spuriousness of the entire Gospel, because the historical narrative in particular claims to be that of St. John, rests upon his testimony, and presents itself to us as the most exact and correct account, even where it seems to differ from the Synoptics.

ORIGIN OF THE SYNOPTIC GOSPELS.

§ 91.

From all the considerations, cumulatively viewed, which we have now advanced, it is, I think, fully proved that the fourth Gospel was certainly the work of the Apostle John. And if this be so, we must not scruple to assert, what is clear from the contemplation of the Gospel itself, and from the comparison instituted between it and the Synoptics, that it presents a true and historical account of the Lord's life,—an account exactly corresponding with the course of events. When, therefore, we would draw up a consecutive and chronological exposition of our Lord's history during His public ministry, we cannot hesitate to make St. John's Gospel the basis of our plan, even in those points wherein there is a seeming discrepancy between it and the Synoptics, and though the Synoptics all three coincide in their narration. The question, however, arises: How comes it to pass that the three first evangelists present such variations and divergencies from St. John, and that they all three agree with one another in these variations, and so closely resemble each other both in the general history and in many particulars?

The affinity subsisting between the first three evangelists has been a topic of much inquiry and controversy since the beginning of the present century;[1] but too little attention has been paid to the relation in which all three stand to St. John's Gospel. Many have supposed that the Synoptics, independently of each other, alike availed themselves of that oral tradition only which had gradually grown up in the Church. This is called the *Tradition* hypothesis. It was advanced by Eckermann, Herder, and Paulus, and most acutely and zealously developed and supported by GIESELER.[2] His opinion is, that without any preconcerted plan, a normal or pattern form of the gospel history formed itself very early among the apostles at Jerusalem,—an oral Syro-Chaldaic Gospel, defined in its contents and its extent, in its arrangement and narration of particulars; and that an oral Greek Gospel was also formed after the same pattern. From these two Gospels, handed down by word of mouth, our first three Gospels were composed, about the middle of the first century. Gieseler, by his able advocacy of this

---

[1] [See the history given of the criticism of the Synoptics in HOLTZMANN, *Die synopt. Evv. ihr Ursprung u. geschichtl. Charakter*, Leipz. 1863, pp. 15–43; HILGENFELD, *Zeitschr. f. wiss. Theol.* 1861.]

[2] GIESELER, *ob.* 1854; *Hist.-krit. Versuch über die Entstehung und die frühesten Schicksale der schriftl. Evv.*, in Keil u. Tzschirner's *Analekten*, vol. iii. 1; separately published and enlarged, Leipz. 1818.

theory, has won for it very wide acceptance; and it has been cleverly espoused by Ebrard, Credner, Neudecker, Guericke, and others.

It is indeed the fact, that oral tradition was the first, and for some time the only, or at least the chief, means of diffusing the gospel history, and that it formed the groundwork of the written Gospels. But this reference solely to oral tradition is not of itself sufficient to explain the relation subsisting between the first three evangelists, and between them and St. John. It furnishes no explanation of the fact that the Synoptics all three, or sometimes two of them, in so many places verbally agree in the expressions they use and the plan they adopt, both in their records of Christ's discourses and in their own narrations. To account for these coincidences on this principle, we should have to suppose a preconcerted arrangement, among those disciples at least who adopted and maintained this sameness of expression in the Greek account, mechanically to learn the traditional Gospel by heart, and to repeat it memoriter word for word; and this even Gieseler himself admits to be quite unnatural. This difficulty is specially apparent in the verbal coincidence and identity of the quotations given from the O. T. (see § 69),—a coincidence traceable even in cases where these quotations verbally differ both from the Hebrew text, and from the Septuagint, which is usually the basis of them. We can explain these coincidences only upon the supposition that the narratives and discourses in which they occur had already been committed to writing, and this in Greek, either by one of the Synoptics or by another writer, and that the form thus given them was followed and retained by the subsequent writers.

This reference to oral tradition further fails to explain the *cycle* or range of events which all three narratives embrace. Had this range of events been defined only by oral tradition, it must have been done solely by the apostles at Jerusalem. But on this supposition, the omission of any notice of Christ's earlier visits to Jerusalem, and of the time and occasion of these visits, would be quite inexplicable: we could not conceive how three evangelists, writing independently of each other, could have all alike omitted this important cycle of events in our Lord's life. Nor could we explain how it is that they alike repeat in the same order the same events and particulars, all alike referring in a merely summary way to other series of occurrences at certain periods of the history. Above all, it would be utterly inexplicable how three different evangelists could all agree in giving an inaccurate account (see § 71, 72), viz. in representing that Jesus spent all His public life down to the last passover in Galilee, that He went direct from Galilee to this feast, and that He was crucified on the 15th of Nisan. We cannot suppose that these inaccuracies had a common origin in an oral tradition defined and established by the APOSTLES.

§ 92.

These phenomena are far more easily explained upon the supposition of *some one earlier connected work written in Greek* upon the life of our Lord, which, though not composed by an apostle, was widely read, and became a sort of pattern or basis for subsequent evangelists, both as to the range or cycle of events noticed, and the manner of combining them into an historical whole. This is the supposition adopted by most critics who have studied the subject, though they differ from each other in details. The question arises, whether this primitive document or *primary Gospel* was one of the Synoptics, or another and different work which has not come down to us. The former hypothesis [called in German *de Benutzungshypothese*] used to be the ordinary one; and (according to the order of the books in the Canon) Matthew was regarded as this primary Gospel. Mark was said to have made use of Matthew, and Luke to have made use of Matthew and Mark. HUG advocates this view with great acuteness; but in order consistently to carry it out, he held that Luke originally contained the sections which occur in Matthew and Mark, between the miraculous feeding of the 5000 and the miraculous feeding of the 4000 (Matt. xiv. 22-xv. 39; Mark vi. 45-viii. 10),—these being left out through a mistake of some copyist, arising from the ὁμοιοτέλευτον of the passages. Hug further maintains, notwithstanding the tradition of the Church, that Matthew originally wrote in Greek; others, however, adopting the same theory, hold that he wrote in Aramæan, and in various ways endeavour to explain the verbal coincidence between our Greek Matthew and the two other Synoptics. (See Bertholdt, § 308; iii. 1117 sqq.)

Other theories have been suggested concerning the chronological relation of the Synoptics to each other. Matthew is put first, Luke next, and Mark third as making use of the two former, or either Mark or Luke is regarded as the primary Gospel. The opinion that Mark's Gospel was the first of the three has been strongly advocated of late. (See § 93.)

Others, again, have attributed the first written basis of our synoptical Gospels to one or more earlier writings; and this view has been maintained with various modifications. Some have supposed that several small independent documents formed the original basis, and this was the view espoused by many earlier critics (see De Wette, § 86). Schleiermacher, too,[1] supposes that Luke's Gospel is based upon a series of small Gospel fragments, written independently of each other, and recording distinct portions of gospel history—fragments which were collected and arranged by the evangelist himself. As the basis of our first Gospel, he supposed an Aramæan collection of the sayings of the Apostle Matthew (see § 40); and as the basis of our second Gospel, an original work of Mark's, mentioned by Papias, and different from our Mark. But these conjectures by no means explain the resemblance and kinship subsisting between the three Synoptics, and their harmony in comparison with St. John.

But in early times, and especially since the last decade of the eighteenth century, *an original document, written in Aramæan*, has been supposed to have formed the common

[1] *Ueber die Schriften des Lukas, ein krit. Versuch*, Berlin 1817; also in his *Theol. Werke*, ii. 1–220.

basis of our Synoptics. This original document is supposed to have been either the Aramæan original of our Matthew, or the Gospel of the Hebrews (see De Wette, § 84, *a*), or a smaller Aramæan work composed according to agreement by the apostles collectively, or as a private work by some unknown writer; and our Synoptics are supposed to have been derived therefrom through various media, such as translations or revisions: what is common to all three, or distinctive of each, indicating, on the one hand, the contents of the original document; and, on the other, the characteristics of the media through which it had passed. Very persevering and painstaking labour has been bestowed upon this hypothesis.[1] But one refrains from thus endeavouring minutely to explain the construction of our Gospels from such an original document, seeing that there must necessarily be a great deal of mere conjecture in the matter. Most critics have contented themselves with a merely general account of the process. SCHWEGLER, for example, like the Baur school generally, regards "the Gospel of the Hebrews" as the primary document, and takes this as the basis of our three Synoptics (*Nachapost. Zeitalter*, i. 199–216). The untenableness of this view is evident from what has already been advanced in § 44. EWALD[2] also has endeavoured to explain the growth of gospel history from its first beginnings down to the composition of our Synoptics; but he does this more by self-confident assertion than by satisfactory evidence. He arranges the written history in the following order: 1*st*, The *earliest Gospel*, containing brief accounts of the main events of the life of Jesus, from His baptism downwards,—a work written in Greek, used by St. Paul, and perhaps written by Philip the deacon. 2*d*, The *Apostle Matthew's collection of*

---

[1] (*a*) By EICHHORN, *Ueber die drei ersten Evv.*, in his *Allg. Biblioth. d. bibl. Litter.* vol. v. 5 (1794), and more elaborately in his *Einl. i. N. T.*; see DE WETTE, § 84, *b* and *d*. (*b*) MARSH, in his notes to Michaelis' *Einl.*; see DE WETTE, § 84, *c*. GRATZ, *die Entsteh. der 3 ersten Evv.*, Tüb. 1812.

[2] *Jahrbb. d. bibl. Wissensch.* ii. 180–224. In the preface to his *Gesch. Christus u. seiner Zeit*, he supposes that an original Gospel preceded our Mark, which was afterwards blended with Nos. 1 and 2 into its present form.

the Lord's discourses, spoken of by Papias. 3*d*, *St. Mark's Gospel*, in the composition of which Nos. 1 and 2 were used, and which was from the first very much the same as we still have it, though it probably had at first a few concluding sections now wanting, the present conclusion (ch. xvi. 9-20) being a subsequent addition, and also ch. i. 2, 3. 4*th*, *The book of the higher history*, akin to No. 1, and enlarging the narratives briefly recorded there. 5*th*, *Our Gospel of St. Matthew*, written in Greek, and based upon Nos. 1-4, especially upon 2 and 3. 6*th*, 7*th*, and 8*th*, *Three other lost works*, the first of which was distinguished for its beauty of detail, the second for its thoroughness and accuracy of representation, and the third as being an Aramæan work. 9*th*, *Our Gospel of St. Luke*, based upon all the others excepting No. 5, and especially upon St. Mark. Ewald has noticed the fact that Luke, between ch. ix. 17 and ver. 18, has omitted the long section given in Mark vi. 45–viii. 27; but he has not explained this omission. In his work *Die drei ersten Evv. übers. u. erkl.*, Gött. 1850, he endeavours in his translation to trace the various sources of each Gospel. [Since the hypothesis that Mark was the first of the three Synoptics has become popular, several have endeavoured to trace back our Synoptics to two primary documents, which themselves are supposed to have arisen partly from written sources and partly from oral tradition; viz. 1*st*, the Gospel of Mark named by Papias (see § 48), either a different Gospel from our Mark or the same; and 2*d*, the collection of λόγια made by St. Matthew, and also spoken of by Papias. Our present Matthew is thus supposed to have been compiled from the original Mark and St. Matthew's collection of λόγια. This is substantially the view taken by WEISSE, MEYER, REUSS (*Gesch. des N. T.*, and in the *Revue de Théologie*, vols. x.-xii., *Nouvelle revue*, vol. ii.), TOBLER (see § 63), WEISS (*Stud. u. Krit.* 1861, pp. 29-100, 646-713), REVILLE (*Études critiques sur l'évangile selon St. Matthieu*, Leyden 1862), HOLTZMANN, WEIZSAECKER, and others. These two main sources are also prominent in Ewald's theory. The first of them is taken as the basis of Matthew and Luke, and indeed of Mark itself, so far as our Mark is regarded as distinct from it. Ewald, Meyer, and Weiss consider the second (*i.e.* St. Matthew's collection) to have formed the basis of all three Synoptics. Reuss takes it to have been the groundwork of Matthew only, and Holtzmann of Matthew and Luke only.]

§ 93.

In order to solve this question, and to discover how far the affinity between the first three Gospels is to be explained by their having a common origin, let us first consider *St. Mark's Gospel in its relation to the other two.* It is evident that the relation in which Mark stands to Matthew and Luke, is different from the relation in which these two stand to one another, and that *either Mark is dependent upon them, or they are dependent upon Mark* (see § 112). There are indeed other views, *e.g.* that of HILGENFELD,[1] who places Mark between Matthew and Luke. But most scholars who trace a relationship between the several works of our evangelists, espouse one or other of the alternative theories which I have named, regarding Mark either as the earliest of our evangelists, or as the latest of all. Among those who regard Mark as the latest, may be named CLEMENS ALEX. (in Euseb. vi. 14), who gives it as a tradition of the earlier presbyters. Hence the inference was easy, that Mark made use of Matthew and Luke. This was OWEN's view (*Observations on the Four Gospels,* London 1764); also that of GRIESBACH (*Commentat. Theol.* i. 360-434); of PAULUS, H. SAUNIER (*ob.* 1825, *Die Quellen des Ev. des Marcus,* Berl. 1825); of DE WETTE, [and of ANGER, *Ratio qua loci V. T. in ev. Matth. laudantur, quid valeat ad illustrandam hujus evangelii originem, quæritur,* Leipz. 1861, 1862]. This also is the theory espoused by most theologians of Baur's school, by STRAUSS,

---

[1] *Das Marcus-Ev. nach seiner Compos.,* etc., 1850 [*Der Kanon u. die Kritik des N. T.,* and elsewhere. According to HILGENFELD, the apostolic germ of the first Gospel was the beginning of gospel history; and this germ was a strongly Judaizing treatise, which received a universalistic colouring in our Matthew].

Schwegler, Zeller, and Baur himself (*Kanon. Ev.* pp. 539-561); [also in Keim's treatise, *Der geschichtl. Christus*, Zurich 1865]. The opposite opinion, that Mark is the earliest of our evangelists, was espoused by Storr;[1] but it did not at the time find much acceptance. It has, however, been very earnestly advocated by Wilke (*Der Urevangelist*, etc.); but in support of his view he has to take many parts of Mark as interpolations (see De Wette, § 82, *c*),—those parts even which clearly belonged originally to Mark only. Bruno Bauer agrees with Wilke (*Krit. d. ev. Gesch. d. Synoptiker*, 1841).[2]

§ 94.

Ever since I began to lecture upon the subject in 1822,[3] I have adopted the view *which places Mark after the two other Synoptics*. The considerations which lead me unhesitatingly to this conclusion, are based, 1*st*, upon a comparison of parallel passages and longer paragraphs, which Mark has in common with Matthew and Luke; and 2*d*, upon the contents of the Gospel in general, and the relation of the discourses given to the facts recorded; and in particular, the selection, order, and connection of the several sections.

[1] *Ueber d. Zweck d. ev. Gesch. u. d. Briefe Joh.*, Tüb. 1786, pp. 274-295; *De fonte Evv. Matth. et Luc.*, Tüb. 1794; reprinted in Velthusen, etc., *Commentatt.* iii. 140 sqq.

[2] [Bruno Bauer, however, regards Mark as a creative evangelist, who himself invented the gospel history.] Many other scholars have advocated the priority of Mark; viz. Lachmann, *Stud. u. Krit.* 1835; Weisse, *Evang. Gesch.*, and *Die Ev.-Frage in ihrem gegenwärtigen Stadium*, Leipz. 1856; Hitzig, *Ueber Joh. Marcus u. seine Schriften*, Zur. 1843, pp. 37-62; Ewald; Ritschl, *Theol. Jahrbb.* 1851; Reuss; Thiersch, *Apost. Zeitalter*, p. 101; Meyer, *Comm. z. den Evv.*, ed. 3; in the first edition he adopted Griesbach's view. [Also Plitt, *De compositione Evv. synopticorum*, Bonn 1860; Weiss, Holtzmann, Schenkel, Weizsaecker, and others. Weiss and Holtzmann, however, admit the secondary character of some portions of Mark as compared with Matthew and Luke; and they variously explain this: see § 92, 112.]

[3] See my *Beitr. z. Ev. Krit.* pp. 72-75, and my *Synoptische Erklärung der drei ersten Evv.*, republished by Holtzmann, 2 vols., Leipz. 1862. De Wette, in his fourth edition, adopts the same view, and vindicates it

As to the first, the comparison of parallel passages, we cannot affirm that the matter is so clear and obvious, as not for a moment to admit of a doubt as to the priority of Matthew and Luke. But I affirm that no instance occurs here which obliges us to regard Mark's Gospel as the primary one; while not a few oblige us to regard it as the latest. This is very manifest in those passages which all three evangelists have in common, where Mark blends, in a manner peculiar to himself, what Matthew and Luke respectively say. Take, for instance, Mark i. 32–34, as compared with Matt. viii. 16 and Luke iv. 40.

MATTHEW.	LUKE.	MARK.
Ὀψίας δὲ γενομένης	Δύνοντος δὲ τοῦ ἡλίου,	32. Ὀψίας δὲ γενομένης, ὅτε ἔδυ ὁ ἥλιος, ἔφερον πρὸς αὐτὸν πάντας τοὺς κακῶς ἔχοντας, καὶ τοὺς δαιμονιζομένους.
Προσήνεγκαν αὐτῷ δαιμονιζομένους πολλούς·	Πάντες ὅσοι εἶχον ἀσθενοῦντας νόσοις ποικίλαις, ἤγαγον αὐτοὺς πρὸς αὐτόν·	
Καὶ ἐξέβαλε τὰ πνεύματα λόγῳ, καὶ πάντας τοὺς κακῶς ἔχοντας ἐθεράπευσεν.	Ὁ δὲ . . . . . ἐθεράπευσεν αὐτούς.	34. Καὶ ἐθεράπευσε πολλοὺς κακῶς ἔχοντας ποικίλαις νόσοις· καὶ δαιμόνια πολλὰ ἐξέβαλε.

against WILKE. ["Instead of St. Mark's narrative being an abridgment of that of St. Matthew or of St. Luke, it is often much fuller. Particulars are introduced, which an abridger, aiming at condensation, would have been certain to prune away, if he had found them in his authority; while the freshness and graphic power of the history, the lifelike touches, which almost put us on the stage with the actors, and his superior accuracy as regards persons, words, times, and places, prove the originality and independence of his work."—Article on Mark by E. VENABLES, in KITTO's *Biblical Cyclop*. These words sum up the more modern views, to which BLEEK's is opposed. BLEEK's argument is founded upon his alternative, that "either Mark is dependent on Matthew and Luke, or they are dependent upon him." And were this the only alternative, BLEEK's view would perhaps be the more probable. But it is now more generally thought that a *via media* is possible, and indeed by far the most probable, viz. the supposition of one primary document, which all three Synoptics made use of in those parts wherein all three coincide. See § 112, by F. BLEEK, junior.—TR.]

Here Mark evidently agrees partly with Matthew and partly with Luke; and his words are incorporated from theirs. This appears most obviously in the first clause, which states the time when the miracles were wrought. If Mark's were the original and primary statement, the inference would be, that Matthew and Luke divided his words between them, Matthew appropriating one portion, and Luke the other. But it is improbable that an independent writer would have used two such expressions side by side to designate the eventide, had he not been led thereto by finding them elsewhere. The likelihood clearly is, that Mark has here blended the expressions of the two other evangelists. The same remark applies to the following clauses. It appears from Matthew's and Luke's account conjoined, that Jesus both cast out devils and healed other sicknesses. In relating this, Matthew names only " many possessed with devils," and Luke " the sick with divers diseases;" Mark blends both in the stronger words, πάντας τοὺς κακῶς ἔχοντας, καὶ τοὺς δαιμονιζομένους. The probability clearly is, that Mark had the two accounts before him, and that when he wrote the words πάντας τοὺς κακῶς ἔχοντας he had before him the following clause in Matthew, where the phrase more naturally occurs: πάντας τοὺς κακῶς ἔχοντας ἐθεράπευσεν, i.e. *all who were brought to Him.*

So also in the cleansing of the leper, Matt. viii. 2, 3, Luke v. 12, 13, Mark i. 40. All three state the leper's request, and the reply of Jesus, how He stretched forth His hand and touched him, in almost the same words; and then Matthew adds, καὶ εὐθέως ἐκαθαρίσθη αὐτοῦ ἡ λέπρα; Luke adds, καὶ εὐθέως ἡ λέπρα ἀπῆλθεν ἀπ' αὐτοῦ; and Mark writes, καὶ εὐθέως ἀπῆλθεν ἀπ' αὐτοῦ ἡ λέπρα καὶ ἐκαθαρίσθη. In the parable of the sower, Matt. xiii. 19, Luke viii. 12, and Mark iv. 15, we have another example. In Matthew we read, The wicked one cometh, καὶ ἁρπάζει τὸ ἐσπαρμένον ἐν τῇ καρδίᾳ αὐτοῦ; in Luke, The devil cometh, καὶ αἴρει τὸν λόγον ἀπὸ τῆς καρδίας αὐτῶν; in Mark, Satan cometh, καὶ αἴρει τὸν λόγον τὸν ἐσπαρμένον ἐν ταῖς καρδίαις αὐτῶν.

At the beginning of the account of Christ's entrance into Jerusalem we read:

LUKE XIX. 29.	MATTHEW XXI. 1.	MARK XI. 1.
Καὶ ἐγένετο ὡς ἤγγισεν εἰς Βηθφαγῆ καὶ Βηθανίαν, πρὸς τὸ ὄρος τὸ καλούμενον ἐλαιῶν, κ.τ.λ.	Καὶ ὅτε ἤγγισαν εἰς Ἱεροσόλυμα, καὶ ἦλθον εἰς Βηθφαγῆ πρὸς τὸ ὄρος τῶν ἐλαιῶν, κ.τ.λ.	Καὶ ὅτε ἐγγίζουσιν εἰς Ἱερουσαλήμ, εἰς Βηθφαγὴ καὶ Βηθανίαν πρὸς τὸ ὄρος τῶν ἐλαιῶν, κ.τ.λ.

Here Mark's words, ἐγγίζουσιν εἰς Ἱερουσαλὴμ εἰς Βηθφαγὴ καὶ Βηθανίαν, which in themselves are neither natural nor clear, are best explained by supposing that he had before him the two other evangelists, and endeavoured to blend their words. The reverse supposition, that they had Mark's words before them, is inadmissible here.

The question which the Jews put to Christ in Mark xii. 14 is in its first sentence (διδάσκαλε, οἴδαμεν ὅτι ἀληθής εἰ καὶ οὐ μέλει σοι περὶ οὐδενός. οὐ γὰρ βλέπεις εἰς πρόσωπον ἀνθρ.) word for word identical with Matt. xxii. 16, the two latter clauses being transposed only; and what follows, ἀλλ' ἐπ' ἀληθείας τὴν ὁδὸν τοῦ Θεοῦ διδάσκεις, corresponds verbatim with Luke xx. 21 (Matthew between the first and second clauses has καὶ τὴν ὁδὸν τοῦ Θεοῦ ἐν ἀληθείᾳ διδάσκεις). Here also Mark's dependence upon Matthew and Luke is beyond comparison more probable than their dependence on him. The same dependence appears in other places; see those cited in DE WETTE, § 80, note *b*, to which many more examples might be added. Though all these passages may not be equally satisfactory, the opposite hypothesis is not more probable in any one of them; and we are therefore justified in taking the more doubtful passage in the same manner as those which clearly leave no room for doubt, and in so taking those passages also which Mark has in common with only one of the other two,—those, *e.g.*, cited in De Wette, § 79, *b*,[1] and others, where a verbal coincidence is traceable; those wherein the priority of Matthew and Luke is probable, and those which in themselves are doubtful.

---

[1] Ch. vii. 6, 7; Matt. xv. 8, 9. Ch. xiii. 20; Matt. xxiv. 22. Ch. xiv. 48; Matt. xxvi. 55. Ch. vi. 41; Luke ix. 16. Ch. xv. 15; Luke xxii. 12.

§ 95.

The same inference may be drawn from the narrations which Mark has in common with Matthew only, with Luke only, or with both. The course of the narrative as a whole, the prominence given to certain parts, and the method of exposition, show, when we contemplate them, and in spite of many exceptions, the dependence of the one Gospel upon the others. When all three evangelists give the same narrative, the resemblance between Matthew and Luke is less striking than that between Mark and either of the other two. In the general outlines of his narrative Mark agrees chiefly with Matthew, and in certain particular touches he coincides strikingly with Luke. This is best explained by supposing that Mark had both Matthew and Luke before him, and used them both. That this is so, can be proved in several instances; for example, in the account of the baptism of Jesus, Mark i. 9–11, Matt. iii. 13–17, Luke iii. 21, 22, especially in what is stated concerning the descent of the Holy Ghost on Jesus. Mark says, that when Jesus came up out of the water, He Himself saw the heavens opened, and the Holy Ghost descending upon Him. But it is not natural that Jesus should thus be described as the spectator, and not the Baptist, who beheld it. In Luke the occurrence simply is named, and no beholder is mentioned. In Matthew's account it is doubtful whether the pronoun αὐτῷ refers to Jesus or to the Baptist: the probability is, that it (as well as the verb εἶδε) refers to the Baptist; for the voice from heaven is not, as in Luke, addressed to Christ, but to others—to the Baptist in the first instance, Jesus being spoken of in the third person, οὗτός ἐστιν . . ., ἐν ᾧ εὐδόκησα; Luke has it, σὺ εἶ . . ., ἐν σοὶ εὐδόκησα. The fact that the Baptist was really the witness of this heavenly sign is confirmed by the account given in John i. 32–34, which harmonizes with that of Matthew. Now Mark's account is evidently in the first instance derived from Matthew, for he took the εἶδε and the preceding αὐτῷ to refer to Jesus. He therefore represents the voice from heaven (ver. 11) as addressed to Jesus, giving the words just as Luke does, σὺ εἶ . . . ἐν σοὶ (thus Lachmann and others read, instead of the received text ἐν ᾧ) εὐδόκησα. Mark doubtless took these last words from Luke; and as, according thereto, Jesus was the person addressed by the voice, he thought that Jesus must also have been the witness of the sight, and that Matthew's account was not altogether accurate.

An example of another kind occurs in the account of the temptation.[1] Both Matthew and Luke give a full and detailed account; the historical circumstances having clearly a moral bearing. But Mark has only a very brief notice of the event (i. 12, 13), saying that "the Spirit driveth Him into the wilderness, and He was there forty days tempted of Satan, and was with the wild beasts, and angels came and ministered to Him." He does not tell what the several temptations were, nor how Jesus withstood them. Now it seems to me quite inconceivable (as nevertheless Weisse, Ewald, Meyer, and Schenkel think) to regard Mark's account as the original, from which the others have been borrowed and enlarged. In my judgment, the original account is that given by Matthew especially, and by Luke; and Mark's is simply a brief summary derived therefrom, and wholly inexplicable without the fuller narrative. We have a similar instance in Mark xvi. 12, 13, which is only a bare reference to a much fuller account, such as that which we actually find in Luke xxiv. 13 sqq. (See De Wette, § 94, c.)

§ 96.

The following considerations lead us to the same conclusion regarding the relation of Mark to the two other Synoptics. The discourses, even those of Christ, and especially the longer ones, are far briefer and more scanty, *i.e.* in comparison of the general history, in Mark than in Matthew or Luke. Now the natural expectation would certainly be, that the discourses of Christ, His sayings and doctrinal teachings, would be the very part of the gospel history earliest recorded and committed to writing. There would not be the same neces-

---

[1] [Here WEISS, p. 61, and HOLTZMANN, p. 68, allow the secondary character of Mark's account.]

sity for committing to writing the more striking facts of His history, because these would be more easily told, remembered, and transmitted by oral tradition. The only two miracles, moreover, which are peculiar to Mark, viz. the healing of the deaf mute at Decapolis (Mark vii. 32–37), and of one blind (Mark viii. 22–26), possess a very peculiar and distinctive character: they resemble each other, but they differ in many features from the miracles recorded elsewhere in the three Synoptics (though in some respects akin to that in John ix.). Now, if Mark were the earliest of our Gospels, or the first independent Gospel written, it would be very difficult to explain how it came to pass that just these two miracles peculiar to him should be of so distinctive a character, and that they alone should have been omitted by Matthew and Luke. We can very easily see, on the contrary, supposing that Mark wrote subsequently, how he would adopt much that was recorded in Matthew and Luke, and would add these two miracles from some other source.

Against such a supposition, however, it has been urged that Mark passes over in silence many events of the Lord's history which are recorded by Matthew and Luke, *e.g.* the whole *Evangelium infantiæ*, several of the Lord's discourses, and many miracles. These, it is urged, he would not have omitted, had he had the other Synoptics before him. Many have regarded the absence of any sketch of the Saviour's infancy and childhood in Mark as a conclusive proof of the priority of his Gospel. It certainly seems most natural to suppose that the earliest written accounts of Christ's life and teaching began with His public ministry, and not with accounts of His birth and childhood. But we are not warranted to expect that, when once the latter were committed to writing and circulated in the Church—when once fuller Gospels giving the history of the Lord's childhood had been written —every subsequent evangelist must necessarily repeat in his history these early portions. St. John's Gospel shows the contrary, for it was composed by the apostle at a later date than Matthew and Luke, and at a time when the accounts of the birth and childhood of Jesus were well known and widely circulated. Now, if St. John could pass over in silence these portions of the history, we can easily conceive that Mark (even with Matthew and Luke before him) might confine his history to Christ's public ministry. We could not fairly infer regarding him, any more than regarding St. John, that he did not know, or did not believe, the miraculous facts of the Lord's birth recorded by Matthew and Luke. On the contrary, it would appear from the very beginning of his Gospel that he did know and recognise them: for without hesitation he describes the Saviour (ch. i. 1) as Ἰησοῦ Χριστοῦ υἱοῦ Θεοῦ; and in ch. vi. 3 he makes the people of Nazareth say concerning Jesus, not as in Matt. xiii. 55, οὐχ οὗτός ἐστιν ὁ τοῦ τέκτονος υἱός; nor as in Luke iv. 22, ὁ υἱὸς Ἰωσήφ; but, οὐχ οὗτός ἐστιν ὁ τέκτων, ὁ υἱὸς Μαρίας, κ.τ.λ., very probably because he shrank, upon reverential and religious grounds, from putting into the mouth even of unbelieving Jews a description of Jesus which represented Him as merely the son of an earthly father.

§ 97.

The circumstance that so many of Christ's discourses, including the longest and the most important in point of doctrine and teaching, are wholly wanting in Mark, is in keeping with the fact of the prominence given to His miracles, and can by no means be taken as a sign that he did not know the Gospels in which those discourses are given in full. Nor can we draw such an inference from his omission of many facts in Christ's life which Matthew or Luke, or both, record. It would be quite unreasonable to set up as a canon, that each subsequent evangelist must incorporate into his work everything which preceding writers had told. The manner, however, in which Mark's Gospel is composed, the cycle of events he records, and the order in which he groups them, strikingly imply a knowledge on his part of the two other Synoptics.[1] This fact really serves to confirm our

---

[1] GRIESBACH has already very ably shown this, and so has SAUNIER and others; see DE WETTE, § 94, d. [See, however, on the other side, HOLTZMANN, p. 117 sqq.; WEISS, p. 680 sqq.]

opinion that Mark made use of Matthew and Luke as his main authorities in writing his Gospel. Both in his selection of events to be narrated, and in the order in which he arranges them, he is evidently guided by these two evangelists; or first by one, and then by the other, when they differ in their arrangement. And when he passes from one to the other, it is not difficult to discover the reason which influenced him; *e.g.*, because in the one which he has been following, a discourse intervenes longer than he is wont to incorporate. Again, when the same facts, which are recorded by the evangelist whom he is following at any time, are narrated also by the other, he makes use of the latter also, to guide him in his manner of description, and even of expression, but still keeps mainly to the former. Mark begins his Gospel with a notice of John the Baptist's ministry, of the baptism and temptation of Jesus, and of the call of the first disciples, the two pairs of brothers (ch. i. 1–20). Herein he follows Matthew, who mentions these events in like manner and in the same order (Matt. iii. 1–iv. 22); and he adopts his mode of narration in the account of the call of the disciples, adopting almost the same words. He here differs somewhat from Luke, who tells the same fact later in the history, and in a different manner (Luke v. 1–11). The account of the Baptist's imprisonment, which Luke subjoins to his notice of his ministry (iii. 19, 20), and the genealogical table which follows his mention of the baptism of Christ (iii. 23–38), are not here given by St. Mark. In Matthew, the Sermon on the Mount, with what we may call the introduction thereto (Matt. iv. 23–vii. 29), follows the temptation; and hence Mark is led to turn to Luke as his guide in narrating the following events:—

MARK I. 21–III. 19 = LUKE IV. 31–VI. 16.

The account in Luke iv. 16–30 of the hostility of the people of Nazareth against Christ, is not here given by Mark; he follows Matthew in giving it later, Luke having inserted it too early: he also omits the call of Peter and the two sons of Zebedee (Luke v. 1–11), having already adopted Matthew's account. The other events narrated in this section by Luke are given also by Mark, who now follows Luke's and not Matthew's order,—recording not only those facts which Matthew as well as Luke gives, but those too which Matthew has omitted. Thus Mark gives the healing of the demoniac at Capernaum, ch. i. 35-39, and the general statement concerning the ministry of Jesus throughout Galilee, i. 35-39. In the narrations which Matthew as well as Luke gives, Mark clearly makes use also of Matthew, but he mainly adheres to Luke's account: see i. 29-34, the healing of Peter's wife's mother, and other sick folk; i. 40-45, the cleansing of the leper; ii. 1-12, the healing of the sick of the palsy; iii. 1-6, the healing of the man with the withered hand. At the end of this section, Mark (iii. 13-19) gives, like Luke (vi. 12 sqq.), the election of the twelve apostles, which took place upon a mountain. This in Luke introduces the Sermon on the Mount (Luke vi. 20-49); and Mark here omits Luke's summary, as he had omitted Matthew's fuller record. He now turns back again to Matthew for further facts of the Lord's ministry, and goes on at once to the account of the charge against Jesus, that He cast out devils by Beelzebub, Matt. xii. 22 sqq. The events which in Matthew intervene between the Sermon on the Mount and this point in His history, are for the most part given by Mark direct from Luke, either in the preceding or in the following sections. Some of them, however, he omits—viz. (*a*) Matt. viii. 5-13, the healing of the centurion's child ($\pi\alpha\hat{\iota}\varsigma$) at Capernaum; (*b*) Matt. ix. 27-38, the healing of two blind men and of a dumb demoniac, with a more general statement immediately following concerning an evangelistic journey which Jesus took, and of the pity which the sad state of the people awoke within Him; (*c*) Matt. xi., the visit of the Baptist's disciples to Jesus. The new section, wherein Mark again takes Matthew as his guide, is

MARK III. 20-IV. 34 = MATT. XII. 22-XIII. 35.

In this section Mark gives three parabolic sayings of Christ (iv. 21-29) which do not occur in Matthew, but the first two of which he may have got from Luke viii. 16–18, where it occurs, as Mark gives it, after the parable of the sower (the second perhaps also from Matt. xiii. 12). The third is a short parable or outline of a parable peculiar to Mark (the only one thus peculiar to him), illustrative of the silent and gradual growth of the kingdom of God. After this, Mark returns again to Matthew,—omitting, however, the parable of the tares (Matt. xiii. 24–30), and giving the shorter one of the mustard-seed (Matt. xiii. 31, 32; Mark iv. 30–32); omitting also the leaven, and concluding with the comment upon Christ's method of teaching by parables, vers. 33, 34, which corresponds with Matt. xiii. 34, 35. The section likewise contains Christ's reply to the charge of being in league with Beelzebub, His meeting with His mother and brethren, and the parable of the sower, with its interpretation. We find these in Luke likewise, but in a different connection. In the parable of the sower, and its interpretation, Mark has evidently made use of Luke, but he mainly adheres to Matthew, and no reference to Luke appears in what precedes. Mark, while following Matthew, is much briefer, and has certain distinctive peculiarities of his own.

In Matt. xiii. 36–52 we have the explanation of the parable of the tares, and some shorter parables. These Mark does not give; having omitted the parable, he of course omits the explanation too. He now returns again to Luke, from whom he had before (vers. 21–25) taken the parabolic sayings of Luke viii. 16–18. But as in Luke (vers. 19–21) there follows hereupon a narrative which Mark had already given (iii. 31–35) from Matt. xii. 46–50, Mark passes on to what further follows in Luke, and keeps company with him in the succeeding narrative—viz.,

MARK IV. 35–V. 43 = LUKE VIII. 22–56.

Of the events which Luke records in the interval between the call of the twelve (vi. 12 sqq.), when Mark parted company with him, and the beginning of this section (viii. 22), Mark had got from Matthew only two, viz. the parable of the sower, and Christ's meeting with His kinsfolk; but he records none of the rest, viz. (*a*) the Sermon on the Mount; (*b*) the healing of the centurion's child at Capernaum; (*c*) the raising of the widow's son at Nain; (*d*) the message of the Baptist to Christ, and Christ's sayings thereupon; (*e*) the anointing of Jesus in Simon's house; (*f*) the mention of a tour which Jesus made, and of women who ministered to Him (ch. viii. 3) : (*c*), (*e*), (*f*) are peculiar to Luke, though (*e*) may possibly be the same with what Mark (following Matthew) records afterwards in his history of the Passion : (*b*) and (*d*) are given also by Matthew, but in places where Mark does not take him as a guide; Mark, accordingly, has omitted them. The new section in Mark, for which he now has Luke again as his guide, contains three events narrated in the same order; viz. (*a*) the stilling of the tempest; (*b*) the healing of the demoniac in the country of the Gadarenes; (*c*) the raising of Jairus' daughter, and the cure of the woman with the issue of blood. Matthew also gives these three; the two first in the same order, but after the healing of Peter's wife's mother (Matt. viii. 23-34), and the third Matt. ix. 18-26. Mark, however, especially in the two latter narrations, manifestly follows Luke, who is fuller; and hardly anything peculiar to Matthew is traceable in him, though in the first of the three events Mark seems to have made use of Matthew as well as Luke.

In Luke ix. 1 there follows the mission of the twelve, and the directions Jesus gave them; next, Herod's observations concerning Christ. Mark also gives these, but he first inserts the account of the hostility of the people of Nazareth against the Saviour, which he adopts from Matthew, who mentions it at the end of his thirteenth chapter, immediately after the succession of parables, the last of which Mark had omitted.

Mark vi. 1-6 = Matt. xiii. 54-58.

Mark here harmonizes almost literally with Matthew, but he is briefer. He takes no notice of the account of the same event which Luke gives in ch. iv. 16-30. Mark next records the two facts above referred to as narrated by Luke.

Mark vi. 7–16 = Luke ix. 1–9.

The discourse to the twelve is given more fully in Matt. x. Mark occasionally seems to refer to this (vers. 7, 10, 11); but he closely follows the shorter epitome of Luke, and he has one or two things peculiar to himself. We find a parallel to Mark vi. 14–16 in Matt. xiv. 1, 2. Mark has here evidently made use of both Matthew and Luke, and has endeavoured to blend the two narratives.

But in this latter paragraph concerning Christ's relation to the Baptist, whom Herod had beheaded, Matthew has inserted an account of the Baptist's imprisonment and martyrdom (Matt. xiv. 3–12). Mark adopts the same course (vi. 17–29), and thus is led again to turn to Matthew as his guide for the remaining facts of the Galilean ministry, the journey to Jerusalem, and the first series of events there.

Mark vi. 17–xii. 37 = Matt. xiv. xxii. 3–46.

This section contains a considerable number of paragraphs (about thirty in all), for which Matthew must be regarded as Mark's guide, though he may have referred to Luke also in those parts which Luke also records. This is the case, for example, in the account of the feeding of the 5000 (Mark vi. 30–34), which we find not only in Matt. xiv. 13–21, but also in Luke ix. 10–17, and Mark has evidently interwoven expressions from both in the account he gives. The following sections which occur in Matt. xiv. 22–xvi. 12—the walking on the sea, and onwards to the feeding of the 4000—are not to be found in Luke. Mark (vi. 45–viii. 21) follows Matthew, and adopts the same order, but he introduces two miracles which are peculiar to him, viz. (*a*) vii. 31–37, the man deaf and dumb—immediately before the feeding of the 4000, where in the corresponding place in Matthew it is simply stated that Jesus healed many sick folk, and that the dumb were brought to Him, and He healed them; and (*b*) viii. 22–26, the healing of one blind. These two do not, however, disturb the parallelism with Matthew. The paragraphs which follow the latter miracle, given in Mark only, and which extend down to the end of the Galilean ministry, occur in Luke as well as Matthew, and in the same order. Mark, however, though he makes use of Luke, adheres still mainly to Matthew. Towards the close, however, he records, in common with Luke, an observation of the Apostle John's, with Christ's reply (Mark ix. 38, 39; Luke ix. 49, 50). Upon this follows the discourse of Jesus upon the strife for precedence among the disciples, which in Mark, as in Luke, is much shorter than in Matthew. Matthew gives here many sayings of Christ which Mark omits (Matt. xviii. 10–35); Mark, too, omits the account of the stater in the fish's mouth (Matt. xvii. 24–27), which is not to be found in Luke.

In his account of the journey to Jerusalem, Mark follows Matthew almost exclusively. He omits almost all that Luke records in that long and interesting section peculiar to him (Luke ix. 51–xviii. 14), which contains many important discourses, and the two last paragraphs in this corresponding section of Luke, viz. about Zacchæus and the parable of the pounds (Luke xix. 1–27). Mark, on the other hand, gives in common with Matthew what Luke omits, viz. (*a*) x. 1–12, Matt. xix. 1–9, concerning divorce; (*b*) x. 35–45, Matt. xx. 20–28, the answer of Jesus to the request concerning the sons of Zebedee. Mark omits here what Matthew records, viz. (*a*) Matt. xix. 10–12, Christ's comment on the question whether it be not better not to marry; (*b*) xx. 1–16, the parable of the labourers in the vineyard. All three evangelists have in common the remaining paragraphs of this part, and in the same order; and Mark uses Luke as well as Matthew, and sometimes preponderatingly, as *e.g.* for Christ's conversation with the rich young man, Mark x. 17 sqq., Luke xviii. 18 sqq., Matt. xix. 16 sqq.

The last part of this section, containing the first occurrences of the sojourn in Jerusalem, is also given by all three: Mark xi. 1–xii. 37; Matt. xxi. xxii.; Luke xix. 29–xx. 44. Here Matthew and Luke relate the same events; and Mark sometimes follows both, but Matthew in the main, giving with Matthew what Luke omits—the cursing of the barren fig-tree (Mark xi. 11–14, 19–26; Matt. xxi. 17–22), and the declaration concerning the highest and greatest commandment (Mark xii. 28-34; Matt. xxii. 34-40)—and omitting what Luke alone records, Luke xix. 39-44. Still he also omits Matt. xxi. 14-16, and the two parables, Matt. xxi. 28-32, xxii. 1-14. There is nothing in this section peculiar to Mark alone. In the last narrative of this part (the question of Jesus, how Christ can be David's son and David's Lord), Mark (xii. 35-37) follows Luke (xx. 41-44) rather than Matthew (xxii. 41-46). This is still more the case in the words concerning the Pharisees which follow, and which in Matthew occupy the whole of ch. xxiii.; whereas Luke (whom Mark (xii. 38-40) mainly follows here, and almost verbally quotes) has only a short warning of Christ's against the pride and covetousness of the scribes. Mark still follows Luke in

MARK XII. 38-XIV. 2 = LUKE XX. 45-XXII. 2.

Here we have, in the same order, (*a*) The words against the Pharisees. (*b*) The widow's mite (Mark xii. 41-44; Luke xxi. 1-4), which Matthew omits. (*c*) A long eschatological discourse (Mark xiii.; Luke xxi. 5-36), which Matthew (xxiv.) also gives, but with many additions, which Mark as well as Luke omits. Mark, however, has evidently made use of both evangelists. The end of the discourse (vers. 33-37) is peculiar to Mark, but he has manifestly endeavoured briefly to give the substance of the various parables in Matt. xxiv. 37-xxv. 30. (*d*) The plotting of the Sanhedrim to kill Jesus (Mark xiv. 1, 2; Luke xxii. 1, 2). Matthew has the same (xxvi. 1-5), and Mark has made use of him. The account of the anointing of Jesus in Simon's house follows this in Matt. xxvi. 6-13. This Luke omits, probably because it was the same or a very similar event to that which he had mentioned earlier (Luke vii. 36-50). Mark tells this story like Matthew, whom he now follows onwards to the resurrection.

MARK XIV. 3-XVI. 11 = MATT. XXVI. 6-XXVIII. 10.

Mark here adheres to the subject-matter and the order adopted by Matthew, who differs in some particulars from

Luke; and he has some historical touches in common with Matthew which are wanting in Luke: *e.g.* Mark xiv. 25, concerning the false witnesses against Jesus; xv. 34, the cry of Jesus upon the cross, and the command of the angel to meet the risen Saviour in Galilee (Mark xvi. 7; Matt. xxviii. 7). Mark does not here adopt what is peculiar to Luke; viz. Luke xxii. 24-30, 35-38; the sending of Jesus to Herod, Luke xxiii. 4-15; the words to the weeping women, xxiii. 27-32; the confession of the penitent thief, xxiii. 39-43; Peter's running to the sepulchre, and looking in, xxiv. 12. Mark has also omitted some things peculiar to Matthew; viz. Matt. xxvii. 3-10, the repentance and suicide of Judas; xxvii. 19, concerning Pilate's wife; vers. 24, 25, Pilate's washing his hands; vers. 62-66, the guard of soldiers set at the sepulchre. Mark here has omitted nothing common alike to Matthew and Luke; the only fact peculiar to him is that (xiv. 51, 52) concerning the young man who, upon the seizure of Jesus, fled away naked.

Upon the last part of this section, which tells how the risen Jesus appeared to the Galilean women (to Mary Magdalene in particular, according to Mark), we have in Matthew the account of the bribing of the watch by the Sanhedrim. Mark, not having mentioned the watch, does not introduce this, and he therefore turns again from Matthew to Luke for the remainder of the history.

MARK XVI. 12-20 = LUKE XXIV. 13-53.

What Mark states, xvi. 12, 13, is only a brief epitome of the full and beautiful account which Luke gives of the two disciples journeying to Emmaus (see § 95); and ver. 14 has reference to the appearance to all the disciples mentioned in Luke xxiv. 33 sqq. Vers. 19, 20 epitomize Luke's account (vers. 50-53) of the ascension. The farewell words of Jesus to His disciples given by Mark (vers. 15-18) are peculiar to him. It is strange that, having recorded the command given the disciples to meet Jesus in Galilee, Mark does not mention this meeting, but seems to imply that Jesus only appeared to His disciples in or near Jerusalem, where, having spoken to them,

He was parted from them and went up into heaven. Supposing (though it is a disputed point) the genuineness of this part of St. Mark, this circumstance is a clear proof that Mark cannot be regarded as an independent writer, but depended upon Matthew and Luke, whose accounts he could not here fully harmonize; so that his own narrative is not altogether self-consistent. This circumstance, therefore, serves to confirm the conviction we have arrived at through this lengthy examination, that Mark, both in particular places and in his composition as a whole, made Matthew and Luke the main sources of his information, and followed them as his guides.

§ 98.

We have now to examine the relation in which the two other synoptic Gospels stand to each other. If our argument thus far be correct, both Matthew and Luke were in existence when Mark's Gospel was composed, and were extant in Greek as we now have them. We accordingly carry on our investigation concerning Luke and Matthew without reference to Mark. The following points may be named as certain:—

1. Matthew and Luke cannot be regarded as writers wholly independent of each other in those portions which they have in common. There are certainly in both of them accounts (even of the same events) derived from sources wholly independent of each other. Besides the history of our Lord's infancy, and His genealogy, we may name the following:—
(a) The account of the unfriendly reception of Jesus in the synagogue at Nazareth, Luke iv. 16–30, Matt. xiii. 54–58 (Mark vi. 1–6 agrees almost verbally with Matthew, but both Matthew and Mark here differ from Luke): (b) The miraculous draught of fishes when Peter was called, Luke v. 1–11, Matt. iv. 18–22 (Mark i. 16–20 agrees with Matthew, and both Matthew and Mark differ from Luke): (c) Luke vii. 36–50, the anointing of Jesus, possibly referring to the same event as Matt. xxvi. 6–13 and Mark xiv. 3–9; but an independent source must be allowed for each, and the like may be true in other cases. But these cases are the exception, and not the rule. It must generally be allowed, that

when Matthew and Luke relate one and the same event, though variations and differences be traceable when we compare them, and when they record the same discourses, though with different amplification and in different connections, still one and the same written conception and narration, and this in the Greek language, lies at the basis of their exposition. Thus, *e.g.*, the section Matt. xii. 22–45, concerning the healing of the demoniac, and Christ's discourse evoked by the charge of the Pharisees against Him, corresponds in general with Luke xi. 14–32. Each evangelist has somewhat distinctive in his account, and differing from the other in certain points, in the sayings of Christ and their position; yet they agree so strikingly and literally in the Greek phraseology used, that it is most natural to infer a common written source in Greek. Compare especially Matthew, vers. 27, 28, with Luke, vers. 19, 20. Matthew runs: καὶ εἰ (Luke, εἰ δὲ) ἐγὼ ἐν Βεελζεβοὺλ ἐκβάλλω τὰ δαιμόνια, οἱ υἱοὶ ὑμῶν ἐν τίνι ἐκβάλλουσι; διὰ τοῦτο αὐτοὶ ὑμῶν ἔσονται κριταί (Luke, κριταὶ ὑμῶν αὐτοὶ ἔσονται; but Lachmann reads, αὐτοὶ ὑμῶν κριταὶ ἔσονται, and in Matthew he reads, αὐτοὶ κριταὶ ἔσονται ὑμῶν). Εἰ δὲ ἐν Πνεύματι Θεοῦ ἐγὼ (Luke, ἐν δακτύλῳ Θεοῦ) ἐκβάλλω τὰ δαιμόνια, ἄρα ἔφθασεν ἐφ' ὑμᾶς ἡ βασιλεία τοῦ Θεοῦ. The discourses in this section, like Christ's discourses generally, were beyond doubt, most of them, if not all, originally spoken in Aramæan. Now in this discourse the two evangelists agree word for word in expression, and even in arrangement of words: and this would be inconceivable upon the supposition that their accounts were severally derived from different sources, or even from oral tradition simply; or that, independently of each other, they each translated from a common Aramæan report of Christ's words. We can explain the coincidence only upon the supposition that they both had the same Greek document before them when they wrote. The only difference between them, viz. that Matthew has ἐν Πνεύματι Θεοῦ, and Luke ἐν δακτύλῳ Θεοῦ, cannot be regarded a merely accidental one, where the literal coincidence is otherwise so complete. The original expression was probably what Luke gives. This Matthew found, but substituted for it the other expression. Compare further, in the same section, Matt. xii. 30 with Luke xi. 23; Matt. xii. 39 with Luke xi. 29; Matt. xii. 41, 42, with Luke xi. 32, 31; Matt. xii. 43–45 with Luke xi. 24–26,—in all which places the coincidence is so great, that it can only be explained in the manner I have indicated. For other examples, see De Wette, § 79, b. The following may also be named: Matt. viii. 3 compared with Luke v. 13 ($\theta \acute{\epsilon} \lambda \omega$ $\kappa a \theta a \rho \acute{\iota} \sigma \theta \eta \tau \iota \cdot$ $\kappa a \grave{\iota}$ $\epsilon \grave{\upsilon} \theta \acute{\epsilon} \omega \varsigma$ . . .); Matt. viii. 5, 8, 9, 10, with Luke vii. 1, 6, 8, 9; Matt. ix. 20b, 24, with Luke viii. 44a, 52b, 53; Matt. x. 26, 27, 30–33, with Luke xii. 2, 3, 7–9; Matt. xi. 21–23 with Luke x. 13–15; Matt. xi. 25–27 with Luke x. 21, 22; Matt. xii. 13 with Luke vi. 10; Matt. xiii. 3–9 with Luke viii. 5–8 (the parable of the sower, especially the beginning and end); Matt. xvi. 24–26 with Luke ix. 23–25; and others. This coincidence is traceable in almost all the narrations which both evangelists have in common, and in the discourses of Jesus which they give. Even when divergences occur, the verbal coincidence is still so great, that we are constrained to infer a common source from which each drew in the Greek language. To this conclusion we are also led by an examination of the quotations (see § 69) which they make from the O. T., and in which the same literal coincidence, with the very same deviations from the LXX., appears.

2. The two evangelists are not independent of each other in their manner of moulding their several narrations into one complete whole (see § 65). Here, as we have seen, many differences are traceable, especially in the parts relating to the Galilean ministry. Matthew's arrangement often differs from Luke's, and he gives the same sayings of Christ's in a different connection. Still it is not a sufficient explanation of the relation between the two evangelists, to suppose that they both had before them certain digests or collections of Christ's sayings in minor writings, in the use of which, as each moulded his Gospel into a complete whole, they were independent of each other. There would still remain the difficulty unaccounted for, that both chose to record, for the

most part, the same events, and the same sayings of Christ's,—a fact which indicates that, when they wrote, one and the same cycle of events and discourses was already defined and fixed in the exposition of the gospel history, and which makes it highly probable that this cycle of events had already been committed to writing, and formed the basis of both Gospels. Had Matthew and Luke been quite independent in the selection of events and discourses to be recorded, considering the great richness, copiousness, and manifoldness of facts and sayings worthy of record which the Redeemer's life afforded, we should naturally expect that each would have shown far greater variety and distinctiveness. For example, the woe Christ utters against the Galilean cities (Matt. xi. 21-24; Luke x. 13-15) shows that not only in Capernaum, but in Bethsaida and Chorazin, Christ had laboured and given proofs of His divine power and glory. Yet though both evangelists record this woe pronounced by Jesus, neither of them tells us anything, or hardly anything, of the mighty works which were wrought in Bethsaida or Chorazin, and which occasioned this anathema.

The manner, moreover, in which the several narratives are linked together by both evangelists, presents (as we have already seen) a striking similarity, leading us still more decidedly to the same conclusion. They both place the temptation immediately after the ministry of the Baptist and Christ's baptism; next, the return to Galilee, where they both represent Christ as remaining till His journey to Jerusalem at the last passover. Now, on referring to St. John's Gospel, we find that this account of the Lord's movements is incomplete (see § 71); we find that He made other journeys to Jerusalem; and this coincidence in Matthew and Luke's selection and arrangement of events cannot have been merely accidental. On the contrary, we are led to the conclusion, that in their account of the gospel history as a whole, and in the historical arrangement of events and discourses, they were not independent of each other.

§ 99.

3. The relation subsisting between our two Gospels cannot be explained upon the supposition that one of them was the primary Gospel, the earliest connected exposition of gospel history, and that the author of the other knew and made use of it, as well as of oral tradition. Were this so, one of the two would certainly bear marks of originality, and signs of being the primary document, both in its exposition of details and its arrangement as a whole; and the formation of the other could be explained, as Mark's Gospel is, by a comparison with it. But the fact is, they stand in such a relation to each other, that now the one and now the other must be regarded as alternately the original and the derived. Matthew, for example, gives the more original account of Christ's baptism, His temptation, of the nobleman at Capernaum (viii. 5-13; Luke vii. 1-10; cf. John iv. 47-54), of Jairus' daughter, and the woman with the issue of blood (ix. 18-26; Luke viii. 40-56); frequently, too, with reference to the sayings of Christ, *e.g.* vii. 11, where the ἀγαθά of Matthew is much more in keeping with the general character of the declaration than the more definite "the Holy Spirit" of Luke (xi. 13); again, Matt. xii. 43-45 (cf. Luke xi. 24-26), about the return of the evil spirit that had been cast out, where Matthew alone shows the point of the declaration by the place in which the narration occurs, and the words added at the close; and other instances might be named. And yet as little can we hesitate in other cases to assign the priority to Luke; *e.g.* in his narratives, viii. 26-39, xviii. 35-43, as compared with Matt. viii. 28-34, xx. 29-34—in the fact at least that Luke speaks of only *one* who was possessed in the country of the Gergesenes, and of *one* blind man, whereas Matthew in both places speaks of two. So also, in his account of Christ's triumphal entry into Jerusalem, Luke speaks of but *one* beast, viz. an ass's colt (xix. 30), but Matthew (xxi. 2 sqq.) of two, the colt and its mother: Luke's account harmonizes with that of John, Matthew's has reference seemingly to the prophecy quoted from Zechariah. So also in the form in which they respectively give some of the

sayings of Christ; *e.g.* the Beatitudes, Luke vi. 20 sqq. as compared with Matt. v. 3 sqq.; Luke xi. 20 compared with Matt. xii. 28 (see § 98); Luke xii. 58, 59, compared with Matt. v. 25, 26, where the proper sense is apparent only in Luke; the Lord's Prayer, Luke xi. 2-4, compared with Matt. vi. 9-13; and other places.

Again, where both give the same discourses, Matthew's account is usually longer than Luke's, many longer or shorter declarations of the Lord being included, which in Luke we find scattered here and there as spoken on various occasions. The probability is, that these were uttered as Luke represents, and that Matthew has collected them on account of a certain affinity between them; for he seems to have had comparatively less regard to the special circumstances which evoked the Lord's words and their chronological order, than for the similarity and affinity characterizing the subject-matter of them. The discourses to which this remark applies are: the Sermon on the Mount, Matt. v.-viii., Luke vi. 20-49; the directions given to the apostles, Matt. x.; the discourse which follows the visit of the Baptist's disciples, Matt. xi.; the series of parables, Matt. xiii.; the declarations which follow Christ's answer to the question, "Who is greatest in the kingdom of heaven?" Matt. xviii.; the discourse against the Pharisees, Matt. xxiii.; the eschatological discourses, Matt. xxiv. xxv. The probability is, that Jesus did not utter these discourses exactly as they are recorded in Matthew—that He did not, *e.g.*, speak a series of parables or of pregnant proverbial sayings one after another at one and the same time, and without any pause or interruption; so that Matthew's arrangement cannot be regarded as the original and primary form wherein these discourses were committed to writing. In like manner, even in Luke we find, though comparatively seldom, that several sayings are linked and blended together into one discourse,—sayings which in Matthew occur in various places and on more appropriate occasions; the probable inference being, that these were not originally recorded as Luke gives them. See, for example, certain parts of the Sermon on the Mount as recorded in Luke vi. 20–49, and of the discourse he gives in ch. xvi., especially vers. 16-18, and others.

We thus are led to the conclusion that both Matthew and Luke were preceded by an earlier written gospel narrative, giving the history connectedly and substantially according to the same pattern or type as their Gospels, and that this formed the basis of their respective narratives.

§ 100.

4. That our canonical Gospels were not the earliest writings in which the attempt was made systematically to set forth the evangelic history, is further evident from what St. Luke himself says in his preface, Luke i. 1-4. He there speaks of "many (πολλοί) who had taken in hand to set forth in order" the gospel history. The language here employed forbids our understanding the reference, as Ebrard does (§ 137; ed. ii. § 135), merely to certain fragmentary scraps of history in circulation among Luke's readers. The words Luke uses show most clearly that he refers to certain consecutive and arranged accounts of a considerable portion at least of gospel facts, to writings essentially the same in character and construction with that which he felt called upon to write for Theophilus. The words ἔδοξε κἀμοί, " it seemed good *to me also,*" obviously imply that his undertaking is a work the same in kind with those of his predecessors to whom he refers; and the terms in which he describes these previous writings, viz. ἀνατάξασθαι διήγησιν, "to set forth in order," clearly correspond and are synonymous with the καθεξῆς γράψαι, "to write unto thee in order," which he applies to his own undertaking. This, of course, does not oblige us to suppose that Luke did not entertain the hope of surpassing his predecessors in the fulness or accuracy of his treatise.[1]

---

[1] [DEAN ALFORD says that the πολλοί can neither mean the writers of our present Gospels, for Matthew and John were eye-witnesses, nor any apocryphal Gospels which have come down to us. "I believe," he says, "the only probable explanation of the words to be, that many persons in charge of Churches, or otherwise induced, drew up here and there statements (*narratives,* διήγ.) *of the testimony of eye-witnesses* and ὑπηρ.

As to the nature of these Gospels to which Luke refers, we may conclude from what he says, that, so far as he knew, they were not the works of apostles, but of other believers, who availed themselves of the communications, written or oral, of eye-witnesses and participators in the events narrated, *i.e.* of the first and most immediate disciples of Jesus. We cannot tell from Luke's words how these several evangelic writings were related to each other. We may, however, reasonably suppose that they were not wholly independent of each other, and that they presented the gospel history generally after the same type as our Synoptics. Here, however, we enter upon a wide field of conjecture, and we cannot expect to be able to set forth anything quite certain, but only what is more or less probable, concerning the nature and range of the pre-canonical evangelic writings. I think, however, that we may with great probability take the following for granted.

(*a.*) Certain shorter narratives, and especially reports of Christ's discourses and sayings, giving at the same time the occasion and circumstances of time and place when they were spoken, formed the beginning or germ of written gospel history. These narratives were written, if not by apostles, certainly by immediate disciples of the Lord, who were themselves eye-witnesses of Christ's works, and hearers of His words, and also perhaps by those who heard these

τ. λ., as far as they themselves had been able to collect them. I do *not* believe that either the Gospel of Matthew, or that of Mark, are to be reckoned among these; or, if they are, that Luke had seen or used them. That such narratives should not have come down to us is no matter of surprise: for (1) they would be absorbed by the more complete and sanctioned accounts of our present evangelists; and (2) Church tradition has preserved very few fragments of authentic information of the apostolic age. It is probable that in almost every Church where an eye-witness preached, his testimony would be taken down, and framed into some διήγησις, more or less complete, of the life and sayings of the Lord" (Alford on Luke i. 1–4). Archbishop THOMSON says, that by the words of St. Luke are intended "partial and incomplete reports of the preaching of the apostles, written with a good aim; and if we may argue from St. Luke's sphere of observation, they were probably composed by Greek converts." (Article on *Gospels* in Smith's *Dictionary of the Bible*.)—TR.]

facts and discourses from the lips of immediate disciples or εὐαγγελισταί, and who wrote down for their own use, and as a help to memory, what afterwards they allowed others to see, and what thus by degrees was more widely circulated. We may suppose (*a*) that the sayings of Christ first thus committed to writing were His parables, and His shorter proverbial declarations; and (β) that in recording them very little notice was taken of their chronological order, for even the εὐαγγελισταί could not easily in their preaching keep this always in view.

(*b*.) Accordingly we cannot tell when or by whom the first attempt was made to compose a connected exposition of gospel history. The probability is, that it was not made by an apostle, but by some other disciple who had not himself been continually in our Lord's company, and who received his information partly from the briefer evangelic writings already in existence, and partly from the oral instructions of immediate disciples. These he moulded into a connected historical work, which for brevity's sake we may call the *Primitive Gospel* (*Ur-evangelium*). It was composed not certainly in Judea, but probably in Galilee or the neighbourhood; and hence it can be understood how prominence was given to the events of the Galilean ministry, and how no notice was taken of Christ's visits to Jerusalem previous to His last passover. The story of Christ's sufferings, death, and resurrection, must have been known to any gospel writer, whoever and wherever he might be, and could not have been passed by in silence in any connected history. Thus probably the events of gospel history onwards from the outset of Christ's public ministry would group themselves under three heads, viz. (*a*) ministry in Galilee and the parts adjacent; (β) history of Christ's sufferings, and the events connected therewith in Jerusalem; and (γ) connecting these, the journey from Galilee to Jerusalem; so that the earlier visits of Christ to Jerusalem would be passed over in silence, or at the most only a few of the facts incorporated with the events of the last journey and last sojourn there.

(*c*.) This Primitive Gospel would be received and circulated first in the neighbourhood where it was written, and afterwards, through the frequent intercourse subsisting between the early Churches, in a wider district; because it gave, not indeed a complete, but as far as it went a true picture of the Lord's person and work, and a true account of the main events of His life. By means of it, moreover, a certain type and character was given to the gospel history, and to the exposition of many facts. It was soon followed by other connected evangelic treatises, written by believers in different parts, for different circles of readers; and these believers, if they could not write independently from their own experience and knowledge, would make the Primitive Gospel the basis of their history, leaving out what did not seem needful for their purpose, arranging certain portions in stricter chronological order, and adding more or less which otherwise had come to their knowledge, but in such a manner as to retain the general type and character of the history, both in generals and in details, as presented in the Primitive Gospel. This was the origin of our first and third canonical Gospels; and their resemblance is thus easily explained, whether their authors used the Primitive Gospel in its original form, or one or more intermediate recensions. As to Luke, however, it is evident from the preface that he was acquainted with, and probably used in the composition of his treatise, several gospel histories related to each other in the way described, and probably resembling each other still more closely than do our synoptic Gospels.

§ 101.

5. We know nothing of the contents of this Primary Gospel, save what we may infer from a comparative survey of Matthew and Luke.[1] We cannot, of course, give an accurate summary of its contents, nor could we even if we were sure that both evangelists had used it. Besides the portions which both have in common, for aught we can tell,

[1] It is clear from § 94-96 that Mark cannot be taken into account in this estimate, as EICHHORN, MARSH, GRATZ, LACHMANN, and others suppose.

the parts peculiar to each may some of them have been in the Primary Gospel, though omitted by the other as needless for his design. There may also have been things in it which neither evangelist has preserved to us. But we are not certain even that the authors of our Gospels made use of this Primitive Gospel in its original form. They may have had before them only revisions of it. Still we may with great probability conclude—

(*a*) As to its language, that it was written, not, as is usually supposed, in Aramæan, but in Greek. Many passages in our Gospels, wherein Matthew and Luke coincide in the Greek words and phrases they use, and even in the choice of unusual words and phrases, in constructions and ideas, prove that they both had in mind one and the same Greek narrative; and in places where they differ there is no indication whatever that they were both translating from the same Aramæan original. Some have endeavoured to account for sundry variations and differences in the Synoptics in this way,[1] but they have failed even to make their explanation probable. The Greek construction in both Gospels and in many passages is of such a character, as to prove it in the highest degree probable that the thought expressed had originally been expressed in Greek, and quite to exclude the notion that it was a translation from the Aramæan. For example, take the expression in the Lord's prayer, ἄρτος ἐπιούσιος (Matt. vi. 11; Luke xi. 3). There is no single Hebrew or Aramæan word answering to ἐπιούσιος, which would sanction the notion that this adjective was chosen by the writer as a translation from an Aramæan treatise. The Lord's prayer was of course originally given by the Lord in Aramæan; but it was probably committed to writing first in Greek, in the form wherein Greek-speaking Christians had adopted it.

The Old Testament quotations, moreover, which both evangelists have in common, prove the same thing. These quotations occur for the most part in the conversations or

---

[1] See HALFELD (*ob.* 1795), *de origine quatuor Evv.*, Gött. 1794, pp. 9-39; EICHHORN, i. § 49, 58; BERTHOLDT, iii. § 320.

addresses of those whom the history brings before us (see my *Beitr. z. Ev. Krit.* pp. 57, 168); and these conversations and addresses were doubtless originally spoken in Aramæan, so that the quotations were made in an Aramæan version from the Hebrew text. Now if the Primitive Gospel, giving these conversations and discourses, were an Aramæan document, which was afterwards translated into Greek, the quotations in question would have been translated direct from the Aramæan; but the passages from the Old Testament, which Matthew and Luke have in common, are given for the most part from the LXX., either literally, and this in cases where the LXX. differs from the Hebrew (*e.g.* Matt. iii. 3, Luke iii. 4), or more freely and with variations—such variations, however, being made without reference to the Hebrew text (with the exception at least of Matt. xi. 10, Luke vii. 28). These facts are best and most naturally explained upon the supposition that the history was originally thought and written in Greek, and not upon the supposition of an Aramæan original.

§ 102.

(*b.*) As to the contents, scope, and arrangement of this Primitive Gospel, we know not whether it began with an *evangelium infantiæ*, nor, if it did, what that *evangelium infantiæ* contained. Neither do we know whether it gave any account of the Lord's ascension. The probability is, that it contained the history of the Redeemer only during His public ministry, and onwards to His death, His resurrection, and His appearances after the resurrection. Apparently it began with an account of John the Baptist's ministry and the baptism of Christ; then followed the temptation, and the statement that Jesus devoted Himself to Galilee as His sphere of labour. It related the main facts of His life and works in Galilee and the parts adjacent, in an unbroken order, onwards to the journey from Galilee to Jerusalem, before the passover at which He was crucified. It probably represented Jesus as going almost direct from Galilee to Jerusalem at the time of this passover, and eating His last meal with His disciples before He suffered, at the ordinary and legally fixed time for the Jewish passover. Bearing in mind the nature, already described, of those more fragmentary records of Christ's parables and other sayings, which the writer of this Primitive Gospel had before him, it is probable that it contained a large number of the Lord's discourses, and gave many of them in their right connection as to time and place, but sometimes without recording all the events which those sayings and discourses referred to. Thus, for example, the woe pronounced upon the Galilean cities (Matt. xi. 20; Luke x. 13-15: see § 98), and the lamentation over Jerusalem (Matt. xxiii. 37, 38; Luke xiii. 34, 35: see § 71), were both recorded, but without the events and teachings which those declarations implied. This circumstance, which the data before us seem to indicate, would appropriately account for the fact that much might have been omitted which we now find in St. John's Gospel—and even some of the most important miracles, such as the opening the eyes of one born blind, and the raising of Lazarus—without this in any degree invalidating the truth and accuracy of St. John's narrative.

The probability is, that this Primitive Gospel contained those discourses and narrations which our Matthew and Luke have in common, and which they record almost in the same words, showing that the same Greek original formed the basis of both. Whether it also contained any of the parts which are peculiar to Matthew and to Luke respectively, we cannot tell: probably not much. As to order and arrangement, in places where Matthew and Luke coincide, we probably have a reflection of the order followed in the Primitive Gospel; and in places where they differ, there is more or less uncertainty how it was in the primary narrative. When Matthew and Luke record the same discourses, but Matthew more fully, and blending together several different sayings which in Luke are dispersed in different places and occasions, we may infer that Luke has adhered more closely to the original account. The primary Gospel, however, probably gave the briefer account of the journey to Jerusalem, which is to be found in Matthew, and did not contain the long section peculiar to Luke in ch. ix. 51–xviii. 14. Matthew and Luke vary in their arrangement of the Galilean events; yet here also they have sufficient affinity to warrant the conclusion that the primary Gospel was the common source from which they drew, and the common link between them. The sending forth of the twelve, the raising of Jairus' daughter, and the healing of the woman with the issue of blood, were probably recorded and placed as we find them in Luke (viii. 40–ix. 6); but what intervenes in Matthew (ix. 27–38) was probably inserted by himself. These narrations in the primary Gospel, as in Luke, probably preceded the stilling of the tempest and the cure of the Gadarene demoniac; and the intervening section in Matthew (ix. 1–17, which in Luke occurs earlier, viz. ch. v. 17–39) was afterwards inserted. The feeding of the 5000 probably followed the opinions of Herod and others concerning Jesus, as in Luke ix. 7–17; while the intervening narrative in Matthew (xiv. 3–12) was put in by this last-named evangelist himself. The facts as given in Luke ix. 18–50 immediately followed the feeding of the 5000, and the intermediate portion in Matthew (xiv. 22–xvi. 12) was afterwards derived from another source. The Sermon on the Mount was not probably recorded in the Primitive Gospel, either as to time of its delivery or its length, as we find it in Matthew, but rather as in Luke (vi. 12 sqq.), after the appointment of the twelve. Matthew records it as he does, at the outset of his account of Christ's public ministry, in order to give an example of His manner of teaching.[1]

[*Note.*—" The preaching of the apostles, and the teaching whereby they prepared others to preach, as they did, would tend to assume a common form, more or less fixed; and the portions of the three Gospels which harmonize most exactly, owe their agreement not to the

---

[1] See, upon this description of the contents of the supposed Primitive Gospel, the remarks of HOLTZMANN in SCHENKEL's *Allgem. Kirchl. Zeitschr.* 1862, p. 91; *Synopt. Evangelien*, pp. 101, 102, 121.

fact that they were copied from each other, although it is impossible to say that the later writer made no use of the earlier one, nor to the existence of any original document now lost to us, but to the fact that the apostolic preaching had already clothed itself in a settled or usual form of words, to which the writers inclined to conform, without feeling bound to do so; and the differences which occur, often in the closest proximity to the harmonies, arise from the feeling of independence with which each wrote what he had seen and heard, or, in the case of Mark and Luke, what apostolic witnesses had told him. . . . The verbal agreement is greater where the words of others are recorded, and greatest of all where they are those of Jesus, because here the apostolic preaching would be especially exact; and where the historical fact is the utterance of certain words, the duty of the historian is narrowed to a bare record of them. How does this theory bear upon our belief in the inspiration of the Gospels? This momentous question admits of a satisfactory reply. Our blessed Lord, on five different occasions, promised to the apostles the divine guidance. . . . He promised them the Spirit of Truth to guide them into all truth, to teach them all things, and bring all things to their remembrance. That this promise was fully realized to them, the history of the Acts sufficiently shows. But if the divine assistance was given them in their discourses and preaching, it would be rendered equally when they were about to put down in writing the same gospel which they preached. . . . Supposing that the portion of the three first Gospels, which is common to all, has been derived from the preaching of the apostles in general, then it is drawn directly from a source which we know from our Lord Himself to have been inspired. The inspiration of an historical writing will consist in its truth, and in its selection of events. Everything narrated must be substantially and exactly true, and the comparison of the Gospels with one another offers us nothing that does not answer this test. There are differences of arrangement of events; here some details of a narrative or a discourse are supplied which are wanting there; and if the writer had professed to follow a strict chronological order, or had pretended that his record was not only true, but complete, then one inversion of order, or one omission of a syllable, would convict him of inaccuracy. But if it is plain—if it is all but avowed—that minute chronological data are not part of the writer's purpose; if it is also plain that nothing but a selection of the facts is intended, or indeed possible (John xxi. 25), then the proper test to apply is, whether each gives us a picture of the life and ministry of Jesus of Nazareth that is self-consistent, and consistent with the others, such as would be suitable to the use of those who were to believe on His Name—for this is their evident intention. About the answer there should be no doubt. We have seen that each Gospel has its own features, and that the divine element has controlled the human, but not destroyed it. But the picture which they conspire to draw is one full of harmony."— Archbishop THOMSON, article *Gospels* in Smith's *Dictionary to the Bible.* In the remarks on inspiration here, there seems to be a confusion between the *truth* of the facts narrated, and the *truthfulness* of the narrator. The latter does not necessarily involve accuracy in detail, but the former does. The latter seems to be the learned author's test of inspiration.— TR.]

In general, we may, I think, take it for granted that St. Luke has retained the narrations which he adopted from the Primitive Gospel, more in the order and connection in which he found them, than has St. Matthew. Some incidents, indeed, are recorded by Luke in less appropriate connections than those in which Matthew puts them; *e.g.* the account of the appearing of Jesus in the synagogue at Nazareth, which Luke (iv. 14-30; see § 55) places too early, and the first miraculous draught of fishes, which Luke (v. 1-11) does not record till after the cure of Peter's wife's mother.[1] But Luke probably derived these facts, as he relates them, not from the Primitive Gospel, but from some other source; and if the last-named document contained them, they were there recorded in the more natural connection and the more appropriate place in which Matthew (xiii. 53-58, and iv. 18-22) puts them.

§ 103.

6. We know nothing whatever concerning the subsequent history of the Primitive Gospel, and those other pre-canonical writings to which Luke in his preface refers. When the two great canonical Gospels based upon them appeared, they gradually were lost sight of, and in time were wholly lost. The canonical Gospels at once, and from a very early date, were recognised and reverenced in the Church; and this could not have happened had they not been known from the outset as more comprehensive, more complete, and more trustworthy writings than those which preceded them. This is confirmed by the circumstance that St. Mark, who wrote at a time when he had at command still further sources of information both oral and written, nevertheless made our two Gospels the basis of his, and obtained from them almost all the materials of his work.

§ 104.

7. From what we have said concerning the language in which the Primitive Gospel was composed, and concerning the sections which our canonical Gospels have in common, it is clear that these last must have been written in Greek, and that St. Matthew's Gospel in particular was so written (see § 42). Other features of this Gospel lead us to the same conclusion. Even in passages which are not parallel with St. Luke, the Greek could not have been what it is if the thoughts expressed had not been conceived in that language.

[1] [BLEEK, however, gives the preference to St. Luke's order in his *Synopt. Erkl. der drei ersten Evv.* i. 214.—B.]

See, *e.g.*, the expressions βαττολογεῖν and πολυλογία in Matt. vi. 7. Also the play upon words and paronomasia, vi. 16, ἀφανίζουσι . . . φανῶσι; xxi. 41, κακοὺς κακῶς ἀπολέσει. These examples of themselves would not be conclusive, for they might be supposed to have come from the pen of a translator. But they confirm the proofs already adduced (see § 101).[1]

§ 105.

8. As to the TIME when our two Gospels, Matthew and Luke, were composed, there are some texts in Matthew indicating that some time had elapsed since the events narrated had taken place. For example, Matt. xxvii. 8, διὸ ἐκλήθη ὁ ἀγρὸς ἐκεῖνος, ἀγρὸς αἵματος, ἕως τῆς σήμερον; xxviii. 15, καὶ διεφημίσθη ὁ λόγος . . . μέχρι τῆς σήμερον. Both these occur in sections which are peculiar to Matthew. See also xxvii. 15, κατὰ δὲ ἑορτὴν εἰώθει, κ.τ.λ. Still it is very likely that St. Matthew's Gospel was written not later than the year of the destruction of Jerusalem. When we compare the prophetic declarations of Christ given us in the Synoptics, concerning the calamities overhanging the country generally, and Jerusalem in particular, and the manner in which these declarations are blended with others concerning the second advent of the Son of man (Matt. xxiv. xxv.; Luke xxi.), we find no little difference in the reports given, showing that the individuality of the writer, and the exact time at which he wrote, have influenced his record. And when we examine the way in which Matthew has given and blended these declarations, — representing Christ's second

---

[1] In my *Beitr. zur Ev. Krit.* pp. 58, 59, I have urged as an argument in favour of a Greek original, Matt. xxvii. 46, the cry of the Redeemer given in Aramæan, with a Greek translation added ('Ηλί, 'Ηλί, κ.τ.λ.), on the ground that in an Aramæan treatise stress would not have been laid on the fact that the Redeemer spoke these words of the Psalm in Aramæan. But I retract this argument as hardly tenable, because in ver. 47 we are told that some standing by said, "Ὅτι Ἠλίαν φωνεῖ οὗτος; and a Greek translator of an Aramæan original might consider it wise to retain the Aramæan words of the cry, and to add the Greek version of them.

coming as immediately ensuing upon the judgments descending on the city and country (Matt. xxiv. 29),—we are led to the conclusion that he wrote either immediately before or immediately after the destruction of Jerusalem; because subsequently the disciples learnt not to indulge the hope of the immediate return of the Lord in the manner here described. The probability is, that this Gospel was written *before* the catastrophe named, and ch. xxiv. 15 seems to indicate this. The words ὁ ἀναγινώσκων νοείτω are not Christ's, as many have supposed, but the evangelist's, who thus calls his readers' attention to the fact, that even then the event which the Redeemer is referring to was being accomplished,—viz. "the abomination of desolation, spoken of by Daniel the prophet, standing in the holy place." It may be doubted whether the evangelist means by this the Roman army, now already besieging the city, or (as HUG thinks, ii. § 5) the wild bands of zealots and Idumæans who established themselves in the city and desecrated the temple. In either case the time is that of the Roman-Jewish war, immediately before the destruction of the city and temple; and this was most probably the time when St. Matthew's Gospel was written. Some have sought a further proof that this was the time in ch. xxiii. 35. Because the evangelist describes the Zacharias of whose martyrdom Jesus speaks (and whom they take to be the Zechariah named in 2 Chron. xxiv. 19–21 as the son of Jehoiada) as the son of Barachias, they fancy he supposed that Zacharias the son of Baruch (who, according to JOSEPHUS, *B. J.* iv. 5, 4, was murdered by the Jewish zealots in the temple shortly before the destruction of Jerusalem by the Romans) was meant. So Eichhorn, Hug, Credner, and others. But the evangelist was clearly thinking of the postexile prophet Zacharias, son of Barachias (Zech. i. 1, 7); and this passage furnishes no proof of the date at which the evangelist wrote.

As to the Gospel of St. Luke, we may with probability conclude that it was written some time after the destruction of Jerusalem. This is evident, not so much from the preface, where the writer represents himself as belonging to the second generation of Christians, and speaks of "many" who had written connected gospel histories before him,—for both these might apply to a time previous to the destruction of Jerusalem,—but rather from the manner in which he records in ch. xxi. Christ's declarations concerning the coming catastrophe, and the prediction concerning the second coming of the Son of man, as compared with the account of these declarations in Matthew. See especially vers. 20-22, compared with Matt. xxiv. 15; Luke in vers. 25-27, with Matthew in vers. 29, 30.

§ 106.

9. In point of composition, the two Gospels are distinguished from each other in the fact that the writer of the first has digested and worked up his materials, comparatively speaking, more thoroughly than the writer of the other; and, both in generals and particulars, has left more fully the impress of his individuality upon his work. This appears in the manner in which he has arranged his subject-matter, and especially the discourses of Christ. He has often with skill and judgment blended together into one discourse several kindred sayings (see § 99); and the same is true of his groupings of facts. Thus, after the Sermon on the Mount, he has in ch. viii. ix. arrayed together a number of miracles, chiefly cures wrought by the Redeemer, in order to show that, when Jesus had gathered around Him a number of disciples, He began to be publicly active not only in teaching, but also in working miracles. And thus the Sermon on the Mount, in ch. v.-vii., and the miracles of healing in ch. viii. ix., illustrate and confirm the general statement of ch. iv. 23: "Jesus went about all Galilee, teaching and preaching the gospel of the kingdom, and healing all manner of sickness and all manner of disease among the people."

St. Matthew, moreover, often does what Luke never does, —namely, he inserts in his narrations reflections of his own bearing upon the facts recorded; and, like St. John, whenever opportunity offers, he refers to the fulfilment of Old

Testament prophecy in the circumstances and events of the history. Thus, for example, in ch. iv. 13–15, he tells how Jesus left Nazareth, and went down to Capernaum, in the region of Zebulon and Naphthali; and he immediately adds, ἵνα πληρωθῇ, κ.τ.λ. (Isa. viii. 23, 24.) And so in other places; see i. 22, 23, ii. 5, 6, 15, 17, 18, 23, viii. 17, xii. 18–21, xiii. 35, xxi. 5, xxvii. 9, 10.

These comments and reflections upon facts are obviously the work of the evangelist himself; for they do not occur in Luke, never in the manner referred to, and not even in the narrations which Luke gives in common with Matthew (*e.g.* Matt. viii. 17, xxi. 5). These references and citations in Matthew differ from those others which he has in common with Luke, when a passage from the Old Testament is quoted or referred to in the course of a discourse or narrative. In those the LXX. is evidently used; but here, in these peculiar to Matthew, we have a direct translation of the writer's own from the Hebrew text, and differing not only verbally, but sometimes in meaning also, from the Septuagint (see viii. 17, xii. 18, 19), the words of the LXX. but seldom appearing in them. This is the case also in Matt. x. 36, xi. 29*b*, where, even in the sayings of Jesus, which Matthew and Luke have in common, we find original versions of Old Testament declarations, which we must regard as inserted by the evangelist himself, and which have not been borrowed from the Septuagint.[1] This fact, again, goes to prove that the primary conception of the narrations which Matthew has in common with Luke, did not belong to the same writer as these citations peculiar to Matthew; and that the writer of the first Gospel found ready to his hand those common discourses in the *Greek*, and not the Hebrew language. Had they been before him in Hebrew, the evangelist, who, as the citations of the other kind show, knew the Old Testament in the original, and was strong in Hebrew, would not have

[[1] See BLEEK, *Beitr.* pp. 57, 58. ANGER, on the contrary, endeavours to prove (see § 93) that this distinction is only an uncertain one, and that all the citations in Matthew have a common resemblance and distinctiveness.]

given the quotations in those passages which he has in common with Luke, and which almost all occur in the Aramæan discourses of Christ and others, according to the LXX., and without reference to the Hebrew text. In other parts, the Greek of the Gospel is of a uniform character, but in these special sections it has distinctive peculiarities; and we infer that the writer has to a certain extent revised and altered the primary narrative he made use of, conformably with his own distinctive style, and that he has done this in a greater degree than Luke.

§ 107.

As to the Gospel of Luke, if we compare the preface with the rest of the Gospel, we shall see how little the writer has impressed his own distinctive style upon the materials he made use of throughout the treatise. The preface is clearly his own, and is written in good and elegant Greek; but throughout the Gospel we find sections which bear the impress of an Hebraistic writer. See, for example, Luke ix. 51: ἐγένετο δὲ ἐν τῷ συμπληροῦσθαι τὰς ἡμέρας τῆς ἀναλήμψεως αὐτοῦ, καὶ αὐτὸς τὸ πρόσωπον αὐτοῦ ἐστήριξε τοῦ πορεύεσθαι εἰς Ἱερουσαλήμ. The language even of the *evangelium infantiæ*, immediately following the preface, is strikingly contrasted with its pure Greek. This might partly be accounted for by the fact that some sections are translations from an Aramæan original. But even apart from those portions which are common to Matthew and Luke, and in which, as we have seen (§ 101), this is certainly not the case, this explanation is not supported by the other parts of the Gospel. The contrary, indeed, is often proveable where this explanation seems to apply. For instance, in the history of the infancy, the prophetic song of Zacharias (Luke i. 68-79) is of a very Hebraistic character. Yet even here the greater probability is, that it was originally committed to writing in Greek; for ἀνατολή in vers. 78, 79 is used in such a manner, that the idea of a constellation rising upwards in the heavens is confounded with that of a branch shooting forth from the parent stem, *i.e.* of a descendant (*i.e.* from David, and = צמח, Zech. iii. 8, vi. 12),—both conceptions being expressed by one and the same Greek word, but not by any common term in Aramæan. The Hebraistic tone, therefore, of this section must be accounted for by supposing that the style is that of a writer who was a Jew by education, and had attained his knowledge of Greek by reading the Greek version of the Old Testament, and thus had formed a Hebraizing manner of writing and speaking Greek. Such a style was by no means natural to Luke; and we must therefore conclude that he found this narrative already embodied in a written form, and that he adopted either the whole, or at least certain parts of it, into his history.

But we certainly have not ground for going so far as SCHLEIERMACHER and others do, who suppose that Luke simply copied from the documents of others all that he records, appropriating the materials before him without any alteration. There are peculiarities of expression and exposition in various parts of the Gospel which reappear in the book of the Acts, and which must be regarded as characteristic of the writer of both treatises. These peculiarities occur even in those sections which he must have found already before him in a written form.[1] And in the case of those sections of his which he has in common with Matthew, if we compare the two evangelists, we find that Luke has by no means retained the narrative in its original form. Still, comparatively speaking, it must be allowed that Luke has not revised, digested, and altered his materials so much as Matthew. His work indicates less cleverness on his part as an historical writer. His Gospel is not so evidently from one fount as is that of Matthew. Many sections differ in a marked manner from each other in their manner of expression and exposition. Thus the longer or shorter portions peculiar to Luke are distinguished from those which he has in common with Matthew in various ways, *e.g.* by the repeated designation of Jesus as ὁ Κύριος even in the progressive his-

---

[1] See MAYERHOFF, *Einl. in die Petr. Schriften*, pp. 27 sqq.; CREDNER, § 59; DE WETTE, § 91, *a*, note *a*.

torical narration (vii. 13, x. 1, xi. 39, xii. 42, xiii. 15, xvii. 5, 6, xviii. 6, xxii. 31, 61); whereas in the other Gospels it occurs only in direct addresses to the Saviour. In these sections, moreover, Christ's twelve chosen companions are called οἱ ἀπόστολοι, or οἱ δώδεκα ἀπόστολοι (ix. 10, xvii. 5, xxii. 14, xxiv. 10); and this does not occur in the other Gospels, except in Mark vi. 30, where it is retained in a parallel passage from Luke. These two peculiarities may be regarded as Luke's own; but he has not adopted them throughout, and they do not so frequently occur in the sections which he has in common with Matthew.

The absence of any thorough distinctive digest and revision of materials in Luke is also apparent from the fact that the various events are recorded more disconnectedly than in Matthew, and almost abruptly one after another (see De Wette, § 91, c, note b). Hence some facts and incidents seem, if we look to their position in Luke only, as if inappropriately placed. For example, the account of Christ's appearance in the synagogue at Nazareth is put at the beginning of His Galilean ministry (Luke iv. 14–30), though the narrative, even as Luke tells it, shows that already Christ had laboured for some time in Galilee. Again, in his account of the healing of Simon's wife's mother (iv. 38, 39), he seems to take for granted that this Simon is already known to his readers, though he had not previously named him. This want of due connection and arrangement is very apparent in that long section peculiar to Luke, ch. ix. 51–xviii. 14. According to its position in the history, it purports to be the first part of the account of the journey from Galilee to Jerusalem. The statement in ix. 51 implies this, and it is often stated that the facts recorded took place on a journey (ix. 57, x. 1, 38, xi. 1), or on this very journey to Jerusalem (xiii. 22, xvii. 11). But the contents of the section show that we cannot regard it as a consecutive and chronologically arranged account of this journey, or even as a narrative of some events which took place during it. In x. 38–42, in the early part of the section, we have the visit of Christ to Martha and Mary at Bethany, close by Jerusalem. The narrative here cannot be regarded as chronologically arranged, for a good way further on (ch. xviii. 35–37) we find Jesus in Jericho, a long way off from Jerusalem, but still on His way thither; and not until ch. xix. 29 are we told of His coming to Bethphage and Bethany. In ch. xiii. 31–33, moreover, we find Jesus still in Galilee; and in xvii. 11 He is still going through Samaria and Galilee, or seemingly on the borders of both. It is doubtful whether Luke himself arranged the various portions of this section as we have them, or whether he found them already thus arranged; but it is probable (though Weisse, *Evang. Geschichte,* i. 88, and De Wette, § 92, deny it) that he found this section pretty much as he gives it—as a written collection of longer or shorter discourses of Christ, spoken at different times, and without special regard to chronological circumstances of time and place. Luke perhaps has added some portions, and omitted others.

§ 108.

10. As to the characteristic religious tone and spirit of these two Gospels respectively, Matthew is usually regarded as bearing the impress of a Jewish Christian, and Luke of a Gentile Christian writer. This is certainly true; but we must not suppose that the two Gospels are thus formally contrasted, as is represented by the *Sächsische Anonymus*,[1] where the truth of the matter is pushed to an extreme. The first Gospel cannot certainly in its spirit and tendency be regarded as Judaizing in the sense of limiting the Gospel, in opposition to the Pauline view, within the range of Judaism. It cannot be denied, however, that the writer keeps chiefly in view the relationship and wants of the Jewish people, and with a Christian consciousness and perception makes what is laid down in the Jewish law and kingdom the starting-point of his exposition of gospel history. The main design of this Gospel is clearly to prove to Jews, whether belonging to Christian Churches or not, that Jesus is the Christ, the Redeemer promised of God to

[1] *Die Evv. ihr Geist, ihre Verf. u. ihr Verhältniss zu einander*, Leipz. 1845.

His people, to whom the Old Testament Scriptures throughout point, and that the prophecies therein contained find in Him their fulfilment. This aim is evident at the very beginning of the Gospel in the genealogy of Jesus, where He is described as the descendant of Abraham and of David, and in various places where notice is taken of the fulfilment of Old Testament prophecy in the history of Jesus. The evangelist gives prominence, moreover, to those parts of Christ's discourses which have special reference to Jewish customs, to the Jewish law and its relation to the law of the new covenant, and to the Jews themselves—their position as God's people, and their claim to the salvation wrought by the Messiah.

But Matthew's Gospel is by no means Judaizing in its tendency, in the sense of putting the law on a par with the gospel, and limiting the kingdom of God to the Jewish nation. Christ's words in Matt. v. 17-19, "Think not that I am come to destroy the law and the prophets; I am not come to destroy, but to fulfil," and, "Whosoever shall break one of these least commandments, and shall teach men so, he shall be called the least in the kingdom of heaven," are immediately followed (ver. 21 sqq.) by a series of declarations showing the contrast between the spirit of the gospel and the Old Testament law, and describing the Jewish standard of morals as not sufficiently high for the kingdom of God. Matthew, indeed, alone gives our Lord's direction to the twelve when He is sending them forth (ch. x. 5), "Go not into the way of the Gentiles, and into any city of the Samaritans enter ye not; but go rather to the lost sheep of the house of Israel;" and he only records the words of Jesus in the account of the woman of Canaan, which Luke wholly omits, "I am not sent save to the lost sheep of the house of Israel," and, "It is not meet to take the children's bread, and to cast it unto dogs" (Matt. xv. 24, 26). But he also records how Jesus granted to this heathen woman her request, when she gave so beautiful a proof of her faith. Again, in the account of the Gentile centurion at Capernaum (ch. viii. 10-12), Matthew records how Jesus said, "I have not found so great faith, no, not in Israel;" and how He added, "Many shall come from the east and west, and shall sit down with Abraham, and Isaac, and Jacob in the kingdom of heaven; but the children of the kingdom (*i.e.* the Jews) shall be cast into outer darkness: there shall be weeping and gnashing of teeth,"[1]—a declaration which does not occur in the corresponding place in Luke (ch. vii.), though he gives what is essentially the same in another place (Luke xiii. 28, 29). Matthew further records the threatening uttered by Jesus against the Jews (ch. xxi. 43), "The kingdom of God shall be taken from you, and given to a nation bringing forth the fruits thereof,"—words which neither Luke nor Mark record, though they give the narrative in which the words occur,— a fact which still proves that Matthew had specially Jewish readers in his mind when he wrote. Matthew further records, in ch. xxiv. 14, that declaration of the Lord which Luke in the same discourse omits, that "the gospel of the kingdom shall be preached unto all nations;" and in ch. xxviii. 19, at the end of his Gospel, the command of the risen Saviour to His disciples, "Go, teach all nations, baptizing them."

As to St. Luke, it has always been remarked, and with truth, that of all our canonical Gospels, his is most in accord with the spirit and teaching of St. Paul; and this is apparent not only in the tenor and tendency of his Gospel generally, but in many particular places which seem to indicate a close connection between the writer and the great apostle. The genealogy of Jesus in St. Luke is in keeping with the Pauline spirit. It is manifestly given in order to prove the human descent of Jesus, not as a Jew merely, but as man. It is not placed at the beginning of his Gospel, but is inserted as if in passing (ch. iii. 23 sqq.); and it traces the

---

[1] [HILGENFELD (*Die Evv.* p. 106; *Zeitschr. f. wiss. Theol.* 1862, p. 62) considers that the contrast and contradiction between Matt. viii. 10 and xv. 24 is so great, that it can only be explained by supposing the blending in the one Gospel of a strong Judaistic primary document with a more universalist recension. See, on the other side, HOLTZMANN, pp. 378–380; KEIM, *Der geschichtliche Christus,* pp. 60–62, who attributes the contrast to a change in Christ's own progressive views.—B.]

descent of Jesus not merely from David and Abraham, the progenitors of the Jews, but from Adam, the progenitor of the human race, and from God Himself, as the Creator of man. His aim obviously was to show how Jesus, by virtue of His humanity, was akin not only to the Jews, but to man as man, to the whole human race; and therefore that other nations had a certain claim, in virtue of their common humanity, to the salvation which Jesus has wrought. Again, Luke alone relates the mission of the seventy (ch. x. 1 sqq.), and this more fully than that of the twelve (ch. ix. 1 sqq.). According to the later Jews, the number of the Gentile nations was seventy (or seventy-two), according to the list of nations in Gen. x. It is therefore very probable that, as the twelve apostles represented the children of Israel according to their twelve tribes (Matt. xix. 28; Luke xxii. 30), so the seventy disciples were intended to represent other nations collectively; and Luke, in mentioning them, intended to show that the Gentiles as well as the Jews were to be sharers of the salvation which the kingdom of God secured. Luke, moreover, in his account of the Lord's discourse in the synagogue at Nazareth, records the words which He spoke concerning the prophets Elijah and Elisha, who were sent not to the widows and lepers of Israel, but the one to the Gentile widow at Sarepta, and the other to the Gentile leper Naaman the Syrian (Luke iv. 25-27).

St. Luke's Gospel, moreover, is strikingly distinguished from St. Matthew's in the manner in which the Samaritans (through whose country Jesus had to pass in going from Galilee to Jerusalem) are spoken of. They were a strictly monotheistic people, and recognised the law of Moses; but the Jews looked down upon them as heathens, and treated them as such. Matthew only mentions them in x. 5, where he records Christ's injunction to the twelve not to go into any Samaritan cities. This direction was doubtless authentic, but was given by Christ with reference only to the first mission of the apostles. Luke accordingly omits it. But he, and he alone, records the parable of the good Samaritan (ch. x. 25-37), and the story of the ten lepers (xvii. 11-19) whom Jesus healed, and of whom only one returned to thank Him, καὶ αὐτὸς ἦν Σαμαρείτης; and the circumstance named in ch. ix. 51–56, how Jesus rebuked the two sons of Zebedee, who would have called down fire from heaven on the inhospitable Samaritan village. Matthew names none of these incidents, and possibly he intentionally omitted them, lest the setting up of Samaritans over against Jews should be a stumbling-block to the latter.

There are several parables, too, peculiar to Luke, teaching that man cannot by any works of his own earn or merit the praise or reward of God; that outward righteousness may co-exist with inward impiety and faithlessness towards God; that humility of heart is an essential virtue; that man must feel himself to be a sinner, and must look for mercy solely from the grace of God, and without raising himself above his fellow-men: see, *e.g.*, xvii. 7–10, the parable of the unprofitable servants, and xviii. 9–14, the parable of the Pharisee and the publican. These remind us of St. Paul, who insists upon the very same truths.

There are also some more minute particulars in which St. Luke corresponds with St. Paul. (*a.*) His account of the institution of the holy communion (xxii. 17–20) closely corresponds with that given in 1 Cor. xi. 23–25, and in the Greek much more closely resembles it than does Matthew's account. Indeed, we may with very high probability conclude that the evangelist had the Pauline account before him, and made use of it. The words of Jesus when He took the cup after He had blessed (Luke xxii. 20), are given by St. Luke in a manner (grammatically viewed) in which they could not have been written, and could not be explained, unless we suppose that Luke had before him two different accounts, viz. that of St. Paul, and that of the Primitive Gospel, which Matthew (xxvi. 28) used, and here blends them. The first clause is verbatim the same as St. Paul's (τοῦτο τὸ ποτήριον ἡ καινὴ διαθήκη ἐν τῷ αἵματί μου); and the second or participial clause (τὸ ὑπὲρ ὑμῶν ἐκχυνόμενον) is added from another source, and in the grammatical form, wherein it lay there, though this was not in keeping with the first clause, for the participle ἐκχυνόμενον clearly refers to the αἵματι, and should have been in the dative. (*b.*) In Luke xxiv. 34 it is said in passing, in the conversation of the eleven disciples, "The Lord is risen indeed, and hath appeared to Simon," *i.e.* before He appeared to the eleven. This fact is mentioned by none of the other evangelists, but only by St. Paul (1 Cor. xv. 5). (*c.*) The command of Christ to the seventy in Luke x. 8, εἰς ἣν ἂν πόλιν εἰσέρχησθε καὶ δέχωνται ὑμᾶς, ἐσθίετε τὰ παρατιθέμενα ὑμῖν, κ.τ.λ., reminds us forcibly of the Pauline precept (1 Cor. x. 27), πᾶν τὸ παρατιθέμενον ὑμῖν ἐσθίετε, though this is meant, perhaps, in another sense.

§ 109.

11. Putting all the circumstances we have named together, we are led to the conclusion that the writer of the third Gospel was a disciple of the Lord, belonging to the second generation of Christians, who composed his Gospel mainly in the Pauline spirit, and was in close connection with the Apostle of the Gentiles. This is in accord with the title of the Gospel and ecclesiastical tradition, which unanimously speak of St. Luke as the writer, who appears in the Pauline Epistles as a friend and companion of the apostle, not belonging to the circumcision (see § 49). There seems to me to be no ground whatever for denying that the Gospel is his. Still we have not warrant to affirm that St. Paul took part in the composition of this Gospel; still less in holding, with the *Sächsische Anonymus* (see § 55 fin.), that St. Paul himself wrote a considerable portion of it; for the date of its composition was probably subsequent to St. Paul's death.

Luke himself states the design of his Gospel in his preface,—namely, to give to Theophilus, who was probably a distinguished Greek or Roman, though not perhaps a member of the Christian Church, a full, accurate, and consecutive narrative, as complete as possible, of the gospel history, of which he had already heard somewhat. As to the relation of St. Luke's Gospel to that of Marcion, see § 51 sqq., where it is shown that the resemblance between the two proves that our third Gospel was already regarded by Marcion and the Church of his time as the work of a Pauline Christian not belonging to the Jewish nation.

INTEGRITY.—Formerly the *evangelium infantiæ*, ch. i. 5 sqq. and ch. ii., were objected to and regarded as a later interpolation (see Meyer, *Krit. Anm.* to ch. ii.), but without sufficient grounds, as is now acknowledged by those who allow the genuineness of the rest of the Gospel. We need not here name the views of Schwegler, Baur, and others, who date the Gospel as we have it after Marcion's time, for we have already referred to them, § 51 sqq.

§ 110.

12. The conclusion at which we arrive concerning the origin of our *first* Gospel is not thus coincident with ecclesiastical tradition. There can be no doubt that the writer was both by birth and education a Jew, and probably a native of Palestine : the intimate acquaintance with the Hebrew text of the Old Testament which his citations indicate proves this amply. The date also of the Gospel falls within the early apostolic age, probably before A.D. 70 ; and it was written in Palestine, probably in Galilee or thereabouts, for the use of Jews and Jewish Christians of those parts, and in order to lead them in that unquiet time to the belief, or to confirm them in the belief, that Jesus of Nazareth was the Messiah promised of God by the prophets of the old covenant, and that all true peace and salvation were to be looked for in Him. Still we cannot take for granted—as ecclesiastical tradition and the superscription of the Gospel (see § 38, 40) represent—that it is the work of an immediate disciple of Christ, *i.e.* of the Apostle Matthew, or that it is a Greek translation of an Aramæan original written by this apostle. I would briefly remind the reader of the facts which, as we have already seen, militate against this. (*a*) Our Gospel was certainly originally composed in Greek ; see § 101, 104. (*b*) It could hardly have been composed by an apostle, for the whole course of the history is against such

a supposition : the day of the month of Christ's crucifixion (see § 72, 73); its silence concerning the earlier journeys to Jerusalem (§ 71), and concerning many important facts which we learn from St. John, *e.g.* the raising of Lazarus, and the opening the eyes of one born blind; the relation in which our Gospel stands to Luke,—the narratives and discourses which both have in common, indicating that both are dependent upon an earlier document; and the circumstance that the exposition given in Matthew is not always the more original in comparison with Luke, but as often seems to be the derived one (§ 99 sqq.). The connection in which many of the discourses in this Gospel stand (see § 99) is also against its apostolic authorship. These things lead us rather to suppose a writer further removed from the events narrated, who found the materials for his history already before him, and made use of them according to his special purpose and personal individuality, and not an apostle who was an immediate witness of and participator in the events recorded.

The Gospel itself nowhere claims to have been the work of an apostle, nor of the Apostle Matthew. The writer never speaks of himself as an immediate disciple of Jesus, nor does he ever claim to have been an eye-witness of the events which he records. In his account of the call of the Apostle Matthew in particular (Matt. ix. 9), he does not give the slightest hint that he, the writer, is this publican Matthew; the account is quite different from what we should expect in such a case. The state of the case, therefore, is not, that being obliged to deny that the Apostle Matthew was the writer, we must pronounce the work a spurious one. This would be the case only if the Gospel itself claimed to be the work of some one whose work it was not; but no such claim is made. We cannot refer to the title as if it were part of the Gospel itself, for it does not accord therewith, and there is no evidence whatever to show that it proceeded from the writer himself. The probability is, that this superscription, like the postscripts to the Gospel which occur in various manuscripts, were added afterwards, and in conformity with the supposition which had sprung up in the Church concerning the author, and which was the prevailing belief in the middle of the second century.

But the question arises, How did this traditional belief that the Apostle Matthew was the author spring up and gain ground in the Church? and what has it to do with the Aramæan treatise of Matthew's mentioned by Papias (§ 40)? In reply to these questions, we can only propose conjectural explanations; but yet, I think, we can do this with great probability, in support of what we advance. As our Gospel was written by a Palestinian for Palestinians, it was from the beginning received and held in esteem by the Jewish Christians there. To meet the wants of those who did not know Greek sufficiently well, an Aramæan translation or collection of it would very soon be made—probably within ten years of its first appearance; and this was the treatise which Papias knew, and which later writers speak of as εὐαγγέλιον καθ' Ἑβραίους, or as the Gospel of the Nazarenes or Ebionites. This Gospel bore very distinct marks of its being a translation from a Greek original (see § 46); still it expressly claimed (at least when Epiphanius and Jerome knew it) to have been an apostolic work, and indeed the work of the Apostle Matthew (§ 45); and it is not improbable that the first Aramæan recensor of it put it forth thus, in order to secure for it higher authority and esteem. We cannot tell what induced him to choose the Apostle Matthew as the author. This would be easily explained, if we might suppose that the name of the writer of the Greek original was Matthew; but though this is quite conceivable, it can only be named as a conjecture. This much, however, is very probable, that the notion of an apostolic origin was transferred in the first instance from the Aramæan translation to the Greek original, and thus it became general in the Church. If the explanation we have suggested be correct, it would involve a lesser difficulty,—viz. to explain how it came to pass that, when these two Gospels were attributed to St. Matthew, the Aramæan should be regarded in the Church, and even as early as Papias, as the original, and the Greek Gospel, from which the other sprung, as merely a translation.

It cannot be denied that, according to this view, our first canonical Gospel, as an historical authority, loses somewhat of the high rank it would assume as an immediate work of an apostle. But this consideration must not prevent our yielding assent to the results to which a scientific and unbiassed investigation has led us. The case is not such that, if we yield to the force of our conclusions, we must give up the authority of our Gospel. It takes its stand, so to speak, a stage lower than St. John, but it still ranks side by side with St. Luke; and it still remains a trustworthy and most valuable spring from which Christian faith may draw, and by which it may be strengthened and confirmed. And though we have not the immediate testimony of an apostle for those facts and aspects of gospel history which are taught us in the Synoptics only, we have for the most of them the concurrent yet independent testimony of three evangelists who all belonged to the apostolic age; and we must thankfully regard this as a special providence of God, while for that portion and aspect of gospel history which are presented to us in St. John we do not need any further witness than the direct testimony of this apostle.

INTEGRITY.—The *evangelium infantiæ* has also been objected to as spurious in St. Matthew's Gospel (see De Wette, § 92, note *a*); but it is now rightly retained as genuine.

§ 111.

As to the *second* canonical Gospel, it follows from what we have already seen (if our remarks as to the relation between Matthew and Luke are correct, § 94 sqq.), that it was written still later than those Gospels, and consequently after the destruction of Jerusalem. Mark indeed probably wrote subsequently to the composition and publication even of St. John's Gospel. Many passages make it probable that he knew the fourth Gospel, and used it, though comparatively seldom, and for special points. Thus, (*a*) Mark vi. 37 reminds us of John vi. 7. It cannot be denied that the manner in which the "two hundred pence" are mentioned in John is more natural and original than in Mark. (*b*)

Mark xiv. 3, νάρδου πιστικῆς πολυτελοῦς; John xii. 3, μύρου νάρδου πιστικῆς πολυτίμου (Matt. xxvi. 7, μύρου βαρυτίμου). Compare Mark, ver. 6, ἄφετε αὐτήν; John, ver. 7, ἄφες αὐτήν: Mark, ver. 5; John, ver. 5. So also in the history of the passion: see Mark xiv. 65, where, to the account given by Matthew and Luke, Mark adds that the servants (ὑπηρέται) struck Jesus with ῥαπίσματα (compare John xviii. 22); Mark xv. 8, 9, where he coincides with John xviii. 39 in representing that Pilate at the outset, and before mentioning Barabbas, asked the people whether he should liberate the King of the Jews; Mark xvi. 9, where the statement has probably been taken from John xx. 14 sqq., that the risen Jesus appeared specially to Mary Magdalene, for this is not mentioned in Luke, and according to Matthew xxviii. 1 sqq. the other Mary was also present. See also Mark ii. 9, 12 (John v. 8, 9), xi. 9 (John xii. 13). These passages, taken together, lead us to suppose that the coincidence arises from the dependence of the one writer upon the work of the other. It certainly is not at all probable, as Baur, Zeller (*Theol. Jahrbb.* 1847, p. 138), and Hilgenfeld (*Hall. Allg. Litt. Z.* 1847, No. 81, and elsewhere) think, that John was depending upon Mark. This circumstance, if it be as we suggest, serves, moreover, to confirm the genuineness of St. John's Gospel (see § 89).

Whether Mark made use of any other written sources we cannot decide. His Gospel contains two narratives peculiar to him (see § 65), and he gives many historical touches peculiar to himself in the parts which he has in common with Matthew and Luke,—touches which bear on the face of them the stamp of truth. They are clearly authentic touches—facts which he must have learned from some other historical source, but whether from written or oral tradition we cannot say. See, for example, Mark xiv. 51, 52, iii. 17, concerning the surname of the sons of Zebedee; xv. 21, the names of the sons of Simon the Cyrenian; x. 46, the name of the blind man, ὁ υἱὸς Τιμαίου Βαρτίμαιος (Luke has merely τυφλός τις, Matthew δύο τυφλοί); ii. 14, where τὸν τοῦ Ἀλφαίου is added to the name (taken from Luke)

Λευίν; xv. 40, xvi. 1, the name Salome given to the mother of Zebedee's children (see § 56), which is mentioned by no other of the evangelists.

If we return to consider the tradition of the Church regarding this Gospel (see § 48), we find ourselves obliged, by the results of our investigation, to reject the opinion that its contents have for their basis the oral instructions of the Apostle Peter. Had these formed the substance of the Gospel, it would by comparison with the others have presented far more that was new and distinctive than it does (see § 65). The opinion is quite irreconcilable with the fact that our other Gospels are seemingly the sources whence the contents, the arrangement, and the exposition of the treatise from beginning to end are drawn (see § 94 sqq.). It is not probable, moreover, that either St. Peter or the other apostles in their oral discourses related the history of the Lord in orderly connection, as in our Gospels. We may, moreover, take it as certain, from what we have already seen, that St. Mark's Gospel was written a considerable time after St. Peter's death; and indeed Irenæus (*Hær.* iii. 1) distinctly affirms that Mark did not write his Gospel until after the death of Peter and of Paul (μετὰ τὴν τούτων ἔξοδον). Ebrard is certainly mistaken when he takes ὁ ἔξοδος to mean merely the departure of the apostles from Rome.

Still there is no sufficient reason for denying that the Gospel was composed by JOHN MARK, to whom ecclesiastical tradition unanimously assigns it. There are, indeed, particulars which confirm this opinion. The Gospel was probably written in the West, in the first instance for Roman Christians, and by a man who, though belonging to the Jewish nation, must have long resided in the West. No one doubts that the author was a Jew; and the fact that he considers it necessary to explain Jewish customs, shows that he did not write primarily for Jewish readers. Thus in ch. vii., in the discourse concerning the washing of hands (which he has taken from Matt. xv. 1 sqq.), he inserts an explanation (vers. 3, 4) which does not occur in Matthew. See also ver. 2, κοιναῖς χερσὶ, τοῦτ' ἔστιν ἀνίπτοις; xv. 42, ἐπεὶ ἦν παρασκευὴ, ὅ ἐστι προσάββατον. Mark, moreover, has generally omitted the remark which Matthew usually makes about the fulfilment of Old Testament prophecy in the life of Christ, even in places where he evidently is making use of this evangelist; *e.g.* Matt. iv. 14–17, viii. 17, xii. 18–21, xiii. 14, 15, 35, xxi. 5. That he had Romans in view as his readers, is indicated in ch. xii. 42, where, after λεπτὰ δύο (from Luke xxi. 2), he adds, ὅ ἐστι κοδράντης, *quadrans*,—a coin in use only among the Romans. Ch. xv. 21 also is not an unimportant testimony, for here he speaks of Simon the Cyrenian as the father of Alexander and Rufus; and from this we may infer that these two were, when Mark wrote, members of the Christian Church, and were known to those for whom he wrote. And thus it is not unlikely that Rufus is the same who is named in Rom. xvi. 13, who was then with his mother in Rome. It may further be remarked, that Mark uses Latin words oftener than other New Testament writers, and in places where Matthew and Luke have not got them. Thus κράββατος, ch. ii. 4, 9, 11, 12 (Matthew, κλίνη; Luke, κλινίδιον), vi. 55 (though this word occurs also in the Acts and St. John's Gospel); σπεκουλάτωρ, only in Mark vi. 27 (not in Matt. xiv. 10); κεντυρίων, xv. 39 (where Matthew and Luke have ἑκατόνταρχος), xv. 44, 45,—the only places where it occurs in the N. T. See also xv. 15, τὸ ἱκανὸν ποιῆσαι. Such Latin words and Latinisms could have become familiar to Mark only during his residence in Rome with St. Paul and St. Peter, and thus they may be adduced in confirmation of the tradition that he was the author. Still we must not attach too much importance to this argument, because several Latin words had at the time been adopted into Greek, and were current among those who had not much intercourse with Latins.

The historical value of this Gospel cannot be quite on a par with that of the others, not even with that of Matthew and Luke, because these two were the main sources from which Mark drew. If the arguments we have advanced (§ 97) concerning its composition be valid, we cannot regard the Gospel as a standard of appeal for the exact chronological order of given events. Mark must be regarded as an independent historical witness only for those narrations, and additions to the narrations of Matthew and Luke, which are peculiar to him; and these are not, comparatively speaking, numerous or important, though they are very interesting as minute touches completing the picture. Very weighty, however, must Mark be as a witness in another respect,—namely, how that, at the time he wrote, the Gospels of Matthew and Luke were already reverenced in the Christian Church as trustworthy histories of the Saviour's life. Had they not been so, such a man as Mark, who must have been within range of hearing and knowing all facts that might be collected concerning the Lord's life, would not certainly have so closely confined himself in the composition of his Gospel to the works of those two evangelists, in relation to which his treatise may be regarded as a pithy and concise epitome or abstract.

As to the *integrity* of this Gospel, its concluding verses, xvi. 9–20, have been the subject of much doubt and controversy, and are regarded as spurious by many modern critics, partly upon external and partly upon internal grounds. It is wanting in Codex B [and ℵ], and down to the fourth century in many MSS., as we have abundant proof. Yet it occurs not only in all other MSS. which have come down to us, but in all the versions likewise, even in the oldest, such as the Vulgate and Peschito, and is quoted in Irenæus and Hippolytus. Again, we cannot well suppose that Mark could have closed his Gospel with the words of xvi. 8, ἐφοβοῦντο γάρ. The concluding verses, moreover, correspond well with what precedes, if we keep in view Mark's method in relation to Matthew and Luke. Hence it seems to me most probable that this concluding portion did originally belong to the Gospel, and was omitted, through some accident, by a copyist. See my *Synopt. Erkl. d. drei ersten Evv.* ii. 500. Reuss (§ 240) regards the opening verses of the Gospel, ch. i. 1–13 [and in his 3d and 4th editions, ch. i. 1–20], as having been prefixed at a later date; but there are no sufficient grounds for this.

§ 112.

[I. Face to face with the so-called hypothesis of GRIES-BACH's adopted in this work (§ 94 sqq.), according to which Mark is dependent upon Matthew and Luke, these two evangelists forming his main sources, the theory is now maintained that he wrote quite independently of them; that in relation to them he is the more original, and that his Gospel is one source—or, as many think, the main source—from which Matthew and Luke both draw. While, according to the first-named view, very little independent historical authority remains for Mark side by side with the other two Synoptics, this historical authority increases in proportion as he is held to be independent of them and before them, and thus the lively interest attaching to this question can easily be understood. For the sake of acquainting the reader with the subject, and not in order to broach any views of my own, I here subjoin a summary of the main arguments and counter arguments advanced on both sides. For the Griesbachian hypothesis I refer to the preceding argument in § 94 sqq., and for the opposite view chiefly to HOLTZMANN and WEISS (*Stud. u. Krit.* 1861).

In proof of the *dependence* of Mark, the following arguments are urged:—

1. The mode of expression and of narration in parallel passages, wherein Mark as a rule is more akin to Matthew and Luke than these are to each other. (*a.*) The expressions used seem often to result from a combination of both sources (see § 94); *e.g.* Mark i. 32, ὀψίας δὲ γενομένης (= Matthew), ὅτε ἔδυ ὁ ἥλιος (= Luke). In answer to this, it has been observed (Holtzmann, p. 113; Weiss, p. 683), that similar cases occur in Luke viii. 25, ix. 5, 11, 13, as compared with the parallel passages; and further, that these emphatic repetitions are distinctive of Mark's style, and in many places are accounted for by the facts of the case; *e.g.* in i. 32, the additional words ὅτε ἔδυ ὁ ἥλιος are explained by the fact that, it being the Sabbath, they dare not bring the sick to Jesus until the sun was set. Again, that we may easily suppose that Matthew and Luke, in making use of

Mark, might unintentionally have divided his fuller expression between them. (*b*) The narrative in parallel passages seems in Mark to be a combination, or a bare abstract from that of Matthew and Luke (§ 95). In answer to this, reference is made to xvi. 9 sqq., which is supposed to be spurious; and for the rest, this is allowed to hold true in some instances, especially in the account of the temptation.

2. With reference to the selection of the subject-matter, stress is laid (*a*) upon the great preponderance of miraculous facts in Mark over the sayings and discourses of Jesus (see § 96). In reply, it is granted that the discourses of Jesus were probably committed to writing before the historical narration; but it is urged that, when Mark wrote, a collection of discourses had already been made (Holtzmann, p. 116). (*b*) As to the two miraculous narrations peculiar to Mark (vii. 32 sqq., viii. 22 sqq.), see above, § 96, and Holtzmann, pp. 116, 117.

3. The composition of the Gospel as a whole can be explained only by a reference to the two other Synoptics, whom Mark took as his guides; for whenever he turns from Matthew to Luke, or from Luke to Matthew, the reason of the change can easily be traced (see § 97). So far as this argument applies to the concluding verses, xvi. 9 sqq., the spuriousness of this portion is urged in reply. For the rest, it is held that such reasons cannot always be discovered,—that in those places where Matthew is said to be the guide followed, the influence of Luke may be said to assert itself, and *vice versa*. Further, it is urged that such trouble on Mark's part was quite superfluous, and that any such turning backwards and forwards from one source to the other would be arbitrary and strange.

In proof of the *independent originality* of St. Mark, the following arguments have been advanced:—

1. The narratives of Mark are very original and striking, full of life and minuteness of detail.

2. With reference to Mark's selection of materials for his work, reference is made to his omission of the early history as given in Matthew and Luke (see above, § 96).

3. Viewing the composition of the work as a whole, it presents a consecutive thread of evangelic history, sustained unbroken throughout.

4. HOLTZMANN, with special reference to Bleek's argument, urges that Bleek's description of the supposed primitive Gospel, which formed the common basis of Matthew and Luke, really corresponds with what we have in Mark. See his remarks, *Synopt. Evang.* pp. 101, 121, and in Schenkel's *Allgem. kirchl. Zeitschr.* 1862, p. 91.

II. While at present the Griesbachian hypothesis has few advocates beyond the range of the Tübingen school, a special preference for the second Gospel has become very general. It must be remembered, however, that few go so far as to recognise in Mark, as we have it, a source from which the other Synoptics drew, or the Primitive Gospel. Almost all espousers of the Mark hypothesis feel themselves obliged to make certain admissions: they allow in many points (over and above the conclusion, xvi. 9 sqq., which they pronounce spurious) its secondary character as a treatise (see *e.g.* Holtzmann, p. 60 sqq.), and they incline to institute a double relationship between our Mark and the other Synoptics. In explanation of this, 1. They assume another document besides our Mark, which either formed its basis, or grew up side by side with it,—namely (*a*) the so-called primary Mark, from which our canonical Mark sprang, or (*b*) the so-called primary Matthew, or "Collection of Discourses," to which is attributed much of the rich material which the two other Synoptics contain, over and above what they found in Mark. 2. It is only consistent on this theory to maintain that *our canonical Mark* was itself also a source from which Matthew and Luke drew, and that these evangelists were dependent upon him. But among the champions of the Mark hypothesis few only maintain this, *e.g.* Meyer and Weiss. They either make out, as Wilke and Bruno Bauer do, later interpolations in our Mark, or they resort to a primary Mark as the source of our Mark. While accordingly the alternative has been stated, as in § 93, that "either Mark is dependent on the other two Synoptics, or these other two on Mark," the effort is increasingly apparent in the latest investigations to devise a *via media*, avoiding this alternative, by the assumption of one primary document which formed the basis of all three Synoptics, and which our Mark very closely resembles, though it be not identical with it.¹—B.]

THE GOSPEL OF ST. JOHN.

§ 113.

We have already sought to establish the authenticity of this Gospel (§ 71 sqq.). Some other points respecting it, however, remain to be briefly discussed, especially the *time* and *place* of its composition. Here all the Fathers agree, either expressly maintaining or taking for granted that it was written during the apostle's residence in Asia Minor, and especially at Ephesus (see § 61); nor is this view contradicted by internal evidence. That it was not written at Jerusalem, or in its vicinity, or indeed anywhere in Palestine, may be inferred with the highest probability from the fact that the evangelist frequently explains circumstances which he could hardly have thought needed explanation, had he expected his readers to be Jews, and particularly Jews of Jerusalem or of any part of Palestine (see *e.g.* i. 39, 42, ii. 6, iv. 9, 25, v. 2, xi. 18, xix. 40; and cf. § 80). Also in ii.

---

¹ [Thus it is that HOLTZMANN knowingly and consistently cuts his way out of the alternative. None of our canonical evangelists, he holds, made use of the others, not even Luke of Matthew; but the "first main source" (Ur-Marcus) formed the basis of all three. He endeavours to reconstruct the "second main source" (= the Collection of Discourses) not only out of our Matthew, but especially out of our Luke (Luke ix. 51–xviii. 14). It may further be mentioned that HOLTZMANN, as he agrees with BLEEK regarding the language in which Matthew was originally written, and in Luke's independence of Matthew, thinks also that in BLEEK's description of the primary Gospel (see above, § 102), and making allowance for the difference on account of the Griesbachian hypothesis, he can find a not unimportant point of coincidence and agreement with his own view. See the remarks of HOLTZMANN above quoted.—B.]

13, v. 1, vi. 4, vii. 2, the feast of the passover and the feast of tabernacles are described as feasts of the *Jews*. Since John nowhere expressly mentions his readers (as Luke does), we may assume that he had none other definitely in his mind besides those among whom he was living, and that he was not then living in Jerusalem, or even in Palestine, but in a country the majority of whose inhabitants were not Jews. To this conclusion we are also led by certain peculiar phrases occurring in the Gospel; as, for example, when the Jews, with whom Jesus had to do, are throughout distinguished as οἱ Ἰουδαῖοι, especially the upper classes, who were His enemies, to some extent, even in contrast with those who were more favourably disposed towards Him; as in vii. 13, ix. 22, also i. 19, ii. 18, 20, v. 10, 15 sqq., vi. 52, vii. 1, 11, ix. 18, xviii. 12, 14 (see above, § 80). Now as, according to the indubitable tradition of the Church, John passed the latter days of his life, after he had left Judea, in proconsular Asia, we are led, for the reasons already stated, to think of this district, and especially of his place of residence, Ephesus, as the place where he wrote his Gospel; and this is exactly what Irenæus asserts (iii. 1). It is also probable that the evangelist, when he wrote, had long been a resident in this district; for assuredly some time would be necessary before he could have so familiarized himself with his new home, and become so much of a stranger to his former one, as his work appears to represent him; and if we are correct in a conjecture we have already tried to establish (see § 56 fin.), that he did not leave Judea before he had been induced to do so by the Jewish war with the Romans, and the disturbances which led to that event, then it is not likely that he wrote before the destruction of Jerusalem.[1] Still there is a passage (v. 2) which apparently favours that opinion, where the pool of Bethesda is spoken of as if it was still in existence at Jerusalem. This, however, is not decisive. We may concede, that if the evangelist wrote after the destruction of Jerusalem, he has here expressed himself inaccu-

---

[1] This is the view adopted by LAMPE, LARDNER, WEGSCHEIDER, *Versuch einer vollst. Einl. in das Ev. Joh.*, Gött. 1806, and others.

rately, and would have been more correct had he written ἦν, and not ἔστι. Still it cannot be maintained that John could not have used the present tense had he written then, because the pool he speaks of might still have been in existence; and at all events, he may not have seen Jerusalem as it lay in ruins after its destruction. The probability, moreover, is, that he would express himself in just such a way as would describe the situation of the pool at the time when he knew it. At any rate, the argument derived from this passage, apart from other reasons, is far outweighed by other passages, in which the evangelist seems to describe the country round Jerusalem as already laid waste and altered. Thus xviii. 1 (he went forth over the brook Kedron, ὅπου ἦν κῆπος), xix. 41, and especially xi. 18 : ἦν δὲ ἡ Βηθανία ἐγγὺς τῶν Ἱεροσολύμων. Here, again, however, we may concede that these passages, taken alone, are not quite decisive, since it may be, as Schott remarks, § 42, 5 (though even De Wette, § 111, does not admit the validity of this argument), that in relating past events, the author, even though the city was still standing, used the imperfect loosely, when describing the scene of a particular transaction. But, on the whole, it is more probable that the evangelist wrote after the conquest of Judea and its capital; and the passages cited lead much more decidedly to this conclusion than v. 2 does to the contrary. To this we may add (leaving out of consideration for the present the relation of John to the Synoptics, or at least to what they embody), that this Gospel, as is plain from what we have already said of the connection in which the last chapter stands with the rest of the book, was not very widely circulated in the Church prior to the apostle's death, and that he wrote it in the later years of his life, having reached to a very great age, as all the early writers agree in testifying, since otherwise Polycarp (*ob. circ.* 167) could not have known him. All these facts render its composition after the destruction of Jerusalem almost a matter of certainty. In some of the Fathers, Patmos is mentioned as the place where it was written; and among modern critics, Hug has adopted this view. But even if we supposed the apostle's residence on that island to have been longer than it was, there would be nothing of importance to urge in support of this opinion, which, moreover, is only found in the *later* fathers (Pseudo-Hippolyt. *de xii. apostolis, Synopsis sc. sacræ;* Simeon Metaphrastes; Theophylact; Nicephorus, ii. 42, and others; cf. § 61).

§ 114.

We now come to consider the *sources* of this Gospel, using the phrase in the sense in which we speak of the sources, *e.g.*, of Luke and Mark. Here we need enter into discussion only with those who deny its authenticity, passing over those with whom, as with ourselves, this is a settled point. As John was in immediate connection with the Lord during that period of His earthly life which he records, we may safely assume that he was in general an eye-witness of what he relates; or where, through some accident, this was not the case, he was yet so intimate with those who had been eye-witnesses, having the whole told him immediately afterwards, that he could speak of the events with as much authority as if he had himself taken part in them. He would not be likely, therefore, to feel the need of collecting the materials for his Gospel from the oral or written communications of others. Still it is a question whether he wrote entirely from memory, or incorporated into this, his larger and more continuous work, memoranda made at an earlier period. With regard to Christ's discourses particularly, it has been thought that at any rate these in part had been taken down by the apostle long before, and probably during the Lord's life, and transferred to our Gospel.[1] Against this notion, Lücke, Hemsen, pp. 152–164, Credner, and others, have expressed themselves decisively, though some of their reasons are not defensible; and the notion itself is not one to be summarily

---

[1] So MICHAELIS, ii. 1129; PAULUS, *Commentar z. N. T.* i. 387 sq., 638 sqq. (2d ed.), iv. 275 sq.; HAENLEIN, iii. 177, and others; especially BERTHOLDT (*Verosimilia de Orig. Ev. Jo.*, Erlangen 1805, and *Einl.* iii. 1302 sqq.); WEGSCHEIDER, p. 269 sqq.; KUINŒL. Even THOLUCK does not reject it.

rejected. It is not, indeed, very probable, that *while the Lord was on earth,* and he had the opportunity of hearing daily and hourly the words of life from His mouth, John should have thought of recording His utterances, in order not to forget them; but he may have done so at a somewhat later period after the ascension, as perhaps other disciples of Christ did in particular cases. Yet even this is not very probable, when we consider the remarkable character of the discourses to be found in his Gospel. Had John recorded these while he was yet at Jerusalem, either for his own use or for that of his immediate friends, he would no doubt, as Bertholdt conjectures, have done so in the Aramæan in which they were spoken, translating them afterwards into Greek for his Gospel; and in this case they would unquestionably have borne more of an Aramæan or Hebraistic character than we find them doing. The characteristics of their Greek cannot be easily explained, if we suppose them to be merely translations from a written Aramæan original; while they may be, if we assume that, though originally spoken in Aramæan, they were thought in Greek by the apostle throughout, and intended for insertion in a work written in Greek. In this way also may we explain the influence which the evangelist's idiosyncrasy appears to have exercised on their form, though at the same time we have every reason to believe he gives us the essence of them, while the form itself is often manifestly much more original in him than in the Synoptics (*vid.* § 77). Many maintain this view, that John took down the Lord's discourses during His lifetime, because otherwise it seems to them utterly impossible that John could have remembered them accurately for so many years. But this idea is refuted by the following considerations, some of which we have already alluded to:—(*a*) We need not at all maintain that these discourses, especially the longer ones, are reproduced *verbally*: it is enough if they are given to us as to their *essence*, in a trustworthy manner. (*b*) Among the ancients, who were not occupied with books and writing, as the educated modern world, the memory would be much better trained, and more tenacious, than it is nowadays.

(c) According to John xiv. 26, Jesus had expressly promised His disciples, that after His departure the Holy Ghost should bring to their remembrance all things whatsoever He had said unto them. We need not indeed interpret this promise so mechanically, or apply it so minutely, as to understand it of *every* word the Lord spoke; but we may safely infer from it, that the Holy Spirit's help should be so given to the disciples, that what the Lord had said to them should be essentially and livingly reproduced in their souls. A promise of this kind would, above all, be fulfilled in one possessed of so receptive a temperament as St. John. The love which led him to cleave so closely to His person, must from the very first have deeply impressed his mind with the Redeemer's words; so that, even after a long space of time, *he* at any rate would be able to realize and reproduce them; and especially (d) if (and this must have been the case with the apostles after the Lord's ascension) he had had at an earlier period repeated opportunities of orally communicating to others the most important of them.

Of the other grounds on which Bertholdt chiefly relies I shall only notice two. He appeals (a) to the vaguer character of the prophecies in John as compared with the Synoptics, and thinks that if John recorded them for the first time long after they were delivered, he would have made them much more definite, and thus more in harmony with their subsequent fulfilment. The relation which on this point exists between John and the Synoptics has been already touched upon, § 78. But the phenomenon noticed by him does not help to prove Bertholdt's conclusions, because the utterances of Christ on His death and resurrection are to be found exactly in those discourses (ch. xiv.–xvi.) which He delivered on the evening prior to His crucifixion; and yet we can hardly suppose John would have written them down the very day after that event. These, therefore, must have been written after the resurrection, and consequently after they had been at any rate partially fulfilled; hence, if Bertholdt's assumption were worth anything, we should have to infer that these prophecies, though thus early recorded, should have been more definite. Again, Bertholdt maintains (*b*) that in Christ's discourses, as we find them in John, utterly unimportant words are introduced, which, even if really spoken by Jesus, have no connection with the discourse; *e.g.* xiv. 31, ἐγείρεσθε, ἄγωμεν ἐντεῦθεν. Now, in his opinion, if this discourse had been transcribed after the lapse of some time, John would have found it hard to remember words which stood in no real connection with its essential contents, and accordingly would have omitted them. We have elsewhere cited this passage—the only one which Bertholdt brings forward, and indeed the only one of the kind in the Gospel, in proof of the historical truth of the evangelist (§ 78). It tells far more against than in favour of Bertholdt's view. For if at some early period John wrote down the discourses of Christ, without at the same time recording the circumstances under which they were spoken, it would hardly be expected that he would record words having no connection with the subject-matter of those discourses, but which would only be naturally introduced in a work which presented them along with the facts accompanying their delivery.

§ 115.

We have now to consider the *design* and *occasion* of this Gospel. The former John himself seems to tell us in his closing words (xx. 31).[1] What he here declares to be his object in writing, viz. to further faith in Jesus as the Christ and the Son of God, and everlasting life in those who believe, may, as thus generally stated, be regarded as the highest object of the other evangelists, and indeed of all Christian teachers whether writers or speakers. But it is one thing to

---

[1] It is still a disputed point with commentators whether this passage refers to the whole Gospel or only to ch. xx., and the signs by which the Lord was shown to have indeed risen again from the dead. The former is by far the most probable opinion. But even if we accept the latter, there would still be no doubt that what John speaks of as his design in the history of the resurrection, especially at the close of his work, would have been his design throughout.

awaken faith, another to confirm and guard it against errors on all sides. Accordingly the authors of the Gospels might have different points of view, and give to their works a correspondingly different form. Their purpose might have been either the furtherance of faith in the Son of God—and this would influence them more or less in their selection of facts, and in the characteristic execution of their task—or they might content themselves simply with the trustworthy relation of occurrences just as they happened. Among the Synoptics, the latter character seems to belong more to Luke and Mark, the former more to Matthew (cf. § 108). But unquestionably this former character belongs in a far higher degree to John, and certainly not simply through pointed references in him to the fulfilment of Old Testament expressions (cf. § 80), and in virtue of his own remarks and observations, but also through his selection of matter for record, especially such as the discourses of the Lord, which refer far more than those in the Synoptics to the person of Jesus as the Son of God and the Messiah. More than any other of the evangelists might John have declared it to be the simple purpose of his writing, that his readers might believe Jesus to be the Christ, the Son of God. Still it would be a very great mistake to argue from this manifest intention in the Gospel against its historical reality and purpose, and to speak of it as purely dogmatic and apologetic, as has so often been done even by the latest interpreters and critics. So far is this from the truth, that if we may treat any one of our Gospels as an historical work, we may emphatically so treat the Gospel of John. We have already seen how, in the statement of external facts, John is frequently more exact than the Synoptics (*vid.* § 71, 72). Not less is his account of events recorded by himself alone distinguished by great precision and clearness, even when he gives prominence to what has manifestly no direct dogmatic significance; *e.g.* the conversation with the Samaritan woman, the healing of the man born blind at Jerusalem, the raising of Lazarus, etc. Especially is the historical character of his Gospel proved by the clearness with which it unfolds, in its gradual development, the catastrophe which terminated in the death of Jesus the Redeemer. Here pre-eminently, from the very beginning of the Lord's public life onwards, care is taken to show how by His deeds and words the Jewish feeling concerning Him was formed, alternating for a long time between approval and dislike, until at last it took such a course as to give up even eagerly to crucifixion Him on whom but a short time before it had joyfully fixed its expectations. Even at the very first passover at which Jesus appeared openly, when He cast out the buyers and sellers from the temple, it is said that many believed on His name because of the miracles He wrought, but that He did not trust Himself to them, because He knew all men (ii. 39 sq.). We are also told that, as one result of His visit to Judea, the Pharisees took notice how He made more disciples than John, and that He therefore left Judea (iv. 1 sqq.). On His next passover-visit to Jerusalem, when He healed the impotent man at the pool of Bethesda, He is said to have been persecuted by the Jews because He wrought this miracle on the Sabbath (v. 16), and still more because He compared His works with God's, and called God His Father, thus making Himself equal with God (v. 18). In Galilee, the miracle of the loaves and fishes makes such an impression on the people, that they say, οὗτός ἐστιν ἀληθῶς ὁ προφήτης ὁ ἐρχόμενος εἰς τὸν κόσμον; and He found Himself compelled to withdraw from them, because He perceived that they wished to take and make Him a king (vi. 14 sq.). Soon after, the Jews again take offence at Him for speaking of Himself as the Bread which had come down from heaven, while they thought that Mary and Joseph were His father and mother (vi. 41 sqq.). Still the popular feeling in Galilee was more favourable towards Him than in Judea, as we read (vii. 1), καὶ μετὰ ταῦτα περιεπάτει ὁ Ἰησοῦς ἐν τῇ Γαλιλαίᾳ· οὐ γὰρ ἤθελεν ἐν τῇ Ἰουδαίᾳ περιπατεῖν, ὅτι ἐζήτουν αὐτὸν οἱ Ἰουδαῖοι ἀποκτεῖναι. Hence He refuses at first the request of His as yet unbelieving brethren to go up to Jerusalem to the feast of tabernacles (vii. 2 sqq.), because His time is not yet come; and afterwards He goes up secretly, ἐν κρυπτῷ (ver. 10). The Jews seek Him, and there is much discussion among the people about Him: some say, ὅτι ἀγαθός ἐστιν, others, οὐ ἀλλὰ πλανᾷ τὸν ὄχλον. No one ventures to speak openly of Him, for fear of the Jews. Again, when during the feast He appears openly, teaching in the temple, repeated attacks are made upon Him by the Jews, though no one lays hands on Him. Of all this we have a lively picture in v. 14–36. When Jesus finally shows Himself on the last day of the feast, many acknowledge Him to be the Prophet or the Christ, while others reject Him, because Christ is not to come out of Galilee, but Bethlehem, and of the stem of David. Hence the people are divided, but none of His opponents will lay hands on Him even yet (vers. 37–44). Even the servants of the Sanhedrim, who are sent to arrest Him, do not carry out their commission, being filled with reverential astonishment at His words; whereupon the chief priests and Pharisees begin to wrangle with them, and especially with Nicodemus, who declares it to be illegal to condemn any man unheard (vers. 45–52). In a conversation which follows, the Jews say, οὐ καλῶς λέγομεν ἡμεῖς ὅτι Σαμαρείτης εἶ σὺ καὶ δαιμόνιον ἔχεις (viii. 48); their malice rises higher when Jesus promises that the man who keeps His sayings shall never see death (vers. 51, 52); and at last, when he says, πρὶν Ἀβραὰμ γενέσθαι, ἐγώ εἰμι, they take up stones to stone Him (ver. 58 sq.). All this, again, is clearly and vividly depicted. The healing of the man born blind gives rise to another division even among the Pharisees: some saying, "He is not of God, because he keeps not the Sabbath;" others, "Can a man who is a sinner do such miracles?" (ix. 16). Even the parents of the man healed dare not bear witness unreservedly to the miracle wrought on their son, because the Jews had agreed that whoever should acknowledge Him to be the Christ should be put out of the synagogue (ver. 22). The closing words of Jesus occasion another division; some asserting δαιμόνιον ἔχει καὶ μαίνεται, while others point to His words and deeds as utterly unlike those of a man possessed (x. 19–21). But the popular bitterness against Him rises to a still higher pitch on the feast of the dedication of the temple, when, as Jesus is walking about with the Jews in Solomon's porch, they ask Him to tell them plainly whether or no He is the Christ. As they connected with this the hope of deliverance from the Roman yoke, the Lord naturally does not answer in the affirmative, but simply says He and His Father are one, and that they are not of His sheep, since they do not hear His voice; whereupon they regard Him as a blasphemer, and again are on the point of stoning Him (vers. 23-39). He therefore withdraws beyond Jordan, whither many follow Him, and believe on Him, confessing that all the Baptist said of Him was indeed true (vers. 40-42). Lastly, we have the raising of Lazarus. On this occasion several Jews were present, of whom many believe on Him because of this miracle, while others go and report it to the Pharisees (xi. 45, 46). An assembly of the Sanhedrim is then convoked, at which great anxiety is shown lest, if they let Him alone, all would believe in Him, and the Romans should come and take away their place and nation. This leads Caiaphas to make the remarkable statement, that it is better one should die for the nation rather than the whole people should perish: ἀπ' ἐκείνης οὖν τῆς ἡμέρας συνεβουλεύσαντο ἵνα ἀποκτείνωσιν αὐτόν (vers. 47-53). Accordingly, Jesus withdraws to the city Ephraim, which was near to the wilderness (ver. 54). This was just before the passover, the time when many Jews came from the country to Jerusalem to purify themselves before the feast: they search for Him, and ask one another if He will come to the feast; but the scribes and Pharisees had already given commandment that, if any knew His place of abode, they should tell it. The latter even endeavoured to put Lazarus out of the way, since many Jews went out to Bethany to see him who had been raised from the dead, and were thus led to believe in Jesus (xii. 9-11). However, this miracle, which they had either seen or heard of, made such an impression on the common people, that, on the entrance of Jesus into Jerusalem on the foal of an ass, they greeted Him with acclamation as the King of Israel, who came in the name of the Lord (vers. 12-18); while the Pharisees saw in all this more cogent reasons for taking measures against Him (ver. 20). Moreover, not only Jews, but Greeks also (proselytes of the gate) who had come to the feast, were seeking to get sight of Him. The popular favour, however, left Him when He hinted at His death, as it was hard to reconcile such an event with the current notions respecting the Messiah (ver. 34). Thus Jesus found Himself again compelled to hide from them, who, in spite of all miracles, continued unbelieving (ver. 36 sqq.). It is indeed said that many believed on Him, even of the higher ranks; but for fear of the Jews they did not confess Him, because they loved the praise of men more than the praise of God (vers. 42, 43).

In this way the whole Gospel shows us how the popular opinion respecting Jesus was formed; how for a long time it swung between approval and dislike; how the people, entirely filled with the Jewish notions respecting the Messiah, sometimes thought He was the One for whom they were waiting, and then again became determined and bitter against Him; how the Sanhedrim resolved to make away with Him, and how this resolution was affected by a real or pretended fear of the Romans. Especially is it from John that we learn how it came to pass (*a*) that the people greeted Jesus on His entrance into Jerusalem with such rejoicings (the fact itself is recorded by the Synoptics; but it is only in this Gospel that we learn its motive, in the raising of Lazarus shortly before); and yet (*b*) that their feeling so quickly altered respecting Him, through the discourse following the entry, from which it could be seen how little He thought of being a Messiah in the Jewish sense of the word. This change of feeling is also related by the Synoptics, but not so as to show very clearly how it was brought about.

§ 116.

With regard to the more immediate occasion of this Gospel, we need not so construe xx. 31 (ἵνα πιστεύσητε, κ.τ.λ.) as to make the passage refer strictly and simply to such only as were still unbelievers, for these would in general be reached rather by preaching; whereas the Gospel narratives were for the most part written for those who either already belonged to the Christian body, or at any rate had lent a willing ear to the truth. Such was the case, doubtless, with John's Gospel. The ἵνα πιστεύσητε may quite as well be understood of the furthering and establishment of faith as of its first awakening (cf. John ii. 11). We have already remarked, that as the apostle does not specify any particular class of persons as those for whom he wrote, these must have been the people among whom he was living, that is, the Christians of Ephesus and the adjacent country, who were principally Greeks (see § 80, 113), though that some were Jews is plain, from his references (*vid.* § 80) to the fulfilment of Old Testament prophecies. But we cannot more definitely limit the circle for whom he wrote. Many have supposed that he addressed himself to men of culture, and especially of philosophical culture.[1] Of such an acknowledged and definite limitation, however, the Gospel itself gives us no hint. That it bears a more speculative character than the Synoptics, and consequently requires more susceptibility and culture in those who would understand it, is due solely to the author's idiosyncrasy. Besides, we may assume that the Churches round about him generally had so long enjoyed the oral apostolical teaching, first from Paul, and then from our evangelist himself, that many of the deeper Christian ideas, with their definite terminology, were already known to them, though strange to others, as they are to catechumens in our own day, and therefore requiring explanation. For instance, in the Pauline Epistles, especially those to the Ephesians and Colossians, we find these ideas set forth, without the question of their intelligibility appearing to occur to the apostle. Moreover, it is very probable that much in his selection of narratives for record might be explained by a reference to what John could take for granted as already known to his readers. The perusal of his Gospel

---

[1] So, with various modifications, GIESELER (133 sqq.), HEYDENREICH (in his and HÜFFEL's *Zeitzsch. f. Predigerwissenschaften*, Bd. i. (1827) p. 28 sq.), SCHOTT, § 40, OLSHAUSEN (*für gnostisirende Mystiker*), and others.

gives us at once the impression that it was not intended to furnish a complete history of Christ's life to those who were utterly ignorant of it. Unquestionably much is assumed as already known to his readers, and is therefore not recorded, but merely adverted to; and this is precisely what we find fully told in the Synoptics. Thus the baptism of Jesus is not recorded, but is assumed as known in i. 32 sq. In i. 46 Jesus is named incidentally as the son of Joseph of Nazareth, and also as son of Joseph in vi. 42 by the Jews, who murmured at Him; while in the preceding parts of the Gospel nothing whatever is said either of His parents or of His father's city: this, therefore, is assumed as well known. So also in ii. 1, who the mother of Jesus was is presupposed as known; and iii. 24, the imprisonment of the Baptist is implied. The passage iv. 44, where Jesus says, "A prophet has no honour in his own country," is somewhat difficult, standing where it does; but it is quite plain, that nothing, properly speaking, is here recorded of the fact and occasion of the expression; the evangelist merely recalls the words as well-known words of Jesus: on the other hand, the Synoptics tell us when and how He came to utter them (Matt. xiii. 57; Mark vi. 4; Luke iv. 24). In vi. 70 Jesus says, οὐκ ἐγὼ ὑμᾶς τοὺς δώδεκα ἐξελεξάμην; and yet the selection of the twelve, and the establishment of their number, are nowhere recorded by John; nor does he mention them all by name, as each of the Synoptics does. In xx. 17 Christ refers to His speedy return to His Father; while nothing is said as to His actual ascension, or the manner of it.

We are thus led to the general question of the relation of John to the Synoptics. All early writers agree that John not only wrote after these, and knew them, but even intended his work to be supplementary to theirs (*vid.* § 61). But here we must leave out Mark, as it is probable that his Gospel was written after John's (*vid.* § 111). As to Luke's, we can hardly decide with certainty whether it was written before or after; but even if the former be the case, we cannot say that, meant as it was at first only for a private person, it was known in proconsular Asia when John wrote. There is much more probability that this was the case with Matthew. But from our previous inquiries we may regard it as a settled point, that before the composition of our three first canonical Gospels, the same cycle of narratives which they exhibit had already been pretty generally made known, partly orally, and partly by writings of earlier date, and of greater or smaller compass, which John might assume to be known to his readers, even if none of our Synoptics had become so. In accounting, therefore, for the special form of his Gospel, it is not of much importance whether he himself knew, or assumed as known, these last, or any one of them. If he could only assume as known a cycle of evangelical narratives such as we find, at any rate partially, in our Synoptics, this would determine him to select from the copious materials ready to his hands whatever had comparatively little circulation, or was less accurately known, while he passed over what had come to the ears of all. To this latter class belong the sayings and parables of Christ which refer to the kingdom of heaven, and the qualifications necessary for a participation in it. It may be for the same reason, too, that John has omitted many events interesting and important in themselves, but which may be credibly learnt from the Synoptics, although he himself took part in them, *e.g.* the raising of Jairus' daughter and of the young man at Nain, the transfiguration, the institution of the holy supper, etc. We may also thus account for the absence in his Gospel of all reference to the whole class of demoniacal healings, although he may here certainly have been influenced exclusively by that special temperament which would make this phase of the Lord's activity less impressive to him, or by a feeling that its prominence was not so needful for the Greek-speaking community to whom his readers would belong. He may also have passed over much which, whatever its value, had little or no clear bearing on the development of the history, or the delineation of the several stages through which it passed on to the final catastrophe.

§ 117.

If we now return to the closing explanation of the apostle himself in xx. 31, and assume that it was addressed to members of the Christian community, the passage hints that all were not remaining firm and immoveable in a peacegiving faith in Jesus as the Christ, and expresses a fear lest some should fall away. The question then arises wherein the peril consisted, and from what side it came,—points which have occupied a good deal of the attention both of ancient and modern critics. Not only those who acknowledge, but also those who deny its authenticity, have found in our Gospel a definite polemical purpose against special tendencies and parties of various kinds, by which they have determined its value. Of the opinions of this class, held by such as deny the authenticity of the Gospel, we have already spoken incidentally, and we shall therefore confine ourselves here to those which have been put forward by persons by whom that authenticity is either admitted or left untouched. Here the oldest is that of a polemical purpose against Cerinthus;[1] but of this there is not the least proof in the Gospel itself. The peculiar notions of Cerinthus were: (*a*) That the world was not created by Almighty God, but by a subordinate being; and (*b*) that Jesus was the son, naturally begotten, of Joseph and Mary, on whom an Æon, the Spirit of God or Logos, descended for the first time at His baptism, becoming permanently allied to His soul, so that the man Jesus became the Christ. This Spirit of God again left the man Jesus on the cross, and was absorbed into the Pleroma. Now in our Gospel there is no direct refutation of these notions; and if there is much that would be available in a controversy against them, it nevertheless appears too seldom, to make it at all probable that its prominence is due to any such supposed polemical purpose on John's part. Rather may particular passages be found which the Cerinthians could with some

---

[1] So IRENÆUS, iii. 11; and JEROME, *de viris illustr.* ix.; EPIPHANIUS. *Hær.* xxi. 12; and even many modern critics, as SEMLER, MICHAELIS, WEGSCHEIDER, STORR (*ut supra*, p. 43 sqq., 180 sqq.), HUG, etc.; so also SCHOTT, § 40, note 7.

plausibility have used in favour of their views, where the evangelist in the case supposed would have expressed himself in a different and more definite manner, *e.g.* i. 32, 46. There is still less ground for the notion held by others, that the Gospel is directed against the Docetæ and Docetism.[1] The texts adduced in support of this view (i. 14, xix. 34, xx. 20, 27) prove nothing; and, indeed, I doubt whether at the time this Gospel was written Docetism had shown itself in any very marked manner. It has certainly been often imagined that the epistles of John were specially written against it; but even this has scarcely any well-founded basis, as we shall see further on. I merely add that Baur thinks Docetism is the doctrine of the evangelist himself. This notion is certainly far less correct than the one just noticed, and scarcely needs refuting. Baur maintains: This Gospel has as its main topic not so much the man Jesus Christ, in whom the Logos became incarnate, but the Logos, who was clothed with a phenomenal body. He relies chiefly on the prologue, and on vii. 10, viii. 59, x. 39. But in none of these passages do we find what he puts into them, and the whole tone and contents of the Gospel are opposed to his view.[2] A polemical purpose against the so-called disciples of John may be alleged with rather more plausibility. Under this term we include not only the then active mystico-theosophic sects (Mendaites, Nazarites, and Sabeans), but also certain disciples of John the Baptist, of whom mention is made in the Acts of the Apostles, who were reckoned among the disciples of Jesus, and yet were not recognised as full members of the Christian community by Paul and other disciples of the Lord, and on their reception into the Church had to be baptized in the name of Jesus (Acts xviii. 25, xix. 1–7). At the time when our Gospel was written, some of these persons may have gone as far in their regard for their Master as

---

[1] So SEMLER (*paraphr. ad Jo.* i. 14), BERTHOLDT, SCHOTT, and especially SCHNECKENBURGER (*Beiträge zur Einl. i. N. T. u. zur Erkl. s. schwierigen Stellen*, Stuttg. 1832, p. 60 sqq.).

[2] Cf. HAUFF (against Baur), *Stud. u. Krit.* 1846, iii. pp. 550–629, especially p. 571 sqq., 607 sqq.

those mentioned in the *Clementine Recognitions*, who looked upon the Baptist as the Messiah.

As it is in every way probable that the evangelist John himself originally came from the school of the Baptist, we might infer that he had it very much at heart to win over to a full faith in Jesus his companions or their pupils, and to keep those of them who were converted from falling away. It might be also assumed that he would therefore give great prominence in his Gospel to the fact that the Baptist repeatedly bore witness to Jesus as the Son of God, and spoke of himself as only appointed to prepare the way before Him; so that he should necessarily decrease while Jesus increased. And yet all this might be explained on the simple hypothesis that he had himself been a disciple of John, without our attributing to him any very distinct motive; or, on the other hand, it may have been that in his day there was much lukewarmness and laxity in the Asiatic Churches, which speedily led believers to put an Ebionitish construction on the doctrine of Jesus, allowing of no true faith in Him as the Son of God; and these persons may have been in the evangelist's mind. A very improbable conclusion is drawn by Credner (and also by Ewald) from the apostle's closing words, to the effect that his Gospel was written for a circle of trusted personal friends; for it is hardly likely that the faith of such would be quite so weak as those words would seem to imply.

§ 118.

INTEGRITY.—On the relation of ch. xxi. to the rest of the Gospel, see § 84. It is evident from external grounds,[1] confirmed by internal, that the section vii. 53–viii. 11 was inserted only after the middle of the fourth century, very

---

[1] [See what Eusebius says of Papias (*H. E.* iii. 39): ἐκτίθεται δὲ καὶ ἄλλην ἱστορίαν περὶ γυναικὸς ἐπὶ πολλαῖς ἁμαρτίαις διαβληθείσης ἐπὶ τοῦ Κυρίου, ἣν τὸ καθ' Ἑβραίους εὐαγγέλιον περιέχει. HOLTZMANN, p. 92 sqq., attributes this section to the *Synoptic Fundamental Document* (Ur-Marcus), and imagines, following in this HITZIG (*Joh. Marcus*. p. 221 sqq.), that its original place was between Mark xii. 17 and 18. Even HENGSTENBERG admits its spuriousness.—B.]

probably from the Gospel to the Hebrews, where the narrative was originally given from a tradition resting probably on a true historical basis (see my *Beiträge*, 28–31). Further, the passage v. 4, with the concluding words of ver. 3 (from ἐκδεχομένων onwards), is not in many of the oldest MSS., and is probably a later interpolation.

UNCANONICAL GOSPELS.

§ 119.

Besides our canonical Gospels, the ancient Church knew several others which have come down to us in larger or smaller fragments. It is not at all probable that any of these reach further back than our Gospels, or belonged in any sense to the writings referred to by Luke (i. 1 sq.). Most of them had not the least influence in the catholic Church, and though a somewhat greater, yet but a very subordinate and temporary one, even among the minor sects with whom they chiefly originated. This was especially the case with the *Gospel of Marcion* (*vid.* § 51 sqq.), which had not the slightest value or authority outside of the sect of the Marcionites. The Church expressed itself less decidedly against the *Gospel of the Hebrews*, which was in exclusive use among the Jewish Christians especially of Palestine, and to which we find references here and there in early ecclesiastical writers.[1] We have already (§ 87, 88) spoken of Tatian's *Diatessaron* and the *Memoirs of Justin*. The former was not, as some have supposed, an independent evangelical work, but a harmony constructed out of our four Gospels. De Wette's supposition (§ 68),

---

[1] See, with reference to it, § 41 sqq., 110; and compare F. FRANCK, *über das Ev. der Hebräer, Stud. u. Krit.* 1848, ii. 369–422, where, in opposition to SCHNECKENBURGER, SCHWEGLER, and others, he proves the secondary character of this Gospel as compared with our Synoptics. [Its priority has been subsequently maintained by HILGENFELD, *Zeitschr. f. wiss. Theol.* 1863, 345–385. This Gospel is also probably referred to under the name τὸ Ἰουδαϊκόν, a work from which various readings are cited on the margin of a New Testament MS. *Vid.* TISCHENDORF, *Notitia editionis Cod. Sinait.* p. 58.—B.]

that Tatian made use also in his work of the *Gospel of the Hebrews*, is untenable; for then the name διὰ τεσσάρων, which undoubtedly, as Eusebius expressly says, *H. E.* iv. 29, came from Tatian himself, would be hard to explain. It leads us decidedly to the conclusion that there were already in the author's days four Gospels which were held in special regard by the Church (see my *Beitr.* 203 sq.). The statement of Epiphanius, *Hær.* xlvi. 1, λέγεται δὲ τὸ διὰ τεσσάρων εὐαγγέλιον ὑπ' αὐτοῦ γεγενῆσθαι, ὅπερ καθ' Ἑβραίους τινὲς καλοῦσι, is not very intelligible; it probably rests simply on a mistake on the part of Epiphanius himself. But with regard to the *Memoirs of the Apostles*, so repeatedly cited by Justin,[1] it is at once quite clear that these were not some single treatise, but a collection of writings differing from one another, and usually called *Gospels*,[2] which Justin alone somewhat capriciously chose to call ἀπομνημονεύματα. Now, since he expressly attributes these writings to the apostles and their coadjutors, we are directly led to conclude that they were the canonical Gospels we have, which ecclesiastical tradition and their very titles assign partly to the apostles, and partly to their fellow-labourers and disciples. The citations made from the *Memoirs* are, at any rate as to the greater part, unquestionably taken from our present Gospels; only, like almost all the Fathers, and according to his own practice in O. T. passages, Justin uses greater freedom in quoting, and mixes together the text of different Gospels, especially Matthew and Luke. Some of his quotations are certainly such as could not have been made from our canonical Gospels;[3] and we are obliged to assume that in their case he had some other document before him, most probably the Gospel of the Hebrews, which, as a Samaritan by birth,

---

[1] For various opinions upon it, see DE WETTE, § 67, *b*.

[2] *Apol.* i. 66: οἱ γὰρ ἀπόστολοι ἐν τοῖς γενομένοις ὑπ' αὐτῶν ἀπομνημονεύμασιν, ἃ καλεῖται εὐαγγέλια, οὕτως παρέδωκαν.

[3] See DE WETTE, § 66, *b*. [*E.g. Apol.* ii. p. 316: Τὰ τεκτονικὰ ἔργα εἰργάζετο ἐν ἀνθρώποις ὤν, ἄροντα καὶ ζυγά· διὰ τούτων καὶ τὰ τῆς δικαιοσύνης σύμβολα διδάσκων καὶ ἐνεργῆ βίον.—P. 267: Χριστὸς εἶπεν· ἐν οἷς ἂν ὑμᾶς καταλάβω, ἐν τούτοις καὶ κρινῶ.]

and from his theological tendencies, he would know and be likely to value. Still the quotations of this kind which occur in him are not expressly cited as from the *Memoirs of the Apostles*. The assumptions of CREDNER, MEYERHOFF, SCHWEGLER, HILGENFELD (*Krit. Untersuchungen über die Evv. Justins*, etc., 7–304), that Justin made use chiefly of the so-called Gospel of Peter, or that this was the only work to which he gave the name ἀπομνημονεύματα, rests partly on the construction which these learned men put on the passage in the *Dial. c. Tryph.* 106,[1] where they understand the pronoun αὐτοῦ of the object, Peter, in the leading clause. But if this construction were even grammatically correct, still no other Gospel is probably meant than our Gospel of Mark, which Justin certainly had in his mind at that place (iii. 16 sq.); and so it is explained by HUG, WINER (*Justinum M. Evv. canon. usum fuisse ostenditur*, Leipz. 1819), BINDEMANN, and others, even LUTHARDT. But it is most probable that the pronoun should be referred not to the object, but to the subject of the clause, as the nearer principal idea (αὐτόν, *i.e.* Ἰησοῦν Χριστόν); so that in this instance the Gospels are not, as is usually the case in Justin, designated after their authors, the apostles, but after Him whose history they narrate, *Memoirs of* CHRIST,—a sense which, moreover, does not occasion the least difficulty (compare my remarks, *Stud. u. Krit.* 1836, iv. 1070 sq.).

§ 120.

The other uncanonical Gospels worth mentioning are:—

1. *The Gospel of Peter.*—This was probably as to its contents very near akin to our Synoptics, and especially to the Gospel of the Hebrews—perhaps one of its various editions. It is certainly not a genuine work of Peter's, and in its definite form and title did not probably originate before the last decade of the second century in Cilicia, where Serapion found

---

[1] Καὶ τὸ εἰπεῖν μετωνομακέναι αὐτὸν ('Ι. Χρ.) Πέτρον ἕνα τῶν ἀποστόλων καὶ γεγράφθαι ἐν τοῖς ἀπομνημονεύμασιν αὐτοῦ γεγενημένον καὶ τοῦτο, μετὰ τοῦ καὶ ἄλλους δύο ἀδελφοὺς υἱοὺς Ζεβεδαίου ὄντας μετωνομακέναι ὀνόματι τοῦ Βοανεργές, ὅ ἐστιν υἱοὶ βροντῆς, σημαντικόν ἦν, κ.τ.λ.

it. Beyond this country, and at a later time, it obtained no further circulation and recognition in the Church at large, none at least so early or so wide-spread as CREDNER and others have supposed (see above, § 119). An εὐαγγέλιον κατὰ Πέτρον was used by the Church at Rhossus in Cilicia at the close of the second century, and was noticed by Serapion, Bp. of Antioch (*post* A.D. 191). At first, having no personal knowledge of it, he did not oppose its use; but when he heard that it countenanced heretical views, he wrote to the Church just mentioned a letter about it, fragments of which are given in Euseb. *H. E.* vi. 12. He says, that on reading the book he certainly found the greater part of it to be according to sound doctrine; but some things were additions (προσδιεσταλμένα, that is, things not to be found in the Church's doctrine, and not in harmony with it; particularly, it would seem, things which favoured Docetism), which he pointed out to them. ORIGEN also refers to this Gospel in his *comment. ad Matt.* xiii. 54-56, as teaching that the brothers of Christ were Joseph's sons by a former marriage. According to THEODORET, *Hæret. fab.* ii. 2, the Nazarites used it. Nothing more about it is definitely known to us. I remark, in addition, that ORIGEN (*Præf. in libr.* i. *de Princip.* § 8, according to Rufinus' translation) quotes a work under the title *Doctrina Petri*, in which Jesus says to His disciples (after His resurrection), *Non sum dæmonium incorporeum*,—an expression quoted also in Ignatius, *ad Smyrn.* iii., and to be found, according to Jerome, *de vir. illustr.* xvi., in the Gospel of the Hebrews. It has sometimes been thought that this *Doctrina Petri* is the same as the Gospel of Peter (so even DE WETTE apparently, § 65 *b*, note *e*). It is much more probable, however, that we have in it, under a Latin name, the work quoted by CLEMENS ALEX. and ORIGEN under a Greek name as κήρυγμα Πέτρου, another apocryphal writing first cited by Heracleon, the contents and form of which are otherwise not known to us with any certainty.

2. The *Gospel of Cerinthus* was probably merely a revision of the Gospel of the Hebrews, drawn up in the interest of the doctrine of the Cerinthians, or for the most part agreeing

VOL. I. Y

with it. According to EPIPHANIUS (*Hær.* xxviii. 5, xxx. 14), Cerinthus or his followers must have used the same Gospel as Carpocrates, that is, the as yet incomplete Gospel of Matthew, inasmuch as they sought to prove from the genealogy with which that Gospel commences that Jesus sprang from Joseph and Mary. We may assume that it did not contain the whole narrative of the infancy which is to be found in Matthew. Nothing more is known about it.

3. The *Gospel of the Egyptians*—κατ' Αἰγυπτίους.[1]—CLEMENT of ALEXANDRIA (*Strom.* iii. pp. 452, 465, ed. Sylburg) is the first to quote by name a Gospel under this title. He, however, distinguishes it from the Gospels received by the Church. It is next referred to by EPIPHANIUS, *Hær.* lxii. 2, who points out that it had a mystical character, and contained discourses of Christ bearing that character; and this is confirmed by the fragments of it which have come down to us. It had also a strong Encratite tendency. The saying of Christ, cited in the first of the passages from CLEMENT of ALEXANDRIA above referred to, occurs also substantially, though not verbally, in CLEMENT of ROME, Ep. ii. 12; and it is possible that the Gospel was known even to the author of that letter. It was used by the Encratites and (according to EPIPHANIUS) by the Sabellians. Very probably it originated in Egypt. We cannot ascertain exactly in what relation it stood to the Gospel of the Hebrews. SCHNECKENBURGER thinks it was either one and the same with the Gospel of the Ebionites, or very near akin to that. At any rate, it had a peculiar character of its own. ORIGEN's assertion (*Homil. in Luc.* i.), that it was one of the works referred to in Luke i. 1 sq., is certainly very arbitrary and unfounded.

4. On other Gospels mentioned by early writers, such as ORIGEN, EPIPHANIUS, JEROME, etc., see notices in DE WETTE, § 63 and 73.

The *Evangelium juxta duodecim apostolos*, or *duodecim apostolorum*, mentioned as a distinct work by ORIGEN (*Homil.* i. *in Luc.*), AMBROSE (*ad Luc.* i. 1), and JEROME (*Præf. in Matth.*),[2]

---

[1] SCHNECKENBURGER, *Ueber das Ev. der Ægypter*, Bern 1834.

[2] [Plures fuisse, qui evangelia scripserunt, perseverantia usque ad

is, according to JEROME, *adv. Pelag.* iii. 1 (see § 41), none other than the Aramæan Gospel of the Hebrews in the form it had, according to EPIPHANIUS, xxx. 13, at least among the Ebionites, where Matthew is introduced speaking in the name of the apostles. By the Gospel of BARTHOLOMEW, mentioned first by JEROME in the former of the passages just cited from him, and elsewhere, we cannot probably be quite sure that we ought to understand the Gospel of MATTHEW, which it was said BARTHOLOMEW left behind him in Aramæan among the Indians (see § 40). More probably it was a Gospel forged at a later time, under Bartholomew's name, to suit this legend. Nothing definite as to its character is now known. It cannot be ascertained whether the statement in the PSEUDO-DIONYSIUS the Areopagite, *de myst. theol.* i., which professes to be a quotation from Bartholomew, is taken from this so-called Gospel of BARTHOLOMEW, or from some other. Of the Gospel of MATTHIAS, mentioned by ORIGEN, EUSEBIUS, AMBROSE, and JEROME, nothing is known to us except the name.

§ 121.

There still remain to us a number of apocryphal Gospels, portions of which are also quoted by ancient writers. They only concern themselves with a part of the Gospel history,—either the first part, the preliminary history, the birth and childhood of Jesus, together with the history of Joseph and Mary, or with the later history of the Lord. They are altogether without any historical worth; and though many of them were more or less used and valued in the Church, they were never put on a level with the canonical Gospels.[1] These apocryphal Gospels are :—

1. The *Protevangelium of James.*—This is in Greek, and professes to have been written by JAMES the Lord's brother

præsens tempus monimenta declarant, quæ a diversis auctoribus edita diversarum hærescon fuere principia, ut est illud juxta *Ægyptios* et *Thomam* et *Matthiam* et *Bartholomæum*, duodecimque apostolorum et *Basilidis* atque *Apellis* ac reliquorum, quos enumerare longissimum est.]

[1] They have been collected by—(1) FABRICIUS, *Codex Apocryphus N. T.*, Hamburg 1703, 2 vols., 2d ed. 1719, enlarged by a third volume ; AND.

at Jerusalem. It is mentioned by ORIGEN, EPIPHANIUS, GREGORY of NYSSA, and others; probably JUSTIN M. made use of it, *Dial. c. Tryph.* 78. It is given in Greek, with a Latin translation, in FABRICIUS and THILO; simply in Greek in TISCHENDORF (complete from seventeen MSS.), in twenty-five chapters. It consists of a very legendary history of the Virgin Mary's early life, her birth and youth, up to the birth of Jesus (ch. i.–xx.), the visit of the Magi, the flight into Egypt, the massacre of the children at Bethlehem, and so on to the death of Zacharias, who is said to have been murdered because he would not deliver up his son John to Herod. This work had a wide circulation in its Greek form. There was also a translation in Arabic, and one in Coptic. Its date is probably the end of the second century, or even earlier. TISCHENDORF ascribes it to a gnostic Ebionite about 150 A.D. There can be no question that it is unauthentic.

2. The *Evangelium Infantiæ* of THOMAS.—This is made up of miserable and fabulous romances on the childhood of Jesus, from His fifth to His twelfth year. It is, as THILO in particular has proved, very probably the work which ORIGEN, EUSEBIUS, and others (even HIPPOLYTUS, *Philosophumena*, ed. Miller, p. 101) speak of as εὐαγγέλιον κατὰ Θωμᾶν, and which was apparently known to IRENÆUS; so that it would seem to have been in existence even in the second century. It has, however, been much altered and corrupted; so that the MSS. present it with great variations. We possess it in four different forms: (*a*) in FABRICIUS (i. pp. 159–167), after a Paris codex; (*b*) in THILO (pp. 275–315), after two MSS. (at Bologna and Dresden); lastly, in TISCHENDORF (pp. 134–149), who gives it also (*c*) from a totally different codex from Mount Sinai (pp. 150–155), and (*d*) from a Latin text in a Vatican codex (pp. 156–170). It is most complete in (*b*), in nineteen chapters, containing

BIRCH, *Auctarium Cod. apoc. N. T. Fabriciani*, Fasc. i., Copenhagen 1804; (2) J. K. THILO, *Cod. Apocr. N. T.*, Part i., Lpz. 1832, clx. and 879 pp. (contains the apocryphal Gospels); (3) TISCHENDORF, *Evv. apocr.*, Lpz. 1853, lxxxviii. and 463 pp.; Ejusdem, *de Evv. apocr. origine et usu*, The Hague 1851.

fifteen narratives, setting forth the wisdom of Jesus, and His miraculous power even in childhood, as shown by His causing the death of such as did not pay Him proper respect, and by His raising the dead to life again. The last chapter contains the account of Jesus when twelve years old, in Luke ii. 41 sqq., but with very many embellishments. The Latin text (*d*) also gives, in fifteen chapters, most of these narratives, but with considerable variations, sometimes abbreviating and sometimes amplifying them very much: the three last are, however, altogether wanting in it (ch. xvii.–xix.); while (*b*) begins with the flight into Egypt, the sojourn there, and the return (ch. i.–iii.), nothing of which is to be found in the other texts. In the Sinaitic Codex (*c*), the six last narratives (xiv.–xix.) in THILO are altogether left out; so also ch. xii. The other stories are substantially the same as in THILO, but told very differently. The shortest text is that given by FABRICIUS, in seven chapters, of which the first six correspond as to contents with ch. i.–viii. in THILO, though here again the tale is told very differently; ch. viii. is a story peculiar to this text, but very fragmentary. A comparison of these texts shows how capriciously the work has been dealt with, none of them exhibiting the Apocrypha as the Fathers knew it; for instance, what Hippolytus quotes (*ut supra*), is not to be found in any of them.

The *History of Joseph the Carpenter*.—This is found in Arabic in two MSS. at Rome and Paris, and in Coptic in a codex in the Borgian Library, and in another codex, which is partly in Sahidic. It was first edited in Arabic, with a Latin translation, by the learned Swede G. WALLIN (Leipz. 1722); subsequently the Latin translation was given in FABRICII *Codex pseudepigr. V. T.* (ii. pp. 309–336); then in Arabic, with a Latin translation by THILO (pp. 1–61), in thirty-two chapters, assisted by RÖDIGER; and lastly, in a Latin translation by TISCHENDORF (pp. 115–133). This work professes to relate, in the form of an account given by Jesus to His disciples, the history of Mary (here it resembles the *Protevangelium* of JAMES, but is simpler), the birth of Jesus, His persecution by Herod, the flight into Egypt, and lastly and specially, the death and burial of Joseph, in his 111th year. With regard to the texts in which we possess this work, it is very probable that the Arabic was a translation from the Coptic, and that it was originally written in Coptic, and at any rate arose in Egypt, probably not before the fourth century, perhaps even later. It is not mentioned by the earlier writers of the Church.

4. An *Evangelium Infantiæ* is found in several MSS. in Arabic, and also in a Syriac MS. in the Vatican Library: the Arabic was probably a translation from the Syriac. The Syriac text has not yet been edited: the Arabic was first by H. SIKE (Utrecht 1697), with a Latin translation; and in this form it is given by THILO (pp. 63-131), but simply in Latin by FABRICIUS (i. pp. 168-211) and by TISCHENDORF (pp. 171-202). In these editions it contains fifty-five chapters. It begins with the birth of Jesus, relates the flight into Egypt, and the miracles there wrought by Him, in which Mary also took part, and which are for the most part very disgusting and unworthy, such as that a youth who had been changed into a mule was disenchanted merely by means of the water in which the child Jesus had been washed, wrought marvellous cures, and so on (ch. i.-xxv.). Of the same character are the narratives in ch. xxvi.-xxxv., referring to the childhood of Jesus, and recording His miraculous healings at Bethlehem, where again the bathing water and swaddling-clothes are represented as having a virtue to cure. Then in ch. xxxvi.-xlix. follow some other wonderful stories of the youth of Jesus, from his seventh year onwards: the latter of these chapters (xliii.-xlix.) relate the same events, only in a different order, and with variations, as are to be found in the *Evangelium Infantiæ* of THOMAS. At the close of this work, as at the close of the Gospel of THOMAS, the visit of Jesus to the temple at Jerusalem, in his twelfth year, is related, but with very many embellishments. This work was undoubtedly composed much later than the Gospel of Thomas, probably not before the fifth century, first in Syriac, and probably by a Nestorian, as it was used chiefly among the Nestorians.

5. *Evangelium de Nativitate Mariæ*, in Latin—in FABRI-

cius (i. pp. 19–38), THILO (pp. 319–336), TISCHENDORF (pp. 106–114); in ten chapters. It treats of Mary's parents, Joachim and Anna; of her birth (ch. i.–v.), childhood, and betrothal to the aged Joseph (ch. vi.–viii.); her conception, and, very briefly, the birth of Jesus (ch. ix. x.). In its contents it bears to some extent a very close resemblance to the *Protevangelium* of JAMES; but the narratives are briefer. It expressly refers to the four (canonical) Gospels, asserting that, in what preceded and followed the birth of Jesus, only such things shall be narrated in it as are not to be found in them. This promise, however, is not fulfilled; and we must therefore conclude that we do not possess the whole of it.

6. *Historia de Nativitate Mariæ et de Infantia Salvatoris*, in Latin.—THILO has edited this (pp. 339–400), after two Paris MSS., in twenty-four chapters, relating the marriage of Joachim and Anna, Mary's birth and childhood, her espousal to Joseph, the birth of Jesus, and on to the sojourn in Egypt. In particular parts it agrees with, or recounts very nearly the same events as, No. 5 and the *Protevangelium* of JAMES, as far as these writings go, though it also amplifies what is in them, or has what is peculiar to itself. All its stories, however, are spun out in a very marvellous and legendary manner. In one of these two Paris MSS. the history is still more enlarged, by including several miracles performed by Jesus when a child, and which are here related in order to magnify His power and wisdom. Most of these occur also in the *Evangelium Infantiæ* of THOMAS, and in the Arabic *Evangelium Infantiæ*. This is the case also with two other MSS. at Rome and Paris, exhibiting in other respects a text with many variations, which TISCHENDORF has collated and edited (pp. 50–105) in this expanded form, under the title *Pseudo-Matthæi Evangelium*. This designation rests on the title of the Vatican Codex, and the forged letters prefixed to it of the bishops CHROMATIUS and HELIODORUS to JEROME, and the answer of the latter, which speaks of the work as a translation made from the Hebrew of MATTHEW by JEROME. These forged letters are very usually, and even by Thilo, referred to the *Ev. de Nativ. Mariæ* (5), which is therefore

printed with them, even in editions of JEROME's works. Lastly, the work we are now speaking of (6) has in both the Paris MSS. a prologue, in which the authorship (as in the case of the *Protevangelium*) is attributed to JAMES, the Lord's brother, and a son of Joseph. This prologue, however, was unquestionably prefixed at a later date, and the letters were originally written for the larger work (6), which narrates, besides Mary's birth, the childhood of Jesus, and evidently presupposes the contents of those pretended letters; whereas the shorter teatise (5), as we now have it, does not do so (see TISCHENDORF, *Ev. apocr. Prolegg.* xxx. sqq., who also in this place, contrary to his earlier view, *de Ev. apocr. origine et usu*, thinks the larger work was the older, and that the shorter was only composed with a reference to it).

Some other apocryphal Gospels treat only of Christ's later history; for example—

7. The *Gospel of* NICODEMUS, *with the Letters of* PILATE. —Justin M. (*Apol.* i. 35, 48) cites as an original authority for some circumstances connected with the Passion, certain Acts of PILATE (τὰ ἐπὶ Ποντίου Πιλάτου γενόμενα ἄκτα); and TERTULLIAN (*Apol.* xxi.), EUSEBIUS (*H. E.* ii. 2), and others, speak of Reports of PILATE to TIBERIUS on Jesus' execution. The designation ἄκτα applied by Justin, who wrote in Greek, renders it probable that they were originally composed in Latin. They were unquestionably forgeries, and are no longer extant, though, as TISCHENDORF thinks, they probably form the basis of the works we have just referred to, since the quotations made from them by the Fathers are to be found in the so-called Gospel of NICODEMUS. This last is a rather clever work. It may be seen in Latin in FABRICIUS (i. pp. 238–298), and in Greek and Latin in THILO (pp. 490–795), in twenty-eight chapters. It professes to have been written in Hebrew by NICODEMUS, and afterwards, about the time of Theodosius II., to have been translated into Greek by a Jewish Christian, ANANIAS. It is not mentioned by the Greek Fathers, at least under this title, nor by the Latin until the middle of the thirteenth century. It consists of two distinct parts. The first part (ch. i.-xvi.) gives a

copious account of the trial of Jesus before Pilate, His condemnation, execution, burial, and resurrection. This part may be seen in TISCHENDORF in Greek (pp. 203-265), entitled *Gesta Pilati*, with the superscription, ὑπομνήματα τοῦ Κυρίου ἡμῶν Ἰησοῦ Χριστοῦ πραχθέντα ἐπὶ Ποντίου Πιλάτου; and in another very different and shorter recension (pp. 266-300); also in Latin (pp. 312-367). The older *Acta Pilati* could have furnished the groundwork of this part only. The second part (ch. xvii.-xxvii.) contains communications on the descent of Christ to hell from the reports of those who, according to Matt. xxvii. 52 sqq., had been raised by Him from the dead, especially the two sons of the aged Simeon (Luke ii. 25 sqq.), who are mentioned by name— *Carinus* and *Leucius*. This is also given by TISCHENDORF (as *Evangelium Nicodemi*, Pars ii., sive *Descensus Christi ad Inferos*) in Greek (pp. 301-311), Latin (pp. 368-395), and in a shorter and very different recension (pp. 396-410). In some Latin MSS. there is also an additional chapter (THILO gives it as ch. xxviii.; TISCHENDORF, in the Latin *Descensus*, as ch. xii. pp. 388-391), according to which Annas and Caiaphas confess to Pilate, on his demand, that Jesus was truly the promised Son of God. Then follows in some MSS. of the Gospel of NICODEMUS a Letter of PILATE to the Emperor TIBERIUS (in THILO, pp. 796-800; in TISCHENDORF, as ch. xiii. of the Latin *Descensus*, pp. 392-395). In this a brief account is given of the injustice of the Jews in giving up Jesus, and of the extraordinary wonders reported concerning Him, especially His resurrection, with a view of preventing the Emperor from believing the lies of the Jews. A second shorter Letter of PILATE to TIBERIUS is given by THILO after the first Letter (pp. 801-802), by TISCHENDORF (p. 411 sq.). In this Pilate states his conviction of the innocence of Jesus, and his regret that he gave Him up to the Jews. In the MSS. it is never found attached to the Gospel of NICODEMUS.

To writings of this class belong also the following:—

(*a*.) A somewhat longer Report (ἀναφορά) of PILATE to TIBERIUS, in Greek, on the miracles attributed to Jesus, and the charge laid against Him by the Jews of working these on the Sabbath-day; also on His death, and the signs accompanying it, especially the resurrection of the dead bodies and His own resurrection: in FABRICIUS (iii. p. 456 sqq.); and after another recension in THILO (pp. 803–813); and after both recensions (as BIRCH had already given it) in TISCHENDORF (pp. 413–419 and 420–425).

(*b.*) The παράδοσις of PILATE, which is given in many MSS. as an appendix to the ἀναφορά just mentioned. It is in Greek, and tells a romantic story of Pilate's being brought to judgment by the Roman Emperor on account of Christ's death, and finally executed, after having been fully converted: in THILO (pp. 813–816), TISCHENDORF (pp. 426–431).

(*c.*) *Mors Pilati*, in Latin; edited by TISCHENDORF (pp. 432–435), after a Milanese codex. This is a very wild legend, telling how, after his condemnation by Tiberius, Pilate made away with himself. Veronica also, with her marvellous handkerchief, whereon the Lord's countenance was impressed, plays a conspicuous part in it, as does also the seamless coat of Christ.

(*d.*) *Narratio Josephi Arimathiensis*, in Greek, first edited by Birch from a Greek codex of the Gospel of Nicodemus; in Tischendorf, with a collation of several MSS. (pp. 436–447). This work pretends to have been written by Joseph of Arimathea, and treats of Christ's arrest and crucifixion, the history of the two malefactors crucified with Him, and especially the conversion and glorification of one of them (here called Demas), both during the crucifixion and after the resurrection. It is altogether mythical.

(*e.*) *Vindicta Salvatoris*, in Latin; in TISCHENDORF (pp. 448–463). This work relates, in an utterly unhistorical and legendary fashion, the severe chastisements inflicted by the Romans on the Jews because of the murder of Jesus; also the miraculous cure and conversion of Titus and Tiberius. Here, again, Veronica and her wonder-working handkerchief figure very prominently.

I may just mention a short apocryphal Report which a certain LENTULUS, said to have been governor of Judea before

Pilate, sent to the Roman Senate on the person of Jesus, especially His external appearance: in FABRICIUS (i. p. 301 sq.). Not one of all these writings has the slightest historical value. So far from agreeing with our canonical Gospels, they are not even derived from historical tradition, but are for the most part mere arbitrary fancies, the unhistorical character of which strikes us at once, from their romantic air, and their distorted or even utterly unworthy representations of the Redeemer. They are, however, very useful in helping to set more definitely before us the value and historical character of our canonical Gospels.[1]

ACTS OF THE APOSTLES.

§ 122.

IT may be seen by its very commencement, that the Acts of the Apostles is a continuation of the third canonical Gospel, and by the same author. It is professedly addressed to the same Theophilus to whom that Gospel was dedicated, and which the author distinguishes from it as a $\pi\rho\hat{\omega}\tau\sigma\varsigma$ $\lambda\acute{o}\gamma\sigma\varsigma$, already presented to his friend. It would seem, therefore, that he wished this work to be regarded as his $\delta\epsilon\acute{u}\tau\epsilon\rho\sigma\varsigma$ $\lambda\acute{o}\gamma\sigma\varsigma$. The title of the book, as given in the Greek New Testament, is $\pi\rho\acute{a}\xi\epsilon\iota\varsigma$ $\tau\hat{\omega}\nu$ $\dot{a}\pi\sigma\sigma\tau\acute{o}\lambda\omega\nu$, that is, Acts of the Apostles. This title is found in the oldest MSS., and occurs in Clemens Alexandrinus and others. Even some of the oldest translations (the Coptic, Syriac, and Arabic of Erpenius) have retained the Greek $\pi\rho\acute{a}\xi\epsilon\iota\varsigma$, though the word is not otherwise known in these languages; and hence it must have been usual from an early time to regard this as the special name of the book. It is not at all likely, however, that such a designation was given it by the author himself; for as his work was addressed to a private person, and doubtless sent to him without any title attached to it,

[1] RUD. HOFMANN, *Das Leben Jesu nach den Apokr. im Zusammenhange aus den Quellen erzählt u. wissensch. unters.*, Leipz. 1851. Also his article, *Apokryphen des N. T.*, in Herzog's Realencykl. xii. 320 sqq.

the writer had not felt himself called upon to find any name for it, the need of which would probably only be felt when the work had obtained more general circulation in the Church, and was adopted into the Canon. Among the Latins the chief names given to it—*Acta* (-orum) or *Actus* (-uum) *Apostolorum*, the former already found in Tertullian, the latter in Augustine—have, since Luther's translation, been blended together in the German *Apostelgeschichte* (English, Acts of the Apostles), which, moreover, fully answers to the Greek title.

With regard to the *contents* of the book, we may remark that it begins where the Gospel of Luke closes, that is, with the Lord's ascension, which it records with greater fulness of detail, and with more precision. It then goes on to give more or less copious accounts of the spread of the kingdom of God through the efforts of the apostles and other Christian teachers, the history of the Church at Jerusalem, the founding of Churches in other places, and the special labours and fate of such persons as showed themselves more than usually zealous in promoting these ends, concluding with an account of the Apostle Paul's voyage as a prisoner from Cæsarea to Rome, and the statement that he abode in the latter city two whole years, preaching the gospel freely and without hindrance to all who came to him. The facts thus recorded cover a space of about thirty years, but are treated very variously: some fully and clearly; others in a very summary fashion; others, again, with the omission of much which would have made the historical picture altogether more distinct. From the title, we might expect to find in the book a history of the apostles collectively; but this is very far from being the case. The first chapter gives us a cursory view of them all; afterwards we hear nothing more of the majority of them, not even their names,—a fact which proves that the title of the book, however old, did not emanate from Luke himself. There are only two apostles of whose history any particulars are given—Peter and, at a later time, Paul. John indeed is mentioned, but only in the first part, and then merely as the companion of Peter; while of James the

Greater we read nothing more than the very brief account of
his execution by Herod (Agrippa I.). With regard to other
Christian teachers besides the apostles, special mention is
made at some length of Stephen's martyrdom, and the evangelistic labours of Philip the deacon. The book, however,
deals most fully with the history of Paul, his conversion, his
missionary travels in various countries of Asia and Europe,
his last journey to Jerusalem and imprisonment there, and
his trial and voyage to Rome. But even here we meet with
much inequality and incompleteness in the narrative; events
belonging to the whole period, and sometimes of great importance, if judged of by the notices of them in the apostle's
own letters, being now and then referred to very briefly
(*e.g.* xviii. 18–23, xx. 1–3), while nothing at all is told us of
the apostle's residence and labours in several districts, where,
according to his letters, he must have lived and worked—
for instance, in Arabia (Gal. i. 17), Illyricum (Rom. xv. 19),
Crete (Tit. i. 5). In like manner the author is silent about
most of the perils enumerated by Paul in 2 Cor. xi. 23-26
as having befallen himself. In this passage the apostle mentions three shipwrecks which he must have suffered on his
missionary travels, but which are altogether unnoticed in
the Acts, the only one mentioned—that on the voyage to
Rome—having occurred after 2d Corinthians was written.
Still more defective is the history of Peter, which breaks off
abruptly with the story of his deliverance from prison in ch.
xii., after which we meet only with a passing reference to
his labours in ch. xv. Paul's history, too, terminates in a
way which may perhaps serve for a pause, but is not a
conclusion properly so called.

§ 123.

The unsatisfactory close of the book has often been
accounted for by the supposition that Luke wrote at the
time when his narrative leaves off, that is, in the second
year of Paul's imprisonment. This, however, is incorrect.
The very expression he uses, ἔμεινεν δὲ διετίαν ὅλην, κ.τ.λ.,
renders it much more probable that Luke wrote not only

after the lapse of the two years, but when, after that period, some change known to him had taken place in the apostle's circumstances. We may add that even the Gospel of Luke was written after this period — perhaps not till after the destruction of Jerusalem (see § 105); consequently the Acts must have been of much later date. Another explanation, however, is that the author purposed to give a history in his work of the spread of Christianity from Jerusalem, the capital of Judaism, to Rome, the capital of heathenism. This, however, is not very probable, though the view has been held, with various modifications, by DE WETTE, *Einleit.* § 113, *a*, note *b*, who finds the theme of the book in the Lord's words recorded in ch. i. 8; more definitely still by MEYERHOFF, *Hist.-krit. Einl. in die Petr. Schriften*, 1–30, *über Zweck, Quellen und Verfass. der Apostelgesch.*; by LEKEBUSCH, *Die Composition und Entstehung der Apg. von neuem untersucht*, Gotha 1854 ; and lastly by MICHAEL BAUMGARTEN, *Die Apg. oder der Entwickelungsgang der Kirche von Jerusalem bis Rom, ein bibl.-hist. Versuch*, 2 Thle., Halle 1852, 2d ed., Braunschweig 1859. The last writer infers from the words in ch. i. 1, περὶ πάντων ὧν ἤρξατο ᾽Ιησοῦς ποιεῖν τε καὶ διδάσκειν, that Jesus, not the individual human teachers who are brought on the scene, is the principal subject even of this book, and that the author's purpose was to give a complete and exhaustive account of His work, pointing out as its goal, even at the very commencement of his narrative, the two years' unrestrained preaching by the Apostle of the Gentiles in the Roman capital, when the Lord's victory over His enemies was achieved, not by their slaughter or annihilation, but by their subjection, through God, to His footstool.[1] All this, however, is very artificial, and so is a good deal in Baumgarten's treatment of details (see Lekebusch, p. 201 sqq.). Indeed, the notion in general, that the Acts of the Apostles was meant to delineate the course of the gospel as far as Rome, is unnatural. Had this been the author's purpose, he would surely not have neglected, above

---

[1] So also, in the main, OTTO, *Die geschichtl. Verhältnisse der Pastoralbriefe*, Leipz. 1860, pp. 172–188.

all things, to tell us when and how Christianity found entrance into that city, of which we read nothing, though that it had been there for some time before Paul's arrival we learn from the Epistle to the Romans, and, in fact, from Acts xxviii. itself.

Since Luke expressly speaks of the Acts as a continuation of his Gospel, we must, in order to get his point of view, go back to what he himself says at the beginning of the latter work. He there announces his intention to be, following the example of others, to give Theophilus an exact account πραγμάτων ἐν ἡμῖν πεπληροφορημένων, connecting therewith trustworthy information on matters he had heard of. So general, however, is his expression, that we cannot precisely say whether he had directly in his mind the history of Christ only, or that of the apostles as well. Very possibly the latter was the case. But if he thought at first only of a history of Christ, and had no very definite intention at the time of carrying his narrative further, we might expect, à priori, that now that he was undertaking a continuation of his work, he would have no other purpose than to give Theophilus as trustworthy and connected an account as possible of the subsequent prosecution of the work begun by the Redeemer during His sojourn on earth. That this is not done with equal fulness of detail throughout, cannot be particularly strange to us, since we find the same peculiarity in the Gospel, where some facts are entirely passed over in silence,—for instance, Christ's earlier visits to Jerusalem, and His travels there and back. So also in the Acts, the gaps in the history of the apostles may be due to Luke's utter ignorance or want of precise knowledge of many events and circumstances connected with it, which would compel him either to omit them altogether, or to notice them very briefly. That he should show a special interest in Paul, and even give us here and there particulars of his personal history and labours, is only natural; for he himself was a Gentile Christian, and, at any rate at a later period of his own life, stood in a close relation to the apostle (§ 49). Even in the Gospel we have several indications of this (§ 108), and especially in various ways of his affinity with the spirit and writings of Paul. But we certainly have not the slightest warrant for attributing to him, as many learned men do, a definite *apologetic* purpose,—namely, to vindicate against the Jews Paul's reception of Gentiles into the kingdom of God.[1] This seems at once to be altogether improbable, when we call to mind his nationality, and that of the friend to whom his work was addressed. It is very likely that neither of them was a Jew. We may assume this, as most have done, even of Theophilus, and then there would assuredly be no need of writing to him an apologetic history in the sense referred to. There is nothing to support SCHNECKENBURGER's opinion, that the dedication to Theophilus was a mere mask, and that the book was primarily written for Jewish Christians, in order to remove their prejudices against Paul and his adherents. Luke, as himself a Gentile Christian, was not the fittest person to exercise any decisive influence on the Judaizing party; and it is not likely, therefore, that he would put forth under his own name a work having this for its special aim. Still less probable is it that he kept to such a purpose, and carried it out in the way Schneckenburger, Schwegler, Baur, and Zeller suppose. According to these writers, he intended, in a subtle and conscious manner, to place the Apostle Paul in such a light as would make him inoffensive to Jewish Christians, or even induce them to regard him as a true apostle. By this intention (they say) he was influenced throughout his work, both in what he selected for record and in his treatment of individual facts; and thus they account for the historical *lacunæ* in the book, and even for its silence

---

[1] So, for the most part, MICHAELIS, PAULUS, J. E. CH. SCHMIDT, and to some extent DE WETTE in his 4th edition. But the view belongs especially to SCHNECKENBURGER, *Ueber den Zweck der Apg.*, Bern 1841; BAUR, first in the *Tüb. Zeitschr. f. Theol.* 1838, iii. p. 142, and afterwards in his *Paulus, der Apostel J. Chr. sein Leben und Wirken, seine Briefe u. seine Lehre—ein Beitr. zu einer krit. Gesch. des Urchristenthums*, Stutt. 1845; SCHWEGLER, *Nachapost. Zeitalter*, ii. 73–125 (exactly as SCHNECKENBURGER); ZELLER, *Die Apg. nach ihrem Inhalt und Ursprung Krit. untersucht*, Stuttg. 1854, from his contributions to the *Theol. Jahrb.* 1849–1851.

with respect to Paul's death. The author, it is said, was certainly one of the Pauline party, but animated by a conciliatory tendency. He proceeds, therefore, on the plan of exhibiting Paul in his private life as a careful observer of the law, and in his official character as acting in harmony with the other apostles and the original Christian community,—always cultivating a dutiful patriotism in respect of the Jewish people. Whatever, accordingly, in Paul's history would be detrimental to this plan is left out; and even in the first part of the work such facts only are recorded, and recorded in such a manner as would exhibit the other apostles, and especially Peter, as acting in harmony with Paul, and preparing the way for his special labours among the Gentiles. The work, says Zeller, is a conciliatory essay offered by a member of the Pauline party to the Judaizers, with a view of obtaining the recognition of Gentile Christianity by concessions to Judaism, and thus exerting an influence on both parties (ZELLER, 357 sqq., 363).

A notion of this kind, however, presupposes such deliberate purpose and calculated cunning on the author's part, as must appear altogether unlikely if we submit without prejudice to the impression a simple perusal of his work makes upon us. Its advocates are often obliged, in supporting it, to have recourse to utterly unnatural or decidedly false combinations, passing over in complete silence much in the book which is quite opposed to their assumptions. We allow at once that in the first part of his work Luke has given prominence to whatever in the history of the earlier Christian teachers appeared to be more directly introductory to the labours of the Apostle Paul in spreading the gospel among the Gentiles. This would be of special interest to himself as a Gentile Christian, and to Theophilus. But that in so doing he had the express design of justifying Paul's conduct, cannot be assumed with the least probability, from the way in which events are recorded by him; still less that, as Baur, Schwegler, and Zeller suppose, he deliberately altered the history to make it fall in with this design. Rather do particular passages show clearly how very far he was, even in the first part of his work, from giving a Pauline hue to everything, in order to establish the glory and apostolical dignity of his leader. Thus, in i. 21 sq., when Peter tells those who had to choose a new apostle that they must select some one who had been associated with the other apostles during the whole time of the Lord's going in and out among them, it is plain that the qualification does not at all apply to Paul, and would certainly not have been mentioned if Luke had written from no other point of view than that attributed to him. So also, in x. 41, Peter says that God showed Christ after His resurrection, not to the whole people, but μάρτυσι τοῖς προκεχειροτονημένοις ὑπὸ τοῦ Θεοῦ, ἡμῖν, οἵτινες συνεφάγομεν καὶ συνεπίομεν αὐτῷ μετὰ τὸ ἀναστῆναι αὐτὸν ἐκ νεκρῶν. Here, if his purpose was as supposed, the writer would probably have expressed himself differently (see Lekebusch, 373, note). Nor could we explain why in ii. 46 the author should have given prominence to the fact that even after the day of Pentecost the disciples met together with one accord in the temple at Jerusalem; and so with other facts. Not less mistaken is it to consider it a proof of the view in question, that in the second part of the book it is made a marked feature of Paul, that he had the observance of the law at heart, and always in his work as a preacher addressed himself first to the Jews, and only when repelled by them turned to the Gentiles; for this was simply the course which events took historically, and is quite in harmony with what we learn of Paul from his letters, full of love for his own people, and earnestly desiring to see them not altogether excluded from the kingdom of God, glorying in being a Gentile to the Gentiles, and a Jew to the Jews. Certainly, in the account of Paul's conduct given us in the Acts—where, moreover, he is not made quite so conspicuous as the learned men I have referred to maintain—we find nothing more than a record of what really took place, so far as it was known to Luke.[1]

---

[1] Some very good remarks, in opposition especially to SCHNECKENBURGER, may be found in E. A. SCHWANBECK, Ueber die Quellen der Schriften des Lucas, Bd. i.; Ueber die Quellen der Apgesch., Darmstadt 1847, pp. 94-104; and particularly in LEKEBUSCH, pp. 236-386.

§ 124.

We now proceed to inquire into the *sources* from which Luke drew the materials for his work. As regards his Gospel, we have already seen that he doubtless derived the greater part of it from earlier writings of more or less compass,—some things also being probably known to him from oral tradition, while there was no reason to suppose he had been an eye-witness of anything he records. But it is usually supposed that the case is very different at any rate with a good part of the Acts. In the latter part—that is, in the account of Paul's journeys—his fellow-travellers are very often spoken of in the *first person* plural; so that there we have unquestionably the report of one of the apostle's companions. Now, since we are nowhere expressly told who this was, it has been thought that very possibly it was Luke himself, and that he was with Paul whenever the narrative runs on in the style alluded to, and had again left him when this is not the case. This supposition, however, is by no means so certain as might at first sight appear. If we bear in mind how Luke in his Gospel seems to have used the earlier writings he relies upon, adopting them into his work as they lay ready to hand, without specially elaborating them, or compressing them together in any such way as would be appropriate to a continuous historical work, we can see how, in the instances referred to in the Acts, we have not necessarily Luke's own report of Paul's travels. He may have had before him that of some other believer associated with the apostle, which had been drawn up perhaps for some Christian friend or society, and afterwards, on its wider circulation, falling into his hands while composing his own work, had been used by him, though he retained its original form so far as even here and there to adopt a style appropriate only to some companion-traveller. Were Luke himself really the narrator in all these cases, we should expect him expressly to mention somewhere or other the fact of his being associated with Paul, and how he came to be so, as well as the time when he left him, and his reasons for taking such a step, especially in a work written for one personally known to him, to whom it must have been interesting to learn what share the author himself had in the events he records. Intimations of this kind, however, are nowhere to be met with; but we have the *first plural*, and shortly afterwards the *third plural* personal pronoun, without the least remark being made on the change, which, if Luke be here the narrator, would certainly be as extraordinary as if he were giving us in these cases partly literal extracts from a report written by some other of Paul's fellow-labourers.[1] What, however, makes the latter hypothesis on the whole more probable, is this. We find the sort of colloquial narrative referred to employed—(1) in the second of Paul's missionary journeys recorded in xv. 36 sqq.; more particularly xvi. 9–17, of the journey from Troas to Philippi, and the events at the latter city up to the account of the soothsayer who was converted by Paul; (2) in the apostle's later European travels, of the return from Philippi over Asia Minor to Jerusalem, xx. 5 sqq.; (3) in Paul's voyage as a prisoner from Cæsarea to Rome, xxvii. xxviii. In all these instances the report is that of an eye-witness and participator in the events recorded. The same person was also very probably with the apostle at Jerusalem and Cæsarea, although the style we are speaking of is not found in connection with events occurring at these places, inasmuch as there would be no need of the testimony of an eye-witness where the account is exclusively of Paul's own personal history. Now, if Luke were the narrator in these cases, and had consequently been at least associated with Paul in the events recorded with the pronoun *we*, he must have stood in a very close connection indeed with the apostle, and that too at a time which, as we shall see, preceded the composition of Paul's collective epistles. But then we should expect—(*a*) that even in his earlier letters, before his imprisonment at Rome, the apostle would have

---

[1] Compare SCHWANBECK, pp. 188–191, who adduces illustrations from historians of the Middle Ages, where these adopt the words of the authors whom they use as authorities, and even retain the *first person plural* in a way which is altogether unsuitable to their own age and point of view.

had occasion to mention him sometimes—for example, in 1st and 2d Thessalonians, or in 1st and 2d Corinthians, whereas he is never named, but only Timothy and Sylvanus; (*b*) that in the letters written during the imprisonment at Rome, where Luke is mentioned, that is, in Colossians and Philemon, he would be made more prominent than others. This, however, is not the case; for in Philem. 24 he is mentioned last of all the συνεργοί, and in Col. iv. 14 after Aristarchus, Marcus, Jesus Justus, and Epaphras, and Paul is even obliged to point out whom he means by the appellation ὁ ἰατρός. But if Luke had been Paul's companion in all those sections in which *we* occurs, he must have had at least as long and close a connection with him as Timothy. This, however, could scarcely have been the case, if we judge from the way in which he is mentioned in those letters in conjunction with the apostle's other co-workers; and it is much more probable that he was only admitted to the apostle's intimacy when the latter was in Rome. In this city he seems to have been settled for some time as a physician, and we may therefore infer that he was there when Paul wrote his letter to the Philippians, whenever this was written, whether before or after those to the Colossians and to Philemon (on which see § 172). But had Luke been the companion of Paul, who narrates his travels, and who went with him from Troas to Philippi, and stayed at the latter place with him, and then again accompanied him to Asia on his later journey from Philippi, he must have been very closely connected with the Church at Philippi; and then we should expect to find him mentioned in the letter to that society. This, however, is not the case; while in i. 1 Paul associates Timothy with himself in the salutation. To this may be added, that in xvi. 10, the manner in which the narrator expresses himself ("*We* endeavoured . . . assuredly gathering that the Lord had called us," etc.) makes it probable that he had not attached himself to Paul for the first time at Troas, as we must suppose to be the case if he were Luke, but rather that he had been for some time with the apostle, so that he could speak of himself as an associate.

The way, too, in which (xx. 6 and xxvii. 9) the date is given according to the Jewish festivals renders it unlikely that these sections were originally written by Luke for Theophilus, who was an uncircumcised Gentile Christian. It is much more probable that they were due to one more closely connected with the Jewish people, and were written for persons in the same position. We are quite justified, therefore, in thinking that in those portions of the Acts referred to, Luke used the report of some other of Paul's fellow-labourers,—keeping, however, often closely to the original form of the narrative; and it is exceedingly probable that in the first of these sections we have a report of Timothy, —that is, in part of the account of the second missionary journey, that from Troas to Philippi, xvi. 9 sqq. Paul was accompanied in his journey from Antioch by Silas (xv. 40); at a later time, at Lystra, Timothy joined them (xvi. 1 sqq.); but we read of no other companions. It is not therefore far-fetched to suppose that what Luke relates of this journey rests on the reports of one of these three—Paul, Silas, or Timothy. It, however, could not have been Paul or Silas, as Schwanbeck supposes; for when anything is related of Paul himself, or of Paul and Silas unitedly—as, for instance, the imprisonment and release at Philippi—they are mentioned by name, the *third person plural* is used, while the colloquial mode of narration is retained in the context. Thus, in xvi. 13, "*We* went by a river," etc.; ver. 16, "*We* went to prayer:" comp. ver. 17, "The damsel followed Paul and us;" ver. 18, "Paul turned;" and ver. 19, "They caught Paul and Silas," and so on. From all this it is most likely that the narrative here is by Timothy, whose account of these events was probably given in a letter to his adherents or fellow-believers at Lystra, or the district about it, and which Luke had before him.

§ 125.

The style referred to is no longer to be met with in the latter part of this journey, from Philippi onwards. We may therefore conclude that here the original authority was not one of Paul's companions, not even Timothy, who, on the departure of Paul and Silas from Philippi, must either have been left behind by the apostle to confirm the converts, or had already gone away; for in what immediately follows, xvi. 40, Paul and Silas alone are expressly mentioned as the heralds of the faith who went about from place to place (cf. xvii. 4, 10). It is only at Berea that Timothy appears to have rejoined them, since at xvii. 14 it is said that when Paul found himself compelled to quit the city, he left Silas and Timothy behind, with a command to come after him as soon as possible. Now we see from 1 Thess. iii. 2, that Timothy at least came to Paul at Athens, and there remained some time with him. Whether, in writing also this continuation of the journey, Luke had any report by Timothy before him, we cannot precisely say. Still it is not improbable that such was the case, at least as regards the fuller account of Paul's labours at Athens, and his speech on the Areopagus, whether Timothy had then rejoined the apostle, or had simply, on his subsequent arrival, heard the facts from Paul's own mouth or from others. On the other hand, we know nothing of any visit of Silas to the apostle at Athens.

Timothy, moreover, was probably the original reporter of the latter part of the Acts, where again the colloquial style occurs. With regard to the narrative of Paul's journey from Macedonia to Jerusalem, where this style prevails, we find, before it begins, an express assertion in xx. 4, that Timothy was one of the apostle's companions. His account may very well begin at ver. 5, where we should understand the οὗτοι προελθόντες ἔμενον ἡμᾶς ἐν Τρωάδι of the Asiatics, named after Timothy just before, Tychicus and Trophimus, which Zeller incorrectly declares to be untenable (*Apgesch.* 459 sq.), though it is evidently by far the most probable explanation. We can very easily imagine, from the relation in which we find him standing to the Apostle Paul in his epistles, that Timothy continued in close connection with him on his arrival at Jerusalem, after the apostle's imprisonment, and again at Cæsarea, and even accompanied him when he went to Rome, and there also remained a long while with him. It quite agrees with this, that we find him actually with the apostle in all the letters written during his imprisonment to the Colossians, Philemon, and the Ephesians, as well as to the Philippians; and always as a confederate who stood in a much closer personal relation to him than Luke. The habit, too, of reckoning the time by the Jewish festivals is far more intelligible in Timothy's case than it could have been in Luke's; since the former, the son of a Jewess, and doubtless from his childhood attached to the Jewish worship of God, had been fully naturalized as a Jew by receiving circumcision at the hands of Paul. The last particular would suit Silas, as he belonged to the Jewish people; but not the other circumstances. If Silas also at a later time, during the apostle's voyage to Rome, had been as closely and constantly connected with him, we should have had every reason to expect that he would have remained with him too for some time in that city, and have been mentioned in the letters written there. This, however, is never the case.

The view here developed on the origin of these reports of the apostle's travels emanated from SCHLEIERMACHER,[1] and was given in his lectures on the Acts of the Apostles. ULRICH has also adopted and published it in the *Stud. u. Krit.* 1837, pp. 369 sqq.; 1840, pp. 1003 sqq.: see also my notice of Mayerhoff's book, *ib.* 1836, pp. 1026 sqq. In Schleiermacher's published *Lectures Introductory to the N. T.* a similar view is exhibited, except that Timothy is not there pointed out as the reporter. DE WETTE even adopts it (see his *Exeget. Handb. zur Apgesch.*, and especially his *Einleit. ins N. T.*, 5th ed.). MAYERHOFF regards the reports in their original form as Timothy's, but at the same time attributes to him the whole of the Acts and the third Gospel. This, however, is untenable, as I have already proved on good evidence as it seems to me, and Mayerhoff himself has retracted this part of his opinion. We cannot

---

[1] The first, strictly speaking, who advanced the opinion that, in his scrupulous use of sources, Luke went so far as even to allow his authority to speak in the first person here and there, is KÖNIGSMANN (of Flensburg): De fontibus commentariorum sacr. qui Lucæ nomen præferunt, deque eorum consilio et ætate, 1798, in POTT's *Sylloge Commentt. Theol.* vol. iii.

conceive how the attribution of the authorship to Luke, if a mistake, could have obtained currency in the Church, when Timothy was so much better known, and occupied a position so much higher than he; for, except as the author of these works, we know scarcely anything more of Luke than that he was connected with Paul when the latter wrote his letters to the Colossians and Philemon. Such a notion as Mayerhoff's must be rejected, because (*a*) many parts of the Acts treat of events at length, while we have repeatedly but very brief and summary notices of Paul's labours in periods during which, as we know from the apostle's letters, Timothy was associated with him, and must have had much that was important to record, for example xx. 1–3; (*b*) Timothy himself is mentioned (xvi. 1 sqq., xix. 22, xx. 4) in a way very unlikely if he had been the author of the whole book, and had written it for a private and intimate friend. On the other hand, if we are right in maintaining that those sections of the Acts in which *we* occurs proceeded originally from Timothy, there can be no doubt that the personal references to him were not made by himself, but by the author of the book, who was a totally different person.

§ 126.

These reports of Timothy, however, were certainly not the only writings Luke availed himself of in the Acts. We see pretty clear indications of a use also of written records to some extent in the preceding portions of the book; *e.g.* in the account of Paul's first missionary tour with Barnabas, ch. xiii. xiv., especially if we compare the form of its commencement with what immediately precedes. We read in xii. 25, "And Barnabas and Saul returned from Jerusalem," etc. Immediately after, xiii. 1, as an introduction to the subsequent setting apart of the two for their missionary work, the Christian teachers and prophets then at Antioch are mentioned in a way which would not have suggested itself easily if the narrator here had been originally the same as in the preceding chapter. We should rather have expected, in that case, to find mention made only of those whom Paul and Barnabas met on their return to Antioch; whereas they themselves are included indiscriminately with the rest. This is best explained on the supposition that Luke found a special record of Paul's first missionary journey, which he incorporated entirely or partially into his work. As he had just related in xi. 30, of Paul and Barnabas, that they had been entrusted by the Christians of Antioch with a collection for the brethren in Judea, it was natural he should notice their return to Antioch before giving the report of their missionary journey, since this speaks of Antioch as the city from which they were sent out on that journey. He has, moreover, left the beginning of the report unaltered, though some slight change would certainly have been an improvement in point of form.

In like manner, Luke had probably before him an earlier report on the transactions of the apostles recorded in xv. 1–33, which had been drawn up quite independently of that on Paul's second missionary journey, xv. 35 sqq. The former closes with the statement in ver. 33, that Judas Barsabas and Silas, who had been commissioned by the apostles in Jerusalem to accompany Paul and Barnabas on their return to Antioch, went back again, after some time, to Jerusalem, to those who had sent them. Then immediately follows, according to the *received text*, in ver. 34, " It pleased Silas to abide there (at Antioch) still." This remark, however, besides being hard to reconcile with ver. 33, is wanting in the oldest and largest number of MSS., and is doubtless, as Lachmann and Tischendorf maintain, a later interpolation. But ver. 33 does not agree with ver. 40, according to which Silas was at Antioch when Paul undertook his second missionary journey. The facts must be explained in the following way: The commencement of this second missionary journey occurred, as may be otherwise proved, some time after Paul's return from Jerusalem to Antioch, and Silas' departure again from Antioch to Jerusalem. We can then easily see how Silas had meanwhile returned from Jerusalem to Antioch (probably with Peter, whose visit, spoken of in Gal. ii. 11, must have taken place then), where he remained until Paul commenced his journey and took him with him. In the report of the apostolical conference at Jerusalem there was no need of stating that, after his mission to Antioch, Silas went back to Jerusalem, and then very shortly afterwards returned again to Antioch. So also, in any report of Paul's second missionary journey, there was no special need of mentioning that Silas, who accompanied him from Antioch, had only returned thither from Jerusalem a short time before. But if both reports had been originally written in connection with one another, we should have expected that, as ver. 33 told us Silas had gone to Jerusalem, so some notice would have been taken of his return thence again to Antioch.

Even in the first part of the Acts, recourse seems to have been had to some extent to written authorities. Much appears especially to have been taken from a history referring particularly to the Apostle Peter.[1] In this way we can see how this part of the Acts gives us minute details of that apostle; while others, such as John and James, are alluded to only cursorily, and just as far as they were in any way connected with Peter and his history. In proof of this we may refer especially to ch. xii. What is said there (ver. 2) of the beheading of James the elder by Herod (Agrippa I.), as well as the preceding general remark (ver. 1) that this ruler "stretched forth his hands to vex certain of the Church," appears to be simply introductory to the following section, which relates circumstantially how Peter was thrown into prison, and miraculously released. Had this section been originally part of a more general work such as the Acts, the design of which was not to give the history of any one apostle only, then in the case of so distinguished an apostle as James the elder—one of the three most trusted disciples of the Lord, whose subsequent activity in spreading the gospel at Jerusalem made him conspicuous among the apostles, and induced Agrippa to put him out of the way rather than any of the others—we should have expected to find fuller details

[1] This opinion has been held by many previous interpreters, and more recently by even SCHWANBECK, and by DE WETTE, § 115, c.

respecting his martyrdom, the particular occasion of his imprisonment, and especially his previous public labours. So also as regards John: it may indeed be true that his more contemplative disposition would render him less publicly active than, *e.g.*, Peter; but that he was a prominent member of the company of the apostles at Jerusalem, is plain from the manner in which Paul refers to him in Gal. ii. 9. Hence it is somewhat surprising that he is mentioned only cursorily in the Acts, as merely the silent companion of Peter. I may add that there is not the least reason for supposing, with SCHNECKENBURGER (p. 159), that a special history of individual apostles during the apostolical period is inconceivable; for it is not at all clear why such should not have been written soon after the death of an influential apostle, recording his labours, and the events which befell him. It is also probable that in the detailed account of Stephen's martyrdom, and the evangelistic labours of Philip the deacon, Luke made use of some earlier work, dealing chiefly with the history and labours of the deacons at Jerusalem. This may be inferred from the manner in which Philip is mentioned (viii. 5), without any attempt to distinguish him more precisely from the apostle of the same name. On the other hand, there is no need to assume, with SCHWANBECK, the use of some special biography of Barnabas (to which are assigned the sections iv. 36, 37, ix. 8–30, xi. 19–30, xii. 25, xiii. 1–xiv. 27, xiv. 28–xv. 4); since we should then expect to meet with a much fuller and more minute account of the by no means unimportant labours of that evangelist. Compare, however, for the contrary view, DE WETTE, § 115, *c*, note *d*.

We cannot speak with any definite certainty of the number and extent of the various works made use of by our author; still less are we able to do so as to what he learnt from oral tradition merely; but we may very probably assign to this last class all those parts of the book which are characterized by great brevity in the records of considerable periods of time. From what we have already said, it would not seem to be at all likely that Luke recorded any particular events with the authority of one who saw and himself took part in them.

§ 127.

The plan adopted by Luke with his written authorities in the Acts was, as far as we can judge, essentially the same as in his Gospel. That he did not simply take the raw materials ready to hand, and put them one after the other, but attempted to fuse them into some sort of homogeneous whole, is shown by the historical connection which, if we do not try him everywhere by very severe critical rules, may be seen in the work, the numerous references in the later sections to the earlier, and again the foreshadowings in the earlier sections of the contents of the later.[1] So also, certain peculiarities of phraseology which different sections of the Acts have in common with one another and the third Gospel,[2] show that Luke treated with some freedom the general outline and particular expressions of the works he made use of. Nevertheless, what is not his own is not revised and dovetailed, one section into the other, as we should look for it to be in a classical or modern historical writer. Parts of his book often exhibit unmistakeable peculiarities of style and colour which distinguish them from one another, and can only be explained as characteristics of the writers to whom they were originally due;[3] and the connection of certain sections is sometimes, as we have already seen, not quite appropriate. We may, however, safely assert that Luke did not in every case incorporate entire into his work such documents as he had before him, but occasionally made abstracts simply from them, on which some amount of revision must have been bestowed by himself. Thus, if it is correct that he made use of a special history of Peter, he could have drawn from it only a few particular narratives; for such a work would certainly have given Peter's history with more continuity and fulness of detail than we find in the Acts of the Apostles. Indeed, in certain narratives, we

---

[1] DE WETTE, § 115, a, note d; LEKEBUSCH, p. 82 sqq.; ZELLER, p. 401 sqq.
[2] DE WETTE, § 115, a, note b; LEKEBUSCH, p. 35 sqq.; ZELLER, p. 388 sqq.
[3] DE WETTE, § 115, c, notes a and b.

meet with indications that Luke had a more copious work before him, which he compressed. Thus, in xix. 16, in the original text, according to Lachmann and Tischendorf, we have ἀμφοτέρων instead of the received αὐτῶν, which certainly does not agree with the preceding context, where seven sons of Sceva are spoken of as seeking to cast out demons in the name of Jesus, while here only two are pointed out as specially engaged in that work. The narrative, then, in all probability, was much clearer in the original and fuller report, and has been obscured by abbreviation. We also feel as if we had a longer report compressed in the section xi. 19–26, which speaks of the spread of God's kingdom at Antioch even among the Grecians, the continuous abode there of Paul and Barnabas for a whole year, and especially in ver. 26, the application to those who confessed the Lord of the name Χριστιανοί. Similarly, also, must we probably explain the reference in xvii. 5 to the house of Jason at Thessalonica, as assaulted by the people who wished to capture Paul and Silas, while no previous hint even is given of the relation in which Jason himself stood to those preachers of the faith. In the original narrative it was probably told that they had put up at Jason's house,—a fact which Luke would omit as of little importance. So also in xiii. 6–8, it is likely that the original record showed more clearly the relation of the names Barjesus and Elymas to one another.

On the other hand, in other parts of the book the narratives are obscured in such a way as can be explained only on the supposition that Luke interpolated something into the document before him; for instance, in vii. 58 sq., on the stoning of Stephen. It had already been said in ver. 58a, καὶ ἐκβαλόντες ἔξω τῆς πόλεως ἐλιθοβόλουν; then, in ver. 58b, "The witnesses laid down their clothes at a young man's feet whose name was Saul;" and again, in ver. 59, καὶ ἐλιθοβόλουν τὸν Στέφανον, κ.τ.λ. Here we must suppose that Luke found in the document before him simply a general statement that they led Stephen out of the city, and stoned him, and then himself added the words in ver. 58b, καὶ οἱ μάρτυρες, on to the second ἐλιθοβόλουν in ver. 59, from another and probably purely oral tradition, on account of what is there said of Saul, of whom he was going to speak more fully afterwards. Properly, we should have expected after the first ἐλιθοβόλουν the addition also of an object; and its omission can be most easily explained only on the hypothesis of an interpolation of the kind referred to. In like manner, in the narrative contained in viii. 1–3, as we now have it, there is a certain obscurity and confusion, since (*a*) what is related in vers. 1 and 3 of the persecution after Stephen's martyrdom is severed by the unnatural division of ver. 2, containing the notice of Stephen's burial, which we should have looked for before any mention of this persecution. And (*b*) vers. 1 and 3 do not appear to agree with one another exactly: for while ver. 1 says that, with the exception of the apostles, all the believers were scattered beyond Jerusalem into Judea and Samaria, ver. 3 speaks as if what is said of Paul's persecuting fury referred to persons still living in their usual place of abode at Jerusalem. Here also Luke probably introduced from some other source the reference to Paul. There is also something remarkable in the way in which at xiii. 9 the name Paul is applied to the apostle. In the preceding narrative he is always called Σαῦλος; here, in the report of his first missionary journey, he is called once for all Σαῦλος δὲ ὁ καὶ Παῦλος, and Παῦλος ever afterwards. It is not likely that the apostle assumed this name for the first time at Cyprus; such a fact would have been pointed out in a different way. Probably the true explanation is, that in the original narrative of this the apostle's first missionary journey he was throughout called Paul. Instead of this, however, Luke at first retained the name Saul, by which the apostle had been hitherto called; but afterwards found it more convenient to keep to Paul, by which he was better known beyond Palestine, and hence, at the passage we have cited, allowed the alteration to appear in the manner indicated.

§ 128.

From what has now been said, some estimate may be formed of the *historical character* and *value* of this book. In this respect it has been very unfairly judged in modern times; for instance, by K. SCHRADER, *der Apostel Paulus*, Thl. v., Leipz. 1836, and GFRÖRER, *die heilige Sage*, Stuttgart 1838, i. 383-452, cf. ii. 244-247,—the latter of whom allows the second part of the book to be historical, but relegates the first to the sphere of legend, while SCHRADER declares the whole to be utterly unhistorical and untrustworthy. The same view is held by SCHNECKENBURGER and the theologians of BAUR'S school—SCHWEGLER, BAUR himself, and especially ZELLER—who affirm that the narratives throughout were designedly written for an *apologetic* purpose. SCHNECKENBURGER at the same time regards Luke as the sole author, and even attributes to him primarily the sections in which *we* occurs; the others place the composition of the book in the second century, Zeller between 110 and 130 A.D., alleging with Baur, that in the latter part of it the author used, with arbitrary alterations, certain reports of Luke, Paul's companion, for whom he wished to pass himself off. He was the same as the author of the third Gospel,—a fact which Zeller argues at length, and satisfactorily (pp. 414-452). It certainly admits of hardly any reasonable doubt that the Acts of the Apostles was written by the same author as that of the third canonical Gospel, whose *second part* it expressly claims to be. It is not at all likely that a late writer would have feigned a relation of this kind to the earlier work, for then there would be very much more of manifest effort to establish it than we find to be the case. Both works not only breathe throughout the same spirit, but, as we have remarked, exhibit the same phraseology. Now, that the writer was Luke, the friend of Paul, rests as to both the Acts and the Gospel of Luke on ecclesiastical tradition, which we have no just ground to doubt. It is true Luke is not mentioned as the author till towards the close of the second century, first by IRENÆUS, and then by CLEMENS ALEX., TERTULLIAN, and others;[1] but then these writers state the fact so unhesitatingly, not even stopping to discuss it, that it is quite clear they must have known it to be universally acknowledged by the Church in their day, and derived from a still older ecclesiastical tradition. No doubt, from the very first, ever since the works had come before the general public, this had been the common opinion in the Church; and to it we owe the statement of the superscription in each case as to the author, which we find invariably in the MSS. of the Gospel, and to some extent in those of the Acts, and even in the oldest translations. The Acts of the Apostles was not indeed received by many heretics of the first century, such as the Ebionites, Marcionites, Manichæans, and Encratite Severians; but it is allowed that its rejection by these sects rested purely on dogmatic grounds, and referred simply to its canonical authority, without at all contesting its genuineness or Luke's authorship; at least we meet with no hint of this kind. Even in the catholic Church the Acts was not so much read as the Gospel. CHRYSOSTOM, at the commencement of his first Homily on it, says, probably with some exaggeration, that it was utterly unknown to many; but here again the simple reason was, that its contents were comparatively less interesting than those of the Gospel. At a much later time, PHOTIUS (ninth century), in his *Amphilochia* (Answers to 308 Questions and Doubts of Amphilochius, Bp. of Cyzicum), Quæst. 105, remarks, τὸν δὲ συγγραφέα τῶν πράξεων οἱ μὲν Κλημέντα λέγουσι τὸν ʽΡώμης, ἄλλοι δὲ Βαρνάβαν, καὶ ἄλλοι Λουκᾶν τὸν εὐαγγελιστήν; but this statement, important as it is, belongs to far too late a period to help us in forming a proper opinion on the tradition and judgment of the Church, particularly the more ancient Church, since we find nothing like it in any earlier writer. So general was the tradition of Luke's authorship in the early Church, that it forms of itself an important testimony to that fact, and finds no inconsider-

---

[1] [In relation to the Acts of the Apostles, see IRENÆUS, *Hær.* iii. 14, 15; CLEMENS ALEX., *adumbrat. in* 1 *Petr. Ep.*, and *Stromata*, lib. v. p. 588 B., ed. Sylburg; TERTULLIAN, *de Jejun.* x. On the Gospel, see § 50.—B.]

able support in the Pauline spirit which prevails in both works, and the writer's personal interest in the apostle (§ 108, 123).

§ 129.

The historical contents of the book are in harmony with the conclusion just stated. The very manner in which, as we have seen, the author uses other historical works, and to some extent such as were written by those who were eye-witnesses of and concerned in the facts related, attests his earnest endeavour to delineate whatever occurred according to its real course and connection, so far as his knowledge allowed. Equal accuracy indeed is not found in every case. If we judge without prejudice, we cannot deny that in many sections the historical narrative is either deficient in clearness, and presents difficulties, or in the history of Paul particularly does not quite agree with the apostle's own statements in his letters, as we shall see in several instances when we come to speak of his life and writings. Passages to the point here are ix. 20 sqq., 27 sqq., xii. 25. In such cases we cannot hesitate to make Paul's own statements our chief authority, and by them to test, complete, and in some degree rectify, what is told us in the Acts. Discrepancies, however, of this kind are not so numerous or so strongly marked as the scholars I have referred to try to make out, that we must on account of them give up the essential credibility of the book, nor are they such as to warrant our doubting its composition by Luke. Our attempts to explain them would be much more difficult, if Luke had been, as is usually supposed, Paul's trusted companion for several years, from the time of the apostle's second missionary journey onwards; since we should then be justified in expecting from him an accurate acquaintance with Paul's history and the whole course of his labours, even the earlier, and much more the later part of it. In like manner also we should expect an accurate knowledge with minute details of Paul's history, and to some extent with the history of the other apostles also, if Luke had been with Paul during the actual composition of his book. If, however, we admit (and to this the Gospel itself leads us) that Luke wrote only after the destruction of Jerusalem, six years and more after Paul's death, and that he only came into personal contact with him during his last years, that is, during his abode at Rome, we can hardly help seeing that, when he subsequently undertook to draw up this connected work primarily for Theophilus, a good deal even of Paul's history might not have been known to him well enough to allow of a clear and complete account of it; and this would be still more true in respect of the other Christian teachers. Especially if he used in the way we have pointed out the reports of others on particular events, or whole cycles of events, we can easily see that he might not have possessed any very accurate knowledge of their chronological and material connection, and therefore in this respect his work might exhibit much vagueness and inexactitude; and this is what we find to be the case not only in the Acts, but in his Gospel in common with the other Synoptics. One thing, however, is quite certain, that whatever of this kind we meet with in the Acts of the Apostles, is due simply to the fact that Luke was not fully informed on some points, not to any intentional falsification of facts for some supposed particular purpose. Had he really had an *apologetic* purpose, he would have worked up his materials in a way very different from that which we find in his work.

§ 130.

Of late years, many have repeatedly denied altogether the historical reality of the speeches attributed in the Acts to particular persons, especially those to the Christian teachers.[1] There is no ground, however, for this; for I remark—

(*a.*) It cannot be denied that there is a good deal of

---

[1] So pre-eminently, first of all, EICHHORN, who thinks these speeches were all fictitious, like those usually found in Greek and Roman historians; MAYERHOFF, to some extent in his work on the Acts, going still further in the latter parts, where he treats of Peter's speeches; SCHNECKENBURGER, BAUR, ZELLER, all of whom assert the speeches to be purely fictitious, and drawn up by the author to suit his apologetic purpose.

similarity in the addresses assigned to different Christian teachers. Thus in xiii. 16 sqq., Paul reverts to the ancient history of the Israelites in the same way as Stephen in vii. 2 sqq.; and again, in v. 35 sqq., he quotes Ps. xvi. 10 as a proof text of Christ's resurrection, just as Peter does in ii. 25 sqq.; and so with other instances. But it does not at all follow that these addresses were drawn up by one and the same person, and are therefore utterly unhistorical. We are naturally led rather to the conclusion that, among the apostles and first Christians generally, interpretations of the Messianic passages of the O. T., and their use in proof of the Christian faith, were formed after a certain common type, to which the different persons in the Church essentially conformed their teaching, without being in other respects dependent on one another. Nevertheless these addresses present in fact much that is characteristic and peculiar, especially Stephen's when compared with others; so that on this ground alone it is utterly unlikely they were composed by one and the same person.

(*b.*) The opinions we have already expressed as to Luke's authorities, and the use he made of them, at once overthrow such a view as that of the free composition of the speeches in the Acts by him, since, as we have seen, there is no need to doubt he has given them essentially as found in the documents before him. Moreover, as regards Paul's speeches, especially those in the sections written by one of the apostle's travelling companions, we cannot fairly doubt that they were recorded just as far as the reporter was able to recall them to mind. But we certainly could not expect to have them in full, or in the speakers' exact words: in all probability they were often curtailed and compressed; and this of itself would exercise some influence on their style and expression, and may help to explain how it is that in Paul's speeches we do not meet with the same style and the same use of words and modes of expression as in his epistles, and yet may be quite sure that we possess them essentially as to their subject-matter and line of thought. This is confirmed also by their accordance with the circumstances under which they were delivered; *e.g.* the speech at Athens, xvii. 22 sqq., and the farewell to the Ephesian bishops, xx. 18 sqq., etc. In the instance last cited, the authenticity is vouched for by ver. 25, "I know that ye all, among whom I have gone preaching the kingdom of God, shall see my face no more." Here the apostle plainly expresses a troubled foreboding that he should this time succumb to the plots of the Jews in Jerusalem, and lose, if not his life, at least his liberty, and not be able to recover it. Since, however, it is probable that Paul did obtain deliverance from that imprisonment, and even visit Asia Minor again (see § 167, 183), it is not at all likely that Luke or any later writer would have allowed him so to speak in a purely fictitious address; though Luke might very well have adopted the report of the speech as we have it, if he found it in the work of any of the apostle's companions, by whom it had been recorded shortly after delivery.

Of the speeches of other Christian teachers, Stephen's [1] has not the least appearance of having been composed for the first time forty years and more after that martyr's death, by some author from merely oral tradition, or arbitrarily out of his own head. Judging from its abrupt character, and its peculiarities as a whole, it may certainly be best explained on the supposition that it was spoken in the main as we find it, and put together and recorded soon after its delivery, as far as memory served, by some one who heard it. Even in the other non-Pauline speeches there are indications which go to prove how exact, even in minute points at times, is the report of the speakers' words, and which are certainly opposed altogether to the notion that the speeches were made up by Luke. For instance, in xv. 14, James refers to the Apostle Peter by his original name *Simeon*. We can easily see how, in addition to Peter, this name also might continue to be applied to the apostle by his colleagues and more immediate personal friends; but had Luke forged the speech in which it occurs, he would certainly have used *Peter*, by which he always designates the apostle in his narratives, or would at least have added it to *Simeon* (as in 2 Pet. i. 1). Again, in Peter's address, ii. 24,

[1] [On Stephen's speech, see FRIED. NITZSCH, *Stud. u. Krit.* 1860.—B.]

the formula is used, λύσας τὰς ὠδῖνας τοῦ θανάτου. The connection clearly shows that here it was intended to draw a picture of bonds and fetters as belonging to death. But the Greek word ὠδῖνες does not answer to these; and we can only explain it by a reference to the Hebrew חֶבְלֵי מָוֶת, which occurs also in Aramæan, and was, we may suppose, used by Peter in his speech, delivered no doubt in Aramæan, with an allusion to O. T. passages, in which it appears in the sense of *cords, bonds* of death. Peter's address was in all probability reported in Aramæan; and the translator, whether Luke or some one else, finding that חֲבָלִים equally means *cords, bonds,* or *pains, woes,* thought of the last idea, and instead of σχοινία, which would have been correct, used ὠδῖνες (just as the Septuagint in Ps. xviii. 5, cxvi. 3). Such a mistake can be easily explained in the case of a translator from a foreign tongue, but cannot be understood if Luke himself drew up the speech in Greek. Zeller's remark to the contrary (502 sq.) is very unsatisfactory here and in the next case. In ii. 33 and v. 31, in Peter's addresses, Christ is said to be exalted τῇ δεξιᾷ τοῦ Θεοῦ. As the expression occurs in Greek, we should be disposed to render it, *through, by means of,* the right hand of God. There can be no doubt, however, that the meaning is *to* the right hand of God; referring to Ps. cx. 1, in respect of which it is quite common in the N. T. to speak of Christ as at the right hand of God. Now the Greek phrase certainly originated simply in a somewhat inaccurate rendering of לִימִינִי by the dative. I may notice further the letter of the apostles on the liberation of the Gentiles from the Mosaic law, xv. 23–29. One sign of genuineness here is, that in ver. 25 Barnabas is named before Paul, while in the rest of the account of the apostolical conference (with the single exception of ver. 12), as also previously, from a time dating soon after the commencement of the missionary journey undertaken by the two in common, the opposite order is the more usual, and certainly would have been used here, if the letter had been a simple forgery of Luke's. From the authority which, according to the narrative in the Acts, was exercised by James the Lord's brother, it would seem that the letter was drawn up by him; and this is considerably strengthened by the Greek salutation χαίρειν in ver. 23, which only occurs among the epistles of the N. T. in that of James (i. 1), both letters being alike distinguished by the selection of a peculiar Greek expression. The authenticity of such a portion of the Acts tends to establish the historical character of the whole.

(c.) As we have not contended for any *ad verbum* report of the speeches in the Acts, we may even allow that there are addresses which owe their special form in a still greater degree to the author of the book. We may always assume this to be the case when the same words are attributed to several persons, or to an assembly of persons. Thus, in ii. 7, the words of the stranger Jews gathered together at the feast of Pentecost; iv. 15, the council of the Sanhedrim on Peter and John; iv. 19, the words of Peter and John; iv. 24, of the assembled apostles; v. 29, of the apostles before the Sanhedrim; vi. 2, of the apostles to the other disciples; xiii. 46, of Paul and Barnabas, and so on. In these cases it certainly cannot be the writer's meaning that all the individual persons, associated with others, uttered the very words attributed to them, but simply that this was the general sense of what they said. A modern writer would use *oblique*, where an ancient, and more especially a Hebrew, author would prefer *direct* narration, even when it was not at all his intention to report the words, but merely the general sentiment. So in like manner with Gamaliel's speech, delivered before the Sanhedrim, after the apostles had withdrawn (v. 34 sqq.). It is not improbable that an authentic report of this speech reached the writer (who would be a Christian), yet a report only as to its general sense and purport, while the form in which we have it would be due to the reporter, very possibly Luke himself; at any rate, it does not belong to a very early period. This is proved simply by the fact that mention is made in the speech of the revolt of one Theudas, as if it took place long before that of the Galilean Judas. Now it is very probable that no one else is meant by Theudas than he whom we read of in JOSEPHUS,

(*Antiqq.* xx. 5, 1), but who, however, arose long after the Galilean Judas, and probably even eight years after this trial of the apostles; so that Gamaliel could not have mentioned him. The case here, however, is unquestionably very different from what it is with the addresses of the apostles and other Christian teachers, against the essential authenticity of which it furnishes no argument. To an unprejudiced critic these are established on valid grounds, as is the historical character in general of this Acts of the Apostles, for the preservation of which we have all the more reason to thank God, since it is the only historical work preserved to us which gives anything like a trustworthy account of the apostolical period after the Lord's ascension. The close of the book is unsatisfactory. Why is this? (See § 122, 123.) Did Luke take it for granted that the subsequent history was known to Theophilus? This is not an adequate explanation. Even if the latter lived at Rome, and knew that some change had taken place in Paul's circumstances after the lapse of the two years, he could hardly have known all the rest of the apostle's history. Most likely Luke intended to carry on his narrative further in a third λόγος.

APOCRYPHAL ACTS OF THE APOSTLES.[1]

§ 131.

As there were apocryphal Gospels, so also there were, and probably at an early date, apocryphal Acts of the Apostles, portions of which have come down to us, though they have as little historical value as the apocryphal Gospels. They owe their origin partly to particular party interests outside of the Catholic Church, partly to a wish to fill up the gaps in the canonical books on the lives and labours of most of the apostles, which, however, they do for the most part in a purely romantic manner. They deal sometimes with the general history of the apostles, sometimes with individuals

---

[1] [HOFMANN, *Apokryphen des N. T.*, in Herzog's Realencykl. xii. 320, 331 sqq.—B.]

among them. According to EPIPHANIUS, *Hær.* xxx. 16, the Ebionites in his time had an Acts of the Apostles of their own, in which James (in contrast to Paul) appears to have played the principal part, while Paul is spoken of in a spirit of deadly enmity. He is represented as having been by birth a Greek, who became a convert to Judaism from attachment to the high priest's daughter; but on failing to obtain the maiden, afterwards became hostile to the Jewish law, to the Sabbath, and to circumcision. Peter's history is a mere romance as we find it in the works attributed to CLEMENS ROMANUS, which have come to us in several recensions. These also originated probably with Jewish Christians, but were afterwards revised by adherents of the Catholic Church. A conspicuous fabricator of apocryphal Acts of the Apostles was a Manichæan named Lucius (or Leucius) Charinus (cf. FABRICIUS, ii. 768-775), whose works were expressly rejected by the Church, and have not come down to us in their original form, though we may perhaps have them as revised. In Fabricius (ii. 402-742) may be found a copious work in Latin (often printed before), *Historia apostolica* (or *Historia certaminis apostolici*), in ten books. This work professes to have been originally written in Hebrew by ABDIAS, said to have been first bishop of Babylon, and subsequently translated into Latin by JULIUS AFRICANUS. There can be no doubt, however, that it was composed in Latin, probably not before the seventh century: it was quite unknown to the early writers of the Church. The history of the individual apostles is always given separately in it, sometimes after the authority of the Acts by Luke, at other times after authorities altogether different. For notices in the ancient writers of several other apocryphal histories of the apostles, see FABRICIUS, 745-832, who also gives fragments of them. Since his day, several of these works in their complete form have been made known, especially by TISCHENDORF, *Acta Apostolorum apocrypha, ex triginta antiquis codicibus Græcis vel nunc primum eruit vel secundum atque emendatius edidit*, Leipz. 1851, lxxx. and 276 pp. This collection consists of thirteen works, *seven* of which were first edited for it by TISCHENDORF himself, *three* had already been so by THILO, while the remaining *three* were known to the learned of former days. These last *three* are:

1. *Acta Pauli et Theclæ*, first edited in Greek, with a Latin translation by GRABE, in his *Spicilegium Patrum*, tom. i. (1698), 2d ed. 1700, pp. 95–119, after a not quite complete codex in the Bodleian Library. TISCHENDORF gives it (pp. 40–63) in full, revised from three Paris MSS. TERTULLIAN, *de Baptismo*, xvii., mentions this work as one fathered upon the apostle by an Asiatic presbyter who, when taken to task for it, alleged affection for Paul as his motive. It contains the legend of Thecla, a noble maiden of Iconium, who there heard Paul in the house of Onesiphorus, and was so captivated by his words that neither her mother nor Thamyris, to whom she was betrothed, could induce her to leave him and marry the latter. Paul was consequently thrown into prison, when she forced her way to him, and being laid on the funeral pile was nevertheless unhurt. Subsequently she again met Paul and accompanied him to Antioch, where she withstood the suit of a distinguished man named Alexander, at whose instigation she was thrown to the wild beasts, but again escaped unhurt and received baptism, and so on.

2. *Acta Barnabæ*: Greek given by TISCHENDORF (pp. 64–74); previously edited by PAPEBROCHE in the *Acta Sanctorum*, tom. ii., Antwerpiæ 1698. It professes to have been written by John Mark.

3. *Acta Andreæ*—in the form of a letter from the deacons and presbyters of the Churches in Achaia to other Christian Churches on Andrew's martyrdom: previously edited frequently in Latin, but for the first time in Greek, with a Latin translation by WOOG (Lepiz. 1749) from a codex; in TISCHENDORF, in Greek, with a collection of two other MSS. (pp. 105–131). Eusebius mentions the πράξεις of Andrew among other works put into circulation by the heretics. So also do other Church writers, who attribute it to Leucius, to whom no doubt it mainly owed its origin, though afterwards revised from an orthodox point of view.

The *three* works first edited by THILO are:

4. *Acta Thomæ*: first edited in Greek by THILO, Leipz.

1823 (from Paris MSS. with learned annotations); TISCHEN-
DORF (pp. 190-234). This work is likewise quoted by
EPIPHANIUS, AUGUSTINE, and others as apocryphal, and in
use among the Encratites, Manichæans, and others, and no
doubt is the same as has come down to us, though not without alterations.

5. *Acta Petri et Pauli*—on the martyrdom of both apostles:
first edited in full by THILO, at Halle, in his Easter Pro-
grammes, 1837, 1838, the last part with the addition of an
ancient Latin translation; in TISCHENDORF, with a collection
of a number of other MSS. (pp. 1-39).

6. *Acta Andreæ et Matthiæ* (or, according to some authorities, *Matthæi*), in Greek: edited by THILO in a Halle Pro-
gramme, 1846, from three Paris MSS., date somewhere about
the eighth century; in TISCHENDORF, who newly collated
these MSS. and two others (pp. 132-166). Here also the
basis is the fiction of Leucius, but the work has undergone
considerable revision.

The following are the *seven* treatises just edited by
TISCHENDORF:—

7. *Acta Philippi*, or, as the title reads in Greek, ἐκ τῶν
περιόδων Φιλίππου τοῦ ἀποστόλου — *ex peregrinationibus
Philippi apostoli;* from two MSS. in Greek (pp. 75-94), on
Philip's martyrdom at Hierapolis, where he is said to have
preached along with Bartholomew, and his own sister Mari-
amne. It is placed among the Apocrypha in the decretal of
Gelasius.

8. *Acta Philippi in Hellade*, Greek, from a Paris codex of
the eleventh century (pp. 95-104): a silly legend on Philip
the apostle's dealings with the philosophers at Athens and
the high priest Ananias, whom they called to their assistance
from Jerusalem, and who, in spite of all the signs Philip
wrought before him and others, continued unbelieving, and
at last went down alive into Hades.

9. *Acta et Martyrium Matthæi Apostoli*, Greek (pp.
167-189), from two MSS. at Paris and Vienna. This is a
continuation of the *Acta Andreæ et Matthiæ* or *Matthæi*
previously (6) mentioned. It relates the martyrdom of

Matthew in the country of the ἀνθρωποφάγοι, in the city of Myrene.

10. *Consummatio Thomæ* (ἡ τελείωσις Θωμᾶ τοῦ ἀποστόλου), Greek (pp. 235–242), from a Paris codex on the martyrdom of the Apostle Thomas by the Indians under king Misdeos, who, however, as his wife and other of his subjects previously, himself was converted after Thomas' death, because a son of his was healed through touching the earth where the apostle was buried. On this point it agrees substantially with what is related in the book of ABDIAS.

11. *Acta* or μαρτύριον of the Apostle *Bartholomew* (pp. 243–260), Greek, from a codex of the thirteenth century, in the Library of St. Mark at Venice: on Bartholomew's preaching and labours among the Indians, whose false gods he overthrew, converting the king Polymius, whose brother Astreges put the apostle to death, and so on. This also agrees substantially, and sometimes even verbally, with the work of ABDIAS.

12. The πράξεις of the Apostle *Thaddæus*, Greek (pp. 261–265), from a Paris codex of the eleventh century, collated with another at Vienna. It contains an account of the labours of Thaddæus at the court of king Abgarus of Edessa, and in other cities of Syria, until his death. The letter of *Abgarus* to Jesus is also given according to another recension in EUSEBIUS, *H. E.* i. 13.

13. The πράξεις of the Apostle *John*, in Greek (pp. 266–276), from a codex at Paris of the eleventh century and one at Vienna. This work dwells particularly on (*a*) the relations of John to Domitian at Rome, before his banishment to Patmos, on which the emperor resolved very reluctantly, from what he had seen and heard of the apostle; (*b*) the longer addresses of John, after his return to Ephesus before his death, in which great stress is laid on his perpetual virginity. In this last part the writer professes to be an eye-witness. The πράξεις of John is mentioned by EUSEBIUS, *H. E.* iii. 25, as one of the works circulated by the heretics; also by EPIPHANIUS, *Hær.* xlvii. 1; AUGUSTINE, *c. advers. leg. et proph.* i. 20, and others. Some, however, regard it as

one of the works of Leucius, and something of this kind may have formed its basis.

THE PAULINE EPISTLES.

§ 132.

WE can bestow only a short notice on the Epistles of Paul, treating them in their chronological order and historical connection with his life and labours. Leaving out his death, and whatever immediately preceded it, our only sources of information here are the Acts of the Apostles and St. Paul's own letters. Of these we possess *thirteen* in the New Testament; for the Epistle to the Hebrews does not of itself claim to have been written by him. The genuineness of several of the rest has been assailed or denied in modern days, foremost the first Epistle to Timothy, then the three Pastoral Epistles generally, and even the Epistles to the Thessalonians, as well as those to the Ephesians and Colossians. Baur goes still further, for he will allow the genuineness of only four; but we shall see that only in the case of one perhaps is there anything like good ground for doubt. It is natural to regard these letters as our most trustworthy authority on the apostle's personal history; and whenever anything like a discrepancy appears between them and the Acts, we may safely assume that the correct account is substantially given in them. And yet we shall find that, though even in what it says about the Apostle Paul the Acts exhibits much incompleteness, and indeed inaccuracy, here and there it is not by any means so unhistorical and untrustworthy as some now-a-days would have us believe.[1]

---

[1] On Paul's life and writings, compare, besides older works and the various Introductions to the N. T., the following of more recent date:— J. T. HEMSEN (*ob.* 1830), *der Ap. Paulus, sein Leben, Wirken, u. seine Schriften,*—a posthumous work edited by LÜCKE, Gött. 1830. K. SCHRADER, *der Ap. Paulus,* Thl. i., *chron. Bemerkk. ü. s. Leben,* Leipz. 1830; Thl. ii., *das Leben des Paulus,* 1832; Thl. iii., *Lehre des Paulus,*

§ 133.

Paul was the son of Jewish parents of the tribe of Benjamin (Rom. xi. 1; Phil. iii. 5), and was born at Tarsus in Cilicia (Acts ix. 11, xxi. 39, xxii. 3). On this last point, Jerome's statement, *de viris illustr.* v., is different. According to this Father, the apostle was born at Gyksala, a small town of Galilee, which, on its being taken by the Romans, his parents left for Tarsus (cf. ejusdem, *Comment. in Ep. ad Philem.*, ver. 23). This, however, is obscure, for we cannot understand why the possession of a Galilean town in Paul's childhood by the Romans should have forced its Jewish inhabitants to emigrate. Jerome is evidently thinking of the devastation of the country in the last Jewish-Roman war, and has fallen into an utter anachronism. Whatever may have led him to say what he does, is of no weight against the repeated assertions of the Acts, especially in the last two passages above quoted, where the words are the apostle's own. Nor does it follow from Phil. iii. 5 and 2 Cor. xi. 22, where Paul speaks of himself as 'Εβραῖος and ἐξ 'Εβραίων, that he was a Palestinian Jew, since the expressions are not used, as Professor Paulus supposes (*des Ap. Paulus Briefe an die*

1833; Thl. iv. u. v., *Erkl. der Briefe des P. u. der Apgesch.* 1835, 1836. J. F. KÖHLER, *Vers. ü. die Abfassungszeit der epist. Schrift. im N. T. u. d. Apokal.*, Leipz. 1830. NEANDER, *Gesch. der Pflanzung u. Leitung d. christl. K. durch d. Ap.*, 2 Thle., Hamb. 1832-33-4, Ausg. 1847, Bd. i. Abschnitt iii. BAUR, *Paulus der Ap. J. C.*, Stuttg. 1845. K. WIESELER, *Chronol. des Apost. Zeitalters bis zum Tode der Ap. Paulus und Petrus, mit einem Anhange ü. d. Br. an d. Hebräer un Excurs. ü. d. Aufenthalt d. App. Paulus u. Petrus in Rom.*, Gött. 1848. RUD. ANGER, *de temporum in Actis Apost. rationes*, Leipz. 1833. WINER, *Real-W.B.*, article *Paulus*. THOLUCK, *Einleitende Bemerkk. in das Studium der Paulin. Briefe, die Lebensumstände, den Charakter u. die Sprache des Apostels betreffend; Theol. Stud. u. Krit.* 1835, ii. pp. 364-393 (in his *vermischt. Schrift.* ii. 274-329). EWALD, *die Sendschreiben des Ap. Paulus übersetzt u. erklärt*, Gött. 1857. The Pastoral Epistles, and that to the Ephesians, are not included in this work, as EWALD does not think they proceeded directly from Paul. [Cf. also his *Gesch. d. V. Israel*, vol. vi., also published under the title *Gesch. d. Ap. Zeit. bis zur Zerstörung Jerusalems*, Gött. 1858; also CONYBEARE and HOWSON's *Life and Letters of St. Paul*, 2 vols. 4to; HOWSON on the *Character of St. Paul*, 1 vol. 8vo.]

Galater u. Römer-Christen, etc., Heidelb. 1831, p. 323), by way of strict contrast with an Hellenistic Jew. His parents, and consequently he himself, had the Roman right of citizenship (Acts xvi. 37 sq., xxii. 25, 29). We do not know how they came to possess it. Possibly his father, or one of his ancestors, had purchased it, or had received it from the Romans on account of some service rendered to them : it is certainly incorrect to say that in Paul's time the town of Tarsus itself had the *civitas*. The apostle's Jewish name was שָׁאוּל. In the Acts he always appears under this name before his conversion, and for some time after sometimes under the form Σαούλ, sometimes as Græcized into Σαῦλος. The latter is found throughout the narrative in vii. 58, and in what follows up to xiii. 9 ; the former in the Greek rendering of Christ's words addressed to him in Aramæan at his conversion, in the address of Ananias, and in ix. 4, 17, where Luke narrates the event, and xxii. 7, 13, where Paul himself speaks of it. Elsewhere in his letters the apostle always calls himself Παῦλος ; and so too he is always called in the history recorded in the Acts subsequent to xiii. 9, where the name is first applied to him, Σαῦλος δὲ ὁ καὶ Παῦλος. On the historical relation of the two names borne by the apostle, various opinions have been held. It was not unusual among the Hellenistic Jews to add to their Jewish a Roman or Greek name, by which they were known in their intercourse with these nations, or to transpose their Jewish name into one in Greek or Latin most closely resembling it, as Jesus into Jason, Dosthai into Dositheus, etc.; and thus Paul would be nearest to Saul. Though quite possible, it is yet not very probable, that the apostle bore the name Paul in addition to his Jewish one from his very childhood; nor is it probable that it was given to him at his conversion, for then we should have found some intimation of the fact in the earlier sections of the Acts. The most probable explanation is, that he himself assumed it when, as the Apostle of the Gentiles, he made his more extended journeys beyond Judea. Some have supposed that it was adopted by him with reference to the conversion of the proconsul Sergius Paulus in

Cyprus (Acts xiii.). So Jerome, *ut supra*, Meyer, Olshausen, Ewald, *Gesch. d. Apost. Zeitalters*, 419 sq., and Baur in his *Paulus*, p. 93, though he regards the proconsul's conversion as a mere poetical legend, intended to account for the alteration in the apostle's name. It is not altogether impossible for the change to have been made on the occasion referred to; and a plausible argument in favour of this opinion is to be found in the fact that the apostle is called Paul immediately after the proconsul's conversion (ver. 9), and retains the name ever afterwards. Still Luke does not give the least hint that he then assumed it for the first time, or, at any rate, that he did so with any reference to the proconsul; and though, as we have remarked, such an explanation is possible, there is no special probability in its favour.

The apostle's native city of Tarsus was in his day not only a celebrated place of commerce, but also a distinguished seat of Greek learning, and could vie with Athens and Alexandria, though not resorted to by foreigners as were the schools of these cities (Strabo, *Geog.* xiv. 5). The schools of the town were doubtless not without their influence on the apostle's early training. The extent of his Greek learning has been much discussed (cf. De Wette, § 119, *b*, note *b*). Some—Schrader, for instance, recently—have rated it far too high, and on grounds which are not very satisfactory. Others, again, have gone too far in denying to him all knowledge of Greek literature—for instance, Thalemann (1769), and Bertholdt, who avers that he never could have been in a position to write Greek,—an unwarrantable assertion if he had been even born in Palestine, of parents who spoke only Aramæan. His letters and speeches exhibit traces of an acquaintance with Greek literature. Thus 1 Cor. xv. 33 was, according to Jerome, a sentence from Menander; Tit. i. 12, according to Clemens Alexandrinus (*Strom.* i. 299, ed. Sylburg.), from Epimenides. We may also compare his speech at Athens (Acts xvii. 28) with what is said by Aratus of Cilicia (*Phænomena*, v.) and by Cleanthes (*Hymn. in Jovem*, v.). From these three passages Jerome infers (*ad Galat.* iv. 24), *Paulum scisse, licet non ad perfectum, sæculares litteras.* He may indeed, as Tholuck, De Wette, and others suppose, have gained this knowledge at a later period of life, some time (say) during his abode in Cilicia after his conversion (Acts ix. 30; Gal. i. 21); but there is no valid reason for denying that the son of a Roman citizen could have learnt something of Greek authors while yet a youth at Tarsus. But let this be as it may, it is quite certain Paul's early education was more Jewish than Greek. Though he appears to have been early destined to the vocation of a learned Jew as a rabbi, he was taught a handicraft,—this being the custom among the Jews, according to their proverb, "Who teaches his son no trade, teaches him to steal." He became a tentmaker,[1] and as such was wont to earn a livelihood when staying longer than usual in any place, and anxious not to become burdensome to the brethren.[2] His education in Jewish learning he received at Jerusalem, to which city, it is plain from his own statements, he must have gone while young. We see this from Acts xxii. 3, and especially xxvi. 4 sq., with which we may compare vii. 58, where he is described at Stephen's execution as a νεανίας. It is therefore incorrect to speak of him, as Eichhorn, Hemsen, and others do, as being in Jerusalem for the first time only in his riper years—his thirtieth, according to Hemsen. On the other hand, it is not likely that he was at Jerusalem in his earliest childhood, or he would not so repeatedly distinguish himself as of Tarsus. The exact time of his coming to the Jewish metropolis cannot, however, be determined; probably it was not before his twelfth year, and most likely at a still later time. Nor do we know whether he was accompanied by his parents, or sent by them to be educated in one of the schools to be found in that city. We can only infer from Acts xxiii. 16 that his sister's son, and probably the sister herself, lived at Jerusalem. While in the city, Paul especially resorted to the school of Gamaliel the Pharisee

---

[1] This is the simple interpretation of σκηνοποιός (Acts xviii. 3)—the manufacturer of tents for travellers, made of cloth or leather.

[2] Acts xviii. 3, xx. 24; 1 Thess. ii. 9; 2 Thess. iii. 8; 1 Cor. iv. 12, ix. 6–15; 2 Cor. xii. 13 sq.

(Acts xxii. 3). Gamaliel was a Jewish doctor, held in high esteem also among the Jews who belonged to the sect of the Pharisees, and was distinguished above many for his learning and liberal spirit, and had even turned his attention to Greek philosophy (cf. JOST, *Gesch. d. Israel. seit der Zeit Maccab.* Thl. iii., Berl. 1822, p. 170 sqq., and the Appendix to the eleventh book, note 39; and THOLUCK, p. 286). He was a grandson of the renowned R. Hillel, a native of Babylon, who, a short time before Christ, was at the head of one of the most famous of Jewish schools, rivalling that of R. Schammai. With the Jewish reports of Gamaliel's character agrees the narrative, in Acts v. 34 sqq., of his wise moderation when the apostles were brought before the high council for judgment. In his school, then, Paul was educated as a legist of the sect of the Pharisees (Phil. iii. 5; Acts xxvi. 5, xxii. 3). According to Acts xxiii. 6, his father also belonged to this sect (υἱὸς Φαρισαίου); or rather, as the more probable reading there is Φαρισαίων, his parents or ancestors generally were Pharisees.

§ 134.

How long Paul continued under Gamaliel's instruction, and in what relation personally he stood to him, we do not know. He certainly does not appear to have followed his master's wise and circumspect moderation. Like so many of the Pharisees, he was a narrow zealot for the observance of the law of his fathers and the pharisaic ordinances, and therefore cherished great dislike and bitterness of feeling towards the Nazarenes, or those who confessed Christ, who seemed to him to be overthrowing the law (Gal. i. 13 sq.; Phil. iii. 6). He is first mentioned in the Acts at the stoning of Stephen, as a young man to whose care those engaged in that dreadful deed committed their clothes, and who himself took delight in what was done (Acts vii. 58, viii. 1, xxii. 20). He speedily showed himself more active in the persecution which soon afterwards arose against Christ's disciples in Jerusalem (viii. 1), in which he took part with fanatical zeal. Commissioned by the Sanhedrim, he began to hale men and women to prison, caused them to be beaten in the synagogues on account of their faith, gave his approval when they were put to death, and sought by terrors to induce them βλασφημεῖν—that is, to deny Christ by blaspheming against Him.[1] Nor was he satisfied with thus treating the believers at Jerusalem. He followed them even to other cities, whither they had fled in consequence of the persecution, and where they had been to some extent successful in spreading the gospel (Acts xxvi. 11). Thus it came to pass that on one occasion, ἔτι ἐμπνέων ἀπειλῆς καὶ φόνου εἰς τοὺς μαθητὰς τοῦ Κυρίου (Acts ix. 1), he was going to Damascus, furnished with letters from the Sanhedrim to the Jewish synagogues in that city, authorizing him to bind any adherents of the new doctrine he might find there, and bring them to Jerusalem. But while on the way, and now near to Damascus, he had such a manifestation of the Lord as wrought a complete change in him. The story of his conversion is told three times in the Acts of the Apostles: first in Luke's narrative (ix. 1-19); and then twice in Paul's own words—to the people at Jerusalem (xxii. 5-16), and, more briefly, before Agrippa and Festus at Cæsarea (xxvi. 12-18). The two last accounts occur in those sections of the Acts which were almost certainly written originally by one of Paul's companions on his journeys from Macedonia to Jerusalem, and at a later time from Cæsarea to Rome. This friend, in our opinion, was Timothy, who was also probably with the apostle when he delivered the speeches in question—at any rate when he delivered the first of them. We have every reason, therefore, for assuming that they are given us, as to all essential points, exactly as they fell from Paul, and that what they relate really happened, and was not at all likely to have been drawn up by Luke merely; and this, indeed, is confirmed if we look at the narrative which Luke himself has given us. This agrees substantially, and to some extent even verbally, with Paul's, especially what he says in xxii., but exhibits occasional variations or amplifications, yet of such a kind that we

---

[1] Acts viii. 3, xxii. 4, 19, xxvi. 9, 11; Gal. i. 13; 1 Cor. xv. 9; Phil. iii. 6; 1 Tim. i. 13.

may infer almost with certainty that Luke made Paul's narrative the basis of his own, without keeping quite strictly to it, probably adding what he had heard of the matter from others.

According to Paul's own account, the event took place thus. He had, with his companions, already got near to Damascus, when at mid-day a bright light shone round about him, so that he fell in fear down to the ground. He then heard the voice of the Lord (according to xxvi. in the Hebrew tongue) calling to him, "Saul, Saul, why persecutest thou me?" The statement in ix. 7, that the men who journeyed with him heard the voice, but saw no man, must be regarded as inaccurate; for in xxii. 9 the apostle expressly says that his companions saw the light (cf. xxvi. 13), but did not hear the voice which spoke to him. We might conclude from this that the light was something more real and substantial, which all present would see, but not so the voice which Paul heard, and which he seems to have perceived, not as some sound audible from without, but simply inwardly, as in a vision; and yet it must have been truly objective and articulate, or he could not have distinguished it as speaking in Aramæan (xxvi. 14). The light had so blinded Paul, that when he arose he could see nothing, and had to be led by his companions to Damascus. In this condition of blindness he remained until (according to ch. ix., on the third day) a pious believer, a Jew by race, named Ananias, was directed by a vision to go to him, at whose word his sight was restored. He received baptism, and henceforth made a full surrender of his life to the Lord's service.

The miraculous character of his conversion, and the reality of the Lord's objective manifestation to him, whereby it was brought about,[1] is confirmed by express allusions in the Pauline Epistles, especially Gal. i. 15 sq., where the

---

[1] [BEYSCHLAG (*Stud. u. Krit.* 1864, pp. 197–264) argues against HOLSTEN (in HILGENFELD's *Zeitschr.* 1860, p. 223 sqq.), who endeavours to prove Paul's conversion, and the manifestation of Christ to him, to have been purely subjective; and against BAUR (*das Christenthum und die christl. Kirche der drei ersten Jahrhundert*, 2d ed. p. 44 sqq.).]

expressions καλέσας (με) διὰ τῆς χάριτος αὐτοῦ, and εὐδόκησεν . . . ἀποκαλύψαι τὸν υἱὸν αὐτοῦ ἐν ἐμοί, refer, as the context shows, in each case primarily to the illumination and call vouchsafed to him near and at Damascus. Again, when in 1 Cor. ix. 1 he says that he had "seen the Lord," he cannot mean during His life and sojourn on earth; for even if he had seen Him then, which is not likely, this would have been no argument for his apostolical authority. He must allude to the event on the way to Damascus, when the exalted Saviour appeared to him. Lastly, in 1 Cor. xv. 8, after referring to the various manifestations of the risen Jesus, he goes on expressly to say that last of all He was seen by him, the persecutor of the Church. We may also compare with the apostle's own words what is said in xxii. 14 by Ananias in describing the event which occurred to him, ἰδεῖν τὸν δίκαιον καὶ ἀκοῦσαι φωνὴν ἐκ τοῦ στόματος αὐτοῦ, and also the expression ὤφθην σοι in xxvi. 16.

Even after this first manifestation of the Lord, special revelations were from time to time vouchsafed to Paul, by which his faith and knowledge were confirmed and enlarged (cf. Acts xxii. 17 sqq., 2 Cor. xii. 1 sqq.; and also Acts xvi. 9, Gal. ii. 2). To these he always appealed to prove that his knowledge of the gospel came not through men, or even through such as were apostles before him, but by direct revelation from Christ Himself, from whom also he had received his apostleship (Gal. i. 1, 11 sqq., 15 sqq., ii. 6; Eph. iii. 2 sq.). Still it is not probable that the revelations spoken of referred to facts connected with the gospel history, or to special doctrines. It is true we find that even in these Paul claims to have been taught by the Lord, and speaks of himself as receiving from the Lord, or uttering the word of the Lord (cf. especially 1 Cor. xi. 23, vii. 10, 25; 1 Thess. iv. 15). We are, however, probably to understand him not of instruction bestowed directly, but through true tradition of what the Lord had said. We cannot well doubt that even before his conversion he knew something of many facts in the life of Jesus, partly through common report, and partly, it may be, through the earlier minor gospel histories, especially the collected discourses, and it is very possible that after his conversion he took great pains to increase and confirm his knowledge of these matters; and yet he may have regarded any trustworthy information that came to him respecting them as something received of the Lord.

§ 135.

For the years immediately subsequent to his conversion we must fill up the narrative in Acts ix. 19–26 by Gal. i. 17 sqq. and 2 Cor. xi. 32 sq. We are told in the Acts that Paul remained some time (ἡμέρας τινάς) with the disciples at Damascus, and at once preached Jesus in the synagogue, to the astonishment of the Jews, who had heard for what purpose he had come thither. After some time had elapsed (ὡς ἐπληροῦντο ἡμέραι ἱκαναί) the Jews resolved to murder him, and for this purpose watched the gates day and night. The disciples, however, contrived to let him down at night by the wall in a basket, and he came to Jerusalem. On the other hand, from Galatians, *ut supra*, we learn : (*a*) that his visit to Jerusalem was not till three years afterwards, that is, three years after his conversion, for this is no doubt the meaning; (*b*) that in the interval he had been to Arabia, and had returned to Damascus before he went to Jerusalem. From what he himself says, it is very probable that his first stay at Damascus was very brief; and possibly he only began to preach in the synagogues of the city during his second visit, after his return from Arabia, though he may indeed have frequented them on his first (cf. Acts xxvi. 20). At any rate, it is much more probable that his deliverance from the plots of the Jews, of which we read in the Acts, took place towards the close of his second visit. There can be no doubt it was the same as that mentioned in 2 Cor xi. 32 sq., where the apostle tells us that the ethnarch under king Aretas, at Damascus, had set a guard to take him, but he escaped, being let down in a basket through a window by the wall. The ethnarch doubtless acted at the instigation of the Jews, who had prejudiced him against Paul. The mention of this person shows, that at the time Damascus was under the sway of the Arabian king Aretas;[1] and the circumstance has been often used to determine the date of Paul's flight from that city, and then that also of his conversion. The conclusions arrived at, however, have been very different, and not very satisfactory. Damascus at this period belonged to the Roman province of Syria; and even its coins are stamped with the likenesses of the Emperors Augustus and Tiberius, as well as Nero and his successors. Its occupation by Aretas could only have been very transitory; but as we have no other historical information respecting it, we can only determine conjecturally and vaguely when it took place. Aretas made war with his son-in-law Herod Antipas, who had divorced his first wife, a daughter of Aretas, in order to marry Herodias. Antipas being defeated, appealed for aid to the Emperor Tiberius, who commanded Vitellius, the Syrian governor, to chastise Aretas. While Vitellius was on his march, he had news of the death of Tiberius (37 A.D. in the month of March), which led him to withdraw his troops (Joseph. *Antiq.* xviii. 5, 3). We may with tolerable certainty conclude that Aretas did not take Damascus before the retreat of Vitellius, but rather, as many have maintained, after that event, in the winter of 37 A.D., retaining possession of it for some short time, at the longest not in all probability beyond 39 A.D. Wieseler, however (*ut supra*, 167-175; and Herzog's *Real-Encykl.*, *Arethas*), thinks that the new Emperor Caligula himself, at the instigation of Agrippa, who was in Rome, conferred the city on Aretas, who held it even after Caligula's death, under Claudius. At any rate, it seems quite clear from the passage in 2d Corinthians, that Paul's flight could not have taken place before the year 37, and therefore his conversion cannot be dated before 34 or 35, whether and how much later we cannot say; but that it could not have been earlier is plain, even if we look simply at the fact that,

---

[1] Looking at Paul's own words, we cannot agree with ANGER, p. 180 sqq., and others, that this ethnarch was at Damascus at the time simply by accident, and either from friendship for the Jews, or enmity against the apostle, excited the Roman authorities to take measures against him.

when it took place, Christianity had already found its way into Damascus.

We cannot determine with certainty from Gal. i. 17 sqq. whether Paul went to Jerusalem directly after his flight from Damascus. He tells us, however, expressly, that his reason for going to that city was to become personally acquainted (ἱστορῆσαι) with Peter, who had hitherto been the most active in spreading the gospel. With him he appears to have taken up his abode; but his stay did not extend beyond some fifteen days, during which the only one besides Peter whom he saw of the more prominent Christian teachers with whom he subsequently came into something like collision, was James the Lord's brother. To these, as well as to the believers at Jerusalem generally, he was, according to Acts ix. 27, introduced by the Hellenist Barnabas. The statement, however, is too vague and loose, that Barnabas brought Paul to the apostles, and was the first to tell them of his conversion, though, in agreement with it, the author of the Acts represents this visit to Jerusalem as immediately subsequent to the apostle's conversion, whereas they were separated from one another by an interval of three years. From what is said in the Acts, we might easily infer that this visit to Jerusalem was of some duration, which is more precisely determined by the apostle's own words. He is spoken of in the Acts as if he had openly appeared in Jerusalem as a preacher of Christ, and had disputed especially with the Hellenistic Jews, though, judging from Galatians, *ut supra*, we should understand in the latter case private discussions confined to former acquaintances, with whom he now again came into contact.

To the time of this visit belongs also what Paul narrates in Acts xxii. 17–21 of the vision he had while praying in the temple, when the Lord showed him he must quickly depart from Jerusalem, because the people there would not receive his testimony. He was to be sent far away among the Gentiles. From the answer which he at first gave to the Lord's words (ver. 19 sq.), it is clear that he could not then have preached openly in Jerusalem; nor from what follows does he seem hitherto, even three years after his conversion, to have preached to the Gentiles. We cannot admit, with Schrader, Wieseler (pp. 162–165, *Comment. über d. Brief P. an die Galater*, Gött. 1859, p. 592 sqq.), that this vision was identical with the rapture mentioned in 2 Cor. xii. 2 sqq., in which Paul heard unspeakable words, for he tells us that this took place fourteen years before; but between the visit to Jerusalem of which we have been speaking and the composition of 2d Corinthians there was a longer interval than fourteen years.

§ 136.

From Jerusalem Paul went (Gal. i. 21) to Syria and Cilicia; and with this agrees the statement in Acts ix. 30, that, in order to rescue him from the plots of the Jews at Jerusalem, the brethren sent him to Cæsarea (Stratonis, on the Mediterranean), and thence to Tarsus, his native city. We are not told how long Paul remained in these regions, the home of his early days: it may have been for a year, or for several years; and we can well believe that during this time he would not be inactive in the cause of the gospel, although we are altogether without any information on his labours. According to Acts xi. 25, Paul was brought away from Tarsus by Barnabas, with whom he went to Antioch, where he remained (ver. 26) a whole year, zealously occupied in Christian teaching. Into this city (ver. 20 sqq.) Christianity had already found entrance among not only Jews, but Greeks, and it was for this reason Barnabas had been sent thither from Jerusalem. He left it for Tarsus, but returned again, bringing Paul with him. There can be no doubt that the preaching of both these men was directed, if not exclusively, at least mainly, to the Greeks at Antioch, and was intended both to excite and confirm Christian faith. Their departure from the city was due to an external cause. On the occasion of a famine in the time of Claudius, which had been predicted by a Christian prophet named Agabus, the Christians at Antioch made a collection for the brethren in Judea, and sent it to the elders at Jerusalem by the hands of

Barnabas and Paul (vers. 27–30). This famine, from which Judea suffered severely, took place, according to Josephus (*Ant.* xx. 5, 2), when Cuspius Fadus, and subsequently Tiberius Alexander, were governors of the province, the former of whom received office after the death of Agrippa I. (44 A.D.); but when the latter died is not certain, though probably at the latest it was in the year 46. In any case, the famine lasted some years. It may have begun with a scarcity in the year 44, and probably was at its worst in 45 A.D., when the first transmission of the collection from Antioch to Jerusalem may have taken place, as Wieseler (pp. 156–161) indeed maintains, though the reasons he gives are not always sound.

On the termination of their mission, we read in Acts xii. 25, that "Barnabas and Saul returned from Jerusalem (to Antioch) when they had fulfilled their ministry, and took with them John, whose surname was Mark" (the evangelist). It would seem, therefore, as if both Barnabas and Paul had been to Jerusalem, though no particulars are given us of their journey and abode there. But, in fact, it is difficult to reconcile a visit at this time to the holy city on Paul's part with Gal. ii. 1 sqq., where the apostle speaks of a journey to Jerusalem which he made with Barnabas "fourteen years after." From the expression he uses (ἔπειτα διὰ δεκατεσσάρων ἐτῶν πάλιν ἀνέβην εἰς Ἱεροσόλυμα), taken in connection with what he says before, I hold it as good as certain that this journey is not to be reckoned from the same time as that of the three years mentioned in i. 18, that is, from the time of his conversion (so many interpreters: Olshausen, Schott, Anger; Fritzsche, *Opusc. Acad.;* Wieseler, p. 177, and on Gal. ii. 1; and others), but from the time of that journey itself, so that it would be seventeen years after his conversion. Now, if we consider the scope and connection of the passage in Galatians, we can hardly doubt that the visit it speaks of was really the second paid by Paul to Jerusalem, and that in the interval he had not been there at all. We seem therefore at first sight almost inevitably led to identify it with that occasioned by the famine under Claudius, of which we read in Acts xi. 27–30 and xii. 25; and this was the view of Tertullian, *adv. Marc.* i. 20, and Eusebius, *Chron.*, which has been adopted by many learned men in modern times. It is, however, unsatisfactory on chronological grounds, for the journey recorded in Acts xi. 12 must have taken place at the latest in the year 46, and therefore could not have been seventeen, or even fourteen, years after Paul's conversion. Besides, from the particulars Paul gives us in Gal. ii. of this journey, and the whole way in which he speaks of it, there can be no doubt that it was the same as that recorded in Acts xv. So Irenæus maintains, *adv. Hær.* iii. 13, and most modern interpreters, including Anger. If this be correct, then, bearing in mind what we have already said, it is plainly utterly improbable that before this journey Paul had been at Jerusalem more than once after his conversion, still less that he had been there three times (as Wieseler maintains, identifying the journey of Gal. ii. 1 sqq. with that of Acts xviii. 22, but on grounds in which there is a good deal of sophistry, pp. 176–201, and his *Galatians*, p. 553 sqq.). We are therefore, on the whole, compelled to conclude that Paul did not go to Jerusalem at the time of the famine, though he is represented to have done so in the Acts, which, however, does not give us any very precise information of the visit. The true state of the case most probably was, that Paul started for Judea with Barnabas to convey the collection from Antioch, but stopped short of Jerusalem, thinking it better perhaps, on account of the bitter feeling against him which he had before experienced from the people there, and which still existed, to remain in some other district of Judea, and leave all further care of the collection to Barnabas, with whom, however, he returned to Antioch, to the Christians of which place it might easily have been unknown that he had not been to Jerusalem.

§ 137.

This journey of Paul and Barnabas, and their absence from Antioch, probably did not take up any very great length of time, though we do not know how long, or how long they remained in Antioch before they undertook their great missionary journey recorded in Acts xiii. xiv. For this mission Barnabas and Paul were set apart by the direction of the Holy Ghost. They took John Mark with them as a companion, but he returned to Jerusalem before the journey was finished (§ 47). The travellers went first to Seleucia, thence by ship to Cyprus, which they crossed from east to west, and then on to Perga in Pamphylia, where Mark left them; thence again to Antioch in Pisidia, Iconium, and other cities of Lycaonia, especially Lystra and Derbe, returning by way of Lystra to the Pisidian Antioch, and then through Pisidia to Perga and Attalia, where they took ship for Antioch in Syria, from which they had started. Luke's account of this journey probably refers to only a part of it (cf. § 127), and is an abstract of some longer report written most likely by one of the travellers, or by some friend who had heard of it from them. It is very summary, and enters into details only in the case of a few towns, such as Paphos in Cyprus, where Paul converted the Roman governor Sergius Paulus, after having at a word smitten with blindness a false Jewish prophet who had tried to seduce the proconsul from the faith (xiii. 6–12); the Pisidian Antioch, where we have given us at length an address delivered by Paul on his first visit on the Sabbath at the synagogue (xiii. 14–52); Lystra, where Paul healed a born cripple, which led the people to regard him and Barnabas as Zeus and Hermes.

The usual practice of the two missionaries on this journey was to go to the Jews—with whom, of course, they were closely connected—in their synagogues; where also they had the opportunity of being heard by Greeks, men, and especially women, who were more or less attached to Judaism, and by means of whom they became known to other Greeks also. We have already remarked (§ 123) how incorrect it is to assert, with Baur and others, that this account of Paul's conduct—that is, that he went first to the Jews—is utterly unhistorical, and originated simply in an apologetic and conciliatory purpose. We see from the Epistle to the Romans, which all Baur's school admit to be genuine, that even in his later years Paul looked upon the Jews as specially interested in the divine promises (i. 16, Ἰουδαίῳ τε πρῶτον καὶ Ἕλληνι); how near to his heart was the conversion of these his own people, and how he hoped to be working himself for this end even by his labours as the Apostle of the Gentiles (xi. 13 sq.); and how convinced he was that some time or other all Israel would be saved (xi. 26). Compare also what he says in xi. 11 of the gospel as having been specially addressed to the Gentiles, because the Jews had rejected it, which exactly corresponds with his own conduct and Barnabas', *e.g.* in Pisidian Antioch (Acts xiii. 46). In very many places the preachers of the Gospel speedily met with violent opposition from the Jews, who, wherever they had not the power themselves to interfere, strove to stir up the heathen against them. Thus we read that in Pisidian Antioch the Jews stirred up against them τὰς σεβομένας γυναῖκας τὰς εὐσχήμονας καὶ τοὺς πρώτους τῆς πόλεως, so that they were driven away from that region; again at Iconium (xiv. 4 sqq.), at Lystra, where, instigated by Jews from Antioch and Iconium, the people even stoned Paul, and drew him out of the city as one dead.

We may now notice the relation of the two preachers to one another, as it appears in the account we have of their common journey. At the commencement, as in the preceding part of the book, Barnabas appears to have a certain priority, and Paul to be subordinate to him, so that Barnabas is mentioned first, xiii. 1, 2, 7 (as also xi. 30, xii. 25). But in the course of the journey this order is changed. Even at xiii. 13 the travellers are distinguished as οἱ περὶ τὸν Παῦλον, and generally afterwards Paul and Barnabas, or Paul with Barnabas (only at xiv. 14, οἱ ἀπόστολοι Βαρνάβας καὶ Παῦλος). No doubt Barnabas had been a member of the Christian community longer, and was also older than Paul; but though so distinguished a teacher, he was nevertheless inferior to Paul in natural and supernatural gifts, especially in the gift of speech, so that in their common work Paul was always more conspicuous both in word and deed. This relation of the two to one another is confirmed by (among other facts) what is said in xiv. 12 of the inhabitants of Lystra, calling Barnabas Zeus, but Paul Hermes, because he was the chief speaker.

How much time was occupied in this first missionary tour we are not told. But if we bear in mind how many provinces and cities were visited by the two preachers, and that it was not their aim to hurry on as fast as possible, but to proclaim the gospel, and to found and establish the kingdom of God in men's hearts, we may certainly allow a couple of years for the whole. As regards many cities of Asia Minor, such as the Pisidian Antioch, Iconium, Lystra, it appears quite clear from the report, either from express statements, or from the circumstances related as occurring in them, that their stay in such places lasted many weeks, or a considerable time, and very likely this was the case also with other places of which we read nothing particular; otherwise they would not have formally set up Churches, and appointed elders for them, as we are expressly told they did in the cities of Lycaonia, and that region generally (Acts xiv. 23).

§ 138.

In Antioch Paul and Barnabas remained some time, χρόνον οὐκ ὀλίγον (Acts xiv. 28), but we cannot with any certainty say how long. We only see from Gal. ii. 1 that their journey thence to Jerusalem (Acts xv.) took place seventeen years after Paul's conversion. The occasion of this journey was as follows. The Christian society at Jerusalem had always consisted almost exclusively of Jewish Christians, either Jews by birth, or such as not only had been previously attached to the Jewish worship, but also by circumcision had been incorporated into the Jewish nation. All these continued as Jews to participate in the temple service, and to observe the ordinances of the Jewish law, just as the Lord Himself while on earth, and His disciples, had done. In this Church there were scarcely any such Gentiles to be found as, like Cornelius, before their conversion had attained to some knowledge of the one true living God, and without being circumcised had attached themselves more or less to Jewish worship as "proselytes of the gate" (גֵּרֵי הַשַּׁעַר, in the Acts σεβόμενοι), on whom were enjoined the so-called seven laws of Noah (WINER, *Real-Wört. B.*, *Proselyten*; LEYRER, in Herzog's *Real-Encykl.* xii. 249 sq., and others). Peter had need of a special revelation to induce him to go to Cornelius, and had to take some pains afterwards to justify himself at Jerusalem for entering into such an association. Now, as these uncircumcised proselytes of the gate were not regarded by the Jews as full Israelites, and the strict legal Jews always hesitated to come into any close contact with them, especially to eat in common with them, fearing lest they should thereby be rendered unclean; so the stricter among the Jewish Christians also hesitated to receive Gentiles into Christian fellowship unless they had become members of the chosen nation by circumcision, and were thus pledged to an observance of the Jewish law. They indeed acknowledged Jesus as the promised Messiah, but maintained the binding obligation of the Mosaic law even after Christ's appearance, not only on such as were Jews by birth, but on all who desired to be of the family of God, and to share in the salvation of Messiah. Without circumcision, they thought one could have no part with God's people, who on their part were only defiled by intercourse with the uncircumcised. On the other hand, in Antioch very many uncircumcised Greeks had for a long time been admitted to the fellowship of the Church, the greater number of whom had doubtless never, even as proselytes of the gate, been connected with the Jewish religion; and this was true to a still greater extent in the case of those Churches which Paul and Barnabas had founded in the course of their missionary journey. After their return to Antioch, then, a controversy arose, occasioned by some Jewish Christians who came thither, and insisted that, if the believers wished to be saved, they must submit to circumcision,—a position which brought them specially into collision with Barnabas and Paul. The Church at Antioch was accordingly induced to send these two trusted servants of Christ along with some others, among whom, according to Gal. ii. 1, 3, was the uncircumcised Titus, to Jerusalem, to consult with the overseers of the Church, the apostles and elders, on the points in dispute. Paul tells us in Gal. ii. that he was moved to undertake this journey (which, according to the Acts, was made through Phœnicia and Samaria) by a divine revelation,—a statement which may easily be reconciled with what we read in the Acts, on some such supposition as that the Church at Antioch resolved upon his mission primarily on the ground of what he himself had told them of the revelation referred to. Indeed, the statements generally in the Epistle to the Galatians and in the Acts, so far from being irreconcilable, as Baur and others suppose, are merely complementary of one another. The Acts gives more prominence to what took place publicly in reference to the demand of the Judaizing party; Paul, in the Galatians, to what concerned himself personally,—the approval of his special teaching by the leaders of the Church at Jerusalem, by James (the Lord's brother), Peter, and John, when they learnt his gifts and call to the apostleship, and the blessing which had followed his labours, and their ready assent ($\delta\epsilon\xi\iota\grave{\alpha}\varsigma$ $\check{\epsilon}\delta\omega\kappa\alpha\nu$ .... $\kappa o\iota\nu\omega\nu\acute{\iota}\alpha\varsigma$) that he and Barnabas should continue to work as hitherto among the Gentiles. From the way also in which Paul speaks, it does not at all look as if those leaders at Jerusalem were themselves influenced by a narrow Judaism, and had only made a few concessions to the Apostle of the Gentiles out of sheer necessity. What Paul says of them is not at all irreconcilable, as Baur and others maintain, with the liberal temper attributed to them in the Acts in their public conduct on this occasion, when Peter and James strongly recommend, even in the Church at Jerusalem, and against the demand of the strict Judaizers, that the Gentile converts should be circumcised, and obey the law of Moses, that no such yoke should be laid upon them. Of these public transactions Paul makes no mention at all; but that the circumcision of the Gentiles was a question discussed at this time at Jerusalem, is quite clear from the prominence he himself gives in ver. 3 to the fact that even Titus, who was a Greek, and who accompanied him, compelled to submit to that rite. From the way in which he speaks, it is not improbable, or rather it is almost certain, that some attempt to bring this about had been made; but taking even the apostle's own words, it is not at all likely that it proceeded from the rulers of the Church at Jerusalem, but rather from others, whom Paul indeed expressly describes as (ver. 4) παρεισάκτους ψευδαδέλφους, οἵτινες παρεισῆλθον κατασκοπῆσαι τὴν ἐλευθερίαν ἡμῶν, κ.τ.λ. According to the Acts, the result of the deliberations at Jerusalem was, that the Church there declared itself in agreement with James' proposal, not to enjoin on the Gentiles circumcision and the whole Jewish law, but only (as in the case of the proselytes of the gate) certain points, the neglect of which would lead their Jewish brethren to be always very scrupulous of any close intercourse with them. These injunctions related to fornication, which among the Gentiles was often held to be quite permissible,[1] tasting flesh sacrificed to idols, blood, and things strangled. The counsel was communicated by a letter to the Gentile Christians at Antioch, and throughout Syria and Cilicia, which was transmitted by two members of the Jerusalem Church, Judas Barsabas and Silas, who accompanied Paul and Barnabas on their return to Antioch. According to Gal. ii. 10, Paul and Barnabas on their part had engaged to bear the poor in mind, and especially to aid the poorer brethren in Judea by collections made among the Gentile Christians. With respect to this apostolical letter, we have already (§ 130) pointed out a few circumstances which go to prove it genuine, and a production of James. It is, however, somewhat remarkable that its contents are given and referred to in the Acts only (xvi. 4, xxi. 25), and not at all in any of St. Paul's Epistles, not even where we might reasonably have expected some allusion to them,—as, for instance, when the apostle is speaking, as in the Galatians and Colossians, of the demand made by the strict Judaizers that the Gentiles should be circumcised, or, as in 1 Cor. viii.–x. and Rom. xiv., of eating flesh offered in sacrifice to idols. This fact, nevertheless, would not justify us in pronouncing, with Baur and his school, the

---

[1] It is quite incorrect to understand by πορνεία, as some have done —even WIESELER, p. 185, note—*incest*, or contract of marriage especially within the degrees prohibited by the Mosaic law, or (Baur, p. 142) a *second marriage*.

letter spurious in its contents as well as its form—a mere forgery of the author of the Acts—depriving the account of the transactions connected with it of all historical truth. Rather indeed does it lead us to conclude that the recommendations of the letter were not regarded as perpetually obligatory on all Gentile converts. They were meant only for such as were members of the Churches in Syria and Cilicia, and especially of the Church at Antioch; and they enjoined the matters specified, not because these were all equally important and essential, but because, where the Churches consisted of Jews and Gentiles, their observance on the part of the latter would restore peace, and dispel all fear of defilement from personal intercourse on the part of the former. Certainly the letter itself nowhere speaks as if what it prescribed was to be always binding on all Gentile Christians in the Churches already founded, or which might hereafter be so; and hence, in such of them as were subsequently founded by the Apostle Paul, and consisted chiefly, if not exclusively, of non-Jewish Christians, it was not thought necessary or proper to refer to the counsel given from Jerusalem, or to press its observance. The apostle had made no engagement to do this, and he may have feared lest the newly-converted Gentiles, if called upon specially to bear in mind what to so large an extent had to do only with externals, should come to regard these as in themselves of very great value, essentially characteristic of the gospel, and necessary to salvation. On the other hand, the strict Judaizing party, especially in Jerusalem, do not seem to have been by any means satisfied with what had been done, but continued to insist that, if the Gentiles would enter fully into the Church's fellowship, they must be circumcised, or the people of God would be defiled by contact with them, especially by eating with them; and these notions appear to have very speedily shown themselves again, even at Antioch.

§ 139.

How long Paul and Barnabas remained at Antioch after

their return from Jerusalem, does not seem to have been accurately known to Luke. He expresses himself vaguely and obscurely, when in xv. 35 he says that they continued there teaching and preaching along with many others, and then again (ver. 36) that μετά τινας ἡμέρας they determined on a new evangelistic journey. We have already remarked (§ 126) that their stay at this time was not of very short duration, and that meanwhile Silas had returned to Jerusalem, and thence again to Antioch, probably with Peter. In that case, there can be no doubt that the event recorded in Gal. ii. 11 sqq. took place during this period, and not, as Neander supposes, at a later time, understanding what is said in Acts xviii. 22 of Paul's subsequent visit to Antioch, after he had again been for a short time at Jerusalem. According to Paul's own account, in his Epistle to the Galatians, it is most likely that his remonstrance with Peter occurred shortly after the events at Jerusalem to which he refers directly before, and not several years after, when he had again been to the holy city, and met with all the apostles there assembled together. The occurrence happened in this way: Peter came on a visit to Antioch, being possibly led to do so by the joyful news which Judas Barsabas and Silas had brought back to Jerusalem, and desiring to rivet the bonds by which recent transactions had united the two Churches of Jerusalem and Antioch. At first he felt no hesitation in associating with the believing Gentiles, and even eating with them; but afterwards, when some came from Jerusalem who belonged to the strict Judaizers,[1] he allowed himself to be influenced by them so far as to withdraw from any very close contact with the believing Gentiles. He even induced other Jewish Christians, including Barnabas even, to follow

---

[1] The ἀπό 'Ιακώβου (ver. 12) does not make it absolutely necessary, though very probable, that in Paul's view these persons were closely connected in some way with James. Probably they had on some occasion or other been sent to Antioch by James, and had gone about professedly to make known his judgment on the controverted points. It does not follow, however, that James approved of everything or anything in their conduct.

his example. Paul was accordingly led to remonstrate most strongly with him.

Of late years much use has been made of this fact to prove that even Peter must have continued to be affected by strict Jewish prejudices, and therefore that the character in which he is made to appear, for example in Acts xv., cannot be historically true. But then the same prejudices must be equally attributable to Barnabas. Now, looking simply at what is said in the Galatians, the real state of the case would seem to have been very different, and it is plain that even Paul considered it so. Peter allowed himself to be influenced by a fear of others, probably by a wish not to repel from Christian fellowship the strict Judaizing Christians. Paul, however, thought him chargeable with unreasonable compliance with false prejudices, by conduct which is described as ὑπόκρισις, since it made it appear as if he held a much stronger opinion on the necessity of observing the Jewish law than his previous conduct would have suggested. As a matter of fact, he was very far from being so strict, for we find Paul charging him (ver. 14) with living "after the manner of the Gentiles," that is, with a lax observance of the various prescriptions of the Jewish law.

§ 140.

During this fourth sojourn at Antioch, Paul resolved on a second and more extensive missionary journey, to visit and confirm the converts made on the first. This was immediately undertaken, and ultimately extended much beyond what had been at first thought of (Acts xv. 36 sqq.). Paul wished to associate Barnabas with himself on this journey. This, however, was prevented by the wish of Barnabas to take his cousin John Mark again with them, to which Paul would not consent, because on their former journey he had left them prematurely at Perga in Pamphylia, and returned to Jerusalem. Very possibly also, the event recorded in Gal. ii. 11 had some effect in severing Paul and Barnabas from one another, and contributed to the difficulty of associating Mark with them. Barnabas, accompanied by his kinsman, sailed to Cyprus. His labours, however, there and subsequently (1 Cor. ix. 6) are not recorded, and throughout the rest of the Acts he is almost altogether lost sight of. Paul, on the other hand, took Silas (or Silvanus) with him, and went through Syria and Cilicia on to Derbe and Lystra in Lycaonia. In the latter city, according to Acts xvi. 1—not at Derbe, as some suppose, from an erroneous interpretation of xx. 4—he met with Timothy, the son of a Jewess, who was a believer, but married to a Gentile. Having, on account of the Jews in that region, previously circumcised him, the apostle took him also as a companion for the rest of this journey. Paul's conduct in the circumcision of Timothy differed from that adopted in the case of Titus (Gal. ii.); but then the former was by lineage half a Jew, and moreover had probably been brought up in the Jewish religion as a proselyte of the gate. That the apostle should not have adopted the same course of conduct in each case, is not so incredible as Baur supposes (*Paulus*, p. 129 sq., note). The report of the journey so far is very brief and fragmentary, and it is still more compressed in the subsequent part (xvi. 6–8), referring to the incidents on the way from Lycaonia, through several other provinces of Asia Minor, and on to Troas. Here the route is somewhat obscurely indicated, and there is also some uncertainty in the text, though this does not directly affect the districts mentioned. Most likely the course lay in the following direction: From Lycaonia they went first north-west to Phrygia, purposing to go thence due west to proconsular Asia (Ephesus). From this, however, they were held back by the Holy Ghost, and were led to betake themselves to Galatia (N.E. of Phrygia); but all that is said of this province is, that they passed through it. We may, however, assume from the Epistle to the Galatians that they remained in it some time, founding Churches in various places, and meeting with a cordial welcome, especially from the Gentile inhabitants, who consisted of immigrant Celto-Germanic tribes, although at the time Paul was suffering from bodily weakness (Gal. iv. 13 sqq.). Even in Phrygia they were doubtless not inactive, but we are left in ignorance of any results of their labours there. At a later time the gospel had found entrance into the S.W. of this province at Colosse, Laodicea, Hierapolis; but Paul had not been personally in these places (Col. ii. 1). From Galatia they went back probably through the north of Phrygia, then farther west towards Mysia, and got ready to go, when strengthened by the Spirit, to Bithynia, to Troas. At this point and onwards the narrative becomes clearer and fuller, since we now have the report of one of Paul's companions, Timothy, as far as Philippi (§ 124, 125). In Troas Paul had a vision by night, in which a call was addressed to him to go to Macedonia, and preach salvation there also. Accordingly they made at once for Samothracia, and thence for Neapolis, a Macedonian seaport on the borders of Thrace, whence again they went to Philippi, a distance of twelve Roman miles.

It would seem that there was no synagogue at Philippi, but merely a place beyond the city by the side of the river Strymon, where the Jews, chiefly proselytes, met together for prayer. Thither Paul went with his companions on the Sabbath. His preaching was followed by some good results, especially in the case of Lydia, a Jewish proselyte and seller of purple from Thyatira, who was baptized, and then received into her house the preachers of the faith. Subsequently, however, they were thrust into prison; and the event was brought about thus: While on their way to the place of prayer, most probably on a later Sabbath, they were followed by a slave-girl, a Gentile, who was wont to practise sooth-saying while in a state of ecstasy (probably somnambulism), and whose gift was used by her masters to procure gain. She called out after Paul and his companions that they were servants of the most high God, who had come to reveal the way of salvation. She continued to act in this way for several days, till at last Paul by his word delivered her from her bondage, by expelling the evil spirit under whose sway she was held. Her masters, being unable any longer to make a gain of her, became enraged, dragged Paul and Silas—Timothy was not so much noticed, being a younger and probably less conspicuous associate—before the (Roman) magistracy, and complained that these Jews preached things strange to the Romans, and contrary to law. Accordingly they were scourged for breaking the peace, and then thrown into prison. Their imprisonment, however, brought about the jailor's conversion, when, the prison-doors being thrown open by an earthquake, the two missionaries did not avail themselves of the miraculous opportunity for flight which presented itself. The jailor received baptism the same night, and on the following morning Paul and Silas were liberated by an order from the magistrates, who were also greatly alarmed when they found that they had scourged Roman citizens. At their entreaty they left the town, after previously meeting the brethren at Lydia's house, and counselling those who through their preaching had already believed (Acts xvi. 12–40; cf. 1 Thess. ii. 2). On this occasion the Church was formed with which, as the epistle he subsequently wrote to them shows, the apostle ever afterwards maintained a close intimacy. The narrative of those events to be found in the Acts rests (§ 124) on the written report of one of Paul's companions, Timothy—even, no doubt, where he had no personal share in them, *e.g.* the imprisonment, and the circumstances connected with it. We may therefore look upon it as true in all essential points. Baur indeed denies this (*Paulus*, pp. 146–166), and pronounces the whole story of Paul's imprisonment and liberation, with the occasion of it, throughout unhistorical, not even legendary, but a deliberate forgery by the author of the Acts, intended as a counterpart to the equally fictitious account of Peter's deliverance at Jerusalem (ch. xii.). We cannot now attempt a more thorough inquiry into this view; but that Paul experienced some special ill-treatment at Philippi is expressly confirmed by 1 Thess. ii. 2, where it is referred to as well known to the Thessalonians.

§ 141.

From Philippi, Paul and Silas went by land through Amphipolis and Apollonia to Thessalonica (Acts xvii. 1). On this journey, and for some time after, Timothy was not with them. He appears to have rejoined them at Berea[1] (§ 125). At Thessalonica they remained several weeks, as we see from Acts xvii. 1–9, and from 1 Thess. ii. 9, 2 Thess. iii. 8, from which we learn that, while with the Thessalonians, Paul earned his living by his own hands, and took up his abode with one named Jason. For three Sabbaths he disputed with the Jews in the synagogue, endeavouring to prove from the Scriptures that Jesus was the Christ. He did not, however, restrict himself to these labours in the synagogue (cf. 1 Thess. ii. 11 sq.), and he may have remained in the city more than three or four weeks. His zeal was not altogether ineffectual. It is true the number of Jews convinced by his words was not very great; but he gained over to the faith many of the Greeks who had previously been attached to the Jewish religion, and especially many women of high rank (Acts xvii. 4). Indeed, judging from 1 Thess. i. 9, we should infer that many converts were made even among Greeks who had no previous connection with Judaism, but were idolaters up to the time of their conversion.[2] Such results, however, of the preaching of the gospel naturally embittered the majority of the Jews. They contrived to gain over a part of the people of the city, and with their aid attacked Jason's house; but not finding Paul and Silas, they dragged Jason himself and certain brethren before the magistrates, accusing them as men who were turning the world upside down, and inciting to civil disobedience, inasmuch as they were seeking to set up one Jesus as king. Jason, however, and the rest of the brethren succeeded in satisfying the magistrates, probably by their possession of the right of citizenship. Nevertheless it was found expedient to send Paul and Silas away by night; and they went to Berea (xvii.

---

[1] Probably Paul, when leaving Philippi, left him behind to strengthen and establish the brethren and to form the Church. That he was not with Paul at Thessalonica, may be inferred from 1 Thess. iii. 2.

[2] This would be the express statement even of the Acts, *ut supra*, if we adopt LACHMANN's reading, σεβομένων καὶ Ἑλλήνων. [In his exegetical lectures on the Acts and 1st Thessalonians, BLEEK treats καί as an interpolation.—B.]

10-15), a celebrated city in the *tertia regio* of Macedonia, lying fifty miles south-west from Thessalonica. Here, again, they remained probably some time, during which Timothy must have come to them. Paul and Silas resorted to the synagogue in the city, and were at first welcomed by the Jews, who compared their teaching with the Scriptures, and were in many cases led to believe, along with a considerable number of men and women from among the Greeks. But when the Jews of Thessalonica heard of this, some of them came to Berea and sought to excite the populace; so that the brethren were induced to bring Paul down to the coast, whence, escorted by a few of them, he went to Athens, very probably by sea, though this is not quite clear from the Acts. Silas and Timothy, on the other hand, continued in Berea; but on Paul's arrival at Athens he sent them word by his returning companions to come to him as soon as possible. From 1 Thess. iii. 1 it seems very probable that Timothy did come to him, but was again sent to confirm the brethren at Thessalonica, which place he subsequently left in order to rejoin the apostle at Corinth, in company with Silas, who had meanwhile remained at Berea, or at any rate in Macedonia. We may infer from 1st Thessalonians, *ut supra*, and from the account in Acts xvii. 16-34, that Paul stayed some time at Athens, where he did not content himself with appearing in the synagogue and disputing with the Jews and σεβομένοις, but sought out persons in the market daily, and especially such as were Stoics and Epicureans. These also induced him on one occasion to give an address on his doctrines in the Areopagus, which Luke has given us, probably from a report by Timothy (§ 125). His preaching was not wholly without result, and Luke mentions among his converts Dionysius the Areopagite, and a woman named Damaris. From Athens he went to Corinth, where, according to Acts xviii. 11, he stayed at least eighteen months, and where, according to ver. 5, Silas and Timothy again met him. Here Paul lived with a Jew from Pontus named Aquila, who carried on the same trade as himself, tentmaking, and is said (ver. 2) to have come to Corinth with his wife Priscilla (both were probably converts of the apostle's) from Italy, on Claudius' edict commanding all Jews to leave Rome. The last fact helps us to determine the chronology here, though not very exactly. Claudius' edict is mentioned by Suetonius (*Claud.* xxv.),[1] but he gives no date. Some have supposed this edict to be the same as that which Tacitus speaks of (*Ann.* xii. 52) as a decree of the Senate *de Mathematicis Italia pellendis*, issued in the year 52 A.D. This, however, is, to say the least, very uncertain, if not improbable. Most likely the edict bearing on the expulsion of the Jews from Rome belongs to the latter part of Claudius' reign (*ob.* 54 A.D.); but if we assume that Luke's expression προσφάτως is tolerably correct, Paul's arrival at Athens could not have taken place before 54 A.D.: indeed, we are inclined to place it earlier. We shall, however, return to this point again. During Paul's stay at Corinth he composed the earliest of his letters—the two to the Thessalonians.

THE FIRST EPISTLE TO THE THESSALONIANS.

§ 142.

The postscript in most MSS., and among them even the oldest, names Athens as the city from which the first (and even the second) epistle was written. This, however, unquestionably only rests on an inference from 1 Thess. iii. 1, which nevertheless rather points to the contrary opinion, that Paul, who had sent Timothy from Athens to Thessalonica, was not, when he wrote, any longer at Athens. Timothy, indeed, had now returned to the apostle from his mission to Thessalonica (*ib.* ver. 6), and Silas or Silvanus was also with him (i. 1). We cannot doubt, therefore, that Paul wrote during his stay at Corinth, after Silas and Timothy had come to him from Macedonia (Acts xviii. 5). How long he had been at Corinth when they arrived, is not clear from the statement in the Acts. But since even the second epistle was written during the apostle's stay there, and yet was not

[1] *Judæos impulsore Chresto assidue tumultuantes Roma expulit.*

written till some time after the first, the latter cannot belong to the later period of this stay, but rather to the earlier, and yet not exactly to its very commencement. It is plain from several passages, that some time had elapsed between the founding of the Christian society at Thessalonica and the writing of this letter. Thus i. 7, 8 speaks of the conversion and faith of the Thessalonians as known to all Macedonia and Achaia; ii. 17, 18 tells of two attempts on Paul's part to visit them, which had been frustrated by Satan; iv. 13 leads to the conclusion that some members of the Church—perhaps, however, only one of them—had died. These circumstances are not irreconcilable with the supposition of an interval of six months or thereabouts; at any rate it is certainly incorrect, on account of these and similar facts, to infer with Köhler (*Abfassungszeit der epistol. Schriften*, p. 112 sqq.), Schrader, Wurm (*Tüb. Zeitschr. für Theol.* 1833, p. 78), that this first epistle was composed at a time considerably after this visit of Paul to Corinth. That no such length of time had intervened, and that Paul had certainly not been a second time to Thessalonica, we can easily see in many ways, and especially from the manner in which he speaks of the conversion of his readers, and of his preaching as the means of it, and also of his frequently unsuccessful attempts to revisit them (i. 9, ii. 2, 17 sq.; and compare, as against Schrader, Schneckenburger, *Beitr. zur Einl. ins N. T.* 165–181; and as against Wurm, the same author's article in the *Studien der Evang. Geistl. Wurtembergs*, vii. 1834, Part i. p. 137 sqq.).

The immediate *occasion* of our present epistle was the report brought by Timothy, on his return from Thessalonica, as to the condition of things there, which was on the whole such as to cause joy. The members of the Church, who were for the most part Gentiles, had had to endure persecutions and afflictions from their fellow-countrymen, yet they continued immoveable in the faith (1 Thess. ii. 14, iii. 3 sq.; 2 Thess. i. 4). Still there were some among them who had not on their Christian profession immediately abandoned practices which, though usually regarded as quite permissible in heathenism, were utterly irreconcilable with the spirit of the gospel, *e.g.* πορνεία (1 Thess. iv. 3 sqq.). Again, there were some who seemed disposed to give up labouring for their own support, and were consequently becoming burdensome to the brethren, and encouraging an irregular mode of life. This disposition was owing in some degree to a belief in the Lord's speedy return in glory, and the consequent passing away of the existing order of things, and setting up of God's kingdom. As this expectation of the second advent was universal and most vivid in the apostolical age, so Paul's own preaching at Thessalonica seems to have pointed to it as the perfecting of God's kingdom, when Christ should reign as Lord and King of all. It was this characteristic in his preaching that gave the Jews occasion to accuse him as they did before the magistrates (Acts xvii. 7). It was, however, to this part of his doctrine that the Thessalonian believers felt chiefly attracted, and the hope of the Lord's speedy return became specially dear to them. In the form it took among them, it was fostered by certain fellow-believers who claimed to be prophets, and whose inspiration was not fictitious, but nevertheless was mixed up with much that was fanatical and carnal (1 Thess. v. 19-21; 2 Thess. ii. 2). Thus the Church became troubled as to what would become of the brethren who should have fallen asleep before the second advent took place. These things, then, Paul had in mind, when, shortly after hearing of them from Timothy, he wrote this first Epistle to the Thessalonians.

In the first half of his epistle (ch. i.-iii.) the apostle expresses his joy and thankfulness to God for the blessing vouchsafed to his preaching among them, and for the stedfastness of their faith amid great tribulations; also his longing to see them, and prayer to the Lord that He would increase their love and establish their hearts in holiness. He then adds (iv. 1-12) exhortations to hold fast in their life the doctrines they had received, especially to flee from all uncleanness, to continue faithfully performing deeds of brotherly love towards one another, to lead a peaceable life, and to earn whatever was necessary for their support by the work of their own hands. Then follow (from iv. 13 onwards) instructions on the Lord's coming, the chief purpose of which is to comfort them as to those who had fallen asleep in Christ. On the times and the seasons, however, he continues (ch. v.), there was no need of his writing to them, since they themselves knew well that the day of the Lord would come suddenly and unexpectedly, and therefore he warns them to be always ready to receive Him (v. 1–11). Some further exhortations follow, partly of a general kind, and partly bearing specially on their existing circumstances and needs (v. 12–24); and then the apostle closes (v. 25–28) by asking their prayers for himself, and charging them to read his letter to all the brethren.

The *authenticity* of this letter was never questioned till recent times, when it was assailed by BAUR.[1] This critic maintains: (1) That the epistle is too vague and unimportant to be a genuine work of Paul's, being made up of reminiscences of his other epistles, especially First Corinthians; (2) That, in common with Second Thessalonians, it is far too apocalyptic in tone, and has much besides that is un-Pauline; (3) That its historical relations will not allow us to regard it as genuine, since its data require it to have been written soon after Paul's first visit to Thessalonica, while this does not agree at all with its actual contents. The last reason alone has any plausibility, but it has been sufficiently refuted by what we have already said. The whole tone of the epistle is such that its forgery by some later author is inconceivable, and its external history points to the same conclusion. It was found in Marcion's Canon, and was universally recognised by the doctors of the Catholic Church towards the end of the second century, whence we may certainly conclude that its genuineness was established in the first half of that century. It is less needful to examine Baur's assertions more particularly, as his fancy does not seem to have met with any acceptance even among the members of his own school. [Compare Hilgenfeld, *die beiden Briefe an die Thessalon. nach Inhalt u. Ursprung*, in the *Zeitschr. f. wiss. Theol.* 1862, pp. 225–264. Hilgenfeld rejects only the second epistle.]

[1] PAULUS. p. 480 sqq.; *Theol. Jahrbb.* 1855, p. 141 sqq.

THE SECOND EPISTLE TO THE THESSALONIANS.

§ 143.

We neither know by whom Paul sent his first Epistle to the Thessalonians, nor from whom he received his subsequent intelligence respecting them, whether from his messenger on his return or from some one else. It led, however, to his writing to them again. This second epistle was certainly not written before the first, as Grotius maintains in his special treatise on 2d Thessalonians, and again in his *Annotatt. in N. T.*, supposing it to have been written before Paul had been to Thessalonica, to Jewish Christians who had fled thither from Judea. The supposition is very arbitrary, and without the least shadow of probability. Ewald,[1] again, affirms that it was written from Berea by the apostle before he had been to Athens and Corinth (so also Laurent). But this is very improbable. The passage ii. 15 (probably also ii. 2) implies the existence of another epistle, which was doubtless our first to the Thessalonians. The connection of the contents of both letters leaves it beyond a question in my own mind that our *second* epistle was written after the *first*, and to the same readers (cf. HOFMANN, *die heil. Schrift neuen Testaments*, i. 365 sq.). Silvanus and Timothy were with the apostle when he wrote this letter (i. 1); and we may therefore infer that he wrote it before his departure from Corinth to Ephesus (Acts xviii. 18), since these two fellow-labourers do not appear to have been then any longer with him, or at any rate to have accompanied him on that journey. From its relation in other respects to First Thessalonians, we are led to conclude that it was written only some two months later than that epistle, and, according to iii. 2, at a time when the apostle was persecuted by unbelieving opponents among Jews and Gentiles. These facts agree with the time of Paul's residence at Corinth, judging from the indications given in Acts xviii. 6, 9 sq., 12 sqq., though we are

---

[1] *Sendschreiben des Paulus*, p. 17 sq.; *Gesch. des apost. Zeitalters*, p. 455; *Jahrb. d. bibl. Wiss.* iii. 250.

not able to decide very precisely as to the date from what is said there. That it should not, however, be put very late— for example, after the second Macedonian journey (Acts xx. 1 sqq.)—is plain from such passages as ii. 5, iii. 8, 10, where the apostle speaks of his abode among them in a way which will hardly allow us to suppose he had often visited them subsequently. A special reason for writing this second epistle so soon after the first, lay in the need of giving the Thessalonians further instruction respecting the Lord's coming. Through the manifold tribulations they had had to bear on account of their faith, the opinion had gained ground among them that the Lord's coming would take place immediately; and this hope was cherished not only by a few who laid claim to the spirit of prophecy, but was thought to be favoured by certain expressions of the Apostle Paul himself (ii. 2). It has been supposed by very many, *e.g.* by Origen, Chrysostom, and nearly all modern critics, that between the composition of the two Epistles to the Thessalonians which we have, a letter had been forged in Paul's name, on the contents of which the Thessalonians based the special views on the Lord's advent above referred to. This letter, it is said, the apostle himself alludes to (ii. 2), and it led him especially to call attention (iii. 17) to the authentication of his writings. It is, however, manifestly improbable that at so early a date any letter should have been falsely attributed to him, especially a letter to a Church with which he stood in so close a personal relation, and that they should have looked upon it as genuine. Had anything of this kind really happened, Paul would certainly have been much more emphatic in his condemnation of it. What he says at ii. 2, makes it much more probable that he refers to a letter really written by himself, that is, to our First Thessalonians, certain expressions in which had been taken by the Thessalonian brethren far more in their own sense than was consistent with the writer's own meaning; while the passage iii. 17 may, at the most, amount simply to this, as Theodoret saw long ago, that since a use had been made of his letter which was by no means what he intended, he feared lest something should be attributed to him which did not at all belong to him, and therefore pointed out the sure token of his genuine letters. It is not at all necessary, however, to adopt even this explanation, since the apostle was accustomed in those letters which he dictated to others to append at the close a salutation with his own hand (1 Cor. xvi. 21; Col. iv. 18), to meet probably the natural desire of his readers for something directly from himself. That he should have drawn particular attention to this in the present epistle, was not so much to warn the Thessalonians against any fictitious letter, as to certify that the letter really came from him, and consequently claimed their obedience as having apostolical authority.

The main *design* of the letter is to warn the Thessalonians against thinking of the day of the Lord and their gathering together to Him as nigh at hand. It refers to the apostle's previous teaching on the events which should precede the second advent, especially the manifestation of Antichrist. It, moreover, takes occasion to warn those who led an idle and irregular life, and thus threw the burthen of their support on others.

With respect to the external history of the letter, we find that it was as well attested an epistle in the early Church as the first to the same Church; and it was universally acknowledged as a genuine work of the Apostle Paul until the beginning of this century. In modern times, doubts have been raised in several quarters on its genuineness and integrity in common with the first epistle. J. E. C. Schmidt was the first to assail, in 1801 (in his *Bibliothek für Kritik u. Exegese des N. T. u. älteste K. Gesch.* ii. 380 sqq.), the genuineness of ii. 1–12; and subsequently, in 1804 (in his *Einl. ins N. T.*), he questioned the whole epistle, though in a very hesitating way. De Wette followed him in the *first* edition of his *Einleitung*, but in his *second* and *third* editions he placed less reliance on the reasons assigned for doubt; while in his *fourth* edition, and in his *Exegetisches Handbuch*, he expresses himself decidedly in favour of the genuineness of the epistle. Against Schmidt's and De Wette's earlier views, cf. REICHE, *Authenticæ posterioris ad Thess. Ep. vindiciæ.* Latterly the epistle has been again assailed by Kern

(*Tüb. Zeitschr. f. Theol.* 1839, ii. pp. 145-214), and by Baur, *Paulus*, pp. 485-492, and *Theol. Jahrbb.* 1855, pp. 141-168, where he maintains the second epistle is the older of the two (more recently, so also Hilgenfeld, *ut supra*). The particular reasons assigned for calling in question the genuineness of the epistle are: (1) The manifest effort it makes to prove itself a genuine work of the Apostle Paul, as compared with other epistles (iii. 17 compared with ii. 15). This objection is refuted by what we have already said. (2) The section on the Parousia of Christ, ii. 1-12. Here it is maintained: (*a*) The subject is treated in too Judaizing a way, and not with the limitation and tone to be looked for in Paul. This, however, is purely a subjective reason, by which nothing is decided. The apostle was led to treat the subject more copiously by the urgently pressing need of bringing the Thessalonians back to a more practical view than that which they were allowing to influence them. Again, it is said (*b*) that this part of the epistle is opposed to the teaching of First Thessalonians, according to which the Lord's coming was nigh at hand, while here such a view is opposed. Our previous remarks, however, show that such an opposition does not really exist between the two epistles. Kern thinks (*c*) this passage assumes the fall or death of Nero, and therefore must have been written after that event, though still probably before the destruction of Jerusalem, and therefore between 68 and 70 A.D. This reason, however, simply rests on a false interpretation of the meaning of the passage.[1] A more correct view leads us to assign it to a time when the idea which arose subsequently, and which we find in the Apocalypse, that the Antichrist would appear in the Roman emperor, and especially in Nero, restored once more to life, had not yet been broached—that is, to a time prior to the persecution under Nero. Paul's manner of expressing himself is irreconcilable with a later time; and indeed the whole tone of the passage is so individual, intuitive, and charac-

---

[1] [According to Kern, the Antichrist is Nero, whose return was expected immediately after his death; and ὁ κατέχων of ver. 7 was Vespasian and Titus.—B.]

teristic, that it is difficult to conceive of it as the forgery of some later author.

§ 144.

CORINTH, from which the two letters to the Thessalonians were written, was one of the most celebrated cities of antiquity, and the metropolis of Achaia. It lay on the isthmus between two bays, and thus became the centre of the commerce of Europe and Asia. After the old brilliant city had been taken by Lucius Mummius, and plundered and burnt, with all its treasures, it lay in ruins for a century, till Julius Cæsar rebuilt it, recalled the descendants of its former inhabitants, and added a colony of Roman *mancipati*. Favoured by its natural position, the city soon regained its former splendour and wealth, and people from various regions flocked to it. It soon became, however, also, as the ancient city had been, a principal seat of the worship of Venus, and very licentious. It was also the chief stronghold of the Greek Sophists. As was usual at the time in the most important cities of commerce, the population at Corinth embraced a large number of Jews. We see this from the sketch given us in the Acts of Paul's eighteen months' residence in the city (xviii. 1–18). We have, however, little told us of his labours during this time. At first he preached chiefly to Jews only in the synagogue; but when these opposed him, he taught in a house hard by the synagogue, belonging to a σεβόμενος named Justus. That the apostle was the first who preached the gospel at Corinth is clear from Acts xviii., but especially from the Epistles to the Corinthians (1 Cor. iii. 6, iv. 15; 2 Cor. i. 19, x. 11). Among the Jews converted by him, mention is made of a ruler of the synagogue named Crispus (Acts xviii. 8); but his heathen converts were much more numerous. The Jews for the most part showed him great hostility; and to this, no doubt, reference is made in the vision he had when the Lord spoke to his strengthening and encouragement (Acts xviii. 9 sq.). We are, however, specially told (ver. 12 sqq.), after mention of the apostle's labours (ver. 11) during his stay of eighteen months, that, when Gallio was proconsul of Achaia, the Jews brought Paul before the judgment-seat, and accused him of persuading men to worship God contrary to their law. Owing to Gallio's fairness and discretion, the only result of this charge was that the populace were embittered against the Jews. We are further told that, after the apostle had remained some further time (ἱκανὰς ἡμέρας) in the city, he took ship to Syria. The Gallio here referred to is known to us as the brother of the philosopher Seneca, who speaks of him with affection and esteem, and whose Ep. civ. informs us that he had been in Achaia. Still we cannot precisely ascertain the date of his entrance upon the proconsular office, so that we cannot make use of it to determine the exact chronology of Paul's stay at Corinth. From what is said in vers. 11 and 12, we must conclude that when Paul came to Corinth, Gallio was not yet proconsul, but only entered on his office after the apostle had been for some time labouring in the city. It almost seems as if the eighteen months of ver. 11 covered the time from Paul's arrival to his accusation in the way above stated. Still it is quite possible it may refer to the whole time of his stay. The phrase ἱκανὰς ἡμέρας gives us but very vague and general information as to the length of the apostle's stay at Corinth after his accusation; but that event does not appear to have had any effect in hastening his departure.

St. Paul went on this journey without Silas or Timothy, who either remained behind, or had already been sent by him on a mission from Corinth. He was, however, accompanied by Aquila and Priscilla, and started after he had fulfilled a vow by having his head shorn at Cenchrea.[1] He first went to Ephesus and visited the synagogue, but remained only a short time in the city, leaving Aquila and Priscilla behind him. These Christian teachers imparted a fuller knowledge of the Lord to Apollos, an Alexandrian Jew well versed in the Scriptures, who thereupon went with recommendations from the Ephesian brethren to Achaia, and especially to Corinth,

---

[1] Unquestionably the remark in Acts xviii. 18 does not refer to Aquila, as some (WIESELER, MEYER, etc.) have supposed.

and there laboured for the gospel with great success, chiefly in his efforts to convince the Jews that Jesus was indeed the Messiah (Acts xviii. 24–28). Paul, on the other hand, went by way of Cæsarea to Jerusalem on his *third visit* after his conversion, and after saluting the Church proceeded to Antioch on his fifth visit after his conversion. Here he remained some time, and then passed through the cities of Galatia and Phrygia, strengthening all the disciples. This journey from Ephesus onwards (Acts xviii. 21–23) is only mentioned in the briefest possible manner, and no particulars are given even on such a point as the route taken from Antioch to those parts of central Asia Minor which formed Galatia and Phrygia, though we may conjecture with some probability that it lay through Cilicia and Lycaonia. Paul is not generally supposed to have visited Jerusalem in the course of this journey. The words in ver. 21, δεῖ με πάντως τὴν ἑορτὴν τὴν ἐρχομένην ποιῆσαι εἰς Ἱεροσόλυμα, with δέ after the following πάλιν, are wanting in several of the most ancient authorities. Lachmann has excluded them, and even others regard them as spurious, some understanding ἀναβάς of the ascent from the haven to Cæsarea, which lay higher up, and τὴν ἐκκλησίαν of the Church in that city. But this construction of ἀναβάς would be very unnatural, even if we adopt the shorter reading: it is much more probable we should understand it of the ascent to Jerusalem, which is confessedly often expressed by the word ἀναβαίνειν. The words in question, however, are most likely genuine, and then we may conclude that this visit to Jerusalem occurred at the time of a Jewish festival, and certainly of a high festival,—*which* we do not know. Anger (p. 61 sq.) and Wieseler (p. 48 sqq.) decide for Pentecost, which however is far from certain.

§ 145.

We are further told in Acts xix. 1, that after Paul had passed through the upper districts (τὰ ἀνωτερικὰ μέρη, by which is probably meant Galatia and Phrygia chiefly, xviii. 23), he came to Ephesus, while Apollos was still at Corinth. In this metropolis of proconsular Asia he settled for some time, his whole stay extending to nearly three years (Acts xix. 8, 10, and xx. 31). The account in the Acts is here somewhat fuller, though, considering the length of the apostle's residence, we have few special details of his labours, and the events which befell him. He appears to have found among the Jews at Ephesus a greater readiness to receive the gospel than was usual. Even on his former visit they had, after he had been to the synagogue, asked him to remain a longer time with them (Acts xviii. 20); while on this occasion he was allowed to hold his discussions even for three whole months in the synagogue itself, and it was only because many opposed him that he was forced at last to separate the disciples, and to hold his subsequent discussions in the school of one Tyrannus. Even here, however, his labours were not confined to the Greeks, but were to a great extent among the Jews of Ephesus and Asia generally (Acts xix. 10, xx. 21). Still there were opponents among these Ephesian Jews, who stiffly, and even with a feeling of personal malevolence, set themselves against him (xx. 19), and no doubt these were a majority of their nation. Many, however, received the word of life gladly, so that the Church at Ephesus contained a larger number of Jewish Christian members than most of the other Churches founded by Paul. This greater inclination of the Ephesian Jews to receive the gospel was doubtless due to the previous activity among them of the Jew Aquila and his wife Priscilla, together with Apollos. The only points connected with this period of the apostle's residence at Ephesus noticed in the Acts are: (*a*) that he conferred on a great number of John's disciples Christian baptism, and the Holy Ghost; (*b*) that many miracles were wrought by him, especially the healing of demoniacs, so that even the Jewish exorcists used in their magical invocations the name of that Jesus whom Paul preached, especially the sons of a certain ἀρχιερεύς named Sceva, to whom, however, the attempt brought only injury, while through the apostle's influence the believers abjured all the magical arts which they had hitherto practised; (*c*) that it was from Ephesus he sent Timothy—who must have been with him at the time, though we are not told when he rejoined him—with Erastus to Macedonia, while he himself stayed in Asia; (*d*) that a riot was excited against him by Demetrius, a silversmith. On this last occasion we find that two Macedonians, Gaius and Aristarchus, were with Paul at Ephesus, though nothing is said of them previously. That during his stay at Ephesus and the surrounding district, the apostle must have encountered much persecution and many perils, he himself expressly says more than once,—for instance, in his speech to the Ephesian elders, Acts xx. 19, and in 1 Cor. xv. 32, εἰ κατὰ ἄνθρωπον ἐθηριομάχησα ἐν Ἐφέσῳ. The last expression is of course figurative, not literally true, or we should have it more particularly mentioned in 2 Cor. xi. 23 sqq. It cannot, however, refer to the affair of Demetrius, since according to ch. xxi. this took place only a short time before Paul's departure, and therefore at a later date than that of First Corinthians. It must therefore, in common with what is said immediately before of his daily peril of death, refer to persecutions of various kinds on the part of rough men. Another passage pointing to his trials is to be found in 2 Cor. i. 8, where the allusion may be to the narrative in the Acts, since it is very probable that here the apostle is thinking of what befell him shortly before his departure from Asia.

In respect of the subsequent period, the Acts is again extremely brief. As we have remarked, we may suppose from xx. 1, that soon after the riot raised by Demetrius, if not directly in consequence of it, Paul was induced to leave Ephesus and go to Macedonia,—a journey which he is said (xix. 21) to have previously designed. After he had passed through Macedonia he went to Greece (Achaia), where he remained three months, the greater part of which we may take it for granted he spent at Corinth. All here, however, is very cursorily noticed; but during this period—that is, during the apostle's stay in Ephesus, Macedonia, and Achaia —were written, of the epistles we now have, the two to the Corinthians, that to the Romans, and very probably also that to the Galatians: the *first* to the Corinthians from Ephesus, the *second* from Macedonia, on the journey from Ephesus to

Achaia; the Epistle to the Romans from Achaia (Corinth); the date of the Galatians is by no means certain.

THE EPISTLES TO THE CORINTHIANS.

§ 146.

The date of 1st Corinthians will appear from the following circumstances :—

(*a.*) It could not have been written before St. Paul's second visit to Ephesus (Acts xix. 1). When Paul arrived at Ephesus the second time, Apollos, who had been converted by Aquila and Priscilla, had already left for Corinth, and there had been very active in spreading the gospel (Acts xviii. 27, 28, xix. 1). But when Paul wrote 1st Corinthians, Apollos had made many disciples there (i. 12, iii. 4-6), had left, and was again at the same place with Paul (xvi. 12).

(*b.*) It is equally clear from several remarks at the end of the epistle (especially xvi. 5, 8, 19), that it could not have been written subsequent to the apostle's departure from Ephesus (to Macedonia, Acts xx. 1). It would appear from 1 Cor. xvi. 8 that the letter was written only a few months before Pentecost, and perhaps, from the allusion of ch. v. 7, 8, shortly before Easter.

The same is evident from the date of the second epistle, which was written on that journey from Ephesus to Achaia, Acts xx. 1, 2; see 2 Cor. ii. 13, vii. 5, ix. 2. According to 2 Cor. ii. 12, St. Paul had come through Troas, and this he would do in a journey from Ephesus. From 2 Cor. i. 15, 16, 23, and other passages, it is evident that the apostle did not visit Corinth in the interval between the first and the second epistle.[1]

Now, according to the history in the book of the Acts, the apostle had paid but one visit to Corinth previous to the writing of both epistles thither. But this does not seem to correspond with certain statements in the letters themselves,

---

[1] Ewald thinks differently (*Jahrb.* ii. 227 sqq.; *Sendschreiben,* p. 226 sq.; *Apost. Zeitalter,* p. 481), but he is certainly mistaken.

especially in 2d Corinthians, according to which it would appear that Paul had already been twice in Corinth before the sending of that, and consequently of this epistle. Thus 2 Cor. xii. 14, ἰδοὺ τρίτον τοῦτο ἑτοίμως ἔχω ἐλθεῖν πρὸς ὑμᾶς· καὶ οὐ καταναρκήσω (*rec. Gr.* ὑμῶν); xiii. 1, τρίτον τοῦτο ἔρχομαι πρὸς ὑμᾶς. The τρίτον τοῦτο in these passages is by many taken to refer merely to an intention to visit them three times, entertained but not fulfilled, and not to any visits actually paid. But the connection of the first passage quite forbids this interpretation, and it is very unnatural, as the words lie, in the second. Again, in 2 Cor. xiii. 2, the only natural rendering is to take the τὸ δεύτερον with the ὡς παρών immediately preceding,—thus denoting the apostle's presence among them a second time previous to the writing of the letter. Further, from ch. ii. 1, xii. 21, it would appear that on his former visit he found the Church in such a state as to require his severe rebuke and admonition; and this can hardly refer to his first visit, but rather to one paid after the Church had been some time formed.[1] We cannot exactly determine the time of this second visit; we cannot tell how long after the first visit, nor how long before the writing of the first epistle. Ewald places it between our two epistles, and supposes that Paul paid a hurried visit by sea from Ephesus to Corinth and back. But 2 Cor. i. 15, 16, 23, contain statements which quite exclude the notion of a visit in the interval between the two epistles. We may suppose that *before* the journey from Corinth to Ephesus

---

[1] Vid. *Stud. u. Krit.* 1830, pp. 614–624. The arguments I there advanced are not only in harmony with many previous expositors, but have since been adopted by SCHRADER (independently of me), SCHOTT, NEANDER, CREDNER, REUSS (ed. ii. and sqq.), ANGER, WIESELER. Not so, however, by DE WETTE (§ 132, *a*, note *a*, and *Exeget. Handb.*). BAUR strongly expresses his dissent from them, *Theol. Jahrbb.* 1850, pp. 139–165. Still I am convinced that an unbiassed consideration of these passages collectively will leave no doubt upon the mind that the apostle had been already twice in Corinth, though the Acts mentions only one visit (ch. xviii.). So CONYBEARE AND HOWSON (ch. xv.), ALFORD, *Prolegg.* 1 *Cor.*, and HACKETT in SMITH'S *Dictionary to the Bible—Corinthians*.

recorded in Acts xviii. 18, 19, the apostle had left Corinth and returned thither again, so that in the Acts the two successive visits are blended into one, just as we have seen is the case with the two sojourns of the apostle at Damascus—the visit to Arabia intervening; so Michaelis, J. E. C. Schmidt, Anger, Schott, and others. We may be sure that St. Paul did not spend the whole of the eighteen months mentioned in the Acts strictly in the city of Corinth, but that he visited and preached in other places in Achaia; for 2d Corinthians is addressed not only to the Church at Corinth, but to "all the saints which are in all Achaia:" see also ch. xi. 10, ix. 2; 1 Thess. i. 7, 8; 2 Thess. i. 4. But as St. Paul thus addresses his second epistle to the Christians in other parts of Achaia, whom he thus unites with the Corinthian Church, and speaks of having visited them twice, we are obliged to suppose a more distant journey, possibly as far as to Illyricum; see Rom. xv. 19, and cf. also 2 Tim. iv. 10, Τίτος εἰς Δαλματίαν, which was a part of Illyria. Again, it is just possible that this second visit of the apostle was paid *after* the journey of Acts xviii. 18: for the account of the apostle's movements in this part of the Acts is very brief; and between that departure from Corinth (Acts xviii. 18) and the journey from Ephesus mentioned in Acts xx. 1, St. Paul may have made another journey to Corinth, either from Antioch before he went to Galatia and Phrygia (Acts xviii. 22)—and this is Neander's opinion—or from Ephesus, and during his three years' residence there, as Schrader, Rückert, Olshausen, Wieseler, Reuss, [Conybeare and Howson, and Alford] think. In 2 Cor. xi. 25, the apostle, enumerating his sufferings, speaks of three shipwrecks, and adds of one of them, νυχθήμερον ἐν τῷ βυθῷ πεποίηκα. Now in the Acts we find no mention of these, and it is possible that one or more of these shipwrecks may have taken place on a voyage from Syria or Asia Minor to Corinth and back. Then it may have been that he went into Illyricum, passing again through Macedonia; still we may rather suppose that his preaching in Illyricum took place when he subsequently visited Macedonia and Greece.

THE FIRST EPISTLE TO THE CORINTHIANS.

§ 147.

The Church at Corinth, founded by St. Paul, consisted, when he left, of both Jews and Gentiles, the latter being the majority as far as numbers were concerned. Both these parties, however, lived in friendship and peace together, because the Jewish Christians, disowned and persecuted by their unbelieving fellow-countrymen in the city, who had been so bitter against the apostle, clung all the more closely to their believing brethren among the Gentiles, and did not hesitate to eat with them, the uncircumcised, who did not observe the Jewish laws concerning meats and purifyings. But now there came to Corinth Jewish-Christian teachers of far stricter principles, like those at Antioch, who had influenced the conduct even of Peter and Barnabas; and they were backed with letters of recommendation (2 Cor. iii. 1), probably from Judea. They endeavoured to persuade the Jewish Christians at Corinth to withdraw from the common tables with their Gentile brethren, on the ground that these latter felt no scruples of conscience in eating meat that had been offered in sacrifice to idols, and that to do this was virtually to connive at and take part in idolatry. These Judaizers attached great importance to the fact of their purely Hebrew origin (2 Cor. v. 12, xi. 18). Their efforts were not without success. Many of the Jewish Christians espoused their views; and as they appealed especially to the authority of the Apostle Peter, or at least boasted of being one with him, the party formed by them was designated a *Petrine* party, as distinct from the rest of the Church, consisting chiefly of Gentile Christians, who were regarded as the *Pauline* party. This latter party, by virtue of this distinction, were led to espouse more fully what was peculiar to St. Paul's teaching and practice, and to give prominence to his doctrine of the perfect freedom of Christians from the trammels of the law. Besides these two parties there was a third, that of *Apollos*, who during his stay at Corinth must have exerted great influence, especially among the Jews. Between him and St. Paul there was hardly any difference of opinion or of teaching regarding the relation of the gospel to Judaism and the Jewish law. But he seems to have been distinguished by a more subtle power of argumentation, and a more oratorical method of exposition, and thus succeeded in winning to Christianity and retaining many among the Jews whom the plain, simple preaching of St. Paul had failed to attract. We cannot tell whether Apollos had been at Corinth before the apostle's second visit, because we know not the precise date when this second visit was paid. But after St. Paul's second visit a distinct party certainly began to be formed, called the *Apolline* party, side by side with the Pauline; because when the apostle wrote this first epistle, he had already been informed by those of the house of Chloe (probably a Christian matron in Corinth, or according to others, a Christian of Ephesus, some of whose family had been to Corinth), that there were these parties among them (1 Cor. i. 11). The whole Church was sadly divided by these parties; but a few seem to have stood aloof, to have refused to call themselves after any human teacher, and, like Paul himself, to hold to *Christ* alone as their common Master and Lord (i. 12). Some have supposed that these last formed a fourth party, whom the apostle designates οἱ τοῦ Χριστοῦ, and blames in common with the rest. Thus even De Wette (§ 131, *c*) and Schenkel (*Diss. de eccles. Corinth. primæva factionibus turbata*, Basel 1838), who think that the expression denotes certain who denied and rejected all apostolic authority, and professed to receive their knowledge of Christianity by direct revelation from Jesus Christ. But it is not likely that any such party existed in the Church: had there been, St. Paul would certainly have warned them specially against such self-deception. Other suggestions[1]

---

[1] [BAUR maintains that the *Christ* party were identical with the *Petrine*. BEYSCHLAG (*Stud. u. Krit.* 1865, pp. 217-277; cf. *de ecclesiæ Corinthiæ primævæ factione Christina*, Halle 1861) distinguishes it from the *Petrine* as a still more ultra anti-Pauline Judaizing party, against whom the strong language of 2 Cor. x.-xii. is directed.—B.]

are equally untenable; *e.g.*, that they were the followers of the Lord's brothers, or (as Ewald, *Sendschr. des P. S.* 103; *Apost. Zeitalter*, p. 467) that they consisted of certain bookish teachers who held to some one evangelic treatise, insisted upon the example of Christ in all its outward circumstances as the rule for Christians, and condemned marriage because Christ had lived unmarried. This is a very arbitrary and improbable explanation. Ch. iii. 22, εἴτε Παῦλος, εἴτε Ἀπολλὼς, εἴτε Κηφᾶς, shows that οἱ τοῦ Χριστοῦ were not a fourth party side by side with the rest, and distinct in itself. St. Paul regarded himself as τοῦ Χριστοῦ, and would never blame any of the Corinthian Christians who rejected all party names, and would designate themselves simply as οἱ Χριστοῦ. They who acted thus might perhaps seem to be a distinct party, just as those who now-a-days prefer to be called neither Lutherans nor Reformed, but simply Evangelical.

These divisions in the Corinthian Church interrupted the peaceful intercourse of the several members, and caused no small discord among them. In the settlement of their private quarrels they had recourse to the heathen magistracy of the city, and thus their inner discords became matter of public observation (1 Cor. vi. 1 sqq.). In the celebration of the holy communion, moreover, irregularities and improprieties prevailed; for instead of celebrating it according to the pattern given by the Lord when He instituted it, and, in harmony with the practice of the apostolic age, as a feast of love for all believers in common, and for mutual edification, each one took care of himself and for his own supper, without troubling himself about his hungry and needy brethren sitting beside him (1 Cor. xi. 17 sqq.). The miraculous gifts of the Holy Spirit were possessed in a double measure and in great variety among them, but they were not always exercised to the edifying of the Church. The charisma of the γλώσσαις λαλεῖν especially, which was manifested in a very agitated manner of speaking upon religious topics in a state of ecstasy, was esteemed by many among them more highly than other spiritual gifts and graces; and those who possessed it took upon themselves to behave in the public assemblies for worship in a way which served not to edify, but to excite and create confusion. To such a degree did disorder prevail, that, contrary to the universal custom of worshipping assemblies, the women were wont to take part (1 Cor. xiv. 34, 35), and to appear in public unveiled and with the head uncovered,—a practice which was looked upon as unseemly, and caused offence (ch. xi. 2 sqq.). With reference also to the relations of the sexes, there were some members of the Church at Corinth (as at Thessalonica) who were not without offence. Finally, some few among them, probably Gentile believers, denied the doctrine of a future "resurrection of the dead" (xv. 12),—a term which probably had reference to the resurrection of believers upon the second coming of the Lord.

St. Paul, when he visited Corinth the second time, found much in the Church there which grieved him, and called for very grave rebuke and extreme measures (2 Cor. ii. 1, xii. 21), though we are not told exactly what this was. Probably it had reference to the immoral conduct of certain members, and the connivance of others in relation thereto. Subsequently, but before 1st Corinthians was written—though not long before, and probably from Ephesus—St. Paul had written a (since lost) epistle, wherein he had warned them not to keep company with fornicators (1 Cor. v. 9), which he here explains as meaning the avoidance of close intercourse with those who, though outwardly belonging to the Christian community, did not abstain from unchastity and such like impurities. The Corinthians had also written a letter to St. Paul (1 Cor. vii. 1), doubtless in answer to his epistle. This letter (which also is lost) was probably handed to the apostle by the men whom he names in 1 Cor. xvi. 17, 18, Stephanas, Fortunatus, and Achaicus. In it the Corinthians had asked questions upon several subjects upon which they desired his advice, especially concerning marriage, and whether a single life were not to be preferred (1 Cor. vii. 1 sqq.); also whether it was allowable for Christians to eat meat offered in sacrifice to idols (viii. 1); further, concerning spiritual gifts, their proper value and use, especially the γλώσσαις λαλεῖν (xii. 1); and once more, concerning a collection which was set on foot in behalf of their poor brethren in Judea (xvi. 1). St. Paul had also heard from other sources—partly from the conveyers of the letter, and partly from those of the house of Chloe—further particulars as to the condition of the Corinthian Church which greatly troubled and distressed him, concerning the divisions among them, and the disorder prevailing in their meetings for worship, especially at the holy Supper (xi. 18); concerning the unchaste practices tolerated within the Church,—in particular, one very offensive case, that of a person living in adultery with his father's wife, his stepmother (v. 1 sqq.); further, that in their private quarrels they had had recourse to the heathen tribunals (vi. 1 sqq.). In our first Epistle to the Corinthians the apostle refers to all these things; and thus it is fuller and more varied in its subject-matter than any other of the Pauline letters, or indeed of the N. T. epistles. This truly grand epistle serves as a type and pattern in dealing with the multifarious tendencies, relations, and disorders of the Christian Church, almost all of which have their counterpart in the Corinthian Church, and are continually repeated with various modifications at various times.

As to the mode of sending the letter, a comparison of ch. iv. 17 and xvi. 10 leads to the probable inference that St. Paul entrusted it for delivery to the care of Timothy. These passages are commonly taken as intimating that Timothy was sent off before the epistle. This is the opinion of Neander and De Wette (§ 132, *c*). The latter supposes that the apostle sent the epistle by the three messengers named in ch. xvi. 17 [so also Ewald, *Apost. Zeitalter*, p. 480]. Upon this supposition, Timothy's journey from Ephesus must have been made but a very short time before, because in the second of the texts referred to it is intimated that he had not yet arrived, and certainly had not left them again before the letter came. To me, however, it seems very probable, judging from the way in which St. Paul expresses himself, that he had it in his mind to send Timothy as the conveyer of the epistle. It is very generally supposed (and by De Wette) that this mission of Timothy is the same with that mentioned in Acts xix. 22, where we read that, before going himself to Macedonia and Achaia, he sent two of his fellow-labourers, Timothy and Erastus, from Ephesus thither. The probability is, however, that this last-named mission took place subsequently, at least after Timothy had returned again to Ephesus, having fulfilled his mission to Corinth. It is at least evident from 1 Cor. xvi. 11 that Paul expected him in Ephesus before he himself left.

The *authenticity* of this epistle has never been disputed, not even by Baur and his school, [but by Bruno Bauer, 1851]. Besides the internal marks of genuineness which the character of the epistle presents, the testimony of tradition and of the earliest writers is unanimous in its favour; for we not only find unmistakeable traces of a knowledge of it in the apostolic Fathers, in Polycarp and Ignatius, but Clemens Romanus (*ad Cor.* xlvii.) expressly quotes it as a work of St. Paul.

THE SECOND EPISTLE TO THE CORINTHIANS.

§ 149.

This epistle, as we have already seen, was written in Macedonia, during the journey from Ephesus to Achaia, and St. Paul had not been again at Corinth in the interval between it and our first epistle. This is generally admitted; and as far as I can see, there can be no doubt of it. It is confirmed by the fact that in many of the old Greek MSS. and versions Philippi is named in the postscript as the place of writing; and this is not improbable, for St. Paul seems to have written the letter soon after his coming into Macedonia; and after calling at Troas, to which place he came from Ephesus (ch. ii. 12), it is very likely that he would at once go to Philippi to visit the Church there, which was the dearest and most closely attached to him of all the Macedonian Churches, and that there he would stay some time.

It is commonly supposed that our 2d Corinthians was the

first letter which the apostle wrote to Corinth since his sending our 1st Corinthians. I, on the contrary, have endeavoured to show [1] that between our two epistles there intervened another letter now lost. This opinion has hitherto received but little favour;[2] still I cannot but think that I am right, and that, to say the least, the opinion is in the highest degree probable. I will here state my reasons for it.

(*a.*) In our second epistle repeated reference is made to a previous letter of the apostle to the Corinthians, both as to its contents and to its effect upon them, which must immediately have preceded this our epistle; and our thoughts naturally turn to our first epistle. But our first epistle by no means answers to the description. For example, in 2 Cor. ii. 3, 4, St. Paul says, "Out of much affliction and anguish

---

[1] *Theol. Stud. u. Krit.* 1830, pp. 625–632.

[2] OLSHAUSEN (*Bibl. Commentar*, iii. 1) acknowledges himself as much inclined towards my opinion, and BILLROTH (*Comment. zu den Br. des P. a. d. Cor.*, Leipz. 1833, p. xxxiv. note) confesses that he has long wavered about adopting it himself. EWALD has declared himself in its favour, *Jahrb.* ii. 227–229, and *Sendschr. des Paulus*, p. 227 sq. Most scholars, however, have declared themselves against it: *e.g.* J. G. MÜLLER (*de tribus P. itineribus Corinthum susceptis de epistolisque ad eosdem non deperditis*, Basel 1831), WURM (*Tüb. Zeitschr. f. Theol.* 1833, i. 66), RÜCKERT (*die Br. P. an die Kor. bearb.* 2 vols., Leipz. 1836), DE WETTE, BAUR, REUSS; also WIESELER, pp. 365–370. [BLEEK's opinion is espoused by NEANDER (*Gesch. der Pflanzung*, 4th ed.; and in his *Auslegg. d. beiden Br. an die Kor.*, edited by BEYSCHLAG, Berlin 1859), though he had previously rejected it (see *Planting and Training*, Bohn's ed. pp. 266–269). Cf. also CREDNER, p. 371. CONYBEARE AND HOWSON (*Life and Epp. of St. Paul*, ii. 105, n.) allow that "it is not impossible that Titus may have carried another letter to the Corinthians." ALFORD (vol. ii. *Prolegg.*) says concerning Bleek's opinion: "This ingenious conjecture, while it might serve to clear up some expressions in 2 Cor. ii. 1–4, which seem too strong for the first epistle, can perhaps hardly be admitted in the absence of any allusion whatever of a clearer character. All we say is, it *may* have been so; and after all that has been written on the visits of Timotheus and Titus, we shall hardly arrive nearer the truth than a happy conjecture." Bp. ELLICOTT, in Smith's *Dictionary of the Bible*, says: "There is a show of plausibility in the supposition of Bleek; but, as has been justly urged by Meyer, there is quite enough of severity in the first epistle (consider ch. iv. 18–21, v. 2 sqq., vi. 5–8, xi. 17) to call forth the apostle's affectionate anxiety."—TR.]

of heart I wrote unto you with many tears; not that ye should be grieved, but that ye might know the love which I have more abundantly unto you;" and this is commonly taken as referring to 1 Cor. v. 1–8, where the apostle censures their connivance towards the incestuous person. 2 Cor. vii. is accordingly taken to refer to the effect of this censure upon the Corinthians. But 2 Cor. vii. 12 presents a serious difficulty in the way of this interpretation. St. Paul there says, that what he had written he wrote οὐχ ἕνεκεν τοῦ ἀδικήσαντος (Lachm. B. al. add. ἀλλ') οὐδὲ ἕνεκεν τοῦ ἀδικηθέντος. Here ἀδικηθέντος cannot (as Billroth and others think) be taken as neuter ("neither on account of the individual sinner, nor of the sin committed by him"), but only as masculine, "neither on account of the injurer, nor of the person injured;" *i.e.* he had no personal motive in writing, he had regard neither to the one nor the other personally. It is accordingly quite unnatural to take "the person injured" as meaning the father of the incestuous person, as most interpreters do: it must refer (as Lachmann's reading ἀλλ' οὐδέ so strikingly brings out the antithesis, but even without the ἀλλ') to the apostle himself. The ἀδικήσας so opposed the apostle that he was regarded as his personal enemy, directly injuring him; and what the apostle had written might have been taken as if it had been directed against that offender personally, or at least for his own sake, and in his own vindication. But any such personal reference is quite inapplicable to the case of the incestuous person named in 1 Cor. v.; and what St. Paul says of him, strong as his language is, could not possibly be construed as implying anything that concerned him personally, or affected his reputation. The reference becomes plain, if we suppose that something further had occurred after the writing of our 1st Corinthians—that after that epistle had been received the individual censured had persevered in his criminal conduct, in open defiance and contempt of the apostle's censure, and had not been immediately checked and condemned by the Church; so that St. Paul was obliged to write again, still more strongly, and even beseechingly, to urge the Church to take the matter up; and this had had a wholesome effect upon the man. Calumniators and opponents might easily have interpreted the apostle's severity as arising from personal pique, as if he had felt himself personally injured by the contemptuous disobedience of the incestuous person. Thus we can better understand the language he uses in 2 Cor. ii. 3, 4 regarding the letter he had written, as applying to a letter written after our first epistle in much stronger and severer terms, and dwelling almost exclusively upon this one special subject. Wieseler allows that I am right in affirming that the apostle's statements in 2 Cor. ii. 3, 4 cannot well refer to our 1st Corinthians, but he thinks that they have reference to the other epistle preceding our 1st Corinthians. But this is quite inadmissible; for that earlier epistle (as we have seen), though it warned the Corinthians to withdraw from πόρνοις, did not treat of that particular case: for the manner in which St. Paul speaks of it in 1 Cor. v. 1, 2 (ἀκούεται ἐν ὑμῖν πορνεία καὶ τοιαύτη πορνεία, κ.τ.λ.) shows that he had only then heard of it. It is clear that the statements in 2d Corinthians refer not to an epistle written long before, but to the last which he had sent; and if this cannot have been our 1st Corinthians, it must have been one written subsequent thereto.

(*b.*) Other passages in 2d Corinthians show that certain opponents of the apostle at Corinth charged him with fickleness and cowardice, on account of his not coming, as if he would not venture to come to them. It is clear that St. Paul had told them of his design to come very soon, and that he had altogether changed his plans; and his opponents made this the ground of a charge against him.[1] This also leads us to the conclusion that the apostle had thus expressed his intention in a letter written subsequently to our 1st Corinthians, for this last-named epistle contains nothing whatever furnishing any ground or pretext for such a reproach; neither does it contain anything that could be laid hold of to give plausibility to the accusation that he spoke of himself, or

---

[1] See 2 Cor. i. 15 sqq., ii. 1 sqq., x. 9 sqq.,—passages which show that during the interval between our two epistles St. Paul could not, as Ewald supposes (see § 146), have been himself to Corinth and back.

boasted of his own authority,—charges which evidently had reference to some statements of his in the previous letter: see 2 Cor. iii. 1, v. 12, 13, xi. 16 sqq. Our 1st Corinthians furnishes no pretext for such a charge; but we may suppose that the apostle, troubled at the account he had received of the continued inaction of the Corinthians, and neglect of the warnings and instructions addressed to them in our 1st Corinthians, wrote again, insisting much more strongly upon his personal claims as an inspired apostle.

(c.) When St. Paul wrote 1st Corinthians, Timothy either had been shortly before sent by him to Corinth, or, as is more likely, was entrusted with that epistle, and commissioned to convey it to them (see § 148). St. Paul, moreover, expected him back again before going himself to Corinth (1 Cor. xvi. 11). Now, when St. Paul wrote 2d Corinthians, Timothy was again with him in Macedonia (2 Cor. i. 1). When and where he joined him we are not told, nor is any intimation given that Timothy had brought any tidings which occasioned the writing of our second epistle. Instead of this, Titus here appears as having come from Corinth to Paul, and as having been the bearer of tidings which prompted the apostle to write (2 Cor. vii. 6 sqq.); and it further appears that St. Paul had not met with him accidentally or unexpectedly, but that he had himself sent Titus to Corinth (2 Cor. vii. 14, xii. 18), and had waited for him at Troas, on his journey from Ephesus to Macedonia (ii. 12, 13). Various explanations of these facts have been proposed. (a) Wieseler divides our second epistle into two parts. The first half was written (ch. i. 1–vii. 1), he thinks, before the apostle met Titus; and the tidings from Corinth to which he in this portion refers, he had received through Timothy. But the second half was (he thinks) written after the meeting with Titus, who had likewise been despatched by Paul from Ephesus to Corinth, after Timothy's departure, and before his return. But the first half of 2d Corinthians does not contain the slightest hint that the tidings received had been brought by Timothy, or were in any respect other than those to which the latter half refers; on the contrary, ch. ii. 5 shows clearly that St. Paul had already received the more favourable news as to the effect of his admonitions upon the evil-doer, of which Titus was the bearer. (β) Others, *e.g.* Schrader, Müller, Billroth, think that Titus had been sent to Corinth before Timothy, and before 1st Corinthians was written, to look after the collection (2 Cor. viii. 6). But apart from the fact (which De Wette, § 133, *a*, note *a*, also observes) that in this case we should have expected to find him mentioned in 1 Cor. xvi., we cannot on this theory understand how it comes to pass that St. Paul makes no allusion whatever to the tidings which Timothy had brought him. (γ) Others, again, *e.g.* Schmidt, Bertholdt, Neander (ed. 3), Credner, Rückert, suppose that Timothy had not been to Corinth, but that Titus had gone in his stead. This is certainly a possible conjecture; but taking all the facts we have named under (*c*) together, and even omitting the considerations (*a*) and (*b*), it seems much more probable that Timothy had really been to Corinth, had brought thither our 1st Corinthians, had discharged the trust committed to him, and, according to the apostle's pre-arrangement, had returned to Ephesus, and had been then despatched with Erastus to Macedonia. Furthermore, that St. Paul, after Timothy's return from Corinth, sent Titus thither with further directions, and with another letter, the effect of which he wished to know before going himself to Corinth; and that, accordingly, he did meet the returning Titus, not indeed, as he had hoped, at Troas, but in Macedonia.

§ 150.

Accordingly, we take the state of the case, and the course of events as they actually occurred, to have been as follows. Our first epistle seems not to have been favourably received by the various parties in the Corinthian Church; and in particular, the apostle's rebuke of their indifference with reference to the incestuous person seems to have failed of its purpose: the man, in contempt of the apostle's injunction, maintained the criminal relationship, and was not hindered in his conduct by the Church. Timothy brought back this information to St. Paul, who at once wrote a much stronger letter bearing expressly upon this matter, upon the indifference manifested by the Church, and their neglect of his apostolic directions. In this letter he endeavoured to establish his apostolic authority against those Judaizing opponents who called it in question, and he had occasion consequently to speak of himself personally. He further told them that, under the circumstances, he would not come to them so soon as he had intended. In 1 Cor. xvi. 5 sqq. he had intimated his purpose to come to them through Macedonia, and in this new (and now lost) letter he probably said that he had intended to come to Corinth first (see 2 Cor. i. 15), but that he had changed his mind. This letter he sent by Titus, who was accompanied by another Christian brother (2 Cor. xii. 18). Hereupon he made the journey by way of Troas to Macedonia, whither a short time before he had sent Timothy and Erastus (Acts xix. 22). We have no means of knowing whether this journey was taken at Pentecost, as he had purposed (1 Cor. xvi. 8), or somewhat later. But we can easily imagine how anxious Paul must have felt to know the effect of that severe letter upon the Corinthians, and to receive tidings concerning them. Upon his arrival in Macedonia, Titus came to him, and his account was upon the whole encouraging. The Christians at Corinth had most of them taken the fatherly admonition in good part, and had excluded the incestuous person from their fellowship, though it does not clearly appear that he was formally expelled (2 Cor. ii. 6 sqq.). The behaviour of the Church towards that offender had a beneficial effect upon him, and had brought him to bitter repentance on account of his crime. Possibly the Church conveyed this information to the apostle by a letter entrusted to the care of Titus; but, at the same time, the Judaizing adversaries of the apostle did not hesitate to make use of this last letter of his against him, depreciating and finding fault with him as a man who vainly prided himself upon possessing an authority belonging only to the apostles at Jerusalem, and who had not the courage to lay claim to that authority in person, but only ventured to do so in his letters. With these facts the contents of our 2d Corinthians, written soon after the arrival of Titus, fully correspond. It also is written in a high-toned and earnest strain. He now begs the Corinthians to show forgiving kindness to the offender, lest he should be driven to despair. But the greater part of the epistle is apologetic, asserting the personal relationship and position of the apostle, especially towards the Corinthian Church; for he felt himself called upon to disprove the accusations of his calumniators, and to vindicate and establish his apostolic authority, which they had called in question, and had endeavoured to undermine.

The apostle sent this epistle also by Titus, who was accompanied by two other brethren (viii. 18, 19, 22), one of whom was perhaps the same person who had accompanied him before, and the other (ver. 22, τὸν ἀδελφὸν ἡμῶν) St. Paul's brother, as Rückert thinks,—an opinion not at once to be rejected. St. Paul expresses his earnest wish that the collection for the saints in Judea should be made among them by these his chosen deputies, so that upon his arrival all would be so far settled, and he would have no reason to be ashamed of them before the Macedonians who were to accompany him. He then admonishes the Corinthians in very strong and earnest words. By this section the epistle is divided into three distinct parts: 1. Ch. i.-vii. treat of his personal relations towards them; and in vi. 14–vii. 1 he warns them against unworthy fellowship with unbelievers, meaning probably connections in marriage among them. 2. Ch. viii. ix. concern the collection. 3. Ch. x.-xiii., wherein he again treats of his personal relations generally, and especially to the Corinthians, and of the falsehoods which his opponents had taken pains to circulate against him. Possibly, when he had written the greater part of the letter, he heard something more from Titus, or some one else, which prompted him to resume his remarks upon his personal circumstances, and to express himself still more strongly than he had done in the beginning of the epistle. But there is no occasion whatever to question the *integrity* of the epistle, or to suppose that two or more letters are in it blended together into one, as Semler, Mich. Weber, and others, have on these and other grounds

supposed (see, on the other side, Bertholdt, vi. 3378-3395).
Nor is there any sufficient reason for supposing, with Ewald
(*Sendschr. des P.* pp. 231, 282), that the section ch. vi. 14–
vii. 7 is a later interpolation from another epistle addressed
to a Church of Gentile Christians by some subsequent apostolic writer. Still less can the *authenticity* of this epistle be
called in question, for it belongs to those Pauline Epistles
whose genuineness has never been disputed. Of all the
epistles of St. Paul which have come down to us, this is
written in the highest tone and strongest feeling, and for this
very reason presents many difficulties to the expositor.

§ 151.

Our investigations thus lead us to the conclusion that at
least two epistles of St. Paul to the Corinthians have been
lost. We have a poor substitute for these in two *uncanonical*
letters,—one professing to be from the Corinthians to St.
Paul, and the other his reply. They are both extant in
Armenian. These were not known in Europe till the beginning of the seventeenth century, and they have been
variously printed; in Armenian and English by Aucher
(**Grammar, Armenian and English*, Venice 1819), in a
German translation by W. F. Rink (*das Sendschr. d. Kor.
an den Ap. P. und dritte Sendschr. P. an die Kor.*, etc.,
Heidelb. 1823), who endeavours in vain to prove them
genuine. In reply to him, Ullmann has established their
spuriousness, *Ueber den . . . dritten Brief P. an die Kor.*, etc.,
reprinted from the *Heidelb. Jahrbb.* 1823. The letters are
very unimportant and very short. The Corinthians ask St.
Paul to come to them in order to refute certain false teachers,
Simon (Magus) and Cleobus, whose doctrines are stated;
and St. Paul, in his reply, endeavours to refute these errors,
but in a manner quite unworthy of the great apostle. We
cannot determine when these letters were written, nor in
what language they were originally composed; probably they
never existed in Greek.

THE EPISTLE TO THE ROMANS.

§ 152.

This epistle was written, subsequently to 2d Corinthians, from Achaia, and probably in the city of Corinth, whither St. Paul had returned from Macedonia (from whence he had sent 2d Corinthians), and therefore during the three months' sojourn in Achaia to which reference is made in Acts xx. 1, 2. These facts are evident from Rom. xv. 23–28, where it is stated that he purposed journeying to Jerusalem "to minister to the saints" there, and to convey to them a certain contribution made in their behalf by the Christians of Macedonia and Achaia. This is the collection which the apostle speaks of in 1 Cor. xvi. 1–3 and 2 Cor. viii. ix., where he exhorts the Corinthians to contribute liberally, and says that, if their contribution was worthy of them and of the object, he would himself convey it to Jerusalem. When the Epistle to the Romans was written, this collection was already completed, so that the letter must have been written after the apostle's coming to Achaia, and indeed after he had spent some time there. From the passage referred to, it is likewise in the highest degree probable that he wrote *before* his journey from Achaia to Jerusalem, which took him again through Macedonia, and not in the course of that journey, or while passing through Macedonia. This is confirmed by the following passages: (*a*) xvi. 1, 2, where he commends to his readers Phoebe, "a deaconess of the Church which is at Cenchrea." Cenchrea was the eastern port of Corinth, and this leads us to infer that the apostle was, when he wrote, in that neighbourhood. (*b*) xvi. 23, where St. Paul sends greeting to his readers from Erastus, whom he had sent with Timothy into Macedonia before his departure from Ephesus (Acts xix. 22). St. Paul describes Erastus in our epistle as ὁ οἰκονόμος τῆς πόλεως,—an expression which implies that the city in which he was, was one well known and distinguished, and thus leading us to think of Corinth; and this again harmonizes with 2 Tim. iv. 20, "Ἔραστος ἔμεινεν ἐν Κορίνθῳ.

(c) xvi. 23, where he sends salutations from a certain Gaius; and this was doubtless the Gaius mentioned in 1 Cor. i. 14 as one of those members of the Corinthian Church whom the apostle himself baptized. In harmony with this are other data of the letter: *e.g.*, (a) according to xvi. 21, Timothy was with him, for Timothy was with him when 2d Corinthians (i. 1) was written, and with him still upon his journey to Macedonia, and his return to Asia, Acts xx. 4; (β) according to xvi. 21, one Sosipater was with him, who was probably the same with the Sopater often mentioned in the Acts as one of St. Paul's companions upon his return to Asia; again, (γ) according to xv. 30-32, in looking forward to his visit to Judea, he feared persecution on the part of the unbelieving Jews there,—a fear which the apostle entertained upon that journey from Achaia to Jerusalem, according to the narrative of the Acts (see especially xx. 22-24). It is by no means out of harmony with this, (δ) that Aquila and Priscilla, who were still at Ephesus when 1st Corinthians (xvi. 19) was written, were now, when the Epistle to the Romans was penned, at Rome (Rom. xvi. 3): they might very well in the interval have returned to Rome, where they before had resided, and whence they had been driven by the edict of Claudius (Acts xviii. 2).[1]

§ 153.

The epistle is addressed to the Christians at Rome collectively (Rom. i. 7); and from the tenor of the letter as a whole, as well as from particular passages in it, it is clear that they were partly Jewish and partly Gentile believers. We have no trustworthy evidence enabling us to decide when and how Christianity was first introduced into Rome.[2] The

---

[1] H. E. G. PAULUS (*de originibus ep. P. ad Rom.*, Jena 1801, and *des Ap. P. Lehrbriefe a. d. Gal. u. Römerchristen*, etc., Heidelb. 1831, p. 342) infers from Rom. xv. 19 that the epistle must have been written in a city of Illyricum; but this is by no means a necessary inference from the verse referred to.

[2] Many (especially Roman Catholic theologians) regard the Apostle Peter as the founder of the Roman Church, and suppose that he visited Rome in the early years of the reign of Claudius. But we may with

probability is, that it was not conveyed thither by any special or prominent teachers or missionaries sent for the purpose, but that residents in the city, Jews and Gentiles, became acquainted with it, and were converted elsewhere, and upon their return made converts among their friends. This may have been the case especially with several of the Jews who were driven from Rome by the edict of Claudius, and who, when this edict was either forgotten or revoked, returned again, or went to reside there for the first time. They may have been converted to Christianity partly by St. Paul's preaching or by that of his companions, or in some of the Churches planted by him, and partly in other places, *e.g.* in Jerusalem itself. From the salutations in ch. xvi. it is evident that there were then in Rome a considerable number of disciples and labourers in the Lord's kingdom who were personally acquainted with the apostle, though he had never been to Rome himself, and who most probably had been converted to the truth of the gospel elsewhere than in Italy. Thus, for example, Aquila and Priscilla (ver. 3) were most probably brought to the knowledge of the truth by the Apostle Paul himself during his first residence at Corinth; so also with Epenetus, ver. 5, τὸν ἀγαπητόν μου, ὅς ἐστιν ἀπαρχὴ τῆς Ἀσίας; again (ver. 7), Andronicus and Junias, or Junia, relations of Paul's "who were in Christ before" him, and had been his fellow-prisoners, and must have been distinguished among the furtherers of gospel truth; ver. 9, Urbanus, and ver. 13, Rufus, whose mother St. Paul calls his own likewise, who was probably the son of the Simon of Cyrene mentioned in Mark xv. 31. All these, with others who had obtained their first knowledge of Christianity among Jewish Christians, and had adopted that aspect of it, would succeed in winning converts among their friends in Rome to the faith of Christ; and we can easily understand how this would be specially the case in such a city as Rome, where many at the time were inclined towards a new religion, and some especially to Judaism.

certainty infer from the epistle before us, that when it was written neither Peter nor indeed any of the apostles had visited Rome.

The manner in which Christianity was thus introduced into Rome, and gained a footing there in various quarters, will account for the probable fact that the believers there were not for a considerable time united formally into a regularly organized Christian fellowship. This probably was not the case even down to the time when our epistle was composed, as J. E. Ch. Schmidt has supposed. There is no mention (as in the Epistles to the Thessalonians, Corinthians, and Galatians) of an ἐκκλησία in Rome, or, as in the Epistle to the Philippians, of the faithful σὺν ἐπισκόποις καὶ διακόνοις, but simply (i. 7) "to all that be in Rome, beloved of God, called to be saints;" and there are no references in the course of the epistle to any settled Church organization or Church discipline. The believers there were probably wont to meet in private houses for mutual edification, at the house of Aquila for example (xvi. 5), and in the dwellings of others, as is intimated in the words of xvi. 14, 15, " Salute Asyncritus," etc., "and the brethren which are with them;" "Salute Philologus," etc., "and all the saints which are with them." But they had not yet formed themselves into a regularly constituted Church, with its bishops, or elders, and deacons. The account, moreover, of St. Paul's arrival in Rome given us in Acts xxviii. makes it very probable that even then, though there were many Christians in Rome, there was no regularly constituted Church. Ewald[1] indeed is of opinion that a Christian Church had already, and some time previously, been formed; but the considerations and references which he adduces do not sanction his view,—not certainly, *e.g.*, xiii. 11, to which he specially refers.

The believers in Rome were probably both Jews and Gentiles, for the apostle sometimes expressly addresses the one or the other separately.[2] But they were divided, not simply on the ground of parentage and nationality, but in virtue of the different views they took of Christian truth. The Gen-

---

[1] *Sendschr. des P. S.* 315.

[2] The Gentile believers, for instance, in ch. xi. 13, 28-30; see also i. 5, 6, 13, vi. 20-22; similarly in ix. 1 sqq., x. 1 sqq., xv. 14 sqq. The Jewish believers in ch. ii. 17, iv. 1, vii. 1, 4 sqq.; comp. ii. 1 sqq., iii. 9.

tile Christians, for the most part, together with some Jewish believers, such as Aquila and Priscilla, who had been in close intercourse with St. Paul, adopted the broader and freer views of this apostle as to the relation subsisting between the Jewish law and the gospel. Most of the Jewish Christians, on the other hand, together with some of their Gentile brethren, adopted stricter and narrower views, and regarded obedience to the Jewish law as necessary to a full participation in the blessings of the kingdom of God.

Olshausen is certainly wrong in supposing that, when the Epistle to the Romans was written, these parties were not in existence among them, and that there was not any strong tendency to Judaizing views. But Baur[1] equally errs in affirming that the Gentile Christians there formed only a very small and insignificant portion of the fellowship, and that the few Gentiles who were among them partook of the prevailing Judaizing and Ebionite character. The passages to which we have referred show very plainly that St. Paul regarded the majority of his readers as Gentiles, who had not therefore been received into the Jewish Church by the rite of circumcision, nor had yielded to the Judaizing Christians even so far as to comply with their prejudices concerning meats, and their laws with regard to eating generally. This may fairly be inferred from ch. xiv. 1 sqq., 20 sqq., xv. 1, 2.

§ 154.

The two opposite tendencies to which we have referred were not so fully developed, nor were the parties respectively adopting them so clearly divided, as in the Corinthian Church. But there were among them clashings of opinion, and dissensions: those who were of Judaizing tendencies kept themselves aloof from their more liberal and free-thinking brethren, fearing that by closer intimacy with them they would be defiled; while the more liberal Gentile Christians would in turn look down upon and despise their Jewish brethren. The apostle had probably been for some time aware of this state

[1] In a dissertation in the *Tüb. Zeitschr.* 1836, pp. 59–178; and still more fully in his *Paulus*, pp. 332–416.

of things, and would have ample opportunity of hearing, during his stay in Corinth, how matters were going on in Rome, for there was a large and continual traffic between these two great centres of commerce. He would, moreover, be in correspondence with Aquila and Priscilla, and would be informed of the state of things in Rome by them; and by others likewise, as the salutations in Rom. xvi. show. No sooner had the gospel gained a footing in Rome, than the apostle with sagacious eye discerned the great importance of the Church in such a centre, and of the tendencies which it adopted as influencing the Church of Christ at large, and how desirable it was that the Christians there should not be disturbed and rent in sunder by internal disputes and party strifes. It was only natural that he should have a strong desire to visit Rome, and that he should plan to do so (ch. i. 10 sqq., 15, xv. 22). But this he could not at once accomplish, for he considered himself bound to convey the collection made in Macedonia and Achaia to Jerusalem. Still he entertained the purpose of making a journey from Jerusalem as far even as Spain (ch. xv. 23 sqq.; Acts xix. 21). It was accordingly most natural that he should now, on his way to Jerusalem, avail himself of the opportunity afforded by the intended journey of Phoebe the deaconess to Rome, to put himself in communication with the Christians there, and to send them a letter containing his apostolic instructions and exhortations. The greater part of the epistle presents the essence of the gospel objectively in its relation both to Judaism and to the world at large; but the apostle evidently has in his mind, as he writes, the false views entertained upon these subjects, not only by the Jews, but by many Jewish Christians even in Rome. He endeavours to show his kinsfolk according to the flesh, who could not understand how it was that the majority of those received into the new kingdom of God were Gentiles, while the great bulk of the Jewish nation was excluded, that this was only natural and right. The fact he tells them—on the one hand that the Gentiles were received without obedience to the Jewish law and without circumcision, and on the other hand that the Jewish nation remained without—was by no means contrary to God's justice and faithfulness, but that the Jews were self-excluded by their wilful disobedience, and in accordance with the original conditions of the covenant, and the prophecies concerning them. This is the main theme of the epistle; and to this end the main doctrines of the depravity of man by nature, of divine grace, and of justification by faith alone, are successively expounded. Besides this doctrinal and apologetic design, the epistle has an harmonizing and conciliatory aim; for the apostle earnestly and affectionately exhorts the more liberal thinkers and the Gentile Christians not to conduct themselves haughtily towards their weaker brethren, reminding them that it is through the grace of God alone that they have become partakers of His kingdom, and that God's purposes towards Israel were still purposes of love, that they likewise should after all be " graffed in." They must not therefore use their liberty to grieve or offend the consciences of their brethren.

The epistle as a whole thus divides itself into three parts. I. Ch. i.-viii., containing a doctrinal and argumentative exposition of the relation of faith to the law, and of justification by faith in Christ alone. II. Ch. ix.-xi., on the relation subsisting between the Jews and the Gentiles, and the connection of both with the kingdom of God. III. Ch. xii. sqq. are of a more practical bearing, containing several exhortations to the exercise of Christian dispositions and the practice of Christian virtues; obedience to the powers that be; mutual love, and the legitimate use of Christian liberty; not to judge and condemn one another; not to despise our weaker brethren; not wantonly to put a stumbling-block or an occasion of offence in our brother's way. These exhortations bring us to ch. xv. 13. What follows is of a more personal nature,—apologies for his freedom of speech in writing, salutations, etc., xv. 14–xvi. fin.

St. Paul dictated the epistle to one Tertius, who describes himself (xvi. 22) as the writer of the letter. Its contents are less varied than those of 1st Corinthians, but it is by no means behind that epistle in its true nobleness and value, and in its significance as bearing upon the doctrine of the evangelical Church. Luther, in his preface to this epistle, calls it "by far the noblest book in the New Testament, containing the purest and clearest gospel, which every Christian man should not only know by heart word for word, but daily study and feed upon as the daily bread of his soul."

Its genuineness has been disputed by an Englishman named Evanson (sometime Rector of Tewkesbury, *ob.* 1805), in a work bearing date 1792, and also by Bruno Bauer in 1852; but this opinion has gained no countenance whatever. The genuineness of the Epistle to the Romans cannot be disputed on any reasonable grounds; it is conclusively established both by its internal character and by external witnesses. It never was suspected in the early Church; on the contrary, we have the earliest traces of its being recognised and used as a work of the Apostle Paul's in Clemens Romanus and Polycarp, and even in the Epistle to the Hebrews, and perhaps in the first Epistle of St. Peter.

As to the last two chapters, some commentators (Semler, Eichhorn, and others) have put forth a theory with various modifications, to the effect that this portion (or at least ch. xvi. 1-20), though proceeding from the Apostle Paul, was not originally written in connection with the epistle itself, and was primarily addressed not to Christians in Rome, but to Christians of some other place. [The following are the arguments used in support of this: 1. The different places in which the doxology (xvi. 25-27) is found in different MSS. 2. The fact that both chapters are wanting in Marcion (according to Origen, *in loc.*); but see above, § 54. 3. The repeated farewell and concluding forms of expression, viz. besides the doxology, ch. xv. 33, xvi. 20, 24, which are' to be explained as successive endings of the epistle. 4. Friends and kinsfolk of St. Paul are named among the persons to whom salutations are sent in ch. xvi., and others whose residence we must almost with certainty suppose to have been elsewhere. But, as Bleek says in his Exegetical Lectures, *in loc.*, "remembering the position which Rome held at the time as the mistress city of the world and the centre of commerce, connected closely as it was with all other commercial cities, it is only natural to suppose that many Christians came to reside there for longer or shorter periods from other countries (see § 153). De Wette also has rightly remarked, that the mention of Narcissus (ver. 11) obviously obliges us to think of Rome. It would be very difficult to give any reasonable explanation of the supposed circumstance, that this section of it was originally intended for quite another place, but came to be joined on and interpolated into the Epistle to the Romans, and incorporated as part and parcel of it."] Ewald indeed, in his *Sendschr. des Paul.* pp. 428–430, still entertains this opinion. Concerning ch. xvi. 3-20 he says: "This is a fragment of an epistle written by Paul in Rome to the Ephesians, and by an inadvertency it has been appended to the Epistle to the Romans." Reuss also supposes that ch. xvi. 1 sqq. was originally addressed to the Ephesians. See also Dav. Schulz, *Stud. u. Krit.* 1829, pp. 609 sqq. Baur and Schwegler (ii. 123-125) consider ch. xv. xvi. as utterly spurious. Baur, indeed, finds in this section "a meagre repetition only of the statements of ch. xiv., and a poor dilution of Pauline views, the object of which was to win the Jewish Christians at Rome towards Pauline Christianity, by making concessions to them, and to represent St. Paul as connected by kinship and friendship with the notabilities of the early Roman Church." The arguments, however, on which these opinions are based are quite untenable and false; and the genuineness of these chapters, and their primary connection with this epistle, must be regarded as certain. See, in answer to Baur, Kling, *Stud. u. Krit.* 1837, pp. 309 sqq.

END OF VOL. I.

Works Published by T. & T. Clark, Edinburgh.

In demy 8vo, price 10s. 6d.,

THE REVELATION OF LAW IN SCRIPTURE:

CONSIDERED WITH RESPECT BOTH TO ITS OWN NATURE, AND TO ITS RELATIVE PLACE IN SUCCESSIVE DISPENSATIONS.

The Third Series of the 'Cunningham Lectures.'

By PATRICK FAIRBAIRN, D.D.,

AUTHOR OF 'TYPOLOGY OF SCRIPTURE,' ETC.

'The theme is one of the grandest that can engage the attention of the most exalted intelligences, and few of our readers, we presume, will be satisfied without reading for themselves this masterly and eloquent contribution to our theological literature, which will not only sustain, but augment the reputation the author has acquired as an eminent theologian.'—*British and Foreign Evangelical Review.*

'It is impossible to give any idea, in a bare notice like the present, of the masterly manner in which, with the true instinct of the metaphysical divine, and the profound scholarship of the biblical interpreter, Dr. Fairbairn establishes his successive positions, and overthrows those of his various antagonists.'—*Evangelical Witness.*

In crown 8vo, price 3s. 6d.,

THE FOUR EVANGELISTS;

WITH THE DISTINCTIVE CHARACTERISTICS OF THEIR GOSPELS.

By EDWARD A. THOMSON,

Minister of Free St. Stephen's, Edinburgh.

'We have not seen for a long time a volume more fresh and scholarly, more suggestive and beautiful.'—*Freeman.*

Just published, in crown 8vo, price 3s. 6d.,

APOLOGETICAL LECTURES ON JOHN'S GOSPEL.

By J. J. VAN OOSTERZEE, D.D.,

Professor of Theology, University of Utrecht.

I. THE AUTHENTICITY OF ST. JOHN'S GOSPEL.
II. JOHN AND THE SYNOPTIC GOSPELS.
III. JOHN'S ACCOUNT OF CHRIST'S MIRACLES.
IV. THE JOHANNEAN CHRIST.
V. TABLE OF APOLOGETICAL LITERATURE ON JOHN'S GOSPEL.

TRANSLATED, WITH ADDITIONS, BY J. F. HURST, D.D.,
AUTHOR OF THE 'HISTORY OF RATIONALISM.'

'The small volume before us is the production of a strong and cultivated mind. . . . . Nothing could be more able, seasonable, and complete.'—*Watchman.*

Works Published by T. and T. Clark, Edinburgh.

Ante-Nicene Christian Library.

A COLLECTION OF ALL THE WORKS OF THE FATHERS OF THE CHRISTIAN CHURCH, PRIOR TO THE COUNCIL OF NICÆA,

EDITED BY THE

REV. ALEXANDER ROBERTS, D.D.,

AND

JAMES DONALDSON, LL.D.

The Volumes of First Year:—THE APOSTOLIC FATHERS, in One Volume; JUSTIN MARTYR and ATHENAGORAS, in One Volume; TATIAN, THEOPHILUS, and the CLEMENTINE RECOGNITIONS, in One Volume; and CLEMENT OF ALEXANDRIA, Volume First;—and the Volumes of Second Year—IRENÆUS, Volume First; HIPPOLYTUS, Volume First; TERTULLIAN AGAINST MARCION, in One Volume; and CYPRIAN, Volume First;—and the Third Year is now ready, viz.: the Completion of IRENÆUS and HIPPOLYTUS, in One Volume, the First Volume of the Writings of ORIGEN, CLEMENT OF ALEXANDRIA, Volume II., and the First Volume of the Writings of TERTULLIAN.

The Subscription for First, Second, and Third Years is now due—£3, 3s.

The Subscription to the Series is at the rate of 21s. for Four Volumes when paid in advance (or 24s. when not so paid), and 10s. 6d. each Volume to Non-Subscribers.

'We give this series every recommendation in our power. The translation, so far as we have tested it, and that is pretty widely, appears to be thoroughly faithful and honest; the books are handsomely printed on good paper, and wonderfully cheap. . . . . . The work being done so well, can any one wonder at our hoping that the Messrs. Clark will find a large body of supporters?'—*Literary Churchman.*

'The work of the different translators has been done with skill and spirit. To all students of Church history and of theology these books will be of great value. . . . . . . We must add, also, that good print and good paper help to make these fit volumes for the library.'—*Church and State Review.*

'We promise our readers, those hitherto unaccustomed to the task, a most healthy exercise for mind and heart, if they procure these volumes and study them.'—*Clerical Journal.*

'For the critical care with which the translations have been prepared, the fulness of the introductory notices, the completeness of the collection, the beauty and clearness of the type, the accuracy of the indexes, they are incomparably the most satisfactory English edition of the Fathers we know.'—*Freeman.*

'It will be a reproach to the age if this scheme should break down for want of encouragement from the public.'—*Watchman.*

'The translations in these two volumes, as far as we have had opportunity of judging, are fairly executed.'—*Westminster Review.*

Works Published by T. & T. Clark, Edinburgh.

ANTE-NICENE CHRISTIAN LIBRARY. OPINIONS OF THE PRESS—*continued*.

'There is everything about these volumes to recommend them, and we hope they will find a place in the libraries of all our ministers and students.'—*English Independent*.

'The translation is at once good and faithful.'—*Ecclesiastic*.

'The translations are, in our opinion, and in respect of all places that we have carefully examined, thoroughly satisfactory for exact truth and happy expressiveness; and the whole business of the editing has been done to perfection.'—*Nonconformist*.

'The entire undertaking, as revealed in this instalment, is nobly conceived. . . . . We can most heartily congratulate the editors on this noble commencement of their voluminous responsible undertaking, and on the highly attractive appearance of these volumes; and we most heartily commend them to the notice of all theological students who have neither time nor opportunity to consult the original authorities.'—*British Quarterly Review*.

'The whole getting up of the work deserves warm commendation, and we conclude by again recommending it to notice, and expressing the hope that it will attain the wide circulation that it well deserves.'—*Record*.

'This series ought to have a place in every ministerial and in every congregational library, as well as in the collections of those laymen, happily an increasing number, interested in theological studies.'—*Christian Spectator*.

'If the succeeding volumes are executed in the same manner as the two now before us, the series will be one of the most useful and valuable that can adorn the library of the theological student, whether lay or cleric.'—*Scotsman*.

'The editing is all that it should be. The translation is well executed, perspicuously and faithfully, so far as we have examined. . . . . There is nothing in English to compete with it. Not only all ministers, but all intelligent laymen who take an interest in theological subjects, should enrich their libraries with this series of volumes.'—*Daily Review*.

MESSRS. CLARK have the honour to include in the Subscription List, amongst other distinguished names, both of Clergy and Laity—

His Grace the Archbishop of Canterbury.
His Grace the Archbishop of York.
His Grace the Archbishop of Armagh.
The Right Rev. the Bishop of Winchester.
The Right Rev. the Bishop of London.
The Right Rev. the Bishop of Oxford.
The Right Rev. the Bishop of Gloucester and Bristol.
The Right Rev. the Bishop of Ely.
The Right Rev. the Bishop of St. David's.
The Right Rev. the Bishop of Kilmore.
The Right Rev. the Bishop of Meath.
The Right Rev. the Bishop of Barbadoes.
The Right Rev. Bishop Eden of Moray.
The Right Rev. Bishop Wordsworth of St. Andrews.
The Rev. Principal, Cuddesdon College.
The Rev. President, Trinity College, Oxford.
The Rev. Canon Mansel, Christ Church.
The Rev. Canon Robinson, Bolton Abbey.
His Grace the Duke of Argyll.
His Grace the Duke of Buccleuch.
The Right Hon. the Marquis of Bute.
The Right Hon. the Earl of Strathmore.
The Right Hon. the Lord Justice-Clerk.

Works Published by T. & T. Clark, Edinburgh.

In Two Volumes 8vo, price 21s.,

THE CHURCH OF CHRIST:

A TREATISE ON THE NATURE, POWERS, ORDINANCES, DISCIPLINE, AND GOVERNMENT OF THE CHRISTIAN CHURCH.

BY THE LATE JAMES BANNERMAN, D.D.,
Professor of Apologetics and Pastoral Theology, New College, Edinburgh.

Edited by his Son.

In crown 8vo, price 3s. 6d.,

THE FOUR EVANGELISTS:

WITH THE DISTINCTIVE CHARACTERISTICS OF THEIR GOSPELS.

BY EDWARD A. THOMSON,
Minister of Free St. Stephen's, Edinburgh.

In demy 8vo, price 10s. 6d.,

THE DOCTRINE OF JUSTIFICATION:

AN OUTLINE OF ITS HISTORY IN THE CHURCH, AND OF ITS EXPOSITION FROM SCRIPTURE, WITH SPECIAL REFERENCE TO RECENT ATTACKS ON THE THEOLOGY OF THE REFORMATION.

The Second Series of the 'CUNNINGHAM LECTURES.'

BY JAMES BUCHANAN, D.D.,
Professor of Divinity, New College, Edinburgh.

'This is a work of no ordinary ability and importance. Quite apart from the opinions of the author, it has a high value, as fairly exhibiting the history of the doctrine of justification at large, but especially in the early church, the mediæval period, and the era of the Reformation. It gives us a most favourable opinion of the Scotch Theological Colleges, that works of such breadth of view, and exhibiting such solid learning, are produced by their professors, among whom Dr. Buchanan has long been distinguished.'—*Clerical Journal.*

'Our readers will find in them an able, clear, and comprehensive statement of the truth which forms the subject, clothed in language "suitable alike to an academic and to a popular audience." We only add, that the copious notes and references, after the manner of the Bampton and Hulsean Lectures, beside which it is worthy to stand, greatly enhance the value of the volume, and constitute it a capital handbook of the doctrine of justification.'—*Weekly Review.*

Works Published by T. & T. Clark, Edinburgh.

In One volume 8vo, price 10s. 6d.,

ANALYTICAL COMMENTARY ON THE EPISTLE TO THE ROMANS,

TRACING THE TRAIN OF THOUGHT BY THE AID OF PARALLELISM: WITH NOTES AND DISSERTATIONS ON THE PRINCIPAL DIFFICULTIES CONNECTED WITH THE EXPOSITION OF THE EPISTLE.

By Rev. JOHN FORBES, LL.D.

In addition to the Text, with Analytical Commentary and Notes on each Chapter, the work contains Dissertations on the 'Son of God,' chap. i. 4. On the 'Righteousness of God;' on the 'Glory of God,' chap. v. 5. On the 'Comparison between Adam and Christ.' On the expressions 'Died to Sin,' 'The Body of Sin,' of 'Death.' On the question 'Who is the husband?' chap. vii. 1-4. On the question 'Is the person described in chap. vii. 13-25, regenerate or unregenerate?' On the 'Meaning of Law,' in chap. vii. 21, 23, 25, viii. 2. On the 'Meaning of the Law of Sin and Death,' in chap. viii. 1-4. On 'Creation Groaning;' on the 'Love of God;' on 'Predestination and Free Will,' etc. etc.

Now ready, in crown 8vo, price 6s., Second Edition, revised and enlarged,

THE TRIPARTITE NATURE OF MAN:
SPIRIT, SOUL, AND BODY.

Applied to Illustrate and Explain the Doctrines of Original Sin, the New Birth, the Disembodied State, and the Spiritual Body.

By the Rev. J. B. HEARD, M.A.

CHAP. I. The Case Stated. II. The Psychology of Natural and Revealed Religion contrasted. III. The Account of the Creation of Man. IV. The Relation of Body to Soul in Scripture. V. Of the Relation of Soul and Spirit in Scripture. VI. Psyche and Pneuma in the light of Christian Experience. VII. The Unity under Diversity of the Three Parts of Man's Nature. VIII. Analogies from the Doctrine of the Trinity to the Trichotomy in Man considered. IX. Of the Pneuma as the Faculty which distinguishes Man from the Brute. X. The state of the Pneuma in Man since the Fall. XI. The Question of Traducianism and Creationism solved by the distinction between Soul and Spirit. XII. Conversion to God explained as the quickening of the Pneuma. XIII. The Question of the Natural Immortality of Psyche considered. XIV. Application of the Doctrine of the Trichotomy to discover the Principle of Final Rewards and Punishments. XV. Intermediate State. XVI. The Resurrection and Spiritual Body. XVII. Summary.

'It will be seen that Mr. Heard's theme is a noble and important one, and he has treated it in a way to afford a high intellectual treat to the Christian philosopher and divine.'—*Clerical Journal.*

'We must congratulate our author on having, from a theological point of view, established satisfactorily, and with much thought, the theory he advocates, and with having treated a subject generally considered dry and unreadable, in an attractive style.' —*Reader.*

In Two Volumes, crown 8vo, price 12s.,

BIBLICAL STUDIES ON ST. JOHN'S GOSPEL.
By Dr. BESSER.

'This book is full of warm and devout exposition. Luther's own rugged words start out, boulder-like, in almost every page.'—*News of the Churches.*

'We now call attention to the great merits of this volume. The character of this commentary is practical and devotional. There are often very exquisite devotional passages, and a vein of earnest piety runs through the whole work. We recommend the book most warmly to all.'—*Literary Churchman.*

'There is a quiet, simple, penetrating good sense in what Dr. Besser says, and withal a spirit of truly Christian devoutness, which the reader must feel to be in beautiful accordance with the inspired teachings which awaken it.'—*British Quarterly Review.*

Works Published by T. & T. Clark, Edinburgh.

In crown 8vo, price 6s.,
APOLOGETIC LECTURES ON
THE SAVING TRUTHS OF CHRISTIANITY.
By C. E. LUTHARDT, D.D., Leipsic.

The Nature of Christianity; Sin; Grace; The God-Man; The Work of Jesus Christ; The Trinity; The Church; Holy Scripture; The Means of Grace; The Last Things.

'We can assure our friends that the work is worthy of being studied.'—*Clerical Journal.*
'Dr. Luthardt is a profound scholar, but a very simple teacher, and expresses himself on the gravest matters with the utmost simplicity, clearness, and force.'—*Literary World.*

By the same Author, in crown 8vo, Second Edition, price 6s.,
THE FUNDAMENTAL TRUTHS OF CHRISTIANITY.

The Antagonistic Views of the World in their Historical Development; The Anomalies of Existence; The Personal God; The Creation of the World; Man; Religion; Revelation; History of Revelation—Heathenism and Judaism; Christianity in History; The Person of Jesus Christ.

'Luthardt is the very man to help those entangled in the thickets of modern rationalism; we do not know just such another book as this; it is devout, scholarly, clear, forcible, penetrating, comprehensive, satisfactory, admirable.'—*Evangelical Magazine.*
'We have never met with a volume better adapted to set forth the evidences of Christianity in a form suited to the wants of our day. The whole of the vast argument is illustrated by various and profound learning; there is no obscurity in the thoughts or in the style; the language is simple, the ideas clear, and the argument logical, and generally, to our mind conclusive.'—*Guardian.*

In crown 8vo, price 5s.,
THE CHURCH:
ITS ORIGIN, ITS HISTORY, ITS PRESENT POSITION.
By DRS. LUTHARDT, KAHNIS, and BRÜCKNER,
PROFESSORS OF THEOLOGY, LEIPSIC.

History of the Old Testament Revelation; The History of Jesus Christ; The History of the Apostolic Church; The Ancient Church; The Mediæval Church; The Modern Church; The Present Condition of the Church, The Present Tasks of the Church; The Present Prospects of the Church.

In crown 8vo, price 4s.,
THE SYMBOLICAL NUMBERS OF SCRIPTURE.
By REV. MALCOLM WHITE, M.A.

CHAP. I. The Time of the End. II. The Time and Times and Half a Time. III. The Numbers Three and a Half. IV. The Number of Beast 666. V. The Number Ten, and the Millennium. VI. The Related Numbers Seven, Three, Four, Twelve. VII. The Number Forty. VIII. The Numbers in the Book of Job. IX. The Number One hundred and fifty-three.

'We heartily thank Mr. White for his able, sober, and suggestive contribution to the right interpretation of the symbolical numbers of Scripture; for, without binding ourselves to every detail, we say with confidence, that he has rendered a good and needful service to the book "one jot or one tittle of which shall in no wise pass away till all be fulfilled."'—*London Weekly Review.*
'We have read this volume with more than ordinary interest, treating as it does of one of the greatest difficulties which the interpreters of Scripture have to encounter. . . . . We bear willing testimony to the general excellence of his work, which is well deserving of a place in the library of every biblical student.'—*Wesleyan Methodist Magazine.*
'The recommendation of Mr. White's researches is, that while he has no sympathy with this presumptuous prying into the future, he yet endeavours to give the right meaning to the symbolical numbers.'—*Clerical Journal.*

Works Published by T. & T. Clark, Edinburgh.

In Two Volumes, 8vo, price 21s.,

THE CHRISTIAN DOCTRINE OF SIN.

TRANSLATED FROM THE GERMAN OF DR. JULIUS MÜLLER,
Professor of Theology in the University of Berlin,

BY REV. WILLIAM URWICK, M.A.

This is *an entirely new translation* of Müller's inestimable work, from the latest edition. No pains have been spared to make it a thoroughly good and reliable translation.

In 8vo, price 10s. 6d.,

CHRISTIAN DOGMATICS.

A COMPENDIUM OF THE DOCTRINES OF CHRISTIANITY.

BY H. MARTENSEN, D.D.,
Bishop of Seeland, Denmark.

TRANSLATED BY REV. WILLIAM URWICK, M.A.

I. Introduction.   II. The Christian Idea of God.   III. The Doctrine of the Father.
IV. The Doctrine of the Son.   V. The Doctrine of the Spirit.

'Every reader must rise from its perusal stronger, calmer, and more hopeful, not only for the fortunes of Christianity, but of dogmatical theology.'—*British Quarterly Review.*

'He enters into the various subjects with consummate ability; and we doubt whether there is in any language a clearer or more learned work than this on systematic theology.'—*Irish Ecclesiastical Gazette.*

'We have seldom seen any theological work, by a foreign author, which combines so profound a reverence for the Bible with such vigour and originality of independent thought.'—*London Review.*

In demy 8vo, price 10s. 6d.,

THE DIVINE REVELATION.

BY THE LATE CARL AUGUST AUBERLEN, PH.D., D.D.,
Professor at Basle.

The Pauline Epistles; The Gospels; The Old Testament; The great intellectual Conflict in the Christian World; The elder Protestantism and Rationalism; The Defeat of Rationalism.

In demy 8vo, price 10s. 6d.,

SYSTEM OF CHRISTIAN ETHICS.

BY DR. CHR. A. VON HARLESS.

Works Published by T. & T. Clark, Edinburgh.

WORKS BY THE LATE WILLIAM CUNNINGHAM, D.D.,
PRINCIPAL AND PROFESSOR OF CHURCH HISTORY, NEW COLLEGE, EDINBURGH.
COMPLETE IN FOUR VOLUMES 8VO, PRICE £2, 2s.

In Two Volumes, demy 8vo, price 21s., Second Edition,

HISTORICAL THEOLOGY:
A REVIEW OF THE PRINCIPAL DOCTRINAL DISCUSSIONS IN THE CHRISTIAN CHURCH SINCE THE APOSTOLIC AGE.

Chapter 1. The Church; 2. The Council of Jerusalem; 3. The Apostles' Creed; 4. The Apostolical Fathers; 5. Heresies of the Apostolical Age; 6. The Fathers of the Second and Third Centuries, 7. The Church of the Second and Third Centuries; 8. The Constitution of the Church; 9. The Doctrine of the Trinity; 10. The Person of Christ; 11. The Pelagian Controversy; 12. Worship of Saints and Images; 13. The Civil and Ecclesiastical Authorities; 14. The Scholastic Theology; 15. The Canon Law; 16. Witnesses for the Truth during Middle Ages; 17. The Church at the Reformation; 18. The Council of Trent; 19. The Doctrine of the Fall; 20. Doctrine of the Will; 21. Justification; 22. The Sacramental Principle; 23. The Socinian Controversy; 24. Doctrine of the Atonement; 25. The Arminian Controversy; 26. Church Government; 27. The Erastian Controversy.

In demy 8vo (624 pages), price 10s. 6d., Second Edition,

THE REFORMERS AND THE THEOLOGY OF THE REFORMATION.

Chapter 1. Leaders of the Reformation; 2. Luther; 3. The Reformers and the Doctrine of Assurance; 4. Melancthon and the Theology of the Church of England; 5. Zwingle and the Doctrine of the Sacraments; 6. John Calvin; 7. Calvin and Beza; 8. Calvinism and Arminianism; 9. Calvinism and the Doctrine of Philosophical Necessity; 10. Calvinism and its Practical Application; 11. The Reformers and the Lessons from their History.

'This volume is a most magnificent vindication of the Reformation, in both its men and its doctrines, suited to the present time and to the present state of the controversy.'—*Witness.*

In One Volume, demy 8vo, price 10s. 6d.,

DISCUSSIONS ON CHURCH PRINCIPLES:
POPISH, ERASTIAN, AND PRESBYTERIAN.

Chapter 1. The Errors of Romanism; 2. Romanist Theory of Development; 3. The Temporal Sovereignty of the Pope; 4. The Temporal Supremacy of the Pope; 5. The Liberties of the Gallican Church; 6. Royal Supremacy in Church of England; 7. Relation between Church and State; 8. The Westminster Confession on Relation between Church and State; 9. Church Power; 10. Principles of the Free Church; 11. The Rights of the Christian People; 12. The Principle of Non-Intrusion; 13. Patronage and Popular Election.

In Two Volumes, demy 8vo, price 21s.,

INTRODUCTION TO THE PENTATEUCH:
AN INQUIRY, CRITICAL AND DOCTRINAL, INTO THE GENUINENESS, AUTHORITY, AND DESIGN OF THE MOSAIC WRITINGS.
BY REV. D. MACDONALD.

'The object of this work is very opportune at the present time. It contains a full review of the evidences, external and internal, for the genuineness, authenticity, and divine character of the Pentateuch. While it gives full space and weight to the purely critical and historical portions of the inquiry, its special attention is devoted to the certainly more profound and more conclusive considerations derived from the connection between the Pentateuch and the great scheme of revelation, of which it forms the basis; and this portion of the work is that upon which the author lays most stress. We entirely agree with him in his view of its importance. The work is singularly complete also in its view of the literature of the subject, as well as in the outline of its plan.'—*Guardian.*

Works Published by T. & T. Clark, Edinburgh.

WORKS OF JOHN CALVIN,

IN 51 VOLUMES, DEMY 8vo.

MESSRS CLARK beg respectfully to announce that the whole STOCK and COPYRIGHTS of the WORKS OF CALVIN, published by the Calvin Translation Society, are now their property, and that this valuable Series will be issued by them on the following very favourable terms:—

1. Complete Sets in 51 Volumes, Nine Guineas. (Original Subscription price about £13.) The 'LETTERS,' edited by Dr BONNET, 2 vols., 10s. 6d. additional.
2. Complete Sets of Commentaries, 45 vols., £7, 17s. 6d.
3. A *Selection* of Six Volumes (or more at the same proportion) for 21s., with the exception of the INSTITUTES, 3 vo's.; PSALMS, vol. 5; and HABAKKUK.
4. Any Separate Volume (except INSTITUTES), 6s.

The Contents of the Series are as follow:—

Institutes of the Christian Religion, 3 vols.
Tracts on the Reformation, 3 vols.
Commentary on Genesis, 2 vols.
Harmony of the last Four Books of the Pentateuch, 4 vols.
Commentary on Joshua, 1 vol.
„ on the Psalms, 5 vols.
„ on Isaiah, 4 vols.
„ on Jeremiah and Lamentations, 5 vols.
„ on Ezekiel, 2 vols.
„ on Daniel, 2 vols.
„ on Hosea, 1 vol.
„ on Joel, Amos, and Obadiah, 1 vol.
„ on Jonah, Micah, and Nahum, 1 vol.
„ on Habakkuk, Zephaniah, and Haggai, 1 vol.
Commentary on Zechariah and Malachi, 1 vol.
Harmony of the Synoptical Evangelists, 3 vols.
Commentary on John's Gospel, 2 vols.
„ on Acts of the Apostles, 2 vols.
„ on Romans, 1 vol.
„ on Corinthians, 2 vols.
„ Galatians and Ephesians, 1 vol.
„ on Philippians, Colossians, and Thessalonians, 1 vol.
„ on Timothy, Titus, and Philemon, 1 vol.
„ on Hebrews, 1 vol.
„ on Peter, John, James, and Jude, 1 vol.

In Two Volumes, 8vo, price 14s. (1300 pages),

THE INSTITUTES OF THE CHRISTIAN RELIGION.

BY JOHN CALVIN.

Translated by HENRY BEVERIDGE.

THIS translation of Calvin's Institutes was originally executed for the Calvin Translation Society, and is universally acknowledged to be the best English version of the work. The Publishers have reprinted it in an elegant form, and have at the same time fixed a price so low as to bring it within the reach of all.

In One Volume, 8vo, price 8s. 6d.,

CALVIN:

HIS LIFE, LABOURS, AND WRITINGS.

By FELIX BUNGENER,

AUTHOR OF THE 'HISTORY OF THE COUNCIL OF TRENT,' ETC.

'M. Bungener's French vivacity has admirably combined with critical care and with admiring reverence, to furnish what we venture to think the best portrait of Calvin hitherto drawn. He tells us all that we need to know; and instead of overlaying his work with minute details and needless disquisitions, he simply presents the disencumbered features, and preserves the true proportions of the great Reformer's character. We heartily commend the work.'—*Patriot*.

'Few will sit down to this volume without resolving to read it to the close.'—*Clerical Journal*.

Works Published by T. & T. Clark, Edinburgh.

MESSRS CLARK *beg to offer a Selection of Eight Volumes from the following List of Works (chiefly forming the* BIBLICAL CABINET, *the first series of translations published by them),*

For ONE GUINEA, remitted with order.

The price affixed is that at which they can be had separately, which is also much reduced.

ERNESTI'S PRINCIPLES OF BIBLICAL INTERPRETATION OF NEW TESTAMENT. Translated by Bishop Terrot. 2 vols., 8s.

PHILOLOGICAL TRACTS. 3 vols., 4s. each.
  Vol. I.—Rossi and Pfannkuche on the Language of Palestine in the Age of Christ; Planck on the Nature and Genius of the Diction of New Testament; Tholuck on the Importance of the Study of Old Testament; Beckhaus on the Interpretation of the Tropical Language of New Testament. Vol. II.—Storr on the Meaning of 'The Kingdom of Heaven;' Storr on the Parables; Storr on the word 'ΠΛΗΡΩΜΑ;' Hengstenberg on Isaiah liii. Vol. III.—Ullmann on Christ's Sinlessness; Rückert on the Resurrection of the Dead; Lange on the Resurrection of the Body; M. Stuart on Future Punishment.

THOLUCK'S COMMENTARY ON THE EPISTLE TO THE ROMANS. 2 vols., 8s.
PAREAU ON THE INTERPRETATION OF OLD TESTAMENT. 2 vols., 8s.
STUART'S SYNTAX OF THE NEW TESTAMENT. 4s.
UMBREIT'S EXPOSITION OF THE BOOK OF JOB. 2 vols., 8s.
STEIGER'S COMMENTARY ON FIRST PETER. 2 vols., 8s.
BILLROTH'S COMMENTARY ON THE CORINTHIANS. 2 vols., 8s.
KRUMMACHER'S CORNELIUS THE CENTURION. 3s.
WITSIUS' EXPOSITION OF THE LORD'S PRAYER. 4s.
ROSENMULLER'S BIBLICAL GEOGRAPHY OF CENTRAL ASIA. 2 vols., 8s.
ROSENMULLER'S BIBLICAL GEOGRAPHY OF ASIA MINOR, PHŒNICIA, & ARABIA. 4s.
ROSENMULLER'S BIBLICAL MINERALOGY AND BOTANY. 4s.
WEMYSS' CLAVIS SYMBOLICA; or, Key to Symbolical Language of Scripture. 4s.
CALVIN ON THE EPISTLES TO GALATIANS AND EPHESIANS. 4s.
GESS ON THE REVELATION OF GOD IN HIS WORD. 3s.
ROSENMULLER ON THE MESSIANIC PSALMS. 4s.
COVARD'S LIFE OF CHRISTIANS DURING FIRST THREE CENTURIES. 4s.
THOLUCK'S COMMENTARY ON THE EPISTLE TO THE HEBREWS, with Dissertations on Citations from Old Testament in New Testament, and on the Idea of Sacrifice and Priest in Old and New Testaments. 2 vols., 8s.
CALVIN AND STORR ON THE PHILIPPIANS AND COLOSSIANS. 4s.
SEMISCH'S LIFE, WRITINGS, AND OPINIONS OF JUSTIN MARTYR. 2 vols., 8s.
ROHR'S HISTORICO-GEOGRAPHICAL ACCOUNT OF PALESTINE IN THE TIME OF CHRIST. 4s.
TITTMANN'S EXEGETICAL, CRITICAL, AND DOCTRINAL COMMENTARY ON ST JOHN'S GOSPEL. 2 vols., 8s.
BARBACOVIS' LITERARY HISTORY OF MODERN ITALY. 2s. 6d.
MY OLD HOUSE; or, The Doctrine of Changes. 4s.
NEGRIS' EDITION OF HERODOTUS, with English Notes. 4s. 6d.
  ,,   ,,   PINDAR,   ,,   ,,   4s. 6d.
  ,,   ,,   XENOPHON, ,,   ,,   2s.
WELSH'S ELEMENTS OF CHURCH HISTORY. 5s.
NEANDER ON THE EPISTLE TO THE PHILIPPIANS AND ON THE EPISTLE OF ST JAMES. 3s.
EDERSHEIM'S HISTORY OF THE JEWISH NATION AFTER THE DESTRUCTION OF JERUSALEM UNDER TITUS. 6s.

Works Published by T. & T. Clark, Edinburgh.

Works from the BIBLICAL CABINET, *etc., continued.*

HOFFMANN'S CHRISTIANITY IN THE FIRST CENTURY. 4s. 6d.
KAHNIS' INTERNAL HISTORY OF GERMAN PROTESTANTISM. 4s. 6d.
ULRICH VON HUTTEN, HIS LIFE AND TIMES. 4s.
NETTLETON AND HIS LABOURS. Edited by Rev. A. Bonar. 4s. 6d.
PATTERSON'S ILLUSTRATIONS, EXPOSITORY AND PRACTICAL, OF THE FAREWELL DISCOURSE OF OUR LORD. 6s.
WILSON'S KINGDOM OF OUR LORD JESUS CHRIST. 7s. 6d.
THORNLEY'S SKELETON THEMES. 3s.
THORNLEY'S TRUE END OF EDUCATION, AND THE MEANS ADAPTED TO IT. 3s. 6d.
ANDERSON'S CHRONICLES OF THE KIRK. 3s. 6d.

The following Tracts, issued in the STUDENT'S CABINET LIBRARY OF USEFUL TRACTS, *are also offered as under :—*

LOWMAN'S ARGUMENT *à priori* FOR THE BEING OF A GOD. 6d.
JOUFFROY ON THE METHOD OF PHILOSOPHICAL STUDY. 1s.
JOUFFROY'S ESSAYS ON HISTORY OF PHILOSOPHY; PHILOSOPHY OF HISTORY; INFLUENCE OF GREECE ON THE DEVELOPMENT OF HUMANITY; AND PRESENT STATE OF HUMANITY. 9d.
JOUFFROY ON SCEPTICISM OF PRESENT AGE; FACULTIES OF HUMAN SOUL; GOOD AND EVIL; ECLECTICISM IN MORALS; AND ON PHILOSOPHY AND COMMON SENSE. 1s.
COUSIN ON THE DESTINY OF MODERN PHILOSOPHY. 6d.
COUSIN'S EXPOSITION OF ECLECTICISM. 1s. 6d.
MURDOCK'S SKETCHES OF MODERN PHILOSOPHY, especially among the Germans. 1s.
EDWARDS' STATE OF SLAVERY IN ANCIENT GREECE. 4d.
EDWARDS' STATE OF SLAVERY IN THE EARLY AND MIDDLE AGES OF THE CHRISTIAN ERA. 6d.
HITCHCOCK ON THE CONNECTION BETWEEN GEOLOGY AND NATURAL RELIGION. 4d.
HITCHCOCK'S HISTORICAL AND GEOLOGICAL DELUGES COMPARED. 2 Parts, 9d. each.
EICHHORN'S LIFE AND WRITINGS OF MICHAELIS. 6d.
STÄUDLIN'S HISTORY OF THEOLOGICAL KNOWLEDGE AND LITERATURE. 4d.
VERPLANCK ON THE RIGHT MORAL INFLUENCE & USE OF LIBERAL STUDIES. 4d.
WARE ON THE CHARACTER AND DUTIES OF A PHYSICIAN. 4d.
STORY ON THE PROGRESS OF LITERATURE, SCIENCE, AND GOVERNMENT. 2 Parts, 4d. and 9d.
LIFE OF NIEBUHR. By his Son. 6d.

LIFE OF MADAME DE STAEL. 9d.
SAWYER'S POPULAR TREATISE ON BIBLICAL INTERPRETATION. 6d.
STUART'S PHILOLOGICAL VIEW OF MODERN DOCTRINES OF GEOLOGY. 6d.
LIFE OF LADY RUSSELL. 9d.
CHANNING ON SLAVERY. 6d.
WARE ON EXTEMPORANEOUS PREACHING. 9d.
CHANNING ON FENELON. 4d.
CHANNING ON NAPOLEON BONAPARTE. 6d.
EVERETT ON THE IMPORTANCE OF SCIENTIFIC KNOWLEDGE. 9d.
SIR JOSHUA REYNOLDS' DISCOURSES TO THE STUDENTS OF ROYAL ACADEMY. 1s. 6d.
CHANNING ON SELF-CULTURE. 6d.
CHANNING ON THE IMPORTANCE OF A NATIONAL LITERATURE. 4d.
NEGRIS' LITERARY HISTORY OF MODERN GREECE. 4d.
REYNOLDS ON THE NECESSITY OF PHYSICAL CULTURE TO LITERARY MEN. 4d.
HITCHCOCK ON THE CONNECTION BETWEEN GEOLOGY AND THE MOSAIC ACCOUNT OF CREATION. 1s.
STORY'S HISTORY OF THE LAW. 9d.
LORD STOWELL'S JUDGMENT IN CASE OF DALRYMPLE *v.* DALRYMPLE. 1s. 6d.
LORD STOWELL'S JUDGMENT IN CASES OF THE 'MARIA' AND 'GRATITUDINE.' 1s. 6d.
LORD LIVERPOOL ON THE CONDUCT OF GREAT BRITAIN IN RESPECT OF NEUTRAL NATIONS. 1s. 6d.
CONTROVERSY RELATIVE TO PRUSSIA'S ATTACHMENT OF BRITISH FUNDS IN REPRISAL FOR CAPTURES. 1s. 6d.
BURKE'S LETTER TO A NOBLE LORD. 6d.
WARNKÖNIG'S ANALYSIS OF SAVIGNY ON THE LAW OF POSSESSION. 6d.

STORIES FOR CHILDREN.

THE FLOWER BASKET. By Schmid. 1s. 6d.
EASTER EGGS, AND ROBIN REDBREAST. By Schmid. 6d.
THE LITTLE LAMB. By Schmid. 6d.

THE LITTLE DOVE. By Krummacher. 4d.
THE MINISTER OF ANDOUSE. By Mowes. 1s. 6d.

Works Published by T. & T. Clark, Edinburgh.

COMMENTARIES ON THE OLD TESTAMENT
BY PROFESSORS KEIL AND DELITZSCH.

In Three Volumes, demy 8vo, price 31s. 6d.,
Biblical Commentary on the Pentateuch.
BY PROFESSOR KEIL.
TRANSLATED BY REV. JAMES MARTIN, B.A.

'There is a life in the criticisms, a happy realizing power in the words, which will make this work most acceptable. The Commentary, while it is verbal and critical, has also the faculty of gathering up and generalizing the lesson and the story, which will add immensely to its value. It aims to be an exegetical handbook, by which some fuller understanding of the Old Testament economy of salvation may be obtained from a study in the light of the New Testament teachings.'—*Eclectic Review.*

'We can safely recommend this work to the clergy and others who desire to study the Bible as the *Word of God.*'—*Scottish Guardian.*

BY THE SAME AUTHOR.
In 8vo, price 10s. 6d.,
Biblical Commentary on Joshua, Judges, and Ruth.

In 8vo, price 10s. 6d.,
Biblical Commentary on the Books of Samuel.

In Two Volumes, 8vo, price 21s.,
Biblical Commentary on the Book of Job.
BY PROFESSOR DELITZSCH.
TRANSLATED BY REV. FRANCIS BOLTON, B.A.

In Two Volumes, 8vo, price 21s.,
Biblical Commentary on the Prophecies of Isaiah.
BY PROFESSOR DELITZSCH.
TRANSLATED BY REV. JAMES MARTIN, B.A.

In Two Volumes, 8vo, price 21s.,
Biblical Commentary on the Minor Prophets.
BY PROFESSOR KEIL.
TRANSLATED BY REV. JAMES MARTIN, B.A.

In Two Volumes,
Biblical Commentary on the Epistle to the Hebrews.
BY PROFESSOR DELITZSCH.
TRANSLATED BY REV. T. L. KINGSBURY.
Volume I. is ready, price 10s. 6d.; Volume II. is in preparation.

In Preparation. In Three Volumes,
Biblical Commentary on the Book of Psalms.
BY PROFESSOR DELITZSCH.

www.ingramcontent.com/pod-product-compliance
Lightning Source LLC
Chambersburg PA
CBHW051859300426
44117CB00006B/455